New England

a lonely planet travel survival kit

Tom Brosnahan

Kim Grant

New England

1st edition

Published by
  Lonely Planet Publications
  Head Office: PO Box 617, Hawthorn, Vic 3122, Australia
  Branches: 155 Filbert St, Suite 251, Oakland, CA 94607, USA
                 10 Barley Mow Passage, Chiswick, London W4 4PH, UK
                 71 bis rue du Cardinal Lemoine, 75005 Paris, France

Printed by
  Colorcraft Ltd, Hong Kong

Photographs by
  Tom Brosnahan   Kim Grant
  Michelle Gagné   Kate Miner

  Front cover: Franconia area barn, New Hampshire, Ric Ergenbright

Published
  September 1996

National Library of Australia Cataloguing in Publication Data

Brosnahan, Tom.
  New England.

  Includes index.
  ISBN 0 86442 265 2.

  1. New England – Guidebooks.
  I. Title. (Series: Lonely Planet travel survival kit).

917.404

text & maps © Lonely Planet 1996
photos © photographers as indicated 1996
climate charts compiled from information supplied by Patrick J Tyson, © Patrick J Tyson, 1996

Tom Brosnahan

Tom Brosnahan was born and raised in Pennsylvania, but took a trip to New England during his high school years and fell in love with the region. He returned to attend Tufts University near Boston, and, after Peace Corps service and graduate study, he came here to live. Though he travels frequently as co-author of Lonely Planet guides to Belize, Guatemala, Mexico and Turkey, he's always happy to return home to Concord, MA. His wife, Jane Fisher, is a management consultant. Lydia, their seven-year-old daughter, got her passport when she was nine months old.

Kimberly Grant

Kimberly Grant grew up in the Boston area and graduated from Mount Holyoke College in western Massachusetts. She has combined her love of travel and photography for her life's work: she is the author of *Cape Cod and the Islands: An Explorer's Guide* and co-author of *Best Places to Stay in New England*. Her travel photos appear in many national and international publications, while her fine art photographs are sold in a half-dozen galleries in the US. She has been working with Tom on writing projects since the mid-1980s.

From the Authors

From Tom As US regions go, New England is small in size and large in possibilities. Half-way into writing this guide, it was clear that New England provided more possibilities than one author could describe. Luckily, I was able to get quick, competent, ever-cheerful assistance from my colleagues Kimberly Grant and Katherine Imbrie.

Kim, an experienced guidebook author and professional photographer, took over the pleasant task of describing the perils and pleasures of Boston, Cape Cod, Nantucket and Martha's Vineyard. Kate Imbrie researched and wrote the greater part of the Rhode Island and Connecticut chapters.

Kate Imbrie spent childhood vacations in the Stonington/Mystic area of Connecticut, and soaked up sunshine on the beaches of Weekapaug, RI. For the past 15 years she's been a feature writer for the *Providence Journal*, covering things to do and places to eat in Rhode Island. She's also written for numerous guides and magazines, including the *Original Guide to New England*, Boston's *New England Guide*, *Travel-Holiday* and *Yankee* magazine. This is her first contribution to a Lonely Planet guidebook.

I'm greatly indebted to the Lonely Planet staff in Oakland, CA, for their constant encouragement and assistance, particularly Caroline Liou, our hard-working editor Michelle Gagné, and LP's incredibly talented cartographers.

Finally, this book is for Jane. "Roses are red, violets are blue; if you marry a redhead, you'll know what I do."

From Kim A month before Tom asked for my help with this first edition, I had just finished writing another guidebook. I had emphatically said to my partner (a one-time travel writer turned civil rights lawyer), "I'm not going to accept any more travel writing assignments for the next month! Don't let me! I need a break!" But when Tom called I couldn't refuse. Other jobs got shuffled; photo shoots were squeezed in between road trips. Now that this is completed, you can be sure I'm off to do another book. This time, though, no one will hear me whimpering about needing a break. I wouldn't have it any other way. Fortunately, my cats and my photo clients have accepted my comings and goings.

From the Publisher
Michelle Gagné was project editor of this 1st edition. Carolyn Hubbard, Tom Downs and Don Gates proofed text and maps.

Hayden Foell, Michelle Gagné, Jen Morris, Sacha Pearson and Scott Summers conducted research and supplied a few nuggets. Special thanks to Laini Taylor, Caroline Liou, Randy and Isha (and little Randy) Clark, Mark Pincus and Robert Aichele for their assistance and contributions.

Map production was directed by Alex Guilbert. Stalwart Hayden Foell composed the bulk of the maps with assistance from Chris Salcedo, Beca Lafore, Cyndy Johnsen and Alex Guilbert.

Scott Summers coordinated book production. Hayden, Hugh D'Andrade and Scott composed the layout. Hugh, Hayden and Mark Butler created the illustrations. Hugh designed the cover and the title page.

Warning & Request
Things change – prices go up, schedules change, good places go bad and bad places go bankrupt – nothing stays the same. So if you find things better or worse, recently opened or long since closed, please write and tell us and help make the next edition better.

Your letters will be used to help update future editions and, where possible, important changes will also be included as a Stop Press section in reprints.

We greatly appreciate all information that is sent to us by travelers. Back at Lonely Planet we employ a hard-working readers' letters team to sort through the many letters we receive. The best ones will be rewarded with a free copy of the next edition or another Lonely Planet guide if you prefer. We give away lots of books, but, unfortunately, not every letter/postcard receives one.

Contents

Map Legend

BOUNDARIES

— · — · — · — · — International Boundary

— · · — · · — · · — Provincial/Department Boundary

AREA FEATURES

Park

NATIONAL PARK National Park

National/State Forest

HYDROGRAPHIC FEATURES

Water

Coastline

Creek

River, Waterfall

Swamp, Spring

ROUTES

Freeway

Primary Road

Secondary Road

Tertiary Road

Unpaved Road

Trail

Ferry Route

Railway, Railway Station

Massachusetts Bay Transportation Authority

ROUTE SHIELDS

(95) Interstate Freeway

(1) US Highway

(3) State Highway

SYMBOLS

✪	NATIONAL CAPITAL	✚	Airfield	🅟	Gas Station	🚂 Picnic Area
◉	State/Provincial Capital	✈	Airport	⌐	Golf Course	★ Police Station
		∴	Archaeological Site, Ruins	✚	Hospital, Clinic	🛏 Pool
●	City	❺	Bank, ATM	❶	Information	✉ Post Office
●	Town	🔲	Baseball Diamond	⚏	Lighthouse	⚡ Skiing, Alpine
		🏖	Beach	✳	Lookout	⚡ Skiing, Nordic
		◆◆	Border Crossing	▲	Mission	⚓ Shipwreck
		⬤	Bus Depot, Bus Stop	▲	Monument	✦ Shopping Mall
■	Hotel, B&B	⊟	Cathedral	▲	Mountain	🏛 Stately Home
⚑	Campground	⌐	Cave	🏛	Museum	✡ Synagogue
⚑	Hostel	✝	Church	←	One-Way Street	☎ Telephone
🚐	RV Park	⚭	Embassy	⬠	Observatory	▣ Tomb, Mausoleum
▼	Restaurant	🐟	Fishing, Fish Hatchery	🅿	Parking	🧍 Trailhead
⛴	Bar (Place to Drink)	⊁	Foot Bridge	▲	Park	✤ Winery
⛾	Cafe	✽	Garden	)(	Pass	🐗 Zoo

Note: not all symbols displayed above appear in this book.

Introduction

The English explorer Captain John Smith, while cruising the coast of North America in 1614, christened the land New England. The name came to be used when referring to the four early British colonies here: Massachusetts, Rhode Island, Connecticut, and New Hampshire.

In the 1700s the states of Maine and Vermont were included. Since that time, the six states have preserved their character as a unique region.

"Early America" is alive and well in New England as in no other part of the USA. The heavily forested region is scattered with picture-perfect villages and towns, small farms, granite mountain ranges and thousands of glacial lakes and ponds. Its dramatic rockbound coast – 6000 miles long – is cut by innumerable coves and bays, and punctuated by sandy beaches.

New Englanders are proud of their history, secure in their regional identity and welcoming – if sometimes reserved – to visitors.

Americans from other regions of the country come to New England for its history, culture, and cuisine, and to feel as though they're "almost in Europe." Europeans and other foreign visitors come to beautiful, refined, stable New England as a contrast to the brash energy of New York City, the machismo of Texas, and the good-natured but bewildering trendiness of California.

Though New Englanders feel a common regional identity, the six states are also quite different in character:

Massachusetts is the powerhouse, with the regional capital, Boston, the major industrial and commercial base, and the lion's share of the vacation resorts.

Rhode Island, the smallest state in the Union, is, like Switzerland, enhanced rather than diminished by its size.

Connecticut's cosmopolitan feel comes from its close proximity to New York City, and its several important coastal cities.

Vermont has far more cows than people, and unspoiled mountains and forests, lakes and towns, which is why "flatlanders" (non-Vermonters) flock there for summer hiking and winter skiing.

New Hampshire, the Granite State, is famous for its right-wing, anti-government, pro-commercial policies, and for the majesty of the White Mountain National Forest.

Maine is New England's last frontier, the largest of the six states, with vast forests, an endless and beautiful coastline, popular Acadia National Park which combines both, and innumerable potato fields.

A traveler setting out to see most of the USA must think of distances in continental terms. Not so in New England. Like its namesake, New England packs a lot of beauty and interest into a relatively small space. From Boston, most points can be reached in a morning's drive, and no point in the region is more than a day's drive.

Other parts of America may be exciting, brawny, dramatic, breathtaking, sordid, bland or dangerous. New England, however, is beautiful, historic, dignified, romantic, self-satisfied and, many visitors say, simply delightful.

Facts about New England

HISTORY

The history of New England is the history of early America. Before the written history brought by the European explorers, the record was kept in oral traditions and art. Though this served the Native American peoples well, it leaves gaps in the written record which are difficult to fill.

Early Times

The first human inhabitants of the Western Hemisphere are thought to have been a Mongolian race who crossed the Bering Strait sometime between 12,000 and 25,000 years ago. With slow gait and tired feet, they reached New England about 10,000 or 9000 BC.

The history of these people has been lost, and we cannot even be sure if they were the ancestors of the Algonquian peoples who inhabited the region when the first European settlers arrived. The peoples of New England led a relatively simple life raising corn and beans, pumpkins and tobacco; hunting turkeys, deer, moose, beaver, squirrels and rabbits; and collecting clams, lobsters and fish from coastal waters.

There was no center of power among the New England tribes as there was in the Iroquois confederacy of New York. Intertribal warfare was common in New England, making a common defense against the encroachments of European settlers impossible.

The Explorers

There are many claimants to the title of first Europeans to reach America. Most historians believe it was the Vikings, but the Spaniards, Irish and Portuguese all claim the honor, some pointing to strange inscriptions on Dighton Rock, in eastern Massachusetts, as proof.

Let's assume, as most scholars do, that it was the Norse who first explored New England around the year 1000 AD, calling

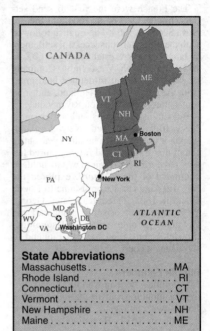

State Abbreviations

Massachusetts	MA
Rhode Island	RI
Connecticut	CT
Vermont	VT
New Hampshire	NH
Maine	ME

it Vinland. However, the Norse colonies failed. The next contingent of explorers to stumble across the continent were the Spanish. Christopher Columbus, an Italian mariner in the service of the Spanish monarchs, reached landfall in the Caribbean in 1492, opening the way for a wave of European explorers.

Upon his return to Europe, the confirmation of the myths of the "western islands" or "Indies" sent other explorers from many nations racing across the ocean in search of adventure and glory. John Cabot (actually Giovanni Caboto, another Italian mariner) claimed the land of New England for his patron, King Henry VII of England, in 1497. In 1534, Jacques Cartier set a cross on the Gaspé peninsula, claiming it for

France. Despite this early claim, little progress was made in exploiting the discovery in the following years.

The French were the first to send settlers, first to Québec in 1604 and then to Nova Scotia in 1608. The English followed with the ultimately unsuccessful settlement at Jamestown, VA, established in 1607. In 1621, the Dutch West India Company received a huge but ill-defined land grant from the government of Holland, and soon sent settlers to the Hudson River Valley.

But English explorers and settlers most successfully colonized New England, though it wasn't until a hundred years after Cabot that England had fully explored her new territories. Bartholomew Gosnold, in command of the *Concord*, explored the New England coast from Maine to Rhode Island in 1602. Three years later, George Weymouth took prisoner a man of the Pawtuxet people named Tisquantum (Squanto) and sailed back to England to show him at court.

Pilgrim Founders

John Smith – the man who had been saved by Pocahontas from execution near the Jamestown, colony – arrived in New England in 1614. He coined the name "New England" for the region, and, upon his return to London, praised its possibilities for settlement. His recommendation was soon acted upon by a group of religious dissenters in search of a place where they could practice their Congregationalist beliefs unhindered by government.

The small ship *Mayflower* set sail from Plymouth (in Great Britain) in late summer 1620, with 102 passengers, some animals, tools, seed, household effects and foodstuffs, bound for New England. After a tedious voyage of two months, these "Pilgrims" made landfall at Provincetown, on the tip of Cape Cod, in November, when the winds of winter had already begun to blow.

Having left England in disagreement with their financial backers, the Virginia Company, the Pilgrims now found themselves without a governing charter. They composed the Mayflower Compact, which defined "majority rule" as their fundamental law.

Unhappy with the exposed position and sandy, unproductive soil of Cape Cod, they spent some time searching the coasts for a more suitable place, and finally decided on Plymouth (MA) arriving there in December.

Though the local people were not bitterly hostile, the New England winter was. The Pilgrims hastily built shelters, but about half of them perished of scurvy, exposure and other privations during the winter of 1620-21. Their first governor, John Carver, died within a year. But the Pilgrim Founders, as this first group is called, had indeed founded a colony.

Prosperity

In the spring of 1621, things began to get better in "Plimoth Plantation."

Squanto, the Pawtuxet who had been taken to England by George Weymouth, had returned to the New World in 1615. Hearing of the new English settlement, he sought out the Pilgrims, and, speaking both languages, facilitated a 50-year treaty of peace between the Pilgrims and Massasoit, *sachem* (chief) of the Wampanoag people in whose territory the Pilgrims settled. Though the Narragansetts who lived farther inland were still hostile, the Pilgrim-Wampanoag alliance secured basic peace.

Squanto also taught the new arrivals essential survival skills: how to plant corn, where and how to hunt deer and other game.

The late John Carver was succeeded as governor by William Bradford, a born leader of strong character and great resourcefulness who continued to lead the colony's development until his death in 1657.

The first summer in New England saw the growth of the colony's first modest corn crop, but this had to be shared with a boatful of new arrivals from England. Even so, at harvest time in the autumn, the colonists celebrated their survival with a three-day feast of Thanksgiving, inviting their Wampanoag neighbors to join them.

This first toehold at Plymouth was followed by the foundation of the Massachusetts Bay colony in 1628. Soon the region could boast several thousand English settlers, with more coming every year.

In 1643, New Englanders attempted a political union as the "United Colonists of New England," joining Massachusetts Bay, Plimoth Plantation, Connecticut and New Haven to promote mutual welfare and defense. Though this New England Confederation broke down a decade later, it was an early example of political union in the region.

Growth of a Nation

The century from the mid-1600s to the mid-1700s saw rapid growth in both the population and wealth of the New England colonies. The region's forests and fields produced food and natural resources in abundance, and New England's many excellent natural ports provided a springboard for the lucrative maritime trade.

As the colonists flooded into New England, the indigenous peoples retreated and died – victims of war, European diseases against which they had little natural immunity, and alcoholism, a disease to which they were genetically susceptible. Within only three generations, the native peoples of the region were reduced to small, relatively powerless groups of survivors.

Though New Englanders still considered themselves subjects of the British crown, they had no representation in Parliament. Nor did they think they needed it. From the first days of settlement in New England, the colonists had governed themselves by majority rule in their own legislative councils, with oversight by governors appointed from London. The colonists saw their affairs as largely separate from the concerns of the old country.

But after the Restoration (1660), English monarchs began to assert more control. The French and Indian Wars (1689-1763) were New World echoes of continental French and British rivalries which cost the colonists dearly. Besides the local battles and Indian depredations brought on by the wars, the expenses of colonial defense provided a rationale for direct taxation of the colonies from London: if the British government was going to spend money defending the colonists, then the colonists could help to pay the bill.

The flaw in this reasoning was that the colonists had no voice in the deliberations over these new taxes. The taxes were

---

Ethan Allen & Vermont

Rural Vermont, distant from Boston, New York and Hartford, was the last corner of New England to be extensively settled. In 1749, Benning Wentworth, royal governor of New Hampshire, issued land grants to Vermont territory for the settlement of towns. This infuriated New York, which also claimed the land, as did the French crown.

Later, in 1764 King George III upheld New York's claim, but before long Vermont farmer Ethan Allen had organized the Green Mountain Boys (1770), who carried out attacks against New York claimants to an extent that prompted the governor of New York to offer a reward of £100 for Allen's capture.

In the Revolutionary War, Allen's Green Mountain Boys and a small force from Connecticut laid siege to Fort Ticonderoga by surprise, prompting its astonished British commander to surrender in a bloodless victory.

During the war the residents of the "New Hampshire Grants" organized a constituent assembly and, in 1777, declared Vermont an independent state. The new state petitioned Congress for admission to the US, but was refused, whereupon Ethan Allen and others plotted to have Vermont come under the aegis of the British crown as an independent state. In 1791, however, Vermont was admitted to the union. ∎

decided in Parliament, which meant taxation without representation.

George III (reigned 1760-1820) and the prime minister, Lord North, pursued taxation of the colonies vigorously. In 1764 Parliament passed the Sugar Act, and in 1765 the Stamp Act, requiring colonial subjects to pay duties on sugar and documents which they used daily. This presumption of authority by the government in London was met first with resistance, and ultimately with revolution.

War & Independence

Tensions mounted, resulting in inflammatory incidents. An angry crowd taunted and threatened a small number of Royal Army sentries in Boston in March of 1770. The sentries, afraid for their lives, fired into the crowd, giving the nascent revolution its first five martyrs in this "Boston Massacre."

In response to the Boston Massacre, many of the repressive Townshend Acts, passed in 1767, were repealed by Parliament, but the tax on tea was retained as a symbol of London's right to tax the colonists directly. The colonists' response was the "Boston Tea Party": in the dead of night on December 16, 1773, a band of colonials masquerading as African and Native Americans forcibly boarded HMS *Dartmouth*, *Beaver* and another ship and dumped their cargos of taxable tea into Boston Harbor.

The response from London was to tighten the screws even further. Parliament passed what were known in the colonies as the "Intolerable Acts," and the colonists, who had traditionally maintained militias against the possibility of Indian attack, began arming and training for war with their erstwhile motherland.

Battles of Lexington & Concord In April 1775, a British spy posing as a carpenter from Maine in search of employment, discovered that the Colonials were stockpiling arms and munitions at Concord, about 18 miles west of Boston. Secret orders were given for an expeditionary force to march under cover of darkness to Concord on the night of April 18, and to make a surprise search of the town.

American spies learned of the plan, and three riders – Paul Revere, William Dawes and Samuel Prescott – spread the word that "the British were coming." Members of the local militias, called "minutemen" because of their ability to be ready for battle on a moment's notice, proved true to their name, turning out, matchlocks in hand, to face the "aggressors."

They could not have been very cheerful. The minutemen, with little training and no experience, were about to face 700 of the world's best professional soldiers, and no one knew what might happen. Word went out beyond Lexington and Concord for reinforcements.

The rhythmic crunch of 1400 British boots in the streets of Lexington must have terrified the 70 minutemen who had lined up in defensive formation on Lexington Green at dawn, but they did not disperse when ordered to do so by Major Pitcairn,

THE
FEMALE COMBATANTS

OR WHO SHALL.
Published according to Act Jany 26 1776. Price 6.

A revolutionary-era cartoon portrays
Great Britain and the American colonies
as two fighting women.
COURTESY THE WALPOLE COLLECTION OF YALE

Massachusetts barn

Sailing away
KIM GRANT

Sleepy central New Hampshire
KIM GRANT

Annual Paul Revere Ride, Boston
KIM GRANT

Country road, Central Massachusetts
KIM GRANT

Squash and gourds
KIM GRANT

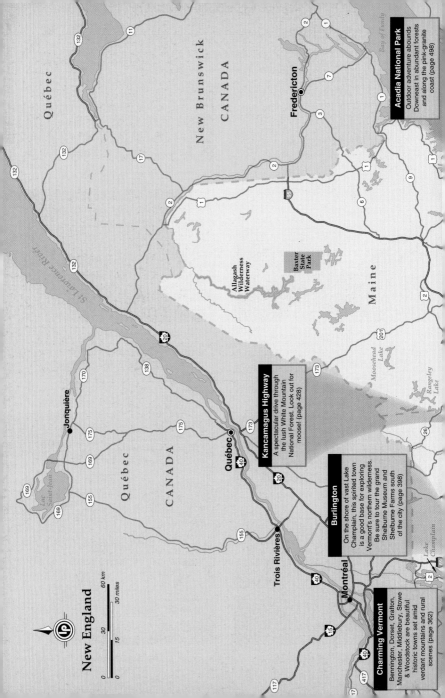

New England

0 15 30
0 30 60 km
30 miles

Québec

CANADA

Québec

New Brunswick
CANADA

Maine

St. Lawrence River

Lake Saint-Jean

Jonquière

Québec

Trois Rivières

Montréal

Fredericton

Allagash Wilderness Waterway

Baxter State Park

Moosehead Lake

Rangeley Lake

Lake Champlain

Bay of Fundy

Acadia National Park
Outdoor adventure abounds Downeast in abundant forests and along the pink-granite coast (page 498)

Kancamagus Highway
A spectacular drive through the lush White Mountain National Forest. Look out for moose! (page 428)

Burlington
On the shore of vast Lake Champlain, this spirited town is a good base for exploring Vermont's northern wilderness. Be sure to tour the grand Shelburne Museum and Shelburne Farms south of the city (page 398)

Charming Vermont
Bennington, Dorset, Grafton, Manchester, Middlebury, Stowe & Woodstock are beautiful historic towns set amid verdant mountains and rural scenes (page 362)

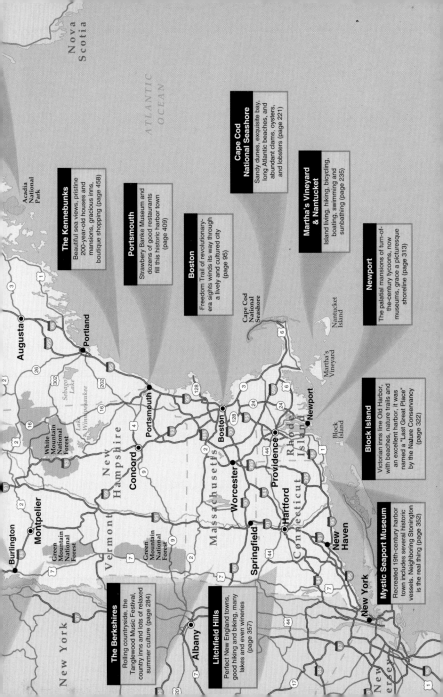

The Kennebunks

Beautiful sea views, pristine 200-year-old houses and mansions, gracious inns, boutique shopping (page 458)

Portsmouth

Strawbery Banke Museum and dozens of good restaurants fill this historic harbor town (page 409)

Cape Cod National Seashore

Sandy dunes, exquisite bay, long Atlantic beaches, and abundant clams, oysters, and lobsters (page 221)

Boston

Freedom Trail of revolutionary-era sights winds its way through a lively and cultured city (page 95)

Martha's Vineyard & Nantucket

Island living, hiking, bicycling, boating, swimming and sunbathing (page 235)

Newport

The palatial mansions of turn-of-the-century tycoons, now museums, grace a picturesque shoreline (page 313)

Block Island

Victorian inns line Old Harbor, with beaches, nature trails and an excellent harbor, it was named a "Last Great Place" by the Nature Conservancy (page 322)

Mystic Seaport Museum

Recreated 19th-century harbor town includes several historic vessels. Neighboring Stonington is the real thing (page 352)

The Berkshires

Rolling countryside, the Tanglewood Music Festival, country inns and lots of relaxed summer culture (page 284)

Litchfield Hills

Perfect New England towns, good hiking and biking, many lakes and even wineries (page 357)

Familiar sights in New England coastal towns

the British commander. Tension mounted, and finally a shot rang out. Many more followed as the "redcoats" overwhelmed the colonial force. Eight minutemen died in the melee.

If the Lexington minutemen had been apprehensive, those assembled at Concord had reason to be scared stiff. Joined by minutemen from surrounding towns such as Acton and Bedford, the Concord group mustered on a hill with a view of the town across the Concord River.

Having been warned well in advance of the British expedition, the arms caches at Concord had been spirited away and hidden elsewhere. Thus the British search for arms turned up only a few wooden gun carriages, which were set afire.

Seeing smoke rising from the town, the minutemen assumed their town was being put to the torch. "Will you let them burn the town down?" shouted one. Emboldened, they advanced down the hill and engaged the British at the North Bridge. The British, having marched to the far side of the bridge to disperse the minutemen, were forced to retreat across it when met with salvos from colonial muskets.

The ranks of the minutemen continued to swell as reinforcements poured in even from distant towns. By noon, now seriously outnumbered, the British force began its retreat from Concord to Boston. But minutemen harried and sniped at the "lobsterbacks" all along the way (at the time not a respectable way to fight), inflicting a shocking number of casualties.

News of the battles of Lexington and Concord spread like wildfire through the colonies, enflaming revolutionary fervor among most Americans, and terrifying those Loyalists who still supported the Crown.

Ticonderoga & Bunker Hill The battles of Lexington and Concord resulted in the gathering of the Second Continental Congress in Philadelphia on May 10, 1775, to decide on defensive measures. On the same day, Ethan Allen led his Green Mountain Boys from Vermont in a successful assault against the British outpost at Fort Ticon-

deroga. The Revolutionary War was well under way.

Boston itself was held by the British. As a challenge, the Americans fortified Breed's Hill, next to Bunker Hill, right across Boston Harbor. The British response was to throw wave after wave of troops up the hill, only to see them mowed down by murderous American fire.

With their ammunition running low, Colonel Prescott, the American commander, was eager to make every shot count and shouted the famous order, "Don't fire until you see the whites of their eyes." His troops obeyed, and when their ammunition was finally exhausted they retreated, leaving over a thousand British soldiers wounded or dying on the slopes of Breed's Hill.

Though it was a British victory, it was an inordinately costly one. As it was being fought, the Continental Congress selected George Washington to lead the American forces against the crown.

Colonial society was torn by divided loyalties. Many colonists remained loyal to the British monarchy despite its injustice; others saw independence as the only solution. All of colonial life was in turmoil, and society broke down in many areas.

Declaration of Independence On May 4, 1776, the colony of Rhode Island and Providence Plantations formally renounced allegiance to King George III, which provoked the British to occupy Rhode Island. By this time it was clear what needed to be done. On July 4, 1776, colonial leaders met in Philadelphia to sign the Declaration of Independence.

The Revolutionary War raged throughout the colonies. Many turning-points (Valley Forge, Yorktown) did not take place in New England, but this is where the war began. Today, April 19 (Patriots' Day), the date of the battles at Lexington and Concord, is a holiday in Massachusetts, and the battles are re-enacted each year.

Early USA

"After the revolution," as they say, "the *real* work begins." The Revolutionary War freed the American colonies from governance by Great Britain, but it did not guarantee America's survival as an independent nation. Americans had no strong, effective central government. It took most of the 1780s to work out the details, but by 1789 the US Constitution had been written, amended and ratified as the basic law of the land.

Freed at last from the restrictions imposed by Great Britain, New England's mariners and merchants built up the young nation's trade in commerce and fishing, to be followed soon after by manufacturing.

19th Century
In the 19th century, New England prospered from another sort of "water power." Designs for textile machinery powered by river flow were smuggled out of England and brought to America. Soon New England's many rivers were bordered by vast brick mills turning out a wealth of clothing, shoes and machinery.

The wealth of the Industrial Revolution, added to that of fishing, whaling and maritime trade, made up for the region's relatively modest agricultural endowments, and allowed 19th-century Boston to

The Underground Railroad
During America's antebellum period, a network of abolitionists subverted slavery laws by forming the Underground Railroad to escort escaped slaves to the northern states, where Blacks were considered "free." After the Fugitive Slave Law of 1851, which stated that escaped slaves found in a free state were to be sent back to their owners, their "promised land" became Canada. Only there could they live free without fear of being pulled back into slavery. Many abolitionists risked imprisonment for harboring slaves, whom they shuttled from safe haven to safe haven. Many New England towns – Farmington, CT, Burlington, VT, Canaan, NH, Portland, ME, and Plymouth, MA, to name a few – were important Underground centers.

Among those most often connected to the abolitionist movement and the Underground Railroad are orator William Lloyd Garrison (1805-1879) of Newburyport, MA, who published the anti-slavery newspaper *The Liberator* and introduced Frederick Douglass (1818-1895) to the world. Douglass

Frederick Douglass

was born into slavery in Maryland, and became a spokesman for the cause throughout New England. Douglass wrote three autobiographies, was the first African-American publisher and served as government minister to Haiti.

Harriet Beecher Stowe (1811-1896) was from a family of abolitionists – including her brother, Reverend Henry Ward Beecher – in Litchfield, CT. She wrote *Uncle Tom's Cabin*, a best-seller when it sold an unheard of 500,000 copies in the US and abroad. The book brought the subject to international prominence.

Harriet Tubman, known as "Moses the deliverer," escaped from slavery in Maryland, only to return for her brethren and her parents (whom she brought to Boston). Her motto was "I can't die but once," and when she did, much later, she was a free woman.

For more information on this subject, see Charles L Blockson's books, *The Underground Railroad: Dramatic Firsthand Accounts of Daring Escapes to Freedom*, or *The Underground Railroad*, which specifically relates to its sites. ■

become one of America's most sophisticated cities, the "Athens of America."

The Industrial Revolution touched the state of Vermont differently; the boom in textile weaving turned Vermont into one huge sheep farm, its forests felled in great swaths to make grazing land.

But no boom lasts forever. As the century drew to a close, New England saw its prosperity threatened on all sides. With the advent of steam power, the great textile factories no longer needed water power, and could move to the Southern states where wages were lower. Steel-hulled, steam-powered ships replaced New England's renowned wooden sailing clipper ships. Petroleum, natural gas and electricity did away with the need for whale oil.

Millions of immigrants who had come from abroad to share in New England's commercial boom – many fleeing Ireland's potato famine – had only minimal skills in a diminishing job market. As settlers moved westward across North America, they opened up vast new farming and grazing lands, producing far greater agricultural riches than the rocky soil and northerly climate of New England would allow.

20th Century

Weakened by these reverses, New England's economy was dealt a final blow by the stock market crash of 1929.

The economic exertions of WWII benefited the economy in some ways, as the shipyards in Maine and Massachusetts, the firearms factories of Connecticut, the naval ports of all the coastal states, and the brain power of New England's universities contributed to the war effort.

The war was followed by recession, which the region felt acutely. But New England still had wealth. During the 1960s and '70s, the children of the postwar Baby Boom crowded its hundreds of colleges and universities. Enchanted by New England's beautiful towns, villages and livable cities, many industrious graduates remained in the region to pursue their careers.

During the 1980s, the boom in comput-

ers, biotechnology and defense spending brought renewed prosperity to the region. Boston housing prices soared as well-educated engineers and technicians were recruited by fast-growing companies such as Data General, Digital Equipment Corporation, Honeywell, Prime Computer, Raytheon and Wang Laboratories. Meanwhile, tourism brought "clean money" to Vermont.

When recession hit the computer industry in the late 1980s, New England's fortunes again turned down, but not for long. Its fundamental strengths in high technology, health care, tourism and other fields soon brought prosperity again.

GEOGRAPHY

The Appalachian Range, which begins in northern Maine and extends as far south as Georgia, was formed some eight million years ago. Over the ages, erosion and geologic pressures reduced these early Alps to much lower hills.

A scant million years ago the earth's temperature dropped, the polar ice caps built and spread toward the equator. This last Ice Age blanketed New England with a river of ice – millions of tons of it.

Pushed slowly southward by the pressure of ice build-up at the North Pole, these glaciers dredged up millions of tons of soil and rock and carried them southward. At the glaciers' southernmost extent, this soil and rock was dumped to form New York's Long Island, a glacial moraine.

Throughout New England, the retreat of the ice 10,000 to 20,000 years ago left glacial deposits such as oblong hills called drumlins (Bunker Hill is one), scooped-out holes which became glacial ponds (Thoreau's Walden Pond) and huge granite boulders ("glacial erratics") in fields and streams.

The resulting landscape has an appealing variety – verdant, winding valleys, abundant forests and a rocky coastline sculpted into innumerable coves and sprinkled with sandy beaches. The mountains lack dramatic height, but because of that they are all the more accessible. Farmers may complain that New England's rocky soil "grows boulders" (they're actually pushed up by the succession of freezing winters), but outdoors enthusiasts will find the New England countryside a perfect place for bicycling, hiking, canoeing, kayaking and boating.

CLIMATE

In 1838, author Harriet Martineau wrote, "I believe no one attempts to praise the climate of New England."

New England's weather conforms to that humorous dictum, "If you don't like the weather, just wait a minute." It is not at all impossible to have hot, muggy 90°F days in July followed by a day or two of cool 65° weather. And the January thaw – when the temperature rises from below freezing to 50°, 60° or even 70°F, is a fervently awaited – if not always dependable – anomaly.

The best weather, cool nights and warm days, is in spring and autumn. See the climate charts in the back of the book for temperature and rainfall information.

Spring

Spring can be very short: "Last year it was on a Tuesday," is the typical joke. If the spring, coming from late April to early June, is a long one, it can be glorious, with apple and cherry trees in bloom, and maple trees being tapped of their sap to make maple syrup. But if spring is short, it may just come on a Tuesday, to be followed on Wednesday by the heat and humidity of summer.

Summer

June can be late spring, with some cold, rainy days, or early summer, with balmy temperatures. July and August are warm to hot, with air temperatures rising above 90°F, and even occasionally above 100°F, with high humidity. Water temperatures, however, never get really high in New England even in the dog days of summer; beaches with gradual slopes are more pleasant. The good weather typically lasts into early September.

Autumn

This is New England's finest season, a reliably pleasant period with daytime temperatures above 60° or 70°F, and cool, sometimes chilly nights. As the weather gets steadily cooler in late September, the foliage begins to change color, and by early October the color of the maples and beeches reaches its peak in northern New England. The wave of color spreads south through mid-October, with Columbus Day (the second Monday in October) making the long weekend when everyone goes out "leaf-peeping."

The color depends upon rainfall and temperature patterns, however, and its timing is not predictable until a few weeks before it happens. It is also uneven: you may travel in late October through country bare of foliage, only to turn into a valley where the trees are ablaze with color. (See the sidebar under Planning in Facts for the Visitor.)

Inns and tourist resorts normally stay open through mid-October; those open in the winter often close in late October or November for staff vacations.

Harvest time includes fresh cranberries on sale in the markets, and "pick-your-own fruit" days and cider-making at orchards throughout the region. By November most of the leaves have fallen from the trees, but a brief period of "Indian Summer" often brings back a week or so of warmer daytime temperatures. By the end of November it's clear that winter is approaching, and by mid-December the bitter winds have begun to blow.

Winter

Winter can be severe or moderate; it is rarely mild. Though the snow can start in November, this is considered early. It's expected in December. Total snowfall may be anywhere from a few inches to the nine feet recorded in the winter of 1995-96. When it's not snowing, however, it's likely to be bright and sunny, with temperatures between 15°F and freezing (32°F), with occasional dips below 0°F. On cold, clear days without wind, the sun warms you, and winter sports such as ice skating, snow-shoeing, skiing and snowboarding can be very enjoyable.

FLORA & FAUNA

For the last 10,000 to 20,000 years, the region has been covered in thick forests of beech, birch, hemlock, maple, oak, pine and spruce. The forest floor harbors many flowers and mushrooms suited to the northerly climate.

The thick forests are populated with white-tailed deer, moose, black bears, rac-coons, beavers, woodchucks (ground hogs), rabbits and porcupines. Many visitors comment on the legions of squirrels (mostly gray, but some smaller red) which hop about on the lawns and paths, and leap from tree to tree in the forest canopy. Chip-munks, smaller and with their character-istic stripes, stay closer to the ground.

The wild turkey is native to New England, as are the pheasant, grouse and many species of songbirds. Hawks and even some eagles favor the mountain areas. The seacoast is crowded with several species of gulls.

Many Canada geese, which once flew over New England on their way south for the winter, have come to stay in recent years. Whales and dolphins play in New England's coastal waters, and provide an alternative livelihood for some of the fishing crews put out of work by the closing of fishing grounds. In fact, the whales seem truly to enjoy sporting for the boats, and captains of whale-watching cruises know their "regulars" by name, and even expect them at certain maritime rendezvous.

GOVERNMENT

The six New England states – Connecticut, Maine, Massachusetts, New Hampshire, Rhode Island and Vermont – are separate governing entities which send representa-tives and senators to Congress in Washing-ton, DC. The governors of the six states, elected by their respective populations, meet as the New England Governors' Council to solve common problems, but this body is unofficial.

New England towns and villages are famous for their town meetings, a form of direct democracy descended from simple beginnings in the rough-and-ready settle-ments of religious congregations.

In the classic town meeting, the entire adult population of a town congregates once or twice a year, often in the spring, to approve ordinances and budgets. Anyone can speak, and many do. Many towns have made practical modifications to the town meeting scheme so that much of the town business during the year is carried out by a board (of selectmen, elders, aldermen, etc) and by professional management staff. But important, and especially budgetary, ques-tions are decided at town meetings.

ECONOMY

Electronic and medical technology, light manufacturing, fishing, tourism, farming and service industries fuel the New England economy.

Historically, New England Yankees have been famous for their technical prowess. In the 19th century, Connecticut was re-nowned for the gadgets, gizmos and firearms turned out in its workshops and factories. Today MA 128, Boston's ring road, is famed as the East Coast counter-part to California's Silicon Valley com-puter realm. Research, programming and electronics manufacturing are all carried out here.

Though the region has a long history of shipbuilding, much of the industry's busi-ness has moved to northern Europe and Asia. Ships (including nuclear submarines) are still built in Groton/New London, CT, and Bath, ME, however.

Farming New England's rocky land has never been easy, but the soil itself can be rich. Some native crops used by the Indians and the first European settlers still have an important role in New England's commercial agricultural economy. Tart, sour, ruby-red cranberries are still har-vested from bogs and wetlands in Massa-chusetts and Rhode Island for juice, sauces, jellies and pies. Blueberries (called huckleberries in other parts of the USA)

Maple Sugaring

The sap of the maple tree is collected during the spring thaw, when nights are still cold but days warm enough to encourage the rising of the sap. During "maple sugar time," metal tubes driven into the sugar maple trunks yield a slow drip of watery sap into buckets. The buckets are collected and the sap poured into big vats, where it is boiled and reduced for hours. The result is a thick, amber-colored syrup with a distinctive flavor which is poured on pancakes or waffles, or crystallized and molded into maple sugar candy. ■

are an important cash crop in Maine and several other states.

New England farmers grow apples, cherries, grapes, lettuce, peaches, pears, plums, rhubarb, several varieties of sweet corn (maize), strawberries, tomatoes and many other vegetables and fruits.

All of the New England states produce maple syrup from the sap of the sugar maple tree. Though Vermont is famous for its maple syrup, New Hampshire's is just as good.

Dairy and sheep farming is important throughout the region, but especially in Vermont. New Hampshire's economy is midway between pastoral Vermont and the manufacturing muscle of Massachusetts and Connecticut.

As an example, in New Hampshire, forests cover 85% of the state, and the north (particularly the White Mountain region) depends largely upon tourism and forest products for its livelihood. Granite-cutting, once an important industry, is still done, but on a small scale.

The fishing industry is on its knees. Overfishing has nearly exhausted the once-rich supply and the lobster industry may be in for a similar fate. During the 1980s, easy bank loans, encouraged by certain government programs, led to investment in more efficient boats and equipment, which led to larger seafood harvests. Belatedly, in 1994, the government changed its policies and

closed the fishing grounds of George's Bank, a mainstay of the New England economy from colonial times. Overfishing had also led to serious imbalances in the food chain, which means that any recovery will be long in coming, and uncertain of ultimate success. Meanwhile, tens of thousands of fishing crews are out of work.

POPULATION & PEOPLE
Native Americans

The New England landscape is dotted with long Native American names such as Connecticut, Massachusetts, Narragansett, Pemigewasset, Penobscot, Winnipesaukee, testifying to the peoples who lived here before the arrival of the Europeans.

Reporting on his discoveries along the New England coast, Captain John Smith wrote of "large fields of corn (maize), and great troops of well-proportioned people."

The Native American population at the time might have been somewhere between 25,000 and 75,000, but no Indian census was taken until 1890. It is thought that 10 major Algonquian tribes, often divided into clans, inhabited the present New England area when the Pilgrims arrived, including the Abenakis, Malecites, Micmacs, Narragansetts, Passamaquoddies, Penobscots, Pequots and the Wampanoags. They lived in villages of about 100 people each, and migrated between summer camps on the coast and winter quarters inland.

Today there are about 12,000 Indians, some living on reservations of ancestral land as at Martha's Vineyard and Mashpee, MA, and Indian Island, ME; many others have assimilated, more or less, into American life.

In several places (notably Connecticut and eastern Massachusetts), tribes have cashed in on the special extraterritorial rights of their reservations to open gambling casinos otherwise forbidden by state laws.

Immigrants

The British and French were the early European claimants to this land, and they have left their mark throughout New

England. The French presence is most obvious in northern and eastern Maine, and northern Vermont and New Hampshire, where many residents are bilingual, but there are colonies of French-Canadian speakers in some of Massachusetts' industrial towns, where they had gone in search of work.

In the 19th and early 20th centuries, Armenian, Greek, Irish, Italian and Portuguese immigrants flooded into the region to provide labor for its factories and fishing boats. There are still many neighborhoods in the region's cities that hold fast to these century-old European ties.

In recent years immigrants have come from around the world to study at New England's universities, work in its factories or manage its high-tech firms. You can hear Caribbean rhythms in Hartford, smell Vietnamese and Cambodian cookery in Cambridge and see signs in Brazilian Portuguese in Somerville, MA.

ARTS

New England looks upon itself as the birthplace of US culture, and has a lot of evidence to prove the point. Many of the greatest early American architects, painters, silversmiths and other artisans were from New England.

Crafts

In colonial times, popular arts such as sewing, quilting, glass-blowing and ironmongery were most common, though furniture-making, painting and other more sophisticated artistic pursuits developed in a fairly short time.

Perhaps the region's most famous early artisan was Paul Revere. Remembered mostly for his midnight ride to warn the minutemen that the redcoats were coming, Revere was in fact a master silversmith. His famous design for the Revere bowl is still followed today.

Scrimshaw The best loved New England art from past centuries is undoubtedly scrimshaw, the carving and engraving of ivory. Ivory teeth and whalebone were readily available from the whaling trade, and whaling voyages allowed for long hours of inactivity. Many sailors became expert scrimshanders, turning out surprisingly fine, delicate carvings. Some objects were utilitarian, such as kitchen utensils, buttons, letter openers and corset stays. Other objects, like cameos, brooches and pins, were made for gifts, and to exhibit the craftsman's abilities. The scenes etched on scrimshaw pieces were often of ships and other nautical scenes. Though scrimshaw is still done, most pieces are replicas on imitation ivory (plastic). The antique pieces are of high value.

Furniture Making Among the most outstanding of New England's artisans in the 19th century were the Shakers (see Religion). At their communal settlements in Maine, New Hampshire and western Massachusetts, they equated work with prayer, and each object was made as a tribute to the Almighty. They worked hard and carefully and well, and their harmonious, pleasant designs continue to be reproduced by artisans today.

Painting

For all its 19th-century wealth, New England society could not fully nurture its renowned artists, most of whom sought training and artistic fulfillment abroad. These included Henry Sargent (1770-1845), of Gloucester, MA, a student of Benjamin West's, and James Abbott McNeill Whistler (1834-1903), of Lowell, MA, who challenged the tradition of closely representational painting by blurring lines and emphasizing the play of light in his work.

An exception was Winslow Homer (1836-1910), who pursued a career as an illustrator for the popular press, but later dedicated his talents to painting. Though a Bostonian, Homer is most famous for his accurately depicted scenes of the Maine coast.

By the turn of the century, however, New England – Boston in particular – was capable of supporting its world-class artists. John Singer Sargent (1856-1925) painted his telling portraits of Boston's upper class, and Childe Hassam (1859-1935) used Boston Common and other New England landscapes and cityscapes as subjects for his impressionist works.

Norman Rockwell (1894-1978), perhaps New England's most famous artist, reached his public mainly through his magazine illustrations, particularly the covers he painted for the *Saturday Evening Post*. His evocative, realistic pictures of common men, women and children involved in the small triumphs, tragedies and comedies of daily life cemented US popular culture and raised the nation's consciousness of what it meant to be an American. Rockwell lived and worked in Arlington, VT, and Stockbridge, MA, which now have major museums of his work.

Highly regarded for her "American primitive" paintings of rural life, Anna Mary Robertson Moses (1860-1961) didn't begin painting until her late 70s. See Bennington, VT, for information on "Grandma Moses."

Sculpture

New England has produced its share of sculptors. Daniel Chester French (1850-1931) designed the Minuteman memorial in Concord, MA, and the seated Lincoln in Washington, DC's Lincoln Memorial. Augustus Saint-Gaudens (1848-1907) was born in Ireland, worked in New York, London and Rome, but finished his career in Cornish, NH. Alexander Calder (1898-1976) made many of his world-famous mobiles and stabiles at his studio in Roxbury, CT.

Architecture

Though not as eager to break with architectural tradition as are some other American regions, New England has its share of dramatic modern structures, from the glass-sheathed air-foil skyscrapers of Boston and Hartford to the radical IM Pei-designed John F Kennedy Library just outside of Boston.

New Englanders are attuned to the conservation of their traditions; most of the region's cities now have well-preserved historic cores where you can inspect good examples of the region's many architectural styles.

At the time of settlement, the Pilgrims in Plymouth built simple thatched-roof log huts – and were glad to have them. As they prospered, wood-frame clapboard houses followed.

The simple life of colonial settlers gradually gave way to a life of greater comfort and worldliness, and more beautiful and elaborate structures were built. The Neo-Classicism of Palladian architecture, as practiced in London by Christopher Wren and Inigo Jones during the latter half of the 17th century, was particularly popular in New England. Called Georgian after the reigning British monarchs, it was – and still is – used extensively: Harvard, Dartmouth and many other New England schools boast a riot of red brick and white cornice in Georgian style. Harvard even has a Georgian firefighters' station built only a few decades ago. The typical tall-steepled New England meetinghouse (church) is a variation on the Palladian design.

When European taste moved on to the Classic Revival aesthetic in the late 18th and the early 19th centuries, American taste followed. Thomas Jefferson's updated Roman temple design used for Monticello influenced New Englanders as well, and soon Greek and Roman temples were appearing as college halls, courthouses and bank buildings. Boston's Quincy Market echoes the Neo-Classicism of London's Haymarket.

State capitols built in the 19th century were designed with Neo-Classical domes, colonnades and arcades, perhaps the best example of which is the Massachusetts State House by Charles Bulfinch (1763-1844). Even when the rest of New England and the nation had succumbed to a fascination with Gothic Revival, Boston architect Henry Hobson Richardson (1838-86) continued to build romantic Romanesque structures like Trinity Church, built from 1872 to 1877, in Copley Square, Boston.

New England's fascination with European styles continued into the 20th century, but was diluted by a riot of local creativity. While modified Cape Cod cottage styles were exported to the Midwest and California, ranch-style houses started popping up in New England.

The lyrical Art Nouveau style of the early part of the century left little impression on the region, and most modern Art Deco buildings have fallen to the wrecker's ball. However, one exceptional example, the Fleet Bank Building, still stands in Providence, RI.

In the 1950s and '60s, cold, modern monumentalism produced huge sterile building complexes such as Boston's Prudential Center and the graceless blocks in the city's West End which, in later years, had to be softened and humanized with gardens and clusters of shops. The sturdy granite warehouses along Boston's Waterfront were slated for destruction, to be replaced by a dull modern shopping center, until saved by the efforts of preservationists.

Richardson's Trinity Church was soon reflected in the glass wall of the John Hancock Tower, designed in 1976 by IM Pei.

Literature

Literature has been in the lifeblood of New England since its earliest times. Even the smallest New England towns have public libraries.

New England's traditional reverence for literature was brought by the Puritans, who believed that through religious education one came to know God. American literature, therefore, was initially ecclesiastical.

The desire for religious education inspired the founding of many of the great colleges and universities here. Amherst, Bowdoin, Brown, Dartmouth, Harvard, Tufts, Williams and Yale were all founded to train candidates for the ministry.

New Englanders' passion for literacy was evident as early as 1828, when Noah Webster (1758-1843) published his *American Dictionary of the English Language*. It sold hundreds of thousands of copies in edition after edition – an astounding

Ralph Waldo Emerson published *Essays* in 1841, which included the "Over-Soul" and "Self-Reliance."

achievement considering the country's population at the time.

By the late 1800s the preoccupation with theological education had been modified to include a passion for secular letters. New England's colleges became magnets for literati of all beliefs and opinions. Some New England towns – notably Concord, MA – nurtured the seeds of 19th-century America's literary and philosophical flowering.

This transition is epitomized in the writings of Ralph Waldo Emerson (1803-82), a founder of Transcendentalism (see Religion) who believed in the mystical unity of all creation. Emerson gained a nationwide – even worldwide – audience for the teachings he promulgated from his home in Concord.

Emerson's friend and fellow Concordian, Henry David Thoreau (1817-62), was among the first Americans to advocate a life of simplicity, lived in harmony with nature. Such beliefs were a radical departure from the prevailing industrial and commercial Protestantism of the time, but they gained a wide and impassioned following. Thoreau is best remembered for *Walden, or*

Life in the Woods (1854), his journal of observations written during his solitary sojourn (1845-47) in a log cabin at Walden Pond, on the outskirts of Concord. He also wrote a treatise on *Civil Disobedience* long before this moral position was put to good use by Mahatma Ghandi. Less well known but equally engaging are Thoreau's travelogues: *The Maine Woods* and *Cape Cod*.

Another Concord author was Nathaniel Hawthorne (1804-64), America's first great short-story writer and author of *The Scarlet Letter*, *Twice-Told Tales* and *The House of the Seven Gables*.

Louisa May Alcott (1832-88), though born in Pennsylvania, lived much of her life in Concord, MA, and wrote to contribute to the family income. She knew Emerson and Thoreau well. Her largely autobiographical novel *Little Women* (1868-69) is her best-known work, but its several sequels *(Little Men* and *Jo's Boys)* are also still read with pleasure by many Americans.

Among New England's classics are many dealing with its maritime past, including *Moby Dick* (1851) by Herman Melville, and *Two Years Before the Mast* (1840) by Richard Henry Dana.

Altogether different are Henry James's *The Bostonians* (1886), and John P Marquand's *The Late George Apley* (1937), novels of Boston parlor society.

Reaching a world audience, few were more prominent than Mark Twain (Samuel Clemens, 1835-1910). Born in Missouri, Twain settled in Hartford, CT, and wrote *Tom Sawyer* and *Huckleberry Finn* there. He also wrote *A Connecticut Yankee in King Arthur's Court* (1889).

Several New England writers were instrumental in the battle against slavery preceding and during the Civil War. Among them were William Lloyd Garrison (1805-79), John Greenleaf Whittier (1807-92), and Harriet Beecher Stowe (1811-96). Ms Stowe's best-selling fictionalization of life on a slave-holding plantation, *Uncle Tom's Cabin* (1852), received acclaim both in the USA and abroad, and helped to hasten the end of American slavery. More information on Stowe is given in the Underground Railroad sidebar, earlier in this chapter.

In 1903 Dr William Edward Berghardt DuBois (1868-1963), of Great Barrington, MA, and Harvard University, wrote *The Souls of Black Folk*, an influential book that sought to change the way Blacks dealt with segregation, urging pride in African heritage.

The Last Puritan (1936) by George Santayana explores what it might be like for someone with 17th-century Puritan ideals to be attending Harvard in the 20th century.

New England's signature poet is, of course, Robert Frost (1874-1963). Though born in California, Frost returned to his New England roots and attended Dartmouth and Harvard. He tried farming at various places in Vermont and New Hampshire (with very limited success). His many books of poetry use New England themes as the vehicles to explore the depths of human emotion and experience.

Henry Wadsworth Longfellow (1807-82) wrote *The Song of Hiawatha*, *Paul Revere's Ride*, "The Village Blacksmith," "Excelsior," and "The Wreck of the Hesperus." Emily Dickinson (1830-86), "the Belle of Amherst," wrote beautifully crafted poems that were largely published after her death. Edgar Allen Poe (1809-49) wrote *The Raven* (1845) while wooing his beloved in Providence, RI. Edna St Vincent Millay (1892-1950) wrote poetry that reflects her native Maine.

Stephen Vincent Benét (1848-1943), the author of *John Brown's Body* about the abolitionist, lived in Stonington, CT.

Playwrights from New England include Eugene O'Neill *(Long Day's Journey into Night)*. O'Neill's house in New London, CT, is now a museum. Arthur Miller, though from New York, wrote *The Crucible*, successfully dramatizing the Salem, MA, witch trials.

Modern Fiction Many of today's books written by New England authors are less political and ethical, but are usually more enjoyable.

For up-to-date thrills set in Boston and New England, pick up any of the "Spenser" thrillers written by Robert B Parker. Many of Stephen King's novels and stories, notably *Dolores Claiborne*, are set in his native Maine.

Jaws, by Peter Benchley, set on Martha's Vineyard, is the novel from which the popular motion picture was made. Little known is that Benchley's grandfather is Robert Benchley, born in Worcester, MA, and famous as a member of New York's Algonquin Round Table.

Annie Proulx, award-winning author of *The Shipping News*, describes rural Vermont in her novel *Postcards*. John Irving, a New Hampshire native, wrote *Hotel New Hampshire, The World According to Garp, Cider House Rules* and *A Prayer for Owen Meany*, all of which are set in New England.

John Knowles, who wrote the affecting *A Separate Peace* (1960), went to Yale. The book is set in a New England prep school.

A group of übermodern authors may not be from New England, but they certainly have been affected by it. Donna Tartt wrote *The Secret History* (1993), whose characters commit murder at a college modeled on Bennington College, where she and author Bret Easton Ellis studied. Jay McInerney of Connecticut attended nearby Williams, and is memorable as the author of *Bright Lights, Big City* (about making the grade in New York City). His 1996 novel *Last of the Savages*, is about two diverse friends who meet at a New England prep school.

RELIGION

New England began its modern history as a haven for religious dissenters, and the tradition of religious freedom and pluralism lives today.

The Pilgrims who arrived at Plymouth in 1620 were "Puritans," believers in a strict form of Calvinism which sought to "purify" the church of the "excesses" of ceremony and decoration acquired over the centuries. The Bible was to be interpreted closely, not to be subjected to elaborate theological interpretation. Their strict and rigorous adherence to religious law served them well in the harsh and unforgiving conditions of early colonial life.

The Pilgrims disagreed early and often on the details of religious belief and church governance. Presbyterians believed in a central governing body for the church, while Congregationalists wanted autonomy for each church community. The common solution to theological disagreements was for the minority group to shove off into the wilderness and found a new community where they could worship as they wished. Human nature and theology being what they are, this resulted in new communities popping up throughout the region: Thomas Hooker and his followers abandoned Cambridge, MA, to found Hartford, CT; Roger Williams and his flock split to found Providence, RI. In many cases the new colonial towns, having more recently suffered intolerance, were more tolerant themselves. Newport, RI, though founded by Puritans, soon had a Quaker meetinghouse and a Jewish synagogue.

Shakerism

Shakerism originated among members of the Society of Friends ("Quakers") in Manchester, England, in the mid-1700s. Guided early on by Jane and James Wardley, leadership was soon taken over by Ann Lee (1736-84), a convert to the sect imprisoned by the English government for her zeal. "Mother Ann," as she came to be known, had a religious epiphany in 1770, and came to believe that she was the manifestation of Christ's "female nature."

In order to pursue her beliefs freely, she emigrated to the New World in 1775 and established a community with her followers in Watervliet, NY. In later years Shaker communities were founded throughout New England. At its height, New England Shakerism could boast some 6000 members.

The name "Shakers" was given to members of the sect by the outside world because their worship ceremony involved a trembling dance to symbolize being possessed of the Holy Spirit. The tenets of Shakerism called for closed communities, set apart from the world, in which men and women lived in separate quarters, coming together only for prayer, dining and work. Shakers were admonished to "put their hands to work and their hearts to God." Work was looked upon as an act of worship, and the result an offering to God, so the Shakers' craft items such as quilts and furniture are possessed of a timeless beauty and flawless quality.

The combined strictures of separation from the world and separation of the sexes spelled the end to Shakerism. Cut off from the world there could be no proselytization, and cut off from the opposite sex there could be no procreation, so the Shakers died out. Their exquisite crafts survive, however, in museums throughout the USA and in the four former Shaker communities that survive in New England as museums in Hancock and Harvard, MA; Sabbathday Lake, ME; and Canterbury, NH.

Christian Science

The 19th century saw the birth of another religion in New England. Mary Baker Eddy (1821-1910) of New Hampshire experienced a miraculously speedy recovery from an accident in 1866. She attributed her cure to the healing powers of God as lived and taught by Christ. She undertook a thorough and devoted study of the Bible and its teachings on the matter of medical science and health, and formulated the tenets of Christian Science. Her findings and beliefs were embodied in the Church of Christ, Scientist, headquartered at the Mother Church in Boston, with "daughter" churches now spread throughout the world in 68 countries. The sect's fame has spread in this century through its excellent newspaper, the *Christian Science Monitor*.

Congregationalism

The basic beliefs of Congregationalists are that each Protestant Christian community should have full control of its own affairs, and that there should be no hierarchy of bishops or pope-like head of the church, because Jesus is the only head needed. When the movement began in England in the 1500s, early proponents, called Independents, were persecuted by the Church of England.

Congregationalism flourished in New England, where conditions were right for its practice. New England's noted early preachers, such as Jonathan Edwards, were all Congregationalists, and the region's most prominent colleges, including Amherst, Harvard, Williams and Yale, were founded by Congregations, though the colleges were non-sectarian.

Unitarianism (see below) and Congregationalism had many points of mutual attraction, and during the 19th century some Congregations adopted Unitarian beliefs.

Self-government does not preclude association, however, and Congregational churches have long formed associations of equals, including the United Church of Christ (1957).

Transcendentalism

Emerson, Thoreau, Bronson Alcott and other prominent thinkers in Concord, MA, during the mid-1800s refined the tenets of Unitarianism into a belief called Transcendentalism. They believed not just that God was inherent in all people, but that each person could "listen" to that God-like part for ethical, moral and spiritual guidance. Furthermore, humans must seek to understand nature and to live in harmony with it. This was no doubt the inspiration for Thoreau's retreat at Walden Pond from 1845 to 1847.

Other Transcendentalist thinkers went even further. In 1841 they purchased Brook Farm in West Roxbury, MA (now an affluent Boston suburb), as a living laboratory for their beliefs. Hawthorne, Melville and other Transcendentalists both famous and unknown lived together at Brook Farm until 1847, when the experiment came to an end. Though it must be counted a failure, the Brook Farm experiment identified an ideal which is perhaps more meaningful today than it was a century and a half ago.

Unitarianism

In its earliest forms, Unitarianism declared the unity of God, which was blasphemy to Christians who believed in the Trinity. In its American incarnation, Unitarianism became a religion based on reason. It has no doctrine; members declare only that "in the love of truth and in the spirit of Jesus, we unite for worship of God and service to Man." Unitarian beliefs were advocated most forcefully by William Ellery Channing (1780-1842), Ralph Waldo Emerson and Thomas Parker.

Unitarianism became popular among the Congregational churches of New England, and today most Unitarian churches have a Congregational form of government.

In 1825 the American Unitarian Association was formed, and in 1865 it held a national convention. In 1961 the American Unitarian Association joined with the Universalist Church of America to form the Unitarian Universalist Association.

Universalism

John Murray arrived in New Jersey from England to preach the Universalist belief that God's purpose was to save every person from sin through the divine grace of Jesus. Murray settled in Gloucester, MA, where he founded the first Universalist church in America.

Universalism spread throughout the region, with each congregation being independent, though all accepted a common doctrine. Though early of a Calvinist cast, Universalism distanced itself from strict Calvinism in the 19th century, and later allied itself closely with Unitarianism.

LANGUAGE

Though the principal language of New England is obviously English, various other languages thrive as well. In northern Maine there are communities of French speakers descended from the Voyageurs (early explorers) of Québec. In Gloucester, New Bedford and other coastal towns there are significant communities of Portuguese speakers from Portugal and the Azores who came to New England to work the rich fishing grounds. In Boston's North End many older people still speak only Italian, and in Hartford you may hear the musical patois of the Caribbean islands. Legal notices in the Boston area are often printed in English, Portuguese, Spanish, Vietnamese and Cambodian in recognition of immigrants who have arrived this century.

New Englanders, and especially Bostonians, are famous for abbreviating many words. Massachusetts Avenue becomes "Mass Ave;" the Harvard Business School becomes "the B School;" "Cape Cod" is "the Cape" and "Martha's Vineyard" is "the Vineyard." Boston's subway system, officially the MBTA Rapid Transit System, becomes "the T" in local parlance.

But the region is most famous for the broad-voweled English commonly called the Boston accent. "Pahk the cah in Hahvahd Yahd" (Park the car in Harvard Yard) is the common joke sentence satirizing the peculiar "r" which is also common to some dialects in England. During John F Kennedy's presidency, his speech was satirized for the "r"s which would disappear in some places – "cah" – and pop in others – "Cuber" (Cuba, pronounced as KYOO-berr) – when it was used for elision (the "bridge") between two vowels.

To the north, the people of Maine and New Hampshire are kidded for punctuating their speech with a meaningless sound – "ayuh" (uh-YUH) – early and often.

Facts for the Visitor

PLANNING

New England is principally a summer destination, with another busy season when the fall foliage reaches its full color. From mid-July through August the summer resort areas are very busy, accommodations are fully booked and restaurants are crowded. Perhaps the best time to travel here is between the weekend of Memorial Day (the last Monday in May) and mid-June, before the schools close and families hit the road; and the early part of September, after the big summer rush but before the "leaf peepers" (foliage tourists) arrive. Especially during the week at these times, hotels and inns are likely to have rooms available, vacant campsites can be found easily, and the hottest restaurants will have tables ready without a long wait.

Because New England entertains a dense tourist population in the summer and fall, the opportunity for special events, festivals and celebrations is endless – and therefore only a few are detailed in this part of the book. For more information on them, see the destination heading in this guide, or call the state division of tourism.

For an overview of each state's attractions, see Highlights, later in this chapter.

When to Go

January New Year's Day (January 1) is a legal holiday. (See December for New Year's Eve or "First Night" celebrations.) Transportation services are crowded several days before and after New Year's Day, but from January 4 to 14 travel services are not heavily used, and traveling is easy and relatively cheap. The weather is usually bitterly cold and snowy, though often there is a welcome "January thaw," a few days of surprisingly mild temperatures.

The third Monday is Martin Luther King Day, a holiday celebrating the civil rights leader's birth (January 15, 1929). This is the unofficial opening of the busy skiing season.

Chinese New Year begins at the end of January or the beginning of February and lasts two weeks. In cities with a significant Chinese population (like Boston), the first day is celebrated with parades, firecrackers, fireworks and lots of food.

Contact ski areas for local snow festivals and ski/snowboard/snowmobile competitions in January and February, especially in Maine and New Hampshire. Stowe, VT, has a popular winter carnival mid-month.

February The weather remains quite cold, and skiing is the big activity this month. Many New Englanders fly off to warm southern islands for a respite.

February 14 is Valentine's Day (not a holiday).

The third Monday is Presidents' Day, a legal holiday commemorating the birthdays of George Washington (February 22, 1732) and Abraham Lincoln (February 12, 1809). Ski destinations are particularly busy.

In Massachusetts, actors dress up as Puritans and Native Americans in Old Deerfield to celebrate Indian House Memorial: 1704 Weekend.

In New Hampshire, Hanover's Dartmouth Winter Carnival has been celebrated since 1911 with games, drink and cultural activities.

In Maine, the Annual US National Toboggan Championship takes place the first week in Camden. Kennebunk, Houlton, Caribou, Searsport, Greenville and other towns celebrate Winter Carnival.

March Cold and snow continues at least until mid-March. In Vermont, March 7 is a public holiday that's known as Town Meeting Day.

St Patrick's Day (March 17, not a holiday) is celebrated in Boston and other cities with large Irish-American populations. Parades, speeches and drinking parties are the order of the day. However, the Boston city government celebrates March 17 (or the Monday closest to it) as Evacuation Day, a public holiday celebrating the day the British pulled out of Boston Harbor in 1775.

In Massachusetts the Spring Bulb Show features thousands of flowers and plants at Smith College in Northampton.

In Maine, toward the start of the month, the week-long Ice Fishing Tournament is held on Moosehead Lake (Rockwood). Maple Sugar Sundays are held in Rockport and statewide when maple sugar houses open their doors to the public.

Late March brings the beginning of "mud time," when the earth thaws. When days are warm and nights cold, farmers tap the maple sap from their sugar bushes (maple tree groves) to make maple syrup.

In some years, Easter (see April) falls in late March.

April Mud time continues, and the chance of a major snowstorm disappears. By Patriots' Day (April 19), nights are still chilly but days can be relatively warm and pleasant. The Monday nearest Patriots' Day is a holiday in Massachusetts with parades and speeches (state government offices and some local businesses close). In Lexington and Concord, MA, the opening battles of the Revolutionary War are re-enacted, and the parades feature troops of "British redcoats," colonial minutemen, fire engines and politicians seeking publicity.

Also in April is the Boston Marathon, which celebrated its 100th anniversary in 1996. In Vermont, the Vermont Maple Festival is held in St Albans, near the start of the month.

Easter often falls in April. Some businesses are closed Good Friday (not a holiday) and transportation services are crowded. Many businesses are closed on Easter Sunday.

New England's hundreds of colleges empty out and close down for "spring break," usually the week leading up to Easter Sunday.

Summer-Long Festivals
Two festivals span the summer months in Massachussetts' Berkshire County. Jacob's Pillow Dance Festival in Lee is the oldest dance festival in the US, presenting ballet, jazz and modern dance. In Lenox, the Boston Symphony Orchestra performs at the Tanglewood Music Festival. ■

In April, ski season is winding down and spring has not really arrived, so many country inns and other vacation lodgings are closed for all or part of the month.

May Weather in May is usually delightful, with cool nights and warm days, though cold rain and even a short freak snowstorm aren't impossible.

Mothers Day, the third Sunday of May, is a commercial celebration that ends up as the busiest restaurant day of the year – reservations are required everywhere.

The weekend of Memorial Day (the last Monday in May) signals the official start of the summer vacation season. The holiday commemorates US veterans with patriotic parades and ceremonies. Many festivals are held during the three-day weekend.

Campgrounds, theme parks, seasonal museums and attractions are all open – and very busy. Have advance reservations for any tourist services (hotel, restaurant, transport) that you may need.

In Massachusetts, Boston's Art Newbury St has galleries hosting special exhibits while musicians perform on sidewalks. Salem's waterfront Seaport Festival is a celebration of the state's seafaring history, artists and craftspeople. The Brimfield Outdoor Antiques Show is a mile-long strip featuring more than a thousand dealers; also held in July and September in Brimfield.

In Connecticut, Mystic's Lobsterfest is an outdoor old-fashioned lobster bake on the banks of the Mystic River, held on Memorial Day weekend.

Over the entire month, Greenville, ME, celebrates Moosemania with "moose related activities and events."

June Early June is an excellent month to travel in New England. Because schools are still in session, local families do not crowd resort areas except on the weekends. Everything's open, but prices are not yet at the high level they will attain in late July and August. The weather is completely unpredictable: a breathlessly hot few days may be followed by a surprising chill, but mostly the weather is quite fine.

After mid-June, when schools adjourn, resorts become much busier on weekdays as well as weekends. You may need to make advance reservations as summer festivals hit their stride.

June 17 is Bunker Hill Day, a Boston holiday that closes some local business. The third Sunday in June is Fathers' Day, a commercial celebration similar to Mother's Day (see May), but without the restaurant angle.

In Massachusetts, Provincetown's Blessing of the Fleet holds family events and a religious celebration honoring fisherfolk. The ACC Crafts Fair in West Springfield brings together more than 350 of the nation's artisans to show and sell their work in the Eastern States' Exhibition.

In Connecticut, The Taste of Hartford festival is one of New England's largest outdoor food fests near the start of the month. Around the same time, Farmington Antiques Weekend is the largest antique event in the state with over 600 exhibitors.

In Rhode Island, the first weekend brings the Festival of Historic Homes, when private gardens and buildings are open to the public in Providence.

Vermont has the Annual Vermont Dairy Festival in Enosburg Falls in the early part of the month, as well as Burlington's Discover Jazz Festival. Waterbury hosts free Concerts in the Park (with free ice cream!) every Thursday night from mid-June to mid-August. Ethan Allen Days – "Fun with the Green Mountain Boys" – with historical re-enactments in Arlington, is held mid-month.

In New Hampshire, the second weekend of June brings Portsmouth's Old Market Square Days, which celebrates food mostly. The last weekend of the month is Portsmouth's Jazz Festival on the waterfront.

In Maine, Rockport celebrates the Annual Down East Jazz Society Festival. At the end of the month, Boothbay Harbor has its Annual Windjammer Days, which has a parade, concerts and more. More unusual is Caribou's Midsomer Dagen, a Swedish-American celebration of mid-summer with a maypole and traditional Swedish dancing.

July Independence Day (July 4) is USA's biggest patriotic holiday, commemorating the signing of the Declaration of Independence on July 4, 1776. It is celebrated on the actual day with parades, cookouts and fireworks displays in every town ranging from the smallest village to large cities like Boston, where the Boston Pops outdoor concert on the Charles River Esplanade is legend. When the 4th of July falls on a Friday or a Monday, resorts and transport are particularly busy as everyone takes off for a long weekend. The weather is warm to hot.

Other notable 4th of July celebrations are at Old Sturbridge Village, MA; Hartford, CT; and Burlington, VT. In Maine, you can find a good one anywhere, but especially in Bar Harbor (plus a Seafood Fest the same weekend), Bethel, Boothbay, Greenville, Kennebunk, Millinocket, Ogunquit and Rangeley.

The eight weeks between the 4th of July and Labor Day (the first Monday in September) are New England's high season for tourism. Everything is crowded, and reservations are required for many services: lodgings, campsites, car ferries, etc.

In the month's second week, Boston's Harborfest is a celebration of maritime history with fireworks, concerts, food festivals and historic reenactments. In New Bedford, MA, the Annual Feast of the Blessed Sacrament is the largest Portuguese festival in the US with a parade, entertainment and a giant midway with rides.

Near the start of the month, in Bridgeport, CT, the Barnum Festival culminates with a giant parade honoring the circus king. In Litchfield, CT, an Open House Tour lets you inside the town's private historic homes and gardens. The Guilford (CT) Handcrafts Exposition, a show featuring items from more than a hundred artisans nationwide, is held toward the end of the month.

In the first week of July, in Brandon, VT, you can take a self-guided tour of the cellars and hiding places once used by slaves fleeing to Canada on the Underground Railroad. The Manchester Music Festival and the Marlboro Music Fest are held from July through August, as is the Champlain Shakespeare Festival, in Burlington, VT, at UVM's Royall Tyler Theatre.

July is a busy month for Maine: the second weekend of the month Crawford has an Annual Breakneck Mountain Bluegrass Festival, Rockland has the Annual Great Schooner Race, and Fort Kent has Summerfest with an arts and crafts fair, barbecue and more. Mid-month brings Camden's Annual Arts and Crafts Show with over 100 professionals attending, and Bar Harbor has a Native American Festival, with crafts, dancing and food. Yarmouth has an Annual Yarmouth Clam Festival good for everyone in the family. Running for two weeks near the end of the month is the Bangor State Fair, the largest of the state, and complete with agricultural exhibits, rides, entertainment and down-home fun.

August The weather is at its hottest in August, often with a week or so of "dog days" when the temperature exceeds 90° or 95°F in high humidity and, despite prevalent air-conditioning, everyone except those at the beach complains. Tourism is at its busiest in August, with prices at their highest.

In Massachusetts, the Gloucester Waterfront Festival has a Yankee lobster bake, pancake breakfast, whale watches and more.

In Connecticut, mid-month brings the Volvo International Tennis Tournament to New Haven, where international stars of men's tennis compete.

In Rhode Island, the Newport Jazz Festival and the Folk Festival are held on alternate weekends near the start of the month.

August 16 is Bennington Battle Day in Vermont, a state holiday that might close some businesses. The battle is reenacted in Bennington.

In Maine, Rockland has its long-running Annual Lobster Festival near the start of the month. Wilton has a Blueberry Festival with many activities for the whole family and Rangeley and Machias also have blueberry festivals toward the end of the month. Mid-month, Perry has "The Gathering, Passamaquoddy Tribe," which includes traditional dance and the lighting of the sacred fire.

September Labor Day, the first Monday, honors workers, and signals the official end to the summer tourism season. It's the busiest vacation weekend of the season – everything is crowded, so advance reservations are essential.

The two weeks after Labor Day are an excellent time to travel in New England. School is in session so the crowds disappear, but almost all services are still open and prices drop somewhat. The weather is summer-like, but without the intensity of heat and humidity.

Mid-September brings the beginning of foliage season. Days are still pleasantly warm but nights are cool. Prices for tourist services rise a bit and inland resorts see a new surge of visitors. The fall foliage color spreads southward from Canada, often reaching its peak in southern New England by mid-October.

In Massachussetts, the Eastern States Exposition (the Big E) is a New England "state fair" in West Springfield. A Taste of the Berkshires in Great Barrington is an outdoor event celebrating the bounty of the area when restaurants offer samples and you can tour local farms. Hancock Shaker Village has the Autumn Farm

Weekend, which is a festival of the harvest in Pittsfield.

Mid-month in Connecticut, the Four Town Fair in Somers is the state's oldest fair with exhibits, a midway and fireworks. At the end of the month the Connecticut Antiques Show takes place in West Hartford.

The biggest Vermont fall festival is probably the Stratton Arts Festival, near Manchester, in which more than 200 artisans participate from mid-month to mid-November. There's also the Vermont State Fair early in the month in Rutland.

In New Hampshire the White Mountain Jazz and Blues Crafts Festival is held early in the month in North Conway.

In Maine, the annual Fiddle Contest and Old Time Country Music Show takes place the second weekend of the month in Kennebunk. Farmington has a Leaf Peeper Festival at the end of the month.

October The first half of October usually finds fall foliage blazing throughout New England. Beach resorts may be open, but are not particularly busy. Columbus Day, celebrated on the second Monday of the month, commemorates the landing of Christopher Columbus in the Bahamas on October 12, 1492. On Columbus Day weekend, country inns and other inland lodgings are all booked up well in advance, at high-season prices. Conventioneers often fill many city hotels. Sunny days are pleasantly warmish ("sweater weather"), but rainy days are chilly; nights are very brisk, with frost possible in northern New England.

After Columbus Day, many resorts, attractions and small local museums close for the winter, but enough services stay open to make travel possible. In fact, with a bit of luck, late October can be a wonderful time to travel. Prices for all services are low, the weather is usually brisk but agreeable and blazing pockets of fall foliage can be found everywhere except in extreme northern regions.

On Halloween (October 31, not a public holiday), children dress in costumes and go from house to house for "trick or treat," soliciting sweet treats and (rarely) threatening tricks if the treats aren't forthcoming. In Salem, MA, Haunted Happenings is a celebration of Halloween that includes events like the Psychic Fair.

Elsewhere in Massachusetts, look for harvest festivals in Westport, South Carver (cranberries!), Plimoth Plantation in Plymouth, and Old Sturbridge Village. In Cambridge (and Boston) the Head of the Charles Regatta is the world's largest single-day rowing event with championship events and races for all ages. In Lexington, it's Colonial Weekend at Minuteman National Historic Park.

In Southington, CT, the Apple Harvest Festival is celebrated over two weekends with entertainment and a carnival.

Vermont also has an Applefest held in South Hero the first weekend in October. The Annual Fall Festival of Vermont Craft Show in Montpelier is the first weekend of the month, with good foliage and outdoor fun. The Springfield Annual Vermont Apple Festival & Craft Show is held the first weekend of the month; Brattleboro also celebrates Apple Days then.

In Maine, Boothbay, York, Machias, Sunday River and Camden have annual Fall Foliage Festivals throughout the month with outdoor activities, craft fairs and entertainment.

November Early November is much like late October for travel in New England. With fall foliage color gone, the New England countryside shows a limited palette of gray shades. Many inns close, as foliage season is past and ski season has yet to begin. Hotel rates and transport fares are often quite reasonable.

The Veterans' Day (November 11, national holiday) remembers war veterans. This long weekend marks the opening of the ski season at resorts with snowmaking capabilities.

Thanksgiving, the fourth Thursday in November, is the busiest holiday of the year for travel throughout the US. Millions crowd highways, buses, trains and airplanes in order to be with relatives and friends for the dinner which recalls the feast the Pilgrims and their Wampanoag Indian neighbors shared in Plymouth, MA, in 1621. Peak travel times are the Wednesday just before Thanksgiving Day, and the Sunday following it. Avoid traveling on those days if possible. If not, have advance reservations, and allow plenty of time for delays.

In Massachusetts, Plimoth Plantation and Old Sturbridge Village celebrate Thanksgiving Day in traditional costume with traditional food and invite everyone.

The Friday after Thanksgiving also marks the beginning of the Christmas shopping season – shopping districts and malls are packed.

By late November, days are chilly and nights cold. The ground in northern New England is frozen hard, and there may be snowfalls anywhere in the region.

December By mid-December, the weather can be bitterly cold, with snowfalls from an inch or two to a foot. If there's freezing weather but no snow, the ice skating can be wonderful on the region's many glacial ponds.

Shopping districts in cities and towns are hectic with the annual pre-Christmas shopping spree. Transportation is crowded during the few days before and after Christmas (December 25), which is a national holiday. Between Christmas and the New Year, many New Englanders take short vacations to New York City.

In Massachusetts, Boston has two Christmas Tree Lightings: one at the Prudential Center downtown and another on Boston Common. There's also a reenactment of the Boston Tea Party. Cape Ann, as well as Nantucket, Stockbridge and Worcester County, celebrate a month-long Christmas Festival

In Rhode Island, Newport's Christmas celebrations start the first week of the month with decorated mansions, festivities and food.

In New Hampshire, Portsmouth's Strawbery Banke Museum celebrates Christmas the first two weekends of the month with activities and music.

Christmas by the Sea is popular in the Maine coastal towns of Livermore, Ogunquit and Thomaston.

On New Year's Eve (December 31), Boston, Burlington, VT, Providence, RI, Stamford and Hartford, CT, and other cities and towns hold First Night celebrations – winter festivals featuring parades, ice and snow sculpture exhibitions, concerts and other performances. New Year's Day (January 1) is a national holiday.

What to Bring
An umbrella or raincoat and hat are good to have any time of year.

From mid-June through early September, have cool summer clothing plus a sweater or jacket for evenings. A windbreaker is good for the mountains and the windy coast. If you plan to dine in fancy restaurants in Newport, Boston or other cosmopolitan centers, have a dress/jacket and tie.

In spring (April to May) and autumn (mid-September to late October or mid-November), there can be chilly mornings and afternoons, and cold nights approaching freezing, so have warmer clothes.

For the winter (mid-November through March) have cold-weather gear: fleece, woolens, waterproof footwear, warm hat and gloves. From mid-December through February, Boston can have several weeks where the temperature does not go above freezing. In northern New England, the cold lasts even longer and is more bitter.

If you take prescription medicines regularly, bring a supply of the medicine, not a prescription for it. Doctors are licensed by state, and their prescriptions are not normally accepted in any state except the one in which they are licensed.

Maps
The most detailed state highway maps are those distributed – usually for free – by state governments. You can call or write the state tourism offices in advance (see Tourist Offices) and have the maps sent, or you can

pick up the maps at highway tourism information offices when you enter the state on a major highway.

Other highway maps with sufficient detail to be useful for normal driving are for sale in fuel stations, bookstores, newsstands and at some shops and lodging places.

Local chambers of commerce usually hand out simple maps of their towns. These vary from useless advertisements to very detailed street maps.

The US Department of the Interior Geological Survey (USGS) topographical maps cover the USA at a scale of 1:24,000, showing every road, path and building (though some of these may be out of date). They are superb close-up maps for hiking or intensive exploration by car. They also publish a variety of other maps, including metropolitan and resort-destination maps at scales between 1:24,000 and 1:100,000, and state topographical maps at 1:500,000.

USGS maps may be ordered from their offices in Denver, CO 80225, or Reston, VA 22092. When you order maps, also request the folder describing topographic maps and the symbols used on them. For faster, easier service, you may order maps by mail from Boston's Globe Corner Bookstore (☎ 617-523-6658, 800-358-6013, fax 617-227-2771, info@gcb.com), 3 School St, Boston, MA 02108. They've posted a catalog of USGS maps on the Internet's World Wide Web at http://www.gcb.com/catalog/.

Hiking trail maps are available from outdoors organizations. See Trail Guides under the Books heading in this chapter.

Atlases

Visitors spending a significant amount of time in the region should get the appropriate state volume of atlases. The DeLorme Mapping series of atlases and gazetteers contain detailed topographic and highway maps as well as very helpful listings of campgrounds, historic sites, parks and even scenic drives. DeLorme doesn't cover all the states of New England, but look for similar atlases (such as Arrow) in good bookstores. Most cost about $20.

SUGGESTED ITINERARIES

There's no "right" way to see New England, but it can help to have sample itineraries. Modify and combine these to suit your interests. Try to visit cities on weekends and country towns and resorts on weekdays in summer or foliage season. This gets you lower prices and fewer crowds.

Less than a Week

With only three to five days, use Boston as your base. Plan to spend at least a half day walking the Freedom Trail (you may spend most of a day, though), and another half day at the Museum of Fine Arts and the Gardner Museum.

Any number of other excellent attractions can fill another half day: the Museum of Science, the New England Aquarium, and the Children's Museum are top picks.

If you're a shopper, schedule at least a half day at Downtown Crossing or strolling past the boutiques on Newbury St. Harvard Square requires a half day for a stroll through Harvard Yard and some shopping, or a full day to also visit Harvard's excellent museums.

For excursions, go west to Lexington (by car) and Concord (car or train), or north to Salem (car, bus or train) and Marblehead (car or bus). You could even do a day-trip to Plymouth (preferably by car or bus tour). In summer, excursion boats sail from Boston to Provincetown and back in a day, which is definitely the best way to go to the tip of Cape Cod on a day-trip, avoiding the long drive.

A Week or More

After spending several days in **Boston**, if you have a week or 10 days, you can really get a good taste of New England. Your itinerary will change depending upon the season, but consider these high points:

Stay at least one night in a fine old **Cape Cod** town. If you can stay two or three nights, spend one day on an excursion to one of the islands, Martha's Vineyard or Nantucket or, better, overnight there. Stop in Plymouth on the way to or from the Cape.

If it's summer or autumn, drive to the **Berkshires** and stay at least one night, stopping midway to tour Old Sturbridge Village. If you have two nights, that's even better. With three nights to spend, take in Williamstown or the Litchfield Hills of northwestern Connecticut.

In **Rhode Island**, spend a long half day in Providence, and at least one night in Newport touring the mansions and strolling the Cliff Walk. With another night to spend you can take in some sun on the Rhode Island beaches. Block Island requires at least a day of its own.

Drive north to New Hampshire's **White Mountains** for a few days of sightseeing, hiking, canoeing, white-water rafting or skiing, spending the nights in campgrounds or country inns. Two nights is the minimum to see central New Hampshire. With three, you can tour Lake Winnipesaukee as well.

Portsmouth, NH, Portland, ME, and the towns of the southern Maine coast are only a few hours' drive or bus ride from Boston, making them accessible for an overnight excursion. With two nights to spend you can take in Boothbay Harbor and even Camden, though you'll want at least a full day and preferably three or five days for a windjammer cruise along the Maine coast.

Two Weeks

With two weeks to spend, you'll have the time to see Boston and other top sights, and also venture to some of the more remote parts of New England, which are of special interest to outdoor enthusiasts.

In **Downeast Maine**, spend two nights on Mt Desert Island exploring Acadia National Park, a night or two (or more) on a windjammer and the rest of your time in any of the beautiful small coastal towns.

Spend three or four days in the wilds of **northern Maine** on a canoe or kayak excursion, or on a white-water rafting expedition, or hiking and camping. Rafting

is most exciting in the springtime when the rivers are at their highest and whitest.

Though southern **Vermont** is only a few hours' drive from Boston, it takes several more hours to get to the northern part of the state. With four or five days to devote to Vermont, spend a day and a half exploring Bennington, Brattleboro and a few of the pretty southern towns such as Newfane and Grafton. Then drive north along VT 100 through the center of the state, camping or staying at inns. There are lots of organized activities at Killington: in winter, downhill skiing, snowboarding and cross-country skiing; in summer, hiking and mountain biking.

Make a detour to beautiful Woodstock, then continue north via Waitsfield to Stowe for a hike on the Long Trail or, in winter, skiing. Finish with a visit to friendly Burlington and the Shelburne Museum.

Take a day or two to visit New Haven and the historic towns of the **Connecticut** coast. After at least a day at Mystic Seaport Museum, head up the Connecticut River Valley. Stop at Hartford for a half day on your way to Lake Waramaug and the Litchfield Hills, or go on via Sturbridge, MA, and Old Sturbridge Village.

HIGHLIGHTS
Boston

Among cities, Boston comes first. Explore the Freedom Trail, major art and science museums, parks and gardens and neighboring Cambridge, home of Harvard University and its museums. Historic Lexington and Concord, Salem and Marblehead, Gloucester and Rockport or Plymouth all make great day trips.

Cape Cod & Islands

Next top sights, at least in summer, are Cape Cod and the islands of Nantucket and Martha's Vineyard.

Central Massachusetts & Berkshires

In central Massachusetts the prime attraction is Old Sturbridge Village, the recreated 17th-century town populated by "interpreters" in period dress. In western

Massachusetts, visit the Berkshires fine old summer vacation resorts, or attend a performance at the Tanglewood Music Festival, Jacob's Pillow Dance Festival or the Williamstown Theater Festival.

Rhode Island

In Rhode Island, Newport is a must-see. Tour the palatial mansions and enjoy the seaside ambiance. Spend at least an afternoon on one of the great beaches or take an excursion (at least a day) to Block Island.

Connecticut

Visit Hartford to see Mark Twain's mansion at Nook Farm. New Haven has Yale University and several excellent museums. Mystic and New London are the centers of the state's maritime activities. Mystic Seaport Museum is a recreated maritime town of the 1800s. New London is the home of the US Coast Guard Academy, and neighboring Groton has a Navy submarine base.

For the prettiest Connecticut scenery, go to the picturesque towns at the mouth of the Connecticut River (Essex, Old Lyme, Ivoryton) or to the Litchfield Hills in the northwestern corner of the state.

Vermont

In northern New England drive and walk in the Green Mountains, preferably along VT 100, which threads its way from south to north through the center of the state. The most charming towns are Bennington, Dorset, Grafton, Manchester, Middlebury, Stowe and Woodstock. The city of Burlington is also worth a stop, or a day trip from Stowe. Be sure to see the vast Shelburne Museum south of Burlington.

New Hampshire

In New Hampshire, you should see Portsmouth and the restored, historic Strawbery Banke on the coast, and perhaps make brief stops at Manchester (for the Currier Gallery of Art) and Concord (the state capital) on your way to Lake Winnipesaukee for water sports and the White Mountain National Forest for hiking and camping. Check out the beauties of Franconia Notch State Park north of Lincoln, then don't miss the scenic drive along the Kancamagus Hwy (NH 112) between Lincoln and Conway. North Conway is the outdoors center of the region.

Maine

Enjoy the beach resort towns along the southern coast, then head to Portland. Go "Downeast," stopping in several of the wonderful coastal towns and villages (Blue Hill, Boothbay Harbor, Camden, Castine, Pemaquid Point) before reaching Bar Harbor and Acadia National Park. Those looking for outdoor adventure should consider an excursion to the lakes and mountains of north-central Maine.

TOURIST OFFICES
State Tourist Offices

State tourism offices will send you excellent detailed road maps, lists of lodgings, festivals and special events, and other materials before your trip.

They also maintain "welcome centers" at major highway entrances to their states. Typically, you drive across the state line into a new state, and the next exit will have a welcome center with toilets, picnic area, vending machines for hot and cold drinks and snacks and an information desk dispensing maps, camping, lodging and restaurant lists and brochures.

Here are the main addresses for state-run tourist offices:

Massachusetts Office of Travel & Tourism (☎ 617-727-3201, 800-227-6277 ext 300, fax 617-727-6525) 100 Cambridge St, 13th floor, Boston, MA 02202 http://ftp.std.com/NE/masstravel.html

Rhode Island Tourism Division (☎ 401-277-2601, 800-556-2484, fax 401-277-2102) 7 Jackson Walkway, Providence, RI 02903 http://www.ids.net/ri/ritour.html

Connecticut Dept. of Economic Development (☎ 203-258-4200, 800-282-6863; fax 203-563-4877) 865 Brook St, Rocky Hill, CT 06067 http://ctguide.atlantic.com/vacguide/

Vermont Travel & Tourism
(☎ 802-828-3236, 800-837-6668, fax 802-828-3233; faxback system 800-833-9756) 134 State St, Montpelier, VT 05602
http://www.genghis.com/tourism/vermont.htm
New Hampshire Office of Travel & Tourism Development
(☎ 603-271-2666, 800-386-4664 ext 145, fax 603-271-2629) 172 Pembroke Rd, PO Box 1856, Concord, NH 03302-0856
http://www.VisitNH.com/
Maine Office of Tourism
(☎ 207-623-0363, 800-533-9595, fax 207-623-0288) 189 State St, State House Station 59, Augusta, ME 04333
http://www.state.me.us/decd/tour/
Maine Publicity Bureau
(☎ 207-287-5711, 800-533-9595, fax 207-287-5701) Box 2300, 97 Winthrop St, Hallowell, ME 04347

Chambers of Commerce

The address and telephone number of each chamber of commerce or other tourist office is given in the Information headings under each town.

Sometimes called convention and visitors' bureaus, these are membership organizations for local businesses: hotels, restaurants, shops and any other commercial establishment. They always provide maps and lots of information that can be very useful. They rarely provide information about establishments which are not chamber members, however, and this sometimes means they don't know about the cheapest or smallest establishments.

Local chambers of commerce usually maintain an information booth at the entrance to the town or in the town center, usually open only during tourist seasons (summer, foliage season, ski season, etc). It may also have a separate business office (ie, not an information office) elsewhere. Some chamber information offices will help you to make reservations at member lodgings.

Tourist Offices Abroad

US Embassies will often have tourist information (see Embassies). The USTTA was, until 1995, the USA's overseas tourism

information office. In that year it lost its government funding. A successor organization, to be funded privately, had not been established when this guide went to press. Until there is another organization, contact your travel agency for options.

In the UK, you can also contact the New England tourism office (☎ 01732 742 777). Or write to Discover New England, Seven Oaks, Kent TN14 5BQ. Be sure to include two letter-mail stamps so they'll send you something back.

VISAS & DOCUMENTS
Visas

Canadians must have proper proof of Canadian citizenship, such as a citizenship card with photo ID or a passport. Visitors from other countries must have a valid passport and most visitors also require a US visa.

However, there is a reciprocal visa-waiver program in which citizens of certain countries may enter the USA for stays of 90 days or less without first obtaining a US visa. Currently these countries are the UK, New Zealand, Japan, Italy, Spain, Austria, the Netherlands, Belgium, Switzerland, France, Germany, Norway, Denmark, Sweden, Finland, Iceland, San Marino, Andorra, Luxembourg, Liechtenstein and Monaco. Under this program you must have a roundtrip ticket that is non-refundable in the USA and you will not be allowed to extend your stay beyond 90 days.

Other travelers will need to obtain a visa from a US consulate or embassy. In most countries the process can be done by mail.

Your passport should be valid for at least six months longer than your intended stay in the USA and you'll need to submit a recent photo (37 x 37 mm) with the application. Documents of financial stability and/or guarantees from a US resident are sometimes required, particularly for those from Third World countries.

Visa applicants may be required to "demonstrate binding obligations" that will insure their return back home. Because of this requirement, those planning to travel through other countries before arriving in the USA are generally better off applying for their US visa while they are still in their home country – rather than while on the road.

The validity period for US visitor visas depends on what country you're from. The length of time you'll be allowed to stay in the USA is ultimately determined by US immigration authorities at the port of entry.

Incidentally, the infamous prohibition against issuing visas to people who "have been members of communist organizations" has been dropped. An anachronism of the Cold War, it still appears on the visa applications although most consular offices have penned a line through the item.

Visa Extensions

If you want to stay in the USA longer than the date stamped in your passport, contact the local office of the Justice Department's Immigration & Naturalization Service (INS) *before* the stamped date. In Boston, call the INS at ☎ 617-565-3879 for information, or ☎ 800-870-3676 for forms. The Boston office is in the John F Kennedy Federal Office Building, 5th floor, Government Center, Boston, MA 02203; take the subway to the Government Center station.

If you remain more than a few days past the expiration date the INS may assume you want to work illegally. At an interview with the INS you will need to explain why you didn't leave by the expiry date and convince the officials you're not looking for work and that you have enough money to support yourself until you do leave. It's a good idea to bring a US citizen with you to vouch for your character and to have some verification that you have enough currency to support yourself.

Photocopies

It's a good idea to make photocopies of your important travel documents and to keep the copies in a different, safe place from the documents themselves. If your documents are lost or stolen, replacing them will be much easier.

International Driving Permit

An International Driving Permit is a useful accessory for foreign visitors in the USA. Local traffic police are more likely to accept it as valid identification than an unfamiliar document from another country. Your national automobile association can provide one for a nominal fee. They're usually valid for one year.

Automobile Association Card

If you plan on doing a lot of driving in the USA, it might be beneficial to join your national automobile association. Members of the American Automobile Association (AAA) or an affiliated automobile club can get lodging, car rental and sightseeing admission discounts with membership cards. See the Useful Organizations section in this chapter for more information.

Hostelling International Card

Most hostels in the USA are members of Hostelling International/American Youth Hostels (HI/AYH). For more information on HI/AYH, see the Useful Organizations section; also see Hostels, under Accommodations in this chapter.

Student Identification

In college towns such as Boston, Cambridge, Hanover or New Haven, your student ID card can sometimes get you discounts. Museums and attractions outside these cities may also give small discounts to students, and you'll need a card to prove you are one.

EMBASSIES
US Embassies & Consulates Abroad

US diplomatic offices abroad include the following:

Australia
  US Embassy: 21 Moonah Place, Yarralumla ACT 2600 (☎ (6) 270 5900)
  US Consulate General: Level 59 MLC Center 19-29 Martin Place, Sydney NSW 2000 (☎ (2) 373 9200)
  There are also consulates in Melbourne, Perth and Brisbane.

Austria
  Boltzmanngasse 16, A-1091, Vienna (☎ (1) 313-39)
Canada
  US Embassy: 100 Wellington St, Ottawa, Ontario 1P 5T1 (☎ (613) 238-5335)
  US Consulate General: 1095 West Pender St, Vancouver, BC V6E 2M6 (☎ (604) 685-1930)
  US Consulate General: 1155 Rue St-Alexandre, Montréal, Québec (☎ (514) 398-9695)
  There are also consulates in Toronto, Calgary and Halifax.
Denmark
  Dag Hammarskjolds Allé 24, Copenhagen (☎ 31 42 31 44)
Finland
  Itainen Puistotie 14A, Helsinki (☎ (0) 171-931)
France
  US Embassy, 2 Rue Saint Florentin, 75001 Paris (☎ (1) 42.96.12.02)
  There are also consulates in Bordeaux, Lyon, Marseille, Nice, Strasbourg and Toulouse.
Germany
  Deichmanns Aue 29, 53179 Bonn (☎ (228) 33 91)
Greece
  91 Vasilissis Sophias Blvd, 10160 Athens (☎ (1) 721-2951)
India
  Shanti Path, Chanakyapuri 110021, New Delhi (☎ (11) 60-0651)
Ireland
  42 Elgin Rd, Ballsbridge, Dublin (☎ (1) 687 122)
Israel
  71 Hayarkon St, Tel Aviv (☎ (3) 517-4338)
Italy
  Via Vittorio Veneto 119a-121, Rome (☎ (6) 46 741)
Japan
  1-10-5 Akasaka Chome, Minato-ku, Tokyo (☎ (3) 224-5000)
Mexico
  Paseo de la Reforma 305, Cuauhtémoc, 06500 Mexico City (☎ (5) 211-00-42)
Netherlands
  US Embassy: Lange Voorhout 102, 2514 EJ The Hague (☎ (70) 310 92 09)
  US Consulate General: Museumplein 19, 1071 DJ Amsterdam (☎ (20) 664-4834)
New Zealand
  29 Fitzherbert Terrace, Thorndon, Wellington (☎ (4) 722 068)
Norway
  Drammensvein 18, Oslo (☎ (22) 44 85 50)

South Africa
  877 Pretorius St, Box 9536, Pretoria 0001 (☎ (12) 342-1048)
Spain
  Calle Serrano 75, 28006 Madrid (☎ (1) 577 4000)
Sweden
  Strandvagen 101, S-115 89 Stockholm (☎ (8) 783 5300)
Switzerland
  Jubilaumsstrasse 93, 3005 Berne (☎ (31) 357 70 11)
Thailand
  95 Wireless Rd, Bangkok (☎ (2) 252-5040)
UK
  US Embassy, 5 Upper Grosvenor St, London W1 (☎ (0171) 499 9000)
  US Consulate General, 3 Regent Terrace, Edinburgh EH7 5BW (☎ (031) 556 8315)
  US Consulate General, Queens House, Belfast BT1 6EQ (☎ (0232) 328 239)

Embassies & Consulates in the USA

All embassies are in Washington, DC. Some countries maintain consulates, honorary consuls or consular agents in Boston and/or New York City. To get the telephone number of an embassy or consulate, call the directory assistance number for the city in which you hope to find a consulate (Boston: ☎ 617-555-1212, New York: ☎ 212-555-1212, Washington: ☎ 202-555-1212).

Australia
  Embassy: 1601 Massachusetts Ave NW, Washington, DC 20036 (☎ 202-797-3000, fax 202-797-3168)
  Boston Consul: Honorary Consul Margaret Stanzier, 20 Beacon St, Boston, MA 02108 (☎ 617-248-8655)
  New York Consulate: International Bldg, 636 Fifth Ave, New York, NY 10111 (☎ 212-245-4000)
Canada
  Embassy: 501 Pennsylvania Ave NW, Washington, DC 20001 (☎ 202-682-1740, fax 202-682-7624)
  Boston Consulate: 3 Copley Place, Suite 400, Boston, MA 02116 (☎ 617-262-3760)
  New York Consulate: 1251 Avenue of the Americas (Sixth Ave), 16th floor, New York, NY 10020-1175 (☎ 212-768-2400, fax 212-768-2440)
Denmark
  Embassy: 3200 Whitehaven St NW,

Washington, DC 20008 (☎ 202-234-4300)
Boston Consul: Honorary Consul Christian G Halby, 419 Boylston St, Boston, MA 02116 (☎ 617-266-8418)
New York Consul: Honorary Consulate, 825 Third Ave, 32nd floor, New York, NY 10022 (☎ 212-223-4545)

Finland
Embassy: 3301 Massachusetts Ave NW, Washington, DC 20008 (☎ 202-298-5800)

France
Embassy: 4101 Reservoir Rd NW, Washington, DC 20007 (☎ 202-944-6000, fax 202-944-6072)
Boston Consulate General: 3 Commonwealth Ave, Boston, MA 02116 (☎ 617-266-1680)
New York Consulate General: 934 Fifth Ave, New York, NY 10021 (☎ 212-606-3699)

Germany
Embassy: 4645 Reservoir Rd NW, Washington, DC 20007 (☎ 202-298-4000)
Boston Consulate General: 3 Copley Place, Suite 500, Boston, MA 02116 (☎ 617-536-4414, fax 617-536-8573)
New York Consulate General: 460 Park Ave, New York, NY 10022 (☎ 212-308-8700)

India
Embassy: 2107 Massachusetts Ave NW, Washington, DC 20008 (☎ 202-939-7000)

Ireland
Embassy: 2234 Massachusetts Ave NW, Washington, DC 20008 (☎ 202-462-3939)
Boston Consulate: Chase Bldg, 535 Boylston St, Boston, MA 02116 (☎ 617-267-9330)
New York Consulate: 515 Madison Ave, New York, NY 10022 (☎ 212-319-2555)

Israel
Embassy: 3514 International Drive NW, Washington, DC 20008 (☎ 202-364-5500)

Italy
Embassy: 1601 Fuller St NW, Washington, DC 20009 (☎ 202-328-5500)
Boston Consulate General, 100 Boylston St, Suite 900, Boston, MA 02116 (☎ 617-542-0483)
New York Consulate General: 690 Park Ave, New York, NY 10021 (☎ 212-737-9100)

Japan
Embassy: 2520 Massachusetts Ave NW, Washington, DC 20008 (☎ 202-939-6700)

Mexico
Embassy: 1911 Pennsylvania Ave NW, Washington, DC 20006 (☎ 202-728-1600)

Netherlands
Embassy: 4200 Linnean Ave NW, Washington, DC 20008 (☎ 202-244-5300)

Boston Consulate: 6 St James Ave, Boston MA 02116 (☎ 617-542-8452)

New Zealand
Embassy: 37 Observatory Circle NW, Washington, DC 20008 (☎ 202-328-4800)

Norway
Embassy: 2720 34th St NW, Washington, DC 20008 (☎ 202-333-6000)
New York Consulate General: 825 Third Ave, 38th floor, New York, NY 10022-7584 (☎ 212-421-7333, fax 212-754-0583)

Sweden
Embassy: 1501 M St NW, Washington, DC 20005-1702 (☎ 202-467-2600, fax 202-467-2699)
Boston Consulate: 286 Congress St, 6th floor, Boston, MA 02210 (☎ 617-350-0111)
New York Consulate: 1 Dag Hammarskjøld Plaza, New York, NY 10017 (☎ 212-751-5900)

Switzerland
Embassy: 2900 Cathedral Ave NW, Washington, DC 20008 (☎ 202-745-7900)

UK
Embassy: 3100 Massachusetts Ave NW, Washington, DC 20008 (☎ 202-462-1340)
Boston Consulate General: Prudential Tower, Suite 4740, Boston, MA 02199 (☎ 617-437-7160)
New York Consulate General: 845 Third Ave, New York, NY 10022 (☎ 212-752-8400)

CUSTOMS

US customs allows each person 21 years of age or older to bring one liter of liquor and 200 cigarettes duty-free into the USA. US citizens are allowed to import, duty free, $400 worth of gifts from abroad while non-US citizens are allowed to bring in $100 worth. Should you be carrying more than $10,000 in US and foreign cash, traveler's checks, money orders and the like, you need to declare the excess amount. There is no legal restriction on the amount which may be imported, but undeclared sums may be subject to confiscation.

MONEY
Cash

Most of the world knows that the US currency is the dollar ($), divided into 100 cents (¢). Coins are of 1¢ (penny), 5¢ (nickel), 10¢ (dime), 25¢ (quarter),

HIV & Entering the USA

Everyone entering the USA who is not a US citizen is subject to the authority of the Immigration & Naturalization Service (INS). The INS can keep someone from entering or staying in the USA by excluding or deporting them. This is especially relevant to travelers with HIV (Human Immunodeficiency Virus). Though being HIV-positive is not grounds for deportation, it is a "ground of exclusion" and the INS can invoke this rule and refuse to admit visitors to the country.

Although the INS doesn't test people for HIV at the point of entry into the USA, they may try to exclude anyone who answers yes to this question on the non-immigrant visa application form: "Have you ever been afflicted with a communicable disease of public health significance?" INS officials may also stop people if they seem sick, are carrying AIDS/HIV medicine or, sadly, if the officer happens to think the person looks gay, though sexual orientation is not legally a ground of exclusion. A visitor may be deported if the INS later finds that they have HIV but did not declare it. Being HIV-positive is not a "ground for deportation" but failing to provide correct information on the visa application is.

If you do have HIV, but can prove to consular officials you are the spouse, parent, or child of a US citizen or legal permanent resident (green-card holder), you are exempt from the exclusionary law.

It is imperative that visitors know and assert their rights. Immigrants and visitors who may face exclusion should discuss their rights and options with a trained immigration advocate within the USA before applying for a visa. For legal immigration information and referrals to immigration advocates, contact The National Immigration Project of the National Lawyers Guild (☎ 617-227-9727), 14 Beacon St, Suite 506, Boston, MA 02108; or Immigrant HIV Assistance Project, Bar Association of San Francisco (☎ 415-267-0795), 685 Market St, Suite 700, San Francisco, CA 94105. ■

50¢ (rare half dollar) and $1. Notes ("bills") are of $1, $2 (rare), $5, $10, $20, $50 and $100.

Credit Cards

Major credit and charge cards are accepted by car rental agencies and most hotels, restaurants, fuel stations, shops and larger grocery stores. Many recreational and tourist activities can also be paid for by credit card. The most commonly accepted cards are Visa, MasterCard (EuroCard, Access) and American Express. However, Discover and Diners Club cards are also accepted by a fair number of businesses.

You'll find it hard to perform certain transactions without one. Ticket buying services, for instance, won't reserve tickets over the phone unless you offer a credit card number, and it's difficult to rent a car without a credit card (you may have to put down a cash deposit of several hundred dollars). Even if you prefer traveler's checks and ATMs, it's a good idea to have a Visa or MasterCard for emergencies.

Lost or Stolen Cards If you lose your credit cards or they get stolen contact the company immediately. Following are toll-free numbers for the main credit card companies.

American Express	☎ 800-528-4800
Diners Club	☎ 800-234-6377
Discover	☎ 800-347-2683
MasterCard	☎ 800-826-2181
Visa	☎ 800-336-8472

ATMs

Cash (cashpoint, debit) cards from many banks may be used to pay at hotels, restaurants, shops, fuel stations, etc, and to obtain cash from Automated Teller Machines (ATMs). Look for ATMs in or near banks, shopping malls, large supermarkets, airports, train stations and on busy streets. Most are available for use 24 hours a day. In urban settings, use caution at ATMs after dark. In order for your card to be useful in New England, the bank that issued it must be a member of one of the large interbank card systems such as Cirrus, Interlink, Plus Systems or Star Systems. Ask at your bank before leaving home whether your card can be used in New England. Contact your bank if you lose your card.

Currency Exchange

Only a few banks, mostly in Boston, are prepared to exchange foreign cash. If you are coming to the US from abroad, you should plan on using your bank cash card (ATM card, cashpoint card, etc) to obtain cash most easily at the most advantageous rate of exchange. Also plan to use your major credit card (Visa, MasterCard/Euro-Card/Access, Diners Club, American Express) often. If you have neither of these kinds of plastic money, plan to buy US dollar traveler's checks before leaving home, or upon arrival in the US.

Nearly all banks will buy and sell Canadian currency; some businesses near the border will offer to accept Canadian dollars "at par," meaning that they will accept Canadian dollars at the same rate as US dollars.

There are Baybanks (☎ 800-451-1809) foreign currency exchange booths at Boston's Logan Airport in Terminals C (☎ 617-569-1172) and E (☎ 617-567-2313). Baybank has 10 other exchange locations in Boston and Cambridge, including its main office in Harvard Square (☎ 617-556-6050) at 1414 Massachusetts Ave, Cambridge. It also has 90 other locations throughout Massachusetts that are prepared to exchange foreign currency. Call ☎ 617-788-5000 for locations.

Exchange Rates

At press time, exchange rates were:

Australia	A$1	=	$0.79
Canada	C$1	=	$0.74
Germany	DM1	=	$0.65
Hong Kong	HK$10	=	$1.30
Japan	¥100	=	$0.95
New Zealand	NZ$1	=	$0.69
UK	UK£1	=	$1.51

COSTS

New England is among the more expensive regions in the USA for travel, but it is worth the expense. You can travel quite cheaply here if you know how.

What you spend depends upon several factors: when and where you travel, how you travel, and your age.

Seasonal Costs

New England's busiest travel seasons are July and August (high summer or in-season), and from late September through mid-October (foliage season, also considered in-season). Prices for hotels, transportation and attractions are generally highest then. (See Planning above.)

City vs Country

Generally speaking, accommodations in cities are more expensive during the week, less expensive on Friday, Saturday and sometimes Sunday nights. In small towns, resorts and the countryside, inns and motels are cheapest during the week, more expensive on weekends. Thus you should plan to visit cities on weekends, and venture out into the country during the week, if possible.

Budget Ranges

Bottom End The cheapest way to see New England is to camp with a tent, share a rental car among four people, and have picnics for lunch. Traveling this way, your daily budget for food, lodging and transport can be as low as $20 to $30 per person; figure $5 to $10 more per day if you plan to spend more time in the big cities or resorts. Remember that it's only practical to camp from May through mid-October.

Middle A couple staying in budget motels, eating breakfast and lunch in fast food places or lunchrooms, dinner in moderately priced little restaurants, and getting around by rental car, can expect to spend between $60 and $75 per person per day. If you spend lots of time in resorts and cities, your costs might be $75 to $95 per person.

Top End Two people touring in a rental car staying at luxury-class hotels, motels and inns and dining as they please should expect to spend $100 to $150 per person per day.

Tipping

Americans are liberal tippers. Occasionally, not giving the appropriate tip may earn you scorn from the untipped service provider. At take-out food counters there may be a jar or other container labeled "tips" into which you may throw a few coins if you like. If you sit down in a restaurant, bar or lounge, be prepared to tip 10% for mundane service, 15% for good service or up to 20% for exceptional service. If you leave under 10%, it will be interpreted as foreign ignorance or a purposeful insult (which may be what you intend). Tip in cash on the table, or add it to your credit card slip in the appropriate space.

Most hotels and inns allow you to find your room and carry your bags up by yourself if you prefer.

Discounts

At some state tourism information centers there are racks of brochures for hotels, motels, inns, restaurants, tours and attractions. Some offer discounts to travelers who have handbills or coupons given out at the information centers. For some lodgings, you must call and make a reservation from the information center to obtain the discount.

Also, call the state tourism office for their brochure, which will come in the mail and often contains coupons for car rental, hotel, motel and restaurant chains.

If you are a member of the American Automobile Association (☎ 407-444-8000, fax 444-8030), 1000 AAA Drive, Heathrow, FL 32746, substantial hotel discounts may be available to you. It's certainly worth calling AAA for more information.

Students Some museums and attractions offer slightly lower rates to college students. Though there are many special student deals available in college towns like Boston, often these special rates for cultural attractions are available only through individual colleges and universities. You must buy your tickets through the university, not at the attraction itself.

Families Virtually all hotels and motels allow one or two children to share their parents' room at no extra charge. If a rollaway bed is needed, there may be a charge (often $10 to $20). Usually, children must be younger than 18 years of age. At country

---

Tipping Guidelines

Bartenders	10% to 15% of the bill
Cinemas, theaters	no tip
Coat checkrooms	75¢ to $1 per coat
Doorman (hotel or restaurant)	$1 at top hotels for calling a cab, getting your car from the parking lot, or other direct service
Drivers who handle your luggage	$1 (not required)
Fast-food restaurants	no tip
Fuel station attendants	no tip
Hairdressers, barbers	about 15%
Hotel housekeepers	$2 to $3 per day in expensive hotels
Luggage porters	75¢ to $1 per piece
Restaurant or nightclub waitstaff	15% to 20% of the bill
Taxi drivers	12% to 18% of the fare
Valet parking	75¢ to $1 if attendant brings your car to you

inns and B&Bs, however, this policy does not usually apply. In fact, many country inns do not allow young children as guests.

Most activities and attractions, including museums, theme parks, whale-watch expeditions, etc, offer reduced admission charges for children. Some offer special family rates; always ask if they do.

Some outdoor attractions (concerts, state parks, beaches, etc) charge admission by the car: one person or seven inside, the charge is the same.

Seniors Older travelers are eligible for discounts at attractions, museums, parks, in many hotels, on rental cars, trains and buses, and other items. The age at which discounts apply varies and you must have photo identification as proof of your age. See Senior Travelers under Useful Organizations, below, for more information.

Taxes
There is no national sales tax (such as VAT) in the USA. Some states levy sales taxes, and states and cities/towns may levy taxes on hotel rooms and restaurant meals. Room and meal taxes are not normally included in prices quoted to you, even though (or perhaps because) they may increase your final bill by as much as 11% or 12%. Be sure to ask about taxes when you ask for hotel room rates.

Taxes on transport services (bus, rail, and air tickets, gasoline, taxi rides) are usually included in the ticket price quoted to you.

POST & COMMUNICATIONS
There's a post office in virtually every town and village, providing the familiar postal services such as parcel shipping and international express mail.

Private shippers such as United Parcel Service (UPS) and Federal Express (FedEx) ship much of the nation's load of parcels and important time-sensitive documents. They ship worldwide as well.

Postal Rates
US postal rates are fairly cheap and fairly stable, changing every few years. The next change, a rise of about 10%, may come in 1997. Currently, rates for 1st-class mail within the USA are 32¢ for letters up to one ounce (23¢ for each additional ounce) and 20¢ for postcards.

International airmail rates (except Canada and Mexico) are 60¢ for a half-ounce letter, 95¢ for a one-ounce letter and 39¢ for each additional half ounce. International postcard rates are 40¢. Letters to Canada are 46¢ for a one-ounce letter, 23¢ for each additional ounce and 30¢ for a postcard. Letters to Mexico are 35¢ for a half-ounce letter, 45¢ for a one-ounce letter and 30¢ for a postcard. Aerogrammes are 45¢.

Sending Mail
Packages must be securely wrapped in sturdy containers to be accepted for international shipment, especially if you expect to insure them. If you want to send a letter or parcel by Registered Mail, be sure it is sealed with glue or paper tape (not cellophane or masking tape) so that the seams can be stamped with the postmark of the originating postal station.

Receiving Mail
Poste restante is called "general delivery" in the US. If you are sending (or expecting) mail to be held at the post office in a certain city or town, it should be addressed:

Taxes			
State	*Meal*	*Lodging*	*Sales*
Massachusetts	5%	5.7%	5%
Rhode Island	6%	11%	6%
Connecticut	8%	8%	8%
Vermont	6%	–	6%
New Hampshire	8%	8%	–
Maine	5%	5%	5%

Your name
General Delivery
(*Optional:* Station Name)
Town, State, ZIP Code
USA

Mail is usually held for 10 days before it's returned to the sender; you might request your correspondents to write "hold for arrival" on their letters.

In large cities it's a good idea to put the optional station name if you know it. If you do not put the ZIP code or station name, your mail will be held at the main station (central post office), which may not be the most convenient one for you, though it will have the longest hours of operation.

When you go to pick up your mail, have some form of photo identification with you. Your passport is best.

Alternatively, have mail sent to the local representative of American Express or Thomas Cook, which provide mail service for their clients.

Telephone

Telephone service is good, convenient and not particularly expensive, but the plethora of private companies, policies and rates is very confusing even for Americans. Some smaller companies charge much higher rates than the large companies; some charge lower rates. In general, the best policy is to use the larger companies such as Bell Atlantic, AT&T, MCI and Sprint. Look for these names and/or logos on the public phone you're calling from.

How to Place a Call Within a city or town (or to dial from anyplace in Rhode Island to any other place in Rhode Island), press the last seven digits of the number. To call to a nearby city or town within the same area code, you may be able to dial only the last seven digits or you may have to dial "1" plus the area code.

Massachusetts has three area codes: 617 for Boston and vicinity, 508 for other towns in eastern Massachusetts and 413 for central and western Massachusetts. Connecticut has two area codes: 860 for most of the state, including Hartford, and 203 for Fairfield and New Haven Counties which include Bridgeport and New Haven in the southeastern corner of the state.

Each of the other New England states has only one area code: 401 for Rhode Island, 802 for Vermont, 603 for New Hampshire and 207 for Maine.

From a town in one area code to a town in another, dial ☎ 1 + area code + the number. This method is used to call from Boston to nearby Lexington, or to California, or to Bermuda and Canada.

For calls to other countries from a public phone, press "0" (zero) for an operator and ask for an international operator.

Cost of Calling Local calls cost from 10¢ to 25¢ for three minutes or more, depending upon the town.

Because of the byzantine rate structure, regional calls (anywhere from two miles to 200 miles) are often the most expensive domestic calls, costing from 60¢ to $1 and up per three-minute call. In some cases it is cheaper to call from Boston to California than from Boston to Worcester.

Long-distance domestic calls can cost as low as 15¢ per minute if dialed from a home phone, but will be more like 25¢ to 75¢ per minute from a public coin telephone. Telephone company credit card calls may cost several dollars for the first minute, but only 25¢ to 35¢ for subsequent minutes.

Foreign calls vary by the country being called, the telephone being used (public or private), the time of day and the day of the week. US rates are generally competitive with, and often cheaper than, public-phone rates in other countries.

Paying for Calls Most public telephones in the USA accept only coins (5¢, 10¢, 25¢); some accept credit cards instead. For local and short calls to other points in the USA, using coins is easy enough. However, there are ways to pay for calls which are more convenient than feeding a stack of quarters into the phone to make an overseas call.

Some telephones in airports and large hotels allow payment by credit card. There may be a slot to slide your card into, or you may have to punch in your credit card number.

Compared to the easy-to-use Japanese and French debit card systems, those in the USA are confusing, cumbersome and expensive. You purchase a telephone debit card from a convenience store, phone company office or at a tourist information office. Cards are usually sold in denominations of $5, $10, $20 and $40 or $50, and offer calls in the USA for about 50¢ to 60¢ per minute; $1.80 per minute to Canada and the UK; $2.40 to Europe; or $3 per minute to Asian and Pacific countries.

The card often has no magnetic stripe or microchip, but rather just an account number. The card should be sealed in paper when you buy it, to keep the number secret. Follow the calling instructions on the card, which usually requires that you punch in 35 or so digits altogether. As you talk, the time on the line is deducted from your account. If someone gets your account number, they can make calls using your money. They don't need the card itself.

Typical of these cards is the AT&T TeleTicket, sold at AT&T Phone Stores. Call ☎ 800-462-1818 for information on the cards and the locations of phone stores selling them. MCI and Sprint have similar phone card schemes.

Email & Fax

A growing amount of communication in the USA is done by email, but there are currently few public facilities where you can send or receive it.

Fax is another matter entirely. Many small businesses such as pharmacies, parcel mailing shops (Mailboxes, Etc and others), printshops (PIP, Alphagraphics and others) have fax machines to and from which you can communicate by fax for a fee. The fee is usually not particularly cheap, perhaps a dollar or two for the first page sent or received, and 50¢ or $1 for each subsequent page, plus phone charges (for outgoing calls).

BOOKS

For literature, see that section in Facts about New England.

Travel Guides

It is hoped that the guidebook you have in your hands can provide you with all of the information you may need on a first, second or later tour through New England. But obviously, no one book can tell all travelers everything they want to know.

For exploring New England's several states in greater detail, the Explorer's Guide series by The Countryman Press is the best. *Cape Cod and the Islands: An Explorer's Guide*, by Kimberly Grant, has 390 pages on that area alone. These guides are available at bookstores in New England, or from The Countryman Press, PO Box 175, Woodstock, VT 05091-0175.

A guide specific to Boston's historic and modern architecture is Susan & Michael Southworth's *The Boston Society of Architects' AIA Guide to Boston*, 2nd edition. It details general walking tours as well as specific buildings not only in the city, but also in Charlestown and Cambridge.

Trail Guides

Excellent, detailed trail guides (with maps) of the Appalachian Trail and the White Mountain National Forest trail system are published by the Appalachian Mountain Club (AMC, ☎ 617-523-0636), 5 Joy St, Boston, MA 02108.

The Green Mountain Club (☎ 802-244-7037), RR1, Box 650, Waterbury Center, VT 05677, publishes some excellent hikers' materials, including the *Guide Book of the Long Trail* ($10), complete with 16 color topographical maps. The Long Trail is a primitive footpath which follows the crest of Vermont's Green Mountains 265 miles from Canada to Massachusetts, with 175 miles of side trails and 62 rustic cabins and lean-tos for shelter.

History

How New England Happened, by Christina Tree (Little, Brown and Co) is the definitive traveler's history of the region.

FILMS

Little Women (1994), Louisa May Alcott's wonderful book about girls growing up in 19th-century Concord, MA, has been made into a movie starring Susan Sarandon as Marmie.

Jaws (1975), the improbable but still terrifying story of a great white shark attacking swimmers on New England beaches, is widely available on video.

On Golden Pond (1981), the story of two lovers in their declining years, was filmed at New Hampshire's Squam Lake, and features fine performances by Henry Fonda and Katharine Hepburn.

John Huston's classic *Moby Dick* (1956), with Gregory Peck and Orson Welles, is a wonderful introduction to New England maritime life in the 19th century.

School Ties, the story of a working-class scholarship student at an elite New England prep school, was filmed at the Middlesex School in Concord, Massachusetts. *The Witches of Eastwick* was filmed in Duxbury, Massachusetts.

Housesitter, with Steve Martin and Goldie Hawn, is a light romantic comedy set in a fictional New England town somewhere west of Boston, but filmed in Concord and Duxbury, Massachusetts.

MEDIA

Radio and TV also support a wide variety of news programs, though most of the reporting tends to center on the USA.

Television & Radio

Your hotel or motel room will have a color TV that receives perhaps several dozen channels, including the major broadcast networks: Public Broadcasting System (PBS), American Broadcasting Company (ABC), National Broadcasting Company (NBC), FOX, and Columbia Broadcasting System (CBS); as well as the many cable networks.

Each radio station follows a format, or programming formula, which may be to play classical music, country and western, rock and roll, jazz, treacly easy-listening music, or "golden oldies." FM stations carry mostly popular music. On the AM (middle wave) frequencies "talk radio" rules: a more or less intelligent or outrageous radio host takes telephone calls from listeners, makes comments and expresses opinions.

National Public Radio (NPR) features a more level-headed approach to news, discussion, music and more. NPR normally broadcasts on the lower end of the FM dial.

Newspapers & Magazines

There are over 1500 daily newspapers published in the USA, with a combined circulation of about 60 million. The newspaper with the highest circulation is *Wall Street Journal* followed by *USA Today*, *New York Times* and *Los Angeles Times*, which are all available in major cities.

The region's major newspaper, on sale throughout New England, is the highly regarded *Boston Globe*, followed by the more popular tabloid *Boston Herald*.

Many smaller cities and large towns have their own local newspapers, some of which are issued weekly rather than daily.

Boston and Cambridge have newsstands which sell many foreign publications. See Bookstores under Boston.

For the frequent traveler to New England, *Yankee Traveler* (published nine times a year – $36 subscriptions or $5 per copy; write to PO Box 37021, Boone, IA 50037-0021) is a newsletter from the travel editors of *Yankee Magazine* (PO Box 523, Dublin, NH 03444). It has an ideal format for those living in and around the area, offering destination recommendations and reviews for the coming months, but isn't available at newsstands. *Yankee Magazine* is available at stores throughout New England.

PHOTOGRAPHY & VIDEO
Photography

All major brands of film are available at reasonably good prices. Every town of any size has at least one photo shop which stocks a good variety of fresh film, cameras and accessories.

In most towns and tourist centers, some shops can develop your color print film in one hour (which really ends up being two or so), or at least the same day, for an extra charge. For regular service a roll of 100 ASA 35 mm color film with 24 exposures will typically cost about $7 to get processed.

There are virtually no restrictions on photography, except within museums and at musical and artistic performances.

Film can be damaged by excessive heat, so don't leave your camera and film in the car on a hot summer's day and avoid placing your camera on the dash while you are driving.

It's worth carrying a spare battery for your camera to avoid disappointment when your camera dies in the middle of nowhere. If you're buying a new camera for your trip do so several weeks before you leave and practice using it.

Video Systems

Overseas visitors who are thinking of purchasing videos should remember that the USA uses the National Television System Committee (NTSC) color TV standard, which is not compatible with other standards (PAL, SECAM) used in Africa, Europe, Asia and Australasia unless converted. It's best to keep those seemingly cheap movie purchases on hold until you get home.

Airport Security

All passengers on flights have to pass their luggage through X-ray machines. Technology as it is today doesn't jeopardize lower speed film, but it's best to carry film and cameras with you and ask the inspector to visually check your camera and film.

TIME

The USA (excluding Alaska and Hawaii) spans four time zones.

New England is on US Eastern Time, five hours earlier than GMT/UTC, and three hours later than US Pacific Time. When it's noon in Boston, it's 5 pm in London and 9 am in San Francisco.

New England observes daylight saving time. Clocks are set ahead one hour at midnight on the last Saturday night/ Sunday morning in April, and back one hour on the last Saturday night/Sunday morning in October.

ELECTRICITY

Electric current is 110-120 volts, 60-cycle. Appliances built to take 220-240 volt, 50-cycle current (as in Europe and Asia) will need a converter (transformer) and a US-style plug adaptor with two flat pins.

WEIGHTS & MEASURES

The USA uses a modified version of the traditional English measuring system of feet, yards, miles, ounces, pounds and gallons. See the inside back cover of this book for conversion charts.

Distances are in feet (ft), yards (yds) and miles (mi). Three feet equal one yard, which is .914 meters; 1760 yards or 5280 feet equal one mile.

Dry weight is measured in ounces (oz), pounds (lb) and tons; 16 ounces make one pound; 2000 pounds make one ton.

In liquid measure, one US pint equals 16 fluid ounces, not 20 as in the Imperial system; two US pints (32 fl oz) equal one US quart. Four quarts make one gallon. The US gallon, at 64 ounces, is 20% less than the imperial gallon at 80 ounces; or, it takes 1.2 US gallons to make an Imperial gallon. Wine bottles, however, tend to be of 70 centiliters or 750 milliliters.

The metric system is used in certain situations. Most commercial products have labels giving their weight, volume or length in metric measure as well as the traditional one. Cars sold in the USA usually have speedometers marked in kilometers per hour as well as miles per hour.

LAUNDRY

Pricier hotels and motels usually provide laundry and dry-cleaning services, but it is often faster and certainly cheaper to find the nearest laundry (self-service coin-operated laundry) or dry-cleaning shop yourself. Check the local yellow pages.

RECYCLING

Traveling in a car seems to generate large numbers of cans and bottles. If you'd like to save these for recycling, you'll find recycling centers in the larger towns. Materials accepted are usually plastic and glass bottles, aluminum and tin cans and newspapers. Some campgrounds and a few roadside rest areas also have recycling bins next to the trash bins so look out for those.

Despite the appearance of many large cities, littering is frowned upon by most Americans. Travelers need to respect the places they are visiting. Some states have implemented anti-littering laws (which impose fines for violation) to try to curb the problem.

HEALTH

Boston is among the world's most highly regarded centers for medical care and research, with a dozen major hospitals and a half-dozen medical schools. The quality of care is generally very high, as are its costs.

All other cities in New England – even small ones – have hospitals. To find one, look on the highways and roads for the standard hospital symbol of a white "H" on a blue background. Many cities also have walk-in clinics where you can show up without an appointment, see a nurse, nurse-practitioner or doctor for a minor ailment or preliminary diagnosis, and pay in cash or by credit card.

Make sure you're healthy before you start traveling. If you are embarking on a long trip, make sure your teeth are in good shape. If you wear glasses, take a spare pair and your prescription. You can get new spectacles made up quickly and competently for well under $100, depending on the prescription and frame you choose. If you require a particular medication, take an adequate supply and bring a prescription in case you lose your supply.

No immunizations are needed unless you are coming from a country that has experienced a recent cholera epidemic.

Health Insurance

Be sure that you have some form of health insurance which will pay your US medical bills in full should you need medical care while in the USA. Bills for an illness that requires hospitalization can easily exceed $1000 per day, and you will be expected to pay even at publicly supported government hospitals unless you can show that you are destitute.

Some policies specifically exclude "dangerous activities" like scuba diving, motorcycling and even hiking. If these activities are on your agenda avoid this sort of policy.

You may prefer a policy which pays doctors or hospitals directly, rather than your having to pay first and claim later. If you have to claim later, keep all documentation. Some policies ask you to call collect (reverse charges) to a center in your home country for an immediate assessment of your problem.

Check whether the policy covers ambulance fees or an emergency flight home. If you have to stretch out you will need two seats and somebody has to pay for it!

Companies offering various sorts of travel insurance, including health insurance, are:

Access America, Inc
   (☎ 212-490-5345, 800-284-8300),
   600 Third Ave, New York, NY 10116
International Underwriters/Brokers, Inc
   (☎ 703-281-9500, 800-394-2500),
   243 Church St W, Vienna, VA 22180
Travel Assistance International
   (☎ 800-821-2828)
Tripguard Plus
   (☎ 800-423-3632, fax 818-892-6576).
   In the UK, apply to Europ Assistance,
   252 High St, Croyden, Surrey CR0 1NF
   (☎ (0181) 680 1234).

Travel Health Guides

Here are a few books on travel health:

Travelers' Health, Dr Richard Dawood (Random House), is comprehensive, easy to read, authoritative and highly recommended, but rather large to lug around.

Travel with Children, Maureen Wheeler (Lonely Planet Publications), offers basic advice on travel health for younger children.

Heat Exhaustion

Dehydration or salt deficiency can cause heat exhaustion. Salt deficiency is characterized by fatigue, lethargy, headaches, giddiness and muscle cramps. Salt tablets may help. Vomiting or diarrhea can also deplete your liquid and salt levels. Always carry – and use – a water bottle on long trips.

Hypothermia

Changeable weather can leave you vulnerable to exposure: after dark, autumn temperatures can drop from balmy to below freezing, while a sudden soaking and high winds can lower your body temperature rapidly. If possible, avoid traveling alone; partners are more likely to avoid hypothermia successfully. If you must travel alone, especially when hiking, be sure someone knows your route and when you expect to return.

Seek shelter when bad weather is unavoidable. Woolen clothing and synthetics, which retain warmth even when wet, are superior to cottons. A quality sleeping bag is a worthwhile investment, although goose down loses much of its insulating qualities when wet. Carry high-energy, easily digestible snacks like chocolate or dried fruit.

Get hypothermia victims out of the wind or rain, remove their clothing if it's wet and replace it with dry, warm clothing. Give them hot liquids – not alcohol – and high-calorie, easily digestible food. In advanced stages it may be necessary to place victims in warm sleeping bags and get in with them. Do not rub victims but place them near a fire or, if possible, in a warm (not hot) bath.

Motion Sickness

Eating lightly before and during a trip will reduce the chances of motion sickness. If you are prone to motion sickness, try to find a place that minimizes disturbance, for example, near the wing on aircraft, near the center on buses. Fresh air usually helps. Commercial anti-motion sickness preparations, which can cause drowsiness, have to be taken before the trip commences; when you're feeling sick it's too late. Ginger, a natural preventative, is available in capsule form.

Jet Lag

Jet lag occurs because many of the functions of the human body (such as temperature, pulse rate and emptying of the bladder and bowels) are regulated by internal 24-hour cycles called circadian rhythms. When we travel long distances rapidly, our bodies take time to adjust to the "new time" of our destination, and we may experience fatigue, disorientation, insomnia, anxiety, impaired concentration and loss of appetite. These effects will usually be gone within three days of arrival, but there are ways of minimizing the impact of jet lag:

- Rest for a couple of days prior to departure; try to avoid late nights and last-minute dashes for traveler's checks, passport, etc.
- Try to select flight schedules that minimize sleep deprivation; arriving late in the day means you can go to sleep soon after you arrive. For very long flights, try to organize a stopover.
- Avoid excessive eating and alcohol during the flight. Instead, drink plenty of noncarbonated, nonalcoholic drinks such as fruit juice or water.
- Make yourself comfortable by wearing loose-fitting clothes and perhaps bringing an eye mask and ear plugs to help you sleep.

Giardiasis

Commonly known as Giardia, and sometimes "Beaver Fever," this intestinal parasite is present in contaminated water and usually affects those who drink untreated water from apparently pristine rushing streams in the backcountry. It's not very common in New England.

Hepatitis

Hepatitis is a general term for inflammation of the liver. There are many causes of this condition: drugs, alcohol and infections are but a few. The discovery of new strains has led to a virtual alphabet soup, with hepatitis A, B, C, D, E and a rumored G. These letters identify specific agents that cause viral hepatitis. Viral hepatitis is an infection of the liver, which can lead to jaundice (yellow skin), fever, lethargy and digestive problems. It can have no symptoms at all, with the infected person not knowing that they have the disease. Travelers shouldn't be too paranoid about this apparent proliferation of hepatitis strains; hep C, D, E and G are fairly rare (so far) and following the same precautions as for A and B should be all that's necessary to avoid them.

Viral hepatitis can be divided into two groups on the basis of how it is spread. The first route of transmission is via contaminated food and water, and the second route is via blood and bodily fluids.

Sexually Transmitted Diseases

Sexual contact with an infected partner spreads these diseases. While abstinence is the only 100% preventative, using latex condoms is also effective. Gonorrhea and syphilis are the most common of these diseases. Syphilis symptoms eventually disappear completely but the disease continues and can cause severe problems in later years. The treatment of gonorrhea and syphilis is by antibiotics.

There are numerous other sexually transmitted diseases, for most of which effective treatment is available. However, there is no cure for herpes and there is also currently no cure for AIDS.

HIV/AIDS

Any exposure to blood, blood products or bodily fluids may put the individual at risk to contract the HIV/AIDS virus. Infection can come from practicing unprotected sex or sharing contaminated needles, including needles re-used for acupuncture, tattooing, or body piercing. HIV/AIDS can also be spread through infected blood transfusions, though the blood supply in the USA is now well screened.

It is impossible to detect a person's HIV status without a blood test. A good resource for help and information is the US Centers for Disease Control AIDS hotline (☎ 800-343-2347). AIDS support groups are listed in the front of phone books.

Ticks

Ticks are a parasitic arachnid that may be present in brush, forest and grasslands, where hikers often get them on their legs or in their boots. The adults suck blood from hosts by burying their head into skin, but are often found unattached and can simply be brushed off.

Always check your body (and especially your child's body) for ticks after outdoor activities in grassy or wooded areas, or near animals. If one has attached itself to you, use tweezers to pull it out, getting a firm grip on the head. If a small chunk of skin comes out along with the head, that's good – you've got it all, and no part of the tick will be left to cause infection.

Deer ticks, which can carry and spread a serious bacterial infection called Lyme disease, are found throughout New England. The ticks are usually very small (some as small as a pinhead), and thus are not likely to be noticed casually – you must look carefully for them. A bite from a Lyme disease-infected deer tick may show a red welt and circular "halo" of redness within a day or two, or there may be no symptoms beyond a minor itch. Mild flu-like symptoms – headache, nausea, etc – may follow, or may not.

In the long term Lyme disease causes mental and muscular deterioration. Early treatment is essential. The best preventative measures are to wear clothing that covers your arms and legs when walking in forests or shrubby areas; use insect repellent containing DEET; and inspect carefully for ticks at the end of each day spent camping or hiking.

TOILETS

The American penchant for euphemism reaches its greatest height in descriptions of public toilet facilities. A public toilet is never called a toilet, but rather a "comfort station," "facility," "rest room" (the most common term), or "sanitary facility." But "toilet" was, in its time, also a euphemism. Some things don't change.

You will find relatively clean public toilets in airports, bars, large stores, museums, state and national parks, restaurants, hotels and tourist information offices. The ones in bus, train and highway fuel stations and rest stops might be clean or might not, but most are still usable. Not all fuel stations have toilets; among those that do, the quality varies considerably. Public toilets in city parks and other public places have mostly been closed due to crime and sexual encounters.

WOMEN TRAVELERS

If you are traveling alone, maintain a little extra awareness of your surroundings. People are generally friendly and happy to help travelers. The following suggestions should reduce or eliminate the chances of problems, but the best advice is to trust your instincts.

In general, you might want to ask for advice at your hotel or telephone the visitors center if you are unsure which areas are considered unsafe, especially when making room reservations.

Avoiding vulnerable situations and conducting yourself in a common-sense manner will help you to avoid most problems. You're more vulnerable if you've been drinking or using drugs than if you're sober; and you're more vulnerable alone than if you're with company. If you don't want company, most men will respect a firm but polite "no thank you."

Don't pick up hitchhikers if driving alone. At night avoid getting out of your car to flag down help; turn on your hazard lights and wait for the police to arrive. Leaving the hood open is a sign that you need help.

Many women protect themselves with a whistle, mace, cayenne pepper spray or self-defense training. If you decide to purchase a spray, contact a police station to find out about regulations. Laws regarding sprays vary from state to state, so be informed. It is a federal felony to carry defensive sprays on airplanes.

Many cities have rape crisis centers established to aid victims of rape. For the telephone number of the nearest center, call directory information at ☎ 411 or 1 + area code + 555-1212.

The headquarters for the National Organization for Women (NOW, ☎ 202-331-0066), 1000 16th St NW, Suite 700, Washington, DC 20036, is a good resource for information and can refer you to state and local chapters. Planned Parenthood (☎ 212-541-7800), 810 7th Ave, New York, NY 10019, can refer you to clinics throughout the country and offer advice on medical issues. Check the yellow pages under Women's Organizations & Services for local resources.

GAY & LESBIAN TRAVELERS

There are gay people throughout the USA. In cities like San Francisco and New York, which have the largest gay populations, it is easier for gay men and women to live their lives with a certain amount of openness. As you travel outside of large cities it is much harder to be open about your sexual preferences and many gays are still in the closet. This matches the prevailing attitude of the country, which prefers that gay people are neither seen nor heard. Gay travelers should be careful – holding hands in public might get you bashed.

Larger US cities often have a gay neighborhood or area. One example is the South End in Boston. Provincetown, on Cape Cod, happens to be a small-town gay mecca. Most cities have a gay or alternative newspaper listing current events or at least provide phone numbers of local organizations.

A couple of good national guidebooks are *The Womens' Traveler*, providing listings for lesbians and *Damron's Address Book* for men, both published by the Damron Company (☎ 415-255-0404, 800-462-6654), PO Box 422458, San Francisco, CA 94142-2458. Ferrari's *Places for Women* and *Places for Men* are also useful, as are guides to specific cities (check out *Betty & Pansy's Severe Queer Reviews* to New York City and Washington, DC). These can be found at any good bookstore.

Another good resource is the Gay Yellow Pages (☎ 212-674-0120), PO Box 533, Village Station, NY 10014-0533, which has a national edition as well as regional editions.

National resource numbers include the National AIDS/HIV Hotline (☎ 800-342-2437), the National Gay/Lesbian Task Force (☎ 202-332-6483 in Washington, DC) and the Lambda Legal Defense Fund (☎ 212-995-8585 in New York City, 213-937-2727 in Los Angeles).

SENIOR TRAVELERS

When retirement leaves the time clock behind and the myriad "senior" discounts begin to apply, the prospect of rediscovering the USA elicits a magnetic draw for foreigners and the native-born alike. Though the age where the benefits begin varies with the attraction, travelers from 50 years and up can expect to receive cut rates and benefits. Be sure to inquire about such rates at hotels, museums and restaurants *before* you make your reservation.

Visitors to national parks and campgrounds can cut costs greatly by using the Golden Age Passport, a card that allows US citizens age 62+ (and those traveling in the same car) free admission nationwide and a 50% reduction on camping fees. You can apply in person for any of these at any national park (the only one in New England is Acadia, in Maine) or regional office of the USFS or NPS or call ☎ 800-280-2267 for information and ordering.

Some national advocacy groups that can help in planning your travels include the following:

American Association of Retired Persons
The AARP (☎ 800-227-7737), 601 E St NW, Washington, DC 20049, is an advocacy group for Americans 50+ and is a good resource for travel bargains. Annual membership for US residents is $8.

Elderhostel
Elderhostel (☎ 617-426-8056), 75 Federal St, Boston, MA 02110-1941, is a nonprofit organization that offers seniors the opportunity to attend academic college courses throughout the USA and Canada. The programs last one to three weeks and include meals and accommodations, and are open to people 55+ and their companions.

Grand Circle Travel
This organization (☎ 617-350-7500, fax 350-6206), 347 Congress St, Boston, MA 02210, offers escorted tours and travel information in a variety of formats and distributes a free useful booklet, *Going Abroad: 101 Tips for Mature Travelers*.

National Council of Senior Citizens
Membership to this group (☎ 202-347-8800), 1331 F St NW, Washington, DC, 20004, gives access to added Medicare insurance, a mail-order prescription service and a variety of discount information and travel-related advice. You needn't be a US citizen to apply; fees are $13 for one year, $30 three years, $150 lifetime.

DISABLED TRAVELERS

Travel within USA is becoming easier for people with disabilities. Public buildings (including hotels, restaurants, theaters and museums) are now required by law to be wheelchair accessible and to have available restroom facilities. Public transportation services (buses, trains and taxis) must be made accessible to all, including those in wheelchairs, and telephone companies are required to provide relay operators for the hearing impaired. Many banks now provide ATM instructions in Braille and you will find audible crossing signals as well as dropped curbs at busier roadway intersections.

Larger private and chain hotels have suites for disabled guests. Main car rental agencies offer hand-controlled models at no extra charge. All major airlines, Greyhound buses and Amtrak trains will allow guide dogs to accompany passengers and will frequently sell two-for-one packages when attendants of seriously disabled passengers are required. Airlines will also provide assistance for connecting, boarding and deplaning the flight – just ask for assistance when making your reservation. (Note: airlines must accept wheelchairs as checked baggage and have an onboard chair available, though some advance notice may be required on smaller aircraft.) Of course, the more populous the area, the greater the likelihood of facilities for the disabled, so it's important to call ahead to see what is available.

There are a number of organizations and tour providers that specialize in the needs of disabled travelers:

Access
    The Foundation for Accessibility by the Disabled (☎ 516-887-5798), PO Box 356, Malverne, NY 11565.
Information Center for Individuals with Disabilities
    Call or write for their free listings and travel advice. Fort Point Place, 1st floor, 27-43 Wormwood St, Boston, MA 02210 (☎ 617-727-5540, TTY 345-9743, 800-248-3737).
Mobility International USA
    Mobility International (☎ 503-343-1284), PO Box 3551, Eugene, OR 97403, advises disabled travelers on mobility issues. It also runs an exchange program.
Moss Rehabilitation Hospital's Travel Information Service
    (☎ 215-456-9600, TTY 456-9602) 1200 W Tabor Rd, Philadelphia, PA 19141-3099.
SATH
    Society for the Advancement of Travel for the Handicapped (☎ 212-447-7284) 347 Fifth Ave Suite 610, New York, NY 10016.
Twin Peaks Press
    Publishes several handbooks for disabled travelers (tel 360-694-2462, 800-637-2256) PO Box 129, Vancouver, WA 98666.
Handicapped Travel Newsletter
    This is a nonprofit publication (☎ /fax 903-677-1260) with good information on traveling around the world and US government legislation. Subscriptions are $10 annually. PO Drawer 269, Athens, TX 75751.

USEFUL ORGANIZATIONS
American Automobile Association
AAA ("Triple-A"), with offices in all major cities and many smaller towns, provides useful information, free maps and routine road services like tire repair and towing (free within a limited radius) to its members. The basic membership fee is $39 per annum, plus a one-time initiation fee of $17 (still an excellent investment for the maps alone, even for non-motorists). Its nationwide toll-free roadside assistance

number is ☎ 800-AAA-HELP, 800-222-4357. Members of its foreign affiliates, like the Automobile Association in the UK, are entitled to the same services.

Appalachian Mountain Club
The AMC (☎ 617-523-0636), 5 Joy St, Boston, MA 02108, sells hiking guides and maps to the White Mountains and other New England backcountry.

Hostelling International/American Youth Hostels
HI/AYH (☎ 202-783-6161, fax 783-6171), 733 15th St NW, Suite 840, Washington, DC 20005, is the successor to the International Youth Hostel Federation (IYHF). For hostel listings in the USA and Canada, get HI/AYH's *Hostelling North America*, the official guide. For a list of New England's hostels and organizations by state, see Hostels under Accommodations.

National Park Service & US Forest Service
The NPS and USFS administer the use of parks and forests. National forests are less protected than parks, allowing commercial use of some areas (usually logging or privately owned recreational facilities).

National parks most often surround spectacular natural features and cover hundreds of sq miles. A full range of accommodations can be found in and around national parks. In New England, there's only Acadia National Park in Maine, but the NPS also administers the Freedom Trail in Boston and other frequently-used places in the area.

National park campground and reservations information can be obtained by calling ☎ 800-365-2267 or writing to the National Park Service Public Inquiry, Dept of the Interior, 18th and C Sts NW, Washington, DC 20013.

Current information about national forests can be obtained from ranger stations. National forest campground and reservation information can be obtained by calling ☎ 800-280-2267, or by writing to the address listed above.

DANGERS & ANNOYANCES

Some major US cities have well-earned reputations for being hotbeds of violent crime. New England's cities – Boston, Burlington, Hartford, New Haven, Portland, Providence, Springfield, Worcester – are among the safer ones, but all suffer to some degree from the crimes of pickpockets, muggers (robbers) and rapists.

As in other cities throughout the world, the majority of crimes take place in the poorest neighborhoods among the local residents. The signs of a bad or dangerous neighborhood are obvious, and pretty much the same as any other country. But you should follow common-sense rules when traveling in New England, particularly in its cities:

- Carry valuables such as money, traveler's checks, credit cards, passport, etc, in a money belt or pouch underneath your clothing for maximum safety from pickpockets. This is usually only necessary in crowded areas such as subways, city buses or concerts.
- Lock valuables in your suitcase in your hotel room when you're not there, or put them in the hotel safe.
- Don't leave anything visible in your car when you park it in a city, particularly at night. Always lock your car when you leave it.
- Avoid walking or driving through poor neighborhoods, especially at night. Don't walk in parks at night. Avoid walking along any empty street at night. Well-lit streets busy with other walkers are usually alright.

EMERGENCY

Most states, cities and towns in New England are connected to the emergency notification system reached by dialing ☎ 911 from any telephone (no money required). Operators who answer 911 calls can fill your need for help from the police, firefighters, emergency medical response teams or other emergency services.

In areas without 911 service (or if dialing 911 does not work), dial ☎ 0 for the telephone operator, who will connect you to the necessary local emergency service.

The Travelers Aid Society (☎ 617-542-7286), 711 Atlantic Ave, Boston, MA 02111, is an organization of volunteers who do their best to help travelers solve their problems. Volunteers are on duty at Boston's Logan International Airport (☎ 617-567-5385, 569-6284) and at Boston's Amtrak South Station (☎ 617-542-9875, 423-7766). For offices in other large New England cities, look in the local yellow pages or call directory assistance at and ask for the Travelers Aid Society.

LEGAL MATTERS

If you are stopped by the police for any reason, bear in mind that there is no system of paying fines on the spot. For traffic offenses, the police officer will explain your options to you. Attempting to pay the fine to the officer is frowned upon at best and may lead to a charge of bribery to compound your troubles. Should the officer decide that you should pay up front, he or she can exercise their authority and take you directly to the magistrate instead of allowing you the usual 30-day period to pay the fine.

If you are arrested for more serious offenses, you are allowed to remain silent and are presumed innocent until proven guilty. There is no legal reason to speak to a police officer if you don't wish. All persons who are arrested are legally allowed (and given) the right to make one phone call. If you don't have a lawyer or family member to help you, call your embassy. The police will give you the number upon request.

Driving & Drinking Laws

The drinking age throughout New England is 21 and you need a photo ID (ironically, Americans use their drivers license) to prove your age.

Stiff fines, jail time and penalties can be incurred if you are caught driving under the influence of alcohol. During festive holidays and special events, road blocks with breathalyzer tests are sometimes set up to deter drunk drivers. Be aware of your alcoholic consumption and drive responsibly.

BUSINESS HOURS

Public and private office hours are normally 8 or 9 am to 5 pm, Monday through Friday. For public holidays, see Planning.

Banks

Customary banking hours are Monday through Friday from 9 am to 3 pm, but most banks have extended customer service hours, until 5 pm (or even 8 or 9 pm on Thursday), and on Saturday from 9 am to 2 pm or later. No banks are open on Sunday except the currency exchange booths at international airports.

Fuel Stations

Fuel stations on major highways are open all the time. City fuel stations usually open at 6 or 7 am and stay open until 8 or 9 pm. In small towns and villages, hours may be only from 7 or 8 am to 7 or 8 pm.

Museums

Museums normally open at 10 am and close at 5 pm, Tuesday through Sunday (closed Monday), but if you want to know for sure, call and confirm the hours in each case.

Some smaller museums and exhibits are seasonal, open only in the warmer months. Many museums and attractions close on Thanksgiving Day (the fourth Thursday in November), Christmas Day and New Year's Day.

Post Offices

Post offices are open Monday through Friday from 8 or 8:30 am to 5 pm; some major post offices in cities stay open until 5:30 or 6 pm. Weekend hours are normally 8 am to noon or 2 pm on Saturday, closed Sunday.

Shopping Hours

Most stores are open Monday through Saturday from 9:30 or 10 am to 5:30 or 6 pm (usually later in big cities). Many stores are also open from 11 am or noon until 5 pm on Sunday.

All cities and many large towns have at least a few "convenience stores" for food, beverages, newspapers and some household items open 24 hours a day. Many highway fuel stations, also open 24 hours a day, have small shops selling snacks, beverages and frequently needed items.

Most city supermarkets stay open from 8 or 9 am to 9 or 10 pm, with shorter hours on Sunday, but some in large cities close only from Sunday evening to Monday morning for maintenance.

CULTURAL & SPECIAL EVENTS

See Planning at the front of the chapter for a breakdown of events by month.

ACTIVITIES

New England's mountains may not be as high as the Rockies, but the region has many virtues as an outdoor paradise. With its hundreds of colleges and universities, and cutting-edge research and technology companies, New England has a large population of young, eager outdoor enthusiasts who support efforts to expand opportunities and preserve natural resources.

New Hampshire's White Mountains, Vermont's Green Mountains and the dense forests of northern Maine offer good mountain hiking and rock climbing, camping, canoeing and white-water rafting. The thousands of miles of rugged coastline are good for sailing, canoeing, sea kayaking, sailboarding, whale watching and even scuba diving. Swimming, canoeing, boating, fishing and water skiing are available on many of the region's thousands of lakes and ponds. Though the waters of the Atlantic are usually chilly, swimming and other beach sports are popular in summer, particularly in the warmer, sheltered waters of Rhode Island and Cape Cod Bay.

Last but not least, New England is relatively small and manageable: it is entirely possible to begin the day with a climb in New Hampshire's White Mountains, and finish it by watching the sunset on a Rhode Island beach.

If you find that one of the following companies gives particularly good service, please write to me and let me know so that I can recommend it in future editions. These tour operators were researched from and recommended by a variety of sources, including tourist boards. Prices go up and good places go bad, so before you part with your hard-earned cash, you should, as usual, get opinions, quotes and advice from as many services and travel agents as possible. Double-check directly with the tour operator or travel agent to make sure you understand the details of the service you're paying for. The travel industry is highly competitive and there are many lurks and perks.

Hiking & Walking

The Appalachian Trail spans New England from its northern terminus at Maine's Mt Katahdin (5267 feet), southward through the Maine woods, New Hampshire's White Mountain National Forest, Vermont's Green Mountains, Massachusetts' Berkshire hills. It then crosses into Connecticut and passes to the north of New York City before continuing south to Georgia.

Shorter but still challenging, Vermont's Long Trail starts at Jay Peak (3861 feet) in the Northeast Kingdom, then follows the Green Mountains south to Bennington.

Besides these long treks, Acadia National Park in Maine has a good system of hiking trails as well as a unique, easier (and bikeable) system of unpaved "carriage roads."

Most of the region's hundreds of state forests, parks and reservations have walking or hiking trails of varying levels of difficulty. Even many cities and towns have simple trail systems meandering through woodlands, parks and city reservations.

Mountain Hiking For mountain hiking and rock climbing, by far the most popular area is the White Mountains' Presidential Range, with Mt Washington (6288 feet) at its apex. Though hardly a challenger to the Rockies or the Alps, Mt Washington has the severest weather in the region, and – please note – at least a few hikers perish or are badly injured on its slopes each year.

Mt Katahdin (5267 feet), in Maine's north country, is for the seriously outdoorsy who want wilder country, more adventure

and fewer people around. It has remained remote backcountry because it is a considerable distance from New England's cities.

In Vermont's Green Mountains, the best hikes are near Stowe and up Mt Mansfield along the Long Trail.

Mt Greylock (3491 feet), the highest mountain in Massachusetts, is an excellent goal for a day's walk from Williamstown, in the northwest corner of the state.

New Hampshire's Mt Monadnock (3165 feet), near Jaffrey just a short distance north of the Massachusetts state line, is the "beginners' mountain," a relatively easy climb up a bald granite bathylith.

Organized Hikes Should you want to see nature with an organized group, Country Walkers, Inc (☎ 802-244-1387), RR 2, Box 754, Waterbury, VT 05676-9742, organizes two- to five-day walking trips in Vermont and Maine, as well as other parts of the world. Tour participants range in age from eight to 80 years old, and are matched so that they keep about the same pace during each day's four- to nine-mile (6.5 to 14.5 km) trek, covered in three to five hours. Luggage is transported by van, not carried. Lodgings are usually at country inns in rooms with private baths. Two-day weekend trips cost about $300, five-day trips about $800. Lodging and all meals are included.

New England Hiking Holidays (☎ 800-869-1049), PO Box 1648, North Conway, NH 03860, runs similar two- to five-day hiking trips throughout New England and other areas, with lodgings and meals at country inns.

Camping

Tent camping is popular in New England, and is done mostly in state and national forests and parks. Private campgrounds usually have a few places for tents, but they make their money catering to huge recreational vehicles (RVs), which require water, sewer and electricity hookups.

For details on camping, see the Accommodations section in this chapter, or see the chapter that deals with your destination.

Bicycling

New England's varied
and visually interest-
ing terrain makes it
a good place for
bicycle touring and
mountain biking.

Thousands of miles
of back roads wander
through handsome
villages and red-brick
towns, far enough
apart to give
cyclers a sense of
being in the country, but close enough to
provide needed services. Parts and supplies
are available in the larger cities and towns,
particularly in college towns.

Bicycle Touring Cape Cod is among the
region's best biking areas, with several
special bike paths (Shining Sea between
Falmouth and Woods Hole, Cape Cod Rail
Trail from Dennis to Wellfleet, and the
paths in the Cape Cod National Seashore
near Provincetown). The *Cape Cod Bike
Book* ($3), with maps and information on
bike rentals, bike paths, rest stops and
other necessities, is sold in bookstores on
the Cape, and may also be ordered by mail
from Cape Cod Bike Book, PO Box 627,
South Dennis, MA 02660, for $3.75.

Getting your car to the islands of
Martha's Vineyard, Nantucket or Block
Island is expensive (and often, without
reservations, impossible). But bicycles
move easily and cheaply on the ferries (no
reservation needed), and each island has a
network of bike paths. The flat terrain and
fine sea views make these among the best
areas for biking. If you don't have a bike,
rent one there.

New England Bicycle Tours (☎ 800-
233-2128, fax 728-4911), Box D, Randolph, VT 05060, runs two-, three-,
five-day and longer bicycle and canoe
tours in New England, tailoring the tours
to varying levels of proficiency and stamina. Prices are about $230 for a three-day
(two-night) tour and $700 to $850 for five-
and six-day tours. The price includes

lodging at inns, breakfast, dinner, maps
and snacks. You can use your own bike, or
rent one from them.

Mountain Biking Many of the region's
forest and mountain trails are open to
mountain bikers. Be sure you know the
rules before heading down the trail. If you
plan a mountain-bike tour during the
autumn foliage season, probably the best
time of the year, reserve your accommodations well in advance.

Several companies run organized bike
tours. The Mountain Bike School (☎ 802-
464-333, 800-451-4211) at Mt Snow in
Vermont, operates on summer weekends,
offering tours of varying difficulty. Your
weekend includes bike rental, two days of
instruction, lunch and swimming for $140
per person; with lodgings and meals, the
price is $300.

Vermont Mountain Bike Tours (☎ 802-
746-8580) of Pittsfield, VT, is for more
adventurous riders. For $115 per person
per day you get a guide, a ride and lodgings and meals at good inns. Bring your
own bike, or rent one of theirs for about
$20 per day.

Craftsbury Sports Center (☎ 802-586-
7767), PO Box 31, Craftsbury Common,
VT 05827, offers similar mountain biking
programs at slightly lower prices: bring
your own bike, opt for an inn room with
shared bath, and provide your own meals,
and you may pay as little as $50 per person
per day. For all the comforts, expect to pay
up to $100 per person per day.

Leaf Peeping

This is what New Englanders call foliage
appreciation: touring by bicycle, car, bus,
train, boat or on foot to enjoy the spectacular colors of the region's fall foliage.
Special tours are organized by many
commercial and nonprofit organizations. A
good source of information on foliage tours
is the tourist information office for each
New England state.

The easiest way to pinpoint where the
peak autumn foliage is on any given September or October day is to call the

states' Autumn Foliage Hotlines. Just call and these lines will give locations for the best viewing:

Massachusetts	☎ 800-227-6277
Rhode Island	☎ 800-556-2484
Connecticut	☎ 800-252-6863
Vermont	☎ 802-828-3239
New Hampshire	☎ 800-258-3608
Maine	☎ 800-533-9595

Swimming & Beaches

The Rhode Island seacoast has excellent beaches. Cape Cod, and the islands of Martha's Vineyard and Nantucket in Massachusetts sport that state's best beaches: Cape Cod National Seashore is a glorious array of dunes making their way to the Atlantic. Maine has a scattering of beaches in its coastal towns including Bar Harbor, but also on a few inland lakes, like Rangeley Lake. Swimming on Lake Winnipesaukee and other of New Hampshire's lake-region bodies of water can be warmer and more enjoyable than the chilly ocean.

Canoeing, Kayaking & Rafting

Canoeing is popular in summer throughout New England in its ponds, lakes, rivers and along the sheltered parts of its coastline. The heart of riverine canoe activity is undoubtedly North Conway, NH, but there are many canoe outfitters in Maine as well.

Downeast Whitewater (☎ 603-447-3002, 800-677-7238, fax 447-6278), PO Box 119, Center Conway, NH 03813, can take you on canoe, white-water rafting and inflatable kayak trips in Maine and New Hampshire.

Eastern River Rafting (☎ 207-672-9238, 800-634-7238), PO Box 66, Caratunk, ME 04925, leads guided canoe, raft and kayak trips on Maine's Kennebec, Upper Kennebec, Penobscot and Dead Rivers.

Either in rigid or inflatable boats, kayaking is popular wherever there's water, from the quiet ponds of Rhode Island and Connecticut to the Boston waterfront and the wilds of northern Maine. Many outfitters provide rentals and instruction. Perhaps the ultimate New England kayak experience is along the rocky, pine-fringed coasts of Maine.

Only 20 minutes by ferry from Portland, Maine Island Kayak Co (☎ 207-766-2373), 70 Luther St, Peaks Island, ME 04108, runs half- and full-day kayak tours among the Diamond Islands in Casco Bay, and more ambitious weekend and five- to 10-day expeditions covering the best reaches of the Maine coast. Nights are spent at low-impact campgrounds on islands along the way. The guides welcome beginners. "If you can walk a few miles," they say, "you can paddle between camps."

White-water rafting is mostly done in the northern New England states, particularly on New Hampshire's Saco River, and on the Kennebec, Upper Kennebec, Penobscot and Dead Rivers in Maine. For adventures

---

White-Water Rafting: How Difficult Is It?

White-water rafting trips are classed according to difficulty:

Class I – slow current, no obstructions in the river, very small rapids and low waves

Class II – faster current, frequent rapids of medium difficulty, but few obstructions in the river

Class III – numerous rapids and large, irregular waves up to four feet in height; the raft needs to be maneuvered by an experienced leader

Class IV – fast current along a course that is not always easy to maneuver, numerous and often dangerous obstacles and powerful waves

Class V – extremely fast and difficult course through long and violent rapids and large, unavoidable and irregular waves

Class VI – maximum difficulty, approaching the unnavigable, with significant risk to life and limb

closer to Boston, contact Zoar Outdoor (☎ 413-339-8596, 800-532-7483, fax 413-337-8436), PO Box 245, Charlemont, MA 01339.

In addition to the companies mentioned above, you can obtain rental craft (canoes, kayaks, rafts) and equipment, instruction and guide service from these companies:

Magic Falls Rafting Co
    (☎ 800-207-7238), PO Box 9, West Forks, ME 04985
Maine Whitewater
    (☎ 207-672-4814, 800-345-6246), PO Box 633, Bingham, ME 04920
New England Whitewater Center
    (☎ 207-672-5506, 800-766-7238), PO Box 21, Caratunk, ME 04925
North Country Rivers
    (☎ 207-923-3492, 800-348-8871, fax 923-3850), PO Box 47, East Vassalboro, ME 04935
Northern Outdoors
    (☎ 207-663-4466, 800-765-7238, fax 663-2244, RAFTING@mint.net), PO Box 100, Route 201, The Forks, ME 04985
Professional River Runners of Maine
    (☎ 207-663-2229, 800-325-3911), PO Box 92, West Forks, ME 04985
Wilderness Expeditions
    (☎ 207-534-2242, 800-825-9453, fax 534-8835, WWLD@aol.com), PO Box 41, Rockwood, ME 04478

Windjammer Cruises

The Maine coast in summer is among the world's finest sail-cruising areas. Tall-masted craft use Camden, Rockport and Rockland as their home ports. A cruise of a few days along the gorgeous Maine coast is a perfect way to forget your daily worries and concentrate on nature for awhile. For details, see the Camden section in the Maine chapter.

Cruising isn't limited to Maine, however. Day cruises are available in many touristy coastal towns such as Gloucester and Rockport, MA, and from the islands: Block Island, RI, Nantucket and Martha's Vineyard, MA.

Out O' Mystic Schooner Cruises (☎ 800-243-0416), 7 Holmes St, PO Box 487, Mystic, CT 06355, runs one-, two-, three-, and five-day schooner cruises every summer from Mystic, CT. You have the choice of lending a hand as part of the crew, or relaxing as a passenger. Shipboard experiences range in price from $89 for 24 hours to $579 for a five-day cruise.

Whale-Watching Cruises

Once known for their prowess in seeking out whales for slaughter, New England's sea captains now follow the whales with boatloads of camera-carrying tourists.

Craft vary from small and old-fashioned fishing vessels to posh, modern double-hulled speedboats. Whale-watching cruises depart from South County, RI; New Bedford, Barnstable, Provincetown, Boston and Gloucester, MA; Portsmouth, NH; and Portland, Boothbay Harbor and Bar Harbor, ME, among other coastal towns.

For a detailed description of whale watching, see the Gloucester section in the Around Boston chapter.

The captains, equipped with electronic sounding gear, radios and long experience in New England waters, usually have no trouble finding marine behemoths such as minke whales, finbacks, right whales and dolphins. If for some reason they fail to sight a whale, most boats will give you a pass for another cruise.

When you go whale watching, be prepared. Unless you're an experienced sailor, pick a day when the sea is calm; stormy days and the day immediately following a storm are usually uncomfortably choppy. If you think you might get seasick (on choppy seas most people do), take ginger capsules (sold at health food stores) before boarding the boat. Don't eat a big meal right before you sail, and avoid alcoholic beverages.

Other whale-watching necessities: a sweater or windbreaker, even on hot days; a hat, sunglasses and sunblock are essential as you will be subject to harsh sunlight both from the sea and the sky.

Skiing

Virtually all ski resorts in New England have substantial snowmaking capacity, and the many gladed trails provide a memorable experience. Smaller, local hills are often cheaper to ski and less crowded, and are ideal for beginners. Before making reservations at a big resort, check for motels around the smaller hills, which might save you a significant sum.

Snowboarding has invaded New England's ski areas as it has others; some ski resorts make special provisions for boarders.

New England's best skiing is in Vermont at Killington, Mt Snow, Stratton, and Stowe; and in New Hampshire's White Mountains at Waterville Valley, the Franconia Notch area (Loon Mountain) and the Mt Washington Valley. Massachusetts' Berkshires, Connecticut, northern New Hampshire and Vermont offer smaller ski areas.

Cross-country (Nordic) skiing is also popular, and especially pleasing in the forests and from village to village or inn to inn. Every town seems to have at least a few marked cross-country trails. Out in the countryside, resort towns such as North Conway, NH, and Stowe, VT, have elaborate systems of well-groomed cross-country trails.

Snowmobiling
Snowmobiling is offered in a number of state parks during the winter. Use of the noisy machines is regulated: you must be at least 16 to operate one, you must stay on approved snowmobile routes and tracks, etc. If you haven't ever ridden a snowmobile before, you should definitely take a safety training course beforehand, as there are special cautions and dangers associated with them.

WORK
There are lots of summer jobs at New England seaside and mountain resorts. These are usually low-paying service jobs filled by young people (often college students) who are happy to work part of the day so they can play the rest. If you want such a job, contact well in advance the local chambers of commerce or businesses

that interest you. You can't depend on finding a job just by coming in the summer and looking around.

In winter, contact New England's ski resorts, where full-time help is often needed.

Foreigners entering the USA to work must have a visa that permits it. These can be difficult to procure unless you can show that you already have a job offer from an employer who considers your qualifications to be unique and not readily available in the USA.

There are, of course, many foreigners working illegally in the country. Controversial laws prescribe punishments for employers employing "aliens" (foreigners) who do not have the proper visas. The Immigration and Naturalization Service (INS) officers responsible for enforcing the laws can be persistent.

ACCOMMODATIONS
New England provides a comfortable array of choices in accommodations. In the countryside the choices range from simple campsites to lavish country inns. In the cities, mid-range and top-end hotels abound, but truly inexpensive accommodations are rare. The most comfortable accommodations for the lowest price are usually to be found in that American invention, the roadside motel.

In order to keep your cost of accommodations down, observe this rule: visit cities on weekends, and the countryside during the week. Most city hotels offer low weekend rates for Friday, Saturday and Sunday nights; most country and resort lodgings reduce their rates by 20% to 45% Monday through Thursday.

At the busiest times, you may have to reserve accommodations well in advance. This is particularly true of B&Bs and inns. When you reserve a room in advance, be conscious of the terms and requirements. Here are some key questions to ask:

• Is smoking allowed? Most B&Bs and inns are "smoke free." You must go outside to smoke.
• Are children allowed? Many inns do not

welcome children under a certain age, perhaps as old as 12 years.
- Are pets allowed? In most cases, they are not.
- Is there a minimum stay required?
- Are meals included or required?
- Can you reserve precisely the sort of room you want ("in the main inn, not in the annex," "with private bath," "with water view"), or must you take whatever is available when you arrive?
- Are there additional charges for service, activities or facilities? How much is the tax?
- Are credit cards accepted? Personal checks? Only cash?
- Is a deposit required? How much? Under what circumstances can the reservation be canceled and the deposit refunded?

Camping

If you don't bring your own camping equipment, you can buy good stuff at good prices at many places in New England. Refer to the Boston chapter under Things to Buy, and also to Freeport in the Maine chapter.

You cannot plan to just stop by the road and camp. With few exceptions, you will have to camp in an established campground. Luckily, New England has lots of these. Unluckily, most of them are full on weekends in July and August, and many fill up during the week as well. You must reserve in advance or arrive early in the day to give yourself the best chance of getting a site.

Rough camping is permitted in the backcountry of some national forests, but often it must be at established sites; these may have simple shelters, and are usually free. Excellent trail guides and maps exist which show and describe these sites. See Books for details.

An inexpensive option is the primitive forest site with only basic services: pit (waterless) toilets, cold running water (perhaps from a pump) and fireplaces. These are generally found in national forests, and cost about $6.

Standard campsites in state and national parks usually have flush toilets, hot showers (for a fee), and often a dump station for RVs. Tent sites are usually shaded, and are sometimes on wooden platforms or grass, with plenty of space between sites. These sites cost between $6 and $18. Most government-run campgrounds only stay open during the summer season from mid-May to early September or late October.

Private campgrounds are usually more expensive and less spacious, with sites closer together and less shade, but with lots more entertainment facilities. Most of the sites are for RVs and have water and electric hook-ups, and perhaps sewage. A small grassy area without hook-ups is usually set aside for tent campers, who are distinctly in the minority and who pay the lowest rate. Sometimes hot showers are free, sometimes not. Private campgrounds usually have small shops and snack bars for essentials. Recreation facilities are usually elaborate, with playgrounds, swimming, game rooms, and even miniature golf courses.

Hostels

Hostelling is not nearly as well developed in New England as in Europe. But some prime travel destinations, including Bar Harbor, Boston, Cape Cod, Martha's Vineyard and Nantucket, have hostels which allow you to stay in $100-per-night destinations for $12 to $17. Needless to say, advance reservations are essential, and may often be made by phone if you have a credit card.

Hostelling International/American Youth Hostels (HI/AYH) has its own toll- and surcharge-free reservations service (☎ 800-444-6111), but not all hostels participate in the service. HI/AYH membership can be purchased through this office, the regional council offices and at many (but not all) youth hostels. The HI/AYH card may be used to get discounts at some local merchants and services.

See Useful Organizations, above, for more on the national council. There are two hostelling councils that cover New England (there are no hostels in Rhode Island):

HI/AYH Yankee Council
(☎ 203-247-6356)118 Oak St, Hartford, CT 06106, is the office for hostels in Connecticut and Vermont.

HI/AYH Eastern New England Council
(☎ 617-731-6692, fax 734-7614, Worldwide Information Line 617-731-5430, Activities Hotline 617-730-8294), 1020 Commonwealth Ave, Boston, MA 02215, is the office for hostels in Maine, Massachusetts and New Hampshire.

Here's a list of New England hostel locations – get in touch with the appropriate hostelling council for more information on these:

Massachusetts
Boston (2), Dudley, Eastham (Cape Cod), Littleton (near Concord), Martha's Vineyard, Nantucket, Northfield, Shelburne Center (near Deerfield), Truro (Cape Cod)
Connecticut
Windsor
Vermont
Burlington, East Jamaica (25 miles north of Brattleboro), Ludlow (near Plymouth), Montpelier, St Johnsbury, Underhill Center (between Burlington and Stowe), Woodford (near Bennington)
New Hampshire
Peterborough
Maine
Bar Harbor, Portland, South Hiram

Motels

Motels range from small, homey, cheap 10-room places in want of paint and wallpaper to lavish resorts with manicured lawns and gardens, vast restaurants and resort-style facilities.

Prices range from $30 to $100 and up. On the highway, or on the outskirts of any but the largest cities, you can get a very comfortable motel room for $50 to $75. The cheapest places are invariably the small local ones which are not members of a national chain, and which are thus most difficult to find out about.

Virtually any motel offers you standard accommodations: a room entered from the outside, with private bath, color cable TV, heat and air-conditioning. Though some smaller, older places may have only twin beds, most motels now have two double beds or larger, or perhaps a queen-size bed and a single bed. In other words, it's easy for a small family (parents and two children) to find one room to accommodate them all. Whether you all want to sleep together is another matter.

Motel rooms often have small refrigerators, and motels always provide free ice for drinks, and usually have a vending machine or two for soft drinks and snacks. Many motels have restaurants attached or nearby; if not, most will provide a simple breakfast of muffins or rolls, fruit and coffee, often at no extra charge. Many motels without restaurants keep menus from local restaurants on hand which you can study to decide where to go for dinner. Most motels (excluding the very cheapest) have swimming pools. Most also provide toll-free reservations lines.

Hotels

City hotels are mostly large and fairly lavish, with few of the small, inexpensive "boutique" hotels to be found in London or Paris. Hotel rooms provide similar services to motel rooms, but are usually a bit more inclusive. Standard hotel services include restaurants and bars, room service for meals and beverages, and exercise rooms ("health clubs"). Many city hotels set aside several floors as special "executive" sections, with more elaborate decoration and a central lounge with an attendant.

Prices range from $80 to $200 and up per night, with most between $100 and $150. Weekend discounts and special weekend packages offer significant savings. Be sure to ask about them when you call to ask prices and make reservations. Virtually all large hotels have toll-free numbers for reservations, but you may find better savings by calling the hotel directly, as some discounts are aimed only at local callers.

Usually, children under 18 may stay for free in their parents' room. In a room with two double beds, then, a family of four could stay for the same price as a couple.

If you are 55+, ask about senior citizen discounts.

B&Bs

Between WWI and WWII, before large-scale automobile production, American resorts had "tourist homes," private residences with several simple rooms to rent to travelers. The tourist home was often the main source of income of the single woman, retired couple or widow who ran it. After WWII, tourist homes were largely replaced by motels.

In the 1960s, young American tourists flooded Europe and discovered the convenient, congenial and above all inexpensive B&Bs, *pensions, gasthofen* and *pensioni*. They took the experience home to America, and the tourist home came to life again. But, as with most imports to America, it was thoroughly Americanized.

Though a minority of American B&Bs match the European model, most are not cheap, simple homes with spare rooms, but rather, small inns. Some are aggressively, even relentlessly adorable, with abundantly frilly decors and theatrically charming hosts. Some have the services and amenities of minor resort hotels, and the prices to match.

The simpler B&Bs in smaller towns and resorts may charge $40 to $75 for single or double rooms with shared bath, breakfast included. Fancier B&Bs in or near the more popular resorts charge $65 to $125 per night for a room with private bath. At peak times from mid-July through early September, and late September through mid-October, and on holiday weekends, prices at the fanciest B&Bs in the most popular resort towns may rise to $150 or even $175.

B&B rooms vary in size, appointments and conveniences. Some have air-conditioning and TVs; most do not.

Breakfast may be store-bought cake or muffins and instant coffee, or fresh-baked pastries and a selection of fresh-brewed stimulants, or a full American-style breakfast of bacon or ham and eggs, toast or muffins, fruit, cereal and milk; or any variation of the above. Usually it's pretty good.

In the most popular resort towns, B&Bs may have restrictive policies: a minimum stay of two or three days may be required on weekends; bills may have to be paid in advance by check or in cash (not by credit card); cancellations may be subject to a processing fee, or worse.

Inns

New England has over 1500 country inns. They vary in size and amenities from small B&Bs (see above) to large rambling old inns which have been sheltering travelers for several centuries. Many inns are historic and authentically furnished, with modernized services. Others aspire to historicity. Many large mansions and summer houses, built by wealthy families a century ago, are now comfortable, even sumptuous inns.

The charm and character of New England's inns are famous throughout the country. New Englanders and those from neighboring regions (New York City, Philadelphia, Montréal, etc) look upon them not simply as lodgings, but as weekend resorts, or places good for a summer's vacation of a week or two. Many inns have excellent dining rooms and taverns, and may also have such services as swimming pools, gardens, hiking trails, or associations with local golf courses or tennis clubs.

Inn rooms are often aggressively decorated in antique styles. Most have private baths, but may not have air-conditioning or television.

Prices range from $75 to $200 and up, depending upon the inn, the particular room, the town, the season, and the day(s) of the week. A room priced at $75 on a weekday night in Lenox, MA, may cost $120 on Thursday, Friday or Saturday night. To this price you may have to add a $5 obligatory maid's fee, $10 if you use that romantic fireplace in your room, and the 9.7% state and local lodging taxes, making your final bill $148.

As with B&Bs, inns may require minimum stays, payment in advance, or have other restrictions.

Rentals
Renting a cottage or condominium for a week or two is popular in New England, but not particularly easy for those who do not live in the region. There is no central registry of vacation rental properties. The best you can do is contact the local chamber of commerce and ask for listings of available properties.

FOOD
A hundred years ago, Boston was famous for baked beans (white/navy beans, molasses, salt pork, and onions cooked slowly in a crock) and New England boiled dinner (beef boiled with cabbage, carrots, and potatoes). Though these dishes regularly show up in nostalgic and touristic accounts of the region, they are not common on menus anymore.

Some traditional foods are still common, and for good reason. New England's seafood is outstanding. Maple syrup is produced in all the New England states. Vermont dairy products – milk, cream, yogurt and cheese – are only slightly less famous than that state's most famous edible: Ben & Jerry's ice cream.

The major cities and the more sophisticated country inns have excellent restaurants serving refined American, continental and international cuisine. It is possible to spend anywhere from $2 to $200 per person for a meal.

Except deep in the forest, you are never far from someplace serving food. Some fast-food restaurants (hamburgers, pizza and doughnuts and coffee) are open 24 hours a day in cities and on highways. The food is often bland, but prices are low.

Breakfast is served in restaurants from 6 or 7 am to 11 am or noon, and in lodgings from about 7 to 9 or 10 am. Some restaurants advertise that they serve breakfast all day. The meal can be a muffin and coffee for under $2, or a hearty meal of fried eggs, or an omelet, bacon, ham or sausage, toast, fruit juice and coffee for $6 or $7.

Lunch is served from 11:30 am to 2 or 3 pm, and in fact many luncheon items are served right through till the evening closing time. A good simple lunch can cost $3 to $12, a fancy one up to $25. If you like good restaurants but can't afford their dinner prices, come for lunch. Portions will be somewhat smaller, but prices may be significantly lower.

Dinner is served in the fancier restaurants from 6 to 10 pm. Normally, a good dinner can be had in a pleasant though not fancy restaurant for $16 to $35, drinks included. In posh big-city restaurants and resorts it is possible (but unusual) to see a bill of $100 per person. Portions are usually large. Some restaurants continue serving from a lighter, less formal ("bar" or "tavern") menu until midnight or 1 am. Some restaurants close on Monday; a very few close on other days of the week.

In almost all restaurants, sections are designated as "smoking" and "nonsmoking." You will normally be asked which section you want. A growing number of restaurants are completely nonsmoking, meaning that you must step outside for a puff. See the sidebar Smoking, under Entertainment.

Fruit
Fruits are among the region's specialties as well. Strawberries come early, from mid-June through July. Local rhubarb is also ripe then, and if you come across a strawberry-rhubarb pie, grab two pieces at least. Late June to mid-July is blueberry season, when pies of fresh blueberries (huckleberries) appear. September brings peaches, plums and apples, as well as fresh-squeezed apple cider. Orchard farmstands are the best places to buy fruits.

Cranberries, a Massachusetts specialty, are also harvested in the autumn. The bright red berries grow in shallow ponds called bogs, and are harvested by amphibious machines. The berries are very tart and sour, but when sweetened make good juice, jelly, sauce, muffins and pies. Tart cranberry sauce is the traditional garnish for a Thanksgiving turkey.

Seafood

Fish Both intensive and illegal fishing have depleted stocks here as in other seas, raising prices on seafood. Still, if you enjoy seafood, you'll enjoy eating in New England.

New England's early commerce was built on fish. It is thought that Scandinavian fishing boats found bounteous harvests in the fishing grounds of Georges Bank even before the arrival of Columbus. In colonial and early American times the trade in codfish was so important that a stuffed codfish was put in a place of honor in the Massachusetts State House. It's still there.

Fish chowder is whitefish, potatoes, corn and milk. It usually takes second place to the more popular clam chowder.

Boston scrod is any bland whitefish. The term is said to have originated at a local hotel restaurant. The chef could never be sure which whitefish (cod, haddock, etc.) would be freshest in port that day, so he invented the word scrod and served the catch of the day sautéed in butter or covered with a cheese sauce. Patrons happily ordered the bland fish filets and didn't notice any difference among fish. Today, scrod usually refers to young codfish.

Bluefish, a full-flavored fish, can be fried, baked, broiled or grilled, or smoked and made into a pâté appetizer.

Monkfish is a large-flaked whitefish. When sautéed in butter it tastes mildly like lobster.

Halibut, swordfish and tuna steaks are excellent charcoal grilled and drizzled with lemon juice.

Oysters & Clams Oysters are available on many restaurant menus. Those harvested in Wellfleet, on Cape Cod, are the region's choicest. They're best eaten raw on the half shell, but may come grilled, fried, baked and stuffed, or in rich, creamy oyster stew.

Attached to the rocks and sea floor, dark purple salt water mussels are abundant along the New England coast. Their flavor is coarser than that of oysters or clams.

New England clams are of two types: soft-shell, with chalky, easily breakable shells; and hard-shell, with shells resembling porcelain.

The most popular soft-shell clams are "steamers." They're cooked in steam, which opens the shells. Extract the clam meat, shuck off the wrinkled membrane from the black "neck," wash off any sand by dipping the clam in the thin clam "broth" provided, dip in melted butter, and eat. After about five clams, you'll be shucking those membranes easily. The clam broth, by the way, is just the water the clams have been steamed in. It's used for dipping, not drinking.

The most common hard-shell clams are named littlenecks and cherrystones. They're best eaten raw on the half shell with a few drops of lemon juice, tomato sauce or horseradish, but they may be steamed or stuffed and baked as well.

Quahogs (KO-hogs) are sea clams larger than your fist. They're usually cut into strips, deep-fried and served as fried clams in seaside clam shacks, or chopped and used to make clam chowder. New England clam chowder is made of sliced or chopped quahogs, potatoes, milk, cream, and perhaps a bit of seasoning. Manhattan clam chowder, by the way, is made with a tomato base, not milk or cream, and is rarely found in New England.

The traditional New England clambake is a feast of steamed clams, boiled or roasted corn on the cob, and steamed or boiled lobsters.

Lobster Maine lobster is perhaps the most famous seafood dish. In fact, the same lobsters are caught off the coasts of Massachusetts, Maine and the Atlantic provinces of Canada, and are shipped around as demand requires. Purists – which are most New Englanders – demand live lobsters cooked to order, usually steamed for 10 to 20 minutes (depending upon size) in a large pot with a few inches of water. Steaming or boiling in seawater gives a distinctive flavor and salty tang. Lobsters may also be split from head to tail and grilled. Many restaurants serve baked stuffed lobster: the meat is removed, mixed with other ingredients, and the shell refilled. Most New Englanders look upon this as a tourist dish for the uninitiated.

Though lobster has a reputation as a luxury food, it was not always so. In colonial times, a governor of the Massachusetts Bay colony was forced to apologize to an important visitor because he had only lobster to serve him, as the cod boats could not go out. Lobsters were then so common they were harvested in great quantity from shallow waters, and used as fodder and fertilizer.

Store prices for lobster range from $4 to $8 and more per pound, depending upon the season; restaurant prices can be as low as $10 for a whole lobster with salad, corn on the cob, bread and butter, or $15 to $20 for "twin lobsters" (two chicken lobsters).

Summer sees the lowest prices for live lobsters. After summer, they're kept alive in seawater tanks for sale in other seasons, and are consequently more expensive. Prices are highest in spring.

Groceries & Markets

Many bakeries, snack shops, cafes and small restaurants in resort areas prepare food to take away. Most supermarkets

How to Eat a Lobster

Lobster is messy to eat. In early summer your lobster may come with a bone-hard shell, and you will have to use a cracker to break the claws. In mid- to late summer they have their new shells, which are soft and easily broken with the fingers. Purists believe (perhaps rightly) that spring hard-shell lobsters have the sweetest meat, and that soft-shell lobsters are not quite as good.

The best place to eat lobster is in a beachfront shack called a lobster "pound" or "pool." Here you can tear the beasts apart with abandon, using your fingers, which is the only way it can be done. To eat only the tail meat is looked upon by New Englanders as a terrible waste of good body and claw meat.

At lobster pounds or pools, live lobsters are cooked on order. They range in size from one pound ("chicken lobsters" or "chicks") to those weighing 1¼ to 1½ pounds ("selects") to "large" lobsters from two to 20 pounds in weight. "Culls," those missing a claw, are sold at a discount, as the claw meat is considered choice. "Shorts," smaller than chicks, do not meet the legal minimum size for harvesting. Do your part to discourage illegal fishing, and question any lobster that looks very small.

When you order lobster, you'll be brought some special tools: a plastic bib, a supply of napkins, a cracker for breaking the claws, a small fork or pick for excavating claws and other tight places, a bowl in which to throw shells, a container of melted butter, a slice of lemon and an alcohol-soaked towelette to wipe your hands after the mess is over.

The lobster may be very hot. Start by twisting off the little legs and sucking or chewing out the slender bits of meat inside. Go on to the claws: twist off the claw, break it with the cracker, and dip the tender claw meat in butter before eating. Each of the joints in the claw leg also has a large, succulent bit of meat in it as well. Use the cracker and pick to get it.

Next, pick up the lobster body in one hand and the tail in the other. Twist the tail back and forth to break it off. Break off each of the flippers at the end of the tail and suck out the meat. Then use your finger or an implement to push through the hole at the end of the tail where the flippers were, and the big chunk of tail meat will come out.

There is delicious meat in the body as well, though it takes work to get it. Tear off the carapace (back shell), then split the body in two lengthwise. Behind the spot where each small leg was attached is a chunk of meat, best gotten with pick and fingers. ∎

Culinary Terms

Here are some culinary terms common or unique to New England:

boiled dinner – a one-dish meal of boiled beef, cabbage, carrots and potatoes

bread pudding – baked pudding made with bread, milk, eggs, vanilla, nutmeg, and diced fruit such as dates, nuts or raisins

clam chowder (New England-style) – chopped sea clams, potatoes and perhaps corn in a base of milk and cream. (Manhattan-style) – same ingredients in a thick, tomato-based soup

clambake – a meal of lobster, clams and corn on the cob, usually steamed

cranberries – very tart, sour water-grown berries from Massachusetts, sweetened and used in juice, sauces, muffins, etc

frappe – pronounced "FRAP," whipped milk and ice cream; called a milkshake in other regions

fried dough – deep-fried pastry dough sprinkled with powdered sugar; served at snack stands and fairs

grinder – large sandwich of sliced meat, sausage, meatballs, cheese, etc, and salad on a long bread roll; called a hoagie, sub(marine), po' boy or Cuban in other regions

Indian pudding – baked pudding made of milk, corn meal, molasses, butter, ginger, cinnamon and raisins

johnnycake – Rhode Island-style pancakes

milkshake – a thin frappe

onion rings – a snack of sliced onion rings dipped in batter and deep fried

oven grinder – a heated grinder (see grinder)

raw bar – place to eat fresh-shucked live (raw) oysters and clams

tonic – soda; sweet carbonated ("fizzy") beverage

---

have delicatessen counters where you can buy cold meats, cheeses, salads, pâtés, dips, spreads and other picnic and quick-meal items.

Vacation cottages and condominiums have kitchens or kitchenettes, as do "efficiencies" – motel rooms equipped for light cooking.

DRINKS
Nonalcoholic Drinks

The familiar soft drinks – Coca-Cola, 7-Up, fruit-flavored fizzy drinks, root beer, ginger ale, etc – are readily available, and are sometimes called "tonic" or "pop" rather than soda or soft drinks. Also popular are bottled fruit juices, iced tea and spring water. Maine's own Poland Spring water is the local favorite. Most drinks are served in cups or glasses filled with ice, so you're paying mostly for frozen water. You might want to order your drinks "without ice" or "with just a little ice."

Tap water is safe to drink virtually everywhere, and usually quite palatable.

Americans are among the world's most frequent drinkers of coffee. Traditionally, American coffee is brewed from a brown-roasted bean, and is weaker than that preferred in Europe. In some parts of New England, "regular" coffee means coffee with sugar and milk or cream, so specify "black coffee" if that's what you want.

Espresso, the strong steam-pressed brew made from black-roasted beans, is easily available, as are American versions of other European favorites such as cafe au lait, cappuccino and caffé latte. True to form, the American versions are often elaborate concoctions with endless variations – with cinnamon, vanilla, raspberry or hazelnut flavoring, for instance – but little regard for the quality of the underlying coffee. Still, cities and most larger towns have specialty coffee shops where beans are roasted frequently, ground shortly before brewing, and brewed by bean variety or origin, to order.

Tea, likewise, comes in bewildering variety, but tends to be weak and less than robust in flavor. Tea is served with lemon unless milk is specified. Herbal teas of many kinds are readily available; decaffeinated tea is sold in stores, but is not commonly served in restaurants. Iced tea with lemon is a popular summer drink.

Alcoholic Drinks
New England has vineyards, wineries and breweries producing palatable, even excellent, regional vintages and beers.

Beverage Laws Alcoholic beverage use is governed by federal, state and local laws. In Maine, New Hampshire and Vermont, liquor may only be bought in state government-operated stores; in Connecticut, Massachusetts and Rhode Island liquor stores are private, and some supermarkets are licensed to sell wine and beer. Retail liquor stores are not permitted to sell alcohol on Sunday, though most restaurants and bars with liquor licenses may serve liquor by the drink on Sunday. The minimum age for drinking is 21 years, and anyone who looks younger than that will be carded – that is, asked to produce a convincing photo ID card bearing their birthdate. A driver's license or passport is accepted in virtually all cases.

A restaurant may have a "full liquor license" (for liquor, wine and beer), a "wine and beer" license, or no license. Some small or new restaurants without liquor licenses allow you to "BYO" (Bring Your Own alcoholic beverages). The restaurant typically offers "set-ups" (ice buckets for wine, glasses, corkscrews, mixers for mixed drinks, etc). A few New England towns (Rockport, MA, and Oak Bluffs, MA, on Martha's Vineyard come to mind) are "dry:" no shop, restaurant or hotel can sell or serve you alcohol, but you can buy wine, beer or liquor in another town, bring it into the dry town, and serve yourself.

You are not allowed to drink alcohol, even beer, in most fast-food restaurants such as hamburger, doughnut, pizza or sandwich shops. When in doubt, look for beer advertisement, such as a neon sign in the window, or ask inside.

Public drinking is also prohibited outdoors. You may not take alcoholic beverages to the park, beach or forest trail, or on a sidewalk or in your car. Indeed, in some states the driver of a car may be prosecuted for drunk driving if any open alcoholic beverage container is found in a car he or she is operating – even if it is being drunk exclusively by the passengers. If you are discreet, you can usually have wine or beer with your picnic.

Wine Grapes grow wild in New England. The Concord grape, a labrusca variety developed in Concord, MA, is used for grape juice, sweet and ceremonial wines, jellies, jams and fillings. Even so, the short growing season and rocky soil are not optimal for fine wine grapes.

Modern growing methods and careful study of micro-climates have allowed vintners in the southern New England states to produce drinkable table wines, white, red and "blush" (the favored euphemism for "rosé," a word now *déclassé*). Some vintage wines from hybrid and even vinifera grapes are of respectable quality and interesting flavor. Eastern Massachusetts, southeastern Rhode Island and northwestern Connecticut have vineyards. Try those made by Sakonnet Vineyards, RI, Chicama Vineyards on Martha's Vineyard, MA, Haight Vineyards near Litchfield, CT and Hopkins Vineyard on Lake Waramaug, CT.

Wines made from other fruits – apples, blueberries, pears, peaches, raspberries, etc – are made in a few wineries. Though without the complexity and body of grape wines, they can be tasty. Nashoba Valley Winery, near Concord, MA, makes good fruit wines, and you may find drinkable blueberry wine in Maine.

Beer The micro-brewery fashion has come to New England, spearheaded by the Boston Brewing Company's excellent Samuel Adams dark lager. The smallest micro-breweries are really brewpubs, serving their beers in only one or two local establishments. Slightly larger micro-breweries may distribute throughout their home state. A few, like Samuel Adams and Harpoon Lager (another Boston beer) are shipped to other states and even to other countries.

Liquor stores stock a bewildering variety of "coolers," flavored sparkling wines and beers, which might best be described as alcoholic soda pop.

Liquor Strong liquors of all kinds, both domestic and imported, are widely available. Favorite mixed drinks on hot days are gin, rum or vodka and tonic water, and drinks made with liquor and fruit or fruit juice, perhaps beaten or blended with ice.

If you're visiting from abroad and you like whiskey, be sure to try some Ken-tucky bourbon. Representative brands are Old Granddad (about $13 for a fifth – ⅘ of a quart or 750 ml), Wild Turkey ($18) and Maker's Mark ($25). Perhaps the best-known American whiskey is Jack Daniels ($16), a sour mash distilled in Tennessee.

ENTERTAINMENT
New England is rich in opportunities for entertainment in music, dance and drama.

Classical Music
The most famous symphony orchestra in the area is the Boston Symphony Orches-tra (BSO) conducted by Seiji Ozawa, but New England's other large cities have their own orchestras as well. The winter

---

Smoking
The USA, which gave the world tobacco, is in the throes of a rebellion against tobacco use. Anti-smoking advocates continue their efforts to banish tobacco advertising from the media, and to banish smokers from public places, while tobacco companies publish advertisements in news-papers and magazines about the anti-smoking "lifestyle police."

Many Americans find smoking an unpleasant and even danger-ous public health problem. Sci-entific evidence has shown that heavy or habitual smoking is unhealthful and harmful not only to the smoker but also to those nearby (particularly children and people with asthma or other pulmonary impairment).

If you are a smoker coming from a country which permits smoking in public places, you should be aware of American regulations and social customs.

Smoking is prohibited in most public buildings such as airports, train and bus stations, hospitals, stores, etc. You must step outside to smoke. (It's now common to see office workers standing outside near a door to their building, puffing away.)

Smoking is also prohibited on all public conveyances (airplanes, trains, buses).

Most cities and towns require restaurants to have nonsmoking sections. There is no requirement that there be smoking sections, and indeed some restaurants are com-pletely "smoke-free." Many hotels offer "nonsmoking" rooms – that is, rooms used only by nonsmoking guests so that the room has no stale tobacco smell.

If you are in an enclosed space (a room or car, for example) with other people, it's polite to ask permission of all others before you smoke, and to refrain from smoking if anyone protests. ■

season runs from September to March, and is followed by a "Pops" season of informal concerts indoors in a music hall atmosphere.

In summer, the orchestras move outdoors: the BSO heads for its Tanglewood series in Lenox, MA. There are other notable chamber music series at Tanglewood, in Great Barrington, MA, in Stowe and Marlboro, VT, and in Blue Hill, ME, among other venues.

There is no major opera house in New England. It is surprising that Boston, with such a rich cultural life and many distinguished musical performance halls, does not have a proper opera house. A converted theater called the Opera House is used for performances when Ms Sarah Caldwell's Opera Company of Boston can raise the funds for a season. Otherwise, local and visiting companies use all-purpose performance halls such as Boston's Wang Center. Some series are "concert opera," where the music is performed in a concert setting without sets or costumes.

Theater

Boston is a proving-ground for Broadway plays and musicals. Many of New England's universities have good theater departments. In summer, local theater companies in resort areas provide good entertainment at low prices, often with well-known stars. The Williamstown Theater Festival in Williamstown, MA, is worth making a special trip for, if you love theater. An evening of Shakespeare at the Mount, the late Edith Wharton's mansion in Lenox, MA, is a delight as well.

Dance

Boston has the most and best dance, with its Boston Ballet Company and a number of modern and experimental dance companies. In summer, the Jacob's Pillow Dance Festival in Lee, MA, in the Berkshires, is the region's premiere dance festival.

Popular Music

Several cities, including Boston, Burling-ton, Hartford, New Haven, Newport, Portland, Providence and Worcester are on the circuit for rock, pop and jazz performers year round. Warm-weather concerts are held outdoors in several cities and resorts, especially in Boston, in Massachusetts' Berkshire hills, on Cape Cod, and in Newport, RI. Sunday band or ensemble concerts are given, usually for free, in many towns. Ticket prices vary widely, from a few dollars for standing room to $50 to $100 for the best seats.

Clubs

Every city and town has at least a few clubs, lounges or bars providing live entertainment such as pop music, jazz, rock and roll, or standup comedy. In the larger cities and summer resorts, the choice and variety are great. Many places require you to pay a cover (admission) charge of a few dollars, or buy a minimum number of drinks, if you're there when the entertainment is on.

Coffeehouses & Bars

In the cities and in college towns, many coffeehouses and bars (which are usually more downscale than clubs) have live entertainment several nights per week. The groups are usually local, but are sometimes regional or even national talent. Prices, which may be a cover charge of $3 to $10, or a minimum order of drinks and/or food, are reasonable. Look in local newspapers and free tourist handouts, or in the cafes and bars themselves, for programs of events.

Cinemas

Boston, Cambridge and New Haven, being university towns, have the most cinemas with the widest range of offerings. Most towns of any size have at least one cinema, usually a "multiplex" or "cineplex" holding several small cinemas showing different movies. Admission ranges from a few dollars for some of the student shows to $6 to $8 for first-run flicks at the big-city cinemas.

SPECTATOR SPORTS

In the fall, regardless of the temperature or class of play, a football game is an exhilarating, fun experience. The same goes for baseball in the spring, summer and fall. Minor-league and college teams are sometimes significantly less expensive and yet more fun than professional teams.

Boston has major-league teams in baseball (Boston Red Sox), basketball (Boston Celtics), football (New England Patriots) and ice hockey (Boston Bruins). Also, Boston's colleges and universities support some excellent National Collegiate Athletic Association (NCAA) sports. See the Boston chapter for details.

In Rhode Island, the Pawtucket "PawSox" are a big minor-league Triple-A baseball draw.

In Vermont, Burlington has a Triple-A baseball team and UVM has a good hockey team; in Connecticut, Hartford has UConn's excellent basketball team and the major-league Hartford Whalers hockey team, Yale in New Haven has an athletic rivalry with Harvard in Cambridge, MA; in Cape Cod, MA, the Cape Cod Baseball League (established 1885) has teams in Brewster, Chatham, Falmouth, Harwich, Hyannis, Orleans and Yarmouth-Dennis.

THINGS TO BUY

Regional gifts and souvenirs include maple syrup and maple sugar candy, silver or pewter items in designs made by Paul Revere, and scrimshaw (carved ivory – but today it's plastic imitation ivory). The Bull & Finch Pub, inspiration for the popular television series *Cheers*, is Boston's most prolific souvenir factory, selling anything from T-shirts to buttons to beer mugs.

Getting There & Away

The two most common ways to reach New England are by air and by car, but you can also get there by train and bus.

AIR

From the mid-Atlantic states or the Midwest, it may make sense to drive your own car to New England. But from elsewhere in the USA, it makes sense to fly, then rent a car or get around by bus, plane and train once you arrive.

Airlines

These major airlines serve Boston and/or New York City:

Aer Lingus	☎ 800-223-6537
Aerolíneas Argentinas	☎ 800-333-0276
Air Canada *	☎ 800-776-3000
Air France	☎ 800-237-2747
Air New Zealand	☎ 800-262-1234
American Airlines *	☎ 800-433-7300
British Airways	☎ 800-247-9297
Canadian Airlines *	☎ 800-426-7000
China Airlines	☎ 800-227-5118
Continental Airlines *	☎ 800-525-0280
Delta Air Lines *	☎ 800-221-1212
Japan Air Lines	☎ 800-525-3663
KLM Royal Dutch	☎ 800-374-7747
LAN Chile Airlines	☎ 800-488-0070
Lufthansa Airlines	☎ 800-645-3880
Northwest Airlines *	☎ 800-447-4747
domestic	☎ 800-225-2525
Qantas Airways	☎ 800-227-4500
Scandinavian Airlines	☎ 800-221-2350
Singapore Airlines	☎ 800-742-3333
Swissair	☎ 800-221-4750
TWA *	☎ 800-221-2000
domestic	☎ 800-892-4141
United Airlines *	☎ 800-241-6522
USAir *	☎ 800-428-4322
Virgin Atlantic Airways	☎ 800-862-8621

* denotes major domestic carriers

A dozen smaller domestic airlines such as Midway Airlines have route systems concentrated in a particular region, with some national flights. Several of these are "discount" airlines that offer lower fares and fewer restrictions on their flights, but usually have fewer flights than the majors. Southwest Airlines (☎ 800-531-5601) serves mostly the western US, but may soon fly to the northeastern states as well.

Small regional "commuter" airlines shuttle passengers from large and intermediate-sized airports like Hartford, CT; Warwick, RI; and Albany, NY, to the airports of smaller cities. Others make short hops across bodies of water, as from New Bedford to Nantucket, MA, or Warwick to Block Island, RI. See the Getting Around chapter for these.

New England Airports

Boston's Logan International Airport is the major gateway to the region, and is easily accessible – usually by nonstop or direct flight – from other major airports in the USA. Several other airports in the region receive limited national and international flights: Albany, NY; Bradley International Airport in Windsor Locks, CT (serving Hartford, CT, and Springfield, MA); Burlington, VT; and Bangor and Portland, ME. The Getting Around chapter has details on these airports.

New York City Airports

New York City has three major airports, of which Newark International is the newest, most efficient and comfortable.

There are numerous flights daily to Boston from each of New York's three major airports, and even some commuter flights from New York's smaller airports (MacArthur, Islip, etc). USAir operates hourly shuttle flights between LaGuardia and Boston; no reservation needed. Continental operates similar flights between

Newark and Boston. Fares vary, but range between $79 and $129 one way for the 40-minute flight.

Scheduled flights connect New York City with these other New England airports: Albany, NY; Bangor, ME; Bridgeport, CT; Burlington, VT; Hartford, CT; Hyannis, MA; Lebanon, NH; Manchester, NH; Martha's Vineyard, MA; Nantucket, MA; New Haven, CT; New London, CT; Portland, ME; Presque Isle, ME; Providence, RI; and Worcester, MA.

Here's ground transportation advice for dealing with New York City. Each of these services also runs buses from the city to airports; all fares are one way. For the latest ground transportation information on any New York airport, call ☎ 800-247-7433.

John F Kennedy International This airport (JFK; ☎ 718-656-4520), 15 miles southeast of Manhattan on Long Island, handles mostly transcontinental and intercontinental flights.

Until 2001, JFK will be undergoing major renovations to terminals (especially the international arrival terminal) and roadways, and will purportedly be adding a major rail link with the Long Island Railroad. Prepare for delays.

The most convenient transport into the city is aboard a Carey Coach (☎ 800-678-1569) bus, which runs every 30 minutes from 6 am to midnight (45 to 65 minutes, $13) to Grand Central Terminal (for trains to New Haven, CT) and the Port Authority Bus Terminal (for buses to Boston and all other New England and US cities) in midtown Manhattan.

To connect with Amtrak trains at Penn Station, take the Carey Coach to the Jamaica Station of the Long Island Railroad (LIRR), then a train to Penn Station. This service operates every hour from 5:30 am to 10:30 pm, takes 60 to 70 minutes, and costs $8 to $10.

The cheapest way to get into Manhattan is also the longest: take the free yellow, white and blue Long-Term Parking Lot Bus to Howard Beach Station, then get on an "A" subway train (☎ 718-330-1234) to Far

Rockaway, connecting with other subway lines to reach your final destination in Manhattan. Trains ($1.50 – have exact change) run every 15 minutes, 24 hours a day.

A taxi from JFK to Manhattan takes 40 to 60 minutes (longer at peak traffic hours) and costs about $30, plus tolls.

LaGuardia LaGuardia (LGA; ☎ 718-533-3400), eight miles northeast of Manhattan, has mostly domestic US flights.

Carey Coach (☎ 800-678-1569) buses run every half hour between 6:45 am and midnight from LaGuardia and Grand Central Terminal (20 to 30 minutes or more, $10) and the Port Authority Bus Terminal (30 to 45 minutes or more, $10). To get to Penn Station for Amtrak trains, take the Carey Coach to the Long Island Railroad's Jamaica Station, as described above under JFK airport.

The Delta Water Shuttle (☎ 800-543-3779) operates between LaGuardia's Marine Air Terminal and Manhattan's 34th Street (East River) and Wall Street (Pier 11) Docks. The trip takes 30 to 45 minutes and costs $20; call for schedules.

The slowest but cheapest way is to catch an M60 bus ($1.25) to 125th St, or a Q33 or Q47 bus ($1.25), to connect with the subway system ($1.25).

A taxi to Manhattan takes 20 to 30 minutes or more, and costs about $20 to $25, plus tolls.

Newark International Newark (EWR; ☎ 201-961-6000), 16 miles southwest of Manhattan, handles both domestic and international flights. This is the most efficient and pleasant of New York City's major airports.

Ground transportation from Newark Airport into Manhattan is cheap and easy. Take a New Jersey Transit (☎ 201-762-5100, 800-772-2222) No 300 Express bus (30 to 40 minutes or more, $7) to the Port Authority Bus Terminal. Olympia Trails (☎ 212-964-6233) Express buses to Grand Central Terminal (30 to 60 minutes or more, $7) or to Penn Station (30 to 40 minutes or more, $7) run from 6:15 am to midnight.

If you're going to lower Manhattan ("downtown" rather than "midtown"), take an Olympia Trails bus to the World Trade Center (20 to 40 minutes or more, $7), or an Airlink/New Jersey Transit No 302 bus to the PATH subway station ($4), then a PATH train ($1).

A taxi from Newark Airport to Manhattan costs about $40 plus tolls, and takes 40 minutes or more.

Inter-Airport Transfers You can get from one airport to another by taking the Carey or Olympia buses into Manhattan, then transfer to an onward bus, but direct airport-to-airport buses and vans are faster, easier and only a few dollars more.

Carey Coaches run between JFK and LaGuardia every 30 minutes from 5:30 am to 11 pm for $10. The trip takes about 45 minutes. A taxi is a bit faster, costs $16 to $20 and makes sense if you share the fare with someone else – better yet, with two someones.

Between JFK and Newark, the Princeton Airporter Van (☎ 609-587-6600, 800-468-6696) runs frequently from 9 am to 10 pm, takes about 90 minutes for the trip and costs $19. A taxi costs $65 plus tolls.

Between LaGuardia and Newark, Marc 1 (☎ 718-352-7070, 800-309-7070) runs vans every three hours between 9:20 am and 9:30 pm (75 to 90 minutes for $18), or you can take a Carey or Olympia bus into Manhattan, then another one out to the airport.

Chicago Airports
Chicago is served by four airports: O'Hare International, Midway, Palwaukee and Merrill C Meigs. As one of the country's major air hubs, it has many daily flights to New England and nearby destinations, including Albany, NY; Bangor, ME; Boston, MA; Burlington, VT; Hartford, CT; Manchester, NH; New York, NY; Portland, ME; Providence, RI; and Worcester, MA. Its most active airlines are American, Midway (☎ 800-446-4392), Northwest, United and USAir.

Canadian Airports
Montréal's Dorval airport, 14 miles southwest of the city center, handles Canadian domestic flights and flights to the USA. Mirabel, 34 miles northwest of the city, handles intercontinental flights. Delta Airlines operates routes from Dorval Airport to Boston and Hartford. When flying to the USA from Toronto or Montréal, you clear US Customs and Immigration right in the Canadian airport before departure.

Buying Tickets
Airfares in the US range from incredibly low to heights that enter the realm of fantasy. While writing this guide I checked the airline computers for summer weekday roundtrip fares between Boston and Washington, DC. There were over four dozen separate fares ranging from $98 to $1838. Think of it: people paying $98 and others paying $1838 are flying on the same airplane.

In the USA, the *New York Times*, *Los Angeles Times*, *Chicago Tribune*, *San Francisco Examiner* and other major newspapers all produce weekly travel sections with many advertisements for discounted

Sample US Airfares
Here are sample discount roundtrip fares from various US and Canadian cities to Boston:

From:	R/T Excursion Fares
Atlanta, GA	$178 to $255
Chicago, IL	$129 to $286
Dallas-Fort Worth, TX	$296 to $459
Denver, CO	$338 to $392
Indianapolis, IN	$159 to $368
Los Angeles, CA	$386 to $528
Miami, FL	$196 to $378
Minneapolis-St Paul, MN	$278 to $398
Montréal, QC, Canada	$159 to $306
New York, NY	$107 to $218
Phoenix, AZ	$318 to $468
San Francisco, CA	$398 to $498
Seattle-Tacoma, WA	$388 to $518
Toronto, ON, Canada	$147 to $387
Washington, DC	$98 to $358

airfares. Council Travel (☎ 800-226-8624) and STA Travel (☎ 800-777-0112) have offices in major cities nationwide, and may offer good fares.

Travel CUTS has offices in all major Canadian cities, and often has fare bargains. The *Toronto Globe & Mail* and *Vancouver Sun* carry ads for low fares; the magazine *Great Expeditions* (PO Box 8000-411, Abbotsford BC, V2S 6H1) is also useful.

The travel sections of magazines such as *Time Out* and *TNT* in the UK, or the Saturday editions of the *Sydney Morning Herald* and *The Age* in Australia, carry ads offering cheap fares. STA, a travel agency which has been dependable in the past, has offices worldwide.

The magazine *Travel Unlimited* (PO Box 1058, Allston, MA 02134) publishes details of the cheapest international airfares and courier possibilities.

Return (roundtrip) tickets usually work out cheaper than two one-way fares – often *much* cheaper.

Discount Tickets If you call a major airline and book a same-day roundtrip flight to Boston from Chicago or Washington, DC, the fare can be as high as $600. If you reserve at least a week in advance and stay over a Saturday night before returning, the roundtrip fare can be as low as $125.

The rules are complex, but buying as far in advance as possible and staying over a Saturday night usually gets you the best fare. Also, certain times of the year are cheaper: mid-January through March and October through mid-December, except for Thanksgiving (see When to Go in the Facts for the Visitor chapter). Also, flights on certain days (Tuesday, Wednesday, Thursday, Saturday after noon and Sunday before noon) may be cheaper than others, and flights at certain times (10 am to 3 pm and after 8 pm on weekdays) may be cheaper as well.

The cheapest tickets are what the airlines call "nonrefundable," even though you may be able to get your money (or at least some of it) back under certain circumstances. A good strategy to use when buying a nonre-fundable ticket is to schedule your return flight for the latest possible date you're likely to use it. In many cases, an airline will allow you to fly standby at no extra charge if you return *earlier* than your scheduled flight; but if you want to fly *later*, you may have to pay a penalty, or buy another ticket entirely.

Holiday Periods At holiday times it can be difficult if not impossible to get the flights you want unless you plan – and reserve – well in advance. These include Christmas, New Year's, Easter, Memorial Day, Labor Day, and *especially* Thanksgiving, the busiest travel time of the year. Not only do the planes fill up early around holidays, but discount tickets are virtually impossible to find.

Special Fares for Foreign Visitors Just about all domestic carriers offer special fares to visitors who are not US citizens. Typically, you must purchase a booklet of coupons in conjunction with a flight to the USA from a foreign country other than Canada or Mexico. Each coupon in the booklet entitles you to a single flight segment on the issuing airline. You may have to use all the coupons within a limited amount of time, and there may be other restrictions, such as a limit of two transcontinental flights (ie, flights all the way across the USA).

Continental Airlines' Visit USA pass costs $479 for three coupons (minimum purchase) and $769 for eight (maximum purchase) in high summer. Changes of itinerary incur a $50 penalty. Northwest has a similar program.

On American Airlines, you must reserve your flights one day in advance.

Delta has two different programs. "Visit USA" grants discounts on certain fully-planned itineraries. "Discover America" allows purchase of coupons good for standby travel anywhere in the continental USA. Four coupons cost about $550, 10 cost $1250. Children's fares are about $40 less.

When flying standby, call the airline one or two days before the flight and make a "standby reservation." This way you get priority over all the others who just appear and hope to get on the flight the same day.

Round-the-World Tickets Round-the-World (RTW) tickets have become very popular in the last few years. Airline RTW tickets are often real bargains and can work out to be no more expensive or even cheaper than an ordinary return ticket. Prices start at about US$1300, A$1800 or UK£850.

RTW tickets are usually offered by a pair of airlines, and permit you to fly anywhere you want on their route systems as long as you do not backtrack. You may also have to book the first sector in advance, and cancellation penalties may apply. There may be restrictions on the number of stops. Tickets are usually valid from 90 days up to a year. An alternative type of RTW ticket is one put together by a travel agent using a combination of discounted tickets.

Although most airlines restrict the number of sectors that can be flown within the USA and Canada to four, and some airlines black out a few heavily traveled routes (like Honolulu to Tokyo) entirely, stopovers are otherwise generally unlimited. In most cases a 14-day advance purchase is required. After the ticket is purchased, dates can be changed without penalty and tickets can be rewritten to add or delete stops for $50 each.

British Airways and Qantas Airways offer a RTW ticket called the Global Explorer that allows you to combine routes on both airlines to a total of 28,000 miles for US$2999 or A$3099.

Qantas also flies in conjunction with Air France, American Airlines, Canadian Airlines, Delta, KLM and Northwest. Qantas RTW tickets, with any of the aforementioned partner airlines, cost US$3247 or A$3099.

Canadian Airlines offers numerous RTW combinations, such as with Philippine Airlines for C$2790 that could include the Philippines, Dubai, Pakistan and Europe; another with KLM that could include Cairo, Bombay, Delhi and Amsterdam for C$3149; and a third with South African Airways that could include Australia and Africa for C$3499.

Many other airlines also offer RTW tickets. Continental Airlines, for example, links up with either Malaysia Airlines, Singapore Airlines or Thai Airways for US$2570. TWA's lowest priced RTW, linking up with Korean Air, costs US$2087 and allows stops in Honolulu, Seoul, Tel Aviv, Amsterdam and Paris or London.

Getting "Bumped" Airlines routinely overbook flights, knowing that there are always numerous "no-shows" (people with reservations who do not take the flight). When no-shows leave empty seats, these become available to standby passengers. When there are few no-shows and there are more people than seats, the airline must "bump" excess passengers onto later flights.

If it appears that passengers will have to be bumped, the gate agent first asks for volunteers. Those willing are booked on the next available flight to their destination, and are also offered an incentive, which can be a voucher good for a roundtrip flight on the airline, or at least a discount on a flight, at a later date. In extreme circumstances, or when faced with a hard bargainer, the airlines may even offer cash, or both cash and a flight pass.

If your schedule is flexible (the next available flight might not be until the next day), getting bumped can be a bonanza. When you check in at the gate, ask if the plane is oversold, and if there may be a call for volunteers. If so, leave your name so you'll get first choice. When it comes time to collect your incentive, keep in mind that you do not have to accept the airline's first offer. You may haggle for a better "reward."

Baggage & Other Restrictions
Baggage regulations are set by each airline, but usually allow you to check two bags of average size and weight, and to carry at least one smaller bag onto the plane. If you are carrying many pieces of luggage, or pieces that are particularly big, bulky, fragile or heavy (such as a bicycle or other sports equipment), check with

your airline about special procedures and extra charges.

Your ticket folder usually gives details of items that are illegal to carry on airplanes, either in checked baggage or on your person. These may include weapons; aerosols; tear gas and pepper spray; camp-stove fuel cannisters; and full oxygen tanks. You may carry matches and lighters on your person, but do not put them in checked luggage.

Smoking Smoking is prohibited on all domestic flights within the USA. Several US airlines have extended the smoking ban to all their flights throughout the world. If you'd like to smoke while you fly, check with the airline before buying your ticket. If you'd like to avoid all smoke, that's worth checking as well.

Travelers with Special Needs

If you have special needs of any sort – a broken leg, dietary restrictions, dependence on a wheelchair, responsibility for a baby, fear of flying – airports and airlines can be surprisingly helpful, but you should let them know as soon as possible so that they can make arrangements accordingly. You should also remind them when you recon-firm your booking (at least 72 hours before departure) and again when you check in at the airport.

Guide dogs for the blind must often travel in a specially pressurized baggage compartment with other animals, away from their owner, though smaller guide dogs may be admitted to the cabin. Guide dogs are not subject to quarantine as long as they have proof of being vaccinated against rabies.

Deaf travelers can ask for airport and in-flight announcements to be written down for them.

Children under two years of age travel for 10% of the standard fare (or free, on some airlines), as long as they don't occupy a seat, but they usually don't get a baggage allowance. "Skycots" may be provided by the airline if requested in advance; these will take a child weighing up to 22 lbs. Children

between the ages of two and 12 can some-times occupy a seat for half to two-thirds of the full fare, and do get a baggage allowance. Strollers must usually be checked at the air-craft door; they are returned to you there right after the aircraft lands.

UK

The Globetrotters Club (BCM Roving, London WC1N 3XX) publishes a news-letter called *Globe* that covers obscure destinations and can help you find traveling companions. Also check the free maga-zines widely available in London – start by looking outside the main railway stations.

Travel Agents Most British travel agents are registered with the ABTA (Association of British Travel Agents). If you have paid for your flight to an ABTA-registered agent who then goes out of business, ABTA will guarantee a refund or an alternative.

Besides the many official fares published by the airlines and sold by them and their travel agencies, there are also "unofficial" bucket shop (consolidator) fares. These seats are sold by the airlines in bulk at a big discount to wholesale brokers, who then sell them to the public and hope to make a profit. If you deal with a reputable shop or agency, these fares can be good value on major airlines. Most such fares are non-refundable (see Discount Tickets under Buying Tickets, above).

London is arguably the world's head-quarters for bucket shops, which are well advertised and can usually beat published airline fares. Two agents for cheap tickets in the UK that have been reliable in the past are Trailfinders (☎ 0171-938-3366), 46 Earls Court Rd, London W8 6EJ, and STA Travel (☎ 0171-937-9962), 74 Old Brompton Rd, London SW7. Trailfinders produces a lavishly illustrated brochure including airfare details.

The very cheapest flights are often adver-tised by obscure bucket shops whose names haven't yet reached the telephone directory. Many such firms are honest and solvent, but there are a few rogues who will take your money and disappear, to reopen elsewhere a month or two later under a new name. If you feel suspicious about a firm, don't give them all the money at once – leave a deposit of 20% or so and pay the balance on receiving the ticket. If they insist on cash in advance, go elsewhere. And once you have the ticket, phone the airline to confirm that you are booked on the flight.

Fares Virgin Atlantic has a roundtrip in-season fare from London to Boston for £396 (US$594), or to New York for £448 (US$672), allowing a one-month maximum stay and requiring a 21-day advance purchase. Off-season (winter) flights from London cost about £192 (US$288) to Boston or £240 (US$360) to New York.

For flights from London to Montréal, Canadian Airlines is a good bet with off-season fares beginning around US$356.

Aer Lingus has direct flights from Shannon and Dublin to New York City, but because competition on flights from London is so much fiercer, it's generally cheaper to fly to London first.

Continental Europe

Virgin Atlantic flights from Paris to New York are substantially cheaper than alternatives; a ticket with seven-day advance purchase ranges from FF3790 (US$733) to FF4530 (US$876). In Paris, Transalpino and Council Travel are popular agencies.

In Amsterdam, a popular travel agent is NBBS Reizen (☎ 20-624-0989).

Lufthansa has nonstop service to Boston from its Frankfurt hub.

Australia & New Zealand

In Australia and New Zealand, STA Travel and Flight Centres International are major dealers in cheap airfares.

Qantas flies to Los Angeles from Sydney, Melbourne (via Sydney or Auckland) and Cairns. United flies to San Francisco from Sydney and Auckland (via Sydney), and also flies to Los Angeles. Connector flights are available to the East Coast.

The cheapest tickets have a 21-day advance-purchase requirement, a minimum stay of seven days and a maximum stay of 60 days. Qantas flies from Melbourne or Sydney to Los Angeles for A$1470 (US$1088) off-season and A$1820 (US$1346) in-season. Qantas flights from Cairns to Los Angeles cost A$1579 (US$1168) off-season and A$1919 (US$1420) in-season. Flying with Air New Zealand is slightly cheaper, and both Qantas and Air New Zealand offer tickets with longer stays or stopovers, but you pay more. Full-time students can save A$80 (US$59) to A$140 (US$103) on roundtrip fares to the USA.

Roundtrip student fares from Auckland to Los Angeles on Qantas cost NZ$1720 (US$1186) in the low season.

Asia

Hong Kong is the discount-ticket capital of the region, but its bucket shops can be unreliable. Ask the advice of other travelers before buying a ticket. STA Travel has branches in Hong Kong, Tokyo, Singapore, Bangkok and Kuala Lumpur.

Japan All Nippon Airways, American Airlines, Japan Air Lines, Northwest and United fly from Tokyo (Narita) to Boston via Chicago, Detroit or Minneapolis/St Paul. Cheapest return (roundtrip) fares range from US$1411 to US$2069.

Southeast Asia Bucket shops in places like Bangkok and Singapore should be able to come up with the best deals.

Flights to Boston from Hong Kong or Singapore are mostly via San Francisco, Los Angeles or Seattle/Tacoma, or via Europe. A normal low fare is around US$2665.

Flights from Bangkok and Kuala Lumpur to Boston are mostly via Europe. Thai International and British Airways fly from Bangkok via Heathrow to Boston for US$2170 to US$2371 and up. British Airways, Virgin Atlantic and Malaysian Airlines/American Airlines have fares from Kuala Lumpur via Heathrow to Boston for US$2435 to US$2879 and up.

Central & South America

Most flights from Central and South America go via Miami, Dallas/Fort Worth or Los Angeles, though go to New York. American, Continental, Delta, Northwest and United all have routes to Mexico, Central and South America. Aeromexico, Mexicana and the airlines of the Central American nations (Aeroquetzal, Aeronica, Aviateca, COPA, LACSA and TACA) have flights to either Miami or New York, with connections to Boston.

Arriving in the USA

As you approach the USA, your flight's cabin crew will hand out a customs and immigration form for you to fill in.

Arriving from outside North America, you must complete customs and immigration formalities at the airport where you first land, whether or not it is your final destination. Choose the proper immigration line: US citizens or non-US citizens. After immigration, pick up your luggage in the customs area and proceed to an officer who will ask you a few questions and perhaps check your luggage. The dog sniffing around the luggage is looking for drugs, explosives and restricted agricultural and food products.

If the airport where you enter the country is not your final destination, you must re-check your luggage.

Leaving the USA

You should check in for international flights at least two hours early. During check-in procedures, you might be asked for photo identification, and you will be asked questions about whether you packed your own bags, whether anyone else has had access to them since you packed them and whether you have received any parcels to carry. These questions are for security purposes.

LAND

Bus

Big, comfortable air-conditioned buses connect most cities and some towns in the USA. However, as the private auto is king,

and air service is faster in this big country, bus service is limited. You can get to New England by bus from all parts of the USA, Canada and Mexico, but the trip will be long, tedious, and ultimately won't be dramatically less expensive than a discounted flight. Bus travel usually only makes sense for those traveling alone, as couples and families can travel more quickly, pleasantly and independently by rented car at about the same expense.

As with planes and trains, New York City is the region's major hub for buses, and many routes from around the country come through New York on their way to New England.

The Port Authority Bus Terminal (☎ 212-564-8484), Eighth Ave and 42nd St in Manhattan, is the city's main bus terminal.

Fares Special travel plans and promotional fares are sometimes offered, and these can reduce fares substantially, especially on the longer trips. Ask about them when you call the bus company.

The table below contains regular one-way/roundtrip fares to Boston.

Bonanza Bonanza Bus Lines (☎ 212-564-8484, 800-556-3815) operates routes to Albany, NY, via the Berkshires (Great Barrington, Stockbridge, Lee, Lenox and Pittsfield, MA) from New York City; and from New York City to Cape Cod (Falmouth, Woods Hole and Hyannis, MA) via Providence, RI. Bonanza also operates buses to Newport, RI, and New Bedford, MA.

Traveling by Bus

From:	Fare	Hours
Chicago, IL	$99/$149	20
Montréal, QC	$40/$75	8
New Orleans, LA	$129/$219	32-35
New York, NY	$30/$55	5
San Francisco, CA	$159/$318	67
Toronto, ON	$75/$109	12
Washington, DC	$43/$80	9

East Coast Explorer The East Coast Explorer (☎ 718-694-9667, 800-610-2680) provides an "alternative" way to travel between Boston, New York City and Washington, DC. Using scenic back routes and passenger vans carrying no more than 14 people, the all-day trip (really a tour) from New York to Boston ($29 one way) makes stops in Guilford and Mystic, CT, among other scenic towns, and gets you to Boston around 7 pm. The return trip follows a different route.

The East Coast Explorer travels its route once a week, though there are plans to expand the service. Pick-up and drop-off points are in areas of the cities convenient to travelers, and reservations are required one day to one month in advance. Contact Larry Lustig for details.

Green Tortoise For travel between the West Coast and New England, Green Tortoise (☎ 415-956-7500, 800-867-8647) buses are more relaxing than Greyhound and *a lot* more entertaining. Foam mattresses and booths with tables replace bus seats, the maximum number of passengers is 38, and food, music and merriment prevail. Tortoise buses leave about every two weeks from their private hostel in San Francisco, and spend either 10, 11 or 14 days winding across country via New York to Boston, and vice versa. Along the way you visit state and national parks, monuments, forests, and anywhere else your fellow passengers agree to stop; flexibility is key. Fares are from $350 to $460, including meals.

Greyhound Greyhound Lines (☎ 212-635-0800, 800-231-2222) operates buses from New York City to Hartford, Springfield, Worcester, New Haven, New London and Providence. Service to Cape Cod is provided in conjunction with Bonanza. The Boston service has a few buses daily.

Vermont Transit Vermont Transit Lines (☎ 802-864-6811, 212-594-2000, 800-451-3292 in New England) serves Montréal, Vermont, Boston, Maine and several points in New Hampshire.

Train
Rail passenger service in the USA is operated primarily by Amtrak (☎ 800-872-7245, 800-USA-RAIL), a quasi-governmental corporation. Service in the "Northeast Corridor" connecting Boston with New York and Washington, DC, is some of the most frequent in Amtrak's system, and yet there are far more airplanes on this route than there are trains.

Several Amtrak routes pass through New York City's Pennsylvania Station (Penn Station), from which about seven trains depart daily for Boston.

Half the trains between Boston and New York are unreserved; the other half are New England Express all-reserved trains with somewhat higher fares. Book with Amtrak or a travel agent.

Smoking is not permitted on most routes; however, on some routes smoking is allowed in private rooms and in the lounge car during specific times.

Fares Amtrak offers special excursion fares, seasonal discounts and rail passes good for unlimited travel during a certain period of time. Children receive discounts as well. The fares listed below are unreserved, coach class, peak-season fares, one-way/roundtrip, to Boston. They're subject to change, and do not include meals. You may buy snacks or meals on board, or take your own food. If you travel 1st class in a club or sleeping car, meals are included.

Washington to Boston Boston is the northern terminus of Amtrak's bustling *Northeast Corridor* train service, connecting Hartford, Providence, New Haven,

Traveling by Train

From:	Fare	Hours
Chicago, IL	$129/$258	21
New Orleans, LA	$172/$202	26
New York, NY	$47/$189	4
San Francisco, CA	$247/$298	72
Washington, DC	$78/$189	8

New York City, Philadelphia, Baltimore and Washington, DC.

New York City to Boston The main line from New York to Boston, the *Shore Route*, follows the coast for much of the way, stopping in New Rochelle, NY; Stamford and Bridgeport, CT, before coming to New Haven, CT (Yale University); Old Saybrook, CT (for Old Lyme, Essex and Ivoryton); New London, CT (US Coast Guard Academy); Mystic, CT (Mystic Seaport Museum); Westerly, RI (for Stonington and Rhode Island beaches); Kingston, RI (for Narragansett, Port Galilee and Block Island); and Providence, RI, before reaching Boston.

The *Inland Route* itinerary follows the main line from New York City as far as New Haven, then runs west up the Connecticut River Valley stopping at Wallingford, Meriden, Berlin (New Britain) and Hartford, CT, then Windsor, Windsor Locks (for Bradley International Airport) and Springfield, MA. One or two trains daily continue past Springfield to Worcester and Framingham, MA, then to Boston. This route takes much longer than the *Shore Route* via Providence.

New York City to Connecticut Trains operated by the Connecticut Department of Transportation *(not* Amtrak), known as Metro North service, link New York City's Grand Central Terminal to New Haven, CT (and stops in between), every hour on the hour from 7 am until after midnight on weekdays, with extra trains during the peak morning and evening hours. Service on Saturday, Sunday and holidays is almost as frequent, with a train at least every two hours. The trip from Grand Central to New Haven takes 1¾ hours. For exact schedule information, call ☎ 212-532-4900 in New York City or ☎ 800-223-6052 in Connecticut.

New York City to Cape Cod During July and August, Amtrak operates special weekend trains from New York City to Hyannis, MA, on Cape Cod.

The *Cape Codder* departs New York's Penn Station in the late afternoon on Friday, stops at Bridgeport, New Haven, New London and Mystic in Connecticut; Westerly and Providence in Rhode Island; and Buzzards Bay, Sandwich and West Barnstable in Cape Cod, terminating in Hyannis. Return trips from Hyannis depart on Sunday afternoon. This train may also serve parts of New Jersey, Philadelphia, PA; Baltimore, MD; and Washington, DC. Call Amtrak for details.

New York City to Vermont The *Vermonter* begins in Washington, DC; runs to Newark, NJ; New York City; Stamford, New Haven and Hartford, CT; Springfield, Amherst, Hartford, MA; and onto St Albans, VT.

New York City to Montréal Two Amtrak trains run daily from Montréal's Central Station (beneath the Queen Elizabeth Hotel) to New York City, a distance of 450 miles.

The *Adirondack*, a day train (10 hours), runs down the Hudson River Valley along the eastern border of New York stopping at Port Kent, NY (ferry to Burlington, VT), and Albany-Rensselaer, NY, before terminating at New York's Grand Central Terminal. Buses connect Albany with southern Vermont and the Berkshires.

The *Montréaler* runs between New York and northern Vermont along the Connecticut River Valley. At the Canadian border, passengers board a bus for the ride to Montréal. Stops include Essex Junction (for Burlington), White River Junction and Brattleboro, VT; Amherst, MA and New Haven, CT.

Chicago to Boston Amtrak's *Lake Shore Limited* departs Chicago's Union Station each evening for Boston, making stops at Toledo and Cleveland, OH; Buffalo, Rochester, Syracuse and Albany-Rensselaer, NY; and Springfield, Worcester and Boston, MA. You can connect with a New York-bound train at Springfield.

Car
Foreign drivers of cars and riders of motorcycles will need their vehicle's registration papers, liability insurance and an inter-

national driver's permit, in addition to their domestic driver's license. Canadian and Mexican drivers' licenses are accepted.

Though the easiest way to get to New England is by airplane, the best way to get around is by car, so you may want to drive. Below are some route suggestions.

From New York City For Connecticut's Litchfield Hills, Massachusetts' Berkshires, southern and western Vermont, take the Henry Hudson Parkway or I-87 north from New York City to the Saw Mill Parkway, which connects with the Taconic State Parkway North. The Taconic is a beautiful non-toll road free of trucks.

For southwestern Connecticut, Hartford, central Massachusetts, Boston, eastern Vermont, New Hampshire and Maine, take the Henry Hudson Parkway or I-87 north to the Saw Mill Parkway, and then north to I-684, which connects with I-84 east via Danbury and Waterbury to Hartford and beyond.

For the Connecticut and Rhode Island coasts (New Haven, New London, Mystic, Providence, Newport), New Bedford and Plymouth, Cape Cod, Martha's Vineyard and Nantucket, MA, take the Henry Hudson Parkway or I-87 north to I-287, then east on I-287 to the Hutchinson River Parkway North. This leads into Connecticut's Merritt Parkway, a scenic toll road not open to trucks. (The alternate route, I-95, has very heavy truck traffic.) The Merritt Parkway in turn leads into the similarly-pleasant Wilbur Cross Parkway, which passes New Haven before heading north to Meriden and Hartford.

For points along Connecticut's southern shore, go east from New Haven on truck-filled I-95. The alternative is the much slower, though more interesting, US 1, which goes through all the coastal towns and their traffic lights.

From Montréal If you're headed for western Vermont, Massachusetts and Connecticut, cross the Pont Victoria or Pont Jacques-Cartier east from Montréal and take CN 15 south to the US border and

I-87. From Gordon Landing (I-87 exit 39) north of Plattsburgh, NY, you can catch a ferry to Grand Isle and follow US 2 to I-89 and Burlington, VT. An alternative route is via Port Kent, NY, farther south, and the ferry (summer only) across Lake Champlain to Burlington. Ferry service is described in the Burlington section of the Vermont chapter.

For Vermont, southern New Hampshire and the southern New England states, cross the Pont Victoria and follow CN 10 (*Autoroute des Cantons de l'Est*) eastward 22 km (13 mi) to CN 35 and QC 133 South. At the US border, follow I-89 south via Burlington and Montpelier to White River Junction, VT, and the junction with I-91. Continue on I-89 to reach Concord and Manchester, NH, and Boston; or take I-91 south to southern Vermont and New Hampshire, central Massachusetts and central Connecticut around Hartford.

If you're traveling from Montréal to northern New Hampshire and Maine, take the Pont Victoria, and follow CN 10 eastward as far as Magog. Turn south on CN 55 to the US border to connect with I-93, which leads straight to New Hampshire's White Mountains. To get to Maine, take US 2 or US 302 eastward from I-93.

Another route from Montréal to Maine, slower, less scenic, and with fewer tourist services, is to continue on CN10 east from Magog and through Sherbrooke. Beyond Sherbrooke, QC 112 is a two-lane road. Follow it to St-Gerard, then follow QC 161 through Lac-Mégantic to the US border. In Maine, follow ME 27 through sparsely-populated forests and mountains to the capital city of Augusta.

From Chicago & Toronto The most direct route is I-80, though the portion between Chicago and Cleveland has heavy truck traffic and is not particularly pleasant. An alternative is I-94 via Detroit into Canada to follow CN 401 to Hamilton before heading down via Niagara Falls to Buffalo and I-90, the New York State Thruway, to Albany and Boston.

From Toronto, the Hamilton; Niagara

Falls; Buffalo, NY; Albany, NY route is the most direct unless you're headed for northern New England, in which case you might want to drive via Montréal.

Drive-Aways

A drive-away is a car that belongs to someone who can't drive it to a specific destination but is willing to allow someone else to drive it. For example, if somebody moves from Denver to Boston, they may elect to fly and leave the car with a drive-away agency. The agency will find a driver and take care of all necessary insurance and permits. If you happen to want to drive from Denver to Boston, have a valid driver's license and a clean driving record, you can apply to drive the car. Normally, you have to pay a small refundable deposit. You pay for the gas (though sometimes a gas allowance is given). You are allowed a set number of days to deliver the car – usually based on driving eight hours a day. You are also allowed a limited number of miles, based on the best route and allowing for reasonable side trips, so you can't just zigzag all over the country. However, this is a cheap way to get around if you like long-distance driving and meet eligibility requirements.

Drive-away companies often advertise in the classified sections of newspapers under Travel. They are also listed in the yellow pages under Automobile Transporters & Drive-Away Companies. You need to be flexible about dates and destinations when you call. If you are going to a popular area, you may be able to leave within two days or less, or you may have to wait over a week before a car becomes available. The routes most easily available are coast to coast, although intermediate trips are certainly possible.

DEPARTURE TAXES

There's a $6 airport departure tax charged to all passengers bound for a foreign destination, as well as a $6.50 North American Free Trade Agreement (NAFTA) tax charged to passengers entering the USA from a foreign country. There may also be smaller airport usage and security fees payable depending upon which airport you fly to or from. Airport departure taxes are normally included in the cost of tickets bought in the USA. If you bought your ticket outside the USA, you may have to pay the tax when you check in for your departing flight.

WARNING

The information in this chapter is particularly vulnerable to change: prices for international travel are volatile, routes are introduced and canceled, schedules change, special deals come and go, and rules and visa requirements are amended. You should check directly with the airline or a travel agent to make sure you understand how a fare (and ticket you may buy) works.

You should also get opinions, quotes and advice from as many airlines and travel agents as possible before you part with your hard-earned cash. The details given in the chapter should be regarded as pointers and are not a substitute for your own careful, up-to-date research.

Getting Around

Without doubt, the best way to get around New England is by car. The region is relatively small, the highways are good, and public transportation is not as frequent or as widespread as in some other countries. Still, there are the alternatives of air, train, bus and boat which may make sense for some routes.

AIR
Regional Airlines

Regional airlines provide commuter service and "puddle jumpers," small aircraft that can shuttle you around some of the larger towns in New England. These include:

Air Tran Airways	☎ 800-247-8726
American Eagle	☎ 800-433-7300
Business Express	☎ 800-221-1212
Colgan Air	☎ 800-272-5488
Continental Express	☎ 800-525-0280
Delta Connection	☎ 800-345-3400
Mohawk Airlines	☎ 800-252-2144
Nantucket Airlines	☎ 800-635-8787
New England Air	☎ 800-464-2460
Northwest Airlink	☎ 800-225-2525
TWA Express	☎ 800-221-2000
United Express	☎ 800-241-6522
USAir Express	☎ 800-428-4322

Airports

Small regional and commuter airlines connect New England's cities and resorts with Boston and New York City. The following airports receive scheduled flights.

Albany County Airport (☎ 518-869-9611), in Albany, NY, on I-90 across the Massachusetts border from Stockbridge, serves the Berkshires and western Massachusetts, as well as Vermont.

Barnstable Airport (☎ 508-775-2020), in Hyannis, MA, serves Cape Cod.

Bradley International Airport (☎ 860-292-2000) in Hartford (Windsor Locks), CT, serves all of Connecticut and greater Springfield, the Pioneer Valley and the Berkshires in Massachusetts, plus Vermont.

TF Green State Airport (☎ 401-737-4000) in Warwick, RI, (near Providence) is that state's largest airport served by commercial and commuter airlines.

Martha's Vineyard Airport (☎ 508-693-7022) serves that island, just as the Nantucket Airport (☎ 508-325-5300) serves Nantucket, MA.

Worcester Municipal Airport (☎ 508-792-0610) in Worcester, MA, serves central Massachusetts and northern Connecticut.

Groton/New London Airport (☎ 860-445-8549) in Connecticut serves the southeastern Connecticut coast. The state's Tweed-New Haven Airport (☎ 203-787-8283) and Igor Sikorsky Memorial Airport (☎ 203-576-7498) also serve the coast with commuter flights.

Burlington Airport (☎ 802-862-9286) is Vermont's major airport, but Vermont is served by those in Albany, NY, Boston, Hartford and Montréal as well.

Augusta, Bangor, Bar Harbor/Hancock County (which serves Acadia National Park), Portland, Presque Isle and Rockland/Knox County Regional Airports in Maine have regularly scheduled flight service. For more on these airports, see the destination headings in the Maine chapter.

BUS

Buses go to more places than airplanes or trains, but the routes still leave a lot out. Except on the most heavily traveled routes, there may be only one or two buses per day.

The major companies with routes which cover several New England states are Bonanza, Greyhound, Peter Pan and Vermont Transit.

Bonanza

Bonanza Bus Lines (☎ 401-331-7500, 800-556-3815), with its hub in Providence, RI, runs buses from New York City via Danbury and Hartford, CT, to

Providence, RI; and via New Milford, Kent and Canaan, CT to Massachusetts' Berkshire hills and Bennington, VT. Other routes connect Providence with Newport, RI, Boston, Fall River, Falmouth, and Hyannis, MA, and Woods Hole on Cape Cod.

Greyhound

Greyhound (☎ 617-526-1810, 800-231-2222) buses connect Boston with Albany, NY; Hartford and New Haven, CT; Newark, NJ; New York City; and the Berkshire hills, Springfield and Worcester, MA, with connecting service to many other parts of the country.

Other Greyhound routes run north via Portsmouth, NH, along the Maine coast with stops in Portland, Freeport, Brunswick, Bath, Wiscasset, Camden, and Bangor. Connecting services can carry you onward to Ellsworth, for Bar Harbor and Acadia National Park; and into New Brunswick and Nova Scotia.

Peter Pan

Peter Pan Bus Lines (☎ 413-781-3320, 800-343-9999), based in Springfield, MA, runs on routes connecting Boston with Albany, NY (with connections as far as Toronto); Amherst, MA; Baltimore, MD; Bangor, ME; Bennington, VT; Bridgeport and Danbury, CT; Greenfield, MA; Hartford, CT; Holyoke and Lee, MA; Middletown, New Britain and New Haven, CT; New York City; Northampton, MA; Norwalk, CT; Philadelphia, PA; Portland, ME; Pittsfield, Springfield and Sturbridge, MA; Waterbury, CT; Washington, DC; Williamstown and Worcester, MA.

Peter Pan buses also run from Springfield, MA, and the Pioneer Valley to Bradley International Airport north of Hartford, CT.

Vermont Transit

Vermont Transit Lines (☎ 802-864-6811, 800-451-3292 in New England), based in Burlington, has routes connecting major Vermont towns with Albany, Binghamton and New York, NY; Boston, MA; Man-

chester and Portsmouth, NH, Bangor, Bar Harbor, Brunswick and Portland, ME; with connections via Greyhound to many other points in New England. There are connections at Burlington with Montréal, Québec, Canada.

Massachusetts Service

Several bus lines operate only within Massachusetts.

American Eagle (☎ 508-990-0000), at Boston's Peter Pan Terminal, operates frequent buses daily between Boston and New Bedford.

Cape Cod Bus Lines (☎ 508-775-5524), based in Hyannis, operates buses among Cape Cod towns from Hyannis to Provincetown.

Englander Bus Lines (☎ 617-423-5810), in Boston's Greyhound Terminal runs buses from Boston via MA 2 to Williamstown.

Plymouth & Brockton Street Railway Co (☎ 508-746-0378, http://www.p-b.com), at Boston's Peter Pan Terminal, goes to Plymouth, Sagamore, Barnstable, Hyannis, Chatham and Provincetown on Cape Cod.

New Hampshire Service

Concord Trailways (☎ 603-228-3300, 800-639-3317), based in Concord, NH, provides most of the bus service in the state, running from Boston up I-91 all the way to Littleton, and also via Laconia and Conway to Gorham and Berlin.

Maine Service

C&J Trailways (☎ 800-258-7111) services Newburyport, MA, Portsmouth, NH and lower coastal Maine, including Kennebunkport, Wells and Ogunquit. Greyhound and Vermont Transit also run buses within Maine.

TRAIN

Amtrak (☎ 800-872-7255) routes throughout New England are covered in the Getting There & Away chapter. Work is under way to restore train service between Boston and Portland, ME. Call Amtrak for an update.

Connecticut is served by two convenient rail lines, Metro North and the Connecticut Commuter Rail Service. Metro North trains (☎ 212-532-4900, 800-638-7646) make the 1½-hour run between New York City's Grand Central Terminal and New Haven, CT. Other branches of Metro North service go north to Danbury, New Canaan and Waterbury, CT.

Connecticut Commuter Rail Service's Shore Line East service (☎ 800-255-7433) travels along the shore of Long Island Sound. At New Haven trains connect with Metro North and Amtrak routes. See Getting There & Away in the Connecticut chapter for details on these routes.

In Boston, North Station serves MBTA Commuter Rail trains (☎ 800-392-6099) that travel out of the city to the west and north, including stops at Concord, Rockport, Gloucester and Manchester. See Boston, Getting There & Away for details.

CAR

Driving is the best way to see New England. If you don't have your own transportation, consider renting a car for at least part of your stay.

Rental

You must be at least 21 years of age (in some cases 25) and have a valid driver's license to rent a car. A major credit card is a practical necessity as well. Without one, you may have to put down a cash deposit of up to $2000.

Well-known, international car rental companies such as Avis, Budget, Dollar, Hertz, National and Thrifty tend to have higher rates, but more efficient service. National firms can be a bit cheaper, but it is the small local companies which are the cheapest. Quality, service and car condition are most variable among the local firms, which often specialize in rentals to people whose own cars are under repair.

National Companies

Reservations can be made with the large rental companies through a travel agent, or by calling the company directly; numbers are listed under Automobile Renting in the yellow pages. Here are some numbers, local to Boston and national:

Alamo	☎ 617-561-4100
	800-327-9633
American International	☎ 800-227-0648
Avis	☎ 617-534-1400
	800-831-2847
Budget	☎ 617-497-1800
	800-527-0700
Dollar	☎ 617-523-5098
	800-800-4000
Enterprise	☎ 617-742-1955
	800-325-8007
Hertz	☎ 800-654-3131
National	☎ 617-661-8747
	800-227-7368
Payless Car Rental	☎ 800-729-5377
Rent-A-Wreck	☎ 617-576-3700
Thrifty	☎ 617-569-6500
	800-367-2277

Local Companies

Some local rental companies and automobile dealerships rent cars as well, often providing good service at cheaper rates. Most should offer free delivery and pickup at the airport or a hotel, unlimited mileage, and quality cars.

Before you rent from a local agency, you might want to check their standing with Boston's Better Business Bureau (☎ 617-426-9000), 20 Park Plaza, Boston, MA 02116, which keeps files of complaints on problem companies. If you find that one of these companies gives particularly good service, please write to me and let me know so that I can recommend it in future editions of this guide.

Agency Rent-A-Car
(☎ 617-783-4470, 800-321-1972)
367 Western Ave, Brighton, MA 02135
Americar Auto Rental
(☎ 617-776-4640, 800-540-4642)
265 Medford St, Somerville, MA 02143
Peter Fuller Rent-a-Car
(☎ 617-926-7511)
43 N Beacon St, Watertown, MA 02172
Snappy Car Rental
(☎ 617-924-7147)
660 Arsenal St, Watertown, MA 02172
U-Save Auto & Truck Rental
(☎ 800-272-8287)
Prospect St, Somerville, MA 02143

Insurance Rental vehicles come with liability insurance so that if you hit another person or property, the damage will be paid for. What is not covered is damage to the rental vehicle itself. The so-called Collision Damage Waiver (CDW) or Loss Damage Waiver on a rental car may cost between $10 and $16 or more per day, significantly increasing the cost of the overall rental. Though it would be foolish to rent without insuring the vehicle in some way, you do not necessarily have to buy the rental company's inflated CDW.

If you own a car registered in the USA, your own auto insurance may cover damage to a rental car; check with your insurance agent to be sure. Some major credit cards may provide coverage for any rental car rented with the card; check your credit card agreement to see what coverage is provided. Note that in case of damage, rental car companies may require that you pay not only for repairs, but also that you pay normal rental fees for all the time that the rental car is off the road for repairs. Your policy should cover this loss as well.

Saving Money The cheapest rates are for the smallest cars, from Thursday noon through Monday noon (or for an entire week or more), returning the vehicle to the place, or at least to the city of rental.

Because of airport taxes, a rental is often more expensive if you pick it up at the airport. A taxi ride to the off-airport office of a local firm may result in a lower price.

You may be offered a choice of "fuel plans:" you can pick up and return the car with a full tank of fuel, or you can pay for the gas that's in the car and return it empty. The full tank is always the better choice. As it's virtually impossible to return a car empty of gas, you will end up turning over several gallons of fuel to the rental company, which will then try to sell it to the next renter.

RV Rental

Most campgrounds are designed to accommodate recreational vehicles, from camper vans to the largest motor homes. Rentals can cost anywhere from $75 to $125 per day, and as they are large vehicles they use lots of fuel. In addition, parking them and sleeping in them overnight outside of camping areas is not allowed in many areas, so you should expect to spend around $10 to $20 per night for a camping place.

Before you decide on an RV rental, read about camping under Accommodations in Facts for the Visitor chapter. For further information, contact the Recreation Vehicle Rental Association (☎ 703-591-7130, 800-336-0355, fax 703-591-0734), 3930 University Drive, Fairfax, VA 22030. Companies which rent RVs are listed in the yellow pages under Recreational Vehicles – Renting & Leasing, Motor Homes – Renting & Leasing and Trailers – Camping & Travel.

Driving Laws

Driving laws are different in each New England state. Generally, you must be 18 years of age to have a driver's license.

Speed Limits The maximum speed on most New England highways is 55 mph, though you're likely to find traffic moving at 65 mph on the major expressways. A few stretches of expressway in Massachusetts and New Hampshire allow speeds up to 65 mph, which means traffic generally moves at around 70 mph. On undivided highways, speed limits vary from 30 to 55 mph. In cities and towns, they are usually 25 to 35 mph, less near schools and medical facilities.

Speed limits are enforced by police patrolling in marked police cars, unmarked cars and by "radar traps" placed so that you won't see them until it's too late. One way to avoid a radar trap is to watch the brake lights of the cars ahead of you. If all the drivers ahead put on their brakes as they pass a certain point, it's likely they've seen a radar trap (too late).

Fines for speeding can run several hundred dollars per offense.

Safety Restraints Some states require the use of safety belts, fining both the driver and the beltless passenger for riding unsecured. Regardless, your chances of avoiding injury in an accident are significantly higher if you wear a safety belt. Buckle up!

In every state, children under four years of age are required by law to be placed in child safety seats secured by a seat belt. Older children may be required by law to wear safety belts. Child safety seats are available from car rental firms, sometimes at a small extra charge.

Fuel

Gas stations can be found everywhere – sometimes on each of the four corners of an intersection – and many are open 24 hours a day. Small town stations may be open only from 7 am to 8 or 9 pm.

At some stations you must pay before you pump, at others you may pump before you pay. The more modern pumps have credit/debit card terminals right in them so you can pay with plastic right at the pump. The most modern pumps have little television screens in them that blast advertisements in your face as you pump the gas. At more expensive, "full service" stations an attendant will pump your gas for you; no tip is expected.

Plan on spending at least $1.30 per US gallon, more around big cities and for higher octane fuels. Leaded gasoline is not sold in the USA.

Accidents Happen

It's important to know the appropriate protocol when involved in a "fender-bender."

• Remain at the scene of the accident until you have exchanged information with the police or the other drivers involved, especially if there has been substantial damage or personal injury. It may be necessary to move your car off the road for safety's sake, but leaving the scene of an accident is illegal.

• Call the police (and an ambulance, if needed) immediately, and give the operator as much specific information as possible (your location, any injuries, etc). The emergency phone number is ☎ 911.

• Get the other driver's name, address, driver's license number, license plate and insurance information. Be prepared to provide any documentation you have, such as your passport, international driver's license and insurance documents.

• Tell your story to the police carefully. Refrain from answering any questions until you feel comfortable doing so (with a lawyer present, if need be). That's your right under the law. The only insurance information needed is the name of your insurance carrier and your policy number.

• If you've hit a large animal, such as a deer or moose, and it's badly injured, call the police to report it immediately. If your car is damaged in any way, report it to your insurance company or rental agency.

• If a police officer suspects that you are under the influence of alcohol, he or she may request that you submit to a breath-analysis test. If you do not, you may have your driving privileges suspended until a verdict is delivered in your court case.

• If you're driving a rental car, call the rental company promptly. ■

Road Maps

Detailed maps are printed and distributed by state tourism offices (see Tourist Offices in the Facts for the Visitor chapter) for free or for a dollar or two. Good commercial maps, like Arrow maps, are sold in gas stations, newsstands, bookstores, convenience and drug stores for $2 to $4.

Parking

Parking is controlled mostly by signs on the street stating explicitly what may or may not be done. A yellow line or yellow-painted curb means that no parking is allowed there. In some towns, a white line is painted along the curb in areas where you may park.

Safety

To avert theft, do not leave expensive items, such as purses, compact discs, cameras, leather bags, or even sunglasses visibly lying around in the car. Tuck items under the seat, or even better, put them in the trunk and make sure your car does not have trunk entry through the back seat; if it does, make sure this is locked. Don't leave valuables in the car overnight.

Some but not all US states have laws requiring motorcycle riders to wear helmets whenever they ride. In any case, use of a helmet is highly recommended.

Breakdowns & Assistance

If your car breaks down and you need help, a few highways in New England have Motorist Aid Call Boxes with emergency telephones posted every few miles along the roadside. On other highways, raise the hood (bonnet) of your vehicle to signal that you need help, and await a police patrol, which often comes within an hour.

The American Automobile Association (☎ 800-222-4357) provides battery charging, short-range towing, gasoline delivery and minor repairs at no charge to its members and to those of affiliated auto clubs. However, even members are liable for long-distance towing and for major repairs.

BICYCLE

Bicycling is a common sport and means of transport both on city streets and on country roads. Several of the larger cities have systems of bike paths which make travel much easier and more pleasant. Some towns have turned disused railroad rights-of-way into bike trails that travel for several miles. The Shining Sea Bicycle Path between Falmouth and Woods Hole, MA, is a prominent example.

Bicycle rentals are available in most cities, towns and resorts at reasonable prices of $15 to $20 per day. Many bike rental shops are mentioned in this guide. For others, look in the yellow pages under Bicycles.

HITCHING

Hitchhiking is not safe, not recommended, and often not legal. Both hitchers and the drivers who pick them up should understand that they are taking a small but potentially serious risk. People who do choose to hitch will be safer if they travel in pairs and let someone know where they are planning to go.

WALKING

Walking and jogging are very popular in New England. Most cities and resort towns have sightseeing trails marked out by signs or shown on brochure maps, and jogging/bike trails along rivers, lakes, or the seashore. In the countryside, several extensive trail systems even allow for interstate hikes. The Appalachian Trail, which stretches from Maine to Georgia, is the most famous, but Vermont's Long Trail is also impressive. See Activities in Facts for the Visitor for more on walking.

BOAT

Boat service is mostly local, and tends to be more for pleasure excursions than transportation. Ferries offer a few exceptions:

- Falmouth Heights, MA, to Edgartown (Martha's Vineyard), MA
- Gloucester, MA, to Provincetown, MA
- Hyannis, MA, to Nantucket Island, MA

- New Bedford, MA, to Woods Hole, MA
- New Bedford, MA, to Cuttyhunk Island, MA
- Woods Hole, MA, to Oak Bluffs (Martha's Vineyard), MA
- Woods Hole, MA, to Vineyard Haven (Martha's Vineyard), MA
- Bridgeport, CT, to Port Jefferson (Long Island), NY
- New London, CT, to Block Island, RI
- New London, CT, to Orient Point (Long Island), NY
- Burlington, VT, to New York state, traversing Lake Champlain
- Bar Harbor, ME, to Yarmouth, NS, Canada
- Portland, ME, to Yarmouth, NS, Canada
- Port Clyde, ME, to Monhegan Island, ME

LOCAL TRANSPORT

City buses and, in Boston, the Ⓣ (subway/underground) provide useful transportation within the larger cities and to some suburban points. Resort areas also tend to have some useful regional bus lines. These are mentioned in the text.

Taxis

Taxis are useful and common in the largest cities. In smaller cities and towns you will probably have to telephone a cab to come and pick you up. Ask at a hotel, restaurant or tourist office, or look in the yellow pages under Taxicabs. Note that a taxi must be licensed by the city in which you board it in order to pick you up, though some companies are licensed to operate in a number of cities.

Taxi drivers are usually willing to take you just about anywhere if you can afford the fare. For longer trips, this may be about $2.50 or $3 per mile.

City taxis have fare meters. Fares usually begin at $1.50, then add a certain price per mile, with possible extra charges for extra passengers, and, as in New York City, an extra 50¢ charge for driving after sundown. On top of cab fare you should add a tip of about 15%. Town taxis may not have meters, but will quote you the fare when you call. The same 15% tip is expected.

Standards of service are generally low. Many drivers speak limited English and many don't know their city well (though they can usually radio to headquarters and get directions).

Many city taxis are rolling wrecks in which the back seat where the passenger rides is separated from the front (driver's) seat by a thick clear plastic barrier. The passenger can easily be forgiven for thinking that he/she is in a jail-on-wheels. Cut into the plastic barrier is usually some sort of hole, chute or sliding door so that the passenger can push money through to the driver at the end of the ride. Although this arrangement makes it more difficult for the passenger to rob the driver, it does not hamper the driver from robbing you by taking an especially long route to your destination. For longer journeys which you are able to plan in advance (such as trips to the airport), you may want to hire a limo instead.

Limousines

Limousines (limos for short) are of two types. The first are luxurious taxis (often Cadillac or Lincoln stretch limos or executive sedans) which take you anywhere you like at either a predetermined or an hourly fare. The cheapest sort – executive sedans – are often not much more expensive than regular taxis, though they cannot be hailed on the street; they must be booked in advance. Standards of service and comfort are far above those of regular taxis. If you can plan ahead and want a more pleasant ride at a modest increase in price, look in the yellow pages under Limousine Service.

The other sort of limo is an airport van or minibus. These hold anywhere from eight to 25 passengers, and usually take them to or from a major airport to suburban communities or major cities as much as an hour or two's ride away. If you don't have your own car, they are often the best means of airport transport from distant points. Fares are usually about the same as a bus. You must reserve your seat in advance. The limo may pick you up at your hotel (or other point), or you may have to meet it at a predetermined stop. For the telephone numbers of airport limos, look in the yellow pages under Airport Transportation Service.

ORGANIZED TOURS
Local Tours
City tours by bus or "trolley" (actually a bus disguised as a light-rail trolley) are popular in the major cities, tourist towns and resort areas. Most are useful for getting a look at the major sights, though the commentary is often bland.

There are some adventurous exceptions, such as the "duck" tours in Boston and Gloucester, MA, a "duck" being a huge military amphibious vehicle that cruises the city streets, then glides into the river or bay for a nautical cruise.

Regional Tours
Regional tours are the way to go if you don't have time to make reservations in many different destinations, or don't have a car. By far the most popular are the autumn foliage tours – they can be a good way to get out of the city. They are often fully booked early on, and may be more expensive than normal tours.

In the mountain towns of Maine, New Hampshire and Vermont, tours by bicycle, canoe, raft and kayak are popular. See the Activities section of Facts for the Visitor for more information.

The company Destinnations (☎ 508-428-5600, fax 508-420-0565), PO Box 1173, Osterville, MA 02655, tailors individual tours according to budget and interests: you could do a "Cape and Island Hop," a B&B & Inns tour, a factory outlet mall tour and more. A five-day seasonal value package could run as low as $500 staying at B&Bs around New England.

The East Coast Explorer provides unique transportation between New York and Boston that cruises the backroads visiting sites many tourists might miss. See Bus under Getting There & Away.

Boston

Most visitors to Boston come to the same opinion: this city is lively, attractive, interesting, educational and perhaps most importantly, it's manageable.

The city's liveliness comes in large part from the huge population of college-age residents. Having 50-odd colleges and universities in greater Boston means that there are always lots of sporting activities, cultural pursuits (cinema, theater, galleries, literary cafes and bars and musical performances for all tastes), shopping and nightlife for a young crowd.

Boston's attractiveness comes in part from its being a wealthy port and commercial city since colonial times. During the 19th century, Boston prided itself on being the "Athens of America" because of its many beautiful buildings, its large population of literati, artists and educators, and its varied cultural institutions of the highest standard.

The Atlantic Ocean, Boston Harbor and the Charles and Mystic Rivers vary the cityscape and provide light and a sense of openness. Urban planning, including a long "emerald necklace" of parks, garden and verdant thoroughfares designed by the great American landscape architect Frederick Law Olmstead, brings a bit of the country right into the city.

Boston suffers a bit by being within a four-hour drive of New York City, the great American metropolis. When they reach the pinnacle of success in Boston, many of the city's top professionals and artists take that final step up the career ladder to New York City. But Boston is cleaner, safer, friendlier and easier to negotiate. It is a city of vibrant neighborhoods, from working-class Charlestown to staid old Beacon Hill to the Italian North End. And in less than 30 minutes, you can be out of Boston among cornfields, vegetable gardens, beautiful colonial towns, paddle-able rivers and cyclable country roads.

HISTORY

Called Trimountain (from its three hills) in its earliest days, Boston took its permanent name from the English town. The vanguard of English settlers led by Reverend William Blaxton arrived in 1624 – less than four years after the Pilgrims arrived in nearby Plymouth.

The colony of Massachusetts Bay was established six years later in 1630 when the elder John Winthrop, official representative of the Massachusetts Bay Company, took up residence. From the beginning this was the center of Puritan culture and life in the New World.

Puritanism was intellectual and theocratic, and so the leading men and women of early Boston society were those who understood and followed Biblical law – and could explain in powerful rhetoric why they did. Thus it comes as no surprise that the Boston Public Latin School was established in 1635 (and continues as an elite public high school today). A year later, Harvard College (now Harvard University) was founded in neighboring Cambridge. By 1653, Boston had a public library as well, and by 1704 the Thirteen Colonies' first newspaper, the *News-Letter*.

Though the New England coast had many excellent natural ports (Essex, Plymouth, Providence, Salem), Boston was blessed by geography with the best of all. By the early 1700s it was well on its way to being what it remains today: New England's largest and most important city.

As the chief city in the region, it drew London's attention. When King George III and Parliament chose to burden the colonies with taxation without representation, the taxes were first levied in Boston. When resistance surfaced, it was in Boston. The Boston Massacre and the Boston Tea Party were significant turning points in the

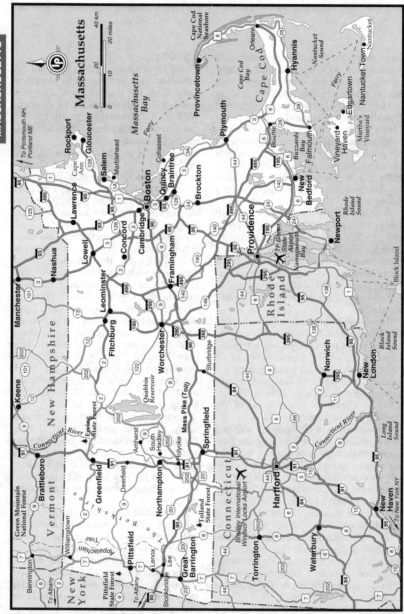

development of revolutionary sentiments, and the Battle of Bunker Hill solidified colonial resolve to declare independence from the British crown.

Following the Revolutionary War, Boston suffered economically as the British government cut off American ships' access to other ports in the British Empire. But as new trading relationships developed, Boston entered a commercial and industrial boom which lasted from the late 1700s until the mid-1800s. Fortunes were made in shipbuilding, maritime trade and manufacturing textiles and shoes. Chartered as a city in 1822, Boston's Beacon Hill was soon crowned with fine mansions built by the leading families, and the Back Bay was filled in to make room for more.

These same prominent families also patronized arts and culture heavily. Though conservative and traditionalist in their general outlook, Bostonians were firm believers in American ideals of freedom, and firm supporters of the abolition of slavery and the activities of the Underground Railroad.

As the 19th century drew to a close, Boston's prominence was challenged by the growth of other port cities and the westward expansion of the national borders, and New England's economic boom turned into a bust when the textile and shoe factories moved to cheaper labor markets in the South.

The Irish potato famine drove thousands of immigrants to the New World, especially Boston, changing the city's ethnic and economic profiles. The new arrivals were soon to be joined by immigrants from Italy, the Ottoman Empire and Portugal.

In the 20th century, Boston has remained an important port, a prominent center for medical education, treatment and research, and USA's premiere university center. Many graduates choose to remain in the Boston area, which has helped to fuel local booming commerce in computer research, development and manufacturing.

ORIENTATION

For a city of its stature, Boston is quite small. The sights and activities of principal interest to travelers are contained within an area that's only about one mile wide by three miles long. It's bounded on the eastern edge by Boston Harbor and the Atlantic Ocean, on the north by the Charles River and Cambridge. Boston proper has about 600,000 people, "greater" Boston about three million.

Most of what you'll want to see in Boston is easily accessible by MBTA ("T") subway trains. Convenient Ⓣ subway stations are given in the text. See Getting Around for more information.

The Central Artery (also known as I-93, the John F Fitzgerald Expressway and simply "the expressway") cuts right through downtown, separating the North End and the waterfront from the rest of the city. The Central Artery, currently undergoing the largest public works project in US history, is being widened and rerouted underground to alleviate the persistent traffic nightmares. The construction, of course, is creating its own set of surface-artery problems (which will remain well into the 21st century). Don't let this deter you from visiting; do, though, think twice about driving in Boston. Currently the hardest hit areas are around South Station and the waterfront.

Most of Boston's downtown streets began as simple colonial cow paths. And as such, they're often winding, one way and narrow. Expect to get a bit lost as you wander the downtown neighborhoods of the small but powerful Financial District (and adjacent Downtown Crossing), the primarily Italian North End, the Brahmin

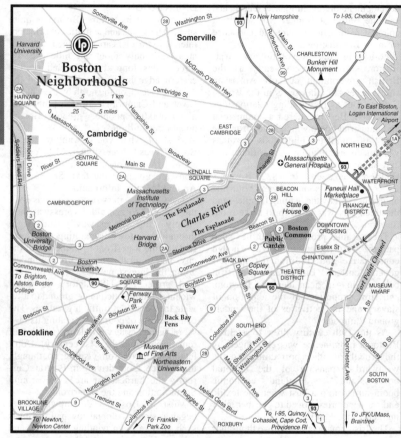

Beacon Hill, the no-nonsense Government Center, colorful and aromatic Chinatown and the Theater District. Boston's neighborhoods are quite distinct, and since all the above areas abut one another, they're best explored on foot.

Beacon Hill, its brick streets lit by gas lanterns and lined with patrician townhouses, is one of the loveliest areas for strolling. It is bounded by Charles, Cambridge and Beacon Sts; two large parks – the Boston Common and Public Garden – lie adjacent to it on the south.

Back Bay, created as a mid-19th century landfill project, is more orderly than the rest of the city. Its streets, lined with lovely brownstones and flowering trees, are laid out east to west in alphabetical order: Arlington, Berkeley, Clarendon and so on to Hereford. Commonwealth Ave (referred to as Comm Ave) is Boston's most grand boulevard, with a grassy promenade running the length of it. Back Bay ends at Massachusetts Ave (known simply as Mass Ave), which runs northeast across the Charles River and into Cambridge and Harvard Square.

West of Mass Ave lies Kenmore Square and the Fenway area. Kenmore Square is home to a vibrant nightclub scene and lots of university students. The Fenway includes a four-mile long grassy byway that leads in one direction to an arboretum, and in the other to two important museums. Fenway Park is the home of the much-loved Boston Red Sox baseball team.

The South End is just south of Back Bay. It lies between Berkeley St and Mass Ave to the east and west, and Huntington and Shawmut Aves to the north and south. This newly gentrified area, thick with restaurants, artsy shops and renovated brownstones, is also nice for walking.

The Charles River, with a popular grassy Esplanade along both banks, separates Boston and Cambridge, which has Harvard University and MIT. The best views of the Boston skyline and Beacon Hill are from the northern banks of the Charles River near the Longfellow Bridge.

To get better oriented with a bird's eye view of Boston, head to the 60th-floor observatory of New England's tallest building: the John Hancock Tower (☎ 617-247-1977), 200 Clarendon St. The ticket booth is at Trinity Place and St James Ave. The observatory will provide a good overview of your neighborhood walking tour. And when you set out walking, remember how compact Boston appeared from high above it. Other observatory bonuses include a topographical map of Boston as it appeared in 1775 and an audio presentation of the Revolutionary War battles that took place in Boston. Admission is $4.25 adults, $3.25 children five to 17. It's open Monday through Saturday from 9 am to 11 pm, Sunday from noon to 10 pm; the last tickets are sold at 10 pm. Ⓣ Green Line to Copley.

The 50th-floor Prudential Center Skywalk (☎ 617-236-3318), 800 Boylston St, offers a spectacular 360-degree view of metro Boston and Cambridge. (The John Hancock Observatory only has views on three sides.) The hours are similar and admission slightly less than the observatory. Ⓣ Green Line to Prudential or Hynes Convention Center.

Maps You can get good maps of Boston and New England at just about any bookstore. (See the Bookstores sidebar.) The AAA map of Boston is good, if a bit large. Look for the smaller, laminated "Streetwise" maps of the city, which are useful for longer stays and cost about $6.

INFORMATION
Tourist Offices
In advance of your visit, write or call the Greater Boston Convention and Visitors Bureau (GBCVB, ☎ 617-536-4100, 800-888-5515, http://www.dvm.com/users/dvm/boston), PO Box 990468, Prudential Tower, Boston, MA 02199. They'll send an information packet.

Once in Boston, drop in at the GBCVB's year-round Visitor Information Center (☎ 617-426-3115), Tremont and West Sts on Boston Common. You can pick up a subway and bus route map, as well as lots of other maps and information. The center (which has public restrooms) is open Monday through Saturday from 8:30 am to 5 pm, Sunday from 9 am. Ⓣ Red or Green Line to Park Street.

In Back Bay, the GBCVB has a booth in the center court of the Prudential Center mall, 800 Boylston St, that's open daily from 8:30 am to 6 pm. Ⓣ Green Line to Prudential or Hynes Convention Center.

The National Park Service Visitor Center (NPS, ☎ 617-242-5642), 15 State St across from the Old State House, has plenty of historical literature, a short slide-show and free walking tours of the Freedom Trail (see the sidebar, Walking Tours). The center is open daily from 9 am to 5 pm, until 6 pm in the summer. Ⓣ Orange or Blue Line to State.

For city and state-wide information, write to or stop in at the Massachusetts Office of Travel & Tourism (☎ 617-727-3201, 800-227-6277, vacationinfo@state.ma.us, http://ftp.std.com/NE/mass-travel.html), 100 Cambridge St, 13th floor, Boston, MA 02202. The office is open weekdays from 9 am to 5 pm. Ⓣ Blue Line to Bowdoin.

In Cambridge, the Visitor Information

Booth (☎ 617-497-1630, 800-862-5678, cambtour@user1.channel1.com), Harvard Square, has plenty of detailed information on current Cambridge happenings and self-guided walking tours. The kiosk is staffed Monday through Saturday from 9 am to 5 pm, Sunday from 1 to 5 pm. (T) Red Line to Harvard.

The Appalachian Mountain Club Headquarters (☎ 617-523-0636), 5 Joy St, is the resource for outdoor activities in Boston and throughout New England. AMC Headquarters, complete with bookstore, is open weekdays from 9 am to 5 pm. (T)Red or Green Line to Park Street.

Foreign Consulates

Countries with diplomatic representation in Boston include the following:

Australia
(☎ 617-542-8655), 20 Park Plaza, 4th floor, Boston, MA 02116, is open by appointment only. (T) Green Line to Arlington.
Canada
(☎ 617-262-3760), 3 Copley Place, Suite 400, Boston, MA 02116, is open weekdays 8:45 am to 5 pm. (T) Green Line to Copley or Orange Line to Back Bay/South End.
France
(☎ 617-542-7374), 31 St James Ave, Suite 750, Boston, MA 02116, is open weekdays, 9 am to 1 pm. (T) Green Line to Arlington.
Germany
(☎ 617-536-4414), 3 Copley Place, Suite 500, Boston, MA 02116, is open weekdays from 9 am to noon. (T) Green Line to Copley or Orange Line to Back Bay/South End.
Ireland
(☎ 617-267-9330), 535 Boylston St, Boston, MA 02116, is open weekdays from 10 am to 4 pm. (T) Green Line to Copley.
Italy
(☎ 617-542-0483), 100 Boylston St, Suite 900, Boston, MA 02116, is open weekdays from 9 am to 12:30 pm. (T) Green Line to Boylston.
Netherlands
(☎ 617-542-8452), 6 St James Ave, Boston, MA 02116, is open weekdays from 10 am to 1 pm. (T) Green Line to Arlington.
UK
(☎ 617-248-9555), 600 Atlantic Ave, Boston, MA 02210, is open weekdays from 9 am to 5 pm. (T) Red Line to South Station.

Money

There are Cirrus and Plus ATM machines all around the city. To exchange foreign currency, head to any BayBank (☎ 617-788-5000).

At the airport, you can exchange currency at the BayBank Foreign Money Exchange at North Terminal C (☎ 617-569-1172), open daily from 8 am to 7 pm and Terminal E (☎ 617-567-2313), open weekdays from 8 am to 9:30 pm, weekends from 11:30 am to 9:30 pm.

Post & Communications

Boston's main post office, the General Mail Facility (☎ 617-654-5326), 25 Dorchester Ave, Boston, MA 02114, is just one block southeast of South Station. It never closes. (T) Red Line to South Station. To find out any zip code, call ☎ 617-654-5767.

Branch post offices are:

Back Bay
(☎ 617-267-8162) 800 Boylston St, in the Prudential Center
Beacon Hill
(☎ 617-723-1951) 136 Charles St
Financial District
(☎ 617-720-5314) 90 Devonshire St
Faneuil Hall Marketplace
(☎ 617-723-1791)
North End
(☎ 617-723-5134) 217 Hanover St
Cambridge
(☎ 617-876-0620) Central Square 770 Mass Ave

Most of these branches are open weekdays from 7:30 am to 6 pm and Saturday mornings.

All general delivery (poste restante) mail must be sent to the General Mail Facility; branch offices cannot accept it.

For internet access, see Internet Cafes under Places to Eat.

Travel Agencies

Budget travel specialists include the Council on International Educational Exchange's (CIEE) Council Travel (☎ 617-266-1926, 800-268-6245), 273 Newbury St. On Thursday from 5:30 to 7 pm, Council

Travel turns off its phones and turns its attention to walk-ins. Ⓣ Green Line to Hynes Convention Center. There is also an office in Harvard Square, 12 Elliot St, 2nd floor, that is open from noon to 4 on Saturdays for walk-ins. Yet another office is on MIT campus in the Stratton Student Center at 84 Mass Ave.

Let's Go Travel (☎ 617-495-9649), 53A Church St, is in Cambridge. Ⓣ Red Line to Harvard.

The Vacation Outlet at Filene's Basement (☎ 617-267-8100), 426 Washington St, offers lots of last-minute deals that tour consolidators couldn't sell. The idea is that they'd rather sell the package at the last minute for some nominal fee than take a complete loss on it. Their loss could be your gain. Ⓣ Red or Orange Line to Downtown Crossing.

Last Minute Travel Services (☎ 617-267-9800), 1249 Boylston St, is in the same business. Ⓣ Green Line to Kenmore.

Media
Local newspapers include *The Boston Globe* (http://www.boston.com), which publishes an extensive and useful Calendar section every Thursday, and the competing *Boston Herald* which has its own Scene section published Friday. The *Boston Phoenix* (http://www.bostonphoenix.com), the "alternative" paper that focuses on arts and entertainment, is published weekly; *Boston Magazine* (http://www.boston magazine.com) is the city's monthly.

Libraries
The venerable Boston Public Library (☎ 617-536-5400, http://www.bpl.org), 666 Boylston St, is the country's oldest free city library; it dates to 1852. Although over two million people visit annually, most bypass the walled-in tranquil garden courtyard (complete with reflecting pool and trees) where you can read Monday through Thursday from 9 am to 9 pm, Friday and Saturday from 9 am to 5 pm and Sunday from 1 to 5 pm. Ⓣ Green Line to Copley.

The grand Boston Athenaeum (☎ 617-227-0270), 10½ Beacon St, is an impressive, independent library, owned by 1049 shareholders who trace their shares back to 1807. One-hour tours of the Neo-Classical reading rooms are offered Tuesday and Thursday at 3 pm, but you must call 24 hours in advance to reserve. Ⓣ Red or Green Line to Park Street.

See below for the JFK Library, which has a Hemingway archive.

Campuses
The greater Boston area has many, many college campuses, too many to mention here. Cultural and sporting events are often open to the public, and this brief listing should help you get further information (see also Spectator Sports). For the Berklee College of Music see Entertainment.

The main gates leading to the quadrangle of the Harvard University campus (☎ 617-495-1000) are across the street from the Red Line T-stop in Cambridge. Free hour-long tours of Harvard Yard (pronounced locally as "Hahvahd Yahd") are given from the information office (☎ 617-495-1573), Holyoke Center, 1350 Mass Ave. The university, founded in 1636, stretches for a few blocks east and west along Mass Ave.

The Massachusetts Institute of Technology (MIT, ☎ 617-253-4795), a world-renowned scientific mecca founded in 1861, is also spread out along Mass Ave in Cambridge, about 1½ miles east of Harvard Square. Free tours of the campus are given weekdays (10 am and 2 pm) from 77 Mass Ave. The number of excellent museums and amount of public art on the campus are impressive. Ⓣ Red Line to Kendall.

About 34,000 students attend Northeastern University (☎ 617-373-2000), Huntington Ave, which boasts one of the country's largest work-study cooperative programs. Ⓣ the "E" branch on the Green Line.

Boston University (BU, ☎ 617-353-2000, 353-2169), Comm Ave west of Kenmore Square, enrolls about 27,000

Bookstores

Boston and Cambridge are a book lovers paradise; there are stores devoted to maps, mysteries, foreign languages and scholarly texts. Although the yellow pages lists over 100 stores, here are a few shops worth searching out. The Harvard Square Visitor Information Booth hands out a free brochure of the square's more than 30 bookstores.

The outstanding Globe Corner Bookstore (http://www.gcb.com/catalog/) has three locations: 3 School St (☎ 617-523-6658), Ⓣ Orange or Red Line to Downtown Crossing; 500 Boylston St (☎ 617-859-8008), Ⓣ Green Line to Arlington or Copley; 49 Palmer St, Cambridge (☎ 617-497-6277), Ⓣ Red Line to Harvard. Specializing in travel books for near and far, Globe Corner also carries hundreds of specialty maps, including topographical maps of New England. See the Globe Corner entry, under Beacon Hill & Downtown.

For more topos, check out the AMC Headquarters, listed in Tourist Offices.

Another excellent choice for travel guides and maps is the Rand McNally Map & Travel Store (☎ 617-720-1125), 84 State St, near Faneuil Hall Marketplace. Ⓣ Orange or Blue Line to State.

The Glad Day Gay Liberation Bookshop (☎ 617-267-3010), 673 Boylston St, is a well-stocked store dedicated to gay and lesbian related titles. The bulletin board outside the 2nd-floor store is packed with useful community information. Ⓣ Green Line to Copley.

In business since the 1930s, the outdoor Copley Square News (no ☎), Boylston St at Dartmouth St, sells hundreds of magazines and many foreign language periodicals. Ⓣ Green Line to Copley.

In Cambridge, Out of Town News (☎ 617-354-7777), Harvard Square, is no ordinary newsstand; in fact, it's a National Historic Landmark, open from 6 am to midnight. It sells papers from virtually every major US city, as well as dozens of cities around the world. Ⓣ Red Line to Harvard.

Schoenhof's Foreign Books (☎ 617-547-8855), 76 A Mt Auburn St, is a national center for foreign-language materials, books, dictionaries covering just about any language. Ⓣ Harvard on the Red Line.

students, has a huge campus and popular sports teams. Ⓣ the "B" branch of the Green Line.

UMass, Boston (☎ 617-287-5000), 100 Morrissey Blvd, is on Columbia Point, surrounded by Dorchester Bay on three sides. It's a commuting campus near the John F Kennedy Library & Museum.

Other well-established universities on the city's fringe include the following list.

On Comm Ave (MA 30) in Chestnut Hill, Boston College (BC, ☎ 617-552-8000) has Gothic towers and stained glass. BC boasts a large green campus, a good art museum and excellent Irish and Catholic ephemera collections in the library. Basketball and football teams are usually high in national rankings. This is also the nation's largest Jesuit community, so mind your Ps and Qs.

Ⓣ last stop on the "B" branch of the Green Line.

Wellesley College (☎ 617-283-2380), a seven-sisters women's college in Wellesley, also sports a green campus and the excellent Davis Museum & Cultural Center. Take the MBTA Commuter Rail plus a 10-minute walk to get there, or drive: MA 16 to MA 135.

Tufts University (☎ 617-628-5000), in Medford, has about 8000 students and a good basketball team. Call for directions.

Brandeis University (☎ 617-736-2000) on South St in Waltham, is a train ride out of Boston; call for directions. The smaller 4800-student campus includes the Rose Art Museum specializing in New England art.

Massachusetts College of Art (☎ 617-232-1555), Huntington Ave, hosts regular exhibitions at their galleries.

The Brattle Book Shop (☎ 617-542-0210), 9 West St, is a treasure, crammed with out-of-print, rare and first-edition books. Ⓣ Orange or Red Line to Downtown Crossing.

One of the most famous poetry bookstores in the USA is near Harvard Square: the Grolier Poetry Bookshop (☎ 617-547-4648), 6 Plympton St.

The Avenue Victor Hugo Bookshop (☎ 617-266-7746), 339 Newbury St in Back Bay, is one of the best used bookstores in the city. You could browse an entire day away here. Ⓣ Green Line to Hynes Convention Center.

British retailer Waterstone's (☎ 617-859-7300, email: wstones@waterstones.com), 26 Exeter St in Back Bay, believes that browsing and buying is an art. Its stores are set up to reflect that – there are plenty of seats. A new location is in the Quincy Market Building (☎ 617-689-0930).

Wordsworth, a general bookstore, has three locations in Harvard Square within a block of each other on Brattle St: the original, plus Wordsworth Abridged and a children's store.

Known simply as "The Coop" the Harvard Cooperative Society (☎ 617-499-2000), 1400 Mass Ave in Harvard Square, carries three floors of books, music and every other "essential" thing a Harvard student could use. But you don't have to be a student to shop here: anyone can buy just about anything emblazoned with the Harvard logo. In 1996 Barnes & Noble took over this store's management, but not the Harvard Book Store (☎ 617-661-1515) which is separate, and called "the premiere intellectual bookstore on the Square."

Barnes & Noble (☎ 617-426-5502), 395 Washington St at Downtown Crossing, is part of a large national chain that offers a 20% to 30% discounts on hardcover books.

The Barnes & Noble at Boston University (☎ 617-267-8484), 660 Beacon St, is one of New England's biggest bookstores, with three floors of books. Ⓣ Green Line to Kenmore.

Borders Books, Music & Cafe (☎ 617-557-7188), 10-24 School St at Washington St in Downtown Crossing, has over 200,000 titles.

See also the Trident Bookseller & Café in Places to Eat. ∎

Cultural Centers

The French Library in Boston (☎ 617-266-4351), 53 Marlborough St, founded in 1946, sponsors regular lectures on travel, cooking and all things French; receptions often follow. The library sponsors an annual Bastille Day celebration during which Marlborough St is closed off. It's open Tuesday through Saturday. Ⓣ Green Line to Arlington.

The Goethe Institute (☎ 617-262-6050), 170 Beacon St, sponsors a cultural program of German events; its library is also well stocked with books, tapes and periodicals. It's open weekdays 10 am to 5:30 pm, Saturdays 2 to 5 pm. Ⓣ Green Line to Arlington.

Medical Services

Massachusetts General Hospital (☎ 617-726-2000) is arguably the city's biggest and best. They can often refer you to smaller clinics and crisis hotlines. Ⓣ Red Line to Charles/MGH.

CVS (☎ 617-876-5519), Porter Square shopping mall on Mass Ave, Cambridge, is the area's only 24-hour pharmacy. Ⓣ Red Line to Porter.

Emergency

The police, ambulances and fire department can be reached by dialing ☎ 911.

Traveler's Aid Society (☎ 617-542-7286), 17 East St (just off Atlantic Ave, across from South Station) is a nonprofit agency that helps travelers in despair. From stolen wallets to practical information to "bedless in Boston," Traveler's Aid is there to help. They also have a booth in South Station (☎ 617-737-2880); both locations are open weekdays 9 am to 5 pm and most holidays. The Logan Airport "Terminal E" Traveler's Aid (☎ 617-567-5385) is usually open daily, noon to 8 pm.

The mayor of Boston staffs a traveler's aid hot line (☎ 617-635-4500) when the Traveler's Aid Society is closed.

Dangers & Annoyances

The Combat Zone, although it continues to shrink every year, extends about a block in each direction from the Chinatown subway station (on the Orange Line) along Washington and Essex Sts. Although all the X-rated movie theaters and topless clubs have recently disappeared from the area, it's still the seediest in Boston. Use caution after dusk.

BEACON HILL & DOWNTOWN

The 50-acre **Boston Common**, bordered by Beacon, Tremont and Charles Sts, is the country's oldest public park established in 1634. During the Revolutionary War, British troops camped here and until 1830, the land was used for cattle grazing. Although there is still a grazing ordinance on the books, today the Common serves picnickers, sunbathers and people-watchers. Colorful characters are often heard spouting off from atop a soap box near the Park Street T station at Tremont and Park Sts. Ⓣ Green Line to Boylston, Green or Red Line to Park Street.

Adjacent to and southwest of the Boston Common is the **Public Garden**, a 24-acre botanical oasis of cultivated flower beds, clipped grass, ancient trees and a tranquil lagoon. You can't picnic on the lawn like you can on the Common, but there are plenty of benches. Pick one in front of the Swan Boats, peddle-powered boats that ferry children (and adults) around the pond while ducks swim alongside begging for bread crumbs. Ⓣ Green Line to Arlington.

The area known as **Beacon Hill** is Boston's most handsome and affluent residential neighborhood. It lies adjacent to Boston Common and the Public Garden.

Beacon Hill extends north to Cambridge St and west to the Charles River. Charles St, which separates the flat and hilly parts of the neighborhood, is lined with shops and eateries. Distinguished 19th-century brick townhouses, lavender window panes, gas lanterns, little courtyards, rooftop gardens and picturesque narrow alleyways: this is the stuff of Beacon Hill. Ⓣ Red Line to Charles/MGH, Blue Line to Bowdoin, Red or Green Line to Park Street.

Specifically, seek out the cobblestone **Acorn St** (the city's often-photographed and narrowest street), **Mt Vernon and Pinckney Sts** (two of the hill's prettiest) and **Louisburg Square** (pronounced Lewis-burg), an elegant cluster of million-dollar homes that face a private park owned by the square's residents.

Beacon Hill was never the exclusive domain of blue-blood Brahmins, though. Waves of immigrants, and especially African Americans, free from slavery, settled here in the 19th century. The **African Meeting House** (☎ 617-723-8863), 8 Smith Court, is the country's oldest African-American meeting house. Abolitionists Frederick Douglass and William Lloyd Garrison delivered passionate speeches here. To visit the Meeting House, check in at the museum for a tour with an NPS guide. Ⓣ Charles/MGH on the Red Line.

Next door, the **Museum of Afro American History** (☎ 617-742-1854), 46 Joy St at Smith Court, housed in the country's first primary school for Blacks, is the best place to learn about the Hill's African-American roots. The museum is open weekdays from 10 am to 4 pm and from late May to early September on weekends also. A donation is suggested.

High atop Beacon Hill stands the golden domed **Massachusetts State House** (☎ 617-727-3676), Beacon and Bowdoin Sts, where the idiosyncrasies of Massachusetts government and politics are played out like a sporting match. The commanding state capitol building was designed by Boston's beloved Charles Bulfinch and completed in 1798. A free 40-minute tour

In addition to organizing pre-revolutionary opposition to British taxation, Sam Adams (1722-1803) also signed the Declaration of Independence and became Governor of Massachusetts (1794-97).

(given weekdays from 10 am to 3:15 pm) includes a discussion of the history, art works, architecture and political personalities as well as a visit to the legislative chambers when it's in session. ⓉRed or Green Line to Park Street.

The bas-relief **Robert Gould Shaw Memorial**, across from the State House at Beacon and Park Sts, honors the nation's first Black Civil War regiment, which was depicted in the 1989 film *Glory*. The soldiers, led by Shaw (the son of a notable White family in Boston), refused their $10 monthly stipend for two years until Congress upped it to $13, the amount White regiments were paid. ⓉRed or Green Line to Park Street.

Walk south on Park St to the **Park Street Church** (☎ 617-523-3383) at the corner of Tremont St. William Lloyd Garrison railed against slavery from the church's pulpit in

1829. This is also where, on Independence Day in 1895, Katherine Lee Bates' hymn "America the Beautiful" was first sung. The church is noted for its graceful, narrow 200-foot steeple. It's open daily in July and August, and by appointment only the rest of the year. Ⓣ Red or Green Line to Park Street.

Adjacent to the church on Tremont St is the **Old Granary Burying Ground**, dating to 1660 and filled with exceptional headstone carvings. Revolutionary heroes including Paul Revere, Samuel Adams and John Hancock are buried here, as are Crispus Attucks (the freed slave who died in the Boston Massacre when British soldiers fired into a group of angry Bostonians in 1770), Benjamin Franklin's parents (he's buried in Philadelphia) and Peter Faneuil (of Faneuil Hall fame). Ⓣ Red or Green Line to Park St.

Continue north to the **King's Chapel & Burying Ground** (☎ 617-523-1749), 58 Tremont at School St. Bostonians were not pleased at all when the original Anglican church was erected in 1688. (Remember, it was the Anglicans – the Church of England – whom the Puritans were fleeing.) The granite church standing today was built in 1754 around the original wooden structure. Then the wooden church was taken apart and tossed out the windows. If the church seems to be missing something, it is: building funds ran out before a spire could be added. The church houses the largest bell ever made by Paul Revere as well as a lovely sounding organ. Recitals are given at 12:15 pm on Tuesdays. The adjacent burying ground contains the grave of John Winthrop, the first Governor of the fledgling Massachusetts Bay colony. The church is open daily mid-June to early September from 9:30 am to 4 pm; mid-April to mid-June, September and October from 10 am to 4 pm on Monday, Friday and Saturday; from 10 am to 2 pm on Saturday the rest of the year. ⓉRed or Green Line to Park Street.

Head south on School St to the **Globe Corner Bookstore** (☎ 617-523-6658), 1 School St. Although it is a superior travel

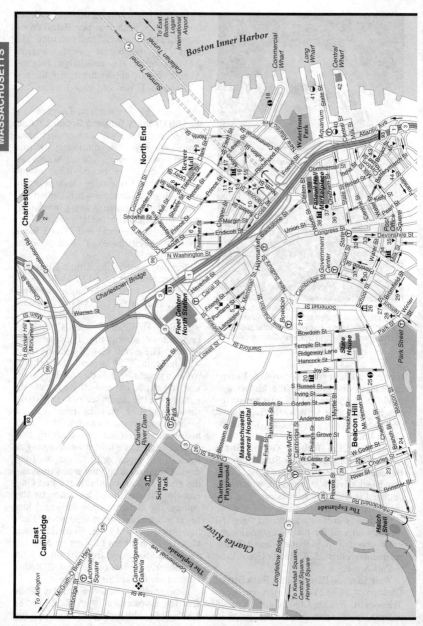

MASSACHUSETTS

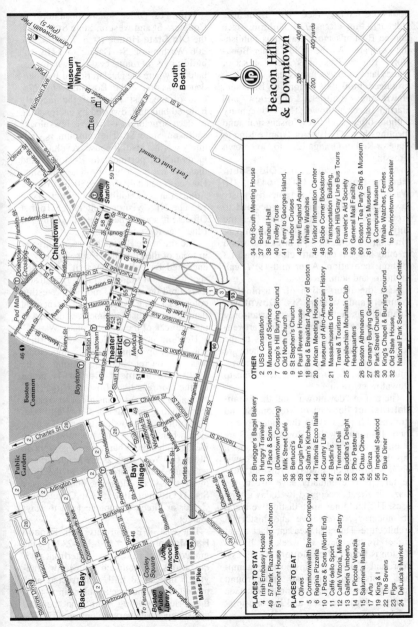

Beacon Hill
& Downtown

PLACES TO STAY
4   Irish Embassy Hostel
49   57 Park Plaza/Howard Johnson
51   Tremont House

PLACES TO EAT
1   Olives
5   Commonwealth Brewing Company
6   Regina Pizzeria
10   J Pace & Sons (North End)
12   Caffè Vittoria, Mike's Pastry
13   Galleria Umberto
14   La Piccola Venezia
15   Salumeria Italiana
17   Artu
19   King & I
22   The Sevens
23   Figs
24   DeLuca's Market
29   Bruegger's Bagel Bakery
31   Hungry Traveler
33   J Pace & Sons
     (Downtown Crossing)
36   Milk Street Café
39   Bertucci's
43   Sultan's Kitchen
44   Trattoria Ecco Italia
45   Country Life
47   Caffè dello Sport
51   Tremont Deli
52   Buddha's Delight
53   Pho Pasteur
54   Chau Chow
55   Ginza
56   Imperial Seafood
57   Blue Diner

OTHER
2   USS Constitution
3   Museum of Science
7   Copp's Hill Burying Ground
8   Old North Church
9   St Stephen's Church
16   Paul Revere House
18   Bed & Breakfast Agency of Boston
20   African Meeting House,
     Museum of Afro-American History
21   Massachusetts Office of
     Travel & Tourism
25   Appalachian Mountain Club
     Headquarters
26   Boston Athenaeum
27   Granary Burying Ground
28   Park Street Church
30   King's Chapel & Burying Ground
32   Old State House,
     National Park Service Visitor Center
34   Old South Meeting House
37   Bostix
38   Faneuil Hall
40   Trolley Tours
41   Ferry to Georges Island,
     Harbor Cruises
42   New England Aquarium,
     Whale Watches
46   Visitor Information Center
48   Globe Corner Bookstore
50   Transportation Building,
     Brush Hill/Gray Line Bus Tours
58   Traveler's Aid Society
59   General Mail Facility
60   Boston Tea Party Ship & Museum
61   Children's Museum
     & Computer Museum
62   Whale Watches, Ferries
     to Provincetown, Gloucester

bookstore today (see the Bookstore sidebar), this circa-1718 building once housed Boston's most illustrious publishing company. As the "Old Corner Bookstore," run by Ticknor & Fields, a set of names later used as a publisher's imprint, it produced books by Thoreau, Emerson, Hawthorne, Whittier, Longfellow and Harriet Beecher Stowe. The 19th-century authors often held lively discussions and meetings here. Ⓣ Blue or Orange Line to State or Red or Orange Line to Downtown Crossing.

Across the street is the **Old South Meeting House** (☎ 617-482-6439), 310 Washington St. After a typically feisty town meeting here, colonists decided to protest the British tea taxation (see the entry for the Boston Tea Party Ship & Museum). The traditional brick and wood meeting house is currently closed for a $4.3 million renovation. After mid-1997, call for hours and admission.

Near the intersection of Washington, Summer and Winter Sts, **Downtown Crossing** is a bustling pedestrian-only shopping area that's home to pushcart vendors and street musicians. Thanks to the volume of nearby office workers, there are plenty of places here for an inexpensive, quick lunch. Ⓣ Orange or Red Line to Downtown Crossing.

The rest of "downtown" and the **Financial District** lies east of Tremont St and stretches all the way to the waterfront (a mere 10-minute walk). Bounded by State St on the north and Essex St on the south, this district was once the domain of cows. Their well-trodden, muddy, 17th- and 18th-century paths eventually gave rise to the maze of streets occupied by today's high rises. The buildings are a distinctive blend of modern, conservative and historical architecture. The most pleasant place to get a feel for the pace of weekday life in Boston is **Post Office Square** (Congress, Pearl and Water Sts). This postage-stamp-size oasis, built atop an underground parking garage, boasts a small cafe (see Places to Eat), fountain and live music at lunchtime in the summer.

From Post Office Square, head north on Congress St and west on State St to reach the **Old State House** (☎ 617-720-3290), 206 Washington St. Dating to 1713, the building is perhaps best known for its balcony where the Declaration of Independence was first read to Bostonians in 1776. One of the best views of the recently restored building, dwarfed by encroaching modern structures, is from a few blocks south on State St. The museum is definitely worth a visit. It houses revolutionary memorabilia pertinent to Boston's (and thus the nation's) history. The Old State House is open daily from 9:30 am to 5 pm. Admission is $3 adults, $1 children six to 18. The NPS Visitor Center (see Tourist Offices) is across the street. Ⓣ Orange or Blue Line to State.

The site of the Boston Massacre, directly in front of the Old State House balcony, is encircled by cobblestones. It marks the spot where, on March 5, 1770, British soldiers fired on an angry mob of protesting colonists, killing five of them. This incident flamed anti-British sentiment, which led to the outbreak of the Revolutionary War.

Heading north on Congress St brings you smack up against a coldly impersonal mass of concrete buildings dating to the 1960s. **Government Center** is home to the fortress-like Boston City Hall. Although there are plans afoot to create a more inviting and humane City Hall Plaza, city politics tend to slow to a snail's pace even when dealing with the most benign ideas for change. What few vestiges remain of the Old West End, as the neighborhood was once called, are found in the little byways between Merrimac and Causeway Sts. Ⓣ Green or Blue Line to Government Center or Green or Orange Line to Haymarket.

Due east of Boston City Hall, **Faneuil Hall Marketplace** (☎ 617-338-2323) is the granddaddy of East Coast waterfront revitalizations. Pronounced "fan'l" or "fanyool," the actual hall, constructed as a market and public meeting place in 1740, is the brick building with the beloved grasshopper weathervane on top of it. The

MASSACHUSETTS

2nd floor is still used for public meetings. Behind Faneuil Hall are three long granite buildings that make up the rest of the marketplace, the center of the city's produce and meat industry for almost 150 years. In the 1970s, the Quincy Market area was redeveloped into today's colorful, festive shopping and eating mecca. It's quietest here in the morning. See also Places to Eat and Things to Buy. Ⓣ Blue or Orange Line to State.

To escape the crowds at Faneuil Hall Marketplace, head to the waterfront park northeast of the marketplace, on the other side of the expressway. The park, complete with benches, grassy knolls, moored sailboats and a trellised archway is a nice place for a picnic.

Northeast of Faneuil Hall on North St, between Union and Congress Sts, are two lifelike bronzes of Boston's former Mayor Curley, a cherished but controversial Irish pol. Just beyond are the four glass columns of Boston's sobering Holocaust memorial, built in 1995.

NORTH END & CHARLESTOWN
The **North End** is separated from the city by the I-93 Expressway, but psychologically the enclave is more like a continent and a century away. Old-world Italians have held court in this warren of narrow, winding streets and alleys since the 1920s. Walk around and you'll soon hear passionate discussions in Italian by old-timers dressed in black. Children run through the streets like they do in Sicilia. Ritual Saturday morning shopping is done at specialty stores selling handmade pasta, cannoli or biscotti, fresh cuts of meat, flowers, a little of this or that – all within a quarter-mile radius of Boston's oldest colonial buildings. When you get tired or hungry, there are a dozen cafes, and more ristoranti per block than anywhere else in the city.

From Faneuil Hall walk north on Union St, past the Union Oyster House (the oldest restaurant in the city, established in 1826) and cross under the expressway at Cross St. Inlaid in the asphalt are bronze casts of vegetables and other detritus of the weekly

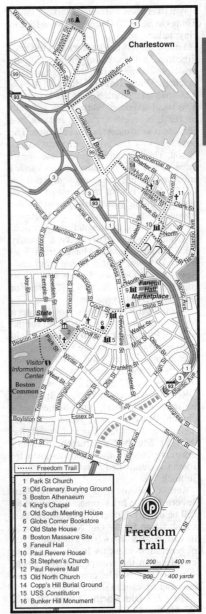

..... Freedom Trail

1 Park St Church
2 Old Granary Burying Ground
3 Boston Athenaeum
4 King's Chapel
5 Old South Meeting House
6 Globe Corner Bookstore
7 Old State House
8 Boston Massacre Site
9 Faneuil Hall
10 Paul Revere House
11 St Stephen's Church
12 Paul Revere Mall
13 Old North Church
14 Copp's Hill Burial Ground
15 USS *Constitution*
16 Bunker Hill Monument

Freedom Trail

Haymarket (see Farmer's Markets under Things to Buy). Ⓣ Orange or Green Line to Haymarket.

Follow the red-brick (or painted red line) Freedom Trail north on Hanover St, the principle commercial thoroughfare, to reach the **Paul Revere House** (☎ 617-523-1676), 19 North Square off Prince St. This small clapboard house, originally built in 1680, is worth a visit – and not just because it's the oldest house in Boston. The hour-long tour also provides a great history lesson. The blacksmith Revere was one of three horseback messengers who carried advance warning on the night of April 18, 1775, of the British march into Concord and Lexington (see those towns in the Around Boston chapter). He lived here for 10 years during the revolutionary period. The house is open daily (except Monday from January through March) from 9:30 am to 4:15 pm, until 5:15 pm from mid-April to late October. Tickets cost $2.50 adults, $1 children five to 17. Ⓣ Green or Orange Line to Haymarket.

At the Paul Revere House you can get a combination ticket that's also good for the adjacent **Pierce-Hichborn House**, built in 1710 and owned by Revere's cousin. It's a fine example of an English Renaissance brick house. Visitation is by guided tour only, usually at 12:30 and 2:30 pm.

Retrace your steps to Hanover St. Across the street is the lovely little St Leonard's Church Peace Garden. Head north on Hanover St for a few blocks to reach the 1804 **St Stephen's Church**, the only remaining church in Boston designed by Boston's renowned architect Charles Bulfinch.

Across the street is the shady **Paul Revere Mall**, a brick prado that might as well be in Italy. Not only does it serve as a perfect frame for the Old North Church to the east, but it's also a lively meeting place for generations of locals. It's also one of the few places in the cramped quarter where you can rest, while contemplating the imposing equestrian statue of Revere.

The 1723 **Old North Church** (☎ 617-523-6676), 193 Salem St, is Boston's oldest church, best known as the place where two lanterns were hung from the steeple on the night of April 18, 1775 as a signal to the three riders that the British were coming by sea. Tall, white box-pews, many with brass name plates of early parishioners, occupy the graceful interior. Look for the little terraces and gardens behind the church. It's open daily from 9 am to 5 pm; Sunday Episcopal services are held at 9, 11 am and 4 pm. A little museum and gift shop are next door. Ⓣ Green or Orange Line to Haymarket.

Head up Hull St to **Copp's Hill Burying Ground**, the city's second-oldest cemetery (1660) from where there are excellent views of the waterfront and Charlestown Harbor. Look for headstones chipped and pocked by Revolutionary War musket fire.

Across the street at 44 Hull St is Boston's **narrowest house**, which measures a whopping 9½-feet wide. The circa-1800 house was reportedly built out of spite: to block light from the neighbor's house and to obliterate the view of the house behind it.

From the vantage point at Copp's Hill Terrace, to the north on Charter St, Charlestown and the last two Freedom Trail sites are visible. If you decide to skip them, retrace your steps to **Salem St**, perhaps the most interesting street in the North End for its collection of specialty markets and restaurants. Stop in at the Bova Italian Bakery, 134 Salem St, which is open 24 hours a day; the aromatic Polcari's Coffee, 105 Salem St; Mottola Pastry Shop, 95 Salem St, for their rich rum cake; and Dairy Fresh Candies, 57 Salem St, for an unsurpassed selection of nuts, chocolates, candies and dried fruit. Around the corner to the right is J Pace & Sons (☎ 617-227-9673), 42 Cross St, a friendly neighborhood Italian grocer where you can pick up fresh cheese, olives, bread and prosciutto. (See Places to Eat for a branch near Downtown Crossing.)

To reach the last two sites, walk a mile or so across the **Charlestown Bridge** from Commercial St and follow the shoreline north to the **USS *Constitution***

(☎ 617-242-5670, http://www.navtap.navy.mil/homepages/constitution), Charlestown Navy Yard.

It's the oldest commissioned US Navy ship (1797), and despite its wooden hull, was nicknamed Old Ironsides for never having gone down in a battle. Outfitted in period uniforms, Navy personnel give free tours of the top deck, gun deck and cramped quarters. In order to maintain the ship's commissioned status, she is taken out onto Boston Harbor every 4th of July, turned around and brought back to the dock. The **Constitution Museum** next door (☎ 617-426-1812) shows an informative film about ship life and the ship's battles. The museum is open daily from 10 am to 5 pm, until 6 pm in the summer. Admission is $4 adults, $2 children six to 16.

The Navy Yard was a thriving ship building center from 1800 until the early 1900s. Although it was closed in 1974, it's been making a slow comeback ever since. Walk around the impressive granite buildings, which have been transformed into shops, residential and office space. There's a good view of Boston from the Navy Yard. Ⓣ Green or Orange Line to North Station. You can also get here by boat, see Boston Harbor Cruises under Organized Tours.

You'll pass through the heart of **Charlestown's** winding, narrow streets lined with colonial houses and gas lanterns to reach the **Bunker Hill Monument** (☎ 617-242-5641), a 220-foot granite obelisk that rises from atop the hill. The neighborhood and two sites (the monument and the *Constitution)* are worth a few hours total – as long as you've been in the city a few days and have done other things first.

Surrounding the Bunker Hill Monument is **Monument Square**, the most impressive spot in Charlestown. It was here, on June 17, 1775, that Colonel Prescott told his revolutionary soldiers, who were running low on gun powder and needed to conserve ammunition, "Don't fire until you see the whites of their eyes." A reenactment of this event takes place every June. Climb the 295 steps for a fine view of Boston; it's open daily from 9 am to 4:30 pm (admission is free). NPS park rangers are on hand in the summer to give talks.

The narrow streets immediately surrounding Monument Square are the most picturesque, lined with restored mid-19th century Federal and Colonial houses. Venture four or five blocks beyond it in any direction and you'll see another side of Charlestown. Many of the homes here are owned by working-class families who've lived here all their lives and not been able to fix up their houses. Indeed, there is a bit of tension between the "townies" and the new, young professionals. The circa-1780 Warren Tavern (☎ 617-241-8142), 2 Pleasant St at Main St in Charlestown, is an atmospheric place for a late afternoon drink. Ⓣ Green or Orange Line to North Station.

CHARLES RIVER ESPLANADE

Boston and Cambridge are graced with grassy banks and paved byways along both sides of the curvaceous Charles River. These paths are perfect for bicycling, jogging and walking. On the Boston side, it's about two miles from the Museum of Science at the Esplanade's eastern end to the Anderson Bridge (which turns into JFK St and leads into Harvard Square).

For one of the best views of Boston, walk, or ride on the Ⓣ Red Line, across the Longfellow Bridge, nicknamed the "Salt and Pepper" bridge because of its towers' resemblance to the shakers.

From Beacon St near Arlington St, cross Storrow Drive (a noisy but necessary auto way) via the Arthur Fiedler Footbridge to reach the Esplanade. This is its most popular and picturesque portion, which includes the **Hatch Memorial Shell**, scene of free outdoor concerts and movies (see Entertainment). On warm days, Bostonians migrate here to sunbathe, sail and feed water fowl gliding along the tranquil riverbank.

The interactive **Museum of Science** (☎ 617-723-2500, http://www.mos.org), Science Park at the Charles River Dam, is an educational ball of fun, especially for kids. Favorite exhibits include the world's largest lightning bolt generator, a full-scale space capsule, a World Population Meter (a baby is born every second or so) and a 20-foot-tall Tyrannosaurus rex dinosaur model. The Skyline Room Cafeteria offers good food and skyline views. The museum is open daily from 9 am to 5 pm, until 9 pm on Friday, and in July and August until 7 pm daily. The cost is $8 adults, $6 children three to 14. (T) Green Line to Science Park.

The museum also houses the **Hayden Planetarium** and **Omni Theater**; combination tickets are available. Generally there are shows on the hour, but call for exact times. The planetarium boasts a state-of-the-art projection system that puts on a heavenly star show and programs about black holes and other astronomical mysteries. The Omni, a four-story, wrap-around theater, makes you feel as if you're experiencing whatever is projected around you: the Grand Canyon, Antarctica or even the human body.

BACK BAY

During the 1850s when Boston was experiencing a population and building boom, Back Bay was an uninhabitable tidal flat. To solve the problem, urban planners embarked on an ambitious and wildly successful 40-year project: fill in the marsh, lay out an orderly grid of streets, erect magnificent Victorian brownstones and design high-minded civic plazas.

Back Bay is one of Boston's most cherished treasures. You could easily spend a half-day here, strolling down shady Commonwealth Ave (known as Comm Ave), window shopping and sipping a latte on chic Newbury St, taking in the remarkable Victorian architecture, popping into grand churches. Although the neighborhood is home to young professionals and blue-blood Bostonians, Back Bay also has a large student population that keeps it from growing too stodgy.

The area is bounded by the Public Garden and Arlington St to the northeast, Mass Ave to the southwest, the Charles River to the northwest and Stuart St and Huntington Ave to the southeast. Cross streets are laid out alphabetically from Arlington St to Berkeley St, and so on, through to Hereford St.

Back Bay is its most enchanting during May when the magnolia, tulip and dogwood trees are in bloom. Marlborough St, one block north and parallel to Comm Ave, is the most tranquil of Back Bay's shady, patrician streets.

To get an idea of what these opulent mansions were like in the 19th century, visit the **Gibson House** (☎ 617-267-6338), 137 Beacon St near Arlington St, a splendid six-story Victorian brownstone. The house is open from May through October, Wednesday through Sunday; November through April on weekends only. Tours are given at 1, 2 and 3 pm. Tickets are $4. (T) Green Line to Arlington.

High-minded **Copley Square**, set between Dartmouth, Clarendon and Boylston Sts, is surrounded by historic buildings. **Trinity Church** (☎ 617-536-0944), 206 Clarendon St, is one of the nation's truly great buildings. Designed by Henry Hobson Richardson in 1877, the grand French and Romanesque building still holds Sunday services. It's open daily from 8:30 am to 5 pm. Across the street, the 62-story **John Hancock Tower**, 200 Clarendon St, constructed with more than 10,000 panels of mirrored glass, stands in stark contrast to Trinity Church. Designed in 1976 by IM Pei, the tower suffered serious initial problems: inferior glass panes were installed and when the wind whipped up, the panes popped out, falling hundreds of feet to the ground. The area was quickly cordoned off and all the panes were replaced. (No one was ever hurt.) There are great views from the observatory; see Orientation. (T) Green Line to Copley

The venerable **Boston Public Library** (☎ 617-536-5400), 666 Boylston St, between Exeter and Dartmouth Sts, lends credence to Boston's reputation as "the Athens of America." See Libraries under Information for details.

Adjacent to Copley Square is the enormous and modern **Copley Place** (see Things to Buy), the largest privately funded development in Boston's history. Another large shopping development, the **Prudential Center** (again, see Things to Buy) lies a few blocks southwest of Copley Place. Like the Hancock Tower, the "Pru" also has an observatory which is detailed in Orientation.

On the subject of shopping, **Newbury St** is to Boston what Fifth Ave is to New York City. International boutiques and galleries get tonier and tonier the closer you get to the Public Garden. Newbury St is perhaps more fun to wander at night when shops are closed but the well-lit windows are dressed to the nines, and when darkness cloaks your less-than-Armani attire. Newbury St is epitomized by its cafe culture and a worldly, haute-couture crowd. Ⓣ Green Line to Arlington, Copley Square or Hynes Convention Center.

The Episcopal **Emmanuel Church** (☎ 617-536-3355), 15 Newbury St near Arlington St, is highly regarded for its musical and cultural offerings. Stop in to see what's scheduled.

Only in Boston could something be called the **New Old South Church** (☎ 617-536-1970), 645 Boylston St. The Italian Gothic structure is quite distinctive, complete with a campanile and multi-colored granite. You can visit weekdays from 9 am to 4:30 pm.

The **Arlington Street Church** (☎ 617-536-7050), 351 Boylston St, was the first public building to be erected in Back Bay. The church features 16 commissioned Tiffany windows, a bell tower and steeple modeled after London's Church of St Martin-in-the-Fields. The Unitarian Universalist ministry is purely progressive. It's open late May through October from 10 am to 4 pm (tours are available) and for Sunday services. Call for winter hours.

Beyond the Pru on the southwestern edge of Back Bay, the **Institute of Contemporary Art** (☎ 617-266-5152), 955 Boylston St, livens up Boston's often conservative art scene by showing the avant-garde art

created by well-known national artists as well as unknown regional artists. The ICA's airy galleries, housed within a renovated 19th-century firehouse, are open Wednesday through Sunday noon to 5 pm (Thursdays until 9 pm). Tickets are $5.25 adults, $3.25 students, $2.25 children under 12; it's free from 5 to 9 pm on Thursdays. Ⓣ Green Line to Hynes Convention Center.

The **Christian Science Church** (☎ 617-450-3793, http://www.csmonitor.com), 175 Huntington Ave at Mass Ave, founded by Mary Baker Eddy in 1866, has its home base in Boston. Tour the grand basilica, which can seat 3000 worshippers, or linger on the expansive plaza with its 670-foot-long reflecting pool. Next door are the offices of the internationally regarded daily newspaper, the *Christian Science Monitor*, an elegant Reading Room and the Mapparium, one of Boston's hidden treasures. The **Mapparium** is a room-sized, stained-glass globe that you can walk through on a glass bridge. Geo-political boundaries are drawn as the world appeared in 1932. The acoustics, which were a surprise to the designer, are a wonder: no matter how softly you whisper in the ear of your companion, everyone in the room will hear it perfectly! The Mother Church (as it's known to adherents) is open Monday through Saturday from 10 am to 4 pm, Sunday 11:15 am to 2 pm. The Mapparium is open from Monday through Saturday 10 am to 4 pm. Both are free. Ⓣ Green Line to Symphony.

Nearby are two architecturally noteworthy buildings. First is **Horticultural Hall** (☎ 617-536-9280), 300 Mass Ave, home to the Massachusetts Horticultural Society. It has the largest independent library in the world devoted to gardening. Head to the 2nd floor for a peek; it's open weekdays. Across the street is **Symphony Hall** (☎ 617-266-1492), 301 Mass Ave, the first concert hall in the world to be designed according to acoustic principles. The pre-eminent Boston Symphony Orchestra plays here; see Entertainment. Ⓣ Green Line to Symphony.

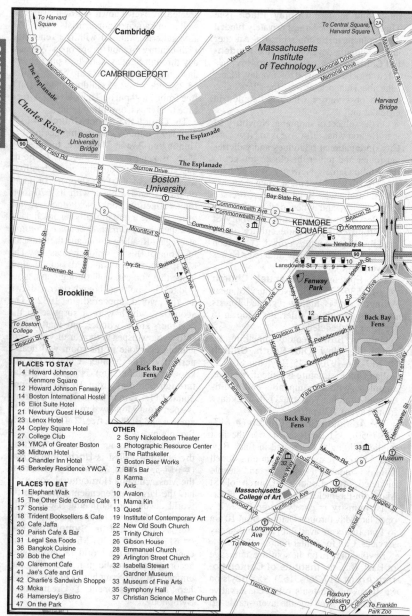

PLACES TO STAY

4 Howard Johnson
   Kenmore Square
12 Howard Johnson Fenway
14 Boston International Hostel
16 Eliot Suite Hotel
21 Newbury Guest House
23 Lenox Hotel
24 Copley Square Hotel
27 College Club
34 YMCA of Greater Boston
38 Midtown Hotel
44 Chandler Inn Hotel
45 Berkeley Residence YWCA

PLACES TO EAT

1 Elephant Walk
15 The Other Side Cosmic Cafe
17 Sonsie
18 Trident Booksellers & Cafe
20 Cafe Jaffa
30 Parish Cafe & Bar
31 Legal Sea Foods
35 Bangkok Cuisine
39 Bob the Chef
40 Claremont Cafe
41 Jae's Cafe and Grill
42 Charlie's Sandwich Shoppe
46 Moka
46 Hamersley's Bistro
47 On the Park

OTHER

2 Sony Nickelodeon Theater
3 Photographic Resource Center
5 The Rathskeller
6 Boston Beer Works
7 Bill's Bar
8 Karma
9 Axis
10 Avalon
11 Mama Kin
13 Quest
19 Institute of Contemporary Art
22 New Old South Church
25 Trinity Church
26 Gibson House
28 Emmanuel Church
29 Arlington Street Church
32 Isabella Stewart
   Gardner Museum
33 Museum of Fine Arts
35 Symphony Hall
37 Christian Science Mother Church

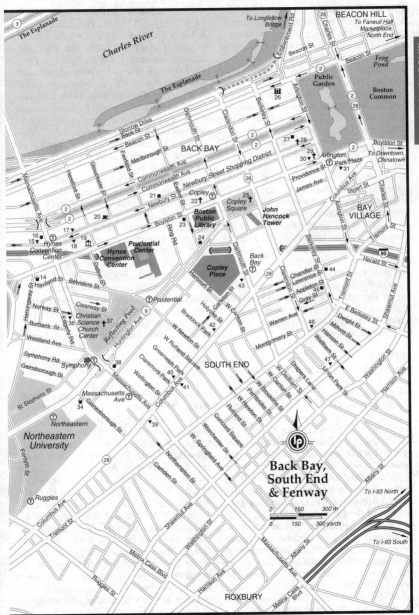

Back Bay,
South End
& Fenway

0   150   300 m
0   150   300 yards

KENMORE SQUARE

West of Back Bay, Beacon St and Comm Ave converge at Kenmore Square, the epicenter of student life in Boston. In addition to the behemoth Boston University (BU, see Campuses under Information), which stretches along Comm Ave, there are more than a half-dozen colleges in the area. Kenmore Square has more than its share of clubs (see Entertainment), inexpensive but nondescript eateries and dormitories disguised as innocuous brownstones. You'll know you're in Kenmore Square when you see the 60-sq-foot Citgo sign. The mammoth neon sign has marked the spot since 1965. ⓣ Green Line to Kenmore.

One block west of Kenmore Square, the **Photographic Resource Center** (☎ 617-353-0700), 602 Comm Ave, is one of the few centers in the country devoted exclusively to this art form. Ever-changing exhibits lean towards the modern and experimental. The PRC is open Tuesday through Sunday from noon to 5 pm, until 8 pm on Thursday. Admission is $3, free on Thursday evenings. The well-stocked library is only open on Tuesdays, Thursdays and Saturdays.

FENWAY

South of Kenmore Square is Fenway, an area wherein the names can be confusing, even to Bostonians. Although The Fenway is a highway and Fenway Park is where the Boston Red Sox play baseball, when people refer to "Fenway," they're generally talking about the **Back Bay Fens**, a tranquil and interconnected park system that extends south from the Charles River Esplanade (at Park Drive or Charlesgate East), along a winding brook to the lush Arnold Arboretum and Franklin Park Zoo. It's part of the Emerald Necklace, a series of parks throughout the city, linked in the 1880s and 1890s by landscape architect Frederick Law Olmstead. Two renowned museums, the MFA and the Gardner, are on The Fenway. It's inadvisable to linger in Fenway after dark, especially near the tall reeds. In recent years there have been a number of gay-bashing incidents here.

The 265-acre **Arnold Arboretum** (☎ 617-524-1717), 125 The Arborway in Jamaica Plain, is a gem. Under a public/private partnership with the city and Harvard University, it's planted with over 14,000 exotic trees, flowering shrubs and other specimens. It's particularly beautiful in the spring. Dog-walking, Frisbee throwing, bicycling and general contemplation are encouraged (but picnicking is not allowed). It's free and open daily from sunrise to sunset. A visitor center is located at the main gate, just south of the rotary at Routes 1 and 203. ⓣ Orange Line to Forest Hills and walk two blocks northwest to the Forest Hills gate.

The 70-acre **Franklin Park Zoo** (☎ 617-442-4896), Peabody Circle at Blue Hill Ave and Columbia Rd, boasts an African Tropical Forest Pavilion, complete with lush vegetation, waterfalls, gorillas, antelopes and crocodiles. It's a well-designed ecosystem with nearly invisible barriers between you and the animals; there are certainly no cages. There's also a three-story free-flight aviary that you can enter. The zoo is open daily from about 9:30 am to 5 pm. Tickets costs $5.50 adults, $4 children four to 11. The lovely park is surrounded by one of the city's poorer and less safe neighborhoods, but as long as you leave by sunset, you'll be fine.

The collections at the **Museum of Fine Arts** (MFA, ☎ 617-267-9300, http://www.boston.com), 465 Huntington Ave in Fenway, are second in this country only to those of New York's Metropolitan Museum of Art. Particularly noteworthy are its holdings of American art, which include major works by John Singleton Copley, Winslow Homer, Edward Hopper and the Hudson River School; American decorative arts are also well represented. The museum has more Asian treasures, including a full-scale Japanese Buddhist temple, than any other collection in the world. European paintings from the 11th to the 20th centuries, including a huge collection of French impressionists, are outdone by only a handful of museums around the globe.

Fenway Park

Boston's most cherished landmark? Site of Boston's greatest dramas and worst defeats? To many Bostonians it's not Bunker Hill or the Freedom Trail, not Harvard or MIT, but tiny Fenway Park, home of baseball's Red Sox, where names like Babe Ruth, Ted Williams, Carl Yastrzemski, Jim Rice and Roger Clemens are uttered and remembered as reverently as any heroes from Boston's colonial history.

Fenway Park has earned the reputation of baseball's mecca, the class of the Major Leagues. Only Wrigley Field in Chicago can rival Fenway's age and uniqueness.

Nestled between the Back Bay Fens and the Mass Pike, Fenway is truly an integral part of downtown Boston. The park is little more than a hundred yards from Kenmore Square, and adjoining Lansdowne St (also known as Ted Williams Way), which sports many of Boston's most popular nightclubs. Even closer to the park are the hearts of the Red Sox fans, who have remained loyal (the Red Sox are a top draw in the Major Leagues) despite the team's failure to win a World Series in close to 80 years.

Much of the team's ill fate is attributed to the "Curse of the Great Bambino," the sale of their best young pitcher Babe Ruth to the hated rival New York Yankees in 1918. The Red Sox have not won a World Series since that season, while Babe Ruth and the Yankees went on to achieve legendary success and fame. Many believe the sale of Ruth to be among the worst transactions in professional sports history.

Baseball played in Fenway is made special by the unique geometry of the park. Thanks to its downtown location, an economy of space gives the fans an intimate proximity to the playing field. The Fenway Faithful claim to feel more a part of the ball game than might be possible in larger, more modern parks. Fenway also has the one and only "Green Monster," a towering wall in left field that compensates for the relatively short distance from home plate. The Green Monster consistently alters the regular course of play – what appears to be a lazy fly ball could actually drop over the monster for a home run, and what appears to be a sharp double into the gap may be played off the wall to hold the runner to a single.

So fabled and important a site as Fenway Park certainly should have protection against urban development, however, that's not the case. Current planners would like to unceremoniously move it to South Boston so that it can abut the "historic" World Trade Center and Expressway areas. The debate continues, as Boston is slow to decide anything.

For more on attending a game at Fenway, see Spectator Sports. ■

When it's time to rest your feet, there is a very good cafe and a tranquil Japanese Tenshin Garden. The entire museum is open from Sunday through Tuesday from 10 am to 4:45 pm, Wednesday until 9:45 pm (when admission is "pay as you wish"); only the West Wing, where special shows are held, stays open until 9:45 pm on Thursday and Friday. Admission is $8 adults, $6 students, $3.50 children six to 17. Ⓣ the "E" branch of the Green Line to Museum.

The **Isabella Stewart Gardner Museum** (☎ 617-566-1401), 280 The Fenway, is a magnificent Venetian-style palazzo built to house "Mrs Jack" Gardner's collection, was also her home until her death in 1924. A monument to one

woman's exquisite taste for acquiring unequaled art, the Gardner is filled with almost 2000 priceless objects, primarily European, including outstanding tapestries, and Italian Renaissance and 17th-century Dutch paintings. Since her will stipulated that her collection remain exactly as it was at the time of her death, nothing in the museum will ever change. That helps explain the few empty spaces on the walls: in 1990 the museum was robbed of nearly $200 million worth of paintings, including a rare and beloved Vermeer. The walls on which they were mounted will remain barren until the paintings are recovered (highly unlikely). The palazzo itself, with a four-story greenhouse courtyard, is a masterpiece, a tranquil oasis, alone worth the price of admission. The Gardner has a lovely cafe that's open for lunch. The museum is open year round Tuesday through Sunday from 11 am to 5 pm. Admission is $8 adults, $5 students ($3 on Wednesdays), $3 children 12 to 17. Ⓣ the "E" branch of the Green Line to Museum.

SOUTH END

Not to be confused with South Boston ("Southie"), which is still remembered for its violent opposition to integrating the Boston public schools in the 1970s, South End is a study in ethnic, racial and economic diversity. South End doesn't have any "sights" per se, but it's worth exploring to get a sense of the promise and vibrancy Boston still holds. Parts have recently been claimed by artists, gays, architects and young professionals, but other parts are less gentrified. Housing projects and halfway houses rub elbows with converted condos. Ⓣ Orange Line to Back Bay/South End.

South of Back Bay and west of the Theater District, this neighborhood is bounded by Huntington, Mass and Shawmut Aves and the Mass Turnpike to the north. Columbus Ave and Tremont St are the principle commercial streets, lined with trendy restaurants.

The **Southwest Corridor**, an almost-five-mile (one way) paved and landscaped walkway, runs between and parallel to Columbus and Huntington Aves. Walk north from Mass Ave for rewarding views of the Back Bay skyline. One block north, St Botolph St is one of the neighborhood's most tranquil.

The South End's side streets, which boast the country's largest concentration of Victorian row houses, have a more British feel to them than other parts of the city. Particularly quaint is the tiny, elliptical **Union Park Square** between Tremont St and Shawmut Ave. Ⓣ Orange Line to Back Bay/South End. Look for Rutland Square, just north of Tremont St, as well.

THEATER DISTRICT

Although the area is tiny by New York standards, Boston has long served as an important pre-Broadway staging area for shows. Thanks to the building boom in the 1980s, many of the landmark theaters received long-needed face lifts. Little more than a sq block, the district is bounded by Boylston, Stuart, Tremont and S Charles St. Don't overlook the smaller venues (see Entertainment) where better value is often found. Ⓣ Orange Line to NE Medical Center or Chinatown.

Off Boylston St is **Boylston Place**, a pedestrian-only alleyway lined with night-clubs (see Entertainment.) As suburban theater patrons spill out of the theaters to head home, a different type of clientele is just beginning to make their way here.

Much of the daytime action takes place within the drearily named **State Transportation Building**, 10 Park Plaza, where you'll find an atrium-like space with eateries, free lunchtime concerts and art exhibits.

Wedged between Stuart, Arlington, Marginal and Charles St South, **Bay Village** is an often-overlooked but charming neighborhood that's certainly worth a stroll. The tiny, early 19th-century brick houses were built and occupied by those who built the Beacon Hill mansions. Today the tight-knit neighborhood is more gay and bohemian than most. Ⓣ Green Line to Arlington.

CHINATOWN

On the eastern edge of the Theater District, the most colorful part of Chinatown is bounded by Tremont, Essex, Kneeland and Kingston Sts. This tiny area is over-flowing with authentic restaurants (many open until 4 am), bakeries, markets selling live animals, import and textile shops and phone booths topped with little pagodas. Don't miss the enormous gate that guards Beach and Kingston Sts. In addition to the Chinese, who began arriving in the late 1870s, the community of 8000 also includes Cambodians, Vietnamese and Laotians. Ⓣ Orange Line to Chinatown.

NEW ENGLAND AQUARIUM

Teeming with sea creatures of all sizes, shapes and colors, the New England Aquarium (☎ 617-973-5200, http://www.neaq.org), Central Wharf off Atlantic Ave, is equally popular with adults and children. Harbor seals within an outdoor enclosure introduce the main indoor attraction: a three-story, cylindrical saltwater tank. It swirls with over 600 creatures great and small – including turtles, sharks and eels. Leave a little time to be mesmerized by the Echo of the Waves sculpture. You can catch whale-watch cruises here too, see Whale-Watching Cruises, below. The aquarium is open year round from 9 am to 5 pm on weekdays, until 8 pm on Thursday, until 6 pm on weekends. Admission is $8.75 for those 12 and over, $4.75 kids age three to 11. Ⓣ Blue Line to Aquarium.

MUSEUM WHARF

South of the aquarium and across Fort Point Channel are the Children's, Computer and Tea Party Museums. The channel is a waterway separating Boston proper from South Boston. This district of old brick warehouses, part of which includes Museum Wharf, contains many artists' lofts and design studios, as well as work-a-day waterfront businesses like seafood markets and shipping docks. Walk to Northern Ave, then east for a few blocks and turn around for a great view of the Boston skyline. Ⓣ Red Line to South Station plus a 10-minute walk.

The delightful **Children's Museum** (☎ 617-426-8855), 300 Congress St, can entertain pre-schoolers to teenagers for an entire day with interactive educational exhibits. There are bubble exhibits, dress-up areas, a two-story climbing gym and an exhibit on what it's like to be a teen in Tokyo. The museum is open from 10 am to 5 pm daily in the summer, and Tuesday through Sunday the rest of the year. On Friday from 5 to 9 pm year round, the admission is reduced to $1 for everyone. (Be forewarned; it's crowded then!) Other-

wise, admission is $7 for adults, $6 children two to 15.

The most popular exhibit at the **Computer Museum** (☎ 617-426-2800, http://www.tcm.org), 300 Congress St, is the enormous, functional Walk-Through Computer. A 250-foot keyboard is hooked up to a 108-foot monitor. There are over 35 other hands-on exhibits where you can explore state-of-the-art devices and pay homage to PC precursors: the abacus, slide rule, punch-card and calculator. The museum is open from 10 am to 5 pm daily in summer, or Tuesday through Sunday the rest of the year. Admission is $7 adults, $5 children over five, half-price on Sunday from 3 to 5 pm.

The **Boston Tea Party Ship & Museum** (☎ 617-338-1773), Congress St Bridge, stands as testimony to the spirited colonists who refused to pay the levy imposed on their beloved beverage. In 1773 they left a town meeting and donned Native American costume as a disguise before boarding the *Beaver* (the *Beaver II*, which you board today, is an approximate replica) and dumped all the tea overboard in rebellion. Costumed guides tell the story, while the adjacent museum offers multilingual information and a complimentary cup of tax-free, Salada tea. The ship and museum are open daily from 9 am to 5 pm, until 6 pm in July and August; admission to both is $7 adults, $3.50 children six to 12.

BOSTON HARBOR ISLANDS

Until recently, Boston Harbor had the unenviable distinction of being the dirtiest harbor in the country. After a massive, multi-million dollar clean-up in the mid-1990s, the harbor is on its way to regaining a healthier reputation. Good thing, too, since it has over 30 large and small islands which offer plenty of history, picnicking, nature walks and fishing. (For information on getting to the islands and camping there, see Places to Stay.)

Georges Island, the jumping-off spot for all the other islands, features a

19th-century fort. Lovell Island is the largest, good for walking along dunes, marshes and meadows. Look for wild raspberries on Bumpkin Island and for a variety of birds on Grape Island.

JOHN F KENNEDY LIBRARY & MUSEUM

The library and museum (☎ 617-929-4500) are out of the way, but worth a visit. It's set on dramatic Columbia Point, near the UMass, Boston campus (see Campuses under Information); together, they take up most of the peninsula, which is nice for strolling.

The JFK museum is the repository for memorabilia related to the 35th US president: papers, video tape, speeches and photographs. Check out the good introductory film about JFK. The museum is open daily from 9 am to 5 pm. Admission is $6 adults, $4 students, $2 children under 16.

Interestingly, the library has an archive of Ernest Hemingway's manuscripts and papers. About 95% of the writer's works can be accessed if you're interested in research, but unfortunately there is no exhibit space. What's the connection? Kennedy was key in helping Mary Hemingway, Ernest's fourth wife and widow, get the manuscripts and papers out of Cuba during the first and most intense days of the embargo. When she died, she willed them here, because the library offers the public better access than most archival libraries.

Next door is the **Commonwealth Museum** (☎ 617-727-9268), which holds exhibits on Massachusetts' people and history. The Massachusetts Archives (☎ 617-727-2816) displays documents from the first days of colonization. It's open 9 am to 5 pm weekdays, 9 am to 3 pm Saturday. Admission is free.

Ⓣ Red Line to JFK/UMass, and catch a free shuttle bus to the museum, or to the university campus. Boston Harbor Cruises runs boats here from Long Wharf mid-May to early October (see Cruises for details).

CAMBRIDGE

Cambridge is known around the globe as the home of intellectual heavyweights Harvard University and Massachusetts Institute of Technology. (See Campuses under Information for details.) With a combined student body of almost 30,000 students from almost 100 countries, Cambridge is a diverse and youthful place, to say the least.

Founded in 1638, Cambridge was home to the country's first college (Harvard) and first printing press, virtually putting an early lock on its reputation as a hotbed for ideas and intellectualism.

Cambridge has always been known for its progressive politics, much of it centering around Harvard Square. Cantabrigians, as residents are called, vehemently opposed the Vietnam War before others did; they embraced the environmental movement before recycling became profitable; they were one of the first communities to ban smoking in public buildings. And when gays were excluded from marching in South Boston's traditional St Patrick's Day parade, Cambridge immediately pledged to hold its own inclusive parade.

You'll find **Harvard Square** overflowing with cafes, bookstores, restaurants, a few protesters and a lot of street musicians. Although many Cantabrigians complain that the Square has lost its edge – once-independently owned shops are continually gobbled up by national chains – Harvard Square is still worth an afternoon.

The "Square" isn't a square at all, but rather a triangle of brick pavement above the Harvard T station. Out of Town News and an information kiosk are also here; see Information. When people refer to the Square, they are referring to the four or five block area that radiates from the Mass Ave and JFK St intersection. Ⓣ Red Line to Harvard.

Most of **Harvard University** lies east of JFK St and east of Mass Ave after it jogs north out of the Square. The gates to famed **Harvard Yard**, a quadrangle of ivy-covered brick buildings, are just across Harvard St

MASSACHUSETTS

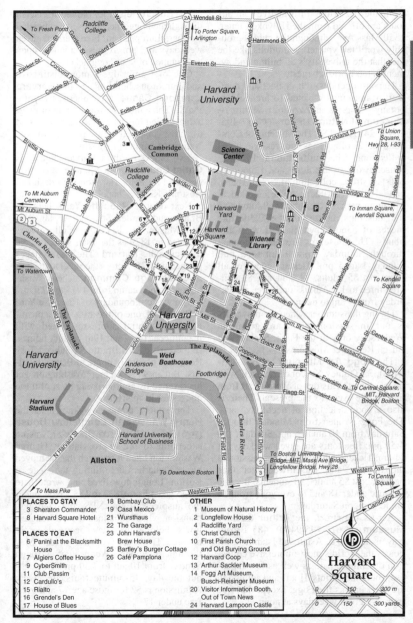

PLACES TO STAY	18 Bombay Club	OTHER
3 Sheraton Commander	19 Casa Mexico	1 Museum of Natural History
8 Harvard Square Hotel	21 Wursthaus	2 Longfellow House
	22 The Garage	4 Radcliffe Yard
PLACES TO EAT	23 John Harvard's	5 Christ Church
6 Panini at the Blacksmith	Brew House	10 First Parish Church
House	25 Bartley's Burger Cottage	and Old Burying Ground
7 Algiers Coffee House	26 Café Pamplona	12 Harvard Coop
9 CyberSmith		13 Arthur Sackler Museum
11 Club Passim		14 Fogg Art Museum,
12 Cardullo's		Busch-Reisinger Museum
15 Rialto		20 Visitor Information Booth,
16 Grendel's Den		Out of Town News
17 House of Blues		24 Harvard Lampoon Castle

Harvard Square

| 0 | | 150 | | 300 m |
| 0 | | 150 | | 300 yards |

from the T-station. Informative campus tours are offered from the Holyoke Center, 1350 Mass Ave, although the guides probably won't tell you tell you tidbits like the fact that the university's $5 billion endowment is the world's largest.

Harvard operates four distinct and noteworthy museums devoted to archeology, botany, minerals and zoology within its **Museum of Natural History** (☎ 617-495-3045), 24 Oxford St. The Museum of Comparative Zoology has impressive fossil collections. The multi-cultural Peabody Museum of Archaeology and Ethnology boasts a strong collection of North American Indian artifacts. The Botanical Museum, perhaps the most well known of the museums, houses over 800 life-like pieces of hand-blown-glass flowers and plants. The museums are open Monday through Saturday from 9 am to 5 pm, Sunday 1 to 5 pm. Tickets, good for all four, cost $5 adults, $4 students, $3 children three to 13. Admission is free on Saturday from 9 am to noon.

During the summer, when the university is not in session, tours are given on Wednesday only at the Fogg, Sackler and Busch-Reisinger Museums.

The **Fogg Art Museum** (☎ 617-495-9400), 32 Quincy St, concerns itself with no less than the history of Western art from the Middle Ages to the present. There is also a good selection of decorative arts. The Fogg is open from Monday through Saturday from 10 am to 5 pm, Sundays 1 to 4:50 pm; free tours are given weekdays at 11 am. Tickets, which include admission to the Sackler and Busch-Reisinger (see below), cost $5 adults, $3 students. It's free to those under 18 and to everyone from 10 am to noon on Saturday.

Across the street, the **Arthur Sackler Museum** (☎ 617-495-9400), 485 Broadway, is devoted to Asian and Islamic art. It boasts the world's most impressive collection of Chinese jade as well as fine Japanese woodblock prints. Hours and admission are the same as the Fogg, except that free tours are given weekdays at noon.

The **Busch-Reisinger Museum**, entered through the Fogg, specializes in Central and Northern European art. Free tours are given weekdays at 2 pm. Admission is free upon presentation of your Fogg ticket.

One of Cambridge's most distinctive and humorous buildings is the **Harvard Lampoon Castle**, Mt Auburn at Plympton St. The namesake student humor magazine, which has its offices here, was said to have inspired the creation of the National Lampoon magazine.

Two blocks north of Harvard Square is **Christ Church**, Garden St near Mass Ave, designed by Peter Harrison who designed Boston's King's Chapel.

Next door is **Radcliffe Yard,** between Brattle and Garden Sts, and Appian Way and Mason St. Radcliffe College was founded in 1879 as the sister school to the then-all-male Harvard. The two colleges merged in 1975. Across the street to the east is **Cambridge Common**, where Washington pitched camp from 1775 to 1776.

The western boundary of Radcliffe Yard is **Brattle St**, one of the area's most prestigious residential addresses, lined with magnificent 18th- and 19th-century homes. In the early 1770s Brattle St, dubbed Tory Row, was generally home to British loyalists. But in 1775 George Washington got his revenge by appropriating most of these houses for his patriots.

The stately home now known as the **Henry Wadsworth Longfellow House** (☎ 617-876-4491), 105 Brattle St, was no exception to the appropriation: George Washington liked it so much that he moved his headquarters here during the siege of Boston. Longfellow lived and wrote here for 45 years from 1837 to 1882. Now under the auspices of the NPS, the Georgian mansion, which contains many of Longfellow's belongings, has been elegantly restored. The house is open from early May through October, Wednesday through Sunday from 10 am to 4:30 pm. Throughout the day, 45-minute tours are given. Admission is $2 for those age 17 and over; free under 17.

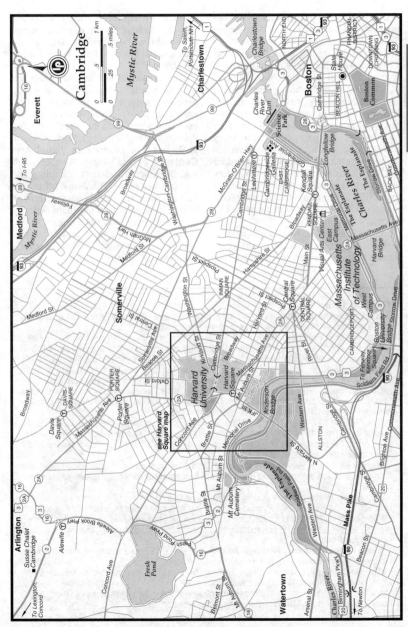

On a sunny day, the **Mt Auburn Cemetery** (☎ 617-547-7105), 580 Mt Auburn St, is worth the 30-minute walk west out of Harvard Square. Developed in 1831, its 170 acres were the first "garden cemetery" in the US. Until then, the colonial notion of moving a body and grave marker around a cemetery was commonplace. Pick up a self-guided map of the rare botanical specimens and of the notable burial plots, including those for Mary Baker Eddy (founder of the Christian Science Church), Isabella Stewart Gardner (of the Gardner Museum), Winslow Homer (19th-century American painter extraordinaire) and Oliver Wendell Holmes (US Supreme Court Justice). The cemetery is open daily.

In East Cambridge, **Kendall Square** at Main St has come alive in recent years thanks to the high-tech industry and the takeover of neglected brick warehouses. The One Kendall Square complex, Hampshire and Broadway Sts, is its nucleus (see Theaters and Places to Eat). Ⓣ Red Line to Kendall.

The campus of **MIT** extends south and west of Kendall Square. Join one of the excellent guided campus tours to best appreciate MIT's contributions to the sciences. Wander around the East Campus (on the east side of Mass Ave), bejeweled with public art. The nearby **List Visual Arts Center** (☎ 617-253-4680), Weisner Building, 20 Ames St, mounts rewarding and sophisticated shows. Admission is free, and the galleries are open Tuesday through Friday from noon to 6 pm (until 8 pm on Thursday), weekends 1 to 5 pm.

From the East Campus, make your way one block south to the Charles River for a great view of Boston.

Walking Tours

Boston is a walker's paradise and is best explored by foot. There are a number of special-interest maps you can pick up that make navigating easier.

The 2½-mile **Freedom Trail** (☎ 617-242-5642) is the granddaddy of walks. Sixteen historically important sites, including colonial and revolutionary-era buildings, are linked by a double row of red sidewalk bricks (or a painted red line) which begins near the MBTA Park Street station, winds through downtown Boston and the North End and ends in Charlestown at the USS *Constitution*. Massive ongoing construction projects downtown have interrupted and obliterated many of the red sidewalk bricks that identify the Freedom Trail, so it's best to use a map. Pick one up at the Boston Common Visitor Information Center or NPS visitor center (see Tourist Offices).

The NPS (☎ 617-242-5642), 15 State St, offers about six free ranger-led walking tours (on the hour from 10 am to 3 pm) along the Freedom Trail from mid-April to late November. In the off-season, it's reduced to twice daily on weekdays, four on the weekends. Ⓣ Orange or Blue Line to State.

The Boston Park Rangers (☎ 617-635-7383), Tremont St on Boston Common, offer free naturalist-led walks around the **Emerald Necklace** of parks. Ⓣ Green or Red Line to Park Street.

The **Black Heritage Trail** encompasses more than a dozen 19th century sites, most of which are on Beacon Hill. Pick up a map at the African American National Historic Site, 46 Joy St (☎ 617-742-5415). Or take a guided walk from late May to early September, daily at 10 am, noon and 2 pm; it departs in front of the Shaw Memorial on Beacon St, in front of the State House.

Maps for the **Women's Heritage Trail** (☎ 617-731-5597) are available from the NPS, which sometimes offers guided walks.

The **Harborwalk**, not surprisingly, follows the shoreline and celebrates Boston's rich maritime past. Pick up a map at the visitor center on Boston Common. Quite honestly, though, this won't be one of the most enjoyable walks for the next couple of years due to heavy Central Artery/Third Harbor Tunnel construction. ∎

BICYCLING

Over 50 miles of bicycle trails originate in the Boston area. One of the most popular circuits runs along both sides of the Charles River, but you can also ride for miles out to the Arnold Arboretum or out to nearby Watertown and back. Although you have to be something of a kamikaze to take to the inner-city streets, people do it. All of the following bike rental places have detailed maps for sale. You can take your bike, by the way, on any of the MBTA subway lines, except the Green Line, during off-peak hours.

Earth Bikes (☎ 617-267-4733), 35 Huntington Ave next to the Copley Square Hotel, rents bikes and organizes tours from March through November. Community Bicycle Supply (☎ 617-542-8623), 496 Tremont St, is also open seasonally. Back Bay Bicycles (☎ 617-247-2336), 333 Newbury St, is open year round. ⓣ Green Line to Hynes Convention Center.

IN-LINE SKATING

The Beacon Hill Skate Shop (☎ 617-482-7400), 135 Charles St South (in Bay Village), rents in-line skates for $5 per hour or $10 per day. Glide over to the Esplanade, or better yet, to Memorial Drive on the Cambridge side of the Charles River, which is closed to auto traffic on Sundays from 11 am to 7 pm in warm weather.

BOATING

The Charles River Canoe and Kayak Center (☎ 617-965-5110), 2401 Comm Ave in Newton, rents boats from April through October for $7 to $9 per hour. The center is across from a tranquil stretch of the Charles River. ⓣ the "D" Branch of the Green Line to Riverside and a 20-minute walk.

Community Boating (☎ 617-523-1038), Charles River Esplanade near the Charles St footbridge, offers experienced sailors unlimited use of 140 sailboats, kayaks and windsurfers for $50 for two days. ⓣ Red Line to Charles/MGH.

KIM GRANT

ORGANIZED TOURS

For walking tours, see the sidebar.

Trolley tours offer great flexibility in sightseeing because you can hop on and off as you like, catching the next trolley that comes along. Trolley operators include the Red Beantown Trolleys (☎ 617-236-2148), who operate Friday through Sunday from January through March and daily from April through December.

The blue Boston Trolley (☎ 617-876-5539) runs daily year round. In the summer, trolleys depart every 10 minutes, but in the off-season, they run every 30 minutes or so. If you don't get off the trolley, the entire trip takes 90 minutes. Tickets are $16 adults, $6 children six to 12.

The rates and schedules for Old Town Trolley (☎ 617-269-7010) are similar. All three trolley companies pick up passengers across from the New England Aquarium, at Atlantic Ave and State St. ⓣ Blue Line to Aquarium.

The Brush Hill/Gray Line bus tours (☎ 617-236-2148, 800-343-1328) offer a mammoth 3½-hour motor coach tour of Boston and Cambridge for $21 from April through November. They depart from the Transportation Building, 8 Park Square, near the Public Garden.

CRUISES

Boston Harbor Cruises (☎ 617-227-4320), 1 Long Wharf off Atlantic Ave, operates 90-minute narrated sightseeing trips around the outer harbor from mid-April through October for $8 adults, $4 children. They also operate sunset cruises and boats that go to the John F Kennedy Library on Columbia Point in Dorchester and USS *Constitution* in Charlestown. (You can get off at both places and catch the next boat back.) Ⓣ Blue Line to Aquarium.

The Charles River Boat Co (☎ 617-621-3001), Cambridgeside Galleria, runs a narrated trip of the Charles River Basin for $8 adults, $5 children. Trips depart on weekends in April, May and September, and daily on the hour from noon to 4 pm from June through August. Meet at the ticket counter near the "food festival" in the mall or on the Boston side of the river, in front of the Hatch Shell on the Esplanade, 10 minutes after the hour.

Bay State Cruises (☎ 617-723-7800), operates boats to Georges Island in Boston Harbor (see Boston Harbor Islands and Camping under Places to Stay) from Long Wharf off Atlantic Ave. Ferries run from early May to mid-October; roundtrip tickets are $7 adults, $5 children. From Georges Island you can catch a free boat to smaller islands. They also run a 30-minute lunchtime harbor cruise at 12:15 pm weekdays in the summer for $1. It's the best and cheapest way to get out onto the harbor. Ⓣ Blue Line to Aquarium.

Boston Duck Tours (☎ 617-723-3825), 101 Huntington Ave at the Prudential Center, offers unusual land and water tours using modified amphibious vehicles from WWII. The narrated tour splashes around the Charles River for about 25 minutes, and then competes with cars on Boston city streets for another 55 minutes. Boats run daily from early April through November; tickets are $18 for adults, $9 for children. Ⓣ Green Line to Prudential.

The AC Cruise Line (☎ 617-261-6633), 290 Northern Ave in South Boston, operates boats to Gloucester from late May to early September. Tickets are $18 adults, $12 children, and include a 2½-hour layover to walk around town. Ⓣ Red Line to South Station and a 15-minute walk.

Whale-Watching Cruises Whale sightings are practically guaranteed at Stellwagen Bank, a fertile feeding ground 25 miles out to sea. Trips take about five to six hours, with on-board commentary provided by naturalists. Boats generally depart on weekends in April, May, June, September and October, and daily in July and August. Dress warmly even on summer days.

Tickets for the New England Aquarium Whale Watching tour (☎ 617-973-5277), Central Wharf off Atlantic Ave, cost $24 adults, $16.50 children three to 11. They offer two trips daily in the summer. Ⓣ Blue Line to Aquarium.

The AC Cruise Line Inc (☎ 617-261-6633, 800-422-8419), 290 Northern Ave, costs $19 adults, $12 children under 12. They do not run boats on Monday in the summer. Ⓣ Red Line to South Station and a 15-minute walk.

SPECIAL EVENTS

Thursday's *Boston Globe* Calendar section has up-to-the-minute details on all events, as does the GBCVB (see Tourist Offices). Remember that accommodations are harder to secure during big events.

February
> Chinese New Year is celebrated with a colorful parade in Chinatown in early February.

March
> The large and vocal South Boston Irish community hosts the St Patrick's Day Parade in mid-March. In recent years it's been marred by the council's decision to exclude gay and lesbian Irish groups from marching. Cambridge now hosts a simultaneous, more inclusive parade.

April
> On the third Monday in April, Patriot's Day is celebrated with a reenactment of Paul Revere's historic ride from the North End to Lexington. In addition, thousands of runners compete in the Boston Marathon, a 26.2-mile run that has been an annual event for more than a century. Starting in Hopkinton to the west of the city, it finishes on Boylston St in

front of the Boston Public Library. Sometime in April the Swan Boats return to the lagoon in the Public Garden.

May

During mid-month's Art Newbury Street, musical ensembles play on the street corners and art galleries host open houses. Magnolia trees bloom all along Newbury St and Comm Ave. Lilac Sunday at Arnold Arboretum celebrates the arrival of spring when over 400 varieties of fragrant lilacs are in bloom. It is the only day of the year that visitors can picnic on the grass at the venerable arboretum.

June

Bunker Hill Weekend includes a parade and battle reenactment at Charlestown's Bunker Hill Monument. The Gay Pride March in Boston draws tens of thousands of participants and spectators to the parade, which culminates in a big party on Boston Common.

July

The 4th of July weekend, extended to a week-long Harborfest, is very big in Boston. The Boston Pops gives a free concert on the Esplanade, attended by hundreds of thousands of people. Fireworks cap off the evening. During Chowderfest, you can sample dozens of fish and clam chowders prepared by Boston's best restaurants for $4 to $6. Italian festivals honoring patron saints run throughout the summer in the North End and are celebrated with food and music.

September

The Cambridge River Festival takes place along the banks of the Charles River.

October

The mid-month Head of the Charles regatta draws more than 3000 collegiate rowers, while cheering fans line the banks of the river, lounging on blankets and drinking beer (technically illegal). It's the world's largest rowing event.

November

The trees that ring Boston Common and the huge Christmas tree in front of the Prudential Center are lit with holiday lights late in the month; they stay on through December.

December

The mid-month Boston Tea Party reenactment involves costumed actors who march from downtown to the waterfront and dump bales of tea into the harbor. First Night celebrations begin early on the 31st and continue past midnight, culminating in fireworks over the harbor. Buy a special button that permits entrance into many events.

PLACES TO STAY

Although it's certainly more convenient to stay downtown, especially considering Boston's notorious traffic problems, if you're willing to spend a little bit of time getting into town, you'll have plenty of moderately-priced options. A few of these require a car; most don't. Remember that it's usually less expensive to stay in city hotels on weekends, when packages are offered.

Places to Stay – bottom end

Campgrounds The *Boston Harbor Islands State Park* (☎ 617-727-7676) consists of almost 30 islands, four of which allow free camping from late May to mid-October. There are about 42 camp sites total; bring your own water for all of them, and facilities are limited to primitive composting toilets. You must write ahead for a permit to the Metropolitan District Commission, 98 Taylor St, Dorchester, MA 02122.

Of these, Lovell Island has a swimming beach; Paddocks is one of the biggest at 183 acres; Grape and Bumpkin Islands are more wooded than the other two. Ferry service is provided by Bay State Cruises (☎ 617-723-7800), Long Wharf off Atlantic Ave. A roundtrip ticket costs $7 adults, $5 children to Georges Island where you catch a free water taxi (another five to 10 minutes) to the smaller islands. Boats run on the hour.

Wompatuck State Park (☎ 617-749-7160), Union St, Hingham, MA 02043, has 400 relatively undeveloped campsites on almost 3600 acres; it's about 30 minutes south of Boston by car. There are excellent bike paths here. Open from mid-May to mid-October, sites cost $6 to $8 for two people. Take I-93 south from Boston to MA 3 south to MA 228 (exit 14). Head seven miles north on Free St to Union St.

Normandy Farms Campground (☎ 508-543-7600, fax 617-543-2785), 72 West St, Foxboro, MA 02035, is a fully developed campground that caters more to RVs than tenters. It's open year round, with a big recreation room and four pools, and

400 open and wooded sites on 100 acres. It's about 50 minutes from Boston by car; take I-93 south to I-95 south to MA 1 south for seven miles; head east on Thurston St to West St. Rates are $21 to $32 nightly.

Boston Hub KOA Kampground (☎ 508-384-8930, 800-621-2280, fax 508-384-8276), 1095 South St (MA 1A), Wrentham, MA 02093, is another developed campground about the same distance from Boston. It has 145 sites ($23 to $28.50) on 22 acres as well as 15 Kamping Kabins that rent for $35 to $42 for two people. It's open from mid-April through October.

Hostels *Boston International Hostel* (☎ 617-536-9455, fax 424-6558), 12 Hemenway St, Boston, MA 02115, is very well run. In addition to offering discount cards to area nightclubs, it also offers a few organized programs daily. Its dorm-style bunk rooms hold three to five people each (segregated by sex). Due to high demand, the 210 beds rent only to HI/AYH members from May to mid-October. You can become a member ($25) on the spot though. Beds cost $16 to $19 nightly, with a five-night minimum during high season. Try to reserve a month ahead of time in the summer, or phone ahead with a credit card. If the hostel is full, they'll guide you elsewhere. The hostel is near the Museum of Fine Arts and Kenmore Square. Ⓣ Green Line to Hynes Convention Center.

The *Irish Embassy Hostel* (☎ 617-973-4841), 232 Friend St, Boston, MA 02114, rents 48 beds (with four to 10 people per room) above its eponymous pub. For $15 nightly, you get free sheets, free admission to hear the live bands in the pub, free barbecue on Sunday and Tuesday in the summer and a pub lunch for $2.95. In the summer the hostel is full by 9 am daily, but they may be expanding a bit. The hostel is near the North End and Faneuil Hall. Ⓣ Green or Orange Line to North Station.

The *Berkeley Residence YWCA* (☎ 617-482-8850, fax 482-9692), 40 Berkeley St, Boston, MA 02116, on the edge of the South End and Back Bay, rents over 200

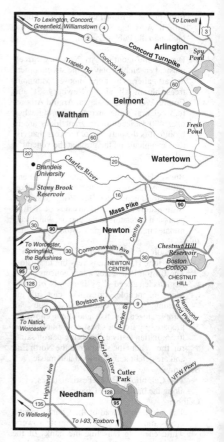

small rooms to women and children age six to 12. Singles ($32), doubles ($46) and triples ($51) are available, as are meals. Breakfast is $2.50, dinner $6.50. Guests can use the library, TV room and courtyard. Ⓣ Orange Line to Back Bay/South End.

The *YMCA of Greater Boston* (☎ 617-536-7800), 316 Huntington Ave, Boston, MA 02115, near The Fenway and Museum of Fine Arts, rents 39 rooms to both men and women. Singles with shared bath cost $38; doubles with shared and singles with private bath cost $56. There are also two

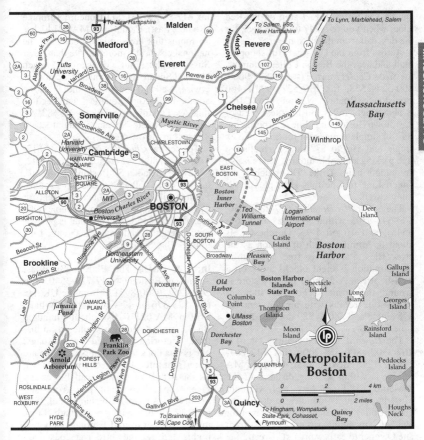

Metropolitan Boston

suites for $86 for four people. Breakfast as well as gym and pool privileges are included. Reserve by mail two weeks prior to your visit or walk-in after noon. Ⓣ the "E" branch of the Green Line to Northeastern University.

Motels Although this *Motel 6* (☎ 617-848-7890, 800-466-8356, fax 617-843-1929), 125 Union St, Braintree, MA 02184, is 15 miles south of Boston, you can be whisked hassle-free into Boston in 30 minutes via public transportation, which is right next door. Singles rent for $46, doubles $52

from mid-May through October; $10 less in the off-season. Ⓣ Red Line to Braintree.

Places to Stay – middle

Motels & Hotels Two *Susse Chalets*, at 800 Morrissey Blvd (☎ 617-287-9100, fax 265-9287) and 900 Morrissey Blvd (☎ 617-287-9200, fax 282-2365), Dorchester, MA 02122, are next door to each other right off the I-93 expressway, five miles south of the city. Between them there are almost 300 standard and drab rooms that rent for $60/$72 single/double in the summer (about $5 less off-season.) The motel has a shuttle van to the JFK T-stop on the Red Line; when you're ready to come back for the day, call from the station.

Across from the Chestnut Hill shopping mall and near the Boston College campus, the *Susse Chalet Newton* (☎ 617-527-9000, 800-524-2538, fax 617-527-4994), 160 Boylston St (Route 9), Newton, MA 02167, is about eight miles (30 minutes) west of downtown Boston on public transportation. Its 144 simple rooms rent for $57 to $65 a single and $62 to $72 double, including free parking and cable movies. There's also an outdoor pool. ⓣ the "D" branch of the Green Line to Chestnut Hill, plus a 10-minute walk.

The *South Bay Hotel* (☎ 617-288-3030, 800-642-0303 within MA, fax 617-265-6543), exit 16 off I-93, Dorchester, is about three miles south of Boston as the crow flies. Parking is free and public transportation is eight blocks away on a well-lit street. A 24-hour grocery store is around the corner. The 100 standard motel-style rooms with air-con rent for $75 single and $80 to $89 double. ⓣ Red Line to Andrew.

The *Howard Johnson Fenway* (☎ 617-267-8300, 800-654-2000, fax 617-267-2763), 1271 Boylston St, Boston, MA 02215, is within walking distance of the Museum of Fine Arts and Gardner Museum, about 10 minutes to downtown on the trolley. The standard rooms rent for $98/$108, including parking ($28 less from late October to early April). ⓣ Green Line to Kenmore.

The *Best Western Terrace Motor Lodge* (☎ 617-566-6260, 800-528-1234, fax 617-731-3543), 1650 Commonwealth Ave, Brighton, MA 02135, three miles west of Kenmore Square, is 30 minutes from Boston Common via public transportation. Some of the 73 rooms have kitchenettes; all have TV, refrigerators and air-con. Rates are $79 to $89 single and $89 to $149, including parking. ⓣ the "B" branch of the Green Line to Mt Hood.

The no-nonsense *Susse Chalet Cambridge* (☎ 617-661-7800, 800-524-2538,

fax 617-868-8153), 211 Concord Turnpike (Route 2 East), Cambridge, MA 02140, has 76 rooms that are similar to others in the national chain. It's more remote than other Susse Chalets, but you can still reach Harvard Square in 10 minutes by car. Otherwise, walk 10 minutes to the T station and be in Harvard Square in another five minutes. Parking is free; rooms are $83/$90 from April to mid-November (about $25 to $30 less in the off-season.)

The central *Chandler Inn Hotel* (☎ 617-482-3450, 800-842-3450, fax 617-542-3428), 26 Chandler St, Boston, MA 02116, has 56 clean, albeit nondescript, rooms. From April through October they rent for $79 to $89 single, $10 more double. Off-season costs $15 less. The hotel is popular with foreigners and gays. ⓣ Orange Line to Back Bay/South End.

Inns & B&Bs The Bed & Breakfast Agency of Boston (☎ 617-720-3540, 800-248-9262, 0800-895128 from the UK, fax 617-523-5761), 47 Commercial Wharf, Boston, MA 02110, lists about a hundred B&Bs, most downtown. Some are in historic Victorian-furnished brownstones; one is in a docked wooden boat; some are waterfront lofts. The agency will give you all the details of what's available at any given time. Expect to pay from $65 nightly for a room with shared bath, $80 to $120 for one with private bath. From mid-November to mid-February, stay two nights and get the third free, based on availability.

The *College Club* (☎ 617-536-9510, fax 247-8537), 44 Comm Ave, Boston, MA 02116, originally a private club for women college graduates in the 1940s, has just nine rooms open to both sexes, renting for $60 single with shared bath, $85 to $105 double with private bath, continental breakfast included. The location couldn't be better: one block from the Public Garden and Newbury St, just three from the grassy Charles River Esplanade. ⓣ Green Line to Arlington.

The *Newbury Guest House* (☎ 617-437-

7666, 800-437-7668), 261 Newbury St, Boston, MA 02116, has 32 rooms with private bath in a four-story, circa-1882 renovated brownstone. Expect to pay $85 to $115 single, $10 more for a double, including a continental buffet breakfast. It's hard to beat the location; there is limited parking for $10. Ⓣ Green Line to Hynes Convention Center.

Places to Stay – top end

Motels The older *Howard Johnson Kenmore Square* (☎ 617-267-3100, 800-654-2000, fax 617-424-1045), 575 Comm Ave, Boston, MA 02215, has 180 comfortable rooms, free parking and an indoor pool. Rates fluctuate widely, from $95 to $175 double, depending on Boston University events. Ⓣ Green Line to Kenmore.

The *Holiday Inn Boston Brookline* (☎ 617-277-1200, 800-465-4329, fax 617-734-6991), 1200 Beacon St, Brookline, MA 02146, is just over the Boston city line, a 25-minute trolley ride from downtown. Rates, including an indoor pool and parking, are $129 to $149 single, $10 more for each additional person. Ⓣ the "C" branch of the Green Line to St Paul.

Hotels Built in 1891, the modest *Copley Square Hotel* (☎ 617-536-9000, 800-225-7062, fax 617-267-3547), 47 Huntington Ave, Boston, MA 02116, attracts a low-key European crowd. The 143 refurbished rooms vary considerably in size and have windows that open. Rooms on the courtyard are quieter than others. Rates are reasonable considering the convenient Back Bay location – singles cost $125, doubles $155 to $175. The hotel's sports bar has all-you-can-eat ribs for $13 on Wednesday. Ⓣ Green Line to Prudential.

The two-story *Midtown Hotel* (☎ 617-262-1000, 800-343-1177, fax 617-262-8739), 220 Huntington Ave, Boston, MA 02115, is on the edge of the South End, just two blocks from the 4½-mile-long Southwest Corridor Park (great for walking). The 159-room hotel fills up with families, business people and tour groups alike. Free

parking and use of the outdoor pool are included for $79 to $149 single, $10 more for double. Ⓣ Green Line to Prudential or Symphony.

Although the *57 Park Plaza/Howard Johnson* (☎ 617-482-1800, 800-468-3557, fax 617-451-2750), 200 Stuart St, Boston, MA 02116, is popular with business travelers. Tourists will appreciate its proximity to the Boston Common. This 24-story hotel has 354 rooms that rent for $100 to $140 a single and $115 to $155 a double, including parking. Added bonuses include private balconies, free movie channels and an indoor swimming pool. Ⓣ Green Line to Boylston.

Right in Harvard Square, the *Harvard Square Hotel* (☎ 617-864-5200, 800-458-5886, fax 617-492-4896), 110 Mt Auburn St, Cambridge, MA 02138, has 73 rooms that rent for $120 to $170. Ⓣ Red Line to Harvard Square.

Within the Theater District near Chinatown and a favorite among actors and stagehands, the *Tremont House* (☎ 617-426-1400, 800-331-9998, fax 617-338-7881), 275 Tremont St, Boston, MA 02116, has 282 smallish guest rooms that are nicely decorated with early American reproduction furniture and prints from the Museum of Fine Arts. The 1925 hotel retains an ornate and elegant lobby, complete with chandeliers and a marble stairway and columns. The Tremont Deli, purveyors of huge New York-style sandwiches, is on the premises. Rooms rent for $89 to $99 from January through March, $149 to $189 the rest of the year. Ⓣ Green Line to Boylston or Orange Line to NE Medical Center.

In Cambridge the *Sheraton Commander* (☎ 617-547-4800, 800-535-5007, fax 617-234-1302), 16 Garden St, Cambridge, MA 02138, is a few minutes' walk from Harvard Square. The 175 rooms on six floors are comfortably decorated; a few have kitchenettes. A multilingual staff caters to many foreign guests. Rates are $125 to $229 from mid-March to mid-November, $109 to $150 in the off-season. Ⓣ Red Line to Harvard.

The European-style, nine-story *Eliot Suite Hotel* (☎ 617-267-1607, 800-443-5468, fax 617-536-9114), 370 Comm Ave, Boston, MA 02215, offers 76 suites and 15 regular rooms on the edge of Back Bay near Kenmore Square. The hotel dates to 1925, but the rooms were elegantly remodeled in the mid-1990s with marble tubs, antiques and French doors separating the living and bed rooms. It's all quite low-key and inviting. Rates are $165 to $225 a single and $185 to $245 a double. Ⓣ Green Line to Hynes Convention Center.

The *Lenox Hotel* (☎ 617-536-5300, 800-225-7676, fax 617-236-0351), 710 Boylston St, Boston, MA 02116, is another turn-of-the-century hotel that's undergone recent extensive renovations. A fancy old-worldish lobby (complete with crackling fireplace) gives way to sound-proofed guest rooms with classical furnishings, high ceilings, big closets and sitting areas. Bright corner rooms with working fireplaces ($250) are favorites. The 214 rooms rent for $180 to $250. Ⓣ Green Line to Copley.

PLACES TO EAT

In recent years the Boston restaurant scene has exploded with dozens of great places to eat, both ethnic and New American. Most restaurants are concentrated in Chinatown, the North End, around Newbury St and Harvard Square in Cambridge. As for the places that seem a bit more difficult to reach, rest assured, they're worth seeking out. In Boston, eating cheaply doesn't have to mean eating badly. Conversely, if you want to splurge a bit, there are memorable places to enjoy an evening.

Remember when assembling a picnic that drinking alcoholic beverages in public is illegal.

Health Food Stores Organic food is sold by weight at the *Harvest Co-Op* (☎ 617-661-1580), 581 Mass Ave in Cambridge's Central Square. There's a good community bulletin board.

The *Nature Food Centers*, 77 Summer St (☎ 617-451-8073) and 343 Washington St (☎ 617-227-4466) in Downtown Crossing, sell organic fruit juices, dried fruits and nuts and vitamins. There are also branches in Back Bay at 342 Newbury St (☎ 617-262-3420) and 545 Boylston St (☎ 617-536-1226). In Cambridge you'll find them at 1731 Mass Ave in Porter Square (☎ 617-492-2599) and within the Cambridgeside Galleria (☎ 617-621-0956).

Bread & Circus (☎ 617-492-0070), 115 Prospect St, two blocks north of Mass Ave in Central Square, is a whole-food supermarket. Although you can find organic produce and other goods in many grocery stores these days, Bread & Circus sells the best (but often priciest).

Delis & Bakeries *DeLuca's Market* (☎ 617-523-4343), 11 Charles St on Beacon Hill, is one of the few places in the area to assemble fixings for a picnic on the Esplanade or Boston Common. It's not cheap, but convenience may be the overriding factor. It's open from 7 am to 10 pm daily.

When you're in the North End, stop in at *Salumeria Italiana* (☎ 617-523-8743), 151 Richmond St, to assemble an Italian-style picnic complete with prosciutto, salami, cheese, bread and olives. It's open Monday through Saturday 8 am to 6 pm.

Before heading off to a little North End park to enjoy your sandwich from Salumeria Italiana, stop at the neighborhood's favorite bakery: *Mike's Pastry* (☎ 617-742-3050), 300 Hanover St. Ask for a ricotta cannoli, which they will make fresh in the back room, rather than opting for an already-filled pastry shell on the counter. It's open daily from 8 or 9 am until 9 or 10 pm (until 6 pm on Tuesday).

J Pace & Son (☎ 617-227-4949), 2 Devonshire Place in the Financial District, pronounced pah-che!, is both an Italian grocery and trattoria, featuring hot pasta dishes, salads, soups and sandwiches. It's open weekdays 6 am to 8 pm, Saturdays 8 am to 4 pm. There's a second location in the North End on Cross St at Hanover.

KIM GRANT

The Longfellow "Salt and Pepper" Bridge is one of nine bridges spanning the Charles River.

In Cambridge, *Cardullo's* (☎ 617-491-8888), 6 Brattle St, carries an impressive assortment of international goodies, but more importantly they make sandwiches-to-go and have over 250 kinds of beer. It's open weekdays 8 am to 8 pm, Saturdays 9 am to 9 pm, with shorter Sunday hours.

Nearby, *Panini at the Blacksmith House*, 56 Brattle St, is well known for its bakery which produces Viennese pastries, German tortes, bûches de Noel at Christmas time and other tasty treats (the scones are particularly good). But you can get light meals at the cafe, too. Outdoor tables are popular in warm weather, while the indoors is cozy. The 1811 house is named for its original resident, the subject of Henry Wadsworth Longfellow's poem "The Village Blacksmith."

Coffeehouses Cambridge's decidedly European *Café Pamplona* (no ☎), 12 Bow St, is the choice among highbrow intellectuals who still enjoy a good face-to-face conversation and who relish the feel of books, pencils and paper. In addition to good coffee, you can also get a few light snacks like guacamole and sandwiches. The outdoor terrace is delightful in the summer. It's open daily.

In Cambridge's Central Square, *1369 Coffee House* (☎ 617-576-4600), 757 Mass Ave, is a bohemian place with good music, serious coffee, a limited snack list and a friendly waitstaff. What more could you want? It's open daily from 7 or 8 am until 10 or 11 pm (until 8 pm on Sunday).

Caffé Vittoria (☎ 617-227-7606), 296 Hanover St in the North End, is the most atmospheric and old-worldish of the many area Italian cafes. It's been here since the 1930s and a few of the Italian-speaking patrons have, too. Come when they do – during daylight hours. It's very loud and crowded as the night wears on. It's open daily from 8 am until midnight.

Caffé dello Sport (☎ 617-523-5063), 308 Hanover St, is the place to be during soccer's World Cup. It's open daily from 6 am until midnight.

The "other side" in *The Other Side Cosmic Café* (☎ 617-536-9477), 407 Newbury St, refers to the other side of Mass Ave, which few crossed before this place opened. The "cosmic" alludes to its funky, Seattle-inspired style. The 1st floor is done in cast iron, while the 2nd floor is softened by velvet drapes, mismatched couches and low ceilings. Vegetarian chili, sandwiches, fruit and veggie drinks and strong coffee are the order of the day. The clientele, some of whom hang out all day and night, are generally in their 20s. The cafe is open daily from 10 am to midnight (from noon on Sunday).

Sonsie (☎ 617-351-2500), 327 Newbury St near Mass Ave, is perhaps the most hip and trendy place to be seen drinking a cappuccino in recent years. The cafe draws a lot of Europeans wearing basic black and dark sunglasses. In warm weather a wall of French doors is flung open making the indoor tables seem al fresco. During busy meal times, cafe tables are reserved for diners. Pizza, pasta and other light dishes are available. The full-fledged dining room in the back, is as pricey as it is good; cuisine leans toward a French and Asian mix. Sonsie is open daily from 7 am to 1 am.

Every time you turn around, another *Starbuck's* coffee shop seems to pop up on another corner in Boston and Cambridge. As of this writing, you'll find the Seattle-based java suppliers at the following locations: 222 Cambridge St (☎ 617-227-2902) near Government Center; 1 Charles St (☎ 617-742-2664) on the northwestern corner of Boston Common; 830 Boylston St (☎ 617-536-7177) near the Arlington

T-stop; 75-101 Federal St (☎ 617-946-0535) and 10 High St (☎ 617-482-4460) both in the Financial District; 441 Stuart St (☎ 617-859-0703); 1662 Mass Ave (☎ 617-491-0442) between Harvard and Porter Squares. They're all open daily and, with the exception of the Financial District locations, they're open until 10 pm.

Internet Cafes *Café Liberty* (tel 617-492-9900, http://www.cafeliberty.com), 497B Mass Ave in Cambridge's Central Square, is bringing cafe culture into the 21st century. At this artsy basement cafe you can surf the Web, while sipping a not-so-virtual espresso. On-line fees are $4.50 per hour, while specialty coffee drinks are about $3. They also have a small selection of soups, sandwiches, scones, bagels and old-fashioned newspapers. It's open daily from 10 am to 1 am.

In Harvard Square, *CyberSmith* (☎ 617-492-5857, http://www.cybersmith.com), 42 Church St, also combines computers and coffee with croissants, cakes and biscotti too. At press time, CyberSmith was getting rewired with more virtual reality experiences, creative stations and the latest technology. There are computers at almost every table, and it's got a more upscale feel, with more emphasis on the coffee, than Liberty. Online fees are about $13 per hour; buy a cybercard and use it until it runs out. It's open daily from 10 am to 11 pm, until 9 pm on Sunday.

Fast Food *Faneuil Hall Marketplace* (Quincy Market, ☎ 617-338-2323), northeast of Congress and State Sts, offers the greatest number of places to eat and the widest variety of food to sample under one roof. You'll find Greek, seafood, Indian, baked goods and ice cream. Purchase your food from the various vendors and head to the center rotunda, which has tables. Food stalls are open Monday through Saturday 10 am to 9 pm, Sunday noon to 6 pm.

Bruegger's Bagel Bakery (☎ 617-357-5577), 32 Bromfield St in Downtown Crossing, has a dozen kinds of bagels and

10 varieties of cream cheese. They'll also slap some deli meats on a bagel, too. Bruegger's has locations around the city: 64 Broad St (☎ 617-261-7115) in the Financial District; 636 Beacon St (☎ 617-262-7939) in Kenmore Square; 83 Mt Auburn St (☎ 617-661-4664) in Harvard Square. All are open daily from early morning to late afternoon.

Hungry Traveler (☎ 617-742-5989), 29 Court Square near Downtown Crossing, is a little-known gem for budget travelers. Hidden on a small side street, this cafeteria serves eggs and sausage and other breakfast staples, as well as cold sandwiches and hot entrees at lunchtime for about $5.50. The service is brusk so you'd better know what you want before getting to the head of the line. Phone ahead to hear the daily recorded menu. It's open Monday through Friday from 5:30 am to 4 pm.

The Garage (no ☎), 36 John F Kennedy St in Cambridge, has about a dozen places to eat under one roof. You're bound to find something fast, filling and cheap.

Seafood There are few rivals to *Legal Sea Foods* (☎ 617-426-4444), 35 Columbus Ave in the Park Plaza Hotel, which has built its reputation and a local empire on the motto: "If it's not fresh, it's not Legal." The menu is simple: every kind of fish, it seems, broiled, steamed, sautéed, grilled or fried. Depending on your appetite, the fried calamari appetizer ($8) could be a main dish. The fish chowder ($4) has been served at Presidential inaugurations. Long lines attest to the high quality. Come for lunch (about $9) rather than dinner ($12 to $22 per entree). There are also branches at the Prudential Center, 800 Boylston St (☎ 617-266-6800), Copley Place shopping mall (☎ 617-266-7775), and 5 Cambridge Center (☎ 617-864-3400) at Kendall Square in Cambridge. All are open daily from about noon to 10 pm.

Vegetarian *Country Life* (☎ 617-951-2534), 200 High St in the Financial District, is worth seeking out for its all-you-can-eat lunch and dinner buffets ($7 on weekdays from 11 am to 2:30 pm). You'll find tasty lasagna, pot pies and lots of different soups, but no meat, dairy or refined grains. The decor is pleasant enough and the self-service keeps the prices reasonable. It's also open for dinner Tuesday through Thursday, as well as brunch and dinner on Sunday. Ⓣ Blue Line to Aquarium.

See also the Asian entries.

Pizza *Baldini's* (☎ 617-695-1559), 71 Summer St in the Downtown Crossing area, is an inexpensive, self-service Italian place where you can get generous pizza-by-the-slice ($1.95), calzones ($3.40 and $4.15) and pasta with meatballs and red sauce ($4.90). It's mobbed at lunchtime, but there is seating upstairs. There are a number of other locations, too: 549 Boylston St (☎ 617-262-2555) near Copley Square; 532 Comm Ave (☎ 617-267-6269) in Kenmore Square; and 304 Stuart St (☎ 617-338-0095) near the Arlington T-stop. They're all open daily with different hours, for lunch and dinner.

Bertucci's (☎ 617-227-7889), 22 Merchants Row next to the Faneuil Hall Marketplace, is one of the most popular places to go for sit-down pizza ($9.25 for a large cheese, $13 for a large "specialty") baked in a brick oven. They also have good salads and calzones. Try not to fill up on the tasty, piping hot rolls. There is also a branch at 21 Brattle St in Harvard Square (☎ 617-864-4748). Both branches are open daily from 11 am to 11 pm.

The Italian North End wouldn't be what it is without the legendary *Regina Pizzeria* (☎ 617-227-0765), 11½ Thatcher St. The crispy, thin-crust pizza – $12.50 for a large with two toppings – is best consumed with a pitcher of beer (about $9). It's open daily from about 11 am to 11 pm. There's also a branch in Faneuil Hall Marketplace (☎ 617-227-8180), but hard-core devotees say it's not as good.

Galleria Umberto (☎ 617-227-5709), 289 Hanover St, certainly rivals its North

End counterpart in quality, but its crust is as thick as Regina's is thin. Furthermore, the 70¢ slices are usually gone by 2 pm, at which time the place closes. It's open daily except Sunday at 11 am.

Figs (☎ 617-742-3447), 42 Charles St on Beacon Hill, excels in fancy pasta dishes, salads and creative pizzas (with whisper-thin crusts) topped with goat cheese, prosciutto and portobello mushrooms for instance. Pizzas run from $11 to $17. Although it's pricier than most, it will feel more like a night out than most pizza joints. It's open weekdays 5:30 pm to 10 pm, weekends from noon to 9 pm. ⓣ Red Line to Charles/MGH. Figs has another storefront eatery at 67 Main St (☎ 617-242-2229) in Charlestown, perfect after a late afternoon of sightseeing. It's open daily for dinner, and offers breakfasts on weekends: try the crab hash with poached eggs.

American *The Sevens* (☎ 617-523-9074), 77 Charles St, is a popular and friendly Beacon Hill neighborhood pub that's crowded from 11:30 am to 1 am. Sit at the bar or in a booth and order a sandwich and beer ($6) or anything else off the menu for about $8.50. ⓣ Red Line to Charles/MGH.

Durgin Park (☎ 617-227-2038), Faneuil Hall Marketplace, is a beloved place, known for no-nonsense waitresses, sawdust underfoot on the old floorboards and family-style dining at large tables. The legendary food hasn't changed much since the restaurant was built in 1827: huge slabs of prime rib, fish chowder, chicken pot pie, Boston baked beans, and strawberry shortcake and Indian pudding for dessert. It's open daily from 11:30 am to 10 pm; expect to pay $7 to $16 for lunch or dinner. ⓣ Orange or Blue Line to State or Green or Blue Line to Government Center.

If you think "Boston, books and breakfast" go together, head to *Trident Booksellers & Café* (☎ 617-267-8688), 338 Newbury St near Hereford St. The shelves are primarily filled with New Age titles, while the tables are crowded with decidedly down-to-earth salads, soups, sandwiches, pasta entrees ($8 or $9) and desserts; breakfast is served all day. It's open daily from 9 am to 11:30 pm. ⓣ Green Line to Hynes Convention Center.

Milk Street Café (☎ 617-542-3663), 50 Milk St, is popular with the Financial District suit crowd, but don't let that deter you from large servings of above-average lunch fare ($6 to $8) such as pastas, salads, soups, sandwiches and pastries. The dairy is kosher. It's open daily 7 am to 3 pm. The Post Office Square location (☎ 617-350-7275) is great in the summer, when cafe tables are set out and diners spill out onto the little park; it's open weekdays 7 am to 5 pm. ⓣ Red or Orange Line to Downtown Crossing.

Blue Diner (☎ 617-338-4639), 150 Kneeland St between Chinatown and South Station, is one of the few places open around the clock on weekends: from 11 am Friday until 4 pm Sunday. Monday through Thursday, it's open daily from 11 am to 8 or 9 pm. It serves up "comfort food" like meatloaf, turkey pot pie and omelets stuffed with corned beef hash for $7. There's plenty of Southern-style dishes like barbecue ribs ($8) on the menu too. The tables are as interesting as the food: glass-topped boxes filled with artists' creations. ⓣ Red Line to South Station.

While you're in the area peek your head into the *Original Beantown Diner*, 178 Kneeland St, a classic chrome-filled diner that's been on this corner since 1947.

Charlie's Sandwich Shoppe (☎ 617-536-7669), 429 Columbus St, is a classic South End coffeeshop frequented by lawyers in three-piece suits and laborers in work boots. It's been serving creative omelets ($6 to $8 with a salad), cranberry French toast and other breakfast platters ($3.50 to $5 with meat) since 1927. For lunch it's turkey hash with two eggs ($5.75), hot pastrami and homemade pies at a few shared tables or the counter. It's open weekdays 6 am to 2:30 pm, Saturdays 7:30 am to 1 pm. ⓣ Orange Line to Back Bay/South End or Green Line to Prudential.

Bob the Chef (☎ 617-536-6204), 604 Columbus Ave, in the South End, serves Boston's best down-home soul food; we're talking barbecue ribs with a side of corn bread or fried chicken with a side of collard greens or black-eyed peas. Sit at the long counter or in a booth. Most meals cost about $10; sandwiches are half that. It's open Monday through Thursday 11 am to 10 pm, Friday and Saturday 8 am to 11 pm. ⓣ Orange Line to Mass Ave.

Parish Café & Bar (☎ 617-247-4777), 361 Boylston St next to the Public Garden, is known for a collection of creative and hearty sandwiches, each designed by a famous local chef. Try this one by Rialto chef Jody Adams: prosciutto and buffalo mozzarella with pesto and a touch of basil oil on grilled white bread ($10) – not your average sandwich. Some sandwiches come with a salad. Other draws include an outdoor patio, a stylish interior, 70 different kinds of beer and 20 wines by the glass. It's open daily from 11:30 am to 2 am. ⓣ Green Line to Arlington.

Moka (☎ 617-424-7768), 130 Dartmouth St between Back Bay and the South End, is a funky little place to hang out, heavily populated with twentysomethings. The outdoor patio is a pleasant spot for an afternoon coffee or a fruit smoothie with a slice of the cheesecake-of-the-day. Otherwise, munch on California-inspired sandwiches like roast turkey on focaccia or bean and veggie burritos ($2 to $4.) Try the homemade granola for breakfast. The cafe is open daily 8 am to 11 pm. ⓣ Orange Line to Back Bay/South End.

In Cambridge, *Bartley's Burger Cottage* (☎ 617-354-6559), 1246 Mass Ave, is *the* primo burger joint, offering at least 40 different burgers. But if none of those suits your fancy, create your own seven-ounce masterpiece topped with guacamole or sprouts. They even make a veggie burger. French fries and onion rings complete the classic American meal. Bartley's is packed with small tables and hungry college students Monday through Saturday from 11 am to 10 pm. You can get out of here for about $10. ⓣ Red Line to Harvard.

A popular haunt for Harvard B-School students, *Henry's Diner* (☎ 617-783-5844), 270 Western Ave at N Harvard St, has basic American food so cheap "it competes with the grocery store." It's out of the way but worth seeking out: pronounce it on-REES (as in the French), order the chicken parm dinner ($4.95) and you'll fit right in.

See also *House of Blues, Commonwealth Brewing Company* and *John Harvard's Brew House* under Entertainment, and *The Other Side Cosmic Café* under Coffeehouses.

Italian *Trattoria Ecco Italia* (☎ 617-261-7458), 274 Franklin St in the Financial District, is a bustling cafeteria-style place that serves pasta dishes with red sauce, tuna and capers or ziti with broccoli and chicken for $5. They have chicken parmesan ($4.25) and other sandwiches too. It's open weekdays for lunch.

Of the more than 50 Italian eateries in the North End, *La Piccola Venezia* (☎ 617-523-3888), 263 Hanover St, consistently provides a great value with huge portions of old-fashioned dishes: eggplant parmagiana ($11 at dinner), spaghetti and meatballs drenched with red sauce ($10) and more unusual but authentic dishes like tripe and gnocchi. It's open daily from 11 am to 10 pm. ⓣ Green or Orange Line to Haymarket.

Although *Artu* (☎ 617-742-4336), 6 Prince St, looks small, its menu of country-style Italian dishes is ambitious and successful. Yes, at lunch you can get roasted chicken or pork sandwiches ($5) and a dozen different pasta dishes for under $7, but you can also order more sophisticated things like seafood stew ($14) or roast leg of lamb with peppers and marinated eggplant ($10). There is also a branch at 89 Charles St (☎ 617-227-9023) on Beacon Hill. Both are open daily from 11 am to 11 pm.

See also *Baldini's*, and other restaurants under Pizza; and Delis & Bakeries.

vegetarians. Choose among noodle soups, tasty tofu dishes and imitation meat dishes like soybean "roast pork". Try a fruit and milk drink for dessert. It's open daily from 11 am to 10 pm. Lunch specials are about $5, dinner is double that.

Imperial Seafood (☎ 617-426-8439), 70 Beach St in Chinatown, is well known for dim sum (Chinese hors d'oeuvres). These little treats are ferried around the room on carts; you pick what looks good and pay based on the number of empty plates at the end of your meal. Classic choices include pork dumplings, quail eggs, duck's feet, tofu and shrimp balls. Dim sum is best shared among a few people; this way you can sample many things and pay about $10 to $15 per person. Dim sum is available daily from 8:30 am to 3 pm.

Bangkok Cuisine (☎ 617-262-5377), 177A Mass Ave, near the Boston International Hostel, was the first Thai restaurant in Boston, and it's still one of the best. The conventional choices of satay (grilled or broiled for $4) and pad Thai ($4.75 at lunch, $6.50 at dinner) are very good. When the menu says hot, it means it. Bangkok Cuisine is open weekdays 11:30 am to 3 pm and 5 to 10:30 pm, Saturday 11:30 am to 11 pm and Sunday 4 to 10 pm. Ⓣ Green Line to Hynes Convention Center.

King & I (☎ 617-227-3320), 145 Charles St, is a good choice for Thai when you're on Beacon Hill. It's a bit more expensive than Bangkok Cuisine at dinnertime (hey, you're in a classy neighborhood), but you'll get good service and ample portions. Seafood dishes and pad Thai ($7.25) are good bets. Vegetables and tofu can be substituted for meat in any of the dishes. Lunch specials are under $6. It's open Monday through Saturday for lunch and dinner, Sunday for dinner only. Ⓣ Red Line to Charles/MGH.

Jae's Café and Grill (☎ 617-421-9405), 520 Columbus Ave in the South End, specializes in Korean food but they have a full pan-Asian menu. Order sushi, satay, pad Thai or vegetarian noodle dishes in this

Asian *Pho Pasteur* (☎ 617-482-7467), 682 Washington St, and 8 Kneeland St (☎ 617-451-0247), serves a full meal in a bowl. Although there are other Vietnamese dishes from which to choose, most people come for the sometimes exotic, always flavorful noodle soup meals ($5.50 for extra large). They're hearty, hot, big, cheap and quick. Both shops are open daily, about 8:30 am to 8 pm. Ⓣ Orange Line to Chinatown.

Chau Chow (☎ 617-426-6266), 52 Beach St in Chinatown, has excellent daily seafood specials and renowned ginger or black bean sauces. Their regular menu, with ample portions, highlights various regions of China. Don't confuse this hole-in-the-wall with the newer and bigger *Grand Chau Chow* (☎ 617-292-5166) across the street; it's your call if newer and bigger are necessarily better. The prices and menu are about the same. Chau Chow is open daily for lunch and dinner until 2 am; lunch is about $5 or $6, dinner $8 to $10.

Buddha's Delight (☎ 617-451-2395), 5 Beach St in Chinatown, will thrill

cozy spot. Expect to wait for dinner unless you arrive by 6 pm. Jae's is open daily for lunch (specials $8 or $9) and dinner (entrees $8 to $12). Ⓣ Orange Line to Mass Ave.

Elephant Walk (☎ 617-247-1500), 900 Beacon St in Brookline just west of Kenmore Square, is highly regarded for its dual menus of classic French and traditional Cambodian cuisine. The large dining room is open daily for lunch 11:30 am to 2:30 pm, nightly for dinner from 4:30 or 5 pm. Make dinner reservations Sunday through Thursday if you can. Lunch is a bargain at $5 to $7; a Cambodian dinner costs about $12, French more like $16.

Ginza (☎ 617-338-2261), 16 Hudson St, is a hip Japanese restaurant in Chinatown, serving some of the best sushi and maki in town. For those who prefer their fish hot, there's always tempura. It's open daily for lunch and dinner from 5 pm. All this excellence doesn't come cheap, though; expect to spend $25 to $30 per person for dinner.

Middle Eastern The storefront eatery of *Café Jaffa* (☎ 617-536-0230), 48 Gloucester St, is a surprising bargain in the middle of blue-blood Back Bay. When was the last time you had real Turkish coffee, shwarma or falafel in a place with polished wooden floors and exposed brick? The servings are large and the prices more than reasonable, from $3.50 to $9.50. Take-out or eat in daily, for lunch and dinner. Ⓣ Green Line to Hynes Convention Center.

Sultan's Kitchen (☎ 617-338-7819), 72 Broad St in the Financial District, is a real find. Line up with the crowds at the fast-moving self-service counter, and take your plate upstairs to dine. You'll be rewarded with sizable portions of complex and delicately flavored Turkish dishes. Standbys include baba ghanoush, stuffed grape leaves, falafel, shish kabobs, salads and baklava. If all else fails, get the sampler plate ($6.75). Too bad it's only open for lunch on weekdays (11 am to 5 pm) and Saturdays (until 3 pm).

Although the service at *Algiers Coffee House*, 40 Brattle St in Cambridge, is less than swift, the faux-Middle Eastern decor makes it a comfortable rest spot. Head up to the airy 2nd floor for a falafel sandwich ($7), a bowl of lentil soup, kibbe (beef with cracked wheat) for $9 or a kebab ($10.50). Algiers is open daily from 8 am to midnight. The one good thing about slow service is that you won't be rushed to finish your pot of Arabic coffee ($2.75) or mint tea.

See also *The Middle East* under Rock Music Clubs and *Club Passim* under Folk Music in Entertainment.

Indian In Harvard Square, the *Bombay Club* (☎ 617-661-8100), 57 John F Kennedy St, is a good choice for lunch because of its bargain buffet ($7, $9 on weekends.) Dinner also features authentic northern Indian dishes like chicken tikka masala ($11).

Cambridge's Central Square, Ⓣ Red Line to Central, has a number of good Indian restaurants. You can't go wrong at *India Pavillion* (☎ 617-547-7463), 17 Central Square at Western Ave. The decor is simple and the dining area tiny, but the excellent and authentic dishes more than make up for it. It's open daily for lunch ($4.50 to $6) and dinner ($9 to $12).

Another prime choice is the *Tandoor House* (☎ 617-661-9001), 569 Mass Ave. The dishes are distinctive tandoori, and the waitstaff is particularly friendly. They're open daily for lunch and dinner; expect to spend about $15 for a complete dinner.

Nearby, *Shalimar of India* (☎ 617-547-9280), 546 Mass Ave, is another great pick, known for its hot and spicy dishes, vegetarian selections and a good all-you-can-eat Sunday buffet ($5.95). It's open daily for lunch and dinner.

Kebab-N-Kurry (☎ 617-536-9835), 30 Mass Ave near Beacon St, is a small, basement place known for consistently good dishes sold at consistently good prices ($6.95 for lunch, $13 for dinner). It's always quite crowded.

Mexican *Casa Mexico* (☎ 617-491-4552), 75 Winthrop St in Cambridge, is the best place for inexpensive and authentic Mexican on either side of the Charles River. The basement dining room is usually crowded with patrons who come for rich mole sauce (as in chicken mole poblano), tostadas and enchiladas. It's been around since the 1970s, so it must be doing something right. Expect to spend about $5.50 for lunch, double that for dinner. It's open daily except Sunday for lunch (noon to 2:30 pm), dinner nightly from 6 to 10 pm.

Eclectic In Harvard Square, *Grendel's Den* (☎ 617-491-1160), 89 Winthrop St, is a long-time favorite among university students, aging hippies, and the budget-conscious. The varied menu jumps from Middle Eastern to Greek to Indian for about $6 or $7 per dish. The salad bar ($4 small, $7 all-you-can-eat) is filling and nutritious, and the downstairs bar is a nice place to hang out. It's open daily from 11 am to 11 pm, until midnight on weekends.

In South End, *On the Park* (☎ 617-426-0862), 1 Union Park, is a friendly neighborhood place that feels a bit like it belongs in New York's Greenwich Village. It's bright, funky, with lots of local art on the walls. The weekend brunch ($6.50 to $12), with champagne and peach drinks, is particularly popular. The food tends towards creative American: marinated pork chops, gingered lamb stew or whole wheat pasta for $10 to $15. It's open nightly for dinner. Ⓣ Orange Line to Back Bay/South End.

Claremont Café (☎ 617-247-9001), 535 Columbus Ave in the South End, is a tiny place but it offers large portions of South American and Mediterranean-inspired cuisine. Rice dishes, paella and roast chicken dishes go for $11 to $18. The cafe draws an artsy group of neighborhood residents, especially in the morning for the terrific scones. It's open for all three meals Tuesday through Saturday, and Sunday 9 am to 3 pm. Ⓣ Orange Line to Mass Ave.

Hamersley's Bistro (☎ 617-423-2700), 553 Tremont St, consistently at the top of every "best restaurants" list, serves French country-American cuisine. The seasonal menu might include grilled filet of beef or hot and spicy grilled tuna. Roasted chicken with garlic, parsley and lemon ($18.50) is a house specialty. The ambiance is urban and cool, but not too cool. It's open nightly for dinner; expect to spend about $100 for two. Reservations are highly recommended. Ⓣ Green Line to Copley or Orange Line to Back Bay/South End.

Just over the Charlestown Bridge from the North End, *Olives* (☎ 617-242-1999), 10 City Square, also draws rave reviews. The creative Mediterranean-New American menu, all of which is prepared in the exposed kitchen, includes spit-roasted meats and an open-face roasted lamb sandwich. Expect to blow a cool $100 for two here, also; entrees are in the $16 to $22 range. There are two drawbacks associated with these prices: it's quite noisy and you'll have to wait unless you arrive very early (at 4:45 pm) or very late. It's open nightly for dinner. Ⓣ Green or Orange Line to North Station.

Rialto (☎ 617-661-5050), within the Charles Hotel, 1 Bennett St in Cambridge, is another top-notch area restaurant. You'll pay handsomely ($100 for two, all inclusive) for dining in this understated, Euro-chic elegance, but it will be romantic and memorable. Mediterranean-inspired dishes include creamy mussel and saffron stew with leeks or seared beef tenderloin with cognac sauce and shellfish paella. The vegetarian entree is always equally creative. Reservations are advised; dinner is served nightly.

See also *Sonsie* under Coffeehouses and *Mercury Bar* under Entertainment.

ENTERTAINMENT

The breadth and depth of cultural offerings in Boston and Cambridge is impressive. There's no doubt that much of it is fueled by the vital university scene. In fact, the Berklee College of Music is one of the nation's premiere jazz and contemporary music colleges (see below).

Note Drinking age for alcoholic beverages in New England is 21, and in most cases you must be 21 to enter a drinking establishment. Some clubs offer "18 & over" nights; check the papers for details. Bars close at 1 am, clubs usually close at 2 am. After 11 pm T service is infrequent, and it stops running at 12:30 pm, so plan ahead and budget funds to take a cab if you think it'll be a late night.

Discount Tickets Half-price tickets to same-day performances are available at Bostix (☎ 617-723-5181), south side of Faneuil Hall in the marketplace. Discounted and full-price tickets are available for theater and dance as well as comedy clubs, sporting events and concerts. Another kiosk is located in Back Bay's Copley Square (☎ 617-723-5181), Dartmouth and Boylston Sts. Both kiosks are open Tuesday through Saturday 10 am to 6 pm, Sunday 11 am to 4 pm; the Copley Square kiosk is also open Monday 10 am to 6 pm.

Cinema Art and foreign films are alive and well in Boston and Cambridge. The *Kendall Square Cinema* (☎ 617-494-9800), 1 Kendall Square in Cambridge, opened with great fanfare in 1995. It has eight screens as well as espresso machines that can churn out a cup of java in 10 seconds. Ⓣ Red Line to Kendall.

In Harvard Square, the *Brattle Theater* (☎ 617-876-6837), 40 Brattle St, is a film lover's cinema paradiso. Film noir, independent films and series that celebrate directors or periods are shown regularly in this 1890 repertory theater. You can often catch a classic double feature for $6.

The *Coolidge Corner Movie Theater* (☎ 617-734-2500), 290 Harvard St in Brookline, is the area's only nonprofit movie house. Documentaries, foreign films and first-run movies are shown on large screens in this Art Deco theater. Ⓣ the "C" branch of the Green Line to Coolidge Corner.

The *Somerville Theater* (☎ 617-625-5700), 55 Davis Square in Somerville, is another classic theater that has survived the megaplex movie house invasion. Second-run films alternate with live musical performances. Ⓣ Red Line to Davis.

In Boston, the *Sony Nickelodeon Theater* (☎ 617-424-1500), 606 Comm Ave, shows independent and foreign films, but most screens are on the smallish side. Ⓣ the first above-ground stop on the "B" branch of the Green Line.

At Harvard University in Cambridge, the *Harvard Film Archive* (☎ 617-495-4700), Carpenter Center for the Visual Arts, 24 Quincy St, screens at least two films per day. Directors and actors are frequently on hand to talk about their work.

The *Museum of Fine Arts* (☎ 617-369-3306 for information, 369-3770 for tickets), 465 Huntington Ave, West Wing entrance, screens a wide variety of films – silent, avant-garde and local – in the Remis Auditorium.

The *French Library and Cultural Center* (☎ 617-266-4351), 53 Marlborough St in Back Bay, shows classic and contemporary French films on Thursdays at 8 pm, Saturdays at 6 and 8:30 pm.

The City of Boston shows free movies under the stars at the *Hatch Shell* (☎ 617-727-9547), Charles River Esplanade, on Fridays at dusk from late June through August. You'll be sitting on the lawn, so bring a blanket and picnic. Ⓣ Green Line to Arlington.

Performance Venues The following venues host big production and pre-Broadway musicals and plays, as well as excellent nonprofit performances.

The lavish 1925 *Wang Center for Performing Arts* (☎ 617-482-9393, 617-931-2000 for tickets), 268 Tremont St, is an enormous hall with one of the largest stages in the country. The Boston Ballet performs here, but the Wang also hosts opera and modern dance productions. Ⓣ Green Line to Boylston or Orange Line to NE Medical Center.

Although the lavish *Colonial Theater* (☎ 617-426-9366), 106 Boylston St, is now enveloped by an office building, it is still resplendent with all the gilded ornamentation, mirrors and frescoes it had in 1900. Ⓣ Green Line to Boylston.

The Beaux-Arts *Emerson Majestic Theater* (☎ 617-824-8000), 219 Tremont St, is owned by Emerson College, a private performing arts school. Since the theater's majesty and luster were restored, it's a fitting space for the excellent nonprofit dance, opera, and theater groups that perform here. Ⓣ Green Line to Boylston.

The *Shubert Theater* (☎ 617-426-4520), 265 Tremont St, is another illustrious venue. Ⓣ Green Line to Boylston or Orange Line to NE Medical Center.

Classical Music Venues The *Berklee Performance Center* (☎ 617-266-7455 information, 266-4998 box office), 136 Mass Ave, hosts jazz concerts given by Berklee College of Music's renowned faculty members and exceptional students for a mere $3 or $4 during the school year. The center also hosts big-name performers at big-buck prices. Ⓣ Green Line to Hynes Convention Center.

The *New England Conservatory of Music* (☎ 617-262-1120 information, 536-2412 box office), Jordan Hall, 30 Gainsborough St, also hosts professional and student chamber and orchestral concerts in the acoustically superlative hall. There are free concerts from Monday through Thursday. Ⓣ Green Line to Symphony or Orange Line to Mass Ave.

The *Hatch Shell* (☎ 617-727-5215), Charles River Esplanade, has frequent free concerts in the summertime. Check the newspapers for evening shows (mid-week) and mid-day shows (on weekends). Ⓣ Green Line to Arlington.

The near-perfect acoustics at *Symphony Hall* (☎ 617-266-1492, 262-1200 for tickets), 301 Mass Ave in Fenway, match the world-renowned *Boston Symphony Orchestra's* ambitious programs. The BSO performs from early October through April. The *Boston Pops* plays popular classical music and show tunes from May to early-July, and again in December for a popular holiday show. For same-day dis-

counted "rush" tickets (one per person), line up at the box office on Tuesday and Thursday at 5 pm for the 8 pm show, Friday at 9 am for the 2 pm show. Another way to beat the high cost of the BSO is to go to open rehearsals on Wednesdays at 7:30 pm, Thursdays at 10:30 am. These $12 tickets can be purchased in advance; otherwise tickets begin at about $22. Ⓣ Green Line to Symphony.

Dance The highly regarded *Boston Ballet* (☎ 617-695-6950), performs classical and modern works at the Wang Center, 275 Tremont St. Tickets begin at about $21, but students can get "rush" tickets for $12 one hour before the performance. Ⓣ Green Line to Boylston or Orange Line to NE Medical Center.

Dance Umbrella (☎ 617-492-7578 for information, 824-8000 for tickets) sponsors renowned international touring companies as well as local contemporary dance troupes. The excellent shows often end with question-and-answer periods with the troupe. Tickets start at about $15, but again, students can get half-price "rush" tickets 30 minutes prior to curtain time.

Theater Boston University's highly regarded *Huntington Theater Company* (☎ 617-266-0800), 264 Huntington Ave, performs five modern and classical plays annually in its Greek Revival theater. Rear balcony seats are usually available for $12. Ⓣ Green Line to Symphony.

Harvard University's Loeb Drama Center (☎ 617-547-8300), 64 Brattle Street, is home to the prestigious *American Repertory Theater* (the ART), which stages new plays as well as experimental interpretations of classics. There isn't a bad seat in the small theater; tickets start at about $18. There's another way to get in, too: each week the theater sets aside 50 tickets on Monday morning for the following Saturday matinee. You literally "pay what you can."

Since 1980 the two-stage Charles Playhouse (☎ 617-426-5225), 74 Warrenton St in the Theater District, has presented *Sheer Madness*, a comical murder mystery with audience participation. It holds the record for the world's "longest-running nonmusical play." ⊤ Green Line to Boylston or Orange Line to NE Medical Center.

The *Boston Center for the Arts* (☎ 617-426-7700), 539 Tremont St, has three distinctive performance spaces (as well as the Mills Gallery, a contemporary art space) perfect for the unusual productions it stages. There's rarely a dull moment at the BCA. ⊤ Orange Line to Back Bay/South End or Green Line to Copley.

The avant-garde performance artists who belong to *Mobius* (☎ 617-542-7416), 354 Congress St, present experimental dance, music and other art-in-progress almost every weekend. Tickets run about $6 to $12. ⊤ Red Line to South Station.

Comedy Clubs The *Comedy Connection* (☎ 617-248-9700), Faneuil Hall Marketplace, is one of the city's oldest and biggest comedy venues. Go mid-week when tickets are about $8, rather than on weekends when it ranges from $14 to $40.

Nick's Comedy Stop (☎ 617-482-0930), 100 Warrenton St in the Theater District near Chinatown, is another place featuring local as well as nationally known jokesters. Tickets are $8 to $12 nightly. ⊤ Green Line to Boylston.

The *Improvisational Center of Boston* (☎ 617-576-1253), 1253 Cambridge St, is actually in Cambridge. This long-running ensemble makes things up as they go along; no two shows are alike. Shows are Friday through Sunday; tickets are $10 to $12. ⊤ Red Line to Central.

Dance Clubs The thriving club scene is fueled by the constant infusion of thousands of students, both American and international. Clubs are fairly stable, although the nightly line-up often changes. Check the *Phoenix* for up-to-the-minute information. Most clubs are along Lansdowne St near Kenmore Square and the Fenway, but there are also some near the Theater District and in Cambridge. Cover charges vary widely, from free (if you arrive early) to $15, but the average is more like $5. Most clubs are open from 10 pm to 2 am.

Man Ray (☎ 617-864-0400), 21 Brookline St in Cambridge's Central Square, is the area's most "underground" club. It encourages creative (ie variations of black) attire and plays progressive, urban and techno rock from Thursday through Saturday (9 pm to 1 am). Thursday is predominately gay.

Esmé (☎ 617-482-3399), 116 Boylston St, in the rear of Mercury Bar (see Bars & Pubs), is an intimate club that's as good for dancing as talking. Settle into a plush alcove filled with brocade cushions and you may never want to go back to the hostel. It's open Thursday through Saturday.

The decor at *Zanzibar* (☎ 617-351-7000), in the alley of 1 Boylston Place in the Theater District, is pseudo-tropical paradise. Dance music tends toward Top 40 and rock and roll, but you can always just watch from the 2nd-floor balcony. Jacket and tie are preferred; the crowd is a bit older here. It's open Wednesday, Friday and Saturday.

The Roxy (☎ 617-338-7699), 279 Tremont St in the Tremont House hotel, plays international, techno and house music from Thursday through Saturday.

Juke Box (☎ 617-542-4077), next door, plays classic rock and roll on Friday, disco on Saturday and Brazilian on Sunday.

Quest (☎ 617-424-7747), 1270 Boylston St in Fenway, is a four-story dance club that plays high energy house music, soul and reggae. College students dominate on Thursday and Friday; a gay crowd rules on Monday (over 18 years old) and Saturday (over 21). It's closed on Tuesday. In warm weather there's a roof deck.

Avalon (☎ 617-262-2424), 15 Lansdowne St, is a huge dance club featuring international, Top 40 and industrial dance music. They also have live concerts. It's open Thursday through Sunday; the cover charge is waived if you arrive between 9:30 and 10:30 pm on the weekends. Sunday night is gay night when the club connects to *Axis* (☎ 617-262-2437), 13 Lansdowne St, which generally attracts a younger crowd, has a few dance floors and also hosts hard rock bands. It's open nightly.

The smaller, 1950s-style *Bill's Bar* (☎ 617-421-9678), 9 Lansdowne St, is open nightly and packed with BU students, with a different theme and music style each night. Call for the current line up.

More formal and upscale, *Karma* (☎ 617-421-9678), 11 Lansdowne St, opened in 1996. It's a different kind of place, decorated with large buddhas. The cover charge is $15 and jackets are required for men.

See also *The Paradise*, below and *Chaps* under Bars & Pubs.

Rock Music Clubs Plenty of nationally known alternative and rock bands got their start in Boston clubs; there are over 5000 bands registered here. Cover charges generally vary from $5 to $10.

Over in Somerville, *Johnny D's* (☎ 617-776-2004), 17 Holland St near Davis Square on the Red Line, is one of the best and most eclectic venues, with a different style of music every night. There's everything from blues and Cajun, to swing and rock and roll. Sunday night blues jams are popular. Weekend jazz brunches are mellow.

In Cambridge's Central Square, *The Middle East* (☎ 617-354-8238), 472 Mass Ave, usually has three different gigs going on simultaneously every night. There's always a free acoustic show in the "Bakery" section. To make matters even more enticing, The Middle East serves pretty good (well-priced) food until midnight.

Mama Kin (☎ 617-536-2100), 36 Lansdowne St, is owned by the members of Boston-based rock legend Aerosmith. The club books a wide variety of bands nightly on three stages. The blues and rock jam sessions on Mondays (at 10 pm) are free, as is the "front room" on most Fridays and Saturdays.

The two-story *The Rathskeller* (☎ 617-536-2750, 536-6508 concert line), 528 Comm Ave in Kenmore Square, more commonly called The Rat, is a bit of a dive frequented by BU students. But it does book a steady stream of up-and-coming rock bands, sometimes two a night, almost every night. You won't go hungry here either; the Rat also serves good ribs until 10 pm.

The Paradise (☎ 617-562-8800), 967 Comm Ave on the "B" branch of the Green Line, is another small club known for its acumen in booking groups from all walks of the musical spectrum. Very few tickets are available without advance purchase. On Wednesday, Friday and Saturday the club plays Euro and techno house music after the concerts finish at 11 pm.

See also *Avalon* under Dance Clubs.

Jazz & Blues Clubs Gritty and smoky *Wally's Café* (☎ 617-424-1408), 427 Mass Ave, is the kind of place that burns in your imagination. Music leans toward traditional jazz, R&B, Latin and Cuban. The fact that it's crowded from 9 pm to 2 am every night has nothing to do with the fact that there's no cover. There are open jams, in essence, every night. Ⓣ Orange Line to Mass Ave or Green Line to Symphony.

In Harvard Square, *House of Blues* (☎ 617-491-2583), 96 Winthrop St, was opened by "Blues Brother" Dan Akroyd and has since become a major force on the national blues scene. The music begins at 10 pm every night and is free during lunch on Friday. The Sunday gospel brunch ($25 all inclusive) is popular.

Marketplace Café (☎ 617-227-9660), North Building, Faneuil Hall Marketplace, has a piano player on weekends and a jazz band the rest of the week. Listening is free; all you have to do is buy a drink.

Ryles (☎ 617-876-9330), 212 Hampshire St in Inman Square, is one of a few great places in Cambridge to hear jazz. It's open nightly from 7 pm, and for a jazz brunch on weekends. Ⓣ Red Line to Central.

In Harvard Square, the *Regattabar* (☎ 617-661-5000 information, 876-7777 tickets), 1 Bennett St in the Charles Hotel, is an upscale club with a yacht-club atmosphere that books internationally known groups, including some of the best jazz acts in town. It's open Tuesday through Saturday. Tickets are $8 to $25. From Tuesday through Thursday you can often stay for the second set for free.

Scullers Jazz Club (☎ 617-783-0811), 400 Soldier's Field Rd in the Doubletree Guest Suites Hotel, is the other big-name jazz club. This one is cozier, but it requires a 15-minute walk from the Central T-stop. There are shows Tuesday through Saturday. Tickets range from $9 to $24, but you often can stay for both sets. You'll have better luck getting tickets to the weekday shows.

See also *Johnny D's* under Rock Music Clubs.

Folk Music Clubs Although other clubs occasionally book folk acts, two Cambridge places are devoted to giving struggling folk singers a venue. Venerable *Club Passim* (☎ 617-492-7679), 47 Palmer St in Harvard Square, is known around the country for supporting the early careers of such notables as Jackson Browne, Tracy Chapman, Nanci Griffith and Patty Larkin. The club is small with only 50 seats; call ahead for the nightly programs and show times. Tickets are about $6 to $10. The club is open until 4 am on Fridays and Saturdays, making it an after-hours oasis. (Remember that the MBTA stops running at 1 am.) Passim is open daily for all three meals. They serve lots of rice and vegetable dishes (with a choice of beef or chicken), with an Middle Eastern emphasis; a full dinner will run you about $11.

Nameless Coffeehouse (☎ 617-864-1630), 3 Church St in Harvard Square within the First Parish Church, is a low-key, volunteer-run place that sponsors acoustic singer-songwriters on most Saturday nights. The suggested donation is $3.

Brewpubs *Commonwealth Brewing Company* (☎ 617-522-8383), 138 Portland St near North Station, with the requisite gleaming copper kettles and pipes, was Boston's first microbrewery. This airy meeting place produces over 10 kinds of English-style suds on premises. And true to tradition, the pints are served at various temperatures. The menu includes appetizers like nachos, ribs and buffalo wings, as well as pub standards like fish and chips. The basement is more of a beer hall, the ground floor more of a restaurant.

Boston Beer Works (☎ 617-536-2337), 61 Brookline Ave near Fenway Park and Kenmore Square, also has exposed tanks and pipes and seasonal brews. About eight different kinds of beer, including Boston Red and Buckeye Oatmeal Stout, are available at any given time. The appetizers and munchies are pretty good too. If you don't like crowds, don't go near this place after a Red Sox baseball game.

Cambridge Brewing Company (☎ 617-494-1994), 1 Kendall Square in Cambridge, has reputable seasonal brews (and samplers too) but beyond the burgers, you'd do better eating somewhere else. This is a convenient place to go after a movie (but it's packed on weekends).

The subterranean *John Harvard's Brew House* (☎ 617-868-3585), 33 Dunster St in Harvard Square, smells and feels more like an English pub than the others and has perhaps the best beer among the crowded microbrewery field. Ale, lager, pilsner and stout: you'll find them all here, plus a sampler rack of all of them. Above average pub grub is available daily at lunch ($6) and dinner ($8 to $10).

Although the *Mass Bay Brewing Co* (☎ 617-574-9551), 306 Northern Ave, is not a brewpub, it is the largest brewing facility in the state. Free hour-long brewery tours and tastings of their popular Harpoon Ale and India Pale Ale are offered on Friday and Saturday at 1 pm. Ⓣ Red Line to South Station and a 20-minute walk over the Northern Ave Bridge.

Bars & Pubs *Mercury Bar* (☎ 617-482-7799), 116 Boylston St in the Theater District, is well known for Spanish tapas, and is the kind of place where you wear black and watch people watching others. It's open nightly from 5 pm to 2 am.

Although *Jullian's Billiard Club* (☎ 617-437-0300), 145 Ipswich St near Fenway Park and Kenmore Square, has more than 50 billiards tables, people also come to play darts, black jack, table tennis and virtual reality games. There are four bars and a full-service menu in this enormous place. It's open daily from 11 am to 2 am.

Wursthaus (☎ 617-491-7110), 4 JFK St in Harvard Square, has an exhaustive beer list and some of the most authentic wurst and schnitzel this side of the Atlantic. It's open daily from 11 am to 11:30 pm and for breakfast on weekends.

Although the *Bull and Finch Pub* (☎ 617-227-9605), 84 Beacon St across from the Public Garden, is an authentic English pub (it was dismantled in England, shipped to Boston and reassembled inside this Beacon Hill townhouse, the Hampshire House), that's not why hundreds of tourists descend on the place daily; the pub served as the inspiration for the TV sitcom *Cheers.* Although it's not a place where "everybody knows your name," the friendly bartender and juicy burgers might lure you in.

Claddagh (☎ 617-262-9874), at Dartmouth St and Columbus Ave in the South End, is a nice neighborhood place open daily for lunch and dinner, serving simple pub grub. Draughts go for the standard $3.25. It gets pretty boisterous on weekends.

Plough & Stars (☎ 617-441-3455), 912 Mass Ave between Central and Harvard Squares in Cambridge, is a friendly Irish bar with the requisite Guinness and Bass on tap, as well as live music nightly from 9 pm to 1 am. There's a cover charge on weekends.

The circa-1780 *Warren Tavern* (☎ 617-241-8142), 2 Pleasant St at Main St in Charlestown, is an atmospheric place for a late afternoon drink.

Chaps (☎ 617-266-7778), 27 Huntington Ave in the South End, is one of the most popular gay men's bars and dance clubs.

SPECTATOR SPORTS

Boston is a big sports town and emotions run high during the various sporting seasons. Be prepared for an impassioned conversation with a local by simply asking, "Hey, what do you think of the Sox this season?"

The *Boston Red Sox* (☎ 617-267-1700 for tickets), 4 Yawkey Way, play in Fenway Park, the nation's oldest ballpark, built in 1912, and certainly one of the most storied (see the sidebar). The season runs from early April to late September. Sit with the "common fan" in outfield bleacher seats for $9 versus about $14 to $18 for regular seats. During sold-out games, there are often first-come, first-served standing-room-only tickets. Head to the ticket windows on Lansdowne St about 90 minutes prior to game time. ⊤ Green Line to Kenmore.

The *Boston Celtics* (☎ 617-723-3200 information, 931-2000 tickets) play basketball from late October through April at the Fleet Center, 150 Causeway St next to North Station. Tickets start at $10, if you're lucky enough to get one; the Celtics have won more championships than any other NBA team.

The *Boston Bruins* (☎ 617-624-1900 information, 931-2000 tickets) play hockey in the same Fleet Center from early October to mid-April. Tickets start at $29. You can also buy Bruins and Celtics tickets in person at the box office, 150 Causeway St.

The *New England Patriots* (☎ 617-543-8200, 800-543-1776), Route 1, Foxboro, play football in Foxboro Stadium about 50 minutes south of Boston. The season runs from late August to late December, and tickets begin at $23. There are direct trains ($7 roundtrip) and buses ($5 roundtrip) from South Station to and from the stadium right before the games; contact the MBTA for exact times.

Many colleges also have spirited, loyal fans and teams worth watching. In April, look for the annual Bean Pot Tournament: college hockey's premier event.

Boston University (☎ 617-353-3838) has a good football team (playing at Nickerson Field) and hockey team (playing at Case

Athletic Center). Both arenas are on Babcock St, off Comm Ave on the "B" branch of the Green Line. Tickets start at about $10.

Boston College (☎ 617-552-3000), Conte Forum at the end of the "B" branch on the Green Line, has a tough hockey team. Tickets are $8 to $10. BC football fans are devoted, so tickets are nearly impossible to get. Basketball is also good here.

End-zone tickets for Harvard University football (☎ 617-495-2211), North Harvard St and Soldiers Field Rd, across the Anderson Bridge south of Harvard Square, go for $5, unless the match is a famous rivalry with another Ivy League school (in which case all the tickets have been snatched up).

THINGS TO BUY

Stores are generally open Monday through Saturday from 9 or 10 am until 6 or 7 pm, unless otherwise noted. Most are also open on Sunday from noon to 5 pm.

Farmer's Markets Touch the produce and you risk the wrath of the Italian pushcart vendors at Haymarket, between the Expressway and Blackstone St. But no one else in the city can match their prices on fruits and vegetables which are ripe and ready. The spectacle takes place every Friday and Saturday year round, and you'll find the best bargains on Saturday afternoon.

Or head to City Hall Plaza, Government Center, on Monday and Wednesday from 11 am to 6 pm July to mid-November.

Copley Square at St James Ave and Dartmouth St, also has a farmer's market from July through November on Tuesday and Friday from 11 am to 6 pm.

Cambridge might seem ripe for a farmer's market, but the plaza at the ritzy Charles Hotel, 5 Bennet St in Harvard Square, hardly seems the obvious site for it. Nonetheless, there is a great market there on Sundays (10 am to 2:30 pm) from mid-June to mid-November.

There is also a large, almost-daily produce market in Downtown Crossing, Washington St in front of the Woolworth's store.

Shopping Districts & Malls Faneuil Hall Marketplace (or Quincy Market, ☎ 617-338-2323), northeast of Congress and State Sts, is perhaps the most well-known shopping area; about 14 million people visit annually. The five buildings are filled with one-of-a-kind shops (catering mainly to tourists), pushcart vendors and national chain stores like Gap, Body Shop and Crate & Barrel. It's expensive and crowded, especially on the weekends, but it's rather festive too. There are lots of outdoor benches to rest your weary feet, fast-food outlets (see Places to Eat) and street performers. Ⓣ Green or Blue Line to Government Center or Orange or Blue Line to State.

Downtown Crossing, a pedestrian mall at Winter, Summer and Washington Sts has more practical shops geared to the everyday Bostonian. You'll find department stores as well as smaller retail outlets. This area, too, is enlivened by street musicians, pushcart souvenir vendors, a few outdoor cafes and benches for people watching. (Look for the aptly named cart Boston's Best Burritos.) Ⓣ Red or Orange Line to Downtown Crossing.

Newbury St, between Arlington St (the western boundary of Boston Common) and Mass Ave, is filled with chic boutiques, cafes and galleries. These eight blocks are great for strolling, but don't get too discouraged about the high prices. By the time you reach Exeter St (walking west), prices begin to drop back into this stratosphere as shops get more youthfully oriented. Ⓣ Green Line to Arlington, Copley or Hynes Convention Center.

Over in Cambridge, Harvard Square boasts about 150 shops within a few blocks. Although there used to be many more independent stores in the square, most have been replaced by national chains. However, there's still much to recommend it, including a spirited street life with plenty of musicians. There is also a cluster of shops within The Garage, 36 John F Kennedy St. Head northwest out of the square on Mass Ave and you'll find an interesting array of shops all the way to Porter Square (about a 30-minute walk).

MASSACHUSETTS

An upscale indoor mall, the Shops at the Prudential Center (☎ 617-267-1002), 800 Boylston St, include about 70 stores and eateries within an atrium-like space. One of the few inner-city grocery stores, Star Market, is on the ground level. Ⓣ Green Line to Prudential.

Copley Place (☎ 617-375-4400), 100 Huntington Ave, an enormous indoor shopping mall, encompasses two hotels, a first-run cineplex, glass walkways, restaurants and dozens of very pricey shops. American consumerism is alive and well here. Ⓣ Green Line to Copley or Orange Line to Back Bay/South End.

Cambridgeside Galleria (☎ 617-621-8666), 100 Cambridgeside Place, just beyond the Science Museum, and near the Lechmere stop on the Green Line, is a three-story mall comprised of about 100 shops, including the bigger and moderately priced department stores of Lechmere and Sears. Ⓣ Green Line to Lechmere.

Art Galleries Newbury St has the most expensive and dense concentration of galleries, but there are also a number of avant-garde galleries in the Leather District, an area near South Station bounded by South and Lincoln Sts, between Essex and Kneeland Sts. There are ways to support local and national artists and artisans without losing your shirt.

The prestigious nonprofit Society of Arts and Crafts (☎ 617-266-1810), 175 Newbury St in Back Bay, was founded in 1897. Within the exhibition and retail space they offer high-quality weaving, leather, ceramics, furniture and other hand-crafted items. There's also a branch in the Downtown Crossing area at 101 Arch St (☎ 617-345-0033).

Artsmart (☎ 617-695-0151), 286 Congress St near South Station, is a funky space with whimsical, interesting and somewhat affordable pieces of functional and not-so-functional art. It's one of the less intimidating galleries.

The Bromfield Gallery (☎ 617-451-3605), 107 South St near South Station, is one of the more accessible, affordable and

reputable galleries on Boston's art scene. It also happens to be the city's oldest cooperative.

Craftspeople double as salespeople at the Cambridge Artist's Cooperative (☎ 617-868-4434), 59A Church St in Harvard Square, which has hand-crafted objects ranging from $3 to $1000.

Antiques Antiques in Boston are extremely pricey, but if you want to do some window shopping head to Charles and River Sts on Beacon Hill. Ⓣ Red Line to Charles/MGH.

Or try the four floors of the Cambridge Antique Market (☎ 617-868-9655), 201 Monsignor O'Brien Hwy, where you might find a little something to take home with you. Ⓣ Green Line to Lechmere.

Camping Supplies Although it's dusty and musty, Hilton's Tent City (☎ 617-227-9242), 272 Friend St near North Station, boasts four floors of tents (most of which are set up to climb around in) and all the camping, backpacking accessories and clothing you'll ever need – all at the lowest prices around.

Eastern Mountain Sports (EMS, ☎ 617-254-4250), 1041 Comm Ave in Brighton, is another good source for hiking and camping gear, books and maps. If you can't find it at Hiltons, you'll find it here. Ⓣ the "B" branch of the Green Line to Babcock.

Clothing The granddaddy of Boston bargain stores, Filene's Basement (☎ 617-542-2011), 426 Washington St in Downtown Crossing, carries overstocked and irregular items at everyday low prices. But the deal gets even better: items are automatically marked down the longer they remain in the store. With a little bit of luck and lots of determination you could find a $300 designer jacket for $30. But it also takes a sense of humor and patience to shop here since customers rip through piles of merchandise, turning the place upside down as if a tornado hit it. It's a sight to be seen. Upstairs from the basement is the conventional Filene's department store.

In 1996 Macy's (☎ 617-357-3000), 450 Washington St, replaced one of New England's oldest full-fledged department stores, Jordan Marsh, which was founded in 1851.

The Original Levi's Store, which sells nothing but the real thing, has three area locations: 101 Arch St (☎ 617-737-2088), within Cambridgeside Galleria (☎ 617-494-0113) and within the Prudential Center (☎ 617-375-9010).

The Eddie Bauer Outlet (☎ 617-227-4840), 252 Washington St in Downtown Crossing, offers irregulars of their popular outdoor wear for 30% to 70% off.

The Gap Outlet (☎ 617-482-1657), 425 Washington St in the Corner Mall, sells jeans and ubiquitous everyday clothing for half of regular retail prices. Banana Republic, owned by the same company, sells its clothing here too.

The Salvation Army Thrift Store (☎ 617-695-0512), 26 West St in Downtown Crossing, has lots of used shirts, shoes, pants, jackets for a few bucks.

GETTING THERE & AWAY

Air Logan International Airport (☎ 800-235-6426), MA 1A, East Boston, is served by most major national and international carriers. Its five separate terminals are connected by a frequent shuttle bus (No 11). The Traveler's Aid Society (see Emergency) maintains a booth at Terminal "E," where all international flights arrive and depart.

Bus Boston has a modern, indoor, user-friendly bus station (no ☎) at 700 Atlantic Ave at Summer St, conveniently adjacent to the South Station train station and above a T stop for the Red Line.

Bonanza (☎ 617-720-4110) serves Hyannis and Falmouth on Cape Cod; Providence, RI; western Massachusetts; Albany, NY and New York City.

Greyhound (☎ 617-526-1810, 800-231-2222) buses depart for New York City throughout the day. Express buses take 4½ hours, but others take as long as seven hours. Fares are $25 one way, $48 roundtrip. Other sample destinations and one-way fares from Boston include: Albany ($24), Hartford ($11), New Haven ($14), Newark ($25) and Springfield ($12).

Plymouth & Brockton (☎ 508-746-0378) provides frequent service to most towns on Cape Cod, including Hyannis and Provincetown.

Peter Pan (☎ 617-946-0960, 800-343-9999) serves Northampton and Williamstown in western Massachusetts (the Berkshires), Hartford and New Haven in Connecticut and New York City.

Concord Trailways (☎ 617-426-8080, 800-639-3317) plies routes from Boston to New Hampshire, and Boston to Portland and Bangor in Maine.

C&J Trailways (☎ 800-258-7111) provides daily service to Newburyport, MA; Portsmouth, NH, and lower coastal Maine, including Kennebunkport, Wells and Ogunquit.

Vermont Transit (☎ 800-451-3292) operates buses to White River Junction and Keene, NH; Portland and Bar Harbor, ME. In Vermont, they go to Burlington, Brattleboro, Bennington and lots of small towns in between.

Train Amtrak (☎ 617-482-3660, 800-872-7245) trains stop at the South Station terminal, Atlantic Ave and Summer St (on the Red Line), as well as Back Bay Station, Dartmouth St (on the Orange Line). Express service (four hours) to New York City costs $49 or $64 one way, depending on the day and time; otherwise the trip takes five hours and costs $43 or $52.

When it was built in 1900, South Station was the world's largest railroad station. Decades of heavy use took their toll, though, until a renovation in the late 1980s brought the magnificent gateway back up to par with the best European stations. Today, the curved, five-story building is alive with pushcart vendors, fast-food eateries, cafe tables, a newsstand and live concerts on many summer afternoons.

By contrast, North Station (☎ 617-722-3200), 150 Causeway St, is a dowdy younger sibling terminal that serves MBTA

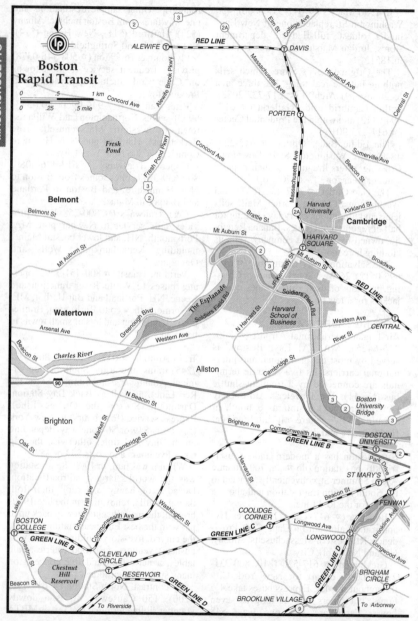

**Boston
Rapid Transit**

0   5   1 km
0   .25   .5 mile

ALEWIFE   RED LINE   DAVIS

PORTER

Fresh
Pond

Belmont

Concord Ave

Alewife Brook Pkwy

Fresh Pond Pkwy

Concord Ave

Belmont St

Mt Auburn St

Mt Auburn St

Brattle St

Mt Auburn St

Watertown

Arsenal Ave

Greenough Blvd

The Esplanade

Soldiers Field Rd

Western Ave

Charles River

Beacon St

Allston

N Beacon St

Brighton

Oak St

Market St

Cambridge St

Lake St

Chestnut Hill Ave

Commonwealth Ave

Washington St

BOSTON
COLLEGE

GREEN LINE B

CLEVELAND
CIRCLE

Chestnut St

Chestnut
Hill Reservoir

Beacon St

RESERVOIR

GREEN LINE D

To Riverside

Elm St   College Ave

DAVIS

Massachusetts Ave

Highland Ave

Central St

Somerville Ave

Beacon St

Massachusetts Ave

Harvard
University

Kirkland St

Cambridge

HARVARD
SQUARE

Broadway

Mt Auburn St

JF Kennedy St

Soldiers Field Rd

Harvard
School of
Business

Soldiers Field Rd

Western Ave   CENTRAL

RED LINE

River St

Cambridge St

Boston
University
Bridge

Brighton Ave   Commonwealth Ave

GREEN LINE B

BOSTON
UNIVERSITY

Park Drive

Harvard St

ST MARY'S

COOLIDGE
CORNER

Longwood Ave

GREEN LINE C

Beacon St

FENWAY

LONGWOOD

GREEN LINE D

Brookline Ave

Longwood Ave

BRIGHAM
CIRCLE

BROOKLINE VILLAGE   To Arborway

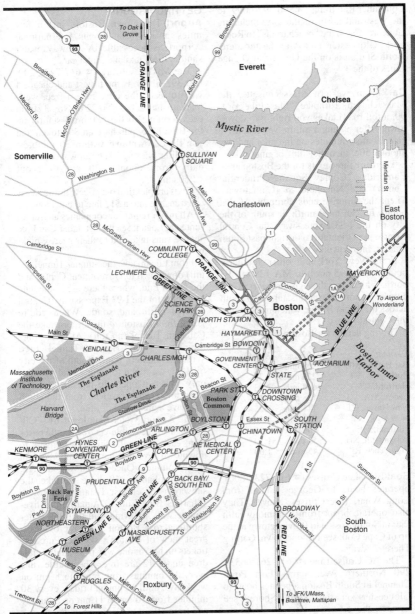

Commuter Rail trains (☎ 800-392-6099) to the west and north of the city, including Concord. Catch the "beach trains" to Rockport, Gloucester and Manchester here. North Station is on the Green and Orange Lines of the T.

Car From western Massachusetts, the Massachusetts Turnpike ("Mass Pike" or I-90, a toll road) takes you right into downtown. After paying a toll in Newton, drive east 10 more minutes on the pike and pay another 50¢; then the "fun" begins.

There are three exits for the Boston area: Cambridge, Copley Square (Prudential Center) and Kneeland St (Chinatown). Then, the turnpike ends abruptly. At that point you can head north or south of the city on the I-93 Expressway (the Central Artery; see Orientation) or right past South Station, into downtown.

From New York and other southerly points, take I-95 north to MA 128 to I-93 north, which cuts through the heart of the city. From northerly points, take I-93 south across the Tobin Bridge which merges into the Central Artery.

Driving details for Boston are:

Destination	Mileage	Hr:Min
Bar Harbor, ME	269 miles	6:30
Burlington, VT	220 miles	4:35
Hartford, CT	108 miles	2:13
Lenox, MA	138 miles	3:10
New Haven, CT	141 miles	3:25
New York, NY	227 miles	4:30
Portland, ME	108 miles	2:15
Portsmouth, NH	57 miles	1:10
Providence, RI	45 miles	1:00

Boat Bay State Cruises (☎ 617-723-7800), operates boats to Georges Island from Long Wharf (see Cruises, above). They also operate boats from Commonwealth Pier in South Boston to Provincetown at the tip of Cape Cod; see Provincetown, Getting There & Away.

The AC Cruise Line (☎ 617-261-6633), 290 Northern Ave, across Fort Point Channel in South Boston, operates boats to Gloucester on the North Shore; see Cruises, above.

GETTING AROUND

Airport Downtown Boston, just a few miles away from Logan International Airport, is accessible by subway, water shuttle, limo, taxi and rental car.

The MBTA subway (☎ 617-722-3200, 800-392-6100), is the fastest and cheapest way to reach the city. Take a free, well-marked shuttle bus (No 22 or No 33) from each terminal to the Airport T-station on the Blue Line, purchase an 85¢ token and you'll be downtown within 30 minutes, including waiting. The subway operates daily from about 5:30 am to about 12:30 am.

Taxis are plentiful but pricey; traffic snarls can translate into a $17 fare to downtown.

All major rental car companies are represented at Logan; see the list under Car. Free shuttle vans take you to their nearby pick-up counters.

From Logan, take the Sumner Tunnel ($1 toll) downtown to Government Center and the North End, where there are immediate on-ramps for the I-93 Expressway (Central Artery) north and south. When you're going *from* Boston *to* the airport, take the Callahan Tunnel (no toll). At press time, the new Third Harbor Tunnel (Ted Williams Tunnel), a mile south of the city off I-93, was open to commercial vehicles only. When it opens to passenger traffic (date unknown), travelers from the south will save a great deal of time.

The Airport Water Shuttle (☎ 617-330-8680), also accessible via free shuttle buses from each terminal, whisks passengers to downtown Rowes Wharf (Atlantic Ave) in seven minutes. Once downtown, though, you'll probably still have to take the subway. (The closest T-station to Rowes Wharf is Blue Line to Aquarium, a five-minute walk.) Having said that, the water shuttle across Boston Harbor provides a great view of Boston's skyline. Purchase tickets on board; one way is $8 adults, children under 12 are free. The shuttle runs every 15 minutes from 6 am to 8 pm on weekdays, until 11 pm on Friday; every 30 minutes from 10 am to 11 pm on Saturday and from 10 am to 8 pm on Sunday.

Light Rail & Subway The MBTA (☎ 617-722-3200, 800-392-6100) operates the USA's oldest subway, built in 1897, known locally as "the T." Stops are easily spotted in this guide by the Ⓣ. There are four lines – Red, Blue, Green and Orange – that radiate from the principle downtown stations. These are Park Street, which has an information booth, Downtown Crossing, Government Center and State. When traveling away from any of these stations, you are heading outbound.

Tourist passes with unlimited travel are available for one week ($18), three days ($9) and one day ($5). You may purchase one at the following T-stations: Park Street, Government Center, Back Bay, Alewife, North Station, South Station, Hynes and Airport. The Visitor Information Center on Tremont St also sells them. For longer stays, monthly unlimited-travel passes are available from around the first of the month to the 15th; subway only passes are $27, subway plus bus passes are $46.

Otherwise, purchase tokens at all stations (85¢ adults, 40¢ children) except those west of Symphony ("E" branch) and Kenmore ("B", "C" and "D" branches) on the Green Line, which are above ground. You must have exact change to board these trains. No fare is collected when heading outbound from an above-ground Green Line station. Some fares heading inbound, though, are higher than 85¢.

The T operates from about 5:30 am to 12:30 am. Call for up-to-the-minute train schedules.

Bus The MBTA also operates bus routes within the city, but these can be difficult to figure out for short-term visitors. The subway goes to 95% of the places you'll want to go.

Car With any luck you won't have to drive in or around Boston. Not only are the streets a maze of confusion, choked with construction and legendary traffic jams, but Boston drivers use their own set of rules. Driving is often considered a sport – in a town that takes its sports very seriously.

Keep in mind that the construction and depression of the Central Artery, scheduled to be completed in 2004, is creating serious traffic problems around the waterfront area.

Two highways skirt the Charles River: Storrow Drive runs along the Boston side and Memorial Drive (more scenic) parallels it on the Cambridge side. There are exits off Storrow Drive for Kenmore Square, Back Bay and Government Center. Both Storrow and Memorial Drives are accessible from the Mass Pike and the I-93 Expressway.

These companies are located at the airport (see also Car Rental in the Getting Around chapter).

Avis	☎ 617-561-3500
	800-331-1212
Hertz	☎ 617-569-7272
	800-654-3131
Budget	☎ 617-497-1800
	800-527-0700
National	☎ 617-569-6700
	800-227-7368
Thrifty	☎ 617-569-6500
	800-367-2277

Pahking the Cah

If you must drive into the city, park at one of the following centrally located garages and walk or take the T from there. Since on-street parking is tricky, expect to pay about $15 daily to park. It's a good idea to ask your lodging place when you make reservations if parking is available, and what it costs.

There are parking lots beneath Boston Common (access via Charles St South) and Post Office Square (access via Pearl St in the Financial District); near Faneuil Hall (via Clinton St) and Government Center (via New Sudbury St); in Back Bay at the Prudential Center (via Boylston St) and Copley Place (via Huntington St); in Cambridge off JFK St. Look for the blue "P" sign around town. There are plenty of small lots, too. ∎

Taxi Taxis are plentiful but expensive. At press time, the initial rates were $2.10 plus $1.60 per mile. Without much traffic, expect to spend about $11 from Harvard Square to Copley Square in Back Bay, $15 or so with lots of traffic. From the North End or Faneuil Hall to Kenmore Square expect about $9 without much traffic.

You'll have trouble hailing one during bad weather and weekdays between 3:30 and 6:30 pm. You can usually get a taxi at Faneuil Hall and major hotels. Recommended taxi companies include: Red & White Cab (☎ 617-242-8000), Checker Cab (☎ 617-497-9000) and Independent (☎ 617-426-8700).

Bicycle Daredevil Bostonians cycle around town, but there are no bike lanes, so use caution if you take to the city streets on two wheels. See also Bicycling.

Boat For information on Boston Harbor Cruises and Bay State Cruises see Cruises, above.

City Water Taxi (☎ 617-422-0392) makes on-demand taxi stops year round at 10 waterfront points, including the airport, Children's and Computer Museums, Long Wharf, Burroughs Wharf in the North End, the USS *Constitution* and the Charlestown Navy Yard. The fare is $5 between any two points, with the exception of the airport ($10 for one person, $8 for two or more).

Boston by Boat (☎ 617-422-0392) plies the waterfront circuit daily during the summer, with stops at the Children's Museum, Aquarium, North End (Burroughs Wharf at Battery and Commercial Sts) and the USS *Constitution*. Hop on and off all day for $5.

See also the Airport Water Shuttle, above.

Around Boston

Colonists who came to Massachusetts Bay did not settle just at Boston and Cambridge. Within a few years other settlements were founded at Lexington, Concord, Salem and other towns.

Part of what makes Boston one of America's most livable cities is its easy access to the countryside. Many of the towns around Boston have beautiful historic centers and offer a variety of things to see and do, including museums, hikes, whale-watching cruises, canoe and bicycle trips. All are reachable by car or bus in under an hour; some are accessible by train as well.

West of Boston

Lexington, about 18 miles northwest of the city center, has a colonial village green and acres of market gardens. Concord, an easy half-hour drive or train ride northwest, is a historic colonial town surrounded by rolling fields, forests and beautiful country roads for bicycling.

LEXINGTON

The roads between Lexington and Boston teem with commuters weekday mornings. But two centuries ago the two towns were a several-hours' horseride apart.

History

On April 18, 1775, Paul Revere, William Dawes and Samuel Prescott set out on their midnight ride from Boston to Lexington and Concord. They rode to warn these communities and others that General Gage, the British commander in Boston, was sending an expeditionary force to search for arms and matériel rumored to be stockpiled at Concord.

Revere, Dawes and Prescott were part of a colonial intelligence and communications network so efficient that the local troops of militia, the minutemen, turned out long before the tramp of British boots was heard on the dirt road approaching Lexington.

When the advance body of 700 redcoats under Major John Pitcairn marched up to Lexington Green just after daybreak, they found Captain John Parker's company of 77 minutemen lined up in formation to meet them.

Captain Parker and his men were here to defend their homes from what they deemed an unreasonable search. The British were here to do their duty. Clearly outnumbered and perhaps fearing capture of his force, Captain Parker ordered his men to disperse peaceably, which they slowly began to do. But the British took this as capitulation and began trying to arrest the "rebels" who had raised arms against them. A shot rang out – from which side has never been clear – and then others, and soon eight minutemen lay dead on the green, with 10 others wounded. Pitcairn regained control of his troops with difficulty and marched them out of Lexington toward Concord.

The skirmish on Lexington Green (now called Battle Green) was the first organized, armed resistance to British rule in a colonial town, and the beginning of the Revolutionary War. Without the bloodshed at Lexington, the Concord minutemen might not have been steeled to offer spirited resistance to the British troops.

Orientation & Information

MA 4 and 225 follow Massachusetts Ave through the center of Lexington, passing by Battle Green. The green is at the northwestern end of the business district.

The Lexington Chamber of Commerce (☎ 508-862-1450), 1875 Massachusetts Ave, maintains a visitors center opposite Battle Green, next to Buckman Tavern. Stop in to see the exhibits that recall the 1775 events. It's open daily from 9 am to 5 pm (10 am to 4 pm in winter).

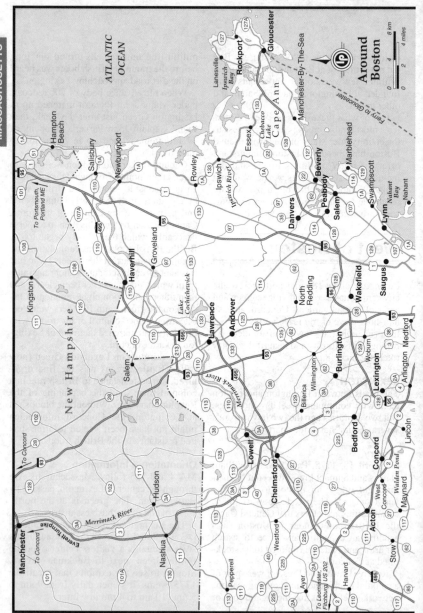

Around Boston

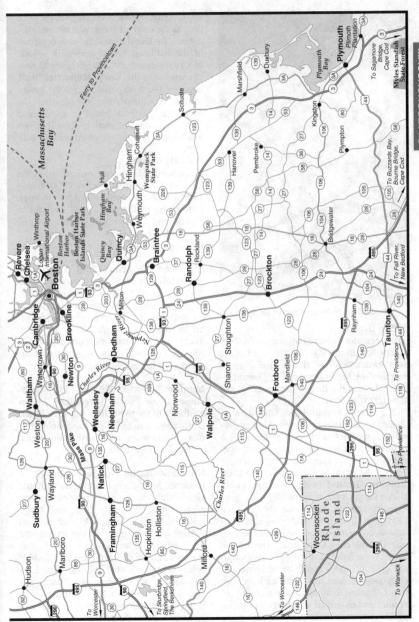

MASSACHUSETTS

KIM GRANT
Minuteman on Battle Green, Lexington

Battle Green

The Lexington minuteman statue (done by Henry Kitson in 1900) stands guard at the southeastern end of Battle Green, commemorating the bravery of the 77 minutemen who met the British here in 1775, and the eight who died.

The green is beautiful and tranquil today, shaded by tall trees and surrounded by dignified churches and stately houses. A boulder marks the spot where the minutemen faced a force ten times their strength. Just off the green by the church is **Ye Olde Burying Ground**, with some fine tombstones dating back as far as 1690.

Every year on April 19th the battle on Lexington Green is re-enacted by local minuteman companies in colonial dress bearing colonial matchlock firearms. The British heavies – somewhat fewer than their original force of 700 – come dressed authentically as well, and the tramp of hobnailed boots, barked commands, explosions of gunfire and clouds of gunsmoke fill the air again. Authenticity is pursued with some

vigor, so the re-enactment starts at the same time as the original event: just after dawn.

For a look at the most famous depiction of the battle of Lexington, walk several blocks southeast of the green along Massachusetts Ave to **Cary Memorial Hall**, between the town offices and the police station. Sandham's famous painting *The Battle of Lexington* hangs in an honored spot, and statues of patriots John Hancock and Samuel Adams are prominent as well.

Historic Houses

Three historic houses are maintained by the Lexington Historical Society (☎ 617-862-1703), and are open mid-April through October from 10 am to 5 pm (Sunday 1 to 5 pm), until 8 pm in high summer. Admission costs $3 per adult for each house (75¢ for kids six to 16), or $6 for all three houses.

Buckman Tavern (1709) Facing the green, this was where the minutemen spent the tense hours between the original midnight call to arms and the dawn arrival of the redcoats. It also served as a field hospital to treat the wounded after the fight. Today it is a worthy museum of colonial life, with instructive tours given by "interpreters" in period costume.

Munroe Tavern (1695) At 1332 Massachusetts Ave, about seven long blocks southeast of the green, this was used by the British as a command post and field infirmary. It's now furnished with antiques and mementos of the battle.

Hancock-Clarke House (1698) At 36 Hancock St, about a block north of Battle Green, this was the parsonage of the Reverend Jonas Clarke in 1775, and it was here that John Hancock and Samuel Adams hid themselves on the fateful day. The original orders given to the British troops had been to arrest these two "rabble rousers," though that mission was later deemed too inflammatory and was changed to a search for munitions. The house was Paul Revere's goal – achieved – as he rode through the night.

Museum of Our National Heritage

The museum (☎ 617-861-6559), 33 Marrett Rd (MA 2A) just off Massachusetts Ave (MA 4 and 225), is over a mile southeast of Battle Green. Founded by the Scottish Rite Masons in 1975, it has four large galleries with changing exhibits of Americana. Call ☎ 617-861-9638 for a recorded schedule of exhibits and events. It's open from 10 am to 5 pm, Sunday from noon to 5 pm, and is free.

Places to Stay

Battle Green Motor Inn (☎ 617-862-6100, 800-343-0235), 1720 Massachusetts Ave, is a motel-style lodging right in the center of Lexington's business district. Modern rooms cost $68 with one double bed, $72 for two beds, with a light self-service breakfast included.

Sheraton Tara Lexington Inn (☎ 617-862-8700, fax 863-0404), 727 Marrett Rd just west of I-95 (follow exit signs for Hanscom Field) has 120 comfortable rooms for $75 to $145 in a full-service facility favored by business travelers. Rooms here are cheapest on weekends.

Places to Eat

Less than a block southeast of Battle Green, the *Yangtze River* (☎ 617-861-6030), 21 Depot Square, just off Massachusetts Ave, features Szechuan and Mandarin cuisine in a daily all-you-can-eat dinner buffet for $11. The luncheon buffet costs $6 (on weekends $7.50).

Ye Olde Burying Ground, Lexington

KIM GRANT

Right in the center of Lexington's business district, the *Versailles Restaurant* (☎ 617-861-1711), 1777 Massachusetts Ave, has a moderately-priced continental menu with several Moroccan dishes as well.

Cafe le Bellecour (☎ 617-861-9400), 10 Muzzey St across from Depot Square, also near the green, specializes in French country, northern Italian and other continental dishes, with prices for lunch (served weekdays) around $12 to $15, dinner (except Sunday) $20 to $30.

Getting There & Away

Take MA 2 west from Boston or Cambridge to exit 54 (Waltham St) or exit 53 (Spring St). From I-95 (MA 128) take exit 30 or 31.

CONCORD

Tall, white church steeples rise above huge old trees in colonial Concord, giving the town a dignity and beauty that makes it a favorite goal for those wanting to get out of the city for awhile. The placid Concord River offers canoeing possibilities, the town's scenic roads are excellent for bicycling and the town's colonial and 19th-century literary history attract visitors from around the world.

Revolutionary History

On the morning of April 19, 1775, after the skirmish on Lexington Green, General Gage's expeditionary force of 700 British soldiers marched to nearby Concord. The colonial intelligence system preceded them, however, reporting that minutemen had died on Lexington Green. This strengthened the resolve of the minuteman companies from Acton, Bedford, Concord, Lexington, Stow and other communities who had turned out to face the "lobsterbacks."

The British marched into Concord around 7 am. The minutemen, still outnumbered, mustered on Punkatasset Hill northeast of the town center and awaited events. The British commander sent seven companies off to the north to seize arms rumored to be stored at Colonel James Barrett's farm, leaving only three of these companies to secure the North Bridge.

The minutemen advanced on the soldiers guarding the bridge, and as they did they saw smoke rising from the town. The British searchers had found nothing but a few gun carriages, which they burned, but the minutemen assumed the worst.

"Will you let them burn the town down?" shouted a minuteman commander. Enraged that the regulars would burn their homes, the minutemen fired on the badly outnumbered British, wounding half of their officers and forcing them back across the North Bridge. Soon the British were on their way back to Boston.

The battle at North Bridge, called "the shot heard 'round the world" by Ralph Waldo Emerson, was the first successful armed resistance to British rule. But it did not end there.

The British lost a number of soldiers, dead and wounded, in Concord. But the true significance of the day's events followed. On their march back to Boston, the British troops were pursued by minutemen who fired at them from behind trees, walls and buildings. Most of this fire did little harm, but occasionally a bullet would find its mark, and in places where the minutemen had defensible positions, British troops fell. They were tired, dispirited and angry when they reached Lexington and met 1000 reinforcements.

These guerrilla tactics were unusual for the time, and were looked upon as cowardly and unfair by the regular troops. Enraged at the locals' resistance, and their ever-mounting casualties, the British troops rioted, murdering innocent colonials whom they encountered along their line of march. At Menotomy (modern Arlington), 5000 men battled one another. By the time the British regained the safety of Boston, they had lost 73 dead, 174 wounded and 26 missing. The American losses were 49 dead, 40 wounded and five missing.

The die had been cast. The situation in the American colonies was no longer one of political and social resistance to rule from London, but of armed rebellion against the forces of the crown.

Henry David Thoreau

19th-Century Literary History

Concord in the 19th century was a very different place. Though still a town of prosperous farmers, it was home to a surprising number of the literary figures of the age, including essayist, preacher and poet Ralph Waldo Emerson (1803-82); essayist and naturalist Henry David Thoreau (1817-62); short-story writer and novelist Nathaniel Hawthorne (1804-64) and novelist and children's book author Louisa May Alcott (1832-88).

Emerson was the paterfamilias of literary Concord, one of the great literary figures of his age and the founding thinker of the Transcendentalist movement. While traveling in Great Britain he befriended Carlyle, Coleridge and Wordsworth. His Concord house is now a museum.

Thoreau took the naturalist beliefs of Transcendentalism out of the realm of theory and into practice when he left the comforts of the town and built himself a rustic cabin on the shores of Walden Pond, several miles from the town center. His memoir of his time there, *Walden, or*

Boston: old & new

Swan Boats

The Old State House

Faneuil Hall

Harvard University, Cambridge

A brisk day in Beacon Hill

Minuteman National Historic Park, Concord, MA

Custom House, Salem, MA

Chestnut St, Salem, MA

Plymouth Rock Monument, Plymouth, MA

Chestnut St, Salem, MA

Transcendentalism

Transcendentalism was a 19th-century American social and philosophical movement that flourished from 1836 to 1860 in Boston and Concord. Though small in numbers, the Transcendentalists had a significant effect on American literature and society.

The core of Transcendentalist belief was that each person and element of nature had within it a part of the divine essence, that God "transcended" all things. The search for divinity was thus not so much in scripture and prayer, nor in perception and reason, but in individual intuition or "instinct." By intuition we can know what is right and wrong according to divine law. By intuition we can know the meaning of life. Living in harmony with the natural world was very important to Transcendentalists.

Bronson Alcott (1799-1888), educational and social reformer and father of Louisa May Alcott, joined Emerson, Thoreau, Margaret Fuller and other Concordians in turning away from their traditional Unitarianism to Transcendentalism.

The Transcendentalists founded a periodical, The Dial, to disseminate their views, and established the community of Brook Farm (1841-47) based on Transcendentalist doctrines of community life and work, social reform and anti-slavery. Hawthorne was a resident for a time, and both he and novelist Herman Melville were influenced by Transcendentalist beliefs.

Bronson Alcott was also a founder of Fruitlands, an experimental vegetarian community in Harvard, MA, established in 1843. He lived here with his family (including 10-year-old daughter Louisa May) and others for a year before abandoning the project. Fruitlands is now a museum open to the public (see Fruitlands, in Concord). ∎

Life in the Woods, published in 1854, was full of praise for nature and disapproval of the stresses of civilized life, sentiments which have found an eager audience ever since. Many of his readers visit the site of his cabin at Walden Pond (see Walden Pond, below).

Hawthorne, author of *The Scarlet Letter, Twice-Told Tales* and *The House of the Seven Gables*, was born and raised in Salem, MA, but lived in Concord at the Old Manse next to the North Bridge for three years just after his marriage. His residence in Concord gave him material for several later stories.

Alcott was a junior member of this august literary crowd, but her work proved more durable than that of the others. *Little Women* (1868-69), her mostly autobiographical novel about a woman's coming of age in Concord, is among the most popular young-adult books ever written. Its several sequels continued her work of portraying family life in Victorian America with keen perception and affection. Her childhood home, Orchard House, is among Concord's most-visited sites (see Historic Houses, below).

Orientation

Concord (population 15,000) is about 22 miles northwest of Boston along MA 2. The center of the sprawling, mostly rural town is Monument Square, marked by its war memorial obelisk. The Colonial Inn stands on the square's north side.

Main St runs west from Monument Square through the business district to MA 2. Walden and Thoreau Sts run southeast from Main St and out to Walden Pond some three miles away.

The MBTA Commuter Rail train station ("the Depot") is on Thoreau St at Sudbury Rd, a mile from Monument Square.

Information

The Concord Chamber of Commerce (☎ 508-369-3120) maintains an information booth on Heywood St between Lexington Rd and Walden St. Approaching Concord from MA 2 and the east along Cambridge Turnpike, look for Heywood St on the left a few blocks before Monument Square. The booth, staffed by volunteers, is open on weekends mid-April through May and daily from June through mid-October.

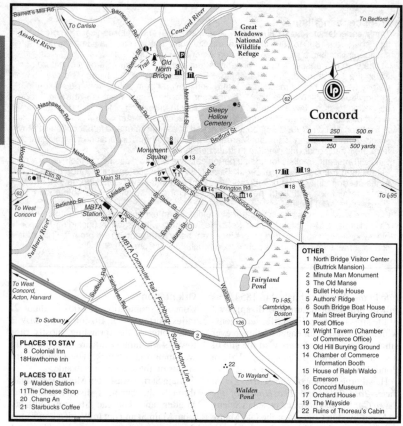

OTHER
1   North Bridge Visitor Center
    (Buttrick Mansion)
2   Minute Man Monument
3   The Old Manse
4   Bullet Hole House
5   Authors' Ridge
6   South Bridge Boat House
7   Main Street Burying Ground
10 Post Office
12 Wright Tavern (Chamber
    of Commerce Office)
13 Old Hill Burying Ground
14 Chamber of Commerce
    Information Booth
15 House of Ralph Waldo
    Emerson
16 Concord Museum
17 Orchard House
19 The Wayside
22 Ruins of Thoreau's Cabin

PLACES TO STAY
8   Colonial Inn
18 Hawthorne Inn

PLACES TO EAT
9   Walden Station
11 The Cheese Shop
20 Chang An
21 Starbucks Coffee

The chamber's main office is in the historic Wright Tavern at Main St and Lexington Rd. They'll answer questions here when the booth is not open.

The Minuteman National Historic Park's Battle Road Visitor Center (☎ 508-371-2687) is on Massachusetts Ave between Lexington and Concord. It's open from mid-April through October. The Concord North Bridge Visitor Center (☎ 508-369-6993), open daily 9:30 am to 4:30 pm in summer, until 4 pm in winter, except Christmas and New Year's Day, is on Liberty St just north of the North Bridge.

Walking Tour

The grassy center of Monument Square is a favorite rest and picnic spot for bicyclers touring Concord's scenic roads. Start here on your walk around historic Concord.

At the southeastern end of the square is **Wright Tavern**, one of the first places the British troops searched in their hunt for arms on April 19, 1775. At the opposite end of the square is the **Colonial Inn** (see Places to Stay), the oldest part of which dates from 1716.

Walk northeast out of Monument Square (keep the Colonial Inn on your left) along

Monument St. It's a 15-minute walk past some of the town's most beautiful colonial houses to Old North Bridge, site of the first battle of the Revolutionary War. Along the way, watch for the yellow **Bullet Hole House** on the right-hand (east) side. British troops fired at the owner of the house as they retreated from the engagement at North Bridge, and a hole made by one of their bullets can still be seen in the wall of the shed attached to the house.

The wooden span of **Old North Bridge**, now part of the Minuteman National Historic Park, has been rebuilt many times but still gives a good impression of what it must have looked like at the time of the battle. Across the bridge is Daniel Chester French's statue "The Minute Man," which is on the way up the hill to the Buttrick Mansion, the park's visitors center.

Walking south and east from Monument Square for five minutes brings you to the **Concord Museum** (☎ 508-369-9609), 200 Lexington Rd, open in summer from 10 am to 5 pm (1 pm to 5 pm on Sunday), in winter from 11 am to 4 pm (1 to 4 pm on Sunday). Admission costs $6 for adults, $5 for seniors, $3 for children and $12 for families. Among the museum's exhibits are one of the lanterns hung in the steeple of Old North Church as a signal to Revere, Dawes and Prescott; Ralph Waldo Emerson's study and the world's largest collection of Thoreau artifacts.

Historic Houses

Across the Cambridge Turnpike from the Concord Museum is the **House of Ralph Waldo Emerson**, 28 Cambridge Turnpike. The house was frequently a meeting place for Emerson's renowned circle of friends, and still contains many of its original furnishings. It's open mid-April through October, Thursday through Saturday from 10 am to 4:30 pm, and Sunday from 2 to 4:30 pm. Admission costs $4 for adults, $2 for kids six to 17.

About a mile east of Monument Square is Louisa May Alcott's home, **Orchard House** (☎ 508-369-4118), 399 Lexington Rd, on the left-hand (north) side as you

come from the center of Concord. Her father, Bronson Alcott, bought the property in 1857, and lived here with his family until his death in 1888. The house, furnishings and his Concord School of Philosophy on the hillside behind the house are open to visitors April through October from 10 am to 4:30 pm (Sunday 1 to 4:30 pm), and in March and November on Saturday from 10 am to 4:30 pm, and Sunday from 1 to 4:30 pm; closed December through March.

A short stroll to the east is **The Wayside** (☎ 508-369-6975), 455 Lexington Rd, another house in which Louisa May Alcott lived, and the one she described in *Little Women*. At another time it was Nathaniel Hawthorne's home, but most of the remaining furnishings are those of Margaret Sidney, author of *Five Little Peppers*. The house is open to visitors mid-April through October from 9:30 am to 5:30 pm, closed Wednesday and Thursday.

Right next to Old North Bridge, **The Old Manse** (☎ 508-369-3909) was built in 1769 by Reverend William Emerson, and owned by the Emerson family for the following 169 years, until it was deeded to the NPS. Today it's a museum filled with mementos of the Emerson family, and of Nathaniel and Sophia Hawthorne, who lived here for three years following their marriage. A guided tour costs $5 for adults, $4 seniors and college students, $3 kids six to 16, $12 for families. It's open mid-April through October from 10 am to 5 pm (Sunday from 1 to 5 pm), closed Tuesday.

Historic Graveyards

Old Hill Burying Ground, with graves dating from colonial times, is on the hillside at the southeastern end of Monument Square. Main Street Burying Ground, at the intersection of Keyes Rd in the commercial center, has the town's oldest tombstones, dating from Concord's founding in the 1600s.

It is in Sleepy Hollow Cemetery, however, that the most famous deceased Concordians rest. Though the cemetery is only a block east of Monument Square along

MICHELLE GAGNÉ
Melvin Memorial in Sleepy Hollow
Cemetery, Concord

MA 62, the most interesting part, Authors' Ridge, is a 15-minute hike (or a shorter drive) further on. Enter the gate from MA 62 and follow signs to Authors' Ridge.

Henry David Thoreau and his family are buried here, as are the Alcotts and Nathaniel Hawthorne and his wife. Ralph Waldo Emerson's tombstone is a large uncarved rock of New England marble, an appropriate Transcendentalist symbol. Down the hill a bit is the tombstone of Ephraim Bull, developer of the famous Concord grape.

Nearby is the Melvin Memorial, a beautiful monument carved by Daniel Chester French in memory of three Concord brothers who died in the Civil War.

Walden Pond

The glacial pond near which Henry David Thoreau spent the years 1845 to 1847 is about three miles south of Monument Square along Walden St (MA 126) south of

MA 2. It's now a state park, with a parking fee payable during the summer. There's a swimming beach and facilities on the southern side, and a footpath that goes all the way around the large pond. The site of Thoreau's cabin, marked by a cairn and signs, is on the northeast side.

Fruitlands

A fast half-hour's drive west of Concord along MA 2 brings you to the town of Harvard and **Fruitlands Museums** (☎ 508-456-3924), 102 Prospect Hill Rd. The original hillside farmhouse, set on spacious grounds with panoramic views, dates from the 1700s, and was used by Bronson Alcott and his utopian "Con-Sociate" family in 1843. Other museums were moved here, including the 1794 Shaker House, an American Indian Museum and a picture gallery featuring paintings by 19th-century itinerant artists and Hudson River School landscape painters.

The estate's grounds are open daily from 10 am to 5 pm. The museums are open mid-May through mid-October (closed Monday, except on holidays) for $3.

The Seasoned Chef at Fruitlands offers luncheon fare ($5 to $10) and beverages from 10 am to 4 pm (Sunday brunch is from 10 am to 2 pm), with outdoor dining to enjoy the excellent views.

Canoeing

The South Bridge Boat House (☎ 508-369-9438), 496-502 Main St (MA 62), a mile west of Monument Square, rents canoes for cruising the Concord and Assabet Rivers from April until the first snowfall. The favorite route is downstream to the North Bridge and back past the many fine riverside houses and the campus of prestigious Concord Academy, a paddle of about two hours. Rental rates are $10 per hour, $40 per day on weekends, with discounts on weekdays and for students.

Places to Stay

The *Concordian Motel* (☎ 508-263-7765, 800-552-7765), 71 Hosmer St, on MA 2 in neighboring Acton, has modern rooms from $49/$54 single/double, light breakfast included. Follow MA 2 west from Concord and look for the motel on the left-hand side.

The *Best Western Concord Motel* (☎ 508-369-6100, 800-528-1234), 740 Elm St at MA 2 near Concord Rotary, charges $67/$80, with light breakfast. Pappa Razzi, a good Italian restaurant, is right next door.

The original building of the *Colonial Inn* (☎ 508-369-9200), 48 Monument Square, Concord, MA 01742, dates from 1716 and has 12 guest rooms, a lobby, dining rooms and tavern. The other 48 guest rooms are in a modern brick annex. Rates are $99 to $165 single or double, plus tax.

The *Hawthorne Inn* (☎ 508-369-5610), 462 Lexington Rd, is about a mile southeast of Monument Square near Orchard House and The Wayside (see Historic Houses, above). The inn has seven rooms with period decor, and prices from $80/$100, breakfast included.

About 13 miles south of Concord lies the town of Sudbury and its *Wayside Inn* (☎ 508-443-8846), on US 20. The inn, dating from 1700, was made famous by Longfellow's poems entitled *Tales from a Wayside Inn*, and now boasts that it is the oldest-operating inn in the USA. It was restored by Henry Ford in the 1920s and still operates as a restaurant and hostelry, with 10 rooms: Nos 9 and 10 are original to the inn and cost $91/$118, tax, service and full breakfast included. The newer rooms cost a bit less.

Places to Eat
For a good, fresh, huge luncheon sandwich for $5 or $6, or for picnic supplies, drop in at *The Cheese Shop* (☎ 508-369-5778), 29 Walden St, a half block southeast of Main St more or less across from the post office.

The cheapest full meal in Concord is the $1.50 daily four-course lunch (beverage included) served at the Northeast Correctional Center (☎ 508-369-4422), off Barrett's Mill Rd and MA 2 near the Concord Rotary. The prison farm, as it's called, is a working dairy farm run by convicts who have served most of their terms in the nearby high-walled prison and are preparing for parole. They cook and serve a filling, tasty meal most days from 11 am to 12:30 pm. Call for reservations.

You can get your morning *Starbucks* jolt at the intersection of Thoreau St and Sudbury Rd, by the railroad tracks.

Across from the Cheese Shop, *Walden Station* (☎ 508-371-2233), 24 Walden St, is a tavern-restaurant with a full menu of luncheon sandwiches and main courses priced from $5 to $15, with slightly higher prices for larger portions at dinner.

Concord's best restaurant is *Aïgo Bistro* (☎ 508-371-1333), 84 Thoreau St, upstairs in the Concord Depot. The New American cuisine is refined, inventive and served every day. Lunch costs about $12 to $20, dinner $40 or $50 per person.

Chang An (☎ 508-369-5288), 10 Concord Crossing, off Sudbury Rd just across the railroad tracks from Thoreau St, has the best Chinese cuisine in town. Lunch usually costs $10 to $16, dinner $15 to $25 per person.

West Concord, several miles southwest of Concord center along MA 62, has a number of restaurants as well. The best value is the *99 Restaurant* (☎ 508-369-0300), 18 Commonwealth Ave, with steak dinners for under $12.

Getting There & Away
Driving west on MA 2 from Boston or Cambridge, it's 20-some miles to Concord. Coming from Lexington, follow signs from Lexington Green to Concord and Battle Rd, the route taken by the British troops on April 19, 1775.

MBTA Commuter Rail trains (☎ 617-722-3200) run between Boston's North Station and Concord and West Concord stations 16 times daily on the Fitchburg/South Acton line. The 45-minute ride costs $3.50, half price for kids five to 11 (under five free). In Concord, buy your tickets at Coggins Bakery, just northwest of the depot building.

North Shore

The entire coast of Massachusetts Bay has a rich maritime history, but no part is richer than the shore north of Boston. Salem was among America's wealthiest ports in the 19th century; Marblehead is among New England's premier yachting ports today and Gloucester is the region's – perhaps the nation's – most famous fishing port.

Trade and fishing brought wealth, which brought on sumptuous houses and great collections of art and artifacts.

Getting There & Away

MBTA Commuter Rail trains (☎ 617-722-3200, 800-392-6100) run from Boston's North Station to Salem, Beverly, Gloucester and Rockport on the Rockport/Ipswich Line about every 30 minutes during the morning and evening rush hours, hourly during the day, with trains every two or three hours in the evening and on weekends. Buy your ticket before you get on the train; there's a $2 surcharge to buy a ticket on the train during the time when tickets are being sold at the station.

Street signage north of Boston is often confusing, making it easy for drivers to get lost. Be prepared to ask the way.

SALEM

To anyone familiar with New England's colonial history, the town's very name brings thoughts of witches and witchcraft. The famous Salem witch trials of 1692 are burned into the national memory even though Salem's true claim to historical fame is its glorious maritime history.

Today Salem is a commuter suburb of Boston with some light industry, though not quite enough to make it wealthy. Visit Salem to see its world-class Peabody-Essex Museum, sumptuous 19th-century ship captains' and merchants' homes, the House of the Seven Gables made famous in Hawthorne's novel of that name and – particularly for the kids – some of the kitschy witch museums.

History

Salem was founded in 1626 by Roger Conant and a band of 20 hearty settlers. Within a century Salem was a port of note, and by 1762 it counted among its residents Elias Hasket Derby, America's first millionaire. Derby and his father Captain Richard Derby built the half-mile-long Derby Wharf, now the center of the Salem Maritime National Historic Site.

During the Revolutionary War, Salem's merchants fitted 158 vessels as privateers – private vessels that preyed on enemy shipping – and held the distinction of sinking or capturing more British ships than all the ships of all the other American ports combined.

After the war, the privateers went into trade. Their traditional British Empire ports abroad being closed to them, they were forced to sail further afield. Elias Derby's ship *Grand Turk* sailed around the Cape of Good Hope, the first Salem vessel to do so, reaching Canton in 1786. Many Salem vessels followed, and soon also navigated around Cape Horn to the East Indies, China and India to bring back rich cargoes of spices, silks and porcelain.

In 1799 they founded the East India Marine Society to provide warehousing services and a central repository for their ships' logs and charts. The new company's charter required the establishment of "a museum in which to house the natural and artificial curiosities" to be brought back by members' ships. The collection, grown to a half-million artifacts, was the basis of the Peabody Museum, now combined with the Essex Institute into the Peabody Essex Museum (see below).

Salem's golden age lasted until the mid-19th century, when New England clipper ships emerged onto the scene. These swift new ships that raced around the world – even carrying New England ice to tropical ports – needed harbors that were deeper than Salem's. As the tall masts gradually disappeared from Salem's harbor, the harbor silted up, ending a chapter in colonial and early American maritime history.

Salem Witch Trials

In the late 1600s it was widely believed that one could make a pact with the devil in order to gain evil powers to be used against one's enemies. The judges of the Massachusetts Bay colony had tried 44 persons for witchcraft before 1692, and three of them had been hanged.

The Reverend Cotton Mather, one of the colony's most fiery preachers, had added his own book on witchcraft to the already considerable literature on the subject. A group of young, poor girls near Salem got hold of a copy and read how the "possessed" were thought to behave. Partly as a prank, they accused a servant of being a witch.

The accused, a half-black, half-Indian woman, confessed under torture and accused two other women of being accomplices in order to save her own life. Soon the accusations flew thick and fast as the innocent accused confessed to riding broomsticks, having sex with the devil and participating in witches' sabbaths. They implicated others in attempts to save themselves. The girls, afraid of being discovered as fakes, kept up their accusations as well.

Governor Phips appointed a special court to deal with the accusations, but its justices were not trained in the rules of evidence, and soon became panicked as the situation careened out of control.

At the end of the summer of 1692, 55 people had pleaded guilty and implicated others to save their own lives, 14 women and five men had been hanged for witchcraft, one man who refused to plead either guilty or not guilty had been pressed to death, and at least four people died in jail of disease.

The frenzy was put down when the accusers began pointing at prominent merchants, clergy and even the governor's wife. The jails were opened, and 150 people accused of witchcraft were released.

Three centuries later, the subject of witchcraft is a Disneyesque amusement in town. The Salem Witch Trials Memorial, off Charter St, honors the innocents who died. ∎

Orientation

The main areas of interest in Salem are the Essex St Mall, a pedestrian way through the heart of historic Salem; Salem Common adjoining the mall and the Derby Wharf a block away (see Salem Maritime National Historic Site, below). All are walkable. The train station is a five-minute walk from Essex St Mall.

The Heritage Trail is a 1.7-mile route connecting Salem's major historic sites. Follow the red line painted on the sidewalk.

Information

The Salem Chamber of Commerce (☎ 508-744-0004), 32 Derby Square in the Old Town Hall building on Essex St Mall, has a visitors center open Monday through Friday from 9 am to 5 pm. The Salem Office of Tourism provides information over its toll-free phone line at ☎ 800-777-6848, or by fax at 508-741-7539.

The NPS Visitor Center (☎ 508-744-4323, 741-3648 on weekends), 2 Liberty St, is open daily from 9 am to 6 pm.

Peabody Essex Museum

The treasure trove of art, artifacts and curiosities brought back from the Far East by ships out of Salem is housed in the Peabody Essex Museum (☎ 508-745-1876, 745-9500 for taped information, 800-745-4054), Essex St Mall at New Liberty St.

This is America's oldest private museum in continuous operation. It has expanded many times since it was first housed in East India Marine Hall in 1824.

The museum includes exhibits from New England's history, including clocks, ceramics, costumes, dolls and toys, military uniforms and weapons, lamps, lanterns and glassware. The town's maritime history is particularly well documented with ship captains' portraits, scale

MASSACHUSETTS

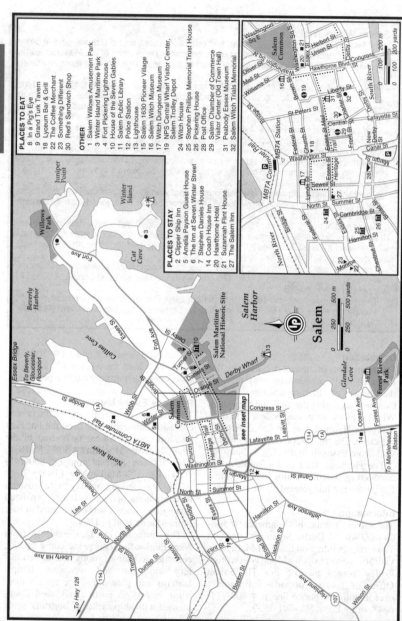

PLACES TO EAT
8   In a Pig's Eye
9   Grand Turk Tavern
18   Lyceum Bar & Grill
22   The Coffee Merchant
23   Something Different
30   Red's Sandwich Shop

OTHER
1   Salem Willows Amusement Park
3   Winter Island Maritime Park
4   Fort Pickering Lighthouse
10   House of the Seven Gables
11   Salem Public Library
12   Police Station
13   Lighthouse
15   Salem 1630 Pioneer Village
16   Salem Witch Museum
17   Witch Dungeon Museum
19   NPS Central Wharf Visitor Center,
       Salem Trolley Depot
24   Witch House
25   Stephen Phillips Memorial Trust House
26   Pickering House
28   Post Office
29   Salem Chamber of Commerce
       Visitor Center (Old Town Hall)
31   Peabody Essex Museum
32   Salem Witch Trials Memorial

PLACES TO STAY
2   Clipper Ship Inn
5   Amelia Payson Guest House
6   The Inn at Seven Winter Street
7   Stephen Daniels House
14   Coach House Inn
20   Hawthorne Hotel
21   Suzannah Flint House
27   The Salem Inn

Salem

models and paintings of ships, 18th-century navigation instruments, scrimshaw (carved whalebone) and carved ships' figureheads. There's even a reproduction of the main cabin of *Cleopatra's Barge*, America's first oceangoing yacht built in 1816 for a member of the East India Marine Society.

The Asian collections cover arts and crafts of peoples native to America, the Pacific Islands and East Asia, including porcelain, paintings, silver, furniture and other arts from China, Japan, Polynesia, Micronesia and Melanesia. The collection from pre-industrial Japan is rated the best in the world.

There are also exhibits on the natural history of Essex County. The *Museum Café* serves lunch and afternoon tea.

The museum is open daily from 10 am to 5 pm (to 8 pm Thursday; Sunday noon to 5 pm), but closed Monday from November through May. Admission costs $7 for adults, $6 seniors and college students, $4 kids six to 18, $18 for families.

Historic Houses

Salem's most famous house is the **House of the Seven Gables** (☎ 508-744-0991), 54 Turner St, made famous in Nathaniel Hawthorne's novel (1851) of that name. The novel brings to life the gloomy Puritan atmosphere of early New England and its effects on the people's psyches; the house does the same. Sound like fun? It's open June through October daily from 9 am to 6 pm, off season from 10 am to 4:30 pm, for $7 for adults, $4 youth 13 to 17, $3 kids six to 12. That fee allows entrance to the site's four historic buildings, the Garden Cafe, and luxuriant gardens on the waterfront.

Furnished in antiques, **Pickering House** (☎ 508-744-1647), 18 Broad St, is said to be the oldest house in the USA continuously occupied by the same family. It's open Monday from 10 am to 3 pm, any other time by appointment, for $4.

House-lovers should also seek out Chestnut St, which is among the most architecturally beautiful streets in the country. It's a block south of western Essex St.

The **Stephen Phillips Memorial Trust House** (☎ 508-744-1551), 34 Chestnut St, is decorated with the family furnishings of Salem sea captains, and includes a collection of antique carriages and cars. Visit from late May through mid-October from 10 am to 4:30 pm, closed Sunday. Adults pay $2, children under 12, $1.

The Peabody Essex Museum owns, maintains and owns several historic homes to the public as well.

Salem Maritime National Historic Site

The Custom House on Derby Wharf is the centerpiece of the national historic site (☎ 508-745-1470). The Central Wharf Visitor Center is the first place to go. The site is open from 10 am to 6 pm in summer, 9 am to 5 pm in winter, for free.

Nathaniel Hawthorne, a Salem native, was surveyor of the port from 1846 to 1849. Other buildings at the site include the Government Bonded Warehouse, containing cargoes typical of the trade in 1819; the Scale House; West India Goods Store, a working store with many items similar to those sold two centuries ago; Derby House, home of the famous shipping family; Hawkes House, used as a privateer prize warehouse during the Revolutionary War; Narbonne-Hale House, a more modest house owned by artisans and their families and the lighthouse on Derby Wharf.

Witch Stuff

The tragic events of 1692 have proved a boon to modern operators of witch-related attractions.

Most authentic of the witchy sites is the **Witch House** (☎ 508-744-0180), 310½ Essex St. This was the home of Magistrate Jonathan Corwin, where some preliminary examinations of persons accused of witchcraft were held. It's open from 10 am to 4:30 pm (until 6 pm in July and August), closed December through mid-March.

The **Salem Witch Museum** (☎ 508-744-1692), 19½ Washington Square North, is on Brown St at Hawthorne Blvd, open 10 am to 5 pm (till 7 pm in July and August), for $4 for adults, $3.50 seniors,

$2.50 kids six to 14. The church-like building holds dioramas, exhibits, audio-visual shows and costumed staff who help you to understand the witchcraft scare.

The **Witch Dungeon Museum** (☎ 508-741-3570), 16 Lynde St, stages recreations of a witch trial based on historical transcripts daily from 10 am to 5 pm for $4 for adults, $3.50 seniors, $2.50 kids. **History Alive!** (☎ 508-927-2300 ext 4747), in the Old Town Hall, 32 Derby Square on the Essex Street Mall, stages a similar re-enactment, "The People vs Bridget Bishop," from mid-June through October for slightly higher prices.

Parks

Less than two miles northeast of Salem center is **Salem Willows Amusement Park** (☎ 508-745-0251), with beaches, children's rides and games and harbor cruises. Just south of it is Winter Island Maritime Park, the site of Fort Pickering and its lighthouse, now a public park and campground.

Forest River Park, on West St less than two miles south of the center, has beaches, picnic areas and a salt-water swimming pool, as well as **Salem 1630** (☎ 508-744-0991), a replicated Puritan village of the 1600s with costumed interpreters, period buildings, gardens, crafts and animals.

Places to Stay

Camping *Winter Island Maritime Park* (☎ 508-745-9430), 50 Winter Island Rd, less than two miles east of the center of town, is open May through October, and has space for 25 tents ($15) and 30 RVs ($18 with electricity). Call and reserve your space in advance.

Motels The *Clipper Ship Inn* (☎ 508-745-8022), at 40 Bridge St (MA 1A) has 60 motel rooms for $62 to $80.

The 130-room *Days Inn* (☎ 508-777-1030, 800-325-2525), 152 Endicott St, Danvers, MA 01923, is four miles from the center of Salem on MA 114 on the northwest side of MA 128. Rooms with one queen-size bed and light breakfast cost $65 single, $75 double.

Inns & B&Bs Salem has at least 10 nice B&Bs from $75 to $150 a night in summer, single or double. All are nonsmoking, and virtually all rooms have direct-dial phones and cable TVs.

The Stephen Daniels House (☎ 508-744-5709), 1 Daniels St, at Essex St two blocks north of the waterfront, must be Salem's oldest lodging, with parts dating from 1667 – before the witch trials – and many period antiques. Several of the five bedrooms adjoin, making them perfect for families, two couples or small groups. Mrs Katherine Gill, the proprietor, charges $40 for a bathless single, $60 to $75 for doubles without bath, $80 to $95 with. Be sure to call for reservations.

Amelia Payson Guest House (☎ 508-744-8304), 16 Winter St, is within walking distance of Salem's sights, and has all the comforts for $85 double with private bath.

Suzannah Flint House (☎ 508-744-5281), 98 Essex St, is a beautiful old 1808 Federal house conveniently located, with private baths and prices of $79 to $109.

The Inn at Seven Winter Street (☎ 508-745-9520), 7 Winter St, is an 1870 Victorian house about four blocks from the center. The rooms, priced from $85 to $115 double, have private baths, a few have kitchens.

The Salem Inn (☎ 508-741-0680, 800-446-2995), 7 Summer St, is a large brick sea captain's house built in 1834. The 21 guest rooms are priced at $119 to $169 single or double on weekends ($10 less during the week), with a light breakfast and all the conveniences. There's a restaurant as well.

The *Coach House Inn* (☎ 508-744-4092), 284 Lafayette St, is about a mile from the center on the route to Boston. Built in 1879, its 11 rooms (nine with bath) cost $70 to $80 double ($10 less without bath).

Hotels Salem's centerpiece is the *Hawthorne Hotel* (☎ 508-744-4080, 800-729-7829), 18 Washington Square West, corner of Hawthorne Blvd and Essex St, right next to the common. This historic

(1920s), full-service hotel right at the center of things charges $102 to $137 for its 89 double rooms, plus almost 10% in tax, with discounts of 8% to 10% off-season. For dining, there's *Nathaniel's*, the formal restaurant serving New American cuisine, and the informal *Tavern on the Green*.

Places to Eat
Breakfast, Lunch & Picnics If you're visiting Salem on a day trip you might just want a sandwich. Try *Red's Sandwich Shop* (☎ 508-745-3527), 15 Central St, with sandwiches and breakfast plates from $2 to $4.

Another good place is *Something Different* (☎ 508-741-8688), 213 Essex St, which has a long list of soups, sandwiches and main-course dinners all packed to take out.

For a blast of gourmet java, it's *The Coffee Merchant* (☎ 508-744-1729), 196 Essex St, which opens at 7 am weekdays (10 am weekends) serving espresso, lattes, scones and bagels.

Restaurants Salem's all-purpose eatery is the historic *Lyceum Bar & Grill* (☎ 508-745-7665), 43 Church St. A varied menu of luncheon sandwiches, salads and main courses carries prices from $6 to $9; at dinner, traditional main-course favorites with New American accents cost $13 to $19.

In a Pig's Eye (☎ 508-741-4436), 148 Derby St at Daniels, has an eclectic menu with Mexican antojitos, Greek salads, vegetarian dishes, pastas and many steak, chicken and seafood main courses priced below $11.

The *Grand Turk Tavern* (☎ 508-745-7727), 110 Derby St at Turner, east of the Custom House, serves a traditional New England menu strong on seafood at moderate prices.

Getting There & Away
The MBTA Commuter Rail (☎ 800-392-6100) train ride to Salem takes about 35 minutes. The ride by bus 450 or 455 from Boston's Haymarket Square (near North Station) takes a few minutes longer.

Salem lies 20 miles northeast of Boston, a 35-minute drive. From Boston, follow US 1 north across the Mystic River (Tobin) Bridge and bear right onto MA 16 (Revere Beach Parkway) toward Revere Beach, then follow MA 1A (Shore Rd) north through Saugus, Lynn (Lynnway) and Swampscott to Salem. MA 1A becomes Lafayette St in Salem, and takes you right to Essex Street Mall and the common.

Coming from MA 128, take exit 25A and follow MA 114 east, which becomes North St, which intersects with Essex St.

Getting Around
The Salem Trolley (☎ 508-744-5469) runs a figure-eight route past all the town's places of interest with a running commentary, departing daily on the hour from 10 am to 4 pm (last departure). From July through October, departures are on the hour and half hour. Your ticket ($8 for adults, $7 seniors, $4 kids five to 12, $20 families) is good all day, so you can hop on and off as you like.

MARBLEHEAD
First settled in 1629, Marblehead's Old Town is a picturesque New England maritime village with winding streets, brightly-painted Colonial and early-American houses, and sleek yachts bobbing at anchor in its well-sheltered harbor. As the great number of boats indicates, this is the North Shore's premier yachting port, and indeed one of New England's choicest moorings.

Orientation
You pass through the modern districts of Marblehead on the way to the Marblehead Historic District, called Old Town, with its network of narrow, winding streets, many of them one way. The small directional signs sometimes help, but Old Town is quite difficult to negotiate by car. Parking is usually a problem in summer, particularly on weekends, so it's best to find a legal parking place inland from the waterfront and explore the town on foot.

Washington St, State St and Mugford St intersect at an open space which is the nearest thing Marblehead's Old Town has

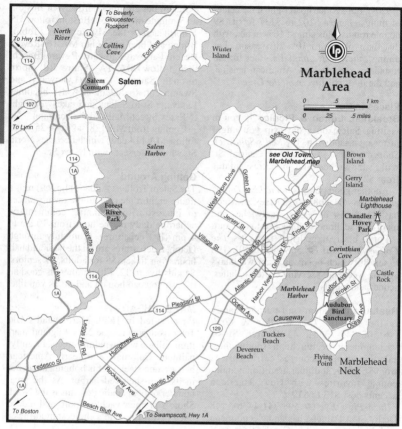

Marblehead Area

0   .5   1 km
0   .25   .5 miles

To Beverly,
Gloucester,
Rockport

North
River

To Hwy 128

Collins
Cove

Fort Ave

Winter
Island

Salem
Common   Salem

To Lynn

Salem
Harbor

see Old Town
Marblehead map

Brown
Island

Gerry
Island

Marblehead
Lighthouse

West Shore Drive

Green St

Chandler
Hovey
Park

Forest
River
Park

Jersey St

Washington St

Front St

Corinthian
Cove

Lafayette St

Village St

Pleasant St

Gregory St

Harbor View

Atlantic Ave

Marblehead
Harbor

Harbor Ave

Castle
Rock

Brown St

Ocean Ave

Audubon
Bird
Sanctuary

Pleasant St

Causeway

Loring Ave

Leggs Hill Rd

Humphrey St

Ocean Ave

Tuckers
Beach

Devereux
Beach

Flying
Point

Marblehead
Neck

Tedesco St

Rockaway Ave

Atlantic Ave

To Boston

Beach Bluff Ave

To Swampscott, Hwy 1A

---

to a main square. It's marked by the Old
Town House, once the town hall.

Southeast of the Old Town House along
Washington and State Sts brings you to the
State Street Landing, the town's main dock,
with views across the harbor to the grand
houses on Marblehead Neck. Marblehead
Neck is a wooded island east of the town
center connected to the mainland by the
Ocean Ave causeway.

Information

The Marblehead Chamber of Commerce
(☎ 617-631-2868, fax 639-8582), 62 Pleasant St, Marblehead, MA 01945, maintains
an information booth on MA 114 (Pleasant
St), corner of Essex and Spring Sts. Look
for it on the right-hand side as you
approach Old Town, and pick up a copy of
their walking tour brochure and map.

Things to See & Do

Every American is familiar with *The Spirit of
'76*, the patriotic painting of a Revolutionary
War drummer, fife-player and flag bearer. It
hangs in the Selectmen's meeting room of
Marblehead's brick-towered **Abbott Hall**
(☎ 617-631-0000), home of the Marblehead

Historical Commission on Washington St. The painting, as well as the deed given by Marblehead's Native American residents to its European settlers in 1694 and several marine life exhibits are on view for free weekdays from 9 am to 4 pm, with extended hours from June to October: until 8 pm on Wednesday, Saturday 9 am to 6 pm and Sunday and holidays 11 am to 6 pm.

The Georgian **Jeremiah Lee Mansion** (☎ 617-631-1069), near the corner of Hooper and Washington Sts, was built on the order of a prominent merchant in 1768, and is now a museum with period furnishings and collections of toys and children's furniture, folk art and nautical and military artifacts. It's open from mid-May to mid-October from 10 am to 4 pm (Sunday 1 to 4 pm), for $4 for adults, $3 college students, $2 youth 10 to 16.

The **King Hooper Mansion** (☎ 617-631-2608), 8 Hooper St more or less across the street from the Jeremiah Lee Mansion, is the home of the Marblehead Arts Association. The historic 1728 house holds four floors of exhibit space, with shows changing monthly. Hours are 1 to 4 pm (closed Sunday). Exhibits are free; the house tour costs $1.

Old Town is perfect for a morning's or afternoon's strolling, cafe-sitting, window-shopping, photo-snapping and picnicking.

A block west of State Street Landing, **Crocker Park** has fine views of the harbor and excellent picnic possibilities.

At the eastern end of Front St, the earthworks of **Fort Sewall** also provide a prime venue for picnics. The fort, built in the 1600s, was strengthened during the Revolutionary War, and is now a park.

On Marblehead Neck's Ocean Ave is an **Audubon Bird Sanctuary**; access is on the southwest side via Risley St.

At the eastern end of Marblehead Neck, **Chandler Hovey Park**, by Marblehead Light, has marvelous views in all directions.

On the southeastern side of Marblehead Neck, a short walk takes you to **Castle Rock**, with views of open ocean and cool breezes for a hot day.

Places to Stay

Marblehead has two dozen small B&Bs charging from $60 with shared bath to $125 with private bath for a double room; the higher prices are for weekend stays. None has more than a few rooms, so reservations are essential. If you have no luck finding a room, or if you want different accommodations, stay in nearby Salem. Try these:

Brimblecomb Hill B&B (☎ 617-631-6366 daytime, 631-3172 evenings), 33 Mechanic St, has a room with shared bath for $60 to $65, another with private bath for $75 to $80 and a private entrance for guests.

The Guest House at Lavender Gate (☎ 617-631-3243, 800-800-6824), 1 Summer St, offers two book-lined suites with private bath and air-conditioning for $75 to $100 double.

The Carriage House (☎ 617-639-1924), 19 Stacey St, has two doubles with shared bath for $55 to $65, living with the family.

Eagle House B&B (☎ 617-631-1532, 631-8177), 96R Front St and 6½ Merritt St, has two suites with sitting room, kitchenette and separate entrance for $100.

Harbor Light Inn (☎ 617-631-2186), 58 Washington St, is Marblehead's "big" hostelry, with 20 rooms priced from $85 to $125. All have private baths, 11 have working fireplaces, five have Jacuzzis. There's a pool as well.

Lindsey's Garret B&B (☎ 617-631-2433, 800-882-3891), 38 High St, has a studio apartment with kitchenette and water-view deck for $80 double.

Sea Street B&B (☎ 617-631-1890, 800-572-7335), 9 Gregory St, has four rooms with private baths and air-con for $65 to $85 double.

Harborside House B&B (☎ 617-631-1032), 23 Gregory St, has two rooms with shared bath for $65 to $75.

Places to Eat

For picnic supplies – fresh breads, baked goods, take-out sandwiches and main courses – head for *Good Tastes* (☎ 617-639-2897), 32 Atlantic Ave, open daily

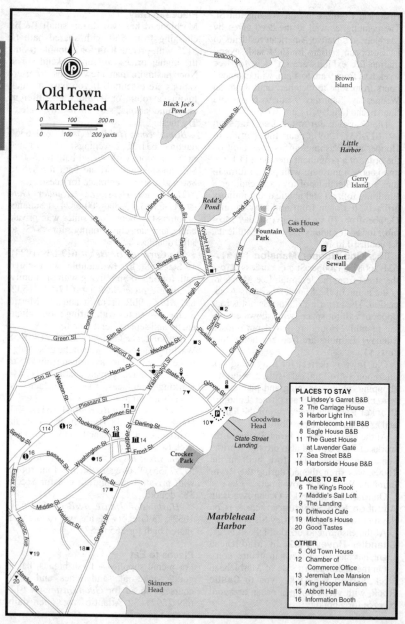

Old Town Marblehead

0   100   200 m
0   100   200 yards

Beacon St

Brown Island

Black Joe's Pond

Norman St

Little Harbor

Gerry Island

Redd's Pond

Peach Highlands Rd

Hines Ct

Norman St

Dunns St

Pond St

Beacon St

Gas House Beach

Fountain Park

P
Fort Sewall

Russel St

Knight Hill Alley

Orne St

Cowell St

High St

■ 1

Franklin St

Pond St

Green St

Elm St

Mugford St

Pearl St

Stacey St

Prokett St

Circle St

Seltman St

■ 2

Mechanic St

■ 3

Front St

Elm St

Watson St

Harris St

Washington St

● 4

State St

● 5

● 6

Glover St

■ 8

Pleasant St

▼ 7

▼ 9

Goodwins Head

11 ■

Summer St

Darling St

P

▼ 10

Rockaway St

13

(114)

❶ 12

Hooper St

Front St

State Street Landing

Spring St

❶ 16

Bassett St

Washington St

14

● 15

Crocker Park

Essex St

Lee St

Middle St

Weldron St

■ 17

Marblehead Harbor

Atlantic Ave

Gregory St

■ 18

Hawkes St

▼ 19

▼ 20

Skinners Head

PLACES TO STAY
1 Lindsey's Garret B&B
2 The Carriage House
3 Harbor Light Inn
4 Brimblecomb Hill B&B
8 Eagle House B&B
11 The Guest House
    at Lavender Gate
17 Sea Street B&B
18 Harborside House B&B

PLACES TO EAT
6 The King's Rook
7 Maddie's Sail Loft
9 The Landing
10 Driftwood Cafe
19 Michael's House
20 Good Tastes

OTHER
5 Old Town House
12 Chamber of
    Commerce Office
13 Jeremiah Lee Mansion
14 King Hooper Mansion
15 Abbott Hall
16 Information Booth

from 7 am to 8 pm (Friday and Saturday until 10 pm).

Four eateries are right near State Street Landing. The most prominent is appropriately named *The Landing* (☎ 617-631-1878), 81 Front St, a full-service restaurant and pub with a long menu (plenty of seafood) and a variety of dining spaces inside and out. Lunches cost $8 to $16, dinners $16 to $30.

Across the parking lot, the low-priced *Driftwood Cafe* (☎ 617-631-1145), 63 Front St, is a Marblehead fixture, serving hearty mariners' breakfasts to the local dawn crew from 5:30 am, closing after lunch at 2 pm (in summer until 5 pm).

The place for the yachting crowd to see and be seen is *Maddie's Sail Loft* (☎ 617-631-9824), 15 State St, a block inland from the landing. Drinks are as important as meals here. Moderately-priced lunches and dinners are served Monday to Saturday.

The King's Rook (☎ 617-631-9838), 12 State St, is a cafe and wine bar good for a cup of joe while reading the news, or a light meal of pizza, pastry, soup and salad, sandwich or rich dessert. They serve wines by the glass, and liqueurs from noon to 11:30 pm; closed Monday evening.

Michael's House (☎ 617-631-1255), 26 Atlantic Ave, was built over three centuries ago, and now serves everything from luncheon fare (11:30 am to 2 pm, $5 to $10) to full Italian and continental meals (5:30 to 10 pm, $16 to $30). Sunday brunch (10 am to 2 pm) is a specialty.

Another good place for fancy coffee, pastry or a light meal is *Caffe Appassionato* (☎ 617-639-3200), 12 Atlantic Ave. Read their newspapers, or use their chess- or checkerboards. They open at 6 am.

Getting There & Away

MBTA buses 441 and 442 run between Boston's Haymarket Square (near North Station) and Marblehead. From Salem, follow MA 114 south and east four miles to Marblehead, where it becomes Pleasant St.

GLOUCESTER

Founded in 1623, just three years after the colony at Plymouth, Gloucester is among New England's oldest towns. To Americans, it's synonymous with fishing. It was founded by fisherfolk, and until the early 1990s it made its living at fishing.

But overfishing by both the boats out of Gloucester and those of other nations imperiled New England fish stocks. Strict government limits on catches in 1994, followed by the closing of most of the once-rich fishing grounds in 1995, dealt Gloucester a terrible economic blow. In only two years, up to 20,000 fishermen found themselves out of full-time work.

Gloucester's industrious workers are presently reinventing the town's economy. The big fish-processing plants are converting to process seafood brought in from other regions, and there's an active search for new industries.

You can still see fishing boats, festooned with big nets and winches, motoring into Gloucester Harbor, with clouds of hungry seagulls circling above.

Orientation & Information

Washington St runs from Grant Circle (a rotary on MA 128) into the center of Gloucester at St Peter's Square, an irregular brick plaza overlooking the sea. Rogers St, the waterfront road, goes east from the plaza; Main St, the business and shopping thoroughfare, is one block inland.

East Gloucester, with the Rocky Neck artists' colony, is on the southeastern side of Gloucester Harbor.

The Cape Ann Chamber of Commerce (☎ 508-283-1601, 800-321-0133), 33 Commercial St, Gloucester, MA 01930, provides information and maps. There's a visitors information office in Stage Fort Park, on the west side of the Annisquam River up the hill.

Walking Tour

The town has organized a Maritime Trail that you can follow with a brochure from the chamber of commerce, or by follow-

TOM BROSNAHAN

Symbol of a once-thriving trade

ing the signs posted around town. Highlights are the Harbor Cove, Inner Harbor, Fish Pier and Leonarde Craske's famous statue, "The Gloucester Fisherman," often called "The Man at the Wheel," and dedicated to "They That Go Down to the Sea in Ships, 1623-1923."

Rocky Neck Artists' Colony
Cape Ann's natural beauty and seaside visual interest have attracted artists for at least a century. The narrow peninsula of Rocky Neck, jutting into Gloucester Harbor from East Gloucester, offered some of the best views. Between the world wars, artists began renting little seaside shacks from local fishers to use as studios. Today many of these same shanties, considerably gentrified, are quaint galleries displaying the work of local artists.

Follow Main St east and south around the northeastern end of Gloucester Harbor to East Gloucester. Turn onto Rocky Neck Ave and park in the lot on the right; parking

farther on, in the village proper, is nearly impossible in high summer. Parking violation tickets are handed out early and often.

It's only a five-minute walk from the parking lot to the galleries and restaurants. Stroll along enjoying the view, poke your head in a gallery or two, then stop for refreshments at one of the restaurants overlooking Smith Cove (see Places to Eat).

Beauport Mansion
Beauport (☎ 508-283-0800), the Sleeper-McCann mansion at 75 Eastern Point Blvd on Eastern Point, East Gloucester, is a lavish "summer cottage" constructed between 1907 and 1934 by Henry Davis Sleeper. Its builder, a prominent interior designer and collector of antiques, worked to make his fantasy palace a showplace of American decor. He toured New England in search of houses about to be demolished, and bought up selected elements from each: wood paneling, architectural elements and furniture. In place of unity, Sleeper created a wildly eclectic but artistically surprising – and satisfying – place to live.

Now in the care of the Society for the Preservation of New England Antiquities, Beauport is open to visitors weekdays between mid-May and mid-October from 10 am to 4 pm, and on weekends from mid-September to mid-October from 1 to 4 pm. Admission costs $5 for adults, $4.50 seniors, $2.50 for children six to 12. Beauport also sponsors programs of afternoon teas, evening concerts and other special events. Call for schedules.

Hammond Castle Museum
Dr John Hays Hammond, Jr (1888-1965) was an electrical engineer whose inventions were important to the development of radar, sonar and radio remote control systems, including torpedo guidance. Despite his genius with things electrical, it was not Dr John but Laurens Hammond (unrelated) who invented the electric organ.

Defense contracts filled his bank account, and with this wealth Dr Hammond pursued his passion for collecting European art and architecture. His eccentric home is an odd castle of four sections, each epitomizing a period in European history: Romanesque, Medieval, Gothic and Renaissance. Furnishings, including an 8200-pipe organ in the Romanesque Great Hall, are eclectic, quirky, at times beautiful, at others gimcrack or even macabre.

The museum (☎ 508-283-7673) is open from 10 am to 5 pm (weekends from 11 am to 1 pm and 1:30 to 5 pm). The 45-minute guided tour costs $6 for adults, $5 for seniors and college students, $4 kids four to 12. For the schedule of concerts and special programs, call ☎ 508-283-2080.

Hammond Castle overlooks several natural features famous in literature. **Rafe's Chasm** is a cleft in the rocky shoreline characterized by turgid and thrashing water. Near it is **Norman's Woe**, the reef on which the ship broke up in Longfellow's poem "The Wreck of the Hesperus."

Beaches

Gloucester has several excellent beaches that draw thousands of Boston-area sun and sea worshippers on any hot day in July or August.

Wingaersheek Beach Perhaps biggest and best of all is Wingaersheek Beach, a wide swath of sand on Ipswich Bay by the Annisquam River. At low tide a long sandbar stretches for more than a half mile out into the bay. At its tip you have a fine view of the Annisquam lighthouse.

On weekends and very hot days in July and August, plan to arrive by mid-morning at the latest. The parking lot fills up by then, and latecomers are turned away. To get there, take the Concord St exit from MA 128 (the exit just before the Grant Circle rotary). Follow Concord St north for several miles, turning at the sign.

Admission costs $15 per car on weekends, $10 on weekdays. There are showers, toilets and refreshments available. If you come too late and the parking lot is full, retrace your route. Several homeowners on the way to the beach rent parking space on their front lawns on busy weekends. The beach is closed at sunset.

Good Harbor Beach Another big beach is Good Harbor, east of East Gloucester off MA 127A on the way to Rockport. Fees, facilities and parking policies are similar to those at Wingaersheek Beach. On hot days and weekends, come early to avoid disappointment.

Long & Pebble Beaches A short distance farther east and north along MA 127A are two smaller beaches, Long Beach and Pebble Beach, in the neighboring town of Rockport.

Stage Fort Park Beach There is a small but usually uncrowded beach down the hill in Stage Fort Park, off Western Ave on the west side of Gloucester. Parking costs $10, but you can park for free on Western Ave, from whence it is a 10-minute walk over the hill to the beach.

Boating

Cape Ann Sea Kayak Company (☎ 508-356-5264), 12 Pleasant St, Ipswich, MA 01938, has a full schedule of kayaking courses and one to three-day sea-paddling adventures.

Whale-Watching Cruises

Gloucester has a particularly good selection of whale-watching cruise boats. If you have not yet gone out in search of the behemoths, you can do it here. See The New Whalers sidebar.

Cruises out of Gloucester cost about $21 for adults, $16 seniors, $12 for children under 16. You can sometimes find discount coupons at the chamber of commerce, or in local publications. Here are some companies:

Capt Bill & Sons Whale Watch
  (☎ 508-283-6995, 800-339-4253), 9 Traverse St, Gloucester, MA 01930. The dock for Capt Bill's boats is off Harbor Loop behind Captain Carlo's Seafood Market & Restaurant. Capt Bill's cruises feature naturalists from the Cetacean Research Unit, Inc.
Cape Ann Whale Watch
  (☎ 508-283-5110, 800-877-5110), Rose's Wharf, 415 Main St (PO Box 345),

Gloucester, MA 01930. Sailings are accompanied by naturalists from the Whale Conservation Institute, and depart from Rose's Wharf, east of downtown Gloucester on the way to East Gloucester.

Yankee Whale Watch
(☎ 508-283-0313, 800-942-5464), 75 W Essex Ave (MA 133), Gloucester, MA 01930. The Yankee Fleet carries naturalists from the Atlantic Cetacean Research Center. Boats leave from the dock next to the Gull Restaurant on MA 133 (MA 128 exit 14).

Seven Seas Whale Watch
(☎ 508-283-1776, 800-238-1776), Rogers St (MA 127), Gloucester, MA 01930. Seven Seas vessels serve alcoholic beverages, and depart from Rogers St in the center of Gloucester, between St Peter's Square and the Gloucester House Restaurant. The cruises are narrated by naturalists from the Marine Education Center of Cape Ann.

Special Events

Gloucester's St Peter's Festival on a weekend in late June brings a carnival to St Peter's Square with rides, snacks, musical performances and special events such as a greased pole climbing competition and boat races. The main event is the procession through the streets of a statue of St Peter, patron saint of fishermen. The cardinal of the Catholic Archdiocese of Boston customarily attends to bless the fishing fleet.

Gloucester's 4th of July parade takes place on the evening of July 3, and is called the Fishtown Horribles Parade. By tradition, children dress up in fanciful costumes (from horrible to humorous) and march, hoping to win a prize for the best. Politicians and local businesses enter floats, and various bands perform.

The New Whalers

A century and a half ago, many New England mariners made their livings – if not their fortunes – hunting the great mammals of the sea. With the discovery of petroleum and natural gas, the importance of whale oil faded away, and with it New England's whaling business.

(Whaling is still a business, of course. As of this writing, Japan and Norway both have active whaling programs even though the hunting of whales is condemned by most other nations. A kilo of whale meat can be worth up to $400 at retail in Tokyo.)

The great whales still produce income for New England mariners, too, but they don't give their lives to do it. Whale-watching cruises are very popular.

Vessels The typical whale-watch vessel is a steel-hulled, diesel-powered boat of 80 to 100 feet in length. Boats are equipped with snack bars, toilets, indoor and outdoor seating areas and full safety equipment. Sonar helps track the schools of fish which often indicate where the whales will be feeding that day. A naturalist accompanies the cruise to provide full information on the species of whales, their habits and even in some cases their "names," as many of the whales are "regulars" known to the crews.

Schedules The typical cruise is a four- or five-hour voyage departing at breakfast-time, mid-morning or just after lunch. Cruises run from late April to late October. From late June through early September many boats make two cruises daily.

Preparations To prepare for your cruise, call ahead and confirm departure times and ticket prices. Ask about maritime conditions: if it's been stormy in the past few days, the seas may still be rough, which means most landlubbers will suffer from seasickness.

Take a warm sweater and/or jacket (a lined windbreaker is perfect) as it will be considerably cooler out on the windy ocean, particularly on morning cruises, even on warm days. Wear rubber-soled shoes.

Sunglasses and sunscreen or sunblock are also necessary, as you will be exposed to direct sunlight as well as the harsh light reflected off the water.

Take your camera and perhaps binoculars. Though not all whale sightings are photogenic, you may be in luck and should be prepared.

Places to Stay

Camping *Camp Annisquam Campground* (☎ 508-283-2992), Stanwood Point, West Gloucester, has 35 tent and trailer sites going for $16 in high summer. *Cape Ann Campsite* (☎ 508-283-8683), 80 Atlantic St, Gloucester, has 300 sites priced at $15, or $18 with hookups.

Hotels & Motels *Anchorage Inn* (☎ 508-283-4788), 5-7 Hawthorne Lane, East Gloucester, MA 01930, is two new buildings in traditional style in a great location: close to Rocky Neck, walking distance to the beach and quietly off of E Main St. Many rooms ($50 to $95) have balconies with harbor views; the most expensive have kitchenettes.

Follow Eastern Point Ave until it becomes Atlantic Rd to find several sea-view motels. Most of these have a large old mansion as the office and dining room, with guest rooms (priced from $65 to $155) built into new motel-type units facing the sea. Prices depend on the size of the room, number of beds, other facilities and views. Most of these motels close from December through March.

There's the *Ocean View Inn* (☎ 508-283-6200, 800-315-7557), 171 Atlantic Rd; the *Atlantis Motor Inn* (☎ 508-283-0014), 125 Atlantic Rd; the *Bass Rocks Ocean Inn* (☎ 508-283-7600, 800-528-1234), 103 Atlantic Rd and the *Back Shore Motor Lodge* (☎ 508-283-1198), 85 Atlantic Rd.

There's also *Gray Manor Tourist Home* (☎ 508-283-5409), 14 Atlantic Rd, not a motel, but rather a large old house which has nine guest rooms with private baths.

Non-alcoholic beverages, snacks and sometimes even light meals are available on board. Only a few boats sell alcoholic beverages or allow them to be served. If the sea is not dead calm, and if you are not an experienced mariner, forget the booze.

Seasickness Prevention If possible, carry capsules of powdered ginger (from a health-food store), and take one or two before departure. Ginger helps to settle the stomach on rocky voyages. There are also anti-seasickness drugs such as Dramamine (ask your doctor or pharmacist). Bring paper napkins and a plastic bag in case these don't work.

If you feel queasy, sit outside, breathe the sea air deeply and look at land or the horizon until the feeling passes. Don't read on a rocking boat (even this guidebook) for long periods, as that is the short, fast route to nausea.

Sightings Your boat motors out to sea for about an hour to where the whales customarily hunt for food, perhaps at the National Marine Sanctuary of Stellwagen Bank. It will then cruise slowly for about two hours looking for whales. Most boats have enviable records, sighting whales over 99% of the time, not to mention sea birds, dolphins and seals. If your cruise fails to sight a whale, the company usually gives you a pass good for another cruise.

The **humpback** whales are baleen (filter-feeding) whales of up to 50 feet in length and weigh 30 tons, with flippers up to 15 feet long. They're the ones most sought because they're big, playful and they tend to "breach" (leap out of the water).

The **finbacks** or fin whales, more slender, longer (up to 70 feet) and heavier (up to 50 tons), are second only to the great blue whales in size. They don't breach, but roll and spout in the water.

The **minke** (MINK-kee) whales are smaller (23 to 28 feet in length) and lighter and do not breach, but roll on the surface.

You might also see **Atlantic white-sided dolphins**, eight or nine feet in length, which have teeth rather than baleen and feed on fish and squid. The dolphins love to leap in the air and sport in boat wakes.

For more details on whales, you can contact the Cetacean Research Unit, Inc (☎ 508-281-6351), PO Box 159, Gloucester, MA 01930. ■

MASSACHUSETTS

Places to Eat

Downtown Gloucester For a snack, grab a slab of pizza ($1) and some cookies at *Virgilio's Italian Bakery* (☎ 508-283-5295), 29 Main St. This is also a good place for picnic supplies. Across the street, *Valentino's* (☎ 508-283-6186), 38 Main St at Short St, serves whole pizzas for $11 to $16. *Mike's Pastry & Coffee Shop* (☎ 508-283-5333), 37 Main St, has excellent Italian pastries and, in summer, cooling lemon ice. *Café Sicilia* (☎ 508-283-7345), 40 Main St at Short St, has Italian pastries and also good, strong espresso.

Halibut Point Restaurant & Pub (☎ 508-281-1900), 289 Main St, is an authentic Gloucester tavern with good food and drink at reasonable prices. Patronized mostly by locals, it serves sandwiches and burgers ($3 to $5), lunch and dinner plates ($6 to $13) in cozy, congenial surroundings.

Captain Carlo's Seafoods (☎ 508-283-6342), right on the water on the street called Harbor Loop, is a seafood market with some picnic tables inside and on a seaside deck. Seafood salads, cakes and fried fish are fresh and low-priced from $3.25 to $7.50. The huge fisherman's platter goes for $11.

The *Imperial Marina* (☎ 508-281-6573), 17 Rogers St near the water and the center of town, serves Cantonese and Szechuan cuisine. Most dinner plates are priced from $7.50 to $13.

Jalapeño's (☎ 508-283-8228), 86 Main St, has more authentic, tasty food at inland prices: pollo con mole for $7.50 at lunch ($11 at dinner). Have a cactus salad followed by the shrimp chipotle (a spicy sauce) for $13.50.

The Gull (☎ 508-281-6060), 75 Essex Ave (MA 133), is a bit out of the way in West Gloucester, but it's worth the trip. It's a bright, upbeat place with large windows overlooking a busy marina. Seafood is the strong point, from excellent lobster rolls ($8) to grilled tuna and swordfish steaks and clambakes ($12 to $22). There's a bar popular with locals.

Barish's (☎ 508-281-1911), a cozy storefront restaurant at 110 Main St, serves seafood dinners (summer only, Tuesday to Saturday from 5:30 pm) with a Mediterranean inspiration. Have the fish Languedoc style, or a crespelle (Italian crêpe) stuffed with seafood. Also have reservations, as the simple but semi-formal dining room fills up early.

Best in town is *The Bistro* (☎ 508-281-8055), 2 Main St at the corner of Washington St, downstairs in the historic Blackburn Tavern. Besides the inevitable (and delicious) seafood, they have interesting dishes like tea-smoked duck, Moroccan lemon chicken and roasted ocean catfish paella. Dinner, the only meal served (5:30 pm on, Tuesday to Sunday), costs $30 to $40.

There's also the *White Rainbow* (☎ 508-281-0017), 65 Main St, serving dinner every day in a cozy brick-lined basement dining room. The menu lists the classic main courses – steak, roast duckling, grilled shrimp – but the appetizers are more adventurous. I like the half wheel of brie baked with lobster meat, and the sautéed soft shell crab. Dinner costs $35 to $40.

Rocky Neck Parking is tight on E Main St and Rocky Neck Ave, so allow a bit of time to find a place.

On the way to Rocky Neck, the *Square Café* (☎ 281-3951), 197 E Main St, is a hip artists' neighborhood bistro right at the turn for the North Shore Arts Association headquarters. Cool music thrums as you dine ($15 to $22) on penne (the "in" pasta these days), quesadillas and artful treatments of chicken and lamb.

The Studio (☎ 283-4123), 51 Rocky Neck Ave, is great for lunch or a light dinner or drink on the deck overlooking the harbor. It's the epicenter of the Rocky Neck dating scene, with a young crowd and a good band. Almost everything on the menu is under $10, and though the drinks are expensive, the view and ambiance are worth it.

Just down the street is *The Rudder* (☎ 508-283-7967), 73 Rocky Neck Ave, known to locals as Evie's. Evie herself, who founded the place four decades ago, shows up nightly around 10 pm to engage in hilarious antics with her colleagues (the menu calls it "spontaneous entertainment"). If you want one of the few tables on the seaside deck, request it when you make your dinner reservation (a good idea on weekends). The simplest dishes are the best choices here. Expect to spend $20 to $35 per person for a full dinner with drinks.

Entertainment

The *Gloucester Stage Company* (☎ 508-281-4099), 267 E Main St, stages excellent small-theater productions of classics, modern works and new plays by acclaimed playwright Israel Horovitz during the summer months. Call for current offerings.

Numerous restaurants and cafes have live entertainment, including the *Rhumb Line* (☎ 508-283-9732), 40 Railroad Ave across from the Gloucester train station; *Dockside* (☎ 508-281-4554), 77 Rocky Neck Ave in East Gloucester and *Cameron's* (☎ 508-281-1331), 206 Main St.

Getting There & Away

Train The MBTA Commuter Rail trains (☎ 508-283-7916, 800-392-6099) stop in West Gloucester off Essex Ave, and in Gloucester on Railroad Ave.

One-way fares from Boston are $3.50 to Manchester-By-The-Sea, $3.75 to Gloucester and $4 to Rockport. Tickets are on sale in Gloucester at the Railroad Variety Store, on Railroad Ave at Prospect St.

Car Driving details for Gloucester are:

Destination	Mileage	Hr:Min
Boston, MA	33 miles	0:50
Portsmouth, NH	50 miles	1:00
Rockport, MA	7 miles	0:15
Salem, MA	16 miles	0:30

Boat There's boat service (☎ 508-283-5110) between Gloucester and Province-town on Cape Cod on Friday, Sunday and Monday from late June through early September. The boat departs Rose's Wharf, 415 Main St, east of the town center, at 9 am, arriving in P-town at 11:30 am. The return trip departs P-town at 3:30 pm, arriving back in Gloucester at 6 pm. Roundtrip tickets cost $33 adults, $28 seniors (60+)

and $16 for kids eight to 15; kids under eight ride free. One-way tickets cost 33% less than roundtrip. You may go Friday and return Sunday. Call for reservations.

AC Cruise Line (☎ 617-261-6633) sails the *Virginia C* from Boston to Gloucester daily in summer. Departure from Boston is at 10 am, arriving in Smith Cove at Rocky Neck (The Studio Restaurant) at 12:30 pm. The return departure from Rocky Neck is at 3pm, arriving back in Boston at 5 pm. One-way tickets cost $12 for adults, $11 for seniors, and $7 for children under 12, or $18, $14, $10 roundtrip. Call for reservations.

ROCKPORT

In the 19th century, Rockport was just that: a sheltered harbor town from which granite blocks were shipped to construction sites up and down the Atlantic coast, and even across the ocean to Europe, often as ship's ballast. Cut at a half-dozen quarries just west of the Rockport Granite Quarry Wharf, the stone was also the favored local building material, and monuments, curbstones, building foundations, pavements and piers all remain as a testament to Rockport's past. The town's several granite buildings are particularly handsome, and sturdy to a fault.

A century ago, Winslow Homer, Childe Hassam, Fitz Hugh Lane and other acclaimed artists came to picturesque Rockport. They painted the hearty fisherfolk who wrested a hard but satisfying living from the fruits of the sea.

The artists told their friends about this pretty town, and those friends told other friends, and today Rockport makes its living from tourists who come to look at the artists. The artists have long since given up looking for hearty fishers because the descendants of the fishers are all running boutiques and B&Bs.

But Rockport is now even prettier and, if anything, more visually appealing than a century ago. In summer it's mobbed with day-trippers. It's got beaches, boutiques, nice walks and drives and a festive air about it. And there are still even some artists.

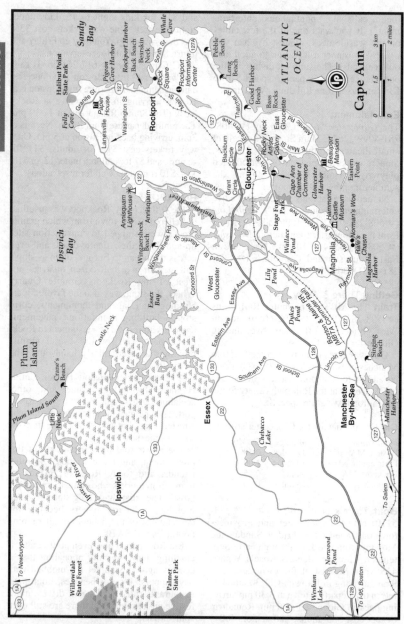

Orientation

The center of town is Dock Square at the beginning of Bearskin Neck. Most everything is within a 10-minute walk of it. The railroad station is less than a 15-minute walk west of Dock Square.

Parking is very difficult on summer weekends. Unless you get here in time for breakfast, you'd do well to park at one of the lots on MA 127 from Gloucester and take the shuttle bus to the center. The few lots in town charge $6 per day, but fill early. Meters (25¢ an hour) are policed vigorously every day; if you overstay your meter it'll cost you $10. Observe the parking regulation signs everywhere, scrupulously.

Information

The Rockport Chamber of Commerce (☎ 508-546-6575, fax 546-5997), PO Box 67, Rockport, MA 01966, has an information office on MA 127 as you enter Rockport from Gloucester, and another in the town center on Pier Ave, just off Main St up from Dock Square. Both are open Monday to Saturday 9 am to 5 pm.

Walking Tours

Rockport is a wandering town. Start at Dock Square and flow with the crowds along Bearskin Neck, window shopping, stopping for coffee, ice cream or a snack and finally emerging at the Breakwater, which overlooks Rockport Harbor to the south and Sandy Bay to the west.

The red fishing shack decorated with colorful buoys is *Motif No 1*. So many artists of great and minimal talent have been painting and photographing it for so long that it well deserves its tongue-in-cheek name. Actually, it should be called Motif No 1-B as the original shack was destroyed by a great storm in 1978 and a brand-new replica erected in its place.

Follow Main St west and north from Dock Square to reach Back Beach on Sandy Bay, which is the nearest beach to the town center.

About a mile north of Dock Square on the water, Wharf Rd heads west out the Rockport Granite Company Wharf, a granite pier from which there are panoramic views of the pretty town and Sandy Bay.

Pigeon Cove, a neighborhood about two miles north of Dock Square, has been preserved as a working fishing and lobsterboat harbor after escaping modern development as a site for luxury condominiums.

For excellent views of the town and the sea, walk southeast from Dock Square along Mt Pleasant St, then east along Atlantic or Heywood Aves to the public footpath marked as the "Way to the Headlands." The walk from Dock Square takes only 10 or 15 minutes and you'll be rewarded with the view.

Halibut Point State Park

Only a few miles north of Dock Square along MA 127, just northeast of the Old Farm Inn, is Halibut Point State Park (☎ 508-546-2997), open daily, for a fee of $2 per person or $5 per carload. A 10-minute walk through the forest brings you to yawning, abandoned granite quarries, huge hills of broken granite rubble and a granite foreshore of tumbled, smoothed rock perfect for picnicking, sunbathing, reading or painting. The surf can be strong here, making swimming unwise, but natural pools can be good for wading or cooling your feet.

Park rangers lead nature walks, explaining the marine life in tidal pools, the working of granite quarries, the local bird life and the area's edible plants. Call for current programs.

Paper House

Inland from Pigeon Cove on Pigeon Hill St is the Paper House, a curiosity begun in 1922 when Mr Elis F Stenman decided something useful should be done with all those daily newspapers lying about. He and his family set to work, folding, rolling and pasting the papers into suitable shape as building materials.

Twenty years and 100,000 newspapers later, the house was done. The walls are 215 layers thick, the furnishings – table, chairs, lamps, sofa, even a grandfather clock and a piano – are all made of newspapers. Some pieces even specialize: one desk is made from reports of Colonel Lindbergh's flight in the *Christian Science Monitor*, the fireplace mantel from rotogravures from the *Boston Sunday Herald* and the *New York Herald Tribune*. On all of the papers, text is still readable.

Cruises

Rockport Schooner Company's *Appledore III* (☎ 508-546-9876), is a 56-foot two-masted schooner built in 1984 which has circumnavigated the globe, and now, in early retirement, takes passengers on 1½-hour sailing cruises of the bay five times daily ($20, kids under 10 half price). The sunset cruise from 7 to 8:30 pm is a favorite. Reserve in advance, then buy your tickets at least half an hour before sailing. Beer is sold on board.

Places to Stay

Rockport has many small inns and B&Bs, and a few motels, almost all of them within an easy walk of Dock Square. Many require two-night minimum stays on weekends (three nights on holiday weekends), some do not accept children under 12, and virtually all are nonsmoking and include at least a light breakfast in the room price.

Motels *Captain's Bounty Motor Inn* (☎ 508-546-9557), 1 Beach St, is right on the beach and only a few minutes' stroll from Dock Square. Its prime location allows it to set rates at $95 to $105 in high summer, without breakfast.

Sandy Bay Motor Inn (☎ 508-546-7155, 800-437-7155), 173 Main St, is a modern motel with a restaurant and enclosed swimming pool less than two miles inland along Main St (MA 127). In summer, rooms cost $92 to $162 without breakfast.

Inns & B&Bs The Victorian *Linden Tree Inn* (☎ 508-546-2494), 26 King St, has a variety of double rooms (18 of them) for $85 to $100; there's one small single that rents for a low $65 as well. Check out the view from the cupola.

Lantana House (☎ 508-546-3535), 22 Broadway, has some of the least expensive rooms in Rockport: double or twin-bed rooms for $65 to $80. Some have kitchenettes and air-con.

Rockport Lodge (☎ 508-546-2090), 61 South St, is a special lodging for women only. Founded in 1906 by the National League of Working Women, it was meant to be a place where women of low or moderate incomes could find a restful vacation from the drudgery of factory labor at affordable prices. It continues to fulfill that mission, offering bed and three meals for $32 to $36 per day on weekdays, $80 for a two-night weekend, to women with annual incomes under $25,000; over that amount a small supplement is payable. Weekly rates are equally reasonable. Linens are provided, but you bring your own towels and soap and tidy up your own room.

Carlson's B&B (☎ 508-546-2770), 43 Broadway, the Victorian home of a prominent local artist, rents double rooms with private bath, private entrance, garage parking and full breakfast for $75.

Sally Webster Inn (☎ 508-546-9251), 34 Mt Pleasant St, is a brick Colonial offering both smoking and nonsmoking rooms for $70 to $100, full breakfast included.

The lovely Greek Revival *Addison Choate Inn* (☎ 508-546-7543, 800-245-7543), 49 Broadway, is among the more charming and historic inns, with a swimming pool and a variety of rooms and suites priced from $85 to $110.

Tuck Inn (☎ 508-546-7260), 17 High St, has nine comfortable rooms priced from $70 to $90, with a four-person suite which goes for $110.

The Inn on Cove Hill (☎ 508-546-2701), 37 Mt Pleasant St, is an early American house (1791) built, so they say, with pirates' gold discovered nearby. Their double rooms, furnished in Federal style with canopy beds, are priced at $53 with shared bath, $68 to $105 with private bath.

The Victorian *Pleasant Street Inn* (☎ 508-546-3915, 800-541-3915), has a hilltop location only a few blocks from the center. All of its rooms have private bath, and are priced from $80 to $100, double.

Old Farm Inn (☎ 508-546-3237), 291 Granite St (MA 127), is a few miles north-east of Dock Square. Built in 1702, it was the original farmhouse for Captain Wood-bury's estate, which encompassed much of the northern tip of Cape Ann. Rooms with buffet breakfast cost $85 to $120 double. It's only a few hundred feet to Halibut Point State Park.

Places to Eat

Remember that Rockport is dry, with no alcohol for sale at all. You can buy bottles in Gloucester or Lanesville, and most restaurants (but not fast-food places) will open and serve them for a corkage fee of about $1.50 per person. Lanesville Package Store, on MA 127 in Lanesville four miles from central Rockport, is open from 8 am to 10 pm (10:30 pm on Friday and Saturday, closed Sunday). In high summer, make reservations for dinner in the better restaurants.

Dock Square, at the beginning of Bearskin Neck, has several good cafes. *Dock Square Coffee & Tea House* (☎ 508-546-2525) is the town's fancy coffee pur-veyor, with excellent brew elaborately concocted and sold for 95¢ to $4 a cup. There are a few outdoor tables.

Rockport Bagel Company (☎ 508-546-6400), 4 Main St, just a few steps uphill from Dock Square, is good for bagels (75¢ to $1.50) and bagel sandwiches ($4), and good Green Mountain coffee from 7 am to 10 pm every day.

Bearskin Neck is crowded with ice cream shops, cafes and eateries. As you walk out you'll pass several places good for a bowl of chowder, fish and chips, cheap lobster or a full and semi-elegant tuck-in.

Arnie's Eatery (☎ 508-546-6900), 28 Bearskin Neck, is a fast-food place serving hot dogs for $2.25 to $3, clam chowder for $4 and fish and chips for $6. There's more seating upstairs, and it's air-con cool in summer.

A bit farther along on the opposite side is the *Roy Moore Lobster Company* (☎ 508-

546-6696), with the cheapest lobster on the 'Neck: as low as $6.50 for a 1¼-pound beast in high summer. With it you get a tray, melted butter, a fork and an wet wipe for cleanup. Claws and shell are pre-cracked for convenience.

Right next door is *Lobster in the Ruff*, which has fairly low prices given its upstairs water-view dining room.

Off to the left (south) on a side street is the *Portside Chowder House* (☎ 508-546-7045), a tiny place specializing in chow-ders, sandwiches and pies. Because there's almost no water view and quarters are cramped (but cozy), prices are low, with a good bowl of clam chowder for only $3. The corn chowder ($2.65) is equally good, and vegetarian.

For a full-fledged restaurant, the *Hannah Jumper* (☎ 508-546-3600), on Tuna Wharf has a long menu and water views from every table. Light meals like soup and sandwich compete with heavy eats like prime rib of beef. A trip to the varied salad bar costs $5.50, with one refill for free. The drinks list (all non-alcoholic, of course) is long and interesting.

My favorite Rockport restaurant is *My Place By the Sea* (☎ 508-546-9667), 68 Bearskin Neck, right out at the end. The location is the best in Rockport, with panoramic views of the bay, indoor and outdoor seating, excellent service and a concise, interesting menu. It's open for lunch (about $8 to $12) and dinner ($25 to $40); have reservations for dinner in high summer.

For coffee or tea and dessert, try *Hel-mut's Strudel*, almost near the outer end, serving various strudels, filled croissants, pastries, cider and coffee. Four shaded tables overlook the yacht-filled harbor.

Getting There & Away

Train Rockport is the terminus for MBTA Commuter Rail trains (☎ 617-722-3200, 800-392-6100) on the Rockport/Ipswich line. The trip from Boston takes about 75 minutes and costs $4 for adults. Trains leave North Station at least every two hours (usually at 15 minutes past the hour) throughout the day.

Car If you're driving, MA 127 makes two loops around Cape Ann, both passing through Rockport. Driving details for Rockport are:

Destination	Mileage	Hr:Min
Boston, MA	40 miles	1:00
Gloucester, MA	7 miles	0:15
Portsmouth, NH	57 miles	1:10
Salem, MA	23 miles	0:40

Getting Around

The Cape Ann Transportation Authority (☎ 508-283-7916) operates bus routes among the towns of Cape Ann. On Saturday, Sunday and holidays from early June through mid-September, its Saltwater Trolleys make nine runs per day on a route connecting Essex, Gloucester, Rockport and their outlying areas. For $4 for adults, $2 seniors and kids five to 12, you can hop on and off anywhere along the route.

MICHELLE GAGNÉ

Chief Massasoit stands above Plymouth Rock.

South Shore

PLYMOUTH

Historic Plymouth, "America's Home Town," is synonymous with Plymouth Rock. Thousands of visitors come here each year to look at this weathered ball of granite, and to consider what it was like for the Pilgrims who stepped ashore in this strange land in the autumn of 1620, seeking a place in which they could practice their religion as they wished without interference from government.

You can see all there is to see of Plymouth Rock in a minute. But the rock is just a symbol of the Pilgrim's struggle, sacrifice and triumph, which is elucidated in many museums and exhibits nearby.

Orientation & Information

"The rock," on the waterfront, is on Water St at the center of Plymouth, within walking distance of most museums and restaurants. Main St, the main commercial street, is a block inland. Some lodgings are within walking distance, others require a car.

The Town of Plymouth's Visitor Information Center (☎ 508-830-1620), 225 Water St, Plymouth, MA 02360, is half a mile north of Plymouth Rock in the old Ocean Spray building next to Cranberry World.

The Regional Information Complex (☎ 508-746-1150) on MA 3 (exit 5), has information on many places in the region besides Plymouth. Look for special discount lodging coupons in the brochure racks.

Plymouth Rock

Though the Pilgrims came from England, Plymouth Rock came from Pangaea, the gigantic continent which split in two to form Europe and Africa on the eastern side and North and South America on the western side, leaving the Atlantic Ocean in between. The boulder is of Dedham granite, a rock some 680 million years old. Most of the Dedham granite went to Africa when Pangaea split; bits were left in the Atlantica terrane, the geologic area around

Boston. About 20,000 years ago, a glacier picked up Plymouth Rock, carried it and dropped it here.

We don't really know that the Pilgrims actually landed on Plymouth Rock; it's not mentioned in any early written accounts. But the colonial news media picked up the story and soon the rock was in jeopardy from its adoring fans. In 1774, 20 yoke of oxen were harnessed to the rock to move it, and split it in the process. Half of the cloven boulder went on display in Pilgrim Hall from 1834 to 1867, the sea and wind lashed at the other half, and innumerable small pieces were chipped off and carried away by thoughtless souvenir hunters over the centuries.

By the 20th century, the rock was an endangered souvenir, and steps were taken to protect it. In 1921 the reunited halves were sheltered in the present granite enclosure designed by McKim, Mead & White. In 1989 the rock was repaired and strengthened to withstand weathering.

Plymouth Rock – relatively small, broken and mended, with the date "1620" cut into it – is a symbol of the quest for religious freedom. It's open to view all the time, for free.

Mayflower II

If Plymouth Rock tells us little about the Pilgrims, *Mayflower II* (☎ 508-746-1622), a replica of the small ship in which they made their fateful voyage, speaks volumes.

As you enter, you'll think it impossible that 102 people with all the household effects, tools, provisions, animals and seed to establish a colony could have lived together on this tiny vessel for 66 days, subsisting on hard, moldy biscuits, rancid butter and brackish water, as it passed through the stormy north Atlantic. But they did, landing on this wild, forested shore in the frigid December of 1620 – eloquent testimony to their courage, spirit and the strength of their religious beliefs.

Mayflower II, moored at the State Pier only a minute's walk north of Plymouth Rock, was built in England in 1955 and sailed across the Atlantic to Plymouth in

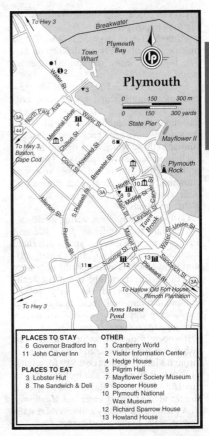

MASSACHUSETTS

PLACES TO STAY
6 Governor Bradford Inn
11 John Carver Inn

PLACES TO EAT
3 Lobster Hut
8 The Sandwich & Deli

OTHER
1 Cranberry World
2 Visitor Information Center
4 Hedge House
5 Pilgrim Hall
7 Mayflower Society Museum
9 Spooner House
10 Plymouth National
    Wax Museum
12 Richard Sparrow House
13 Howland House

1957. The ship is open to visitors from 9 am to 5 pm (until 7 pm in July and August); closed December through March. Admission costs $6 for adults, $4 for kids under 12; discounted combination tickets at $19 and $11 permit entrance to Plimoth Plantation as well.

Plimoth Plantation

During the winter of 1620-21, half of the Pilgrims died of disease, privation and exposure to the elements. But the survivors were joined by new arrivals in 1621, and by 1627, just before another influx of Pilgrims founded the colony of Massachusetts Bay,

Plymouth colony was sturdily built and on the road to prosperity.

Plimoth Plantation (☎ 508-746-1622), a mile or so south of Plymouth Rock on MA 3A, is an authentic recreation of settlements from 1627.

Everything in the 1627 Pilgrim Village – costumes, implements, vocabulary, artisanry, recipes and crops – has been painstakingly researched and remade. Even the animals have been back-bred to be very similar to those which the Pilgrims had.

Hobbamock's (Wampanoag) Homesite replicates the life of a Native American community in this area at the same time: their crafts, costumes and huts made of wattle and daub.

Costumed interpreters, acting in character, explain the details of daily life and answer your questions as you watch them work and play. In the Crafts Center, artisans weave baskets and cloth, throw pottery and build fine furniture using the techniques and tools of the early 1600s. Exhibits explain how these manufactured goods were shipped across the Atlantic in exchange for colonial necessities.

It's open from 9 am to 5 pm (until 7 pm in July and August), closed from December through March. Tickets cost $19 for adults, $11 for kids five to 12, and include entry to the 1627 Pilgrim Village, Hobbamock's Homesite, the Crafts Center and *Mayflower II*. A picnic area, bakery and several restaurants provide modern sustenance.

Pilgrim Hall

This museum (☎ 508-746-1620), 75 Court St at Chilton St, boasts that it is the oldest continually-operating public museum in the USA, having been built in 1824. Its exhibits are not reproductions, but the real things the Pilgrims and their Wampanoag neighbors used in their daily lives, right down to Miles Standish's sword. Monumental paintings in the museum's collection depict scenes of Pilgrim life.

Pilgrim Hall is open from 9:30 am to 4:30 pm, closed in January and on Christmas. Admission costs $5 for adults, $4.50 seniors, $2 for kids six to 15.

Plymouth National Wax Museum

This museum (☎ 508-746-6468), 16 Carver St, across the street and up the hill from Plymouth Rock, is a good place to show children scenes of Pilgrim history. The life-sized wax figures – 180 in 26 scenes – recount the progress of the Pilgrims as they left England for Holland, then set sail for, and arrived in, America. The museum is open from 9 am to 5 pm (until 9 pm in July and August), closed from December through February. Admission costs $5 for adults, $4 seniors, $2 kids five to 12.

Historic Houses

As New England's oldest European community, Plymouth has its share of fine old houses, some very old indeed.

The **Richard Sparrow House** (☎ 508-746-1240), 42 Summer St, the oldest house in Plymouth, was built by one of the original Pilgrim settlers in 1640. It's open from 10 am to 5 pm (closed Wednesday), for $1.

The **Howland House** (☎ 508-746-9590), 33 Sandwich St, built in 1667, began as the residence for a family that had come over on the *Mayflower*. You can take a tour between 10 am and 4:30 pm, from late May to October, for $2.50 for adults, $2 seniors and college students and 50¢ kids six to 12.

The **Mayflower Society Museum** (☎ 508-746-2590), 4 Winslow St, dates from 1754, and shows how wealthy a town Plymouth had become in a little over a century. Note especially the house's flying staircase. Visit any day from July to early September from 10 am to 4 pm; in June, and from early September through mid-October, Friday through Sunday at the same hours.

The Plymouth Antiquarian Society (☎ 508-746-0012) maintains three historic houses and staffs them with costumed interpreters who can tell you all about Pilgrim life. The houses span a century and a half of Plymouth architectural history:

The **Harlow Old Fort House** (1677), 119 Sandwich St, shows you how the second generation of Plymouth colonists lived. **Spooner House** (1747), 27 North St, was occupied by the same family for more than two centuries, which accounts in part for its very rich collection of period furnishings. **Hedge House** (1809), 126 Water St, is in the Federal style.

Cranberry World

Soon after the Pilgrims arrived, they discovered the tart red berries which filled the sandy bogs near Plymouth and south to Cape Cod. Cranberries made it onto that first Thanksgiving menu, and have been there ever since. You can learn all about the sour but appealing and healthful fruit at Cranberry World (☎ 508-747-2350), 225 Water St, north of the town wharf on the waterfront. It's open daily May through November from 9:30 am to 5 pm. Admission is free, as are sample cranberry refreshments.

Places to Stay

Camping The nearest state facility is *Myles Standish State Forest* (☎ 508-866-2526), about 16 miles due south of Plymouth; take MA 3 exit 5, or MA 58 to Carver. There are 16 miles of bike trails, hiking trails, nine ponds (two with beaches and bathhouses) and 475 campsites priced at $6 per site, $8 with electricity.

Wompatuck State Park (☎ 617-749-7160), off MA 228 in Hingham, is 25 miles north of Plymouth. The 2900-acre park has six miles of bike trails, hiking trails and 400 campsites priced at $6 per site, $8 with electricity.

The private campgrounds in the area charge about twice the fees of the state parks and forests. *Pinewood Lodge Campground* (☎ 508-746-3548), 190 Pinewood Rd (US 44) in Plymouth, is among the closest to the town center.

Sandy Pond Campground (☎ 508-759-9336), 834 Bourne Rd, has 30 sites with electricity and sewer connections, 80 with electricity only, two sand beaches and hiking trails.

Plymouth Rock KOA Kampground (☎ 508-947-6435), on US 44 in Middleboro, is farther away.

Motels *Governor Bradford Inn* (☎ 508-746-6200, 800-332-1620, fax 747-3032),

98 Water St, is convenient and charges $89 to $124 for its double rooms; those with sea views are the more expensive ones.

John Carver Inn (☎ 508-746-7100, 800-274-1620, fax 746-8299), 25 Summer St, has three categories of rooms, smoking and nonsmoking, ranging from $79 to $99 in summer, a bit higher during foliage season.

Pilgrim Sands Motel (☎ 508-747-0900, 800-729-7263, fax 746-8066), 150 Warren Ave, only about a half-mile south of Plimoth Plantation, charges $53 to $90 for its rooms in summer.

Places to Eat

Fast-food shops line Water St opposite the *Mayflower II*. For better food at lower prices, walk a block inland to Main St, the attractive thoroughfare of Plymouth's business district.

The Sandwich & Deli, 65 Main St at North St; has clam chowder, bacon, lettuce and tomato sandwiches for $2.50; huge reuben and pastrami sandwiches for $3.50 and many other quick-lunch plates priced in between.

For a meal with a view of the sea, try the *Lobster Hut* (☎ 508-746-2270), on the town wharf five short blocks north of *Mayflower II*. Big plates of fried clams and fish and chips are priced below $10. Seating is both indoors and out.

Getting There & Away

Bus Plymouth & Brockton buses (☎ 508-746-0378) connect Boston and Logan airport with Plymouth (1 to 1¼ hours) and Hyannis (45 minutes), running over a dozen buses daily in summer. The P&B terminal is in North Plymouth's Industrial Park off MA 3 at exit 7, but buses stop in the center of Plymouth as well.

Car Driving details for Plymouth are:

Destination	Mileage	Hr:Min
Boston, MA	41 miles	0:55
Hartford, CT	141 miles	3:00
Hyannis, MA	37 miles	0:50
New York, NY	205 miles	4:00
Providence, RI	39 miles	0:50
Provincetown, MA	83 miles	1:50

NEW BEDFORD

During its heyday as a whaling port from 1765-1860, New Bedford commanded as many as 400 whaling ships. This vast fleet brought home hundreds of thousands of barrels of whale oil to light America's lamps. So famous was the town's whaling industry that Herman Melville set his great American novel, *Moby-Dick; or, The Whale* in New Bedford. (At the time, he lived in Pittsfield, MA.) If you're interested in whaling history, this is the place to find it.

When whale oil was supplanted by petroleum and electricity for light, New Bedford turned to fishing, scalloping and textile production for its wealth. In the early 20th century, the textile industry headed south, then offshore, in search of cheaper labor, and in recent years New England's Atlantic fishing grounds have been exploited to near extinction, so New Bedford is again in search of a source of wealth.

Orientation

The center of town is the restored historic district around Melville Mall, about a mile south of I-195 via MA 18 (take the Downtown exit).

Information

The New Bedford Visitors Center (☎ 508-991-6200, 800-508-5353), 47 N 2nd St, New Bedford, MA 02740, is on Melville Mall. It's open from 10 am to 4 pm (Sunday noon to 3 pm). They'll help find you a room for the night. Walking tours depart the center daily at 9:30 and 11:30 am and 3 pm; on Sunday there's only one tour, at noon.

Mid-July brings the Whaling City Festival; for more information on this and other special events contact the New Bedford Area Chamber of Commerce (☎ 508-999-5231), 794 Purchase St, PO Box 8827, New Bedford, MA 02742.

Whaling Museum

The New Bedford Whaling Museum (☎ 508-997-0046), 18 Johnny Cake Hill, actually includes seven buildings situated between William and Union Sts. To learn what whaling was all about, you need only tramp the decks of the *Lagoda*, a fully rigged, exact-half-size replica of an actual whaling bark. The onboard tryworks was where huge chunks of whale blubber were rendered to release the valuable oil. Old photographs, and a 22-minute video of an actual whale chase, bring this historic period to life.

Don't miss the 100-foot-long mural depicting sperm whales, and also the exhibits of delicate scrimshaw, the carving of whalebone into jewelry, notions and beautiful household items.

The museum is open daily from 9 am to 5 pm (Sunday 1 to 5 pm, but in July and August 11 am to 5 pm). Admission costs $4.50 for adults, $3.50 seniors, $3 for childen six to 14.

Seamen's Bethel

This small chapel (☎ 508-992-3295), on Johnny Cake Hill across from the Whaling Museum, was a refuge for sailors from the rigors and stresses of the maritime life. Melville, who himself suffered under terrible conditions on a whaling ship, immortalized it in *Moby-Dick*. You can visit for free (donations accepted) from May through mid-October from 10 am to 4 pm (Sunday noon to 4 pm).

New Bedford Fire Museum

Antique fire trucks and fire-fighting equipment fill this museum (☎ 508-992-2162) in a century-old building right next to a working New Bedford fire station on Bedford St at 6th St. Kids love the old trucks, uniforms, pumps and fire poles, all on display from 9 am to 3:30 pm in summer; shorter hours in winter. Admission costs $2 for adults, $1 kids six to 16.

Rotch-Jones-Duff House & Garden

New Bedford's grandest historic house (☎ 508-997-1401), 396 County Rd, was designed in Greek Revival style in 1834 by Richard Upjohn (1802-1878), first president of the American Institute of Architects. The English-born architect later rebuilt New York's Trinity Church (1839). You can tour the grand house from 10 am to 4 pm (Sunday 1 to 4 pm; closed Monday) in summer. From September through May it's open Tuesday through Friday only.

Places to Stay & Eat

New Bedford is not thick with lodging possibilities, to put it mildly. Contact the visitors center if you're in a jam.

Try *Cynthia & Steven's B&B* (☎ 508-997-6433), 36 7th St, which has three rooms, all with private bath, for $50 to $65, breakfast included.

The historic district contains several simple restaurants and snack shops which can fill the need for sustenance.

Getting There & Away

Bus American Eagle (☎ 508-993-5040) operates buses between New Bedford and Boston's South Station about every two hours on weekdays and Saturday; it runs every three hours on Sunday.

Car Driving details for New Bedford are:

Destination	Mileage	Hr:Min
Boston, MA	57 miles	1:10
Fall River, MA	15 miles	0:25
Hartford, CT	103 miles	2:10
Hyannis, MA	43 miles	1:00
New York, NY	206 miles	4:20
Plymouth, MA	38 miles	0:50
Providence, RI	32 miles	0:50
Provincetown, MA	93 miles	2:00

Boat Cape Island Express Lines, Inc (☎ 508-997-1688) operates the passenger boat MV *Schamonchi* on the route between New Bedford and Vineyard Haven on Martha's Vineyard. In summer there are three voyages in each direction daily for $8.50 for adults, $4.50 kids under 12. Roundtrip fares are $15 and $7.50.

FALL RIVER

Fall River has a good harbor, rivers for water power and a humid climate well suited to working woolen thread, so it was natural that it became one of New England's most important textile production centers during the 19th century.

Thousands of tons of the local granite were hewn to build the huge textile mills which are still the most prominent feature of Fall River's cityscape.

But Fall River was the victim of its own success. Industrial wealth led to inflation, and higher costs. After the turn of the century the textile trade moved to cheaper labor markets in the southern states, and then overseas, leaving Fall River's great mills empty.

Today the great granite buildings are busy again. Fall River has become an off-price shopping mecca, the "largest factory-outlet shopping center in New England," as the signs say. Most of the spacious mills are again filled with textiles – not goods made here, but imported from the Far East and Latin America.

Factory Outlet Stores

The concept of the factory outlet store began a century ago when flawed but still usable products would be sold at very low prices to locals. Today, in some factory stores, prices are much the same as in city department stores and specialty shops. But in Fall River, cheap rents in the old mills allow real cost savings for all.

Over a hundred merchants have set up shop in the mills selling everything from cut-price jeans to designer dresses only a little bit out of fashion. You'll find accessories, baskets, belts, books, candy and nuts, carpets, children's clothing, cosmetics, crystal and glass, curtains, furniture, gift wrap and greeting cards, handbags, kitchenware, leather goods, linens, lingerie, luggage, toys, raincoats and overcoats, shoes, sweaters, ties, towels and even wallpaper.

Battleship Cove

Take I-195 exit 5 at the Braga Bridge, then follow the signs, to reach Battleship Cove (☎ 508-678-1100, 800-533-3194), a quiet corner of Mt Hope Bay which holds several well-preserved WWII-era vessels you can visit. The exhibits are open daily from 9 am to 5 pm, for $8 for adults, $4 kids six to 14.

The 46,000-ton battleship USS *Massachusetts*, longer than two football fields and taller than a nine-story building, carried a crew of 2300 and was the first and last battleship to fire her 16-inch guns in WWII.

The USS *Joseph P Kennedy, Jr*, named for President John F Kennedy's older brother, did battle in the Korean and Vietnam Wars, and is now a museum.

The USS *Lionfish* is a WWII submarine still in full working condition.

There are also two PT boats, a landing craft, a Japanese attack boat and other craft. The **Old Colony Railroad Museum** holds full-size historic railroad passenger cars, model trains and railroad memorabilia.

Food is available at the site. You can even dine in the *Massachusetts'* wardroom if you like.

Just past the battleship, the **Marine Museum at Fall River** (☎ 508-674-3533), 70 Water St, is especially strong in intricate ship models, including a scale model of the *Titanic* used in the 1950s movie on the subject. Admission costs $3 adults, $2 for children. The museum is open from 9 am to 5 pm (weekends noon to 5 pm) in summer; in winter until 4 pm daily except Monday and Tuesday when it's closed.

Homestead, Martha's Vineyard

Gay Head, Martha's Vineyard

A calm day in a Martha's Vineyard harbor

Beach cottages, Truro, Cape Cod

Nauset Lighthouse, Cape Cod

Whalebone Gateway, Eastham, Cape Cod

Wellfleet, Cape Cod

Provincetown, Cape Cod

Provincetown, Cape Cod National Seashore

Cape Cod

Mariner Bartholomew Gosnold (1572-1607) sailed the New England coast in 1602, naming natural features as he went. The sandy, 65-mile-long peninsula that juts eastward from mainland Massachusetts into the Atlantic he called Cape Cod.

When the Pilgrims first set foot in the New World in November, 1620, it was at the site of Provincetown at the tip of Cape Cod. They rested only long enough to draw up rules of governance (the Mayflower Compact) before setting sail eastward in search of a more congenial place for their settlement, which they found at Plymouth.

After that first visit by the Pilgrims, later settlers founded fishing villages along the coasts. The fishing industry drew boat builders and saltmakers. Soon there were farmers working the cranberry bogs as well, and whaling ships bringing home rich cargoes of oil and whalebone.

In the mid-19th century, Henry David Thoreau made a walking tour of Cape Cod, reporting on the peninsula just before it became a popular vacation destination for wealthy families from Boston and Providence.

In 1879, Cape Cod was connected to Europe by an undersea telephone cable which ran from Orleans to Brest, France, a distance of 4000 miles. Early in the next century Guglielmo Marconi (1874-1937) set up a wireless telegraph station on the beach in South Wellfleet to communicate with Great Britain.

At the beginning of the 20th century, the US government financed construction of the Cape Cod Canal (1909-14), which joined Buzzards Bay and Cape Cod Bay, cutting long hours off any voyage between Boston and Providence and New York, and also cutting the Cape off from the mainland. Cape Cod is now really an island.

"The Cape," as it is universally called by locals, thrives on farming, fishing and light industry, and is among New England's favorite summer vacation destinations. Vacationers come for the beaches that cover much of its 400 miles of shore, though the sea water is usually chilly to downright cold. There is real New England beauty in the Cape's dune-studded landscapes cloaked in scrub oak and pine, its fine stands of tall sea grass, and the grace and dignity of its colonial towns.

Cape-wide information may be found at the Massachusetts Tourist Information Center (☎ 508-746-1150) in Plymouth at exit 5 off MA 3 (for those heading from Boston to Cape Cod). The well-stocked and staffed building is open daily year round from roughly 8:30 am to 4:30 pm.

Once on Cape Cod, stop at the Cape Cod Chamber of Commerce information office (☎ 508-362-3225) at the Cape end of the Bourne Bridge just past the large traffic circle on the southwest side of MA 28. There's another office in Hyannis off US 6 exit 6. (Write to PO Box 16, Hyannis, MA 02601.) In addition, all towns have their own information bureaus. In an emergency call ☎ 911.

Getting Around

The Sagamore (northeast) and Bourne (southwest) Bridges span the Cape Cod Canal, linking the Cape to the mainland. Take the Bourne to Falmouth and Woods Hole (for Martha's Vineyard). Use the Sagamore for the rest of the Cape. The bridges are only four miles apart via US 6.

Locals use a somewhat confusing nomenclature for the various districts on Cape Cod. The "Upper Cape" is the region near the canal and the mainland. "Mid-Cape" is roughly from Barnstable and Hyannis eastward to Orleans. The "Lower" (or Outer) Cape is the long, narrow extension of the peninsula north and east from Orleans to Provincetown.

Main roads on the Cape include MA 28, which heads south from the Bourne Bridge

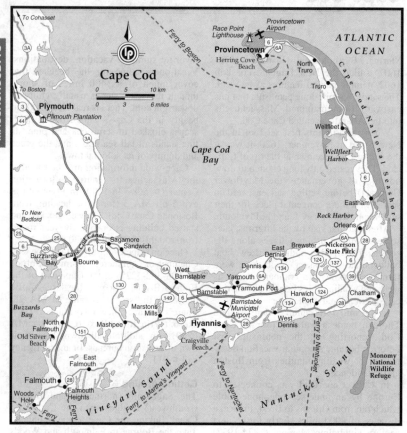

Cape Cod

0   5   10 km
0   3   6 miles

to Falmouth where it takes a sharp turn east and runs along the southern edge of the Cape through Hyannis and into Chatham, where it takes a northern jog before it ends in Orleans. Between Falmouth and Chatham MA 28 is over built with strip malls, fast food joints and motels; it's quite congested in the summer.

The Cape's main transit route is US 6, also called the Mid-Cape Hwy, a four-lane divided highway that runs inland from the canal to Orleans, where the Cape begins to narrow as it heads north. US 6 is the only through-road to Provincetown and traffic

on this part of US 6 is usually free-flowing, if heavy in summer.

The coastal alternative to the Mid-Cape Hwy, highly recommended if you have the time, is MA 6A, a rural and scenic two-lane road between Sandwich and Orleans, offering occasional views of Cape Cod Bay.

FALMOUTH

The Cape's second-largest town, which is quite spread out, is noted for its picturesque village green, attractive Main St area, beaches and nature preserves. Cape Cod doesn't get more quintessentially New

England than the village green: a white picket fence surrounds a large triangle of grass bordered by fine 19th-century houses and a Congregational church with a white steeple. The church's bell was cast in 1796 by patriot Paul Revere. This is a nice place for a picnic.

From Falmouth you can catch a passenger ferry (no cars) to Martha's Vineyard (see Martha's Vineyard, Getting There & Away). Car ferries to the Vineyard depart from nearby Woods Hole.

Orientation

MA 28 leads to Main St and the town green, the center of activity for inns, dining and shopping. Further east on MA 28, college students flock to the Falmouth Heights area on Grand Ave and Falmouth Heights Rd, known for inexpensive lodging and beachside activities. The town's best beach, Old Silver Beach, is five miles north of the town center, off scenic and tranquil MA 28A.

Information

The Falmouth Chamber of Commerce (☎ 508-548-8500, 800-526-8532) has two locations. The main office at 20 Academy Lane, off Main St, is open from 9 am to 5 pm daily mid-May to mid-October; the rest of the year it's open weekdays from 9 am to 5 pm.

A smaller office at 322 Palmer Ave (off MA 28 north of the town center) is open daily from 9 am to 5 pm mid-May to mid-September, with slightly longer hours on Friday night.

The Market Bookshop (☎ 508-548-5636), 15 Depot Ave, is the best bookstore in the area, bar none.

Falmouth Hospital (☎ 508-548-5300), 100 Terheun Drive, off MA 28 just north of town, is open 24 hours a day.

Historic Houses

The Falmouth Historical Society (☎ 508-548-4857) operates three historic buildings just off the village green.

The **Julia Wood House**, 55-65 Palmer Ave, features exhibits related to Falmouth's history. Since the lovely old house was once home to a doctor, one room is also set up as a physician's office.

The **Hallet Barn** behind the Wood House contains 19th-century tools and farming equipment. Next door, the **Conant House** has a room dedicated to Katherine Lee Bates, the town resident who wrote the popular patriotic hymn "America the Beautiful."

The houses are open weekdays from 2 to 5 pm, mid-June to mid-September. Admission to all buildings is $2 for adults, 50¢ for children.

Nature Reserves

Ashumet Holly and Wildlife Reservation (☎ 508-563-6390), off Route 151 from MA 28 in East Falmouth, is an Audubon bird sanctuary with eight nature trails and dozens of varieties of holly trees and bushes. The sanctuary is open year round, Tuesday through Sunday from 9 am to 4 pm; admission costs $3 for adults, $2 for children.

Waquoit Bay National Estuarine Research Reserve (☎ 508-457-0495), off MA 28 in East Falmouth, contains over 2500 acres of barrier beach and fragile estuary. Pick up a trail map and head out or simply spread out a picnic overlooking the

The wren, one of many birds to see on the Cape.

estuary. The reserve is open daily during daylight hours except during spring and fall hunting season. Admission ($2) is only charged between late June and early September.

Lowell Holly Reservation (☎ 508-921-2944), off Route 130 from MA 28 in neighboring Mashpee, is a 130-acre oasis of woodlands, holly trees and wildflowers. A trail runs along the edge of two freshwater ponds. The preserve is open daily from 10 am to sunset May through October; parking is $6 on summer weekends.

Beaches

Old Silver Beach, off MA 28A in North Falmouth, is the town's most popular beach. Parking costs $10 a day, which you don't pay if you bicycle in or walk. The crowds are young and the beach is long and sandy. Facilities include changing rooms and a snack bar serving fried clams, sandwiches and the like. Old Silver makes a nice destination for a bike ride.

Town Beach, at the end of Shore St from Main St, is usually quite crowded because of its central location.

Parking at Menauhant Beach, off Central Ave from MA 28 heading east, costs $5 weekdays and $8 on weekends.

The South Cape Beach State Park (☎ 508-457-0495), off Great Neck Rd from MA 28 in East Falmouth, has nature trails and snack stands, as well as a two-mile-long sandy beach that looks towards the Vineyard. Parking is $5.

Windsurfing & Boating

The New England Windsurfing Academy (☎ 508-540-8106), at Old Silver Beach, offers lessons to adults and children from May through September. Prices vary with the height of the season and with the length of lesson. Old Silver Beach is one of the Cape's best for windsurfing.

Edward's Boatyard (☎ 508-548-2216), 1209 MA 28 in East Falmouth, rents canoes from May to mid-October for paddling around Waquoit Bay National Estuarine Research Reserve (see above).

Bicycling

Bicycling is a good way to get around Falmouth because the town is so spread out, and because car traffic slows to a snail's pace in summer. In addition, admission fees at most beaches are per car; if you're on a bike, you usually get in free.

Pick up a map with various bicycling routes at the chamber of commerce. It gives detailed information about rental shops, routes and parking information.

The **Shining Sea Bike Path**, which follows a former railroad bed, is a very popular and pleasant seven-mile (round-trip) excursion from downtown Falmouth to Woods Hole (see below). This path also connects to other bicycle routes that lead to smaller beaches and harbors. Head toward the wooded Sippewissett area and the tranquil West Falmouth and Quissett Harbors (off MA 28A north of town) to get away from the crowds.

Cruises

Patriot Party Boats (☎ 508-548-2626), 227 Clinton Ave, offers two-hour sightseeing and sailing trips off the coast in an 18th-century replica schooner. Tickets cost $17 for adults, $12 for children 12 and under.

Places to Stay

Guest houses and motels on Grand Ave, which runs alongside Falmouth Heights Beach, tend to be less expensive than those in the middle of town, but they're also noisier and often full in the summer.

Camping The *Sippewissett Family Campground* (☎ 508-548-2542), about two miles north of town on Palmer Ave off MA 28, has 100 wooded campsites and a few camping cabins spread out over 13 acres. Although the campground caters to RVs, you won't feel out of place in a tent. It's open from mid-May to mid-October and features a free shuttle to the beaches and to the Martha's Vineyard ferry in Woods Hole. Rates for two people are $26 in the summer, $18 in the off-season. Cabins rent for $290 to $650 weekly in the summer.

Motels *Falmouth Heights Motor Lodge* (☎ 508-548-3623), 146 Falmouth Heights Rd, a bit more than a mile from the center of town and within walking distance of the beach and Vineyard ferry, has 23 standard motel rooms. Rates range from $72 to $85 in July and August, to about $20 less in the off-season and it's open from May to mid-October.

The *Mariner Motel* (☎ 508-548-1331), 555 Main St, a 10-minute walk from the center of town, has an outdoor pool and 30 motel-style rooms with refrigerators. Open year round, rooms cost $69 to $79 in July and August, less in the off-season.

Across from the beach, the *Park Beach Resort Motel* (☎ 508-548-1010), at 241 Grand Ave off Falmouth Heights Rd from MA 28, is about two miles from town. Most of the 50 rooms have ocean views; some have refrigerators. In the summer doubles rent for $80 to $95, off-season they drop to $39 to $59 double.

Inns & B&Bs *Mostly Hall* (☎ 508-548-3786), at 27 W Main St just off the town green, has six large and airy guest rooms. The B&B has a lot going for it: congenial innkeepers, full breakfasts, a comfortable living room and loaner bikes. In-season, rooms cost $110; off-season they're $80 to $95. The inn is closed in January.

The *Elm Arch Inn* (☎ 508-548-0133), Elm Arch Way off Main St in the center of town, offers 24 Colonial-style guest rooms, many with shared baths and in-room sinks. The rambling inn dates to the early 19th century but there's a modern annex too. There are lots of common rooms as well as a pool. The inn is open year round; summer rates are $50 to $60 single, $60 to $70 for a double.

The *Palmer House Inn* (☎ 508-548-1230), on the village green at 81 Palmer Ave, is a turn-of-the-century Victorian house with eight guest rooms decorated with period antiques. A full breakfast is included with these rates: $95 to $160 double in the summer, about $20 less the rest of the year.

The *Grafton Inn* (☎ 508-540-8688), 261 Grand Ave, across the street from a beach that's popular with college-age visitors, has 11 rooms with private bath. Rates ($95 to $135 double) include a full buffet breakfast.

The *Gladstone Inn* (☎ 508-548-9851), 219 Grand Ave, is also across from the beach and has 16 rooms that rent for $60 double with shared bath, $85 to $95 double with private bath, $33 single. A buffet breakfast is included. There is also an apartment over the garage that rents for $77 nightly.

Places to Eat
Coffee Obsession (☎ 508-540-2233), 110 Palmer Ave, is a great place to hang out and enjoy a cup of strong coffee and a baked snack. Jazz fills the rafters and interesting conversations can often be overheard.

The *Flying Bridge* (☎ 508-548-2700), 220 Scranton Ave, is a huge restaurant with great views from the deck overlooking Falmouth's busy inner harbor. The extensive menu includes pasta, seafood, burgers and sandwiches for $6 to $15 per dish. It's open year round for lunch and dinner.

The *Wharf* (☎ 508-548-2772), 281 Grand Ave, is popular with the volleyball crowd that plays on the beach below the back porch. Inexpensive fish and chips, sandwiches and burgers ($5 to $22) rule the lunch and dinner menu. The Dry Dock Bar, within the Wharf, is quite popular.

The *Clam Shack* (☎ 508-540-7758), 227 Clinton Ave, is a classic of the genre: tiny, with picnic tables on the back deck, and lots of fried clams for a few bucks. The "shack" is open from late May to mid-September.

Domenic's (☎ 508-540-5243), 188 Main St, is a reliable in-town place with a salad bar and deli sandwiches.

Laureen's (☎ 508-540-9104), 170 Main St, is a more upscale deli with fancy sandwiches, cold pasta salads, rich desserts and good coffee.

If you're tired of fish, the *Peking Palace* (☎ 508-540-8204), 452 Main St, serves remarkably good Cantonese, Szechuan

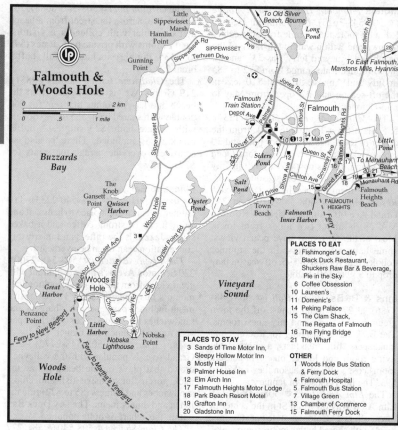

Falmouth & Woods Hole

0   1   2 km
0   .5   1 mile

PLACES TO EAT
2   Fishmonger's Café,
    Black Duck Restaurant,
    Shuckers Raw Bar & Beverage,
    Pie in the Sky
6   Coffee Obsession
10 Laureen's
11 Domenic's
14 Peking Palace
15 The Clam Shack,
    The Regatta of Falmouth
16 The Flying Bridge
21 The Wharf

PLACES TO STAY
3   Sands of Time Motor Inn,
    Sleepy Hollow Motor Inn
8   Mostly Hall
9   Palmer House Inn
12 Elm Arch Inn
17 Falmouth Heights Motor Lodge
18 Park Beach Resort Motel
19 Grafton Inn
20 Gladstone Inn

OTHER
1   Woods Hole Bus Station
    & Ferry Dock
4   Falmouth Hospital
5   Falmouth Bus Station
7   Village Green
13 Chamber of Commerce
15 Falmouth Ferry Dock

and Mandarin dishes until 2 am nightly in the summer.

The Regatta of Falmouth (☎ 508-548-5400), 217 Scranton Ave, has an enviable location overlooking the mouth of the inner harbor. Fortunately the food lives up to the view: the creative continental cuisine is by far the best in the area. Dishes might include grilled fish with a three mustard sauce or boneless rack of lamb. The fancy but unstuffy restaurant is open from mid-May to mid-October for dinner and from June to mid-September also for lunch. Expect to spend about $40 per person for a complete dinner with wine.

Entertainment

Casino-By-The-Sea (☎ 508-548-0777), on Grand Ave in Falmouth Heights, features dancing on the outdoor deck, an indoor nightclub, late-afternoon happy hours, live bands and Saturday afternoon beach parties.

Sea Crest (☎ 508-540-9400), 350 Quaker Rd in North Falmouth, has DJs, live bands, karaoke and comedy in the summer.

College Light Opera (☎ 508-548-0668), Depot Ave, a collegiate company of singers and musicians, performs nine productions from late June through August. Call for schedules.

Getting There & Away

Bus Bonanza buses (☎ 800-556-3815) serve Falmouth from Boston, MA; Providence, RI; and New York, NY. At least 12 buses a day go from Boston to Falmouth; the ride takes 80 minutes and costs $12 one way. The bus stops on Depot Ave, near the center of town.

Car From the Bourne Bridge, take MA 28 South into town; in the center of town MA 28 makes a left turn and heads east towards Hyannis and Chatham. The directional names for MA 28 can be confusing: even though you are heading due east toward Hyannis, West Dennis and Chatham, the road signs say MA 28 South.

Driving details for Falmouth are:

Destination	Mileage	Hr:Min
Boston, MA	75 miles	1:30
Bourne Bridge, MA	15 miles	0:20
Hyannis, MA	23 miles	0:45
Providence, RI	71 miles	1:25
Provincetown, MA	50 miles	1:15
Woods Hole, MA	6 miles	0:12

Boat See Martha's Vineyard, Getting There & Away, for information about getting to the Vineyard.

Getting Around

The Whoosh Trolley, which operates daily from 10 am to 9 pm late May to mid-October, costs 50¢ per ride. It makes a loop between the major points of interest in Falmouth and the Martha's Vineyard ferry in Woods Hole. Pick up a schedule of current locations and departure times at the chamber of commerce. See also Bicycling, above.

WOODS HOLE

Woods Hole is a world-famous center for marine research and exploration. The only places to visit in this picturesque village are a few small maritime exhibits. Most travelers passing through here are headed for the Steamship Authority's big car ferries to Martha's Vineyard.

Orientation & Information

From MA 28 in Falmouth, Woods Hole Rd leads directly to the ferry terminal. Water St, the main road, branches off Woods Hole Rd and leads to restaurants and the research institutions.

The chamber of commerce in Falmouth has information on Woods Hole.

Things to See & Do

The **National Marine Fisheries Service** (☎ 508-548-5123) was founded here in 1871 to study and promote the well-being of USA's fisheries. It was followed in 1888 by the **Marine Biological Laboratory** (☎ 508-548-3705, ext 423), set up to do basic biology research based on marine life forms.

In 1930, the **Woods Hole Oceanographic Institution** (☎ 508-457-2100) was established to pursue deep-sea research using funding from the Rockefeller Foundation.

In the 1960s, these three were joined by the USGS's Branch of Marine Geography (☎ 508-548-8700). Most recently, the **Sea Education Association** (☎ 508-540-3954) was formed in 1975. If you want to know anything about the oceans, this is where you'll find the information.

The National Marine Fisheries Service **aquarium** (☎ 508-548-7684) is open daily mid-June to mid-September from 10 am to 4 pm, (closed weekends in winter), and is free. Show up at 11 am or 3 pm if you'd like to see them feed the seals.

Nobska Lighthouse, on Church St off Woods Hole Rd, is dramatically situated on a point overlooking Vineyard Sound. It's a great place for a picnic or to watch the sun slowly set.

The **Shining Sea Bike Path** runs between Falmouth and Woods Hole. See Falmouth for details.

Places to Stay & Eat

The *Sands of Time Motor Inn* (☎ 508-548-6300, 800-841-0114), 549 Woods Hole Rd, is a 10-minute walk from town and overlooks the harbor. There are 20 modern motel rooms as well as 10 inn-style guest rooms in the Victorian house next door (some with fireplaces) that rent for $90 to $115 in July and August, $60 to $95 in the off-season (closed November through March).

The *Sleepy Hollow Motor Inn* (☎ 508-548-1986), also on Woods Hole Rd just out of town, has 24 basic rooms for $82 in the summer, $52 to $62 in the off-season (closed November through April).

All of Woods Hole's eateries overlook the water. The first one you see as you enter the village along Water St is the *Fishmonger's Café* (no ☎), 56 Water St. It's just what you'd expect: rustic, atmospheric, with lots of good food for all three meals. Lunch ranges from $5 to $7, dinner from $8 to $22.

The *Black Duck Restaurant* (☎ 508-548-9165), 73 Water St, just a few steps away on the opposite side of the street, also has a good menu and decent prices.

Shuckers Raw Bar & Beverage (☎ 508-540-3850), tucked away at 91A Water St behind the Woods Hole Oceanographic Institution's News and Information Offices, has fresh-shucked clams and oysters as well as a good selection of light meals and, in the evening, full dinners.

Pie in the Sky (☎ 508-540-5475), 10 Water St, is the place to go for coffee, pastries and sandwiches while you wait for the ferry.

Entertainment
The Woods Hole Folk Music Society (☎ 508-540-0320), at the Community Hall on Water St, hosts performances on the first and third Sunday of each month between October and May.

Getting There & Away
Bus Bonanza buses (☎ 800-556-3815) discharge passengers at the ferry terminal in Woods Hole from Boston, Providence and New York. In theory, bus schedules are designed to coincide with ferry departures and arrivals, but in practice, neither waits if the other is late. So it's better not to rely on the last connection of the day.

Car Driving details for Woods Hole are:

Destination	Mileage	Hr:Min
Boston, MA	81 miles	1:45
Bourne Bridge, MA	21 miles	0:32
Falmouth, MA	6 miles	0:12
Hyannis, MA	29 miles	1:00
Provincetown, MA	56 miles	1:30

Boat See Martha's Vineyard, Getting There & Away, for details on how to get to the island. Note that you will need advance reservations to take your car; and that the parking lots in Woods Hole fill up early and often in summer. There are satellite lots in Falmouth, with shuttle bus service.

Getting Around
Woods Hole is tiny, so your feet will serve you well. For a nominal fee, the Whoosh Trolley (see Falmouth) connects the ferry terminal to points of interest in Falmouth. See also Bicycling in Falmouth.

SANDWICH
The Cape's oldest town (founded in 1637) is also the first one you'll encounter across the Bourne Bridge. Among its many attractions are a quaint village center complete with duck pond and grist mill, fine historic houses, a famous glass museum, a renowned horticultural park with indoor collections of Americana and an adequate town beach. After exploring the village, head east out of town on MA 6A, the prettiest road on the Cape.

Orientation & Information
Cross the Sagamore Bridge to US 6 East to Route 130 North (also called Water St) into the center of town. Or take MA 6A after crossing the bridge and take Main St into town.

Water, Main and Grove Sts converge in the small village center. Tupper Rd, off MA 6A, leads to the marina and town beach.

The Cape Cod Canal Region Chamber of Commerce (☎ 508-759-3122), 70 Main St (MA 6A), is in the village of Buzzards Bay, on the mainland side of the Bourne Bridge. The office (open weekdays from 9 am to

5 pm year round) contains information on Sandwich, the village of Bourne and activities along the Cape Cod Canal.

If you're visiting during the summer, skip the main office and head to the seasonal booth (no ☎) on Route 130 North.

Titcomb's Book Shop (☎ 508-888-2331), 432 MA 6A, is the best bookstore on the north side of the Cape.

Museums

The **Heritage Plantation of Sandwich** (☎ 508-888-3300), on Grove St about a mile from the center, has a number of fine collections (vintage automobiles, crafts and folk art, firearms and miniatures) spanning various American periods. The lovely grounds include 76 acres of naturalized plantings and an outdoor cafe. The museum is open daily from 10 am to 5 pm early May to late October; admission is $7 for adults, $3.50 for children six to 18.

The **Sandwich Glass Museum** (☎ 508-888-0251), 129 Main St, celebrates Sandwich's famous glassmaking heyday from 1825 to 1888. There are fine examples of molded, blown and etched glass, as well as dioramas that show how the glass was formed and a video that recounts the dramatic rise and fall of the industry. The museum is open April through October daily from 9:30 am to 4:30 pm, and from November through March (closed in January) from Wednesday through Sunday about the same hours. Admission is $3 adults, 50¢ children six to 12.

The **Dexter Mill** (no ☎), near Main and River Sts, stands at the edge of a picturesque mill pond. Originally built in 1654, the present one was rebuilt in 1961. Today, in addition to touring the small mill, you can purchase bags of freshly ground corn meal. It's open daily mid-May to early September from 10 am to 5 pm. Admission is $1.50 adults, 50¢ children.

The **Hoxie House** (☎ 508-888-1173), 18 Water St (Route 130), is the best of Sandwich's many historic houses. The restored circa-1675 house is filled with period antiques. It's open mid-June to mid-October from 10 am to 5 pm Monday through Saturday and 1 to 5 pm on Sunday. Admission is the same as at the mill, but you can purchase a discount ticket good at both the Hoxie and the mill.

At Main and River Sts, **Yesteryears Doll Museum** (☎ 508-888-1711) has hundreds of centuries-old dolls, dollhouses and miniatures from around the globe. Housed in a somewhat dilapidated 1833 church, the museum is open from 10 am to 4 pm Monday through Saturday mid-May to mid-October. Admission is $3 adults, $1.50 children under 12.

The **Thornton W Burgess Museum** (☎ 508-888-4668), 4 Water St, is dedicated to the Sandwich native, naturalist and children's book author. Children enjoy the "see-and-touch" room, story hours and Peter Rabbit puzzles and games. It's open from 10 am to 4 pm Tuesday through Saturday year round, with additional open days in the summer. A nominal donation is requested.

Green Briar Nature Center

This conservation area (☎ 508-888-6870), a few miles east of town off MA 6A, has 57 acres of land with walking trails and wildflower and herb gardens. The center hosts lectures and natural-history classes, but for some the big draw is the old-fashioned kitchen that makes and sells jams. The kitchen is open from 10 am to 4 pm Tuesday through Saturday year round, with additional open days in the summer.

Cape Cod Canal

The canal, which effectively separates the Cape from "mainland" Massachusetts, took five years to dig and was opened in 1914, just a couple of weeks before the Panama Canal. Every year it saves thousands of ships from having to sail an extra 135 miles around the tip of the Cape at Provincetown, a treacherous route studded with constantly changing sand bars.

You can take a boat ride up the 17-mile-long canal with Cape Cod Canal Tours (☎ 508-295-3883), off US 6 and MA 28 at the Onset Bay Town Pier, a few miles west of the Bourne Bridge. Tours are $6.50 to $8 per person, depending on the length.

Beaches

Off Tupper Rd from MA 6A, Town Neck Beach is a long pebbly beach, best visited at high tide if you want to swim. There are restrooms, and parking costs $5.

Bicycling

Each side of the Cape Cod Canal has a well-maintained bike trail. In Sandwich rent bicycles at Sandwich Cycles (☎ 508-833-2453), between MA 6A and Tupper Rd. Near the canal try P&M Cycles (☎ 508-759-2830), 29 Main St (MA 6A) in Buzzards Bay.

Places to Stay

Camping *Shawme Crowell State Park* (☎ 508-888-0351), off Route 130 from MA 6A (about two miles from the center of town), has 280 wooded sites scattered over almost 3,000 acres. Open May to mid-October, the fee is $12 double.

Scussett Beach State Reservation (☎ 508-888-0859), off MA 3 on the mainland side of the canal just before the Sagamore Bridge, has 98 sites adjacent to the Cape Cod Canal. Fees and opening dates are similar to Shawme.

Peter's Pond Park (☎ 508-477-1775), off Cotuit Rd from Route 130 South, is more developed than the other camping options. There are 500 sites (mostly shaded, some along the pond) on 100 acres with walking trails and a pond for swimming. It's open mid-April to mid-October and costs $16 for two.

Motels About five miles east of town, the well-maintained *Spring Garden Motel* (☎ 508-888-0710), 578 MA 6A, has 11 rooms and two efficiency apartments. Rooms overlook a tranquil salt marsh and tidal creek and rent for $68 in the summer, $45 to $51 in the off-season (closed December through April).

The nicely landscaped and shaded *Shadynook Inn & Motel* (☎ 508-888-0409, 800-338-5208), 14 MA 6A, has 30 clean, simple and large rooms that go for $89 nightly in the summer. Efficiency units with a microwave rent for $100. It's open

year round and rooms rent for $55 to $65 in the off-season.

The *Sandy Neck Motel* (☎ 508-362-3992), 669 MA 6A at the entrance to Sandy Neck Beach (see Barnstable), has standard rooms that rent for $70 in the summer, $45 to $55 in the off-season; the motel is closed in January and February.

Inns & B&Bs *Wingscorton Farm Inn* (☎ 508-888-0534), 11 Wing Blvd off MA 6A, is an 18th-century farmhouse set well back from MA 6A. The house has been authentically restored and is furnished with antiques and four-poster beds. Each of the suites can accommodate four. A separate carriage house has a complete kitchen and plenty of space to stretch out; it's great for longer stays. The farm is home to free-range chickens (breakfast eggs are fresh) and other small animals. Suites are $95 for two; $150 in the carriage house.

The *Summer House* (☎ 508-888-4991), 158 Main St in the center of town, has five simple but nice guest rooms, one of which has a private bath. Whimsical common space takes up the 1st floor, where a full breakfast is served. English tea is served on the back porch or in the back garden. Rooms are $65 to $75 from late May to mid-October, after which the inn closes.

The *Dillingham House* (☎ 508-833-0065), a mile or so out of town at 71 Main St, is a circa-1650 Cape house with simple rooms. Both living rooms are comfortable, stocked with books, well-worn couches, a piano and a wood stove. A continental breakfast is included for $65 to $75 nightly, year round.

The *Captain Ezra Nye House* (☎ 508-888-2897, 800-388-2278), nearby at 152 Main St, has six carpeted guest rooms, most with private bath, one with a working fireplace. One of the living rooms has a TV and VCR. A full breakfast is included in the rates of $60 to $95; it's open year round.

Places to Eat

The *Sagamore Inn* (☎ 508-888-9707), 1131 MA 6A, is a friendly place owned and staffed by locals. The interior is classic "old Cape Cod" with tin ceilings, wooden floors, wooden booths and country curtains. In addition to a beloved Yankee pot roast, the kitchen serves up hearty Italian and seafood dishes ($7.50 to $10.50) daily except Tuesday from 11 am to 9 pm April through November.

The *Bee-Hive Tavern* (☎ 508-833-1184), 406 MA 6A, is popular with the locals who come for value-conscious servings of pasta, fried seafood, burgers and sandwiches. You can also get more complete meals like chicken teriyaki. It's open daily for lunch and dinner ($5 to $14) year round and for breakfast on weekends in the off-season.

The *Dunbar Tea Shop* (☎ 508-833-2485), 1 Water St, is one of two places to eat in the village center. Operated by a British couple, you'll find ploughman's lunch, soup, quiche and Scottish shortbread on the menu at lunch time. Otherwise, folks come for an authentic English tea ($6 per person) in a country setting. Because it's good and almost the only place in town, it's usually packed.

The *Marshland Restaurant* (☎ 508-888-9824), 109 MA 6A, is a small roadside place that serves coffee and muffins at breakfast and $4 lunch specials like meatloaf or baked stuffed shells. Eat at a booth or take-out. Open for breakfast on Sunday, breakfast and lunch on Monday, and all three meals the rest of the week.

Captain Scott's (☎ 508-888-1675), 71 Tupper Rd, serves basic Italian dishes, fried seafood and simply prepared fish for $4 to $15 in casual surroundings that draw the locals. It's open daily from 11:30 am to 8:30 pm except in the off-season when it's closed Mondays.

The *Dan'l Webster Inn* (☎ 508-888-3622), 149 Main St, is the fanciest place to eat in town. Have lunch ($5.75 to $10) in the sunny solarium filled with potted plants and retreat to the tavern for lighter meals and drinks in the evening. Or dress neatly but not formally for early-bird continental dinner specials (less than $18) before 6:15 pm in the main dining room. The restaurant is open daily for three meals, with the exception of the winter when breakfast is served only on the weekends.

Things to Buy

Since 1837, Pairpoint Glass Works (☎ 508-888-2344, 800-899-0953), 851 MA 6A, has been renowned for its glass-blowing techniques and original designs. You can watch artisans at work on weekdays year round from 9 am to 4:30 pm. The sales showroom is open daily year round.

Getting There & Away

Bus Plymouth & Brockton buses (☎ 508-746-0378) do not serve Sandwich but they stop nearby in Bourne. Call for specifics about the inconvenient location.

Train See Hyannis for details on Amtrak's summer weekend train, the *Cape Codder*, which makes stops at the Jarves St station.

Cape Cod Scenic Railroad (☎ 508-771-3788), Jarves St off MA 6A, departs twice daily for a two-hour return journey to Hyannis, passing cranberry bogs, salt marshes and small villages along the way. If you take the first train, you can hop out in Hyannis, wander around a bit, and take the later train back. The train runs Tuesday through Sunday from June to mid-October and on weekends in May, November and December. Adults cost $11.50, children $7.50.

Car Driving details for Sandwich are:

Destination	Mileage	Hr:Min
Boston, MA	64 miles	1:10
Chatham, MA	32 miles	0:45
Hyannis, MA	16 miles	0:22
Providence, RI	68 miles	1:20
Provincetown, MA	62 miles	1:15
Sagamore Bridge, MA	4 miles	0:08

Getting Around

The center of town is perfect for strolling but the Glasstown Trolley (no ☎) takes people to a few of the more distant places like Heritage Plantation and Pairpoint Glass Works. You can travel the hour-long circuit daily from 9 am to 5 pm in the summer. An adult ticket costs $5, children age four to 12 cost $3; tickets are valid all day.

MASSACHUSETTS

BARNSTABLE

Barnstable's section of MA 6A lives up to its reputation as the most picturesque road on Cape Cod. It's a tranquil winding route affording glimpses of the ocean and salt marshes. It's also dotted with antique stores, art galleries, craft shops and pricey B&Bs. Take practically any northern turn off of MA 6A and you'll reach the shores of Cape Cod Bay. Perhaps the best thing about Barnstable is Sandy Neck Beach, a six-mile-long stretch of barrier beach and dunes.

Orientation & Information

MA 6A runs from Sandwich through Barnstable, Yarmouth, Dennis and Brewster. If you're in a hurry take US 6 to exit 5 for West Barnstable, exit 6 for Barnstable.

The town of Barnstable includes seven distinct villages and stretches the width of the Cape, from Cape Cod Bay on the north shore to Nantucket Sound on the south. But the most interesting section of town follows historic MA 6A, which is also referred to as Main St and Old King's Hwy.

The Cape Cod Chamber of Commerce (☎ 508-362-3225), conveniently located just off exit 5 from US 6, has information on Barnstable and the entire Cape. It's open weekdays from 8 am to 5:30 pm year round, with additional weekend hours (9 am to 4 pm) from late May to mid-October.

Things to See & Do

The **West Parish Meetinghouse** (☎ 508-362-4445), on Route 149 between US 6 and MA 6A, dates to 1717. Its members belong to the oldest Congregational parish in the country and trace their origins back to London's First Congregational Church.

The **Donald Trayser Memorial Museum Complex** (☎ 508-362-2092), 3353 MA 6A, served as the Old Customs House from the mid- to late 1800s when Barnstable Harbor was the busiest port on the Cape. (It silted up in the early 20th century.) The museum contains a random assortment of items: the custom keeper's office, imported ivory, Sandwich glass, a bicycle dating to 1900 and a late 17th-century jail cell. It's open from 1:30 to 4:30 pm Tuesday through Saturday in July and August; donations are requested.

At Barnstable Harbor off MA 6A, **Hyannis Whale Watcher Cruises** (☎ 508-362-6088, 800-287-0374) offers trips for $18 to $22 per person, $10 for children four to 12, from April through October. Although the whales frolic much closer to Plymouth and Provincetown, making the boat trip from those harbors much shorter, take the trip from here if you're not going to either of those places.

Beaches

Sandy Neck Beach is Cape Cod's best beach; it's six miles long and backed by a rather extensive network of high dunes. Facilities include a changing room, restrooms and a snack bar; parking is $8. To reach it take Sandy Neck Rd off MA 6A on the Sandwich-Barnstable town line.

A nine-mile (roundtrip) nature trail begins at the parking lot and heads into the dunes and salt marshes. It's well worth the four-hour walk, if you have the time.

Places to Stay

MA 6A is lined with former sea captains' houses that have been turned into romantic B&Bs. If you have a bit of money to spare, you'll find a few places to spend it here.

The *Charles Hinckley House* (☎ 508-362-9924), Scudder Lane at MA 6A, is an 1809 Federal-style house with four lovely and comfortable rooms, each with a fireplace and period antiques. The full breakfast is one of the best on the Cape. Rates are $119 to $149 year round.

The circa-1750 *Crocker Tavern* (☎ 508-362-5115), 3095 MA 6A, is a historic hostelry with three spacious but sparsely decorated period-style guest rooms with private bath. Rates are $75 to $95 year round.

Beechwood (☎ 508-362-6618), 2839 MA 6A, is a Victorian inn with a wide wrap-around porch and large back yard. Each of the six guest rooms has a private bath and refrigerator; two have a fireplace. The light and airy rooms are filled with period antiques and rent for $110 to $140 from May through October ($95 to $140 the rest of the year.)

Places to Eat

Mill Way Fish Market (☎ 508-362-2760), at Barnstable Harbor, packs up fish sandwiches, French fries and fish chowder to take to the harbor for $3 to $8.

Barnstable Tavern (☎ 508-362-2355), 3176 MA 6A in the center of the village, serves lunch ($5 to $11) and dinner ($10 to $22) from June through October. You'll find standard pub fare like burgers and sandwiches, but you can also get hummus, stuffed grape leaves and grilled rainbow trout.

Entertainment

The *Benefit Coffeehouse* (☎ 508-775-5165, 428-1053), in Liberty Hall on Main St in Marstons Mills, sponsors acoustic-folk and folk-rock benefit concerts. Call to see what's playing; tickets are $8 to $10. To reach the village of Marstons Mills, take Route 149 south from US 6.

Getting There & Away

Bus The Plymouth & Brockton bus (☎ 508-746-0378) from Boston stops at the commuter lot on US 6 in Barnstable, a few miles from anything of interest in town.

Car Driving details for Barnstable are:

Destination	Mileage	Hr:Min
Boston, MA	77 miles	1:25
Hyannis, MA	5 miles	0:10
Provincetown, MA	53 miles	1:15
Sagamore Bridge, MA	17 miles	0:25
Sandwich, MA	12 miles	0:15
Yarmouth, MA	4 miles	0:08

Getting Around

MA 6A is winding and narrow so it's not well-suited to bicycles; car travel is safer.

HYANNIS

Hyannis is the commercial and transportation hub of Cape Cod. The recently rejuvenated waterfront and Main St area make it a pleasant place to wait for a ferry or a bus.

Hyannis also draws crowds of summer college workers for their one night off per week, and also attracts Kennedy fans: Hyannisport is the summer home to this US political family.

Orientation

From US 6, take Route 132 South (exit 6) to the airport rotary to Barnstable Rd to Main St. From Falmouth or Chatham, take MA 28 directly to Main St.

Main St (one way) is the principal shopping and dining thoroughfare. North and South Sts run parallel to it on either side. Ocean St runs south from Main St to a town park and beach; Gosnold St connects Ocean St to Sea St, where there is another decent beach. Both ferry terminals (the Ocean St Dock and the South St Dock) are about a 10-minute walk from the bus station, which is just one block north of Main St.

Information

The Hyannis Area Chamber of Commerce (☎ 508-775-2201, 800-449-6647), about a mile south of US 6 at 1481 Route 132, is generally open from 9 am to 5 pm Monday through Saturday year round. From late May to early September it is also open on Sundays.

The Cape Cod Hospital (☎ 508-771-1800), 27 Park St, a few blocks from the center of town, is open 24 hours a day.

In an emergency call ☎ 911; for Hyannis police, call ☎ 508-775-0387.

John F Kennedy Hyannis Museum

This museum (☎ 508-775-2201), 397 Main St, celebrates JFK's life in Hyannis through an exhibition of more than 100 heartwarming photographs. John F Kennedy, the 35th president of the US, and his family summered in Hyannisport (an exclusive section of Hyannis) from the early 1930s until he was assassinated in 1963. Many Kennedy family members still have family homes here. The "Kennedy Compound," as it is called, is just a group of private houses (albeit lovely ones), surrounded in most cases by tall fences. The museum is open

MASSACHUSETTS

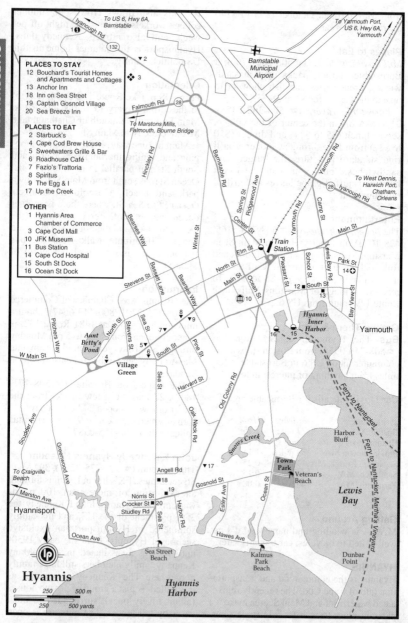

PLACES TO STAY
12 Bouchard's Tourist Homes
   and Apartments and Cottages
13 Anchor Inn
18 Inn on Sea Street
19 Captain Gosnold Village
20 Sea Breeze Inn

PLACES TO EAT
2 Starbuck's
4 Cape Cod Brew House
5 Sweetwaters Grille & Bar
6 Roadhouse Café
7 Fazio's Trattoria
8 Spiritus
9 The Egg & I
17 Up the Creek

OTHER
1 Hyannis Area
   Chamber of Commerce
3 Cape Cod Mall
10 JFK Museum
11 Bus Station
14 Cape Cod Hospital
15 South St Dock
16 Ocean St Dock

Hyannis

daily from March through November and from Wednesday through Saturday the rest of the year. Admission costs $2; kids under six get in free.

A simple JFK memorial was erected off Ocean St overlooking the harbor where he often sailed.

Beaches

Sea Street Beach, off Sea St from the western end of Main St, is a narrow but decent beach with restrooms and a bathhouse; parking is $8.

Kalmus Park Beach, off Ocean St, has a restroom, bathhouse and good windsurfing conditions; parking is $8.

Veteran's Beach, off Ocean St at the town park, is as much a park as it is beach. Families come to picnic and barbecue (there's a snack bar too), play paddle ball on the beach, and swim in shallow waters.

West Hyannisport has Craigville Beach, the largest on Cape Cod.

Activities

Cape Water Sports (☎ 508-771-9755), on Lewis Bay at Dock A, offers sailing lessons and rents boats and sailboards of all sizes and shapes.

Eastern Mountain Sports (EMS, ☎ 508-775-1072), 233 Stevens St in the Village Marketplace, rents kayaks and offers twice weekly instructional clinics throughout the year on everything from using a compass to discussing specific bicycling itineraries.

Cruises

The *Eventide* (☎ 508-775-0222), Ocean St Dock, offers a variety of voyages designed to suit laid back sailors who want to maximize wind power and minimize motor noise as much as possible. *Eventide* sails far into Nantucket Sound, around the bay at twilight, and along the coast in front of the Kennedy compound too. Prices vary but average $16 for adults and $6 for children from mid-April to late November.

Hyannisport Harbor Cruises (☎ 508-778-2600), from the Ocean St Dock, offers hour-long sightseeing trips of the harbor and bay, during the day and at sunset, from late April through October. Adults pay $8, $3.50 for children 12 and under.

Organized Tours

Hyannis Air Service (☎ 508-775-8171), Barnstable Municipal Airport at the Route 132 rotary, offers 30- and 60-minute sightseeing trips in twin-engine propeller planes high above this fragile strip of land. Fly over the lighthouse at Chatham or the Cape Cod Canal ($49 for two people) or out to Provincetown ($89 for two people). It's a great way to fully comprehend and appreciate the unique geology and topography of the Cape. The grand tour ($169 for two) lasts two hours and takes you over the islands as well.

Places to Stay

Motels The *Anchor Inn* (☎ 508-775-0357), 1 South St, about a half mile from the ferries, rents 43 simple rooms most of which have balconies overlooking the harbor. Rates are $79 to $105 in the summer, $39 to $69 the rest of the year.

Hyannis Travel Inn (☎ 508-775-8200), 18 North St, has 83 rooms and an indoor and outdoor pool. Doubles in the summer cost $50 to $99; in the off-season they are $36 to $69. It's closed December and January.

The *Seacoast on the Towne* (☎ 508-775-3828, 800-466-4100), 33 Ocean St, is right in the middle of the action. The 26 cheery rooms, some with refrigerator, cost $55 to $78 double in the summer, $20 less in the off-season. The motel is closed from November through April.

Cottages *Captain Gosnold Village* (☎ 508-775-9111), 230 Gosnold St at Sea St, a block from Sea Street Beach, offers motel rooms, fully-equipped cottages and efficiency apartments that can sleep up to eight people. This is a good place for longer stays and for families, since there is a playground, pool and plenty of wooded space between units. Summertime rates begin at $75 double, and increase with the size of the cottage. It's closed December through March.

MASSACHUSETTS

Inns & B&Bs The *Inn on Sea Street* (☎ 508-775-8030), 358 Sea St, was the first B&B in town and it's still the best. Two of the nine rooms have shared bath; all are decorated with tasteful Victorian or English country antiques. If you want to splurge, and you're lucky enough to get a vacancy, rent the simple, all-white cottage which has a complete kitchen. A home-baked breakfast is included in the rates of $70 to $98 ($110 for the cottage). It's closed from mid-November through March.

Bouchard's Tourist Homes and Apartments and Cottages (☎ 508-775-0912), 83 School St, has a number of buildings with a variety of accommodations, from simple rooms with sinks and shared baths in the hall, to family suites, to apartments designed for week-long stays. In the summer a single (twin-bed) room with shared bath goes for $40 to $55, a double with private bath for $55. It's open year round.

The *Sea Breeze Inn* (☎ 508-771-7213), 397 Sea St, has 14 clean and pleasant motel-style rooms (all with private bath) within a sandal shuffle of the beach. A few rooms have ocean views. Summertime rates are $55 to $95, $45 to $75 the rest of the year.

Places to Eat

There are more than 60 places to eat in town, so you'll be able to find something that suits your wallet and taste buds.

Spiritus (☎ 508-775-2955), 500 Main St, serves up good strong coffee, pizza by-the-slice and filling sandwiches. The funky storefront cafe is a popular hang-out.

The *Cape Cod Brew House* (☎ 508-775-4110), 720 Main St, is a popular micro-brewery where you can munch on onion rings, burgers and chili – all made with the same beer you'll be drinking. Dishes at lunch and dinner cost $5 to $12.

Starbuck's (☎ 508-778-6767), Route 132, is open for lunch and dinner and serves a wide selection of dependable standbys: burgers, pasta, Tex-Mex, shrimp, and chicken sandwiches. Star-

buck's is also known for frozen cocktails and other 20-ounce libations, but keep in mind that this pleasant place serves as many families as it does drinks. Meals are in the $6 to $12 range.

At *Up the Creek* (☎ 508-771-7866), 36 Old Colony Rd, you'll find value for the money you spend. Get a fish, chicken or steak lunch special for about $6 or a broiled seafood platter at dinner for $13.

The Egg & I (☎ 508-771-1596), 521 Main St, is open when other places aren't: from 11 pm to 1 pm. After other night spots close, the Egg & I gets going, serving hearty dishes like fried steak sandwiches. And in the morning, locals stop in for eggs, pancakes and corned beef hash. You won't have to spend more than $6 here unless you want to.

The *Roadhouse Café* (☎ 508-775-2386), 488 South St, suits many moods. It has an espresso bar which also stocks over 40 kinds of beer, outdoor tables where you select from a light cafe menu and an indoor dining room where you choose from a full menu of Italian seafood dishes and New England standards. Come for lunch, which you can get for under $10; dinner will cost at least $20 but there are better places to spend $20.

Fazio's Trattoria (☎ 508-771-7445), 586 Main St, feels like an authentic Italian trattoria decorated with Chianti bottles and red and white checked table cloths. Pizza, pasta, grilled meats, soups and foccaccia sandwiches can be had for $5 to $8 at lunch, $10 to $15 at dinner.

Sweetwaters Grille & Bar (☎ 508-775-3323), 644 Main St, features Southwestern dishes like black bean soup, burritos and chicken fajitas for $9.50 to $13.50 at dinnertime. Lunch is also served on summer weekends.

Entertainment

Coconuts Comedy Club (☎ 508-775-6600), at the Holiday Inn on Route 132, hosts well-known comedians from MTV and New York City on Saturday nights from May to mid-November.

Jammer's (☎ 508-775-2922), MA 28, is the Cape's largest dance place with three dance floors, two stages for separate bands and popular happy hours.

The *Cape Cod Melody Tent* (☎ 508-775-9100), W Main St, hosts big name musicians and comedians under a giant outdoor tent in the summer.

Outdoor movies are shown on the village green, at the corner of Main and South Sts, on Thursday nights in July and August.

Getting There & Away
Air The Barnstable Municipal Airport (☎ 508-775-2020), at the rotary intersection of MA 28 and Route 132, is served by regional carriers of USAir, Delta's Business Express and Continental Express. You can get to Hyannis from Boston on Cape Air (☎ 508-775-8171, 800-352-0714), as well as from Newark, NJ, and New York's LaGuardia Airport on Colgan Air (☎ 800-272-5488).

See also Getting There & Away in Martha's Vineyard and Nantucket.

Bus The Plymouth & Brockton bus (☎ 508-746-0378), at the corner of Center and Elm Sts, connects Boston to Hyannis and other Cape points between Hyannis and Provincetown. There are 15 daily buses from Boston to Hyannis ($11 one way) and two daily buses from Hyannis to Provincetown ($9 one way).

Bonanza buses (☎ 800-556-3815) operate from New York City and Providence to Hyannis. From New York there are about five buses daily that make the six-hour trip ($40 one way).

Train Hyannis is the terminus for Amtrak's summer train from New York City, the *Cape Codder*. It runs to the Cape on Fridays in July and August, making the return trip on Sunday afternoons. Other stops on the route include West Barnstable, Sandwich and Buzzards Bay, in Cape Cod; Providence and Westerly, RI; and coastal points in Connecticut including New Haven. Sometimes the service runs to

Philadelphia, PA; Baltimore, MD; and Washington, DC; check with Amtrak.

The Cape Cod Scenic Railroad (see Sandwich) runs between Hyannis and Sandwich. The train departs Hyannis three times daily.

Car Hyannis is one of the few places on Cape Cod where you can pick up a rental car. Hertz (☎ 800-654-3131), National (☎ 800-227-7368) and Avis (☎ 800-331-1212) are all at the airport. U-Save (☎ 508-790-4700) and Trek (☎ 508-771-2459) are just two blocks away.

Driving details for Hyannis are:

Destination	Mileage	Hr:Min
Boston, MA	79 miles	1:35
Bourne Bridge, MA	23 miles	0:35
Chatham, MA	19 miles	0:40
Falmouth, MA	23 miles	0:45
Provincetown, MA	50 miles	1:15
Sandwich, MA	17 miles	0:25

Boat See Getting There & Away in Martha's Vineyard and Nantucket.

Getting Around
Summertime traffic congestion can be time-consuming. From the town center, you can walk almost anywhere of interest in 20 minutes, so it's best to park and walk. Park for free (there are no meters) along North St.

The Hyannis Shuttle (☎ 508-775-2201) runs along Main St and the waterfront area daily during the summer, every 30 minutes from mid-morning until 9 pm or so.

The Yarmouth Easy Shuttle (no ☎) runs from the Hyannis bus station along MA 28 (including to the beaches) and into neighboring Yarmouth. Both shuttles depend on state funding, so the continuation of their existence from year-to-year remains an open question.

Sea Line buses (☎ 800-352-7155) operate between Hyannis and Woods Hole, with stops along MA 28 in small Barnstable villages, Mashpee and Falmouth. Sea Line begins at the Plymouth & Brockton terminal (at Center and Elm Sts) in Hyannis and ends at the ferry terminal in Woods Hole. The fare varies with the distance traveled, but is usually between 75¢ and $4 one way.

YARMOUTH

The north side of Yarmouth along MA 6A is quiet and dignified, lined with shady trees, antique shops and former sea captains' homes. Along MA 28 on the south side, Yarmouth is thick with low-slung motels built right on the narrow beaches.

Orientation & Information

Take US 6 exit 7 (Willow St) into Yarmouthport, or exit 8 for Yarmouth and South Yarmouth. Better yet, keep wending your way along MA 6A. The villages of Yarmouthport and Yarmouth are on MA 6A; South Yarmouth and West Yarmouth are on MA 28. Everything you'll need is on or just off these two roads.

The Yarmouth Chamber of Commerce (☎ 508-778-1008, 800-732-1008), 657 MA 28 in South Yarmouth, is open from 9 am to 5 pm (with slightly shorter hours on Sunday) daily from late May to mid-October and from 9 am to 5 pm on weekdays the rest of the year.

The Parnassus Book Service (☎ 508-362-6420), 220 MA 6A, is perhaps the best antiquarian and used bookstore on the Cape. An outside wall is lined with shelves of books through which you can browse anytime of day or night; pay on the honor system when the store is closed.

Things to See & Do

The **Winslow Crocker House** (☎ 508-362-4385), 250 MA 6A, is a lovely Georgian house filled with notable antiques from the 17th, 18th and 19th centuries. Tours ($4 adults, $2 children five to 12) are given on the hour from noon to 4 pm daily except Monday and Friday from June to mid-October.

The **Captain Bangs Hallet House** (☎ 508-362-3021), behind the post office off MA 6A, was once home to a prosperous sea captain who made his fortune sailing to China and India. After touring the house, take a short walk on the nature trails behind

it. The house is only open from 2 to 4 pm on Thursday, Friday and Sunday in July and August; and also on Sundays in June and September.

The historic store **Hallet's** (☎ 508-362-3362), 139 MA 6A in Yarmouthport, has a revered place in Yarmouth's history. It began as an apothecary in 1889 and has also served as a post office and town meeting hall. It still boasts its original soda fountain, complete with swivel stools. Stop in for coffee, ice cream or a sandwich. Upstairs is a wonderfully nostalgic little museum chock full of items collected over the last 100 years.

Beaches

Grey's Beach (also known as Bass Hole Beach), off Centre St from MA 6A, isn't known for great swimming but it does have a long boardwalk that stretches out into the tidal marsh and across a creek.

Seagull Beach, off S Sea Ave from MA 28, is Yarmouth's best south side beach. The lovely approach is alongside a tidal river. Parking is $8; there is a bathhouse.

Places to Stay

Motels The *All Seasons Motor Inn* (☎ 508-394-7600), 1199 MA 28 in South Yarmouth, is an attractive two-story motel with 114 modern motel rooms (with refrigerators), two pools (one indoor), saunas and a whirlpool. Rooms rent for $69 to $99 in the summer, $49 to $89 the rest of the year.

The *Beach 'n Towne Motel* (☎ 508-398-2311), 1261 MA 28 in South Yarmouth, has 21 standard rooms that rent for $58 to $62 in the summer, $34 to $50 the rest of the year.

The *Thunderbird Motor Lodge* (☎ 508-775-2692, 800-443-8881), 216 MA 28 in West Yarmouth (two miles from the ferries in Hyannis), has 140 rooms, most of which have two double beds. Doubles rent for $54 to $68 in the summer, $26 to $52 in the off-season; it's closed from mid-October to mid-February.

B&Bs The *Wedgewood Inn* (☎ 508-362-5157), 83 MA 6A in Yarmouthport, is one of the loveliest B&Bs along MA 6A. Its six rooms (a couple with private screened-in porches) are spacious and filled with antiques, oriental carpets and fireplaces. A full breakfast is included with the rates: $105 to $150 from June through October, $90 to $135 the rest of the year.

The circa-1710 *Lane's End Cottage* (☎ 508-362-5298), 268 MA 6A in Yarmouthport, is a small English-style B&B surrounded by flowers and tucked back in the woods. The three rooms, all with private bath, are simple; the brick patio, where a full breakfast is served, is ringed with potted plants. Rates are $80 to $95 year round.

Places to Eat

Jack's Outback (☎ 508-362-6690), 161 MA 6A in Yarmouthport, is a no-frills, pine-paneled place that serves good, cheap American food for all three meals, daily year round. Pour your own coffee, write your own order and pick up your plate when it's ready. Jack's has been doing things this way for years and patrons love it. You'll get out the door well-fed for $5 to $10.

Fiesta Grande (☎ 508-760-2924), 681 MA 28 in West Yarmouth, is owned by a Mexican family that prepares authentic, home-style flautas, enchiladas suizas and tamales. Remarkably, kids eat for free all the time; it's open for all three meals in the summer and for dinner year round.

You can't miss the *Lobster Boat* (☎ 508-775-0486), 681 MA 28 in West Yarmouth, an oversized and hybridized pirate ship-cum-lobster boat. Come for daily specials like twin lobsters for $13, or early bird specials. It's open from 4 to 10:30 pm daily from early April to late October.

Clancy's (☎ 508-775-3332), 175 MA 28 in West Yarmouth, has a pleasant country-tavern atmosphere and a more-than-adequate menu of burgers, sandwiches, peel-and-eat shrimp and chicken fingers. Prices range from $5 to $14 for lunch, dinner and Sunday brunch.

If you're in the mood for a creative meal served in sophisticated but unpretentious surroundings, head to *Abbicci* (☎ 508-362-

3501), 43 MA 6A in Yarmouthport. Contemporary Italian dishes like ravioli stuffed with game or duck breast with mustard sauce are served in a 1775 house modernized with track lighting, contemporary art and an upscale bar. Sunday brunch costs $14 and there are early bird dinner specials during the week. It's open for lunch and dinner, about $14 to $26 per main course.

Getting There & Away

Bus The Plymouth & Brockton bus (☎ 508-746-0378) stops in the center of Yarmouthport at Hallet's on MA 6A on the way from Boston and Hyannis to Provincetown.

Car Driving details for Yarmouth are:

Destination	Mileage	Hr:Min
Barnstable, MA	4 miles	0:08
Boston, MA	80 miles	1:30
Bourne Bridge, MA	20 miles	0:30
Dennis, MA	4 miles	0:08
Hyannis, MA	4 miles	0:10
Provincetown, MA	45 miles	1:00

Getting Around

See Hyannis, Getting Around, for information on the Yarmouth Easy Shuttle.

DENNIS

Similar to Yarmouth's sprawl, Dennis stretches from Cape Cod Bay to Nantucket Sound. Along MA 6A you'll find cranberry bogs, salt marshes and lots of antique stores and artisans shops (including the recommended Scargo Pottery). Dennis also has a museum dedicated to area artists, a highly regarded summer theater, an art cinema and a fine lookout point.

Orientation & Information

To reach most of town, continue along MA 6A or take exit 9 from US 6 (north to MA 6A or south to MA 28). The villages of East Dennis and Dennis are located on MA 6A; West Dennis and Dennisport are along MA 28. Route 134 runs north-south (through South Dennis), linking MA 6A to MA 28.

The Dennis Chamber of Commerce (☎ 508-398-3568, 800-243-9920), at the junction of MA 28 and Route 134 in South Dennis, is open daily from 9:30 am to 4 pm late June to early September (10 am to 2 pm on weekdays the rest of the year).

Things to See

The **Cape Museum of Fine Arts** (☎ 508-385-4477), MA 6A, represents Cape artists, both living and dead, famous as well as up-and-coming, who work in a variety of media. The airy museum, part of which is housed in an old barn, is open from 10 am to 5 pm Tuesday through Saturday and 1 to 5 pm on Sunday. Admission is $2 for adults, free for children under 16.

From **Scargo Tower** (from MA 6A take Old Bass River Rd to Scargo Hill Rd) you can see all the way to Provincetown on a clear day. The high vantage point gives you a good idea of just how delicate the ecology of this little peninsula really is. Directly below is Scargo Lake, one of the Cape's 365 freshwater lakes.

Beaches

Chapin Memorial Beach, off MA 6A, is a long, dune-backed beach with a gently sloping grade. As with all bay-side beaches, at low tide you can walk for a mile out onto the tidal flats. Parking is $8.

West Dennis Beach, off MA 28 in West Dennis, is a narrow, mile-long beach on Nantucket Sound. It's quite popular (the parking lot – $8 – holds 1000 cars); facilities include a snack bar and restrooms.

Bicycling

The paved **Cape Cod Rail Trail** follows the flat railroad bed of the Old Colony Railroad for 20 miles from Dennis to Wellfleet. Along the way you'll pass ponds, forests, a country store or two, ocean vistas, beaches and salt marshes. It's one of the most pleasant excursions on the Cape.

Park at the trailhead on Route 134 in South Dennis, just south of US 6. You can rent bikes nearby at All Right Bikes (☎ 508-394-3544), 118 MA 28.

Cruises

The schooner *Freya* (☎ 508-385-4399, 896-2433), Sesuit Harbor off MA 28 in East Dennis, takes two-hour sails into Cape Cod Bay and hour-long sunset trips for $12 to $16 per adult, less for children.

Water Safari's *Starfish* (☎ 508-362-5555), at the Bass River Bridge on MA 28, offers narrated trips on flat-bottom boats up the largest tidal river on the East Coast. Tickets cost $7.50/$4.50.

Cape Cod Waterway Boat Rentals (☎ 508-398-0080), on MA 28 in Dennisport, allow you to explore the much smaller (but interesting nonetheless) Swan River from the vantage point of a canoe or kayak from June through September.

Places to Stay

Motels In summer, the *Sesuit Harbor Motel* (☎ 508-385-3326), 1421 MA 6A, has 19 rooms that rent for $60 to $85 nightly and six efficiency units that are rented weekly for $475 to $650. The motel is open year round but the room rates drop only about $10 nightly in the off-season.

The *Holiday Hill Motor Inn* (☎ 508-394-5577), 352 MA 28, has 56 large rooms with refrigerators for $39 to $69 in the summer, $28 to $42 in the off-season; the motel is closed from mid-October through April.

The *Huntsman Motor Lodge* (☎ 508-394-5415), 829 MA 28, has 29 simple rooms and nine efficiencies. In the summer rates are $54 to $69 for two ($10 more in an efficiency); in the off-season doubles are $35 to $69; it's closed November to mid-April.

Inns & B&Bs The *Isaiah Hall B&B Inn* (☎ 508-385-9928, 800-736-0160), 152 Whig St off MA 6A in Dennis, offers 11 unpretentious rooms (most with private bath) in a 19th-century house and an attached, newly renovated barn. In addition to lovely gardens, an enthusiastic host and plenty of common space both inside and out, the inn is a 10-minute walk from the beach. Rates are $74 to $102 from mid-June to early September ($57 for the shared bath), slightly less in the off-season. The inn is closed from mid-October through March.

A Victorian sea captain's mansion, now called the *Captain Nickerson Inn* (☎ 508-398-5966, 800-282-1619), 333 Main St in South Dennis, has five guest rooms and is delightfully off the beaten path. A full breakfast is included with the rates: $60 to $85 double (the lower price is for shared bath) from mid-May to mid-October; $50 to $55 the rest of the year.

The *Four Chimneys Inn* (☎ 508-385-6317), 946 MA 6A in Dennis, has eight spacious rooms, most with private bath and high ceilings. Rates are $55 to $95 from mid-June to early September, slightly less in the off-season. The inn is closed from mid-October through April.

Places to Eat

McGuirl's Roadstand (☎ 508-394-5882), 189 Lower County Rd (south of and parallel to MA 28) in Dennisport, is just that: a roadside stand in a gravel parking lot that sells hot dogs, chowder, grilled sandwiches and shish kebobs for just a few bucks. It's open for lunch and dinner daily from mid-April to late October.

Of the Cape's ubiquitous clam shacks, *Captain Frosty's* (☎ 508-385-8548), 219 MA 6A in Dennis, is better because it offers more than fried clams and burgers. You might also order a daily special like grilled shrimp with a salad. Open from early April to mid-September, you'll spend $3 to $11 for a meal here.

If you feel like eating indoors, try *Bob Briggs' "Wee Packet"* (☎ 508-398-2181), on Depot St in Dennisport. The simple, diner-style place is usually packed with people who appreciate moderately priced meals ($3 to $12). The menu extends from broiled seafood, sandwiches and quiche to homemade desserts. The Wee Packet is open for lunch and dinner from early May to late September and also for breakfast in the height of summer.

Gina's By The Sea (☎ 508-385-3213), 143 Taunton St off MA 6A in Dennis, is popular with locals. Arrive early (no reservations are taken), put your name on the waiting list and go for a walk on the beach, just steps away. The northern Italian menu features traditional garlicky dishes for $9 to $20. The interior is pleasant, with knotty pine paneling, exposed ceiling beams and a small bar. It's open for dinner from April through November, and also for lunch in July and August.

The *Scargo Café* (☎ 508-385-8200), on MA 6A in Dennis, is popular and a pleasant place for lunch and dinner. Polished wood and plenty of natural light complement specials like grilled lamb, shrimp and pasta, and chicken with ginger sauce. Lunches vary from $5 to $12, dinners from $10 to $18 per main course. Early bird specials and pre-matinee lunches are popular with the theater crowd.

After the curtain comes down, actors and theater-goers head to the *Green Room Restaurant* (☎ 508-385-8000), 36 Hope Lane behind the Cape Playhouse, for a glass of wine or a coffee at the espresso bar.

The *Red Pheasant Inn* (☎ 508-385-2133), MA 6A in Dennis, serves creative regional American cuisine in a romantic 200-year-old renovated barn. Expect to spend $26 to $45 per person for a full meal; in the off-season the chef experiments with dishes and offers moderately-priced specials. It's open for dinner year round.

MASSACHUSETTS

Entertainment

The *Cape Playhouse* (☎ 508-385-3838, 385-3911), on MA 6A in Dennis, is generally regarded as the Cape's best summer theater. Well-known actors and rising stars perform in a different production each week between July and early September. There are shows every evening except Sunday, and matinees on Wednesday and Thursday; an average ticket costs about $20.

The *Cape Cinema* (☎ 508-385-2503), on MA 6A in Dennis, shows foreign, art and independent films Friday through Monday year round except January. From the exterior it looks like a Congregational church, but it was built to be a cinema in 1930 and the Art Deco ceiling was painted with a huge mural depicting heaven.

Getting There & Away

Bus The Plymouth & Brockton bus (☎ 508-746-0378) stops on MA 6A at the Dennis Post Office and at Player's Plaza in East Dennis on its way from Boston and Hyannis to Provincetown.

Car Driving details for Dennis are:

Destination	Mileage	Hr:Min
Boston, MA	86 miles	1:40
Bourne Bridge, MA	26 miles	0:35
Brewster, MA	6 miles	0:10
Hyannis, MA	8 miles	0:15
Provincetown, MA	45 miles	1:00
Yarmouth, MA	4 miles	0:08

Getting Around

The section of MA 6A that passes through Dennis is only three miles long and MA 28 is about the same, so there isn't much problem with navigating. From MA 6A, it's a mile east to Scargo Tower and two miles west to Chapin Memorial Beach.

BREWSTER

Brewster is another of the tranquil little towns on MA 6A. In addition to an excellent natural history museum, a state park with camping, Brewster also has arguably the best restaurant on the Cape.

Orientation & Information

From US 6 take exit 10 (Route 124 North) into town or continue along MA 6A; everything of interest is on or just off of MA 6A.

Brewster doesn't have an official chamber of commerce but you can pick up information at the Town Hall Annex (no ☎), off MA 6A, a half mile east of Route 124. It is open from 9 am to 3 pm daily in the summer.

Things to See & Do

The mission of the **Cape Cod Museum of Natural History** (☎ 508-896-3149, 800-896-3867), 869 MA 6A, is to "educate, enlighten, and entertain" people about the Cape's unique natural history. To that end, you'll find a series of photographs that show how a storm changed a coast line, fish tanks, whale displays and three short nature trails that cross cranberry bogs, salt marshes and beech groves. The museum ($3.50 adults, $1.50 children six to 14) is open daily except Monday from April to mid-October.

The **Old Grist Mill and Herring Run**, at Setucket and Stony Brook Rds (both off MA 6A), is one of the Cape's most tranquil and lush spots. If you visit from mid-April to early May you'll see thousands of herring migrating from the ocean to fresh water in order to spawn. As for the mill, the water wheel still turns the machinery that grinds the corn meal (which you can buy). The mill is open from 2 to 5 pm on Thursday through Saturday in May and June, and from 2 to 5 pm on Friday in July and August.

With 2000 acres, **Nickerson State Park**, was a local businessman's hunting and fishing estate in the early 1900s. It boasts eight ponds, a network of trails for bicycling and walking, picnic sites and sandy beaches. And it can all be enjoyed for free. The Cape Cod Rail Trail (see Dennis, Bicycling) runs through here.

The Idle Times Bike Shop (☎ 508-896-9242), just west of the park entrance on MA 6A, rents bikes. Jack's Boat Rentals (☎ 508-896-8556), on Flax Pond within the park, rents canoes, kayaks and other floatation devices.

Places to Stay

Camping *Nickerson State Park* (☎ 508-896-4615 for reservations, 896-3491 for information), 3488 MA 6A, has the best campsites on the Cape. There are 418 wooded sites, some with pond views, that cost $6 nightly. Advance reservations are taken for only 150 sites; the rest are rented first-come, first-served. In the summer, you may have to wait a day before getting a site. Although it's open year round, there are no toilet facilities nor running water in the winter months.

If Nickerson is full try the *Shady Knoll Campground* (☎ 508-896-3002), at MA 6A and Route 137. The 100 sites cost $15 to $20 nightly from mid-May to mid-October.

Inns A former girls' school, the *Old Sea Pines Inn* (☎ 508-896-6114), 2553 MA 6A, has rooms that range from small to moderately roomy. Some have antique iron and brass beds; others in the rear annex are more motel-like but quite pleasant. The living room is spacious and the front porch set with rockers. Rooms range from $43 to $95, depending on the time of year and the size.

The early 19th-century *Ruddy Turnstone* (☎ 508-385-9871), 463 MA 6A, has three unpretentious guest rooms and a more expensive suite, all furnished with comfortable antiques, oriental carpets and feather beds. The large living room has a fireplace, while the backyard has a hammock and views of Cape Cod Bay. Rooms rent for $75 to $135 from April through December.

Places to Eat

The *Brewster Coffee Shop* (☎ 508-896-8224), on MA 6A, is a no-frills place where you can get pancakes, eggs and grilled cheese sandwiches for $2 to $6, from 6 am to 2 pm year round.

Just off the Cape Cod Rail Trail, order the requisite fried seafood platter at *Cobie's* (☎ 508-896-7021), 3260 MA 6A, and take it to one of the outdoor picnic tables. It's open from lunch through dinner from late May to mid-September.

The *Box Lunch* (☎ 508-896-6682), on Underpass Rd (off Route 137 from MA 6A), is also just off the Rail Trail. This outfit specializes in inexpensive sandwiches rolled up in pita bread. Look for this chain of counter-top restaurants around the Cape.

The "more" at *Pizza & More* (☎ 508-896-8600), 302 Underpass Rd, includes sandwiches, grinders, pasta and Greek salads for $3 to $12 at lunch and dinner.

The *Brewster Fish House* (☎ 508-896-7867), 2208 MA 6A, is highly regarded for its simple, well-prepared seafood at moderate prices in pleasant surroundings. Expect to wait if you arrive after 6:30 pm for dinner. It's open for lunch ($6 to $8) and dinner ($13 to $20 per main course) from mid-April to mid-December.

Chillingsworth (☎ 508-896-3640), 2449 MA 6A, is regarded as the Cape's best French restaurant, and perhaps the Cape's best restaurant, period. A seven-course, fixed-price dinner will set you back $40 to $52 per person, but there are ways to have a Chillingsworth experience without losing your shirt. Come for the à la carte lunch ($8 to $11.50 per dish) or select from the bistro dinner menu in the less formal but still upscale Garden Room. It's open from late May to late November.

Entertainment

The *Woodshed* (☎ 508-896-7771), on MA 6A, is a rustic bar and restaurant where the locals hang out listening to local bands on most nights during the summer.

The *Cape Rep Theatre Co* (☎ 508-896-6140), 3379 MA 6A, stages creative outdoor productions in a natural amphitheater surrounded by trees.

Things to Buy

The Great Cape Cod Herb, Spice & Tea Co (☎ 508-896-5900), 2628 MA 6A, stocks almost 200 herbs. This section of MA 6A is thick with art galleries and antique shops of varying degrees of quality.

The Brewster Store (☎ 508-896-3744), at MA 6A and Route 124, is an old-fashioned country store that's managed to stay in operation since 1866. Upstairs is a little museum of sorts.

Getting There & Away

Bus The Plymouth & Brockton bus (☎ 508-746-0378) stops at the Brewster Store on MA 6A on its way from Boston to Hyannis and Provincetown.

Car Driving details for Brewster are:

Destination	Mileage	Hr:Min
Boston, MA	90 miles	1:45
Bourne Bridge, MA	30 miles	0:45
Chatham, MA	9 miles	0:15
Dennis, MA	6 miles	0:10
Orleans, MA	5 miles	0:10
Provincetown, MA	34 miles	0:45

HARWICH

There's not much to recommend in Harwich, but if you're passing through from Hyannis to Chatham, you'll find a waterfront restaurant, a homey B&B and an alternative ferry to Nantucket along with one of the most picturesque harbors on the Cape. Tranquil Wychmere Harbor, with a convenient grassy picnic spot overlooking the enclosed harbor, is right on MA 28.

The Harwich Chamber of Commerce (☎ 508-432-1600, 800-441-3199), on MA 28, is open daily from 9 am to 5 pm mid-June to mid-September and on weekends only for the month before and after.

The *House on the Hill* (☎ 508-432-4321), 968 MA 28, is a homey throw-back to the 19th century. Set up on a knoll off the busy road, the farmhouse has three simple guest rooms with private bath that rent for $55 to $65 in the summer; it's open year round.

Thompson's Clam Bar (☎ 508-432-3595), 23 Snow Inn Rd just off MA 28, sits right on the harbor channel, and from some tables you can reach out and almost touch the boats passing by. Open and airy but still clubby, at Thompson's you'll munch on clam chowder, fish and chips, and all manner of seafood. Lunch ($6.50 to $14) costs half of what dinner does.

See Nantucket, Getting There & Away, for ferry information.

CHATHAM

Chatham is the patriarch of Cape Cod towns. A genteel, refined reserve is evident along its pretty Main St; the shops are upscale and expensive, the lodging-places toney. Though the bulk of the town's summer residents are regulars, there is a small but ardent tourist trade.

Orientation

From US 6, take Route 137 South (exit 11) to Old Queen Anne Rd to MA 28 and Main St.

From Hyannis and points west, continue on MA 28 North (you're actually heading due east) into the center of town. From Orleans and points north, take MA 28 South into town to Shore Rd, which runs south along the shore, past the Fish Pier, the lighthouse and onto Morris Island. Main St is about a mile long from the MA 28 rotary to Shore Rd.

Chatham is something of a peninsula, surrounded on three sides by water.

Information

Chatham's Information Booth (☎ 508-945-5199, 800-715-5567 for recorded information), 533 Main St, is a tiny little place with knowledgeable staff, and it's crammed with everything you could ever want to know about the town. The booth is open from 10 am to 6 pm Monday through Saturday and noon to 6 pm on Sunday from late May to mid-October.

Things to See

The **Chatham Light** viewing area on Shore Rd, with an expansive vista of sand and sea, is the town's most visited "attraction." The break in Nauset Beach (the long spit of sand is now broken by a channel of water) was caused by a ferocious storm in 1987; residents are still talking about the environmental consequences. The present light, by the way, dates to 1878 and is visible 15 miles out to sea. There is free parking and a fine beach below (see Beaches below).

Head to the **Fish Pier** on Shore Rd every mid-afternoon to watch the fishing fleet come in with its daily catch. Chatham's boats haul in some of the freshest fish around because they're small and cannot stay out overnight. On Chatham menus, the term "daily catch" really has meaning!

The **Railroad Museum** (no ☎), 153 Depot Rd from Old Harbor Rd north off Main St, is fashioned from an 1887 depot and features a 1910 wooden caboose. The museum is open mid-June to mid-September, from 10 am to 4 pm Tuesday through Saturday; admission is free.

The **Old Atwood House** (☎ 508-945-2493), 347 Stage Harbor Rd (off the western end of Main St from the rotary) contains a historical collection of over 2000 items pertaining to Chatham's past. It's open June through September from 2 to 5 pm Tuesday through Friday; admission is $3 adults, $1 for children 12 to 18.

The 2700-acre wildlife refuge on **Monomoy Island** is a haven for offshore birds, only accessible by boat. You'll be well rewarded for the additional effort it takes to reach it. For information on bird-watching tours call the Wellfleet Bay Wildlife Sanctuary (☎ 508-349-2615) or the Cape Cod Museum of Natural History (☎ 508-896-3867).

Beaches
Chatham Light Beach, directly below the lighthouse on Shore Rd, is a long, wide sandy beach. It's best to walk or bicycle here since parking at the lighthouse is limited to 30 minutes.

Desolate and long North and South Beaches are accessible only by shuttle boat. It's worth the added expense of getting there. See Getting Around, below.

Bicycling
If you want to keep your feet on the ground (sort of), Chatham's side-streets and shady lanes are well-suited to bicycling. You can rent bikes at Monomoy Sail & Cycle (☎ 508-945-0811), 275 MA 28 in North Chatham.

Cruises
Chatham Harbor Tours (☎ 508-255-0619), at the Fish Pier on Shore Rd, offers four daily narrated cruises (from mid-June through September) of Pleasant Bay and the North Beach area. Adults pay $15, children $10.

Organized Tours
The Cape Cod Flying Circus (☎ 508-945-9000, 945-2363), at the Chatham Municipal Airport on George Ryder Rd from MA 28 in West Chatham, offers 20-minute sightseeing flights over the immediate coastline, bays and inlets for $50; there is also a flight over the narrow corridor of the Outer Cape for $30 to $85, depending on the length of the flight.

Places to Stay
Chatham's lodgings are both upscale and expensive.

Motels In addition to a private beach, the *Hawthorne Motel* (☎ 508-945-0372), 196 Shore Rd, has 27 standard rooms and efficiency units overlooking the ocean. There is a four-night minimum stay in the summer. Rates are $110 to $130 nightly from mid-May to mid-October.

Two miles west of town, the *Chatham Motel* (☎ 508-945-2630), 1487 MA 28, has 26 rooms set back from the highway in a pine grove. Rates are $85 to $135 in the summer, $65 to $105 in the off-season; it's closed from November through April.

Three miles west of town, the *Seafarer of Chatham* (☎ 508-432-1739), MA 28 at Ridgevale Rd, has 20 rooms and efficiency units that rent for $110 to $130 in the summer, $68 to $95 in the off-season; closed from December through March. Ask about minimum stay requirements in the summer.

Inns & B&Bs The gracious 19th-century *Cyrus Kent House* (☎ 508-945-9104, 800-338-5368), 63 Cross St, boasts 10 antique-furnished, canopy-bedded rooms in a beautifully restored sea captain's house. A block from the center of town, rooms rent for $125 to $165 in the summer, $75 to $125 the rest of the year.

Toward the end of Main St, the *Cranberry Inn* (☎ 508-945-9232, 800-332-4667), 359 Main St, is a completely renovated early 19th-century hostelry that has fancy wallpaper, antiques and canopy beds in the 18 guest rooms. Most rooms have fireplaces, some have little decks. Rooms start at $125 in the summer, $85 the rest of the year. A full breakfast buffet is included.

Resort Hotel The *Chatham Bars Inn* (☎ 508-945-0096, 800-527-4884), Shore Rd, is the Cape's grande dame of hotels. Rooms are generally overpriced at $160 to $375 double in the summer, but you may want to inquire about off-season packages which start at $90 nightly in the winter. Facilities include an ocean-side pool, tennis courts and a private beach. In any event, it's an impressive place to see, especially from a rocking chair on the expansive veranda.

Places to Eat
The *Chatham Squire* (☎ 508-945-0945), 487 Main St, is the town's most popular all-purpose tavern. The restaurant (to the left) is busy all year, serving lunch and dinner at moderate prices. The lounge (bar, to the right) serves the same menu, but the noise level is louder. The lunch menu is long and varied. At dinner, try the cod cheeks and shrimp over angel hair pasta ($15), a house specialty.

Only a half-block away, the *Impudent Oyster* (☎ 508-945-3545), 15 Chatham Bars Ave, is a bit more upscale and reserved, with an extensive seafood menu, fresh-shucked oysters and a loyal following. Lunch is reasonable ($6 to $10); dinner main courses are more than double that.

Upstairs at Christian's (☎ 508-945-5033), 443 Main St, serves home-style meals like meatloaf with gravy and chicken with biscuits, but it's also a fine pub-style place to come for a beer and a large order of Cajun French fries. In warm weather, eat lunch and dinner on the outdoor deck for $5 to $15 per main course.

The *Beach House Grill* (☎ 508-945-0096), Shore Rd across from the Chatham Bars Inn, is a tad expensive ($7 to $15) for what you get (gussied-up burgers, fancy salads and lobster rolls) but you're paying for the privilege of eating on the beach. It's open for breakfast and lunch from late May to early September.

Bread Harbor (☎ 508-945-4556), 410 Main St, is a fine small place to go for an inexpensive sandwich, soup, a sweet or coffee. You can also assemble a picnic of homemade bread and imported snacks. There are a few indoor tables and a few more on the back deck.

Carmine's (☎ 508-945-5300), 595 Main St, serves hot slices of pizza and cold scoops of gelato in a faux old-fashioned ice cream parlor setting.

If you're tired of sandwiches, stop at *Marion's Pie Shop* (☎ 508-432-9439), 2022 MA 28, and pick up a chicken pot pie.

Entertainment
Most Cape towns have summertime outdoor concerts, but Chatham has the granddaddy of them all. Thousands of folks have gathered every Friday at 8 pm since the mid-1930s to listen and dance to big band music from the gazebo. Follow the crowds to Kate Gould Park off Main St.

The *Monomoy Theatre* (☎ 508-945-1589), on MA 28 towards Harwich, is one of the Cape's best-known Equity playhouses. A new production is staged by Ohio University students every week from late June to early September.

Getting There & Away
Bus There is no bus service to Chatham.

Car Driving details for Chatham are:

Destination	Mileage	Hr:Min
Boston, MA	95 miles	1:50
Brewster, MA	9 miles	0:15
Hyannis, MA	19 miles	0:35
Orleans, MA	9.5 miles	0:15
Provincetown, MA	38 miles	0:50
Sagamore Bridge, MA	35 miles	0:50

Getting Around

Chatham is best explored on foot; it's about a 15-minute walk from one end of Main St to the lighthouse on Shore Rd and another 15 minutes from the lighthouse to the fish pier.

To reach Monomoy Island or North Beach, take the Water Taxi (☎ 508-430-2346) from the Fish Pier's South Dock. A roundtrip ticket costs $10 for adults, $2 to $6 for children depending on their age. The Water Taxi also offers harbor and sunset tours.

Outermost Marine (☎ 508-945-2030), off Morris Island Rd, offers transportation to South Beach ($9 for adults, $4.50 children) as well as seal-sighting trips.

ORLEANS

To some, Orleans is simply the place where MA 28 and US 6 converge and US 6 heads north to Provincetown. Many others know that Nauset Beach is exceptional and that Nauset Marsh has a rich ecosystem worth exploring. Some are keenly aware that there are lots of good restaurants here. But fewer know that Orleans has a military history: the British fired upon Orleans during the War of 1812 and a German submarine fired a few torpedoes at it during WWI.

Orientation & Information

US 6, MA 6A and MA 28 all converge at the rotary on the northern edge of town.

Main St, which intersects with MA 6A and 28, runs northwest to picturesque Rock Harbor and east to East Orleans center and Nauset Beach (where it turns into Beach Rd). The stretch of MA 28 that heads south through Orleans, past Pleasant Bay, is particularly scenic.

The Orleans Chamber of Commerce (☎ 508-240-2484), Eldrege Park Way off MA 6A just north of US 6, maintains a seasonal information booth that's open late May to mid-September from 9 am to 8 pm Monday through Saturday, with slightly shorter hours on Sunday.

The Compass Rose Bookshop (☎ 508-255-1545), Main St, is the best bookstore in town. On Wednesday and Saturday from 10 am to 2 pm doors are thrown open to the 40%-off bargain basement.

Things to See & Do

The **French Cable Station Museum** (☎ 508-240-1735), MA 28 at Cove Rd, stands as testimony to late 19th-century technology. This former station contains the equipment used to transmit the first communications via a 4000-mile underwater cable laid between Orleans and Brest, France. Among the messages relayed: Lindbergh's arrival in Paris and Germany's invasion of France. The museum is open from 2 to 4 pm Tuesday through Saturday in July and August; admission is free. Orleans also has more than its share of artisans, galleries and antiques shops.

You can rent bicycles to explore the quiet back roads at Orleans Cycle (☎ 508-255-9115), 26 Main St.

Beaches

Nauset Beach, at the end of Beach Rd from Main St in East Orleans, is one of the best beaches on the Cape for walking, sunning and body surfing. It's a sandy nine-mile-long barrier beach on the Atlantic Ocean with good facilities, including restrooms, changing rooms and a snack bar; parking is $8, though it's usually free in the off-season.

Cruises

Seashore Park Boat Tours (☎ 508-240-3100), behind the Orleans Inn near the US 6 and MA 28 rotary, narrates tours of Nauset Marsh and the barrier beach twice daily from June to mid-October. The cost is $10 for adults, $7 for children; an evening trip in the summer is a bit less.

Places to Stay

Motels In the middle of town but apart from the bustle, *The Cove* (☎ 508-255-1203, 800-343-2233), 13 MA 28, has 47 very nice motel rooms, some of which are right on Town Cove, and all of which have access to a bit of private shoreline. Outside are barbecue grills and a heated pool.

Inside, rooms have refrigerators, coffee makers and free movies. Rates ($90 to $173 in July and August) include a free boat tour of Nauset Marsh. Doubles rent for $50 to $119 the rest of the year.

The *Orleans Holiday Motel* (☎ 508-255-1514, 800-451-1833), at MA 6A and 28, offers a free shuttle across Nauset Marsh to Nauset Beach. The 2-story motel, with a large pool and picnic area, has 45 modern rooms connected by a balcony-walkway. Rates are $87 to $105 in the summer, $53 to $79 the rest of the year.

Efficiencies *Kadee's Gray Elephant* (☎ 508-255-7608), 216 Main St in East Orleans, has 10 fancifully painted, artsy efficiency apartments carved out of a 200-year-old sea captain's house. Each rents for $110 to $120 in the summer, $70 nightly during the rest of the year. It's about a 30-minute walk to Nauset Beach from here. See also the Parsonage Inn, below.

Inns & B&Bs The *Nauset House Inn* (☎ 508-255-2195), Beach Rd in East Orleans, is one of the best B&Bs in the area. The innkeepers are friendly, the rooms comfortable, the common areas plentiful (including a greenhouse conservatory) and the location excellent – it's about a 10-minute walk to Nauset Beach. Afternoon snacks and drinks are included in the rates but the fabulous breakfast is not: $65 to $105 from April to late October. A few rooms have shared baths.

The rambling late 18th-century *Parsonage Inn* (☎ 508-255-8217), 202 Main St in East Orleans, has eight simple rooms all with private bath that rent for $75 to $95 from June through September and $60 to $85 the rest of the year. There is also a studio apartment that rents for a bit more.

The *Ship's Knees Inn* (☎ 508-255-1312), 186 Beach Rd in East Orleans, has a few nice inn-style rooms but many more plain, colonial-style motel rooms. Rooms with shared bath are at the low end of the range at $60 to $110.

Places to Eat

The *Hot Chocolate Sparrow* (☎ 508-240-2230), MA 6A, has the best espresso around, as well as muffins, chocolate and other treats.

The *Wheel Haus Kaffee* (☎ 508-240-1585), Academy Place at MA 28, owned by a German couple, is part Bavarian pastry shop, part outdoor Euro-cafe.

New York Bagels (☎ 508-255-0255), 125 MA 6A, has real bagels and everything else you'd expect to find at a Jewish deli in Brooklyn.

Frequented by locals, *Land Ho!* (☎ 508-255-5165), on MA 6A in the center of town, is part bar, part restaurant. Patrons come for inexpensive ($3 to $6.25) sandwiches, fried seafood platters and burgers. The atmosphere is informal with wooden floors, old business signs on the walls and newspapers hanging on a wire that separates the tables from the bar. It's open daily year round.

The *Binnacle Tavern* (☎ 508-255-7901), 20 MA 28, is a popular and cozy tavern that's particularly well-known for pizza, but it also offers other Italian dishes ($6 to $9) like eggplant parmigiana. It's open nightly for dinner from April to mid-October.

Cap't Cass Rock Harbor Seafood (no ☎), 117 Rock Harbor Rd, is a little harborside seafood shack that's more quaint than most. Go for a generous lobster roll, clam chowder or one of the daily blackboard specials. Lunch ($5 to $10) and dinner are served from late May to mid-October.

Filled with nautical paraphernalia, the *Lobster Claw* (☎ 508-255-1800), MA 6A, is an informal place with wooden booths and menus shaped like lobster claws. Lobsters, mixed seafood plates and all kinds of fish: it's all on the menu for $6.25 to $14.50. A raw bar and regular bar are upstairs. The restaurant is open daily from 11:30 am to 9 pm April through November.

The *Old Jailhouse Tavern* (☎ 508-255-5245), 28 West Rd just off MA 6A from

Cape Cod National Seashore

With the backing of President Kennedy, who appreciated the Cape's uniqueness and considered it his home, Congress established the Cape Cod National Seashore (CCNS) in 1961. The CCNS includes the whole eastern shoreline of the Lower (or Outer) Cape, from South Beach in Chatham all the way to Provincetown. It covers more than 42 sq miles in all, including at least half (and often more) of the land mass in Eastham, Wellfleet, Truro and Provincetown. The seashore is known for its pristine and virtually endless beaches, crashing waves, dunes, nature trails, ponds, salt marshes and forests.

Everything of interest is on or just off of US 6, the only highway from Orleans to Provincetown.

The Salt Pond Visitor Center, (☎ 508-255-3421), off US 6 in Eastham, anchors the southern portion of the CCNS. There are excellent exhibits and films about the Cape's geology, history and ever-changing landscape. Check the daily list of ranger- and naturalist-led walks and talks, which are usually free. There are two short walking trails that lead from the visitor center.

The Province Lands Visitor Center (☎ 508-487-1256), Race Point Rd in Provincetown, has similar services and exhibits; you can also pick up local trail and bike maps here. It's open daily 9 am to 4:30 pm from mid-April through November, and 9 am to 6 pm daily from late May to early September. ■

Skaket Corners, has something for everyone: fish and chips, burgers, seafood, salads and lots of appetizers. It's always crowded because the prices ($5 to $15.50) are quite reasonable. It's open daily from 11:30 am to 1 am year round. Dine within the walls of the old jail, at the boisterous bar or on the enclosed greenhouse-like terrace.

At *Kadee's Lobster & Clam Bar* (☎ 508-255-6184), 212 Main St in East Orleans, you again have a choice of places to dine: in a rustic dining room, at outdoor tables or anywhere you like (there's a take-out window). It's all fresh and it's all seafood: oysters, seafood stew, lobster, scallops. Kadee's is open for lunch and dinner ($10 to $16 per main course) from late May to early September.

Off-The-Bay Café (☎ 508-255-5505), 28 Main St, serves regional American dishes like duck with cranberry and beach plum compote. The storefront setting is quite pleasant, with wooden booths, brass lights and tin ceilings. Come for lunch (about $10); it costs half what dinner does and you won't have to wait in line.

Entertainment

The outdoor deck of the *Orleans Inn* (☎ 508-255-2222), at the MA 28 and US 6 rotary, is a great place for an après-beach or sunset drink.

The *Academy Playhouse* (☎ 508-255-1963), 120 Main St, stages a variety of dramas, musicals and comedies in the 1873 former Town Hall.

Getting There & Away

Bus The Plymouth & Brockton bus (☎ 508-746-0378) stops at the CVS drugstore on MA 6A on its way from Provincetown to Hyannis and Boston.

Car Driving details for Orleans are:

Destination	Mileage	Hr:Min
Boston, MA	87 miles	1:45
Brewster, MA	5 miles	0:10
Chatham, MA	10 miles	0:15
Falmouth, MA	42 miles	1:00
Provincetown, MA	29 miles	0:40
Sagamore Bridge, MA	37 miles	0:45

Getting Around

It's about three miles from Orleans center to Nauset Beach, about half that in the opposite direction to Rock Harbor.

EASTHAM

Eastham, home to the Cape's oldest wind-mill, is one of the Cape's quietest, most compact towns, just three miles wide from bay to ocean, and six miles long. It's perhaps best known for what happened in 1620: the Pilgrims first "encountered" Native Americans on a stretch of land now aptly called First Encounter Beach. The meeting was less than friendly, though there were no fatalities, and the Pilgrims didn't return to the area for another 24 years.

Orientation & Information

The Eastham Chamber of Commerce (☎ 508-255-3444), on US 6 just north of the Fort Hill Area, is open daily 10 am to 5 pm from late May through September, with slightly longer hours in July and August.

For more tourist information, go to the CCNS Salt Pond Visitor Center.

Things to See & Do

The **Fort Hill area**, east of US 6, provides a high vantage point from which to survey the extensive and fragile Nauset Marsh. There is a short but lovely walking trail here.

The **Edward Penniman House** (☎ 508-255-3421), at Fort Hill, is a mid-19th-century sea captain's house that's being slowly restored to its former grandeur by the NPS. Visiting hours are limited to 2 to 4 pm on weekdays, and 11 am to 1 pm on Saturdays from late May through September.

The **Old Schoolhouse Museum** (☎ 508-255-0788), across from the visitor center, houses the Eastham Historical Society. Its entrance is marked by a huge set of whale jaw bones. Admission is free and it's open on weekdays from 1 to 4 pm in July and August.

The **bike trail** from the visitor center to Coast Guard Beach takes you across a dramatic salt marsh and through a pretty forest. You can rent bikes across from the visitor center at Little Capistrano Bike Shop (☎ 508-255-6515).

Beaches

Coast Guard Beach, east of the visitor center on the Atlantic Ocean, is a long sandy beach backed by tall, undulating dune grasses. Facilities include restrooms, showers and changing rooms. In the summer a bus shuttles people from a parking lot near the visitor center to the beach for $5.

Nauset Light Beach, north of Coast Guard Beach, is also great. Its features and facilities are similar to Coast Guard Beach, but you can park at the beach for $5. Nauset Lighthouse, a picturesque red and white striped tower, guards the shoreline.

Places to Stay

Camping The *Atlantic Oaks Campground* (☎ 508-255-1437), US 6 just north of the Salt Pond Visitor Center, has 100 mostly shaded sites shared by tenters and folks in RVs. Rates are $15 to $20 nightly for two from May through October.

Hostel Eastham has the *Mid-Cape Youth Hostel* (☎ 508-255-2785), 75 Goody Hallet Drive, Eastham, MA 02642, open from mid-May to mid-September. The 50 beds in eight cabins go for $12. Reservations (by mail, or by phone with credit card) are essential in July and August. Off-season, reserve by writing to 1020 Commonwealth Ave, Boston, MA 02215 (☎ 617-739-3017). From US 6 and the Orleans rotary, follow Harbor Rd to Bridge Rd to Goody Hallet Drive.

Motels & Cottages The *Midway Motel & Cottages* (☎ 508-255-3117), US 6, are set back from the highway and shaded by pine trees. Cottages are rented by the week in the summer ($500 to $650); rooms are $68 to $74 nightly in the summer and reduced to about half that in the off-season. The complex is closed from November through January.

The *Saltaway Cottages* (☎ 508-255-2182), Aspinet Rd off US 6, are thankfully well off the highway. The seven well-maintained and homey efficiency units rent for $360 to $660 in the summer, $300 to $390 in the off-season (closed from mid-October to mid-May).

The *Captain's Quarters* (☎ 508-255-5686, 800-327-7769), on MA 6A, has 75 large rooms, a heated pool and tennis courts. Rates are $78 to $100 in the summer, $50 to $64 in the off-season (closed December through March).

Hotel The *Sheraton Ocean Park Inn* (☎ 508-255-5000, 800-533-3986), US 6, is expensive in the summer, but in the off-season you might be able to get a room for as little as $59. Half the rooms overlook the indoor pool; some have refrigerators.

Inns & B&Bs The *Overlook Inn* (☎ 800-356-1121), across from the CCNS Salt Pond Visitor Center, is set back from the road and offers 10 light and airy guest rooms furnished with antiques. There are several slightly eccentric but charming common rooms, including a billiards room. Rates, including a full breakfast are $95 to $110 in the summer, $65 to $95 the rest of the year.

The *Whalewalk Inn* (☎ 508-255-0617), 220 Bridge Rd off the Orleans-Eastham rotary, is the best Outer Cape B&B. If you want to splurge a bit, there are five private suites in detached buildings (most with kitchen) that are on the high end of the rates: $95 to $165 from April through November. Common rooms are sophisticated country-elegant, and the full breakfast served on the flagstone patio is a real eye-opener.

Places to Eat
The *Eastham Lobster Pool* (☎ 508-255-9706), 4360 US 6, offers informal indoor and outdoor dining on lobsters (surprise!), tasty clam chowder ($2.25) and fish cooked practically any way you'd like ($14 to $16) daily from 11:30 am to 9 pm April through November.

Arnold's Lobster & Clam Bar (☎ 508-255-2575), 3580 US 6, is similar to the Eastham Lobster Pool but also has a raw bar and lunch specials for as low as $3.

Entertainment
The little yellow chapel known as the *First Encounter Coffee House* (☎ 508-255-5438), Samoset Rd off US 6 from the windmill, hosts acoustic and folk performances on the first and third Saturday of each month.

Getting There & Away
Bus The Plymouth & Brockton bus (☎ 508-746-0378) stops at the Town Hall in Eastham and the village green in North Eastham (both on MA 6) on its way from Boston and Hyannis to Provincetown.

Car Driving details for Eastham are:

Destination	Mileage	Hr:Min
Boston, MA	100 miles	1:50
Hyannis, MA	24 miles	0:35
Orleans MA	5 miles	0:10
Provincetown, MA	25 miles	0:35
Sagamore Bridge, MA	40 miles	0:50
Wellfleet, MA	11 miles	0:15

WELLFLEET
Like most Lower Cape towns, Wellfleet is relatively untouched by development and rampant commercialism. Although Wellfleet in the summertime is full of professional people who have taken up residence for the season, day-trippers are lured by art galleries, fine beaches, quiet scenic roads and the famous Wellfleet oysters. The town is very quiet from early September to late June.

Orientation & Information
Main and Commercial Sts run parallel to each other in the center of town. Continue west along either road to scenic Chequessett Neck Rd. West of US 6, Pilgrim Spring Rd is also scenic; from the end of it there is a nice view of the harbor. East of US 6, LeCount Hollow Rd leads to Ocean View Drive and Atlantic Ocean beaches.

The Wellfleet Chamber of Commerce (☎ 508-349-2510), just off US 6 in South Wellfleet, is open daily from 9 am to 6 pm in July and August and on weekends in the spring and fall.

Things to See

The 1000-acre Audubon **Wellfleet Bay Wildlife Sanctuary** (☎ 508-349-2615), west off US 6, boasts walking trails that crisscross tidal creeks, salt marshes and a Cape Cod Bay beach. The visitor center is open daily from 9 am to 5 pm year round (except closed on Monday from November through April).

The **Marconi Wireless Station**, east off US 6 in South Wellfleet, was the first place in the US to transmit messages across the Atlantic Ocean. Little remains today except for interpretive plaques. There is an expansive vista from here, a walking trail and a fine beach.

Beaches

Marconi Beach, off US 6, is a narrow Atlantic beach backed by high dunes. Parking is $5 daily; facilities include changing rooms and showers.

Cahoon Hollow and White Crest Beach, both of which are also on the Atlantic Ocean, are excellent but parking is more expensive at $10 daily. White Crest is popular with hang-gliders.

Hiking

The eight-mile **Great Island Trail**, off Chequessett Neck Rd, requires four hours, lots of sunscreen, water and a bit of stamina since you'll be walking on soft sand out to a spit of sand that curves around into Wellfleet Bay. The lack of human presence more than compensates for the extra effort. The road to Great Island Trail is narrow, hilly and winding.

Bicycling

The **Cape Cod Rail Trail**, which begins in Dennis 25 miles southwest, ends at LeCount Hollow Rd, a couple miles from two good beaches. You can rent bikes at the Idle Times Bike Shop (☎ 508-349-9161) on US 6 from mid-June to mid-September.

Places to Stay

Camping *Maurice's Tent & Trailer Park* (☎ 508-349-2029), US 6 just north of the Eastham town line, reserves about a quarter of its 225 sites for tents. Sites cost $18 for two people from mid-May to mid-October.

Motels & Studios The *Even'Tide Motel* (☎ 508-349-3410, 800-368-0007 in-state), on US 6, is about four miles north of the CCNS Salt Pond Visitor Center and set back in a grove of trees. There are 31 rooms and a few studio apartments that rent for $72 to $102 in the summer, $45 to $79 the rest of the year. Other pluses include an indoor heated pool, a nearby trail to Marconi Beach and the Cape Cod Rail Trail, which runs right behind the motel.

The *Wellfleet Motel & Lodge* (☎ 508-349-3535, 800-852-2900), US 6, is across from the wildlife sanctuary and has two pools and 65 above-average rooms. Each has a refrigerator, coffee maker and free movies for $70 to $133 in the summer, $50 to $80 in the off-season; it's closed from December through March.

Ocean Pines Motel and Cottages (☎ 508-349-2774), US 6, has the cheapest beds in town at $62 to $69 double. Cottages rent by the week: $375 for a double in the summer.

Inns & B&Bs The *Holden Inn* (☎ 508-349-3450), Commercial St, is an old-fashioned hostelry that hasn't changed much since the current family purchased it in the mid-1920s. The sparsely furnished guest rooms are housed in three buildings. You can't beat $58 to $68 a double for an in-town location and a rocking chair on the front porch.

The nicest rooms at *Inn at Duck Creeke* (☎ 508-349-9333), Main St near US 6, are in the cottage and carriage house. Otherwise the inn rooms are adequate for $65 to $90, depending on the bath situation.

Brehmer Graphics Bed & Breakfast (☎ 508-349-9595), Commercial St, has just two shared-bath rooms decorated with comfortable Victorian furnishings. With a full breakfast included in the price ($70 in the summer, $45 off-season, closed January through March), it's worth trying to get a room here. The living room doubles as a shop for Brehmer's work.

Places to Eat

The *Lighthouse* (☎ 508-349-3681), Main St, is one of the few places in town open year round, and for all three meals too! It's nothing fancy, just decent food at good prices: omelets ($4.75), sandwiches ($4 to $7), burgers, fish ($6.50 to $12) and Guinness on tap. Try to get a table in the glassed-in dining room; it's quieter.

The *Captain Higgins Seafood Restaurant* (☎ 508-349-6027), on the Town Pier, is an informal seafood place near the water for lunch ($7 to $11) and dinner ($11 to $15) from mid-June to mid-September. Try the lobster rolls, native bluefish and especially the Wellfleet oysters.

The *Bayside Lobster Hutt* (☎ 508-349-6055), Commercial St, is an informal self-service place where patrons dine on indoor picnic tables and dig into their food (lobsters, corn on the cob and clams) with their hands. It's open daily from 11:30 am to 10 pm in July and August and for dinner only in June and September. Bring your own beer or wine if you wish.

Celeste's Depot Café (☎ 508-349-9533), Commercial St, is a cheery little spot that's open daily for breakfast and lunch from June to mid-October. Eggs, sandwiches and salads ($3 to $6) can be taken outside to the tables overlooking Duck Creek.

The *Box Lunch* (☎ 508-349-2178), Briar Lane, serves deli meats and salads rolled up in pita bread ($4 to $5). It's open daily year round.

Above Wellfleet's fanciest and best restaurant, Aesop's Tables, *Upstairs Bar at Aesop's Tables* (☎ 508-349-6450), Main St, has an old-world feel to it with velveteen chairs, comfortable couch groupings and low lighting. It's a nice place to go for a meal (steak sandwiches or barbecue ribs cost about $10), dessert or an after-dinner drink.

Entertainment

The *Beachcomber* (☎ 508-349-6055), at Cahoon Hollow Beach off Ocean View Drive, is an indoor-outdoor, all-in-one restaurant, bar and nightclub on the beach. It's the best area hang-out for live music at night, but the club is also known for Sunday afternoon concerts and happy hours with drinks poured to a reggae beat.

The *Tavern Room* (☎ 508-349-7369), Main St, is a fine place to listen to live jazz, folk and Latin music. You can also get a light snack in this dark and cozy place with beamed ceilings.

The *Wellfleet Drive-In* (☎ 508-349-7176, 800-696-3532), US 6, is one of the few remaining drive-in theaters in New England. Catch first-run movies from May through September.

The *Wellfleet Harbor Actors Theater* (WHAT, ☎ 508-349-6835), Kendrick Ave off Commercial St, stages contemporary, sometimes experimental plays from mid-May to mid-October.

Things to Buy

Wellfleet has over 20 galleries selling both fine art and tourist art. Most galleries host receptions (with free food and drink) on Saturday nights in July and August.

The Wellfleet Flea Market (☎ 508-349-2520, 800-696-3532), at the drive-in theater on US 6, is the Cape's biggest venue for both treasure and junk. It's open on weekends from mid-April to mid-October and on Wednesdays and Thursdays in July and August.

Getting There & Away

Bus The Plymouth & Brockton bus (☎ 508-746-0378) stops at the D&D Market in South Wellfleet (MA 6) and the Town Hall in Wellfleet center (off MA 6) on its way from Boston and Hyannis to Provincetown.

Car Driving details for Wellfleet are:

Destination	Mileage	Hr:Min
Boston, MA	110 miles	2:05
Eastham, MA	11 miles	0:15
Hyannis, MA	36 miles	0:45
Provincetown, MA	15 miles	0:20
Sagamore Bridge, MA	51 miles	1:05
Truro, MA	7 miles	0:09

Getting Around

The center of Wellfleet is best explored by foot and bike since there is very little parking.

TRURO

An odd collection of elements co-exist peacefully in Truro: strip motels and cookie-cutter cottage complexes, huge homes built in the hills and dales to the west of US 6, and undeveloped forests and beaches to the east. There's very little to do in this sleepy little town, but there is good camping and beach-going.

Orientation & Information

Truro is about 10 miles long and only a few miles wide, with no town center per se. Everything you'll need is on or just off of US 6. In North Truro, MA 6A veers off US 6 and is chock-a-block with motels as it heads into Provincetown. Take any winding road east or west of US 6, get lost a bit and soak in the scenery.

The Truro Chamber of Commerce (☎ 508-487-1288), US 6 in North Truro, is open from late June to early September from 10 am to 5 pm daily, with additional (albeit shorter) hours on weekends for the month before and after that.

Things to See & Do

The Highland Light, also known as **Cape Cod Light**, east of US 6 in North Truro, replaced the Cape's first lighthouse, which was built on this spot in 1798. Nearby is the Cape's oldest golf course.

Once a summer hotel, the **Truro Historical Museum** (☎ 508-487-3397), just before the lighthouse, is now an interesting local museum dedicated to Truro's farming and maritime past. It's open daily (adults $2, children under 12 free) from mid-June to mid-September.

The **Pilgrim Heights Area**, east of US 6, has two short trails with splendidly expansive views. One trail leads to the spot where the Pilgrims purportedly tasted their first spring water in the New World.

A four-mile **bike path** runs along the ocean from Head of the Meadow Beach (see below), past the Pilgrim Heights Area, to the end of Highhead Rd.

Beaches

Head of the Meadow Beach, east off US 6, is a wide, dune-backed beach with lots of parking for $5. There are restrooms and changing rooms.

Corn Hill Beach, off US 6 on Cape Cod Bay, is nice for walking at low tide and windsurfing at high tide. Head up the street above it for a great view of the rolling dunes. Parking is $5.

Places to Stay

The *North of Highland Camping Area* (☎ 508-487-1191), Head of the Meadow Rd, is open from mid-May to mid-September and has 237 sites shared by tents and RVs. It's a short walk to the beach from here and costs $16 for two.

The *North Truro Camping Area* (☎ 508-487-1847), Highland Rd, reserves about 100 of its 350 mostly wooded sites for tents. It's open all year and sites cost $14 for a double.

The *Little America AYH Hostel* (☎ 508-349-3889), N Pamet Rd, North Truro, MA 02666, is open from late June to early September and costs $12 nightly. Reserve by mail or by phone with credit card; in the off-season write to 1020 Commonwealth Ave, Boston, MA 02215 or call ☎ 617-739-3017. This former Coast Guard station (now with 42 beds) has a dramatic location amid dunes and marshes, just a five-minute walk to the beach.

The *Sea Gull Motel* (☎ 508-487-1215), MA 6A in North Truro, has 32 above average motel rooms with refrigerators ($78 to $85 double) and a few studio and efficiency apartments rented weekly in-season ($625). The motel is closed from mid-October through April.

Places to Eat

Open from late May to early September, *Jams, Inc* (☎ 508-349-1616), off US 6 in "downtown" Truro, has fancy picnic foods like rotisserie chicken, salmon pâté and imported cheese. The espresso is rich and strong.

Adrian's (☎ 508-487-4360), US 6 in North Truro, has big picture windows that take advantage of a commanding view atop a bluff overlooking the dunes and ocean.

Try the huevos rancheros or frittata at breakfast; at dinner an Italian menu ($7 to $15) with brick-oven pizzas and pasta dishes reigns. It's open Thursday through Monday from mid-May to mid-October and daily in summer.

Nondescript from the outside, *Terra Luna* (☎ 508-487-1019), MA 6A in North Truro, is a little bistro-like place with local art lining the walls. Dishes ($7 to $15) lean toward New American and Italian; try the tofu strudel or spinach tortellini with crab. Terra Luna is open for breakfast and dinner from mid-May to mid-October.

Getting There & Away

Bus The Plymouth & Brockton bus (☎ 508-746-0378) stops at Jam's in Truro center and Dutra's Market in North Truro (both just off MA 6) on its way from Boston and Hyannis to Provincetown.

Car Driving details for Truro are:

Destination	Mileage	Hr:Min
Boston, MA	120 miles	2:20
Chatham, MA	31 miles	0:45
Hyannis, MA	44 miles	0:50
Provincetown, MA	8 miles	0:10
Sagamore Bridge, MA	60 miles	1:20
Wellfleet, MA	7 miles	0:09

PROVINCETOWN

Provincetown is Cape Cod's most lively resort town and New England's gay mecca. Painters and writers, Portuguese-American fishermen and solitude seekers and their families make up this tolerant year-round community of 3500. Walking down Commercial St on any given day, you may see cross-dressers, children eating saltwater taffy, leather-clad motorcyclists, barely clad rollerbladers, women strolling hand in hand and middle-America wondering what they've stumbled into on their way to a whale-watching ferry.

At the very tip of the Cape, this outpost also appeals to those who appreciate long stretches of pristine beach, dramatic sand dunes, contemporary art and one-of-a-kind shops and boutiques. Beyond the main thoroughfare, there are also 4000 acres within the protected CCNS through which to bicycle, walk or gallop.

"P-town," as it's known, is jam-packed from late June to early September as its seasonal population swells to 40,000. Even though there are hundreds of rooms to rent, it's essential to arrive with lodging reservations during the summer. Because of special events, it also remains very crowded on weekends through the end of October. From January through March Provincetown is a desolate but hauntingly beautiful place to visit; just enough restaurants and guest houses remain open to service visitors.

Orientation

Three exits off of US 6 lead into town: Snail Rd leads to the quieter East End, Conwell St leads to the center of town and MacMillan Wharf, Shank Painter Rd leads to the West End.

There are two routes to the CCNS beaches and dunes: take Race Point Rd north off US 6 or follow US 6 to its end and head north on Province Lands Rd.

Commercial St is the town's main drag, lined with shops, restaurants, places to stay, entertainment venues and a few museums and historic houses. About three miles long from end to end, the one-way street runs parallel to the shoreline and functions as the town's boardwalk. Bradford St runs parallel to Commercial St and receives less foot but more auto traffic. Quiet guest houses line the dozens of little streets that link Bradford and Commercial Sts. Parking within the center of town is difficult and the driving slow, but there are numerous public parking lots. Provincetown is eminently strollable, but you'll share Commercial St with kamikaze rollerbladers and convertibles cruising the strip at five mph.

Information

The chamber of commerce (☎ 508-487-3424, fax 487-8966) maintains an information office at 305 Commercial St on MacMillan Wharf, open daily in the summer from 9 am to 5 pm and daily April

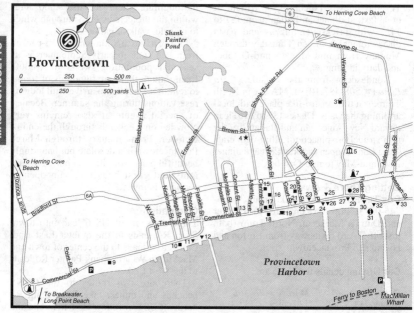

through December from 10 am to 4 pm. The Province Lands Visitor Center (☎ 508-487-1256), Race Point Rd is open daily from 9 am to 4:30 pm from mid-April through November and daily from 9 am to 6 pm late May to early September.

Outer Cape Health (☎ 508-487-9395), Harry Kemp Way off Conwell St from US 6, is open weekdays 9 am to 5 pm and Saturdays 9 am to noon year round.

There are public toilets behind the chamber of commerce information office and on the 2nd floor of the Town Hall.

Art Museums & Galleries

Provincetown began attracting artists in the early 1900s shortly after the Cape Cod School of Art was founded in 1899 by Charles Hawthorne. By the 1920s artists drawn to the clear light had created a fashionable art colony, much like those in Taos, NM; East Hampton, NY and Carmel, CA.

Provincetown remains a vital center on the American arts scene with more than 20 galleries representing artists of various persuasions, from avant-garde to representational.

The **Provincetown Art Association & Museum** (☎ 508-487-1750) at 460 Commercial St was organized in 1914 and is one of the country's foremost small museums. Paintings from the permanent collection are rotated throughout the year; exhibits may show works by Marsden Hartley and Milton Avery, as well as emerging local artists. The museum is open weekends from noon to 5 pm throughout the year and in the summer also on weekdays from noon to 5 plus Friday and Saturday evenings; admission is $2.

Pick up a copy of the *Provincetown Gallery Guide* for the very latest offerings. Well-established galleries include the Long Point Gallery (☎ 508-487-1795), 492 Commercial St; Berta Walker Galleries (☎ 508-487-6411), 208 Bradford St and the Harvey Dodd Gallery (☎ 508-487-3329) at 437 Commercial St.

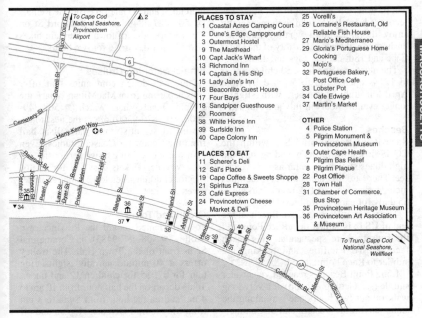

To Cape Cod National Seashore, Provincetown Airport

Race Point Rd
Cowell St
Cemetery St
Harry Kemp Way
Railroad Arch St
Brewster St
Center St
Johnson St
Pearl St
Law St
Dyer St
Priscilla Alden
Miller Hill Rd
Bangs St
Cook St
Howland St
Anthony St
Franklin St
Kendall St
Durham St
Conwell St
Commercial St
Allerton St
Bradford St

To Truro, Cape Cod National Seashore, Wellfleet

PLACES TO STAY
1 Coastal Acres Camping Court
2 Dune's Edge Campground
3 Outermost Hostel
9 The Masthead
10 Capt Jack's Wharf
13 Richmond Inn
14 Captain & His Ship
15 Lady Jane's Inn
16 Beaconlite Guest House
17 Four Bays
18 Sandpiper Guesthouse
20 Roomers
38 White Horse Inn
39 Surfside Inn
40 Cape Colony Inn

PLACES TO EAT
11 Scherer's Deli
12 Sal's Place
19 Cape Coffee & Sweets Shoppe
21 Spiritus Pizza
23 Café Express
24 Provincetown Cheese Market & Deli
25 Vorelli's
26 Lorraine's Restaurant, Old Reliable Fish House
27 Mario's Mediterraneo
29 Gloria's Portuguese Home Cooking
30 Mojo's
32 Portuguese Bakery, Post Office Cafe
33 Lobster Pot
34 Cafe Edwige
37 Martin's Market

OTHER
4 Police Station
5 Pilgrim Monument & Provincetown Museum
6 Outer Cape Health
7 Pilgrim Bas Relief
8 Pilgrim Plaque
22 Post Office
28 Town Hall
31 Chamber of Commerce, Bus Stop
35 Provincetown Heritage Museum
36 Provincetown Art Association & Museum

Provincetown Heritage Museum

This museum (☎ 508-487-0666) at Commercial and Center Sts is topped with a 162-foot steeple that has served since 1861 as a landmark for fishermen sailing into port. It houses the world's largest indoor model of a fishing schooner, which was built at Flyer's Boatyard down the road and assembled upstairs in the museum. Other artifacts celebrating Provincetown's maritime history include an offshore whaling boat, 19th-century fishing artifacts and a trap fishing boat. Adults and children over 12 pay $3.

The Pilgrims

In their search for a place to settle and freely practice religion, the Pilgrims first set foot on American soil in 1620 at Provincetown. A plaque marks the spot at the western end of Commercial St near the Provincetown Inn. The Pilgrims anchored here for five weeks in search of fresh water and fertile ground; when they failed to find

adequate supplies of either, they forged on to Plymouth.

In spite of their short stay, the Pilgrims did make history here. The **Pilgrim Bas Relief**, on Bradford St behind the Provincetown Town Hall, commemorates the Mayflower Compact, which the Pilgrims drew up while anchored in the harbor. The compact, a predecessor to the US Constitution, was designed to quell brewing insurrection by the indentured servants on board by granting them full rights in the new land.

The **Pilgrim Monument & Provincetown Museum** (☎ 508-487-1310, 800-247-1620), on High Pole Rd off Winslow St from Bradford St, is modeled after the Torre del Mangia in Sienna, Italy. Climb the 116 stairs and 60 ramps for a great view of town, the beaches, the spine of the Outer Cape and even Boston on a clear day (it's only 30 miles away as the crow flies).

The museum showcases artifacts from the pirate ship *Whydah*, which sank in 1500 feet of water off Wellfleet in 1717 and was recovered in 1985. Children especially enjoy dioramas of a whaling captains' onshore life, the natural history of the Outer Cape and 18th-century toys and dolls.

The museum ($5 adults, $3 children four to 12) is open 9 am to 5 pm daily from April through November, with slightly longer evening hours in July and August.

Beaches

Race Point Beach, off US 6 within the CCNS, is known for its pounding surf and high dunes stretching as far as the eye can see. There are lifeguards on duty; facilities include restrooms and showers. Parking is $5 daily for cars, $2 for bicycles.

The water at Herring Cove Beach, at the end of US 6, is calmer than Race Point and the sunsets more spectacular (this beach faces west). Facilities and parking are similar to Race Point.

Long Point Beach is reached via a water shuttle (see Getting Around) or a very long walk (about two hours one way along the stone jetty at the western end of Commercial St). There are no facilities out here; pack a picnic and lots of water and sunscreen before heading to Cape Cod's most absolute remote grains of sand. It's well worth getting to because of the relative lack of fellow human beings.

Horseback Riding

Nelson's Riding Stables (☎ 508-487-1112) at 43 Race Point Rd offers one-hour guided Western-style rides on CCNS trails traversing dunes and woods. Rides cost $25 per person from April through October and off-season when weather permits. More experienced riders can gallop along the beach at sunset ($50 per person, not available in July and August).

Bicycling

There are seven miles of paved bike trails within the CCNS; two spur trails lead to the Herring Cove and Race Point beaches. You can rent bicycles at Arnold's (☎ 508-487-0844) in the center of town at 329 Com-

mercial St and at Galeforce Bicycle Rentals (☎ 508-487-4849) at 144 Bradford St on the western edge of town. Mountain bikes cost $16 per day or $6 for two hours.

Whale-Watching Cruises

Of the half-dozen companies that offer trips departing from MacMillan Wharf, the Dolphin Fleet Whale Watch (☎ 508-349-1900, 800-826-9300) offers the best tours. On-board scientists and naturalists hail from the Center for Coastal Studies. Even on a warm day, bring a sweater for the 3½ hour voyage. Tickets cost $17 for adults, $15 for children seven to 12, children under seven are free.

Organized Tours

To get oriented, board the Provincetown Trolley (☎ 508-487-9483), on Commercial St in front of the Town Hall. The trolley offers a 40-minute narrated sightseeing tour for $7, $5 for children 12 and under. Tours depart on the half hour from 10 am to 4 pm and on the hour from 5 pm to 8 pm from May to mid-October. Hop on and off at various points including the Provincetown Art Association and the CCNS Province Lands Visitor Center.

Rambling Rose Carriage Co (☎ 508-487-4246), on Commercial St in front of the Town Hall, offers horse and buggy rides around town from May to mid-October. Prices vary according to the distance traveled and number of people, but generally start at $15 for two people.

Art's Dune Tours (☎ 508-487-1950, 487-1050) at Commercial and Standish Sts offers hour-long, narrated, 4-WD dune tours within the CCNS from mid-April to mid-October. Fares are from $9 to $10 per person; reservations are recommended for the sunset trip.

Places to Stay

Camping As the name suggests, *Dune's Edge Campground* (☎ 508-487-9815) is just off US 6 on the edge of the dunes. Open from May through September, the

100 pine-shaded campsites for both RVs and tents go for $22 for two people.

Coastal Acres Camping Court (☎ 508-487-1700), on Blueberry Rd off Bradford St on the western edge of town, is open longer, from April through October. Tent sites are $19.

Hostel The *Outermost Hostel* (☎ 508-487-4378), 26-28 Winslow St off Bradford St, is a privately run hostel with five cabins housing six bunks each that rent for $14 per night. Common space includes a kitchen, living room and barbecues and picnic tables in the yard.

Motels The *Surfside Inn* (☎ 508-487-1726), 543 Commercial St, is perhaps the least attractive building in town, and one of the only ones made of concrete. But since it has 84 rooms, it's likely to have a vacancy when others don't. Half the rooms have balconies overlooking the bay; others overlook the pool and Commercial St. Rooms cost $95 to $125 double in the summer, $65 to $95 in the off-season; closed mid-October through April.

The *Cape Colony Inn* (☎ 508-487-1755), 280 Bradford St, has 54 rooms that rent for $72 to $92 double in-season, $46 to $88 off-season; closed November through April.

Guesthouses, Inns & B&Bs Provincetown has perhaps a hundred small inns and guesthouses that provide the most interesting accommodations. Most guesthouses have a mix of rooms with private or shared bath. In summer, most will also be booked in advance. If you can't make a reservation in advance, arrive early in the day and ask the chamber of commerce to help you find a vacant room for the night. Better yet, try to visit either before June or after early September.

The *White Horse Inn* (☎ 508-487-1790), 500 Commercial St, rents 12 simple rooms, each decorated with original local art and most with shared baths for $60 to $70 in summer, $40 off-season. There are also six far more interesting bohemian, bungalow-style apartments that rent for $100 to $110 in the summer, but they have a three-night minimum.

Among Provincetown's most pristine and beautiful guesthouses is the *Beaconlite Guest House* (☎ 508-487-9603, 487-4605), 12 and 16 Winthrop St. Very comfortable, harmoniously decorated rooms cost between $80 and $160 in summer. Each room is different, so call for descriptions and reservations.

The *Sandpiper Guesthouse* (☎ 508-487-1928, 800-354-8628 outside Massachusetts), 165 Commercial St, is nicely-kept and conveniently located. The frilly parlors are comfy, and the front porch is good for people-watching. Rooms cost $85 to $130 double in the summer.

Four Bays (☎ 508-487-0859), 166 Commercial St, facing the Sandpiper, is perfectly kept and congenial, with rooms costing $60 to $100 double in summer. The *Captain & His Ship* (☎ 508-487-1850), 164 Commercial St, is another good choice right next door for about the same prices.

The *Richmond Inn* (☎ 508-487-9193), 4 Conant St, is a clean and well-kept place on a quiet street, yet convenient to the center of town. In the summer the 12 rooms go for $45 to $75 with shared bath, $80 to $100 with private bath, less the rest of the year.

Roomers (☎ 508-487-3532), 8 Carver St, is comfy and stylish with interesting artifacts and art objects in the public rooms. Rooms with bath cost around $100 in summer, $65 off-season.

Lady Jane's Inn (☎ 508-487-3387), 7 Central St, is among the area's larger and more attractive guesthouses, built in 1986 with a small courtyard and rooms on two floors. Continental breakfast is included in the rates: $80 in summer, $60 off-season.

Efficiencies About a mile west of the town center, *The Masthead* (☎ 508-487-0523, 800-395-5095), 31-41 Commercial St, is right on the bay. A variety of room configurations are available: multi-room apartments, cottages, studios and simple motel rooms. With the exception of the motel rooms (which are overpriced in the summer), units are rented weekly in July and August starting at $893. The rest of the year they rent for $50 to $175 nightly.

Capt Jack's Wharf (☎ 508-487-1450, 487-1673 in the winter), 73A Commercial St, consists of a series of connected apartments and studios built on a wharf. In a few of them you can see right between the floor boards to the tide beneath you. They're as airy, funky and bohemian on the inside as their exterior suggests. The wharf is lined with bistro tables and draped with colorful buoys. Units rent for $625 to $800 weekly, $480 to $640 off-season, $69 to $92 nightly with a three-night minimum; closed late September to late May.

Places to Eat

Delis No matter where you are on Commercial St, you'll never be far from one of these three delis. From east to west on Commercial St they are *Martin's Market* (☎ 508-487-4858) at No 467, *Provincetown Cheese Market & Deli* (☎ 508-487-3032) at No 225 and *Scherer's Deli* (☎ 508-487-3303) at No 93. Of these, Scherer's is the fanciest, offering sandwich fixings and cold salads like penne with potatoes, and peppers stuffed with prosciutto, but it's only open from early May to mid-October; the others are open year round.

Cafes The tiny *Café Express* (☎ 508-487-3382), 214 Commercial St, is one of the few places in town with outdoor tables, and only a few of them at that! It serves light dishes like salads, soups and sandwiches.

Not only does *Cape Coffee & Sweets Shoppe* (☎ 508-487-6176), 205-209 Commercial St, open before everyone else (at 8 am), they also make the best cappuccino in town.

Without a doubt, *Spiritus Pizza* (☎ 508-487-2808), 190 Commercial St, is the place to go for a late-night slice of pizza. Strong coffee and a pastry will jump start you in the morning.

Restaurants In addition to a decent selection of moderately priced eateries and takeout joints hawking sandwiches, burgers, pizza, pasta and seafood, Provincetown has a surprising number of fine but pricey restaurants. Dining options range from Portuguese to fried seafood to Italian to New American.

Provincetown's favorite snack is a big wad of hot, sugar-dusted fried dough ($1.50) from the *Portuguese Bakery* (☎ 487-1803), 299 Commercial St. The simple bakery-lunchroom, which has been here for a century, also sells the town's cheapest breakfasts and sandwiches.

Every town has one and Provincetown is no exception: *Mojo's* (☎ 508-487-3140), Ryder St at MacMillan Wharf, is P-town's classic clam shack. It's open from 11 am to midnight in the summer.

Café Edwige (☎ 508-487-2008), 333 Commercial St, is the most popular breakfast place among locals and repeat visitors. For $3.25 to $6.75 you can choose from frittatas, tofu casserole, broiled flounder and fruit pancakes. Expect to wait unless you arrive by 8:30 am. At dinnertime the cafe is transformed into a romantic and sophisticated bistro offering New American dishes like planked codfish with baby potatoes and vegetables or Asian-style sesame noodles for $12 to $17 per main course. The solicitous service and creative cuisine make it one of the top two or three places to dine.

Sal's Place (☎ 508-487-1279), 99 Commercial St, serves simple but good southern Italian dishes at outdoor tables on the bay or indoors in a classic trattoria. Dinner ($9 to $20 per main course) is served from mid-May to mid-September.

There's a reason why lines form outside *Lobster Pot* (☎ 508-487-0842), 321 Commercial St. Inside you'll find fresh seafood and fish, chowder, a bakery, tables overlooking the harbor and fast service. A filling lunch costs $7 to $13, dinner $13 to $19. It's open daily except in January.

Lorraine's Restaurant (☎ 508-487-6074), 229-R Commercial St, is down an alley toward the harbor. A small but cozy restaurant, it features Mexican and South-west cuisine with a New England accent. Local littleneck clams are served in a cilantro lime broth with roasted garlic, shallots and scallions; fresh sea scallops are served with tomatillos in a green chile sauce, flambéed with tequila. Lunch costs about $10 to $12, dinner about $18 to $30.

Farther down the alley from Lorraine's is the *Old Reliable Fish House Restaurant* (☎ 508-487-9742), a simple place with low prices, water views and outdoor tables. There are usually several luncheon seafood specials for around $5.

The *Post Office Café* (☎ 508-487-3892), 303 Commercial St, is a good, year-round (well, almost, it's closed from mid-January to mid-February) stand-by for soups, sand-wiches, seafood platters and chicken dishes. It's open for all three meals; prices range from $3.75 to $14.

Gloria's Portuguese Home Cooking (☎ 508-487-0015), 269 Commercial St, across from the Town Hall, has the common menu items as well as fresh pizzas and calzones.

Right next door, *Mario's Mediterraneo* (☎ 508-487-0002), 267 Commercial St, will serve you an Italian sandwich, or cup of soup and a slice of pizza for $4, which you can eat at one of the cafe tables in the front. They serve delicious pastries here as well. In the back is a dining room with a long menu and tables overlooking the beach.

Vorelli's (☎ 508-487-2778), 226 Com-mercial St, has an old-time menu of steaks, veal parmigiana and linguine marinara. Lunches cost around $8 to $12, dinners $18 to $30.

Entertainment
The *New Art Cinema* (☎ 508-487-9222), 214 Commercial St, shows new films.

Inside *Club Euro* (☎ 508-487-2505, 487-2501), 258 Commercial St, deep sea murals provide a back drop for the latest dance videos. At the outdoor bar/cafe you'll hear world-beat music that changes every night.

The *Crown & Anchor* (☎ 508-487-1430), 247 Commercial St, has something for everyone: it's a disco, leather bar and venue for cabaret and drag shows.

The waterfront *Pied Piper* (☎ 508-487-1527), 193A Commercial St, is the women's bar in town. The *Atlantic House* (☎ 508-487-3821), 4 Masonic Place, is more commonly referred to as the A-House, and is the men's equivalent.

The *Boatslip* (☎ 508-487-1669), 161 Commercial St, is known for its wildly popular afternoon tea dances (from 3:30 to 6:30 pm) and two-steppin' dance parties.

Things to Buy
Commercial St is lined with the most cre-ative specialty shops on the Cape. You'll find almost anything that could suit your fancy, from leather implements of torture to rubber stamps, from cutting-edge women's clothing to artsy T-shirts, from sculpture to hand-crafted jewelry.

One shop you shouldn't miss is Marine Specialties (☎ 508-487-1730, 800-274-7124), 235 Commercial St, a cavernous store filled to the rafters with random, surplus Army and Navy stuff and other odd items, all priced to sell.

Getting There & Away
Air Cape Air (☎ 508-487-0241, 800-352-0714) provides daily year-round service from Boston to Provincetown's Municipal Airport, about four miles from town and reached via taxi. Summertime fares range from $138 to $158 roundtrip.

Bus The Plymouth & Brockton bus (☎ 508-746-0378), which stops in the center of town in front of the chamber of commerce, provides two daily buses (3½ hours; $19 one way) between Province-town and Boston with stops in Truro, Well-fleet, Eastham, Orleans, Brewster, Dennis, Yarmouth, Hyannis and West Barnstable.

Car Here are the driving details for Provincetown (assuming you don't get bogged down in heavy traffic!):

Destination	Mileage	Hr:Min
Boston, MA	128 miles	2:30
Chatham, MA	37 miles	0:50
Hyannis, MA	46 miles	1:00
New York, NY	300 miles	6:00
Providence, RI	128 miles	2:30
Sagamore Bridge, MA	63 miles	1:15
Woods Hole, MA	71 miles	1:30

Boat You can get to and from Provincetown by passenger ferry from Boston. The Bay State Cruise Company (☎ 508-487-9284 in the summer, 617-723-7800 year round) links Provincetown's MacMillan Wharf and Boston's Commonwealth Pier on Northern Ave (see Boston). The three-hour voyage costs $16 one way; boats depart once daily from Provincetown at 3:30 pm and from Boston at 9 am in the summer and on weekends from late May to late June, and from early September to mid-October.

Getting Around

A Summer Shuttle (☎ 508-487-3353, 240-0050) travels up and down Bradford St with a detour to MacMillan Wharf between 8:15 am and midnight in the summer; flag the bus down and hop on and off anywhere along the three-mile route. Another bus departs on the hour (between 10 am and 6 pm) from MacMillan Wharf for Herring Cove Beach. Fare is $1.25.

Flyer's Shuttle (☎ 508-487-0898) at 131A Commercial St ferries sunbathers across the bay to remote Long Point from mid-June to mid-September. The fare is $5 one way, $8 roundtrip.

Martha's Vineyard & Nantucket

Islands are special places. The geographical confinement of an island means that people know their neighbors better and have more community spirit.

In the 18th century, the islands off New England's coast were maritime vanguards, havens for whaling vessels and merchant fleets. With the coming of the Age of Steam in the 19th century, they became vacation resorts, charming places where city-dwellers could escape the summer's heat and find a cool, constant sea breeze.

For most of this century, Martha's Vineyard and Nantucket have been pleasure destinations for New Englanders of all social classes. But recently these two charming islands have gone noticeably upscale: President and Mrs Clinton chose Martha's Vineyard for vacation in 1992 and

'93, along with many other rich and famous celebrities. But generally, Martha's Vineyard attracts a more ethnically and economically diverse holiday crowd than Nantucket, whose visitors are more conservative, more blue-blood types.

Nantucket's small airport experiences over 200 takeoffs and landings of private jets each week in summer. The airport has also enjoyed that ultimate American recognition of chic: it is the setting for a television sitcom (Wings).

Most everything is more expensive on the islands, even more expensive than on Cape Cod. But these two special places are charming, historic and beautiful, and there are ways of all kinds to visit Martha's Vineyard and Nantucket without hemorrhaging money.

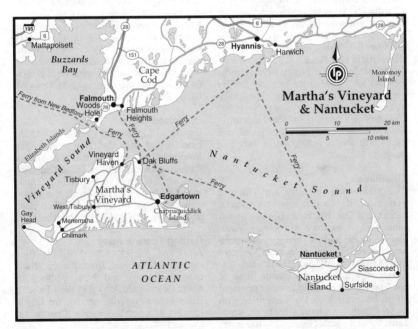

Martha's Vineyard

In the early 1600s, mariner Bartholomew Gosnold cruised the coast of New England, charting it for later exploration. It is thought that he found wild grapes when he stopped at this island and named it Martha's Vineyard in honor of his daughter.

Today there actually is a working vineyard on the island, which you can visit. There are also lots of beaches, bike paths, charming towns, open spaces, restaurants, and inns. To visitors from eastern Massachusetts, it's simply "the Vineyard," as in "Why don't we go to the Vineyard for the weekend?"

History
Prior to 1640 there were 3000 Wampanoag Indians living on the island. Over the next century English settlers colonized the Vineyard and converted the Wampanoags to Christianity. Many Wampanoags died from diseases imported by the English and by the mid-1700s there were only 300 native islanders left. Today, many of their descendants live in Gay Head.

Vineyarders are a proud, fiercely independent lot, relishing the fact that they're separate from the mainland. They have strong opinions on everything. Nevertheless, they've opened their island to a thriving tourist trade: the year-round population of 11,000 swells to 90,000 in July and August.

Orientation
The main ports of entry are Vineyard Haven, the island's year-round commercial center, and Oak Bluffs, a seasonal, somewhat honky-tonk town with ornate Victorian houses and a history of racial integration. It's three miles from Vineyard Haven to Oak Bluffs along Beach Rd.

Edgartown, the pricey grande dame of the Vineyard, is the island's other principal town. Its lovely back lanes are filled with houses built by whaling captains, separated by white picket fences. It's five miles along the shoreline from Oak Bluffs to Edgartown.

Chappaquiddick, an untouristed spit of land within a stone's throw of Edgartown, is reached via a five-minute ferry from Edgartown center. It has pristine beaches.

The island's other towns – West Tisbury, Chilmark, Menemsha and Gay Head – are relatively undeveloped and collectively referred to as "up-island." The western tip of the island belongs to the colorful cliffs of Gay Head, 21 miles from Edgartown or Vineyard Haven.

Information
The Martha's Vineyard Chamber of Commerce (☎ 508-693-0085), Beach Rd (PO Box 1698, Vineyard Haven, MA 02568), is just off Main St. There is also an office (and public toilets) in the ferry terminal. The chamber publishes a visitor's guide, distributes maps and offers other practical advice.

In Vineyard Haven, Bunch of Grapes Bookstore (☎ 508-693-2263), 68 Main St, has a great reputation for carrying a wide selection of books. Pick up the weekly *Martha's Vineyard Times* or *Vineyard Gazette* for a current calendar of events.

Martha's Vineyard Hospital (☎ 508-693-0410) is off the Vineyard Haven-Oak Bluffs Rd.

Organized Tours
Gay Head Sightseeing (☎ 508-693-1555) buses depart from the ferry terminals in Vineyard Haven and Oak Bluffs from May through October. Buses are timed with ferry arrivals, more or less. The 2½-hour island-wide tour takes in all the major towns and stops at Gay Head. Tickets costs $11.50 for adults and $3 for children.

Getting There & Away
Air Cape Air (☎ 800-352-0714) flies throughout the year from Boston, Nantucket, Hyannis and New Bedford to Martha's Vineyard Airport in West Tisbury. Other airlines offering service are USAir Express and, in the summer, Continental Connection.

Boat By far the cheapest and most popular way to get to Martha's Vineyard is by boat.

From Woods Hole & Falmouth Car ferries (which also take passengers) operated by the Woods Hole, Martha's Vineyard & Nantucket Steamship Authority (☎ 508-477-8600), PO Box 284, Woods Hole, MA 02543, operate daily in the summer from Woods Hole to Vineyard Haven (10 trips) and Oak Bluffs (three trips). In other seasons, all 13 daily trips go to Vineyard Haven. In the summer make auto reservations weeks, even months in advance.

Roundtrip fares from mid-May to mid-October are $76 for cars, $9.50 for adults, half price for kids five to 12, $6 for bicycles. Thus it costs $95 roundtrip for one car and two adults. In the off-season, cars cost $36 to $48 roundtrip. The trip takes about 45 minutes.

If you're not bringing a car, two passenger-only ferries operate out of Falmouth. The Falmouth Ferry Service (☎ 508-548-9400), 278 Scranton Ave, docks in Edgartown three times daily from late May to mid-October. Roundtrip fares are $22 for adults, $16 children, $6 bicycles.

The *Island Queen* (☎ 508-548-4800), Falmouth Heights Rd, docks in Oak Bluffs. Service begins in early May and costs $10 adults, $5 children under 13 and $6 bicycles.

From Hyannis Hy-Line Cruises (☎ 508-778-2600 in Hyannis, 508-693-0112 in Oak Bluffs) runs three or four boats daily from the Ocean St Dock to Oak Bluffs late May to early September. For the month before and after that, there's only one boat per day. Fares are $22 adults, $11 children, $9 bicycles. The trip takes under two hours.

From New Bedford The Martha's Vineyard Ferry (☎ 508-997-1688) operates from mid-May to mid-October, running four boats per day during the summer, but at other times there are only one or two. The trip takes one hour. Roundtrip tickets cost $18 adults, $9 children, $5 bicycles.

KIM GRANT

From Nantucket See Nantucket, Getting There & Away.

Getting Around

Bus Island Transport (☎ 508-693-0058) operates between Vineyard Haven, Oak Bluffs and Edgartown (about $2 one way, $3 roundtrip) from early May to late October. In the summer they're supposed to run every 15 minutes between 8 am and 7 pm. If you need to be sure, call the hotline (☎ 508-693-1589) for the current schedule.

They also operate buses (late June to early September) from Edgartown to Up-Island, stopping at the airport, the youth hostel, West Tisbury, Chilmark and Gay Head. Roundtrip fare is $8.

Beach Shuttle South Beach Shuttle, from Edgartown to South Beach (also known as Katama), runs daily (well, on fair weather days) from mid-June to mid-September. The shuttle departs from the Edgartown visitor center every 15 minutes between 9 am and 5:30 pm.

Car A car is nice for longer stays and for exploring up-island, although it is by no means necessary. It costs about the same to rent a car on-island for two days as it does to bring your own car over.

For rentals, Budget (☎ 508-693-1911, 800-527-0700) has offices in Oak Bluffs and Vineyard Haven; Hertz (☎ 508-627-4728) has an office in Edgartown. Cars cost about $50 a day.

Adventure Rentals (☎ 508-693-1959), Beach Rd, Vineyard Haven, has dune buggies, mopeds and 4WD vehicles, as well as cars. All-Island Rent-a-Car (☎ 508-693-6868) is based at the airport but has a free shuttle from the three major towns that brings people there.

Bicycle & Moped Vineyard Haven, Oak Bluffs and Edgartown all have plenty of rental shops with competitive prices. (See Bicycling in each section.) The only destination for which you might want a moped is Gay Head; it's quite hilly out there and it's 20 or so miles from Edgartown or Vineyard Haven. Give yourself a day for that trip by bike.

Expect to spend $8 to $18 per day for a bike, and $25 to $50 per day for a moped. Mopeds, by the way, are banned in Edgartown center.

VINEYARD HAVEN
Although this is the commercial center for the island, it isn't lacking in charm. Its harbor is filled with more wooden boats than any harbor of its size in New England. And its back streets, especially William St, are lined with lovely sea captains' homes. It's the most mellow of the three principal towns – the most "real," if you will. It's a year-round community, so if you're coming off-season, this is the place to stay.

Orientation
The principal part of Vineyard Haven is just four or five blocks wide by about a half mile long.

The Steamship Authority ships dock at the end of Union St, a block from Main St. From the terminal, Water St leads to Beach Rd and the infamous "Five Corners" intersection: five roads come together and no one really has the right of way. Traffic here is a problem in the summer.

From the Five Corners, Beach Rd heads to Oak Bluffs along the ocean. For a picnic place, head west on Main St to Owen Park, a nice patch of lawn that slopes down to the harbor.

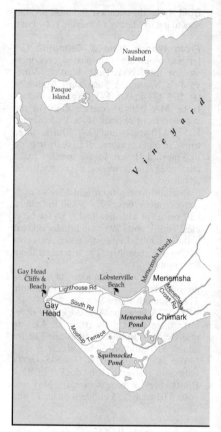

Things to See
The **Old Schoolhouse Museum** (☎ 508-693-3860), 110 Main St at the corner of Colonial Lane, served as the island's first schoolhouse in 1828. Today it houses artifacts depicting early island life. It's open from 10 am to 2 pm weekdays from mid-June to mid-September; donations are requested.

The **State Lobster Hatchery and Research Station** (☎ 508-693-0060), off Beach Rd between Vineyard Haven and Oak Bluffs, is the world's oldest hatchery. Thousands of tiny crustaceans are fed

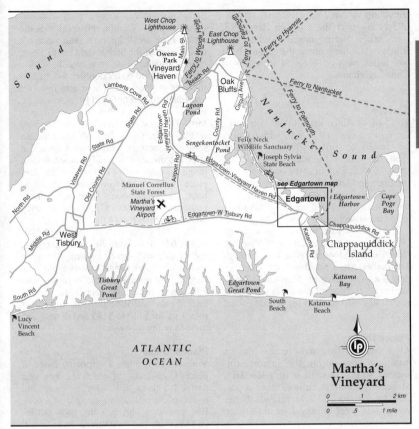

shrimp bits until they're mature enough to survive the Atlantic (that is, to be caught and served for dinner). The hatchery is free and open weekdays from 1 to 3 pm.

Making wine is not easy in New England, but **Chicama Vineyards** (☎ 508-693-0309), about 3½ miles out of town off State Rd towards West Tisbury, does a credible job, and it only seems right that there be a working vineyard on the Vineyard. Stop by for a free tour and tasting from mid-May to mid-October, Monday through Saturday from 11 am to 5 pm (1 to 5 pm on Sunday).

Beaches
Head up-island or to Edgartown.

Activities
Wind's Up (☎ 508-693-4252), Beach Rd, rents sailboards ($14 to $20 per hour or $40 to $60 for a half day), small sailboats, catamarans, canoes and kayaks ($12 to $18 per hour or $40 to $50 for a half day). They also give lessons.

MV Parasail and MV Ski Waterskiing (☎ 508-693-2838, locations change yearly) offer lessons, waterskiing, parasailing and innertubing.

Bicycling Vineyard Vehicle Rentals (☎ 508-693-1185), near the ferry on Beach Rd, rents bikes. Before heading out to Oak Bluffs (a flat route along the ocean), head two miles west on Main St to see West Chop Lighthouse.

Cruises

The 54-foot Alden ketch (a wooden boat), the *Laissez Faire* (☎ 508-693-1646) takes passengers on full ($100) and half-day ($60) sails around the island and into Nantucket Sound. Stop in at the owner's B&B, the Lothrop Merry House at Owen Park, to sign up for a trip. It's crewed by the amicable owners; besides, it seems a fitting way to see the shoreline.

The square topsail schooner *Shenandoah* (☎ 508-693-1699) sets sail out of Vineyard Haven every Monday from June to mid-September for a six-day trip. The ship may put in at Newport, Nantucket, Cuttyhunk and/or Block Island. Day sails are sometimes offered. Call for schedules and prices.

Places to Stay

All across the island, most places require a minimum stay during the summer (in-season), so plan to settle in for a few days. Make reservations as far in advance as possible for summer and fall weekends. Better yet, go mid-week in May, June or October.

Camping *Webb's Camping Area* (☎ 508-693-0233), off Barnes Rd, is the preferred campground because of its wooded sites, some reserved specifically for backpackers, some with pond views. It is open from mid-May to early September; sites go for $22 to $24.

Martha's Vineyard Family Camping (☎ 508-693-3772), Edgartown Rd, has wooded sites for tenters but also has cable TV hookups for RVs, too. It's open from mid-May to mid-October.

Motels The *Vineyard Harbor Motel* (☎ 508-693-3334), 28 Beach Rd, has 40 uniformly modern rooms, each with air-conditioning, TV and a refrigerator. Some rooms have small kitchens, and since it's on the edge of the harbor (and town), some rooms also have water views. In-season rates are $90 to $105 double; $45 to $70 the rest of the year. There are also two apartments that rent for $110 in-season.

Inns The *Lothrop Merry House* (☎ 508-693-1646), at Owen Park off Main St, is a snug 18th-century house with a lawn that stretches down to the sandy harbor. Rooms range from one with a harbor view and fireplace to a small and simple one with shared bath. The seven rooms (four with private bath) rent for $119 to $185 in the summer, $68 to $165 the rest of the year.

The 1843 *Captain Dexter House* (☎ 508-693-6564), 100 Main St, has eight large rooms (all with private bath), furnished with a mix of Victorian, colonial and New England antiques. A couple of rooms have a fireplace, some have four-poster canopy beds. From mid-June through September rooms go for $110 to $185 and drop to $55 to $145 in the off-season.

Places to Eat

Vineyard Haven has a surprising range of places to eat, many of which are open year round. It's also a "dry" town, so no alcohol is served in restaurants or sold in stores. But you can "bring your own bottle" (BYOB) to the restaurant and they'll uncork it for you for a nominal charge.

The *Black Dog Bakery* (☎ 508-693-4786), Water St, is often the first place people go as they disembark from the ferry. Good coffee and freshly baked sweets are perfect any time of the day. Black Dog T-shirts are sold here; you'll see them worn all over the island.

90 Main St Delicatessen (☎ 508-693-0041), 90 Main St, is dedicated to providing coffee, salads and sandwiches at decent prices year round.

La Patisserie Française (☎ 508-693-8087), 96 Main St, is owned by the same folks who own Le Grenier, but this is a more casual place, with some outdoor tables. Concentrating on breakfast, brunch and lunch, the lighter bistro fare of salads, soups, breads and pastas costs $5 to $15.

The *Cafe at the Tisbury Inn* (☎ 508-693-3416), Main St, serves a very good New American menu at sidewalk tables under an awning. You can get away with spending less than $10 at lunch, but dinner will cost three times that. They're also open for breakfast.

Louis' Tisbury Cafe & Take-Out (☎ 508-693-3255), less than a mile out of town at 102 State Rd, is popular with the locals because it's a great value. Vegetarian dishes, pasta, pizza, lasagna and other Italian dishes like shrimp diavolo are the reason for coming. As the name suggests, everything is prepared for take-out, too, starting at 11 am. For dinner, try to arrive before 7 pm if you don't want to wait.

A visit to the *Black Dog Tavern* (☎ 508-693-9223), on the Beach St Extension on the harbor, has become synonymous with a visit to the island. The food is good but pricey – about $20 to $24 for main courses. The American menu is weighted towards fresh seafood and locally grown vegetables. Desserts are made around the clock at their bakery next door. Reservations are not accepted and the lines are usually quite long, so try to arrive before 6 pm for dinner. It's open year round for all three meals.

Le Grenier (☎ 508-693-4906), 96 Main St, is the loveliest place in town. It serves traditional and exceptional French cuisine for dinner only, from mid-March through December. Entrees range from $16 to $29.

Entertainment

The *Wintertide Coffeehouse* (☎ 508-693-8830), Five Corners, is the place to go for live folk music and jazz. They do a bit of improv and cabaret, in addition to serving light meals. It bills itself as a "chemical free" (that is, no smoking or alcohol) spot, but that rule doesn't extend to coffee.

The *Capawock* (☎ 508-696-7469), Main St, shows movies year round.

OAK BLUFFS

Oak Bluffs is the island's summer fun center: informal, downscale, even gaudy. Brightly colored Victorian "gingerbread houses" line several streets, and there's an old-fashioned carousel that claims to be the oldest in the country.

Orientation

The *Island Queen* ferry from Falmouth docks at the end of Circuit Ave Extension, which is lined with inexpensive outdoor eateries. The Steamship Authority docks ships at Sea View and Oak Bluffs Aves.

Oak Bluffs Ave (lined with bike and car rental shops) turns into Lake Ave, which runs parallel to the harbor. Keep going west in this direction to reach Vineyard Haven. Sea View Ave, also called the Oak Bluffs-Edgartown Rd, heads south out of town, along the shore, to Edgartown.

Circuit Ave is the main drag. To the left and right of it on side streets are the gingerbread houses for which the town is famous.

Public restrooms are next to the Steamship Authority off Water St and on Kennebec Ave, a block west and parallel to Circuit Ave.

Gingerbread Houses

Wesleyan Grove is bounded by Lake, Sea View and Dukes County Aves and sliced in the middle by Circuit Ave. It contains the renowned Victorian gingerbread cottages that look like they're dripping with icing. Bold colors and whimsical ornamental woodwork characterize what is known by architects as the Carpenter Gothic style.

In 1835, when the Methodist Campmeeting Association began holding summer revival meetings here, the congregation camped in tents. As the meetings grew, participants who returned year after year began putting up bigger tents. Then they pitched their tents on wooden platforms, which evolved in to small cottages. Every year they adorned their cottages with more and more fanciful wooden trim. Voilà! A Carpenter Gothic village.

This neighborhood is no museum: members of the religious congregation still live here, so note the posted rules, especially no "rude or loud behavior." Services are still held in the 1879 wrought-iron Trinity Park Tabernacle.

The **Cottage Museum** (☎ 508-693-0525), 1 Trinity Park, is typical of the 300 or so tiny 19th-century cottages in Oak Bluffs. It's open daily from mid-June to mid-September, 10:30 am to 4 pm.

Flying Horses Carousel

This merry-go-round, at Circuit and Lake Aves, is said to be the oldest operating carousel (1876) in the country. Rides cost $1; more adults ride it than you might guess.

Joseph Sylvia State Beach

On Beach Rd (Oak Bluffs-Edgartown Rd), this is a narrow, two-mile-long stretch of white sandy beach backed by low dunes. It's also referred to as the Bend-in-the-Road Beach. Park along the road.

Bicycling

Since lots of ferries pull into town, discharging lots of passengers, there are lots of places renting lots of bicycles. Try Anderson Bike Rentals (☎ 508-693-9346) on Circuit Ave Extension and Vineyard Bike & Moped (☎ 508-693-6886) on Oak Bluffs Ave.

The Oak Bluffs-Edgartown Rd straddles the ocean, a good beach and a salt water pond for much of the route. It's a lovely five-mile ride, but the bike path also runs parallel to the heavily traveled road.

Also, head up to the bluff where the East Chop Lighthouse is situated: take Lake Ave towards Vineyard Haven, turn right on Commercial St (along the water) and continue on Highland Ave.

Places to Stay

Of the following lodgings, only Surfside is open year round; most others in Oak Bluffs are open from April through mid-October. Rates are highest from June to September.

Motel & Hotel *Martha's Vineyard Surfside Motel* (☎ 508-693-2500, 800-537-3007), Oak Bluffs Ave, is right in the middle of things so it can get noisy at times. Of the 32 rooms, the more expensive ones have refrigerators and water views. In-season rooms go for $95 to $155, the rest of the year for $45 to $95.

The *Wesley Hotel* (☎ 508-693-6611), 1 Lake View Ave, is a gracious three-story, turn-of-the-century hotel. A long veranda dotted with rocking chairs faces the marina. Half of the 82 comfortably furnished rooms have water views. Rooms with shared bath rent for $65 ($45 off-season); the rest go for $125 to $165 ($80 to $105).

Inns & B&Bs The gingerbread-style *Attleboro House* (☎ 508-693-4346), 11 Lake Ave, has eight basic rooms, all with shared bath. (A few rooms have a sink in them and some can handle an extra person or two.) The house has unobstructed views of the protected marina from the front porch rocking chairs. Open from June through September, doubles cost $65 to $95, singles $55.

The *Oak Bluffs Inn* (☎ 800-955-6235, 508-693-7171), Circuit Ave, has nine guest rooms decorated with bright and fanciful cottage-style furniture. Since the inn is on the edge of Wesleyan Grove, most rooms have picturesque views of the camp meeting houses. The inn is open from mid-May to mid-October and rooms rent for $110 to $150 in-season.

The *Admiral Benbow Inn* (☎ 508-693-6825), 520 New York Ave, is on the edge of a well-traveled road into town. Its seven rooms, all with private bath, are decorated with Victorian furnishings and cost $100 to $150 double in-season, $55 to $100 off-season.

Rooms at the *Oak House* (☎ 508-693-4187), on the corner of Seaview and Pequot Aves, are filled with oak furniture, oak walls, oak ceilings. It's all quite Victorian, cozy, nicely put together and expensive. Most of the 10 rooms have water views (some have private balconies), half have air-conditioning. A big afternoon tea is included in the rates ($140 to $250). Subtract 20% for spring and autumn rates.

Places to Eat
Oak Bluffs has plenty of inexpensive summer resort eateries offering the standard menu of burgers, sandwiches, shrimp and lobster. If you're ready to splurge, there's also one fine choice.

Linda Jean's (☎ 508-693-4093), 34 Circuit Ave, is the town's best all-around inexpensive restaurant. A three-egg omelet filled with vegetables costs $6, a bowl of chowder $3, burgers $3.50 and a platter of fried seafood is as expensive as it gets at $14. Linda Jean's is open from 6 am to 8 pm year round.

Giordano's (☎ 508-693-0184), at Circuit and Lake Aves, is doing something right: it's been in business since 1930. Large portions of homestyle Italian-American food are served for $5.50 to $13, from 11 am to 11 pm. Their fried clams are some of the island's best. Arrive early or wait in line for a while.

Papa's Pizza (☎ 508-693-1400), 158 Circuit Ave, a pleasant storefront eatery with a central location, is a nice place to sit down, but you can also get your pizza to go. (Take it to Ocean Park and listen to an old-fashioned band concert.) Thankfully, this place is open daily year round.

Jimmy Sea's Pan Pasta (☎ 508-696-8550), 32 Kennebec Ave, serves "upscale" pasta dishes, cooked to order and served in the skillet. It's a small casual place that offers up large portions to locals who know a good thing when they find it. Come to dinner with an appetite and be prepared to spend $7 to $19 per entree.

The *Oyster Bar* (☎ 508-693-3300), 162 Circuit Ave, dishes up creative New American seafood that tastes as good as the place looks: high tin ceilings, a strip of neon here, a faux marble column there, linen tablecloths and a chiseled waitstaff. For all the island celebrities who pop into town, this is the place to see and be seen. But you don't have to be famous to get a great meal here; you just have to have some money ($40 per person should do it, including wine).

Entertainment
Oak Bluffs is the island's most lively town; walking around after dark is sometimes entertainment enough.

There's always something going on (year round) at the *Atlantic Connection* (☎ 508-693-7129), at 124 Circuit Ave. Long-time islander Carly Simon and relative newcomer Billy Joel have been known to come to the nightclub for a listen. There's live music Wednesday through Saturday, and comedy, a DJ or karaoke the other nights.

The *Ritz Cafe* (☎ 508-693-9851), Circuit Ave, is a popular bar with live jazz and blues on the weekends.

David's Island House (☎ 508-693-4516), 120 Circuit Ave, is more mellow, featuring David's very good piano playing. It would not be unusual for some of the musical Taylor clan – James, Livingston, Hugh or Kate – to play along.

The Strand, Oak Bluffs Ave Extension, and the *Island Theatre*, Circuit Ave, both show first-run movies seasonally.

EDGARTOWN
Patrician Edgartown is the island's architectural showpiece. Its 18th- and 19th-century whaling captains' houses are perfectly maintained, with clipped lawns, blooming gardens and white picket fences. Though it's crowded in the summer, Edgartown is downright quiet between October and April.

Orientation & Information
You'll probably come into town on Main St, which extends down to the harbor. Water St runs parallel to the harbor and N Water St leads out to the Edgartown Lighthouse.

The Edgartown Visitors Center (no phone), around the corner from the Old Whaling Church on Church St, is open daily from June to early September (9 am to 5 pm). There are public restrooms and a post office here. The shuttle bus (see Getting Around, near the beginning of this chapter) stops here.

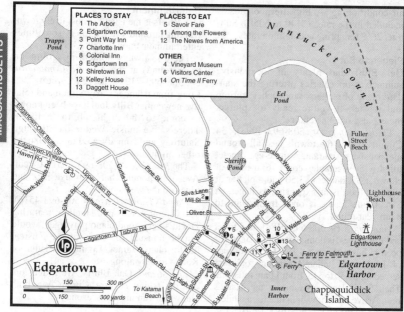

PLACES TO STAY
1 The Arbor
2 Edgartown Commons
3 Point Way Inn
7 Charlotte Inn
8 Colonial Inn
9 Edgartown Inn
10 Shiretown Inn
12 Kelley House
13 Daggett House

PLACES TO EAT
5 Savoir Fare
11 Among the Flowers
12 The Newes from America

OTHER
4 Vineyard Museum
6 Visitors Center
14 On Time II Ferry

Edgartown

Special Event

Of all the Vineyard's various seasonal events, the "Possible Dreams Auction," usually held in Edgartown at the Harborside Hotel, is the most unique. Every August, nationally known celebrities with second homes on the island throw a creative auction to benefit island community services. Highest bidders might win a tour of the *60 Minutes* studios in New York by anchor Mike Wallace or a personal performance by singer Carly Simon.

Vineyard Museum

This museum (☎ 508-627-4441), at Cooke and School Sts, occupies several buildings, including the 1765 Thomas Cooke House. Home to the Dukes County Historical Society, the island's most interesting museum has whaling and maritime relics, scrimshaw and the huge Fresnel lens from the Gay Head Lighthouse. It's open daily from 10 am to 4:30 pm July to early September, with shorter hours the rest of the

year. Adults pay $5, children $3; less in the winter.

Chappaquiddick Island

There are very few houses on the island, and no shops or eateries. The prime "attractions" are the 500-acre **Cape Poge Wildlife Refuge** and the 200-acre **Wasque Reservation**, both unspoiled and unfrequented stretches of sand. It's beautiful out here.

Chappaquiddick is perhaps most widely known for the tragic incident that involved US Senator Edward Kennedy in 1969. A passenger in his car drowned when the car he was driving plunged off a small wooden bridge. Not much remains of the bridge these days, but that doesn't prevent hundreds of people each season from seeking it out.

A six-car ferry, *On Time II* (☎ 508-627-9794), at the corner of Daggett and Dock Sts, takes people and cars to the island. "Chappy" is only 200 yards or so away and the ferry leaves whenever there are people who want to go; that way, it's always "on time."

Felix Neck Wildlife Sanctuary

This Audubon sanctuary (☎ 508-627-4850), off the Edgartown-Vineyard Haven Rd, is crisscrossed with six miles of trails that traverse woods, meadows, marshes and the beach. The visitor center is open June through October daily from 8 am to 4 pm, and closed on Monday the rest of the year. Trail access costs $3 adult, $2 child.

Manuel E Correllus State Forest

The 4400-acre state forest (☎ 508-693-2540), also off the Edgartown-Vineyard Haven Rd, occupies a huge chunk of the island's mid-section. It has walking and biking trails.

Beaches

Katama Beach (extending west as South Beach), off Katama Rd, is three miles long, with moderate surf. There's a big parking lot, which means there are usually a lot of people. A shuttle bus also services Katama (see Getting Around).

Lighthouse Beach, at the end of N Water St, is a nice, easily accessible beach where you can watch the boats put into Edgartown Harbor.

Fuller Street Beach, at the end of Fuller St near Lighthouse Beach, is where a lot of the college kids and summer workers tend to hang out.

See also Chappaquiddick and Joseph Sylvia State Beach in Oak Bluffs.

Bicycling

RW Cutler Bike (☎ 508-627-4052), 1 Main St, and Wheel Happy (☎ 508-627-5928), 8 S Water St, both rent bicycles. The Correllus State Forest has bicycle trails.

Places to Stay – middle

Efficiencies The *Edgartown Commons* (☎ 508-627-4671, 800-439-4671), Pease Point Way to Plantingfield Way, is suited to longer stays. Just a couple blocks from the town center, it's actually a complex of seven buildings with studios and multi-bed apartments. Guests (most of whom are families) also have access to outdoor barbecues and a pool. Rates (for two to six people, depending on the apartment size) are $135 to $205 in the summer, $75 to $125 in the spring and fall.

Hotel The *Kelley House* (☎ 508-627-7900, 800-225-6005), 23 Kelley St, has a pool and 59 nicely maintained modern rooms, each with air-conditioning and TV, some with harbor views. It's right in the thick of things and can get loud at night. Doubles start at $195 in the summer, $125 in the spring and fall. Special off-season packages are sometimes offered.

Inns & B&Bs The *Arbor* (☎ 508-627-8137), 222 Main St, is a 10-minute walk from the harbor, so its location keeps the prices reasonable. Most of the 10 guest rooms have a private bath and rooms are furnished with a combination of antiques and modern pieces. Doubles cost $95 to $145 in-season.

The *Edgartown Inn* (☎ 508-627-4794), 56 N Water St, has 20 simple rooms, all with private, modern bath. The two airy rooms in the Garden Cottage are the nicest. Doubles rent for $80 to $175 in the summer, $50 to $100 in the fall and spring.

The centrally located *Shiretown Inn* (☎ 508-627-3353, 800-541-0090), N Water St, has simple but adequate rooms in the motel-like Carriage House behind the main house. There are also "housekeeping units" (with kitchenette) and some rooms with period furnishings and private entrances. Doubles range from $79 to $259 in the summer, but in the spring and fall you can get a housekeeping unit for $735 weekly.

Places to Stay – top end

Inns & B&Bs The *Daggett House* (☎ 508-627-4600), 59 N Water St, has 20 rooms and three suites, all with private bath, in three separate buildings. One cottage is right on the harbor; more modern rooms are across the street. (The lawn stretches down to the harbor, so wherever you stay you can sit on the harbor.) The main house served as the island's first tavern in the 17th century (this is where the full breakfast is served). Rates start at $140 in-season, $75 the rest of the year.

The *Point Way Inn* (☎ 508-627-8633), 104 Main St, formerly a whaling captain's house, has 15 rooms, many with four-poster canopy beds and fireplaces. The owners have an extra car which they loan to guests (on a first-come, first-served basis) for free. Doubles cost $150 to $260 in the summer, $85 to $185 the rest of the year.

The hotel-like *Colonial Inn* (☎ 508-627-4711), 38 N Water St, is a three-story rambling inn right in the middle of the action. Its 43 rooms, all with private bath, are comfortable, with TVs and air-conditioning. Price is based on size and view: $140 to $225 in summer, $65 to $145 in the off-season. The inn is closed from mid-December to mid-April.

The *Charlotte Inn* (☎ 508-627-4751), 27 S Summer St, caters to a well-heeled crowd. The 24 rooms, connected by English gardens and brick walkways, are furnished with practically priceless antiques. If you don't think you'll feel too out of place, the cheapest room rents for $250 in the summer, $165 in spring and fall, and $125 in the winter. The Charlotte Inn really does deserve its reputation as one of the finest inns in New England. If you're going to go all the way, it has an outstanding (and equally expensive) French restaurant, too: L'Étoile.

Places to Eat
Although there are lots of places to eat, restaurateurs seem to come and go quite a bit. Have a look around; see where the lines are forming and get there earlier the next night.

At *Among the Flowers* (☎ 508-627-3233), 17 N Water St, there are only a few tables outdoors. But don't let that deter you from getting an omelet, soup, salad or a quiche, especially since it will only cost you $4 to $9. The cafe is open throughout the day from April to mid-November.

The Newes from America (☎ 508-627-7000), 23 Kelley St, open from 11 am to midnight daily year round, is better than a good-old standby. Traditional pub grub as well as modern variations like grilled eggplant sandwiches or hummus in a pita pocket are standard fare ($5 to $16). It's a dark and cozy place, with a low-beamed ceiling. The clientele may seem on the preppy side, but they're a fun-loving, boisterous crowd.

Savoir Fare (☎ 508-627-9864), 14 Church St, is always a pleasure. The bistro is a bit on the chic side but thankfully unpretentious, and the food is creative New American, with a few vegetarian and pasta choices. You'll probably spend $10 to $22 for lunch and dinner entrees but you won't be disappointed.

Entertainment
The house specialty at The Newes from America (see above) is a "rack of beer," a sampler with five unusual brews. The entire beer menu, in fact, is worth a sample.

The Wharf (☎ 508-627-9966), Dock St, is a popular pub on the wharf with live music on most summer evenings.

UP-ISLAND
This is the truly pastoral side of the island life. The landscape is a patchwork of rolling fields, lined with stone walls and private dirt roads and dotted with barns and grazing sheep. There's very little to do up-island, except enjoy the scenery by car or bicycle, and head to the beach.

Orientation
From West Tisbury all roads – South, Middle and North – lead to Menemsha. But take South Rd (it's the prettiest) to "Beetlebung Corner," which is the center (just a crossroads really) of Menemsha. To reach the harbor, follow Menemsha Cross Rd and look for signs to Dutcher's Dock.

Only South Rd leads to Gay Head from Menemsha. At one particularly high point you can see Menemsha Harbor to the north.

There are public restrooms near the parking area at Gay Head Cliffs.

Alley's General Store

This local gathering place, in West Tisbury center, has served up-island residents since 1858. It was in danger of succumbing to the pressures of modern retailing in 1994, until a group of locals created a foundation to save it and overhaul it – another example of islanders pulling together to save their community culture.

Menemsha

This quaint little fishing village was used as the setting for the movie *Jaws*. There's a nice beach and good restaurant here, and the sunsets are spectacular, too.

Gay Head Cliffs

The multi-colored clay cliffs were formed by glaciers over 100 million years ago. Rising 150 feet from the ocean, they're dramatic any time of day. The Wampanoag Indians own the cliffs, a National Historic Landmark, and it's illegal to bathe in the mud pools that form at the bottom of the cliffs and to take clay. The brick lighthouse standing precariously at the edge of the bluff was built in 1844.

Wildlife Sanctuaries

The **Cedar Tree Neck Sanctuary** (☎ 508-693-5207), off Indian Hill Rd in West Tisbury, has a few trails and covers over 300 acres of bogs, fields and forests.

The 600-acre **Long Point Wildlife Refuge** (☎ 508-693-7662), of the Edgartown-West Tisbury Rd, has just a few short trails but one leads to a deserted stretch of South Beach. Parking costs $5, and each adult (15+) pays $2.

Beaches

Gay Head Beach is five miles long. Head north for the cliffs; the further you go in this direction the less clothing you'll see. To the south the beach is wider but it's technically restricted to residents only. Stick to the water's edge and you'll have no problem.

Menemsha Beach, northeast of Dutcher's Dock and the harbor, is pebbly but

the water is calm. Across the "cut" of water, to the southwest, is Lobsterville Beach, popular with families because of the gentle and shallow water. In the summer there is usually a little ferry that takes people and their bikes across the cut. (It's a good thing, because parking at Lobsterville is restricted to residents.)

Lucy Vincent Beach, off South Rd about a half mile before the junction with Middle Rd, is open to Chilmark residents only. That's unfortunate because it's the loveliest stretch of sand (complete with dune-backed cliffs) on the island. You shouldn't have trouble using the unmarked beach in the off-season.

Bicycling

It's a long and hilly ride from Edgartown to Gay Head (21 miles one way), but you'll be rewarded with expansive vistas and the quiet details of island life up close. With the exception of the path that borders the state park, you'll be riding on narrow winding roads with all the other traffic.

Cruises

The catamaran *Arabella* (☎ 508-645-3511), docked in Menemsha Harbor, makes a daily run to nearby Cuttyhunk Island (from 11 am to 5 pm; $55) and an evening sunset trip around the cliffs ($35).

Places to Stay

Unless you stay at the hostel, it's impractical to stay up-island without a car.

Hostel The *Manter Memorial AYH Hostel* (☎ 508-693-2665, 800-444-6111 for reservations; 617-739-3017 for off-season information), on the Edgartown-West Tisbury Rd in West Tisbury, has 78 beds ($12 to $15) and is open from April to mid-November. The building was designed to be a hostel, so it's got a great kitchen.

The hostel sponsors a couple of programs per week in the summer on such topics as stargazing, the environment, budget travel and the Wampanoags. Advance reservations are essential in the

summer. Bike or hitch to the hostel; although you can use the Gay Head shuttle (see Getting Around), don't rely on it. It's an eight mile ride (via State, then Old County Rd) from Vineyard Haven.

Inns, B&Bs & Cottages The 17th-century *Captain Flanders' House* (☎ 508-645-3123), North Rd in Chilmark, is tranquilly set on 60 acres of rolling farmland overlooking a pond. Accommodations include six guest rooms (two with private bath) in the main house and two snug, romantic cottages. From late May to mid-October rates (including a coveted pass to Lucy Vincent Beach) are $70 to $170, and $50 to $90 in the off-season.

Menemsha Inn and Cottages (☎ 508-645-2521), North Rd in Menemsha, offers 12 simple and tidy cottages, each with a kitchen and fireplace, that go for $725 to $975 per week in the summer. There are also nine rooms that rent for $115 to $130 in the summer, $85 in the off-season. Reserve in advance if you can; otherwise, hope someone cancels. Guests get passes to Lucy Vincent Beach.

The *Outermost Inn* (☎ 508-645-3511), on Lighthouse Rd in Gay Head, is great for a romantic splurge. Beds have down comforters and cotton sheets, and the airy rooms are trimmed with rich woodwork. Large picture windows overlook the bluff and ocean beyond. Six rooms and one suite rent for $190 to $285 (including a full breakfast) from May through October. The

dining room, open for dinner only, is quite popular despite the remote location. Reserve early if you can.

Places to Eat
The *Chilmark Store* (☎ 508-645-3739), in the center of Chilmark, will satisfy your need for a quick energy fix and a thirst quencher if you're bicycling to Gay Head. You can also assemble a picnic, though it will cost a bit more than if you'd done it in Edgartown.

By the way, there's also a tiny store in Menemsha, but nothing in Gay Head.

The Galley (☎ 508-645-9819), at Menemsha Harbor, is a little shack with picnic tables that sells meaty lobster rolls and a small selection of fried seafood for $8.

Home Port (☎ 508-645-2679), also on the harbor in Menemsha, is very good; make reservations or be prepared to wait. Better yet, go to the back door and order the same food that everyone else is getting – fresh seafood and surf-and-turf combos – and take it to the dock and watch the sunset. Inside, a fixed-price dinner costs $20 to $26; à la carte from the back door will be less. Home Port is open from 5 to 10 pm daily from May to mid-October.

The *Aquinnah* (☎ 508-645-9654), on the cliffs at Gay Head, is open throughout the day during the summer. It has great views and decent food, like chowder, burgers and simple sandwiches, from $7.

The *Feast of Chilmark* (☎ 508-645-3553), on State Rd at Beetlebung Corner in Chilmark, is an upscale bistro-cum-art gallery serving sophisticated New American dishes at dinnertime. Entrees cost $14 to $26.

Things to Buy
West Tisbury Farmer's Market takes place at the West Tisbury Agricultural Hall (in the center of town – you can't miss it) from 9 am to noon every Saturday from June through September.

A flea market at the Chilmark Community Church, in the center of Menemsha, is held every Wednesday and Saturday during the summer. It runs from about 7 am to 2 pm.

Nantucket

Thirty miles (50 km) south of the Cape Cod coast lies Nantucket, a beautiful island of grassy moors, salt bogs, blueberry fields, warm-water beaches and charming villages.

History
The Pilgrims landed at Plymouth in 1620 after a brief stop at the tip of Cape Cod, and within 40 years there were White settlers living on Nantucket, going out in boats and hunting whales. By 1686 one of these whalers, a certain Jethro Coffin, had made a fortune large enough to afford a grand house built of brick. The house still stands.

Throughout the 1700s, Nantucket grew ever richer from the whaling trade. The wealthy island's contribution to the Revolutionary War effort was exemplary: around 2000 Nantucketers lost their lives, and more than 100 whaling vessels were lost in battle.

Though ultimately victorious in the war, Nantucketers were economically defeated by the peace. Before the island could recover from these huge losses, the War of 1812 began and robbed them of yet more men and ships. By the mid-19th century, the great age of the sailing ship was over, supplanted by steam. With the advent of coal and petroleum as fuels, the trade in whale oil suffered a fatal decline.

The same steamships that robbed Nantucket of its whaling wealth brought a new means of prosperity: tourism. Nantucket's mariners abandoned whaling and took up cruising, shuttling visitors between the coast and the island. In the late 19th century, huge rambling wood frame hotels were built to house vacationers, and the island settled into a comfortable, seasonal trade. In the early 1960s, islander and developer Walter Beinecke, Jr, began to

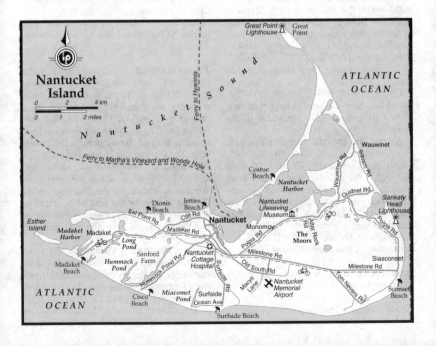

revitalize the waterfront. He convinced merchants, restaurateurs and innkeepers that since the island had finite resources, it was far better to attract a moneyed crowd than folks with just a few dollars to spend. The theory continues to drive the island: you'll see more upscale jewelry and craft stores than T-shirt shops.

The brash, booming 1980s saw the advent of direct jet flights from New York City to Nantucket, allowing the chic and trendy to fly up for the week, the weekend, or just for dinner before returning to the city.

Getting There & Away

Air Nantucket's Memorial Airport is served by a number of national and local carriers. With the exception of the evening rush hour, just show up at the airport in Hyannis New Bedford or Martha's Vineyard, buy a ticket for the next flight and you'll be on the island in less than 45 minutes.

Cape Air (☎ 508-228-7695, 800-352-0714) and Nantucket Airlines (☎ 508-790-0300, 800-635-8787) offer daily flights to and from Boston ($154 to $186 roundtrip in the summer), Hyannis ($60), New Bedford ($119) and Martha's Vineyard ($68).

Island Air (☎ 508-228-7575, 800-248-7779) also operates from Hyannis; flying time is 15 minutes.

Colgin Air (☎ 508-325-5100, 800-272-5488) flies from LaGuardia airport in New York City (about $250 roundtrip in the summer).

Among the national carriers, Business Express/Delta Connection (☎ 800-345-3400) and Continental Express (☎ 800-525-0280) offer connecting flights from Boston, LaGuardia and/or Newark airports. Flights serving Boston and JFK airport are handled by USAir, TWA, Delta, American and Continental.

Northwest Airlink (☎ 800-225-2525) has connecting flights from Hyannis.

Boat The cheapest and most popular way to get to Nantucket is by boat.

From Hyannis The Steamship Authority (☎ 508-477-8600 for advance car reserva-tions, 508-771-4000 for day-of-sailing information), South St Dock, carries people and autos to Nantucket year round. Make car reservations as early as possible (months in advance for the summer, if you can); reservations are not necessary for passengers or bicycles. The authority runs six ferries per day from mid-May to mid-September, and three the rest of the year. Roundtrip fares are $20 for adults, $10 for children five to 12 and $10 for bicycles. Cars cost $180 from mid-May to mid-October and $140 off-season. The trip takes 2¼ hours. Parking in Hyannis is $7.50 per calendar day.

In 1996 Hy-Line (☎ 508-778-2600), Ocean St Dock, inaugurated a "hi-speed" passenger service that reaches Nantucket from Hyannis in less than one hour. Since the boat accommodates only 40 passen-gers, advance reservations are recom-mended. The boat makes six trips a day in the summer, five the rest of the year. A roundtrip ticket costs $52 adults, $39 chil-dren 12 and under, $9 for bicycles.

Regular 2¼-hour service costs $22 adults, $11 children, and $9 for bicycles. There are six boats daily.

From Harwich Freedom Cruise Line (☎ 508-432-8999), on Route 28 at Saqua-tucket Harbor in Harwichport, offers daily morning, noon and evening ferries from mid-May to mid-October. The first two ferries permit you to explore the island for about 6 hours before catching the return boat. The trip takes 2¼ hours and costs $27 for adults, $15 for children 12 and under, and $9 for bicycles. Advance reservations are recommended for the first two boats. Parking is free for the first 24 hours, then it's $8 per day. The advantage of this boat is that you can avoid the traffic in Hyannis.

From Martha's Vineyard Hy-Line Cruises operates three daily inter-island passenger ferries in each direction from early June to mid-September. The trip takes 2¼ hours and costs $22 for adults, $11 for children five to 12, and $9 for bicycles. The ferry docks in Oak Bluffs on the Vineyard

(☎ 508-693-0112) and on Straight Wharf in Nantucket (☎ 508-228-3949).

There is no inter-island car ferry.

Getting Around
Airport It's a $7 taxi ride from Nantucket town.

Bus Across from Nantucket Visitor Services on Federal St, Barrett's Tours (☎ 508-228-0174) operates beach buses on a regular schedule. The only problem is that it's impossible to predict what beaches they will serve. Check in at their booth.

The NRTA Shuttle (☎ 508-228-7237) delivers passengers to Madaket, Surfside and 'Sconset for $1 each way in the summer. Some buses have bike racks on the back. The bus stops between Candle and Union Sts, just off Main St in Nantucket town.

Taxi Taxis are plentiful, especially on Lower Main St and at Steamboat Wharf. Fixed rates to every point on the island are posted in the taxi. Rides cost $4 for one person within town limits, $11 to 'Sconset. A nominal charge is added for each additional person in the taxi, and another additional charge is added after dark. Most taxi drivers can give you a personal tour of the island; you'll have to negotiate a price.

Car In the summer the center of town is choked with automobiles. You don't need a car unless you're staying a week or longer.

Nantucket Windmill Auto Rental (☎ 508-228-1227) is based at the airport but they offer free pick-up and delivery. In town, head to Young's (☎ 508-228-1151) on Steamboat Wharf, or Affordable Rental (☎ 508-228-3501) on S Beach St. Expect to pay $60 per day for a car in the summer, $40 in the off-season. A 4WD jeep will cost $140 in the summer, $80 off-season.

Bicycle & Moped Virtually every able-bodied person takes a bicycle or moped ride while on-island. Bicycling is the best way to get away from the summertime crowds (don't try it on the cobblestones of

Main St), savor the island's natural beauty, and reach much of the protected conservation land. Besides, the generally flat island has honest-to-goodness bike paths, a rarity on the mainland.

There are thousands of bikes to rent from at least a half-dozen shops. Try Young's Bicycle Shop (☎ 508-228-1151) on Steamboat Wharf, which rents them for about $20 per day in-season ($14 off-season); mopeds go for $25 to $35.

Organized Tours There's no better way to orient yourself and get a quick overview of the island's main attractions that to take one of these 90-minute tours.

Gail's Tours (☎ 508-257-6557) offers the unique perspective of a seventh-generation islander. Gail is full of interesting island trivia and also allows guests to hop out of the van to take photos. Tours depart year round at 10 am, 1 and 3 pm in front of the information bureau on Federal St. Call ahead in the off-season.

Barrett's Tours (☎ 508-228-0174), 20 Federal St, and Nantucket Island Tours (☎ 508-228-0334), on Straight Wharf, offer five or six daily tours from April through October. Many buses are timed to depart after the ferry arrives. All tours are $10 per person.

NANTUCKET TOWN
The only town of any size on the island, Nantucket town boasts quaint cobblestone streets shaded by towering elms and lined with gracious 19th-century homes. The whole town is, in fact, a National Historic Landmark, with the largest concentration of houses built prior to 1850 in the country. In the summer Nantucket's Main St is always busy with shoppers, strolling day-trippers and cyclists walking their wheels (riding over cobbles is uncomfortable).

Orientation
There are two ferry terminals, Steamboat Wharf and Straight Wharf, both about a block off Main St in the center of town. Both are within walking distance of most lodgings.

MASSACHUSETTS

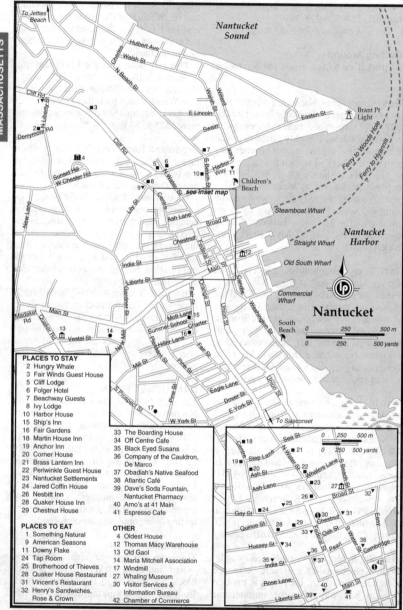

Nantucket Sound

To Jetties Beach

Hulbert Ave

Walsh St

N. Beach St

Cliff Rd

E Lincoln

Swain

Brant Pt Light

Easton St

Ferry to Woods Hole

Ferry to Hyannis

Liberty St

N. Rd

Derrymore Rd

Cliff Rd

Sunset Hill

W-Chester Rd

Harbor Way

Children's Beach

Steamboat Wharf

Nantucket Harbor

New Lane

Lily St

Ash Lane

Broad St

Chestnut

Federal St

Straight Wharf

Old South Wharf

Nantucket

India St

Liberty St

Gardner St

Main St

Madaket Rd

Quaker Rd

Vestal St

Commercial Wharf

South Beach

0   250   500 m
0   250   500 yards

Mott Lane

Summer School

Charter

Hiller Lane

Fair St

Pine St

Eagle Lane

Dover St

E York St

W York St

To Siasconset

PLACES TO STAY
2 Hungry Whale
3 Fair Winds Guest House
5 Cliff Lodge
6 Folger Hotel
7 Beachway Guests
8 Ivy Lodge
10 Harbor House
15 Ship's Inn
16 Fair Gardens
18 Martin House Inn
19 Anchor Inn
20 Corner House
21 Brass Lantern Inn
22 Periwinkle Guest House
23 Nantucket Settlements
24 Jared Coffin House
28 Nesbitt Inn
28 Quaker House Inn
29 Chestnut House

PLACES TO EAT
1 Something Natural
9 American Seasons
11 Downy Flake
24 Tap Room
25 Brotherhood of Thieves
28 Quaker House Restaurant
31 Vincent's Restaurant
32 Henry's Sandwiches,
   Rose & Crown

33 The Boarding House
34 Off Centre Cafe
35 Black Eyed Susans
36 Company of the Cauldron,
   De Marco
37 Obadiah's Native Seafood
38 Atlantic Café
39 Dave's Soda Fountain,
   Nantucket Pharmacy
40 Arno's at 41 Main
41 Espresso Cafe

OTHER
4 Oldest House
12 Thomas Macy Warehouse
13 Old Gaol
14 Maria Mitchell Association
17 Windmill
27 Whaling Museum
30 Visitor Services &
   Information Bureau
42 Chamber of Commerce

Sea St

Centre

Step Lane

N. Water St

Whalers Lane

Beach

Ash Lane

Gay St

Quince St

Hussey St

India St

Rose Lane

Whalers Lane

Broad St

Chestnut

Federal St

Oak St

Pearl

N. Water St

Cambridge

Main St

0   250   500 m
0   250   500 yards

In fact, the majority of tourist/visitor facilities – restaurants, inns, bicycle rental shops, stores – are within a 10-minute radius of Main St and the wharves. These principal areas are bounded by Main, Centre, Broad and S Water Sts. If you walk 30 minutes in any direction from the wharves, you will be on the outskirts of town.

Information
The tourism industry on Nantucket is a well-oiled machine. The official Nantucket Chamber of Commerce (☎ 508-228-1700), 48 Main St, is stocked with plenty of information on seasonal activities and special events. In the summer they are open weekdays 8:30 am to 5:30 pm and Saturdays 10 am to 2 pm (the rest of the year weekdays 9 am to 5 pm).

The Nantucket Visitor Services & Information Bureau (☎ 508-228-0925), 25 Federal St, is the place to go for up-to-the-minute information on room availability and bus schedules. Visitor services is open daily throughout the year (in the summer from 9 am to 9 pm). Visitor services also maintains seasonal kiosks at both ferry terminals and at the airport.

There are public restrooms at the information bureau, the Steamship Authority Ferry Terminal and at the end of Straight Wharf.

Nantucket Cottage Hospital (☎ 508-228-1200) is on the edge of town, at S Prospect St and Vesper Lane. It's open 24 hours.

Mitchell's Book Corner (☎ 508-228-1080), 54 Main St, and Nantucket Bookworks (☎ 508-228-4000), 25 Broad St, have very good selections. The Hub (☎ 508-228-3868), at the corner of Main and Federal Sts, is the source for magazines and newspapers.

Walking Tours
Since practically every building you see in Nantucket town is a historical showpiece with an anecdote to tell, take an organized walking tour to get the most out of a visit. Longtime islander Roger Young (☎ 508-228-1062) leads highly recommended walking tours from mid-May to mid-

October. These two-hour strolls cost $10 per person.

Otherwise, take one of three self-guided walks published by the Nantucket Historical Association (☎ 508-228-1894). Pick up maps at their office at 2 Whaler's Lane or at the chamber of commerce.

For bird-watchers, the Maria Mitchell Association (☎ 508-228-9198), 2 Vestal St, offers birding walks all over the island, depending on where the birds are at any given time, from mid-June to mid-September, for $7 adults, $4 children.

Historic Houses & Museums
The Nantucket Historical Association (☎ 508-228-1894), 2 Whaler's Lane, oversees eight of the island's most important historic buildings. Together, these buildings and their contents represent island life from its farming beginnings to its prosperous whaling days. A special combination pass ($8 adults, $4 children five to 14) allows you unlimited visits during your stay. Most buildings are open 10 am to 5 pm daily in the summer; off-season hours are posted.

The most deservedly famous property, the **Whaling Museum** (☎ 508-228-1736) on Broad St, memorializes the island's principle industry, the original source of its prosperity. The **Thomas Macy Warehouse** on Straight Wharf is the best introduction to Nantucket's various historical periods.

Other buildings worth a look include the island's oldest house on Sunset Hill Rd, built in 1686 as a wedding present for Jethro Coffin and Mary Gardner Coffin. On the corner of S Mill and Prospect Sts stands a working windmill built in 1746. The Old Gaol, 15R Vestal St, was the island prison from 1805 to 1933. The first prisoner to escape was also the last.

Maria Mitchell Association
This association (☎ 508-228-9198), consisting of five buildings headquartered at 2 Vestal St, is devoted to the island's foremost astronomer (1818-1889). In 1847 Mitchell discovered an uncharted comet and went on to become the first woman admitted into the American Academy of

Arts and Sciences and the country's first female professor of astronomy.

The association consists of the Science Library; the Hinchman House, a natural science museum where naturalists lead walks and talks; an observatory open only on clear Wednesday evenings in the summer; Mitchell's birthplace, which has lovely wildflower and herb gardens; and a waterfront aquarium. Check in at the headquarters for a complete schedule of opening times and offerings. One ticket ($4.50 adults, $1.50 children) allows passage to all buildings.

Beaches

You'll have to pedal, hitch or take a bus to the island's prime beaches, but to quickly feel sand between your toes head to Children's Beach, off S Beach St just north of Steamboat Wharf, and South Beach, a few blocks south of the wharf.

Jetties Beach, a 20-minute walk or a short bus ride, is popular because of its location, off Bathing Beach Rd from N Beach Rd. It's good for walking, as well as activities like volleyball, tennis and sailing.

Activities

Force 5 Watersports (☎ 508-228-5358), on Jetties Beach and at 37 Main St, rents kayaks, Sunfish, boogie boards and wind surfers. Some lessons and clinics are also offered.

The Sunken Ship (☎ 508-228-9226), at Broad and Water Sts, is a full-service, year-round dive shop.

Sea Nantucket (☎ 508-228-7499), Washington St Extension, offers half- and full-day tours of the scallop-shaped harbor on nonrollable sea kayaks. Half-day trips cost $25 for a single kayak, $45 for a double. On choppy days, kayaks can be delivered to quieter inland ponds.

Striped bass and bluefish "run" off Nantucket's shores. A half-dozen or so charter boats dock at Straight Wharf, including the *Herbert T* (☎ 508-228-6655).

Bicycling All bicycle rental shops have good, free island maps with routes high-lighted. See Bicycle & Moped under Getting Around for more information.

The **Cliff Road Bike Path** is a short, in-town route that takes you past big summer houses on the edge of town.

The island's pace and terrain are well-suited to bicycling (see Getting Around). The three-mile **Surfside Bike Path** to the beach is flat; the ride takes 15 minutes. The seven-mile **'Sconset (or Milestone) Bike Path** begins east of the historic district and passes forests, bogs and moors. It takes 30 minutes if you're cruising. **Polpis Road Bike Path** is lined with millions of daffodils in the springtime. The circular loop from town to 'Sconset and back via Polpis is about 17 miles.

To reach the western end of the island, take the **Madaket Bike Path**, a hilly and winding six-mile path that passes beautiful terrain.

Cruises

Nantucket Whalewatch (☎ 508-283-0313, 800-322-0013) on Straight Wharf offers day-long trips with an on-board naturalist. The boat departs every Tuesday morning from mid-July to mid-September and costs $65 adults, $35 children.

The Friendship Sloop *Endeavor* (☎ 508-228-5585), Slip 15, Straight Wharf, offers four daily harbor sails, a sunset cruise and trips to Coatue from mid-April through October. Prices, from $15 to $30, vary with the length of the sail.

Places to Stay

Staying overnight in Nantucket is generally not cheap. To get around this, it's best to visit in the spring or fall (or even the winter if you don't mind gray, windy days). It's difficult to find a room in July and August without advance reservations. In addition, many places require a two-night minimum and do not accept credit cards. Although not all places are open year round, enough places are. Camping (or sleeping under the stars or in your car) is not permitted on the island. This policy is strictly enforced.

Places to Stay – bottom end & middle
Hostel The *Nantucket Youth Hostel* (☎ 508-228-0433, 800-444-6111 for reservations, 617-739-3017 for off-season information), 31 Western Ave, is about three miles from the center of town on Surfside Beach. The island's first lifesaving station, an architectural gem, now has bunk rooms accommodating a total of 50 people. The hostel is open from late April to mid-October. Advance reservations are absolutely essential in the summer, but there is usually plenty of room in the spring and fall. Beds cost $12 to $15 nightly.

Hotel The *Folger Hotel* (☎ 508-228-0313, 800-365-4371), 89 Easton St, is a 10-minute walk from Main St. The turn-of-the-century, rambling summer hotel has 60 simple but clean rooms, one-third of which have shared bath. Singles rent for $50 to $85 and doubles go for $95 to $150.

Inns & B&Bs The centrally located *Nesbitt Inn* (☎ 508-228-0156), 21 Broad St, has 13 rooms with shared bath which rent for $42 single, $65 to $75 double and $85 triple. A real bargain and a favorite among Europeans, the 1872 house has many original Victorian furnishings. This is a real find!

Mrs Ven Johnson's *Hungry Whale* (☎ 508-228-0793), at 8 Derrymore Rd in a quiet residential neighborhood about 12-minutes' walk from the center, is a pleasant traditional Nantucket house. The five rooms (one with private bath) rent for $65 to $70, which includes a good breakfast served on the umbrella-shaded deck. Excellent value!

The best bargains at *Beachway Guests* (☎ 508-228-1324), a few blocks from the center at 3 N Beach St, are the shared-bath rooms that rent for $80.

The *Ivy Lodge* (☎ 508-228-0305) is a 10-minute walk from the center of town at 2 Chester St. The 200-year-old house has eight rooms, five with private bath, that rent for $75 to $110.

The antique-filled *Corner House* (☎ 508-228-1530), 49 Centre St, has lovely historic rooms, all with bath. The least expensive, smaller rooms on the 3rd floor are quite nice. Afternoon tea is served on the brick patio or sun porch. In-season rates ($95 to $175) drop to $65 to $100 in the off-season.

The *Anchor Inn* (☎ 508-228-0072), a sea captain's house dating to 1806, is right across the street. Its 11 nicely appointed rooms (all with bath) cost $95 to $155 in the summer, $55 to $95 off-season.

The *Martin House Inn* (☎ 508-228-0678), just down the street at 61 Centre St, is elegantly furnished and comfortable, with canopy beds, antiques and fireplaces in the rooms. At the low end of rates ($80 to $150) are a few bargain rooms with shared baths. They also have singles for $50 in-season.

The *Cliff Lodge* (☎ 508-228-9480), 9 Cliff Rd, is a converted 1771 sea captain's house 10 minutes from Straight Wharf. Its 10 fresh, light and airy rooms and an apartment ($225) are decorated in English-country style. In-season they rent for $125 to $165 double, $85 single.

The *Fair Winds Guest House* (☎ 508-228-1998), 29 Cliff Rd, is a comfortably restored old house. There are commanding views of the harbor from the more expensive rooms which are at the high end of the range: $125 to $175 double ($70 to $140 in the off-season).

In the center of the historic district, the *Quaker House Inn* (☎ 508-228-0400), 5 Chestnut St, has eight rooms decorated simply but comfortably. They're priced at $150 double in-season, $75 to $95 off-season.

The *Ship's Inn* (☎ 508-228-0040), 13 Fair St, is a 10-minute walk from Straight Wharf on a quiet residential street. This 1831 whaling captain's house has 10 large, airy and comfortable rooms for $125 double with private bath, $50 single with shared bath.

Nearby *Fair Gardens* (☎ 508-228-4258, 800-377-6609), 27 Fair St, has 10 rooms with private bath for $105 to $170 in-season. The house features an English-style garden and patio.

The *Brass Lantern Inn* (☎ 508-228-4064, 800-377-6609), 11 N Water St, a few blocks from the waterfront, has 18 traditionally furnished and modern rooms (some with bath) that rent for $115 to $180 double, almost half that in the off-season.

In the middle of town, the *Chestnut House* (☎ 508-228-0049), 3 Chestnut St, has four suites and one room, all with private bath and refrigerator, which rent for $130 to $165 double. A full breakfast is included at two nearby recommended restaurants.

The *Periwinkle Guest House* (☎ 508-228-9267, 800-673-4559), 7-9 N Water St, has 18 rooms just a few minutes from Steamboat Wharf. Rooms come in a variety of sizes and shapes; singles and doubles, with and without bath, go for $50 to $175.

Studios *Nantucket Settlements* (☎ 508-228-6597, 800-462-6882) has studios and apartments all over town with kitchenettes and complete kitchens suited to longer stays. The main office is at 8 N Water St. Accommodations range from $980 to $1155 weekly in the summer, and from $60 to $140 nightly in the off-season.

Places to Stay – top end
Hotel The *Harbor House* (☎ 508-228-1500, 800-475-2637) on S Beach St has 112 contemporary rooms in its main hotel and in townhouse-style buildings that resemble Nantucket cottages. For $165 to $265 in-season you'll get a room with TV, private bath, upscale furnishings and an outdoor pool. In the off-season prices drop to the double digits, a real value.

Inns & B&Bs The centrally located *Jared Coffin House* (☎ 508-228-2405, 800-248-2405), 29 Broad St, is the island's most famous and historic lodging place. Sixty rooms, all with private bath, are located in a 1845 Federal-style brick mansion and the five buildings adjacent to it. Colonial-style reproduction furniture is the norm; most

rooms have a TV. In-season rates vary from $85 to $175 single, $145 to $200 double. For historical value, it can't be beat, but for the price, there are more elegant places to stay. It's open year round.

The *Wauwinet* (☎ 508-228-0145, 800-426-8718) is the ultimate island splurge when price is no object. Set on a dramatic and narrow strip of land between the harbor and Atlantic Ocean, about eight miles from town, the inn's 25 luxuriously appointed guest rooms start at $150 in the spring, $220 in the fall and $270 in the summer. Free jitney service shuttles guests to and from town. Service is exceptional here.

Places to Eat
Nantucket town has plenty of inexpensive sandwich and bistro-style places, all generally creative and inventive. Nantucket is also renown for its dense concentration of exceptional restaurants, so if you've been waiting to splurge this may be the place to do it, but you'll have to be careful not to burn a hole through your pocket. Reservations are advised for the moderate and expensive restaurants in the summer. Unless noted, most places are open from mid-May to mid-October, but you won't go hungry in the off-season.

Places to Eat – budget
The *Espresso Cafe* (☎ 508-228-6930), 40 Main St, serves strong coffee, breakfast pastries, vegetarian dishes, hearty soups and cold salads year round for about $3 to $7. There's a quiet patio in the rear.

Henry's Sandwiches (☎ 508-228-0123), on Steamboat Wharf, makes huge sandwiches and grinders and hearty soups for $3 to $4.

The tiny *Downy Flake* (☎ 508-228-4533), on Children's Beach, purveyors of doughnuts and blueberry pancakes, has been a local institution since the 1960s.

Dave's Soda Fountain (☎ 508-228-4549), inside Congdon's Pharmacy at 47 Main St, and the *Nantucket Pharmacy* (☎ 508-228-0180) next door are classic drugstore soda fountains with swivel stools and cheap coffee, peanut butter and jelly sandwiches and the like for a couple bucks. They're open year round.

Something Natural (☎ 508-228-0504), at 50 Cliff Rd on the way to the beach at Madaket, prepares sandwiches and natural snacks to take to the beach.

Foood for Here and There (☎ 508-228-4291), 149 Lower Orange St on the way to 'Sconset and Surfside, bakes specialty pizzas, quiches and the like for about $5, year round.

Black Eyed Susans (☎ 508-228-2212), 10 India St, usually has a long line of customers waiting for reasonably priced and creative dishes; breakfast averages $5 to $10 and dinner $9 to $19. Try the veggie scramble made with eggs or tofu for breakfast, or try sourdough-crusted cod on a bed of roasted vegetables for dinner. One nice feature is half-portion entrees that you can mix and match.

The *Brotherhood of Thieves*, 23 Broad St, a dark tavern lit by candles even during the day, is a friendly and boisterous place frequented by locals. They come to chow on chowder, burgers and sandwiches for $5 to $16. There's always a long line in the summer and you'll be seated at long tables with fellow patrons for lunch and dinner year round.

The *Off Centre Cafe* (☎ 508-228-8470), 29 Centre St, is usually open for all three meals, served at a few tables indoors or on the patio, which is great for people-watching. Get a simple yogurt with fruit or huevos rancheros for breakfast, soup and salad for lunch ($5.50 to $8). At dinner, it's strictly burritos and enchiladas (about $10), the closest the island comes to ethnic food. Off Centre closes from January through April.

Arno's at 41 Main (☎ 508-228-7001) is open throughout the day and serves decent portions of well-priced food in pleasant surroundings. Sandwiches, Thai peanut noodles, fish and chips, and a few vegetarian dishes will set you back $9 to $16; breakfasts of banana pancakes and eggs Benedict cost less. It's closed in January.

The family-friendly *Vincent's Restaurant*

(☎ 508-228-0189), 21 S Water St, offers plain and fancy pasta dishes, pizzas and seafood for lunch ($6 to $9) and dinner ($7 to $15). The decor is classic Italian-American, with Chianti bottles hanging from the ceilings and red and white checked table cloths. It's closed in January and February.

The *Atlantic Cafe* (☎ 508-228-0570), 15 S Water St, is a casual and fun year-round place (which gets louder and louder as the night wears on). It serves generous portions of noshing food like nachos, buffalo wings, chowder and burgers for $8 to $15.

The pub-style *Rose & Crown* (☎ 508-228-2595), 23 S Water St, offers similar dishes at lunch and dinner (for similar prices) in a large barn-like room that was formerly a livery stable.

The *Gaslight Theatre Cafe* (☎ 508-228-4479), 1 N Union St, serves breakfast (about $6) and burgers and seafood for lunch ($8 to $12). For the money ($15 to $25) there are better places to have dinner. The small outdoor terrace is usually packed.

Places to Eat – middle

The *Quaker House Restaurant* (☎ 508-228-9156), 31 Centre St, is one of the island's best values. The homey and charming dining room serves fixed-price dinners, like shrimp scampi or beef burgundy, that range from $14 to $21. Baked apple pancakes and vegetable omelets at breakfast are also very good. The dining room only seats 40 people, so arrive early or be prepared to wait in line.

The *Tap Room* (☎ 508-228-2400) in the basement of the Jared Coffin House, 29 Broad St, is a cozy, year-round 19th-century tavern serving hearty and traditional American dishes. You can also dine on the shaded terrace. Lunch dishes hover around $10 to $12, while dinner is more like $14 to $17.

As the names implies, *Obadiah's Native Seafood* (☎ 508-228-4430), 2 India St, highlights the local catch. What the name doesn't tell you is that it's very reasonably priced for Nantucket: lunches run about $10, while dinner entrees like grilled tuna and broiled scallops are $15 to $19. Dine in the exposed-brick basement, courtyard or covered patio.

Places to Eat – top end

The Boarding House (☎ 508-228-9622), 12 Federal St, offers innovative American cuisine for lunch and dinner. Entrees like grilled lobster tail and pan-roasted salmon ($16 to $24) are served in a cozy basement setting or outdoors on a brick patio, great for people-watching. The bar, where a less expensive bistro-style menu is served, is very popular with locals. It's open almost year round.

The *Company of the Cauldron* (☎ 508-228-4016), 7 India St, offers a table d'hôte, fixed-price dinner for $40 per person, plus wine. The creative New American menu, served at two seatings in a romantic setting, changes nightly and might go like this: roasted red and yellow pepper soup, Nantucket greens, baked jumbo shrimp stuffed with crab and a chocolate tart to finish up.

American Seasons (☎ 508-228-7111), 80 Centre St, celebrates the four corners of the country with an eclectic menu that highlights jazzed up dishes inspired by the Wild West, Pacific Coast, Down South and New England. The dining room features lots of folk art and the artfully presented entrees range from $14 to $22.

De Marco (☎ 508-228-1836), 9 India St, offers Northern Italian cuisine for dinner only, in elegant but simple dining rooms. Entrees like rack of lamb or lobster with angel hair pasta will set you back $14 to $28, not including a choice from the outstanding wine list.

Entertainment

Pick up a copy of the *Nantucket Map & Legend* or *Yesterday's Island*, free weeklies, for up-to-the minute listings of concerts, theater productions and festivals.

You'll find live music and dancing at the boisterous *Rose & Crown* and a more refined crowd at the Harbor Hotel's *Hearth*. Live folk music is featured at *The Brotherhood of Thieves* and live piano or guitar at the Jared Coffin House's *Tap Room*. The

Atlantic Cafe is a popular place to hang out later in the evening. (See Places to Eat for information.)

The *Dreamland Theater* (☎ 508-228-5356), 19 S Water St, shows first-run movies, while the *Gaslight Theatre* (☎ 508-228-4435), 1 N Union St, shows art films.

Things to Buy

Locally grown produce is sold from the backs of trucks parked on Main St every day except Sunday during the growing season.

There are dozens and dozens of pricey antique shops, clothing boutiques, jewelry stores, art galleries and specialty shops that carry the island's trademark woven "lightship baskets," which can cost between $300 and $3000.

AROUND THE ISLAND

The island measures about 14 miles by three miles and is ringed by sandy beaches, almost all of which are open to the public. Great Point and Coatue Point are narrow strips of beach only accessible by 4WD vehicle. Since over one-third of the island is protected conservation land, there is plenty of space in the interior of the island to walk and enjoy nature.

The only other town of note is Siasconset, referred to locally as 'Sconset. Head out of Nantucket town on Milestone Rd, which takes you directly into the village. The four or five other towns you'll see on the map are really just residential communities with very little going on except new house building.

'Sconset

The charming residential village of 'Sconset is definitely worth a detour. In the summertime the houses are awash with blooming roses. In the 17th century, fishermen and whalers lived in the tiny weathered cottages, adding "warts" (equally tiny rooms) when their families came out to stay with them. By the late 1800s 'Sconset was fashionable with New York City actors who summered here. 'Sconset is seven miles from Nantucket town; the best way to reach it is by bicycle, although you can take a bus (see Getting Around).

Places to Eat The *Siasconset Market* (☎ 508-257-9915) and *Claudette's* (☎ 508-257-6622), both next to the post office in the tiny center of town and open seasonally, have picnic supplies and sandwich fixings after the long bike ride or for the beach.

The *'Sconset Cafe* (☎ 508-257-4008), Post Office Sq, serves an eclectic lunch menu with creative soups and salads ($7). If you pedal out for breakfast you'll be rewarded with cranberry and blueberry pancakes ($4.50). They also serve fancier New American dinners in the same airy setting, surrounded by local artwork.

The *Chanticleer Inn* (☎ 508-257-6231), 9 New St, is arguably the island's best restaurant. The setting is elegant and romantic, in the courtyard of a rose-covered cottage or in small dining rooms overlooking the courtyard. The exquisite French cuisine is a bargain at lunch ($6 to $20), while the memorable fixed-price dinner costs $60 per person, $14 to $30 for à la carte entrees.

Conservation Land
Much of the island's wetlands, moors and grasslands are protected from development and are a naturalist's delight. If you plan to be on-island for any length of time, stop by the Nantucket Conservation Foundation (☎ 508-228-2884), 118 Cliff Rd, in Nantucket town, for an up-to-date map ($3) of their ever-expanding holdings.

Sanford Farm, Ram Pasture and the Woods, off Madaket Rd, are collectively a former 900-acre farm with walking and biking trails.

The Moors
Off Polpis Rd to the south is the island's highest point, Altar Rock, from which there are expansive views of the moors, heather and cranberry bogs. The Moors, criss-crossed with walking trails and rutted dirt

roads, are spectacular in the autumn and are lovely at dawn or dusk throughout the year.

Lighthouses
As you might expect, the island is ringed with working lighthouses. Brant Point Light guards the entrance to the harbor.

Around the island, Great Point Light is accessible only by 4WD vehicle. Its remote location, worth the expense it takes to get there, makes it all the more stately and grand. 'Sconset's Sankaty Light, visible 30 miles out to sea, stands on the edge of a rapidly encroaching 90-foot bluff.

Nantucket Lifesaving Museum
The museum (☎ 508-228-1885) on Polpis Rd displays lifesaving boats and photographs and accounts of dramatic sea rescues. On the edge of a pond, it's nicely situated for a picnic. It's open to visitors from mid-June to mid-October, 10 am to 5 pm Tuesday through Sunday.

Beaches
Dionis, about three miles from Nantucket town off Eel Point Rd from the Madaket bike path, is the island's only beach with dunes. It's good for swimming (the water is relatively calm) and shelling.

Surfside Beach, three miles from town and accessible by frequent shuttle bus, is popular with the college and twentysomething crowd. It's a wide beach with moderate-to-heavy surf.

Madaket Beach, at the end of the namesake bike path, is the most popular place to watch sunsets. Strong currents and heavy surf make for less than ideal swimming conditions.

Cisco Beach, about four miles from town off Hummock Pond Rd from Milk St, is popular with surfers.

'Sconset Beach is long and narrow (it's suffered much erosion in recent years), with a good deal of surf and undertow. It's about seven miles from town on the island's eastern shore.

Central Massachusetts & Berkshires

To many visitors, Massachusetts means Boston and Cape Cod to the east, and the Berkshires to the west. In fact, central Massachusetts saw some of the region's earliest settlement, and during the 19th century, some of its most explosive industrial growth.

The Connecticut River, navigable from Long Island Sound to Vermont in colonial times, was the early settlers' highway into the interior, and the route back out for the ships they built full of the crops and products they produced. The Pioneer Valley, as it's called in Massachusetts, has an interesting mix of colonial, early American and 19th-century industrial villages and towns. It is home to five colleges and universities, bringing a youthful, cosmopolitan spirit to several of its towns.

Getting There & Around

Air Worcester's airport receives flights by major national and regional airlines, though the air traffic hub of the region is Boston's Logan International Airport. Springfield and the Pioneer Valley towns are served by Bradley International Airport across the state line in Windsor Locks, CT.

Bus Peter Pan Bus Lines (☎ 617-426-7838, 800-343-9999), a Trailways affiliate, has its hub in Springfield, and runs buses daily to Albany, NY; Amherst, MA; Bennington, VT; Boston and Logan Airport; Deerfield; Hartford, CT; Holyoke; Hyannis; Lee; Lenox; New Haven, CT; North Adams; Northampton; Pittsfield; Providence, RI; South Hadley; Sturbridge; Toronto, Ontario; Williamstown; Windsor Locks, CT and Worcester.

Bonanza Bus Lines (☎ 212-947-1766, 800-556-3815) runs buses daily between New York City's Port Authority Bus Terminal (Adirondack Trailways ticket plaza) and Bennington, VT, via Great Barrington, Stockbridge, Lee, Lenox, Pittsfield and

Williamstown. There's service between Albany, NY and Pittsfield connecting with the service between Pittsfield and New York City. Another service connects Providence with Springfield, the Berkshire towns and Albany.

Train The Boston section of Amtrak's (☎ 800-872-7245) *Lakeshore Limited* departs Boston's South Station (☎ 617-482-3660) in the afternoon, stopping at Worcester, Springfield and Pittsfield before reaching Albany-Rensselaer in the evening. There it links up with the *Lakeshore* section from New York City (☎ 212-582-6875), and the full train continues to Chicago.

The *Vermonter* runs daily during daylight hours between New York City and St Albans, VT, via Springfield, with connecting bus service to Montréal from St Albans.

The *Adirondack* runs between Montréal and New York City's Grand Central Terminal daily during daylight hours. The closest it gets to Massachusetts is a stop at Albany-Rensselaer, from whence you must continue by bus.

In addition, Amtrak trains traveling between Boston and New York City on the inland route pass through Wellesley, Framingham, Worcester and Springfield, as well as Hartford and New Haven, CT.

Car The Massachusetts Turnpike (I-90, a toll road known as the Mass Pike) and MA 2 are the major east-west roads connecting Boston with central and western Massachusetts. It takes about three hours to drive all the way across Massachusetts from Boston to Lenox on the Mass Pike.

MA 2, between Boston and Williamstown, is mostly four-lane (but not always limited-access) between Cambridge and I-91 at Greenfield. West of Greenfield to Williamstown it's a scenic two-lane road.

Central Massachusetts

Central Massachusetts includes two major north-south highways and two busy east-west highways making getting around by car easy and quick.

WORCESTER
Though blessed with several excellent museums, one of America's best concert halls and numerous institutions of higher learning, Worcester suffers from being in the shadow of Boston, only an hour's drive to the east. It was not always so.

History
Once the home of the Nipmuck Indians, Worcester was incorporated as a town in 1722, and as a city in 1848. During the 19th century, Worcester was one of the inland

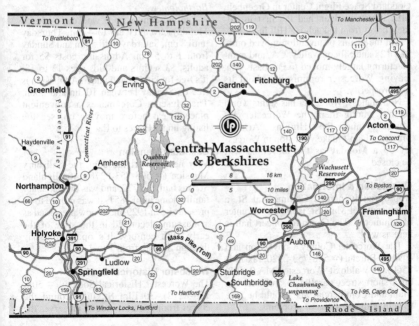

cities and towns of Massachusetts and Connecticut that boomed with industry and invention. All sorts of new devices, implements and conveniences were thought up in these cities' small workshops and passed on to the water-powered mills nearby for large-scale manufacture. Worcester produced machines that were the first to weave carpets, fold envelopes and turn irregular shapes on a lathe. Worcester citizen Esther Howland (1828-1904) was the first person to produce and market Valentine cards in quantity. And in 1887 Sam Jones made the first lunch wagon big enough for customers to step inside – the precursor to that American culinary icon, the diner.

During its heyday, Worcester hosted the first national convention on women's suffrage (1850) and saw the foundation of almost 11 colleges and universities including Clark, Holy Cross, Worcester Polytechnic Institute, as well as several significant museums. One of its native sons, Dr Robert Goddard (1882-1945), for whom the Goddard Space Flight Center in Greenbelt, MD, is named, launched the first liquid-fuel rocket from Pakachoag Hill in 1926.

But the genius of invention moved on to MA 128 and Silicon Valley, CA, and manufacturing largely moved to Far East Asia, leaving Worcester reminiscing about its lost prosperity.

Nonetheless, Worcester has sights worth seeing, among them the Worcester Art Museum and the Higgins Armory Museum. Don't make your stop in Worcester on a Monday as the museums will be closed.

Orientation & Information
Appropriately named Commercial St, a block south of Main St, is the city's center of commerce. The Centrum concert hall is here as well.

The Worcester County Convention and Visitors Bureau (☎ 508-753-2920, fax 754-8560), 33 Waldo St, Worcester, MA 01608, on a short street parallel to and between Main and Commercial Sts, should be able to help with questions or problems.

Worcester Art Museum
When Worcester was rich, its captains of industry bestowed largesse upon the town and its citizens. The Worcester Art Museum (☎ 508-799-4406), 55 Salisbury St, off Park and Main Sts (follow the signs), is one of the most generous and impressive bequests.

This small regional museum has a surprisingly comprehensive collection, ranging from ancient Chinese, Egyptian and Sumerian artifacts through European masterworks and those of Japanese *ukiyo-e* painters to great American paintings and primitives. The museum's collection of more than 2000 photographs spans the history of the medium, from Matthew Brady to Winogrand.

The museum boasts a good number of world-famous masterpieces. Edward Hick's *Peaceable Kingdom* is perhaps the most easily recognizable, but you can also see Cassatt's *Woman Bathing*, Gauguin's *Brooding Woman* and Rembrandt's *St Bartholomew*.

The museum is open weekdays (closed Monday) from 11 am to 4 pm, Thursday until 8 pm, Saturday until 5 pm and Sunday from 1 to 5 pm. Admission costs $5 for adults, $3 seniors and kids ages 13 to 18; it's free for kids 12 and under. Admission is free on Sunday between 10 am and noon. The Museum Café makes a convenient place to eat before moving on, see the listing under Places to Eat.

Salisbury Mansion
Very near the art museum, the Salisbury Mansion (☎ 508-753-8278), 40 Highland St, was built in 1772 and was the Salisbury family home until 1851. It was moved to its present site in 1929 and is now preserved as a museum, decorated in the style of the early 19th century. It's open Thursday through Sunday from 1 to 4 pm.

Worcester Historical Society
The Worcester Historical Society (☎ 508-753-8272), 30 Elm St, just around the corner from the art museum, preserves the

record of Worcester's history, particularly its 19th-century golden age. The museum ($2.50) is open from 10 am to 4 pm, Sunday 1 to 4 pm, closed Monday.

American Antiquarian Society
If you're interested in doing research in the largest single collection of printed source materials relating to the first 250 years of US history, the American Antiquarian Society (☎ 508-755-5221), 185 Salisbury St, a few blocks from the art museum, is a must-see. The society was founded in 1812, and the documents in its library cover all aspects of colonial and early American culture, history and literature. It's open for research weekdays from 9 am to 5 pm; free tours are given Wednesday at 2 pm.

Higgins Armory Museum
John Woodman Higgins, turn-of-the-century president of the Worcester Pressed Steel Company, loved good steel. Medieval armorers made good steel, so he collected it: over 100 full suits of armor for men, women, kids and even dogs. His collection got so big that in 1929 he built a special armory to house it – this Art Deco building with Neo-Gothic accents inside is the Higgins Armory Museum (☎ 508-853-6015), 100 Barber Ave off W Boylston St (MA 12). Children will like the Quest Gallery where they can try on "castle clothing" and replica suits of armor. It's open from 10 am to 4 pm (Sunday noon to 4 pm); it's closed Monday except in July and August. Admission costs $4.75 for adults, $4 seniors, $3.75 kids six to 16.

Mechanics Hall
Mechanics Hall (☎ 508-752-5608), 321 Main St, was constructed in 1857 on the orders of the Worcester County Mechanics Association, a group of artisans and small business owners who typified Worcester's inventive and industrial strength in the mid-19th century. The hall boasts superb acoustics and is regarded as America's finest standing pre-Civil War concert hall. Thoreau and Emerson spoke here, as did Dickens, Twain and Theodore Roosevelt.

Restored in 1977, the hall is still used for concerts, lectures and recording sessions. Call for information on when you can visit, or call the box office (☎ 508-752-0888) for tickets to a lecture or performance.

Places to Stay
Worcester has a number of business hotels. Most of the tourist lodgings in this area are about 20 miles southwest, in and around Sturbridge. The biggest concentration of motels is near I-290 exit 20, a few miles northeast of the city center.

The 48-room *Econo Lodge* (☎ 508-852-5800, 800-446-6900), 531 Lincoln St, at I-290 exit 20, has serviceable rooms for $42 to $52. More or less across the street, the *Days Lodge* (☎ 508-852-2800), 50 Oriol Drive, has 114 better rooms for $63 to $75.

The *Holiday Inn* (☎ 508-852-4000, 800-465-4329), 500 Lincoln St at I-290 exit 20, charges $109 a single for its very good rooms and $10 for every additional adult.

The 58-room *Beechwood Inn* (☎ 508-754-5789, 800-344-2589), 363 Plantation St, east of the town center along MA 9 near the Massachusetts Biotechnology Park, is a cylindrical building with a good reputation, friendly service and luxury rooms priced from $109 to $139 single, $109 to $149 double.

Worcester Holiday Inn Crowne Plaza (formerly the Marriott, ☎ 508-791-1600), 10 Lincoln Square, is well placed between the Centrum and the art museum, with luxury rooms priced at $129 single, $149 double.

Places to Eat
As Worcester was the home of the first diner, you should have at least a snack in one. Prices are generally low. There are three of them around Shrewsbury St alone: the *Boulevard Diner* (☎ 508-791-4535), 155 Shrewsbury St; *Miss Worcester Diner* (☎ 508-752-1310), 300 Southbridge St and the *Parkway* (☎ 508-753-9968), 148 Shrewsbury St. The city has a half-dozen others as well. Most do not serve alcohol.

The *Museum Café* (☎ 508-799-4406) in the Worcester Art Museum at 55 Salisbury St, is a good choice for light meals and moderate prices at a location you'll probably visit in any case. It serves soups, salads and sandwiches for $5 to $15, is open daily except Monday for lunch, and Thursday it's open for dinner.

Legal Sea Food (☎ 508-792-1600), One Exchange Place a block south of the Centrum, is always bustling, its long menu of seafood, a raw bar, moderate prices and good quality drawing in the crowd. Lunch might cost $10 to $15, dinner $12 to $30.

El Morocco (☎ 508-756-7117), 100 Wall St, serves up Lebanese cuisine and live jazz, with moderate prices and good views of the city.

Entertainment
Worcester has made a name for itself by attracting big-name musical performers to its three high-quality venues: *Mechanics Hall* (☎ 508-752-0888) for classical and jazz performers, the huge *Centrum* (☎ 508-798-8888; for tickets 617-931-2000) for rock and other big-crowd acts and the *New Aud* (☎ 508-799-1250), formerly the Worcester Memorial Auditorium, for some of each and more. Check the newspapers or call for current offerings.

Getting There & Away
Air Worcester Municipal Airport (☎ 508-792-0610), several miles due west of the center of town along MA 122 (Chandler St) is served by Northwest, USAir Express, TWA, Delta, American and Continental Airlines.

Bus Peter Pan Bus Lines (☎ 508-753-1515, 754-4600, 800-343-9999), 160 Southbridge St, has direct services between Worcester and Albany, Amherst, Bennington, Boston (and Logan Airport), Deerfield, Hartford, Holyoke, Hyannis, New York City, Northampton, Pittsfield, Plymouth, South Hadley, Springfield, Sturbridge, Toronto and Williamstown.

Train Amtrak (☎ 508-755-0356, 800-872-7245), 45 Shrewsbury St, stops here on its Inland Route between New York City and Boston. MBTA Commuter Rail (☎ 617-722-3200, 800-392-6100) operates several trains daily between Boston and Worcester as well.

Car Driving details for Worcester are:

Destination	Mileage	Hr:Min
Boston, MA	40 miles	1:00
Hartford, CT	63 miles	1:30
Lenox, MA	90 miles	1:45
New York, NY	172 miles	3:30
Northampton, MA	54 miles	1:15
Springfield, MA	51 miles	1:00
Sturbridge, MA	22 miles	0:30

STURBRIDGE
The small, central Massachusetts town of Sturbridge kept much of its colonial character until after WWII. When the Mass Pike and I-84 were built just south of the town, change came all at once.

Sturbridge reclaimed its past in a unique way. To take advantage of the handy highway transport, the town became host to one of the country's first "living museums." Old buildings were moved here from throughout the region, and others were replicated as needed to recreate a typical New England village of the 1830s. Instead of labels, this museum had "interpreters," people who dressed in costume, plied the trades and occupations of their ancestors from that time and explained to visitors what it was they were doing and why.

The concept of the living museum was new when Old Sturbridge Village was built. It has now spread throughout New England and the world, but this remains one of its best exemplars.

Sturbridge is very busy with visitors in summer and the autumn foliage season. Traffic increases exponentially during the three times per year (early May, early July and early September) when the Antiques and Flea Market is held in Brimfield, five miles east along US 20.

Orientation & Information
There are actually three Sturbridges. The first one you see is the least attractive, the commercial strip along US 20 (Main St)

just south of I-90 exit 9. The second is Sturbridge as it used to be, best seen at the Town Common, backed by the historic Publick House Inn, on MA 131, a half mile southeast of US 20. The third is Old Sturbridge Village, entered from US 20.

Most accommodations and restaurants are along US 20, as is the Sturbridge Area Tourist Association information office (SATA, ☎ 508-347-7594, 800-628-8379), opposite the entrance to Old Sturbridge Village at 380 Main St. It's also the Peter Pan/Trailways bus station. The SATA is a division of the Tri-Community Area Chamber of Commerce, whose name you will see on the sign.

Old Sturbridge Village

In the beginning two brothers, Albert Wells and J Cheney Wells, lived in Southbridge and carried on a very successful optics business. They were enthusiastic collectors of antiques – so enthusiastic, in fact, that by the end of WWII their collections left no free space in their homes.

They bought 200 acres of forest and meadow in Sturbridge and began to move old buildings to this land. Opened in 1946, Old Sturbridge Village (OSV, ☎ 508-347-3362) is an authentically recreated New England town of the 1830s, with 40 restored structures filled with the Wells' antiques.

Authenticity is the watchword here: the country store is stocked with products brought from throughout the world by New England sailing ships. Trades and crafts are carried out with authentic tools and materials. The livestock has even been back-bred to approximate the breeds of animals – smaller, shaggier, thinner – that lived on New England farms a century and a half ago. The OSV library has over 20,000 manuscripts and books describing various aspects of early 19th-century life in the region.

Plan at least a day for your visit. OSV is open every day from April to early November from 9 am to 5 pm; in March, the rest of November and December it's closed Monday, but open other days from 10 am to

4 pm. Admission costs $15 for adults, $13.50 seniors 65+, $7.50 kids six to 15; children under six are free. Admission is good for two consecutive days. Food services in the village include the Bullard Tavern, with buffet and à la carte service for full meals, light meals and snacks; and a picnic grove with grills and a play area.

St Anne Shrine

Monsignor Pie Neveu, a Roman Catholic Assumptionist bishop, ministered to a diocese in Russia from 1906 to 1936. While at his post, Bishop Neveu collected valuable Russian icons, a hobby no doubt made easier by the fall of the old order and the advent of secularist communism. Bishop Neveu's collection was augmented by acquisitions from the Assumptionist fathers who served as chaplains at the US Embassy in Moscow between 1934 and 1941, and ultimately brought to the USA. The collection was installed at the St Anne Shrine in 1971.

Since WWII, it has been illegal to export icons from Russia, so the collection of 60 rare works preserved at the St Anne Shrine (☎ 508-347-7338), 16 Church St, is a treasure. The icon museum, open daily from 9 am to 6 pm (free admission, donations accepted) is one building in the shrine complex just off US 20 at the western end of Sturbridge, in the neighborhood sometimes called Fiskdale. Watch for the sign just east of the intersection with MA 148.

Mellea Winery

Ten miles southeast of Sturbridge along MA 131 in West Dudley, just north of the Connecticut state line, is Mellea Winery (☎ 508-943-5166), 108 Old Southbridge Rd.

Joe Compagnone, a local chemist-industrialist, has planted vinifera and French-American hybrid vines on a gravelly south-facing hillside, and produces a variety of wines from table-grade to premium using his own grapes and others imported from southeastern Massachusetts, Long Island and Oregon. White wines are favored, but there are drinkable reds as well.

Come for a free tour and tasting from late May through December, Wednesday through Sunday from noon to 5 pm.

Brimfield Antique Shows

Six miles west of Sturbridge along US 20 is Brimfield, a mecca for collectors of antique furniture, toys, tools and implements, and those categories of goods known as "collectibles." Buyers and sellers come from a dozen states and beyond to do business here, the largest outdoor antiques fair in the USA. The town has numerous shops open year round, but the major antiques and collectibles shows are held in early to mid-May, early July and early September, usually on the second weekends in those months. Actually, there are 20 separate fairs set up in fields surrounding the town. Admission to the grounds costs about $3 on weekdays, $5 on the weekend.

If you're interested, call the Brimfield Antique Show Promoters' Association (☎ 203-763-3760) or the SATA (☎ 508-347-7594, 800-628-8379) for dates and details. Be sure to have advance hotel reservations.

Places to Stay

Many lodgings fill on weekends in summer and, especially, in autumn. When the Brimfield Antiques and Flea Market is in progress (see that entry, above), lodging prices rise substantially and you need advance reservations.

Camping The closest campground is *Yogi Bear's Sturbridge Jellystone Park* (☎ 508-347-9570), with 400 sites, two pools, a hot tub, waterslide and other entertainment. The basic rate for two people in a tent is just under $30. Take I-84 exit 2 and follow the camping signs.

Wells State Park (☎ 508-347-9257), on MA 49 (Mountain Rd) in Sturbridge north of I-90, has 59 wooded sites for $6 or $7 for up to five people, the higher price being for a lakefront site. You can reserve your site in advance with a two-night deposit.

There are also several private campgrounds in Charlton, south of US 20 about

eight miles east of Sturbridge: *Applewood Campground* (☎ 508-248-7017), 44 King Rd, with 60 sites and *The Wood Lot Campground* (☎ 508-248-5141, 800-255-4153), Stafford St in Charlton City, with 92 sites.

Motels If you don't have a reservation when you arrive in Sturbridge, go to the SATA information office (see information above) and look through the motel brochures. Some include coupons that are good for special rates or discounts.

The cheapest lodgings are the smaller motels off US 20, such as the *Sturbridge Heritage Motel* (☎ 508-347-3943), a mile west of OSV, which charges $42 to $47 for its eight relatively quiet rooms. When the Brimfield antiques fair is in session, prices rise to $75. The *Village Motel* (☎ 508-347-3049), more or less across the road and down an unpaved lane, is as cheap and even quieter.

Three other budget motels are about two miles from OSV on MA 131 southeast of the Publick House, up the hill and past the Sturbridge Plaza shopping center. *Green Acres Motel* (☎ 508-347-3496), just past Rom's Restaurant at Shepard Rd; *Pine Grove Motel* (☎ 508-347-9673) and *Sir Francis Motel* (☎ 508-347-9514), 140 Main St, a bit farther along, are similar in comfort and price.

Sturbridge Motor Inn (☎ 508-347-3391), on Haynes St, between the Common and OSV, has a variety of rooms priced from $55 to $70; the more expensive rooms are larger and quieter, with king-size beds.

Carriage House Inn (☎ 508-347-9000), 358 Main St just off I-90 exit 9 at MA 131, is as central as you can get, less than a half mile east of OSV. It has outdoor adult and children's pools, and 79 rooms priced at $72, light breakfast included.

Holiday Inn Express (☎ 508-347-5141, fax 347-2034), 478 Main St (US 20), less than a mile west of OSV, has 64 comfortable rooms at $73, light breakfast included.

Econo Lodge (☎ 508-347-2324, 800-446-6900), two miles west of OSV on US 20, charges $75 for its 48 rooms, with pool, playground and coin-op laundry.

Quality Inn Colonial (☎ 508-347-3306, 800-228-5151, fax 347-3514), on US 20 east of I-84, has 67 comfortable rooms, a large pool and two tennis courts. Rates are $78 in summer.

American Motor Lodge – Best Western (☎ 508-347-9121), a half mile east of OSV on US 20, just off I-90 exit 9 and I-84 exit 3-B, has 55 rooms and all services including a heated pool, saunas and coin-op laundry for $83 in summer. *Old Sturbridge Village Lodges & Oliver Wight House* (☎ 508-347-3327, fax 347-3018), US 20 next to the entrance to OSV and administered by it, is a modern 47-unit motel in updated colonial style. Rooms cost $85 per night in the lodges, and $100 per night in the Oliver Wight House, an adjacent white clapboard inn built in 1789.

Sturbridge Coach Motor Lodge (☎ 508-347-7327), 408 Main St, an attractive and quiet motel on a hill above the highway just west of OSV, has 54 rooms priced at $80 to $95.

Inns & B&Bs The SATA (☎ 508-347-7594, 800-628-8379) can direct you to B&Bs which are members of the association, and may make same-day reservations if you stop in at the information office. Folkstone Bed & Breakfast Reservation Service (☎ 508-480-0380, 800-762-2751), 51 Sears Rd, Southborough, MA 01772, can help you find a room in central Massachusetts for $50 to $150 per night, breakfast included.

Publick House Inn (☎ 508-347-3313, 800-782-5425, fax 347-1246), MA 131, on the Common, is Sturbridge's most famous old inn built in 1771, now a mini-industry with frequent weekend theme programs, several dining rooms and 17 comfortable guest rooms for $85 to $150. Nearby is *Country Motor Lodge* (same phone), with rooms and suites considerably cheaper at $55 to $125. Also run by the Publick House is *Colonel Ebenezer Crafts Inn*, an eight-room B&B priced slightly less than the inn.

Commonwealth Cottage (☎ 508-347-7708), 11 Summit Ave, is a big Queen Anne Victorian in a quiet location with three guest rooms (one with private bath) priced from $62 to $112, breakfast and afternoon tea included. Follow US 20 west and, just past the MA 148 intersection, turn left onto Commonwealth Ave. Bear left at the Heritage Green sign.

Sturbridge Country Inn (☎ 508-347-5503, fax 347-5319), 530 Main St, is a stately Greek Revival mansion about a mile west of OSV on US 20 in the commercial district. Its nine sybaritic rooms all have fireplaces, whirlpool baths, TV and air-conditioning, and cost $119 to $159. There's a bit of traffic noise in front.

Places to Eat

US 20 is sprinkled with the usual fast-food outlets. For a local effort, try the *Heritage Family Restaurant & Pizza* (☎ 508-347-7673) where you can fill up with a pizza, grinder, calzone, salad or fish and chips for $5 or so.

For a full restaurant, there's *Rom's* (☎ 508-347-3349), on MA 131 a mile or so southeast of the Publick House, across from the shopping center. This Sturbridge institution serves big portions of traditional Italian-American fare (and drinks) for moderate prices – about $15 to $20 for a full meal.

The much advertised *Publick House* (☎ 508-347-3313) has a decent dining room with traditional American dishes; try the lobster pie. Full three-course dinners with drinks can be had for $28 to $40, less at lunch. The special turkey dinner costs $25. *Ebenezer's Tavern* is the venue for less formal meals. Lighter meals are served on the terrace in good weather, where, if you're lucky, there may be a cellist to serenade you.

Try also the *Fieldstone Tavern* (☎ 508-347-7603), a restored rustic barn attached to the Sturbridge Country Inn, 530 Main St.

The *Whistling Swan* (☎ 508-347-2321), at 502 Main St about a mile west of OSV, serves a more adventurous menu of American and continental dishes in a Greek Revival mansion dating from 1855. The restaurant's *Ugly Duckling* loft is less formal, with lighter dishes and prices.

Just west of the Sturbridge Coach Motor

Lodge, off US 20, *Le Béarn Restaurant Français* (☎ 508-347-5900), 12 Cedar St, serves traditional French cuisine at dinner daily for $35 to $45 per person.

If you're up for a drive, follow US 20 two miles west from OSV to MA 148 North; seven miles along, turn left (west) onto MA 9 and go five miles to the *Salem Cross Inn* (☎ 508-867-2345) in West Brookfield. The tranquil inn, built in 1705 and set on 600 acres of farmland, is a welcome respite from the vehicular and commercial fury of Sturbridge. Traditional New England meals are served Tuesday through Friday from noon to 9 pm, Saturday from 5 to 10 pm, Sunday and holidays from noon to 8 pm, closed Monday (except holidays). A typical dinner costs $35 to $45 per person, drinks, tax and tip included.

Entertainment
In summer the *Stageloft Repertory Theater* (☎ 508-347-9005), 530 Main St, at the Sturbridge Country Inn, mounts modern plays such as Ira Levin's *Veronica's Room* and Robert Harling's *Steel Magnolias*, with tickets priced at $10 and $12.

For drinks and conversation, the Sturbridge Country Inn's *Fieldstone Tavern* is right next door.

Getting There & Away
Bus Peter Pan Bus Lines (☎ 800-343-9999) runs one-day excursion buses right to OSV from Boston (☎ 617-426-7838), via Worcester and from New York City (☎ 212-564-8484) via Hartford and Springfield. For other bus routes you must connect at Boston or Springfield. The Peter Pan bus stop is opposite the entrance to OSV, at the SATA information office.

Car Driving details for Sturbridge are:

Destination	Mileage	Hr:Min
Boston, MA	65 miles	1:20
Hartford, CT	42 miles	0:55
Lenox, MA	73 miles	1:30
New York, NY	165 miles	3:30
Springfield, MA	32 miles	0:45
Worcester, MA	18 miles	0:25

Pioneer Valley

The Connecticut River valley is known as the Pioneer Valley because of its early settlement. Within a few years after the Pilgrims landed at Plymouth in 1620, fur-traders and settlers were making their way up the great river deep into the region. Springfield and other valley towns later became pioneers of technical advancement.

SPRINGFIELD
Springfield, the largest city in western Massachusetts, is at the region's transportation nexus, where the traditional east-west route from Boston to Albany crosses the Connecticut River valley. Its 19th-century industrial might brought its residents the wealth to build several excellent museums (closed Monday and Tuesday), a library and a grand symphony hall. Basketball players all over the world pay tribute to Springfield with every shot: the game was conceived here. Its long and eventful history is typical of most New England crossroads towns.

Like nearby Hartford, CT, Springfield is a city of commuters. The stately Romanesque buildings around Court Square and the nearby modern office blocks are populated with workers who flee the city center in cars at the end of the work day. There is little nightlife, making Springfield perfect for a stop during the day on your way to Northampton, Amherst or the Berkshires. You may also choose to stay in Northampton or Amherst and visit Springfield on a day trip.

History
By 1636, pioneers and settlers had come up the Connecticut River to Springfield to trade for furs with the Omiskandoagwiak ("Wolf People," the Connecticut Valley Indians) and to farm the valley's fertile alluvial soil. Later, industry sprang up here because the river provided cheap water-power and transport to the markets of Hartford, New York and Philadelphia.

Shays's Rebellion

In 1786, the American Revolutionary War had been won, but the new nation suffered a severe economic depression. The paper money issued to fund the war was still in circulation, but rarely accepted at face value.

Boston's merchants and traders, for whom "sound money" was essential, led a movement to adopt a gold standard. Public officials, with fat salaries, and Boston lawyers acting on behalf of the rich, went along. But farmers in western Massachusetts, who could pay in kind, were opposed to a gold standard. Country people were burdened with heavy land and poll taxes, the foreclosure of mortgages on their farms and debtors' prison; those without property could not vote at all.

The discontent broke out in rebellion on August 29, 1786 when Daniel Shays (1747?–1825), formerly a captain in the revolutionary army, led armed men to prevent the sitting of the courts in Northampton that were handing down judgments against debtors. Shays and his followers planned their moves in an Amherst tavern. Their action forced even the state supreme court to adjourn its session in Springfield.

Early in 1787, Governor Bowdoin sent General Benjamin Lincoln and 4400 men to put down the rebellion. As they marched to Springfield, Shays and his 1200 men attacked the federal armory on January 25, but were repulsed by its federal guards and suffered several casualties.

Put on the defensive, they retreated to Petersham, where Lincoln's troops routed them in February, capturing many. Shays himself escaped to Vermont.

Shays's Rebellion woke up Boston to the dire conditions in the western part of the state. Bowdoin was driven from office, and the senate became more sensitive to the needs of the rest of the state. Governor John Hancock later pardoned Daniel Shays and other rebellion leaders. Similar rebellions in other states influenced public opinion in the direction of a strong federal government capable of preserving public order. ∎

Springfield's prosperity was assured in 1777 when General George Washington and his chief of artillery, Colonel Henry Knox, decided upon this spot for the USA's first arsenal. Though centrally located and easy to access, it was safely distant from the major theaters of the Revolutionary War. Muskets, cannons, and other arms were manufactured here and paper cartridges were manufactured for them. After independence was won, Springfield continued to be the new country's major arsenal.

During the 1780s, poor, debt-ridden farmers in western Massachusetts were losing their land to court-ordered foreclosures. One of the farmers, Daniel Shays, led a rebellion intent on closing down the state and county courts. Shays and his followers marched on Springfield in 1787 to seize the arsenal, but were decisively defeated by the Massachusetts militia, armed from the repository at Springfield. Shays's Rebellion so alarmed wealthy landowners in the region that they worked for the passage of the US Constitution, which mandated a more powerful federal government.

Orientation

Take I-91 exit 6 northbound or exit 7 southbound, follow it to State St (east) then Main St (north), and you'll be at Court Square in the heart of Springfield, a good place to start your explorations. Museum Quadrangle is a few blocks east, the Springfield Armory is a 10-minute walk east and the Basketball Hall of Fame is a 10-minute walk southwest.

Information

Questions are most easily answered by calling Springfield Central (☎ 413-732-7467), the Downtown Happenings Hotline (☎ 413-734-2745) for performances and scheduled events and the Spirit of Springfield (☎ 413-733-3800). The Greater Springfield Convention and Visitors Bureau (☎ 413-787-1548), at Court and Main Sts,

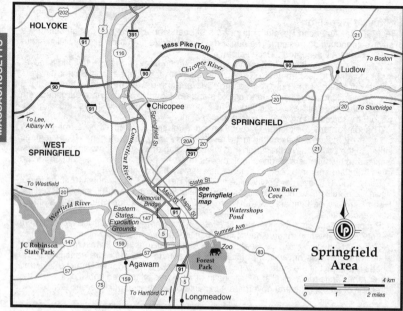

Springfield, MA 01103, has an office in the modern Bank of Boston building facing Court Square. Pick up an excellent informative map from the rack in the lobby of City Hall, the grand Corinthian palace with the tall campanile facing Court Square. The post office is on Main St at the corner with Liberty St.

Court Square

Court Square is surrounded by fine buildings, including Symphony Hall, the First Congregational Church (1819) and the granite Hampden County Superior Courthouse by Henry Hudson Richardson, inspired by Venice's Palazzo Vecchio. William Pynchon, who led the group of Puritans who settled here in 1636, and incorporated the town five years later, is honored with a statue.

Museum Quadrangle

The Springfield Library and Museums (☎ 413-739-3871) are gathered around Museum Quadrangle, two blocks northeast of Court Square. Look for Merrick Park, at the entrance to the quadrangle, and Augustus Saint-Gaudens' statue, *The Puritan*. All of these museums are open Wednesday to Sunday from noon to 4 pm. Admission costs $4 for adults, $1 for those aged six to 16, free for kids under six.

The **George Walter Vincent Smith Art Museum** (☎ 413-733-4214) was founded by a man who amassed a fortune manufacturing carriages, and then spent his money on works of art and artifice. There are fine 19th-century American and European paintings, textiles, ceramics and works in several other media. The Japanese armor collection is among the finest outside of Asia.

The **Museum of Fine Arts** (☎ 413-732-6092) has more than 20 galleries filled with lesser paintings of the great European masters and the better works of lesser masters. Among the masterworks here is Erastus Salisbury Field's *The Rise of the*

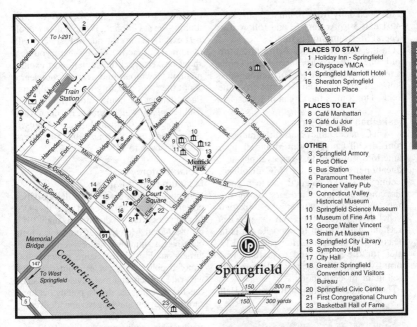

PLACES TO STAY
1 Holiday Inn - Springfield
2 Cityspace YMCA
14 Springfield Marriott Hotel
15 Sheraton Springfield
   Monarch Place

PLACES TO EAT
8 Café Manhattan
19 Café du Jour
22 The Deli Roll

OTHER
3 Springfield Armory
4 Post Office
5 Bus Station
6 Paramount Theater
7 Pioneer Valley Pub
9 Connecticut Valley
  Historical Museum
10 Springfield Science Museum
11 Museum of Fine Arts
12 George Walter Vincent
   Smith Art Museum
13 Springfield City Library
16 Symphony Hall
17 City Hall
18 Greater Springfield
   Convention and Visitors
   Bureau
20 Springfield Civic Center
21 First Congregational Church
23 Basketball Hall of Fame

American Republic, hung above the main stairway. In the impressionist and expressionist galleries, look for Monet's *Haystacks*, and works by Degas, Dufy, Gauguin, Pissarro, Renoir, Rouault and Vlaminck. In the contemporary gallery there are works by George Bellows, Lyonel Feininger, Georgia O'Keeffe and Picasso. Modern sculptors featured include Leonard Baskin and Richard Stankiewicz.

The **Springfield Science Museum** (☎ 413-733-1194) is a good place for children. The Dinosaur Hall has a full-size replica of *Tyrannosaurus rex*. The African Hall has many exhibits about Africa's peoples, animals and ecology. The historic Seymour Planetarium has eight weekly shows (which cost a few dollars).

The **Connecticut Valley Historical Museum** (☎ 413-732-3080) has exhibits on the decorative and domestic arts of the Connecticut River valley from 1636 to the present. There are collections of furniture, pewter and glass, as well as four rooms

decorated authentically in period styles: a 17th-century kitchen, a Federal-period dining room and two rooms from an early 19th-century tavern.

The **Springfield City Library** (☎ 413-739-3871), at the corner of State and Chestnut Sts, is open from noon to 5 pm (closed Monday), and has over a million books, records and videos in its system.

Springfield Armory

The Springfield Armory National Historic Site (☎ 413-734-8551), 1 Armory Square, Federal St at State St, a 10-minute walk from Court Square, preserves what remains of USA's greatest federal armory. During its heyday in the Civil War, 3400 people worked in the armory turning out 1000 muskets a day. Springfield Technical Community College now occupies many of the former firearm factories and officers' quarters, but exhibits in several of the old buildings recall the armory's golden age quite effectively.

It's open daily from 10 am to 5 pm. Take I-291 exit 3 to Armory St and follow it to Federal St. Admission is free.

On the site, the **Small Arms Museum** holds one of the world's largest collections of firearms, including lots of Remingtons, Colts, Lugers and even weapons from the 1600s. Don't miss the Organ of Rifles.

Basketball Hall of Fame

Born in Canada, James Naismith graduated from McGill University in Montréal, then came to Springfield to work as a physical education instructor at the YMCA College. Feeling the need for a good, fast team sport that could be played indoors during the long New England winters, he took two bushel baskets (emptying out the peaches first) and nailed them to opposite walls in the college gymnasium. He wrote down 13 rules for the game, and basketball was born. Twelve of Naismith's rules are still used in the modern sport.

The Naismith Memorial Basketball Hall

KIM GRANT

At the Basketball Hall of Fame, walk through the Shoe Tunnel exhibit which displays the variety of shoes used throughout basketball history.

of Fame (☎ 413-781-6500), 1150 W Columbus Ave at Union St, is one mile south of I-91 exit 7, on the east side of I-91. The hall of fame is an active place where you can shoot baskets, feel the center-court excitement in a wraparound cinema and learn about the sport's history and great players. Plan at least an hour's stop, though you could easily stay all morning. It's open from 9 am to 5 pm (6 pm in July and August). Admission costs $7 for adults, $4 seniors and kids seven to 14.

Indian Motorcycle Museum Hall of Fame

Springfield claims the birth of the gasoline-powered motorcycle, invented here in 1901. Motorcycles were produced here until 1953 by the Indian Motorcycle Company, which once had a sprawling factory complex that turned out motorbikes, large motorcycles, armored police motorcycles, military cycles with rifle holsters and motorcycles with sidecars for sweeping the streets, putting out fires, carrying paying passengers and delivering merchandise. They also made cars, aircraft engines, air-conditioners and, in 1947, the "snowboat," a precursor of the snowmobile.

The last of the company's buildings, once the engineering division, is now the museum (☎ 413-737-2624), 33 Hendee St, with the largest and finest collection of Indian motorcycles and memorabilia in the world. There are other makes as well, and lots of funky period mementos. All of the machines are in working order (note the oil-drip pans underneath), and are taken out and run every three months. If you like bikes, don't miss this place.

It's open daily March through November from 10 am to 5 pm and December through February from 1 to 5 pm. Admission costs $3 for adults, $1 for kids six to 12. To find the museum, take I-291 to exit 4 (St James Ave) then follow the signs north on Page Blvd to Hendee St. The museum is a low brick building in an industrial area.

Forest Park

Forest Park (☎ 413-787-6440), two miles south of the Springfield shopping center off

Pioneers of Invention

In 1794 President George Washington selected Springfield as one of two federal armories that would manufacture muskets for the US army. The first musket produced here in 1795 was a copy of the French "Charleville" popular with US soldiers during the Revolutionary War.

During the 19th century, Yankee ingenuity went to work at Springfield. In 1819 Thomas Blanchard invented a wood-turning lathe to produce identical gun stocks quickly and cheaply. Percussion ignition replaced the flintlock, and breech-loaders replaced muzzle-loaders. The Model 1903 Springfield rifle was what American doughboys carried into battle in WWI, and the M-1 Garand, again built in Springfield, armed the troops in WWII.

After WWII, the armory evolved into a design and testing laboratory for small arms, machine guns, grenade launchers and similar armaments, but these were built elsewhere by private contractors. Finally, in 1968 the Department of Defense decided to close down the armory. It had served the military needs of the nation for almost two centuries.

Arms were not Springfield's only contribution to American life and world culture. It was here, in 1891, that Dr James Naismith conceived the game of basketball, now played and loved around the world. Appropriately, Springfield is home to the Naismith Memorial Basketball Hall of Fame.

Springfield's impressive list of inventions goes on: the monkey wrench, steel-bladed ice skates, USA's first planetarium and the gasoline-powered motorcycle (1901). Another invention was the first practical internal-combustion engine automobile, built in 1894 by the Duryea brothers Charles and Frank on the top floor of the building at 41 Taylor St. For a short time in the 1930s the world's most elegant auto, the Rolls-Royce, was also assembled in this city. ∎

Sumner Ave (MA 83), is an 800-acre swath of lawns, woods, gardens, ponds, fountains and amusements such as walking and horse trails, swimming pools and tennis courts. Walkers and bikers are admitted free; cars must pay a small admission charge. The Zoo at Forest Park (☎ 413-733-2251), open daily from 10 am to 5 pm for a small fee, has over 200 animals, a miniature train and educational field trips.

Special Event

"The Big E" In mid-September, sleepy West Springfield, on the west bank of the river, explodes into activity with the annual rebirth of "The Big E," the Eastern States Exposition (☎ 413-737-2443, fax 787-0271, 800-334-2443 for ticket orders), 1305 Memorial Ave (MA 147). The fair goes on for two weeks, with farm exhibits, horse shows, carnival rides, regional and ethnic food, parades, Wild West and high-diver shows, a circus, petting zoo and country and pop music performances. Each of the six New England states has a large pavilion with its own exhibits as well.

Admission to the fair costs $8 for adults, $6 kids six to 12, under six free; two-day adult passes are $12. Once you're in the fairgrounds, all the shows are free; carnival rides cost extra. Hotels fill up when the Big E is in session, particularly on weekends.

Places to Stay

Cityspace YMCA (☎ 413-739-6951), 275 Chestnut St at Liberty St, two long blocks east of the Peter Pan bus terminal, has 124 simple rooms for $25 to $30, an exercise room, swimming pool and coffee shop.

Econo Lodge (formerly Friendship Inn; ☎ 413-783-2111), 1356 Boston Rd, just over five miles east of the center, has a swimming pool and 110 rooms priced at $55, light breakfast included.

Holiday Inn – Springfield (☎ 413-781-0900, 800-465-4329), 117 Dwight St at Congress, just over a half mile north of Court Square, has 252 rooms for $78 to $105.

Greater Springfield Bed & Breakfast (☎ 413-268-7244) will help you make a reservation at a small B&B in a historic neighborhood of Springfield such as Maple Hill or Forest Park. Rooms cost $50 to $100 double, breakfast included.

The city's top two hotels are right in the city center facing one another across Boland Way, at I-91 exit 6 northbound or exit 7 southbound, a block north of Court Square. They're the 304-room *Sheraton Springfield Monarch Place* (☎ 413-781-1010), with rooms priced at $80 to $150 per night and the 264-room *Springfield Marriott Hotel* (☎ 413-781-7111), with rooms for $145 to $155.

Places to Eat

As a commuter town, downtown Springfield has few good restaurants. Other than those in the big hotels, there are only small lunch places facing Court Square or on nearby streets.

The Deli Roll (☎ 413-827-7007), 17 Elm St, on the south side of Court Square, sells sandwiches and light ,hot luncheon plates for $4 or $5. Most customers come for takeout, but there are several tables inside, and more on the sidewalk in front. *Café du Jour*, 1369 Main St, is just north of Court St.

Pioneer Valley Pub (☎ 413-732-2739), 51-59 Taylor St at Main St, is Springfield's Art Deco brewpub and bistro, serving its own beer and a full lunch and dinner menu at dining room and courtyard tables.

A bright spot in the dismal food picture is *Café Manhattan* (☎ 413-737-7913), 301 Bridge St at Barnes St, an upscale storefront bistro 2½ blocks north of Court Square serving traditional American and continental cuisine for lunch and dinner daily except Sunday. Special luncheon plates are priced around $7 or $8, dinners a bit more.

Entertainment

Recitals and concerts by the members of the *Springfield Symphony Orchestra* (☎ 413-787-6600) are held year round in grand Symphony Hall, just off Court Square.

For theater, try the *Stage West* company (☎ 413-781-2340) in Columbus Center, Bridge St off Main St.

The modern building east of Court Square is the *Springfield Civic Center* (☎ 413-787-6600), 1277 Main St, venue for exhibits, rock concerts and athletic events. A smaller venue for musical and stand-up comedy performances is the restored *Paramount Theater* (☎ 413-734-5874), 1700 Main St.

Pioneer Valley Pub (see Places to Eat) serves up its own brews. Pick up a copy of *The Valley Advocate*, a free weekly newspaper, for entertainment listings.

Getting There & Away

Air Springfield is served by Bradley International Airport in Hartford (Windsor Locks), CT, 18 miles to the south. See Getting There & Away in the Hartford section for details.

Bus Springfield is the home of Peter Pan Bus Lines (☎ 413-781-3320, 800-343-9999), which serves Massachusetts and beyond. The bus station (☎ 413-781-2900, 781-1500), is at 1776 Main St at Liberty St, a 10-minute walk north of Court Square. There are daily buses from Springfield to Albany, Amherst, Bennington, Boston, Deerfield, Hartford, Holyoke, Lee, Lenox, New Haven, New York City, North Adams, Pittsfield, South Hadley, Williamstown and Worcester.

Peter Pan's service connecting the college towns of the Pioneer Valley (Amherst, Holyoke, Northampton and South Hadley) with Springfield and Boston is frequent, with 15 buses daily. Buses run from each town to Springfield almost hourly from 5 am to 6 pm, with two additional late evening buses. From Springfield, frequent connecting buses go on to Boston. There are also direct buses between the Pioneer Valley towns, Springfield and Hyannis via Boston.

Bonanza Bus Lines (☎ 800-556-3815) runs a route connecting Providence, Springfield, Lee, Lenox, Pittsfield, Williamstown and Bennington.

Train Amtrak's (☎ 800-872-7245) *Lakeshore Limited* and Inland Route trains between Boston and New York City serve Springfield. The railroad station (☎ 413-785-4230) is at 66 Lyman St, a 10-minute walk north of Court Square. See the beginning of this chapter for details of trains.

Car Driving details for Springfield are:

Destination	Mileage	Hr:Min
Albany, NY	82 miles	1:40
Amherst, MA	24 miles	0:40
Boston, MA	87 miles	1:45
Hartford, CT	25 miles	0:30
Holyoke, MA	9 miles	0:15
Lenox, MA	40 miles	0:55
New York, NY	134 miles	2:45
Northampton, MA	18 miles	0:25
South Hadley, MA	15 miles	0:23
Sturbridge, MA	32 miles	0:45
Worcester, MA	52 miles	1:00

Getting Around
For airport transport, contact Airport Service of Springfield (☎ 413-739-9999), My Limo (☎ 413-736-7928) or the bus station (☎ 413-781-2900).

The Pioneer Valley Transit Authority (PVTA, ☎ 413-781-7882), 1500 Main St, between Bridge and Boland Sts a block north of Court Square, operates local buses throughout Springfield and vicinity. Most sights in Springfield are an easy walk from Court Square.

SOUTH HADLEY
North of Springfield is Hampshire County, the central region of the Pioneer Valley, sometimes called the Five College area because it is home to Amherst College, Hampshire College, Mount Holyoke College, Smith College and the University of Massachusetts at Amherst.

The quiet town of South Hadley, 15 miles north of Springfield on MA 116, is the most southerly of the Five College towns with USA's oldest college for women at its center.

With their views of hills, fields and old tobacco barns, MA 116 between South Hadley and Amherst, and MA 47 between Hadley and South Hadley, are among the prettiest drives in the Pioneer Valley. For bicycling information see Activities under Amherst.

Information
The Chamber of Commerce (☎ /fax 413-532-6451) is at 362 N Main St, South Hadley, MA 01075. Worth a stop out of your way is the Odyssey Book Shop (☎ 413-534-7307), 9 College St.

Mount Holyoke College
Founded in 1837 by teacher Mary Lyon, Mount Holyoke College is the country's oldest women's college, presently with an

---

Metacomet-Monadnock Trail
The Metacomet-Monadnock Trail is part of a 200-mile greenway footpath which extends from Connecticut along the Connecticut River valley to New Hampshire's Mt Monadnock, and beyond.

In Connecticut, the trail is named for Metacomet (the Indian commander who waged war on the colonists in 1675). It enters Massachusetts near the Agawam/Southwick town line to become Massachusetts' 177-mile-long Metacomet-Monadnock Trail. From the state line, the trail proceeds north up the river valley through public and private lands, ascends Mt Tom, then heads east along the Holyoke Range through Skinner State Park and Holyoke Range State Park before bearing north again.

After entering New Hampshire, the trail ascends Mt Monadnock, where it joins the Monadnock-Sunapee Greenway.

The easiest access to the trail for day hikes is in the state parks, where leaflets and simple local trail maps are available. For longer hikes, it's good to have the *Metacomet-Monadnock Trail Guide* (8th ed, 1995), published by the Berkshire Chapter Trails Committee of the AMC, PO Box 9369, North Amherst, MA 01059. It's also available through the AMC's main office (☎ 800-262-4455), 5 Joy St, Boston, MA 02108, and at bookshops and outdoor stores. ■

enrollment of about 2000 students. Campus tours (☎ 413-538-2222) can be arranged any day.

The great American landscape architect Frederick Law Olmstead laid out the center of Mount Holyoke's park-like 800-acre campus in the latter part of the 1800s. Among the college's other 19th-century legacies is the chapel's hand-crafted organ, one of the last built by New England's master organ-maker, Charles B Fisk.

In the present century the college has added a multi-million-dollar sports complex, a Japanese garden and teahouse and an equestrian center.

Besides a walk around the lovely campus, you can enjoy the **College Art Museum** (☎ 413-538-2245), open year round.

Skinner State Park
This park (☎ 413-586-0350), north of South Hadley off MA 47 in Hadley, is at the summit of Mt Holyoke. The Summit House affords panoramic views of the Connecticut River, its oxbow curve and its fertile valley. There are hiking trails and a picnic area as well.

Holyoke Range State Park
This park (☎ 413-253-2883), a few miles north of South Hadley on MA 116, has trail walks ranging from 0.75 to 5.4 miles along the Metacomet-Monadnock Trail and side trails (see the sidebar).

Places to Stay & Eat
Lodgings are in Amherst, Northampton and Springfield. For a meal, try *Woodbridge's Restaurant* (☎ 413-536-7341), right at the intersection of MA 47 and 116, on the common in the center of South Hadley. Main courses at dinner range from $10 to $14; Sunday brunch (10:30 am to 2 pm) is $10. The front terrace tables are the best in good weather.

Entertainment
The *Mount Holyoke Summer Theater* (☎ 413-538-2406), stages evening performances under canvas, Tuesday through Saturday on the common.

Getting There & Away
Springfield is the long-distance transportation center. PVTA buses (see Getting Around in Springfield) can bring you to South Hadley.

Driving details for South Hadley are:

Destination	Mileage	Hr:Min
Amherst, MA	7 miles	0:12
Northampton, MA	11 miles	0:18
Springfield, MA	15 miles	0:25

NORTHAMPTON
Northampton, settled in 1654, is an eminently livable and visitable place, described by "the Swedish Nightingale," Jenny Lind, as the "Paradise of America" during her visit in 1850. As the Hampshire County seat and the home of highly regarded Smith College, it has a sophistication, a low crime rate and a list of services that might be envied by cities twice its size. Northampton is also the dining center of the region, with a gratifying array of moderately priced restaurants.

The presence of college students and staff gives the town liberal political and sexual instincts, with an active and outspoken lesbian community. The strong influence adds a female sensibility to the college-town lineup of shops, banks, bookstores, cafes, copy shops and pizza parlors.

For bicycling, see the Activities listing under Amherst.

Orientation & Information
The center of town is at the intersection of Main St (MA 9) and Pleasant St (MA 5). Restaurants, banks, shops and other services are within a few blocks' walk, with one exception: lodgings are on the outskirts.

The Greater Northampton Chamber of Commerce (☎ 413-584-1900), 62 State St, Northampton, MA 01060, maintains an information office on Pleasant St across from the Hotel Northampton, open Tuesday through Sunday, June through August, from 9 am to 5 pm. On Monday, when the booth is closed, go to the main chamber office at the northwestern end of Center St.

Smith College

Smith College, at the western end of the downtown area, was founded "for the education of the intelligent gentlewoman" in 1875 by Sophia Smith. The student body, numbering about 2700, continues to consist largely of women, with a sprinkling of men. The wooded 125-acre campus along Elm St holds an eclectic architectural mix of nearly 100 buildings, as well as Paradise Pond.

Visitors are welcome at the **Lyman Plant House** (☎ 413-585-2740), a collection of Victorian greenhouses that are the venue for the Bulb Show and Chrysanthemum Show (see below). You should also take a look at the **Smith College Museum of Art** (☎ 413-585-2770), Elm St at Bedford Terrace, which has a good collection of 17th-century Dutch, and 19th- and 20th-century European and American paintings, including works by Degas, Winslow Homer, Picasso and Whistler. It's open from noon to 4 pm (closed Mondays); from September to June it's also open Tuesday, Friday and Saturday mornings from 9:30 am and Thursday evenings until 8 pm. Admission is free.

Guided campus tours can be arranged through the Office of Admissions (☎ 413-585-2500), or you can guide yourself using the good campus folder available for free at the college switchboard in College Hall, or from the Office of Admissions.

Special Events

Flower-lovers should check out Smith College's renowned Annual Bulb Show in mid-March, and Chrysanthemum Show in November held at the Lyman Plant House.

Springfield has the Big E, but Northampton has the Three-County Fair (☎ 413-584-2237) starting on the Friday of Labor Day weekend. The fair, first held in 1818, features agricultural and livestock exhibits, horse races, food and rides. The Three-County Fairgrounds on MA 9 just west of I-91 exit 19 North or 20 South, is also the site of the New England Morgan Horse Show, held each July.

Places to Stay

It's usually easy to find a room during the summer. At other times of year, room price and availability depend on the college schedule of ceremonies and sporting events.

Cheapest is the *Econo Lodge* (☎ 413-584-9816, fax 586-7512), 237 Russell St (MA 9), formerly the Friendship Inn, four miles northeast of central Northampton in Hadley. Rooms (some with kitchenettes) cost $45 to $60 in summer; the higher price is for weekends. There's a swimming pool.

Days Inn (☎ 413-586-1500, 800-325-2525), 117 Conz St at I-91 exit 18, two miles south of the town center, has an outdoor pool and 60 rooms priced at $85, continental breakfast included.

Autumn Inn (☎ 413-584-7660), 259 Elm St (MA 9), has a swimming pool and an inn-like ambiance despite its motel-like layout. The 34 rooms cost $68 to $78 single, $88 to $100 double.

The 72-room *Hotel Northampton* (☎ 413-584-3100, fax 584-9455), 36 King St, behind the county courthouse, has been receiving Northampton's important guests since 1916. Renovated and upgraded in 1987, it charges $120 to $180 for its comfortable, centrally-located rooms.

Places to Eat

After the high prices of Boston and Cape Cod, Northampton's restaurant prices are a joy. There are plenty of cafes on Main St near City Hall. *Java Net Café* (☎ 413-587-3400), 241 Main St, is Northampton's cybercafe, serving up coffee, tea, baked goods and the Internet.

The Coffee Connection, 211 Main St, is a favorite with java aficionados. Order it by bean variety and sip it at a sidewalk table.

Bart's (☎ 413-584-0721), 235 Main St, specializes in ice cream, but also serves coffee, pastries and light lunches.

Haymarket Café (☎ 413-586-9969), Cracker Barrel Alley (there's an entrance on Main St as well), is a basement place for the literary set, who buy used books with their espressos.

Bakery Normand (☎ 413-584-0717), 192 Main St, across from Haymarket, serves rich pastries, cakes, tarts and coffee mostly to go, but there are two small tables as well.

Curtis & Schwartz Café (☎ 413-586-3278), 116 Main St, has a good assortment of fresh breakfast items (try the homemade granola, $2.75, or blintzes, $6) and light lunches (smoked turkey sandwich, $6) served daily until 3 pm.

Most Northampton restaurants offer some vegetarian fare and alcoholic drinks.

Playing on Northampton's nickname of Paradise, *Pizzeria Paradiso* (☎ 413-586-1468), 12 Crafts Ave, is a wine bar masquerading as a traditional wood-fired brick-oven pizza restaurant. Dinner, the only meal served, can cost from $8 to $16.

Paul and Elizabeth's (☎ 413-584-4832), 150 Main St in Thornes Marketplace, is the town's premier natural foods restaurant, serving lunch and dinner every day. The cuisine is vegetarian, but there's seafood as well. A three-course meal with wine can cost up to $22, but you're more likely to spend $10 or $12, even less at lunch. There's another entrance on Crafts Ave.

La Veracruzana (☎ 413-586-7181), 44 Main St between Pleasant and Strong Sts, has down-home, down-market Mexican food such as 99¢ bean tacos, and tamales, enchiladas, tostadas and fajitas plates for $2 to $7.

Cha Cha Cha! (☎ 413-586-7311), 134 Main St, has a few tiny tables set out among the huge columns of the old Northampton National Bank building. The mood is young, hip and informal, and a meal of burritos or quesadillas with a glass of wine costs about $10.

For fancier fare, head for *La Cazuela* (☎ 413-586-0400), 7 Old South St, off Main, a good Southwest/Mexican restaurant and cantina, with a pleasant terrace dining area for good weather. Meals cost $12 to $25, margarita included.

Northampton Brewery (☎ 413-584-9903), 11 Brewster Court (the main entrance is actually on Hampton Rd), one long block south of Main St, is a modern brewpub with excellent beer, a good menu of light meals and nouvelle cuisine daily

specials. A pint and a sandwich costs under $10. Dine in the pretty beer garden in good weather.

Mulino's Trattoria (☎ 413-586-8900), 21 Center St, is a storefront bistro with a long list of homestyle Italian dishes, including pizza from a wood-fired oven ($6 to $7), panni (Italian sandwiches, $5 to $6) and pasta, meat and fish for $10 to $12. It's open daily for dinner only.

Eastside Grill (☎ 413-586-3347), 19 Strong Ave, a half block south of Main St, has a vast and eclectic menu listing everything from Louisiana fried oysters and chicken étouffée to steaks and pecan pie. The tenderloin costs $15, everything else is several dollars less. The clientele is well dressed. Lunch and dinner are served daily; the wine list is good and reasonably priced.

Many people rate *Spoleto* (☎ 413-586-6313), 50 Main St, as Northampton's best restaurant. The classic dishes such as veal scaloppine and chicken saltimbocca are prepared with California accents. Vegetarians should try the eggplant rollatini. A full dinner (the only meal served) costs from $20 to $30 per person, drinks included.

Entertainment

Northampton is the center of nightlife in the Five College area. For listings of what's happening throughout the Pioneer Valley, pick up a copy of *The Valley Advocate*, a free weekly newspaper.

Theater The *New Century Theatre at Smith College* (☎ 413-585-3220) stages modern works in July and August at the Hallie Flanagan Studio Theatre in the Mendenhall Center for Performing Arts, on Green St on campus.

Music The *Iron Horse Music Hall* (☎ 413-584-0610), 20 Center St a half block off Main St, is the prime folk and jazz venue. Call for the current program, then look for the small storefront with the line waiting to get in.

Pearl St (☎ 413-584-7771), 10 Pearl St at the corner with Strong Ave, is the best dance club, drawing local, regional and national performers and enough loyal patrons to produce a line any weekend night. Wednesday is gay night, Thursday is 18+, Friday is retro and Saturday is for modern rock.

Fire & Water Vegetarian Café & Performance Space (☎ 413-586-8336), 5 Old South St, features folk, jazz, blues and new talent in a funky atmosphere.

The *Academy of Music* (☎ 413-584-8435), 274 Main St, is a cinema, but also hosts performers who draw the biggest crowds when they come to town.

Pubs *Northampton Brewery* (☎ 413-584-9903), 11 Brewster Court, has a lively pub atmosphere every evening, and live music some evenings.

Packard's (☎ 413-584-5957), 14 Masonic St just off Main St, is a lively pub with billiard tables on the 3rd floor rentable by the hour.

FitzWilly's (☎ 413-584-8666), 23 Main St at Strong Ave, is a longtime favorite, a lively centrally located tavern and restaurant with an extensive medium-priced menu.

Getting There & Away
See Springfield for information on air, bus and train service.

Driving details for Northampton are:

Destination	Mileage	Hr:Min
Amherst, MA	7 miles	0:12
Boston, MA	108 miles	2:20
Deerfield, MA	16 miles	0:25
Lenox, MA	61 miles	1:25
South Hadley, MA	8 miles	0:16
Springfield, MA	18 miles	0:25

AMHERST
The town of Amherst is best known as the home of prestigious Amherst College, but in fact the major academic presence here is the University of Massachusetts at Amherst, and the minor one Hampshire College, on the outskirts. The town has produced its share of famous people, among whom poet Emily Dickinson, "the belle of Amherst," is perhaps the best known.

Orientation & Information
The center of Amherst is the town common, a broad New England green framed by churches, inns and other grand buildings.

The Amherst Chamber of Commerce (☎ 413-549-7555), 33 Pray St, Amherst, MA 01002, maintains a summer information booth on the common facing S Pleasant St, directly across from the Peter Pan bus station. The post office (☎ 413-549-0418) is on N Pleasant St at Kellogg Ave. There's a Council Travel agency (☎ 413-256-1261) at 44 Main St. For books, the Jeffrey Amherst Bookshop (☎ 413-253-3381) at 55 Pleasant St is recommended.

Dickenson Homestead
Emily Dickinson (1830-86) was raised in the strict Puritan household of her father, a prominent lawyer. When he was elected to Congress she traveled with him to Washington and Philadelphia, then returned to Amherst and this house to live out the rest of her days in near seclusion. Some say she was in love with Reverend Charles Wadsworth, a local married clergyman. Unable to show her love, she withdrew from the world into a private realm of pain, passion and poignancy.

Dickinson wrote finely-crafted poems on scraps of paper and old envelopes and stuffed them in her desk. She published only seven poems during her lifetime, and no one recognized her as a major talent. After her death more than 1000 of her exquisite poems were discovered and published. These verses on love, death, nature and immortality made her one of America's most important poets.

Emily Dickinson's former home (☎ 413-542-8161), 280 Main St, has several rooms open for touring May through October, Wednesday to Saturday from 1:30 to 3:45 pm; in April and from November to mid-December on Wednesday and Saturday only. The guided tour costs $3; call for reservations.

Hampshire College
The region's newest and perhaps most innovative center of learning is three

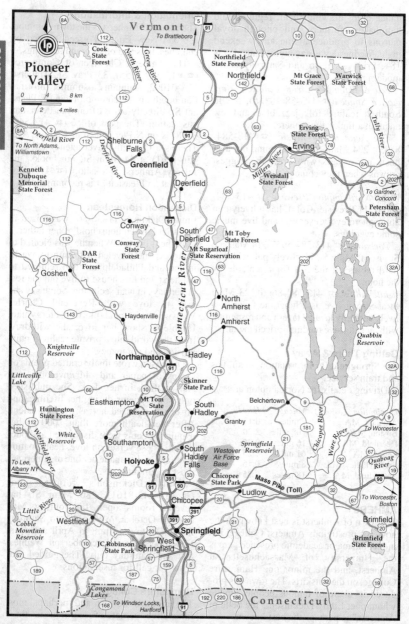

miles south of Amherst center on MA 116. It has a lovely campus and you can schedule a tour through the Admissions Office (☎ 413-582-5471).

Amherst College

Founded in 1821, Amherst has retained its character and quality partly by maintaining its relatively small size (1575 students); thus its prestige has grown. The main part of the campus is just south of the common. The information booth has a map and brochure for self-guided walking tours, or you can ask questions at Converse Hall (☎ 413-542-2000).

University of Massachusetts at Amherst

Over a century old, this UMass extension (☎ 413-545-0111) was founded in 1863 as the Massachusetts Agricultural College. It's now part of the official university system of the Commonwealth of Massachusetts. About 24,000 students study at UMass' sprawling Amherst campus, northwest of the common. A free PVTA bus line serves the campus, allowing for easy transport.

Atkins Farms Fruit Bowl

This recently expanded farm produce center (☎ 413-253-9528), offers maple sugar products in spring, garden produce in summer and apple-picking in autumn. Other activities, like a scarecrow-making workshop in October, take place throughout the year. A full deli and bakery sells picnic supplies, and Atkins Farms will ship gift baskets too.

Activities

See the South Hadley section for information on hiking in the Holyoke Range, south of Amherst.

The **Norwottuck Rail Trail** (nor-WAH-tuk) is a foot and bike path which follows the former Boston & Maine Railroad right-of-way from Amherst to Hadley and Northampton, a distance of 8.5 miles. For much of its length, the trail parallels MA 9. Parking and access is available on Station

Rd in Amherst, the Mountain Farms Mall on MA 9 in Hadley and Elwell State Park on Damon Rd in Northampton.

Biking the trail is particularly enjoyable. Bicycles can be rented for the day from Valley Bicycles (☎ 413-256-0880), 319 Main St, and Bicycle World (☎ 413-253-7722), 63 S Pleasant St in Amherst; or try Competitive Edge Ski & Bike Outlet (☎ 413-585-8833) on MA 9 in Hadley and Northampton Bicycle (☎ 413-586-3810), 319 Pleasant St, or Peloton Sports (☎ 413-584-1016), 15 State St in Northampton. Some of these shops are closed on Sunday.

Places to Stay

There aren't many campgrounds in this region. The *White Birch Campground* (☎ 413-665-4941), 122 North St, Whately, has 40 sites open May through November. Follow MA 116 north through North Amherst and Sunderland to South Deerfield, then go southwest to Whately.

Motels & Hotels

Amherst Motel (☎ 413-256-8122), 408 Northampton Rd (MA 9), on the south side of MA 9 just over the town line behind Domino's Pizza, charges $48 to $55 for a room in summer, light breakfast included.

A bit farther along MA 9 is *Howard Johnson Lodge* (☎ 413-586-0114, 800-654-2000), 401 Russell St, Hadley, with a pool, restaurant, and rooms for $97.

University Motor Lodge (☎ 413-256-8111), 345 North Pleasant St (MA 116), is only a few blocks north of the town common, with rooms for $89.

Campus Center Hotel (☎ 413-549-6000, fax 545-1210) is in the highrise tower of the Murray D Lincoln Campus Center at UMass off N Pleasant St. Rooms rent for $54/$64/$75 a single/double/triple.

Inns & B&Bs

Allen House (☎ 413-253-5000), 599 Main St, just over a half mile east of Pleasant St, is a prim Queen Anne Victorian cottage charging $45 to $95 for its air-conditioned, bath-equipped rooms, full breakfast included. Main St has some traffic noise during the day.

Lincoln Avenue B&B (☎ 413-549-0517), 242 Lincoln Ave, a half mile west of Pleasant St in a quiet residential neighborhood, has three bedrooms with shared baths for $45 to $70, breakfast included.

The 49-room *Lord Jeffrey Inn* (☎ 413-253-2576), 30 Boltwood Ave, facing the town common, is the classic college-town inn: colonial, collegiate, cozy and comfortable. Rooms are priced at $68 to $108, and the location couldn't be better.

Places to Eat

As a college town, Amherst has lots of places serving pizza, sandwiches, Mexican *antojitos* and fresh-brewed coffee.

Café Bonducci (☎ 413-256-1390), 63 S Pleasant St, is convenient to the common and the bus station, with coffee, soups and sandwiches from the lowly peanut butter and jelly ($1.60) to roast beef ($4).

Antonio's Pizza by the Slice (☎ 413-253-0808), 31 N Pleasant St, is Amherst's most popular pizza place, which is saying a lot. No cheap-cheese-on-cardboard here: the variety of toppings, flavorings and spices is vast.

Bueno y Sano Burritos (☎ 413-253-4000), 1 Boltwood Walk, cooks up Mexican snacks with all-natural ingredients for $2 to $3.

Café Mediterranean (☎ 413-549-7122), 1 E Pleasant St, in front of the Amherst Carriage Shops off N Pleasant St, is the place to go for coffee and European-style pastries.

The Raw Carrot (☎ 413-549-4240), 9 E Pleasant St, in the Amherst Carriage Shops, is a juice bar serving light meals (all-natural) as well.

Judie's (☎ 413-253-3491), in a converted house at 51 N Pleasant St, has an eclectic menu of original – some would say odd – dishes and concoctions. Lunch costs $10 to $16, dinner $12 to $24. Alcohol is served.

Amherst Chinese Food (☎ 413-253-7835), 62 Main St, one long block east of Pleasant St, has been serving Chinese dishes success-fully for decades. Main courses are $6 to $10 at dinner, less at lunch.

Lord Jeffrey Inn (☎ 413-253-2576), 30 Boltwood Ave facing the common, is where parents go when they need a fancy meal. Besides the formal dining room ($16 to $45), there's *Elijah Boltwood's Tavern* ($6 to $20) for breakfast and light meals.

For a meal and a view, try the *Top of the Campus Restaurant* (☎ 413-545-0636) in the Murray D Lincoln Campus Center at UMass. The food is traditional, prices are moderate and the view is luxurious. Lunch is served weekdays and dinner is Tuesday through Saturday.

Entertainment

UMass' *Fine Arts Center* (☎ 413-545-2511) has a full program of concert programs, shows, folk, jazz and rock. *Black Sheep* (☎ 413-253-3442), 79 Main St, is the most popular folk club.

Getting There & Away

See Springfield for air, bus and train information. Amherst's connection to the outside world is through the Peter Pan Amherst Center Bus Terminal (☎ 413-256-0431), 79 S Pleasant St, just south of Main St. Tickets are also sold at the Campus Center Hotel and the Southwest Hampden Dining Common on the UMass campus.

Driving details for Amherst are:

Destination	Mileage	Hr:Min
Boston, MA	80 miles	2:00
Deerfield, MA	16 miles	0:30
Hartford, CT	49 miles	1:10
Lenox, MA	64 miles	1:25
New York, NY	158 miles	3:25
Northampton, MA	7 miles	0:15
Springfield, MA	24 miles	0:40

Getting Around

UMass Transit Service (☎ 413-586-5806) runs free buses up and down MA 116 (Pleasant St) between the center of town and the UMass campus.

DEERFIELD

At Deerfield, 16 miles northwest of Amherst on US 5, the fertile river valley was settled in the 1660s. But these were the borderlands of colonial settlement, and open to Indian attack.

Massasoit (1580?-1661), great sachem of the Wampanoags, signed a treaty of peace with the Pilgrims at Plymouth in 1621, and scrupulously observed it until his death. In the four decades after the founding of Plymouth, English settlers poured into the region. The Wampanoags and other native peoples became dependent on English goods, and found themselves yielding their lands in exchange for English cloth, kitchen utensils and firearms.

Upon Massasoit's death his son Metacomet (called "King Philip" by the English) became sachem, and though he preserved peace for several years, he and his people were increasingly agitated by the colonists' steady encroachment.

In 1671 the English government, suspicious of Metacomet's motives, brought him in for questioning, levied a fine and demanded that the Wampanoags give up their arms. They did.

Still, friction increased, and when three Wampanoags were tried and executed for the murder of a Christian Indian who had been an English informer (1675), war broke out.

King Philip's War, as it was called by the English, brought devastation to frontier settlements such as Deerfield. In the autumn of 1675 an Indian force a thousand strong massacred 64 residents here.

The survivors rebuilt the town, only to have the Indians attack again in 1704, with almost 50 residents killed and the rest marched off to Canada; many others died along the way. But the survivors returned and rebuilt the town once again.

Later in the 18th century, when the region had returned to peace, settlers returned to farm the rich bottomlands.

Orientation & Information

The modern commercial center is at South Deerfield, and the original settlement of Deerfield, six miles to the north, has been preserved and restored to something like its appearance in those earlier, dangerous times.

For information before you arrive, contact Historic Deerfield (☎ 413-774-5581), PO Box 321, Deerfield, MA 01342. When you arrive, ask at the information desk at the museum across from the Deerfield Inn. It has maps, brochures and a short audiovisual show which gives you an overview of the Historic Deerfield Village.

Historic Deerfield Village

The main street of Historic Deerfield Village (☎ 413-774-5581) escaped the ravages of time and change and now presents a noble prospect: a dozen houses dating from the 1700s and 1800s well preserved and open to the public.

The **Wright House** (1824), has collections of American period paintings, Chippendale and Federal furniture and Chinese export porcelain. The **Flynt Textile Museum** (1872) has textiles, costumes and needlework from Europe and the US. There's also the Henry N Flynt Silver and Metalwork Collection (1814). The furnishings in **Allen House** (1720) were all made in the Pioneer Valley and Boston.

The **Stebbins House** (1799-1810) was the home of a rich land-owning family, and is furnished with typical luxury items of the time. In the **Barnard Tavern**, many of the exhibits are touchable, making this a favorite with children. The rooms of the **Wells-Thorn House** (1717-51) are furnished according to period from colonial times to the Federal period.

The **Dwight House**, built in Springfield in 1725, was moved to Deerfield in 1950. It now holds locally made furniture and a period doctor's office. **Sheldon-Hawks House** (1743) was the 18th-century home of the Sheldons, wealthy Deerfield farmers. Contrast its furnishings with those in the Stebbins House, built and furnished a half century later.

The local parsonage, or minister's residence, was the **Ashley House** (1730). The **Ebenezer Hinsdale Williams House** has recently been restored to how it looked when it was built between 1816 and 1838.

The **Memorial Hall Museum** (☎ 413-774-7476), at the corner of Memorial St and US 5 and 10, was the original building (1798) of Deerfield Academy, the prestigious preparatory school. It's now a museum of Pocumtuck Valley life and history. Puritan and Indian artifacts include carved and painted chests, embroidery, musical instruments and glass-plate photographs (1880-1920). Don't miss the **Indian House Door**, a dramatic relic of the French and Indian Wars. In February, 1704, the house of the Sheldon family was attacked by Indians. The attackers chopped and bashed at it, but it wouldn't yield. Finally they hacked a hole through the center, and did in the inhabitants with musket fire.

The museum is open daily from May through October from 10 am to 4:30 pm (12:30 to 4:30 pm on weekends). It costs nothing to stroll along the street; for a half-hour tour of the buildings, the fee is $10 for adults, $5 for kids six to 17. Guides in the houses provide commentary; hours are 9:30 am to 4:30 pm daily.

Cruises

The *Quinnetukut II* (☎ 413-659-3714) glides along the Connecticut River on 12-mile, 1½-hour cruises daily in summer. A lecturer fills you in on the history, geology and ecology of the river and the region. It's a good idea to call for reservations. Tickets are on sale at the Northfield Mountain Recreation and Environmental Center on MA 63 north of MA 2, open Wednesday through Sunday from 9 am to 5 pm. Take I-91 north to exit 27, then MA 2 east, then MA 63 north.

Places to Stay

Erving State Forest (☎ 413-544-3939), on the north side of MA 2A in Erving, has 32 campsites about 16 miles east of Greenfield.

Barton Cove Campground (☎ 413-659-3714), off MA 2 in Gill, has 23 family tent sites on a mile-long wooded peninsula on the Connecticut River. The nature trail takes you to dinosaur footprints and nesting bald eagles. Take I-91 exit 27, then MA 2 east four miles and look for the sign on the right.

The *Deerfield Inn* (☎ 413-774-5587, 800-926-3865, fax 773-8712), The Street, Deerfield, MA 01342, has 23 modernized, comfortable rooms right at the head of Historic Deerfield's main street. Rooms cost $137 to $155 double with breakfast, $208 to $228 with dinner as well. The inn, built in 1884, was destroyed by fire and rebuilt in 1981.

The Tea House (☎ 413-772-2675), also on The Street in Deerfield, has two rooms with shared bath for $85 to $95 double with full breakfast; credit cards are not accepted.

Getting There & Away

There is air, rail and bus service to Springfield (see that entry), and bus service to Greenfield.

Driving details for Deerfield are:

Destination	Mileage	Hr:Min
Amherst, MA	16 miles	0:30
Boston, MA	90 miles	2:10
Greenfield, MA	3 miles	0:07
Hartford, CT	60 miles	1:15
Lenox, MA	79 miles	2:00
New York, NY	165 miles	3:20
Northampton, MA	16 miles	0:25
Springfield, MA	39 miles	0:55

The Berkshires

The Berkshire hills dominate the landscape and the mindset of western Massachusetts. Extending from the highest point in the state – Mt Greylock (3491 feet), near North Adams – southward to the Connecticut state line, the Berkshires have been a summer refuge for over a century. On summer weekends when it's hot in Boston, New York and Hartford, crowds of city-dwellers jump in their cars and head for the cool shade and breezes of the Berkshires.

Besides the temperature, they come for culture. The Boston Symphony Orchestra's summer concert series at Tanglewood, near Lenox, draws the biggest crowds.

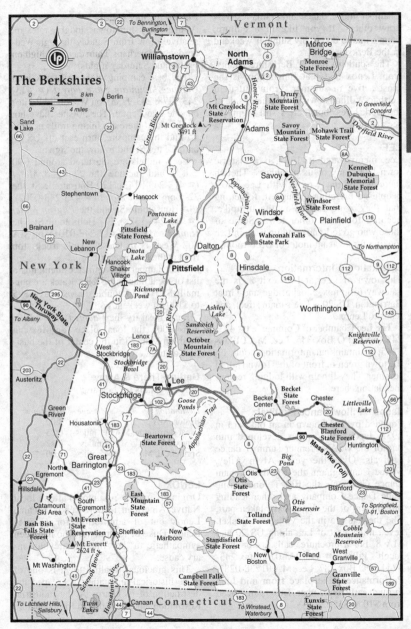

The Berkshires

Chamber music, dance and drama festivals draw others. If you like high culture, there's lots to do on any summer weekend in the Berkshires.

The southern half of Berkshire county, from Lenox to Great Barrington, is the most active in summer. From Pittsfield north to Williamstown is the quieter side of the Berkshires, but there's still plenty to see and do.

LEE
Lee, incorporated in 1777, is a historic town like many of its neighbors. Though there is nothing wrong with Lee, most people go barreling through it, forgetting that they're no longer on the turnpike, heading for some other town. Some of those who go to Lenox end up back in Lee looking for a vacant motel or B&B room.

Orientation & Information
The town of Lee, at I-90 exit 2, is the gateway to Lenox, Stockbridge and Great Barrington. US 20 is Lee's main street, and leads to Lenox.

The Lee Chamber of Commerce (☎ 413-243-0852), PO Box 345, Lee, MA 01238-0345, maintains an information booth on the town green in front of the Town Hall in summer. They'll help with lodging recommendations here.

Jacob's Pillow Dance Festival
Founded by Ted Shawn in an old barn in 1932, Jacob's Pillow has developed into one of the USA's premier summer dance festivals. Over the years Alvin Ailey, Merce Cunningham, the Martha Graham Dance Company, the Bill T Jones/Arnie Zane Dance Company and other leading interpreters of the dance have taken part. The theaters are in the village of Becket, seven miles east of Lee along US 20 and MA 8. For a brochure, call, fax or write Jacob's Pillow (☎ 413-243-0745, fax 243-4744), PO Box 287, Lee, MA 01238-0287. Performances take place from mid-June through early September. Tickets are priced from $10 to $35.

Places to Stay & Eat
As in all Berkshire towns, lodging rates are relatively low from Sunday through Wednesday and perhaps Thursday, and high on Friday and Saturday nights.

The best camping close to Lenox is at *October Mountain State Forest* (☎ 413-243-1778, 243-9735), on Woodland Rd just outside Lee Center. The 50 sites have hot showers and there are hiking trails nearby. To find the campsite, turn east off US 20 onto Center St and follow the signs.

Lee's motels are clustered around I-90 exit 2 and include the *Super 8 Motel* (☎ 413-243-0143), 170 Housatonic St, the 22-room *Sunset Motel* (☎ 413-243-0302), 114 Housatonic St and the *Pilgrim Motel* (☎ 413-243-1328), 127 Housatonic St. The *Hunter's Motel* (☎ 413-243-0101), on MA 102 West, is in Diesel Dan's truck stop right at the turnpike exit.

The chamber of commerce maintains a list of local inns and B&Bs. Rates are normally $50 to $75 double on weekdays, $95 to $100 on weekends.

For a meal try the *Cactus Café* (☎ 413-243-4300), the local place for Mexican food, on Main St in the center of the business district.

Getting There & Away
Driving details for Lee are:

Destination	Mileage	Hr:Min
Boston, MA	134 miles	3:00
Great Barrington, MA	11 miles	0:25
Lenox, MA	5 miles	0:12
Springfield, MA	45 miles	1:00

LENOX
Originally named Yokuntown after a local Native American leader, Lenox became Lenox out of admiration for Charles Lenox, Duke of Richmond, who had been sympathetic to the American revolutionary cause.

This gracious, wealthy town is one of those historical anomalies: it escaped the destruction of its charm by the Industrial Revolution, and then, prized for its bucolic peace, became a summer retreat for those wealthy families (like Andrew Carnegie's) who had made their fortunes by building factories in other towns.

Today Lenox is almost synonymous with the Tanglewood Music Festival, the town's premier summer event since 1934.

Orientation & Information

It's easy to get around Lenox on foot, though some of the many inns are a mile or two from the center. Tanglewood is 1½ miles west of Lenox center along West St (MA 183).

The Lenox Chamber of Commerce (☎ 413-637-3646), 75 Main St (PO Box 646), Lenox, MA 01240, is the local source of information, open Tuesday through Saturday from 10 am to 6 pm, Sunday until 2 pm, Monday until 4 pm. They'll help with same-day room reservations. Pick up a copy of the pamphlet *Walking through Lenox History* detailing the interesting buildings from Lenox's past.

Simply called The Bookstore (☎ 413-637-3390), 9 Housatonic St, this is the place to stop for that map, atlas or summer novel you need.

Church on the Hill

Much of Lenox's architecture, especially its many palatial houses, reflects its wealthy history. But there was a Lenox here before the Industrial Revolution. Perhaps the best example of this is the Church on the Hill, easily visible at the northern extent of Main St. This classic New England meetinghouse was constructed in 1805, and served as a model for others in the region.

Berkshire Scenic Railway Museum

This museum (☎ 413-637-2210), on Willow Creek Rd, 1½ miles east of Lenox center, is a nonprofit museum of railroad lore set up in Lenox's 1902 railroad station.

The museum's two elaborate model railroad displays are favorites with kids, as is the short train ride in a full-sized train on the museum grounds. Admission is free; the train ride costs $1.50 adults, $1 children.

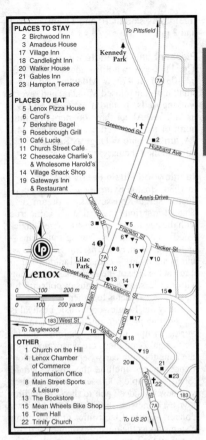

The Mount

Novelist Edith Wharton (1862-1937), a close friend of Henry James', spent summers at her palatial mansion, The Mount, before moving permanently to France. The main reason to visit The Mount is to enjoy the plays staged by Shakespeare & Company (see below). You can tour The Mount (☎ 413-637-1899), at Plunkett St and US 7 on the outskirts of Lenox, daily except Monday in summer, and on weekends through mid-October. Admission costs $6 for adults, $5.50 seniors, $4.50 kids 13 to 18 (12 and under free); tours start at 10 and 11 am, noon, 1 and 2 pm.

Pleasant Valley Sanctuary

The 1112-acre wildlife sanctuary (☎ 413-637-0320), at 472 W Mountain Rd, has a small museum (closed Monday) and several walking trails. To find it, go north on US 7 or MA 7A. About three-quarters of a mile north of the intersection of US 7 and MA 7A, turn left onto W Dugway Rd and go 1½ miles to the sanctuary.

Tanglewood Music Festival

In 1934, Boston Symphony Orchestra conductor Serge Koussevitzky's dream of a center for serious musical study came true with the acquisition of the 400-acre Tanglewood estate in Lenox. Young musicians – including Leonard Bernstein, Seiji Ozawa and many others – came to Tanglewood to study at the side of the great masters. Along with the lessons came music: concerts by masters and students together.

Today the Tanglewood Music Festival is among the premier music events in the world. Symphony, pops, chamber music, recitals, jazz and blues are performed from late June through early September. Performance spaces include the coyly named "Shed," a simple 6000-seat concert shelter with several sides open to the surrounding lawns. The newest space is the Seiji Ozawa Concert Hall. Electronic amplification systems boost the music's volume for those seated on the lawn, making it easier to hear, but less worth hearing.

The Boston Symphony Orchestra concerts on weekends in July and August are the most popular events at Tanglewood. Most casual (as opposed to devoted) attendees – up to 8000 of them on a typical summer weekend evening – arrive three or four hours before concert time. They stake out good listening spots on the lawn outside the Shed or the Concert Hall, then relax and enjoy elaborate picnic suppers until the music starts.

Contemporary star performers include greats such as Midori, Itzhak Perlman,

Anne-Sophie Mutter, Yo-Yo Ma and André Watts. Besides classical stars, such notable popular performers as Frank Sinatra, James Taylor, Wynton Marsalis (in jazz mode), Manhattan Transfer, Joshua Redman Quartet and New Black Eagles Jazz Band have given Tanglewood concerts.

Tickets Tickets range from $10 to $21 per person for picnic space on the lawn to $76 for the best seats at the most popular concerts. If you pay for general admission to the lawn and it rains during the concert, you get wet. (Sorry, no refunds or exchanges.) For information, call ☎ 617-266-1492 in Boston; ☎ 413-637-5165 in Lenox (after June 10), or ☎ 413-637-1666 for weekly program information. Tickets may be bought at the box office at Tanglewood's main entrance, or through the Ticketmaster service (subject to a service fee). Ticketmaster's numbers are ☎ 617-931-2000 in Boston; ☎ 413-733-2500 in the Berkshires; ☎ 212-307-7171 in New York City; or ☎ 800-347-0808 from other areas. If you arrive two or three hours before concert time you can often get lawn space; Shed and Concert Hall seats should be bought in advance.

Parking Ample concert parking is available. Keep in mind that parking – and, more importantly, *unparking* – 6000 cars can take time. It's all organized very well and runs smoothly, but you will still have to wait awhile in your car during the exodus.

Organized Tours You can take a walking tour of Tanglewood grounds on Wednesday at 10:30 am, or Saturday at 1:15 pm, starting from the visitors center.

Several tour companies operate special Tanglewood concert buses which take you directly to the concert, then back home. In Boston, call K&L Tours (☎ 617-267-1905) or Colpitts World Travel (☎ 617-326-7800); in New York City call Biss Tours (☎ 718-426-4000) or Parker Tours (☎ 718-428-7800).

Other Concerts

The renown of Tanglewood has drawn other musicians and audiences to Lenox. The Armstrong Chamber Concert series (☎ 413-637-3646; off-season 203-868-0522) sponsors performances in Lenox's Town Hall Theatre from April through November.

The Berkshire Opera Company (☎ 413-243-1343) stages full-dress productions of classic and modern operas in the Cranwell Opera House on US 20.

The National Music Center (☎ 413-637-4718 for schedules and tickets, 637-1800 for information), 70 Kemble St, sponsors concerts of pop, folk, blues, country and jazz in its 1200-seat state-of-the-art theater.

Shakespeare & Company

Among the most enjoyable cultural events of a Lenox summer are the performances of the bard's great plays staged on the grounds of Edith Wharton's lavish estate, The Mount (see above), by Shakespeare & Company (☎ 413-637-1199; fax 637-4274). There are several performance spaces, including small theaters in the mansion itself and in the stables, but for the "Mainstage" the lawn is the stage, the forest the backdrop, and *A Midsummer Night's Dream* really comes to life. Plays are staged daily except Monday. Tickets cost $12.50 to $30.

Activities

This is excellent country for biking if you don't mind a few hills. Main Street Sports & Leisure (☎ 413-637-4407), 102 Main St, rents road, mountain and kids' bikes ($20), in-line skates, canoes ($25) and tennis racquets ($10). They have brochures for self-guided road and trail rides.

Mean Wheels Bike Shop (☎ 413-637-0644), 57A Housatonic St, specializes in mountain bikes and bikes for women.

Places to Stay

Lenox has no hotels and only a few motels – the *Susse Chalet* (☎ 413-637-3560, fax 637-3218) and the *Quality Inn*

(☎ 413-637-4244) – on US 7 two miles north of the town center. However, there are lots of wonderful inns.

Because of Tanglewood's weekend concerts, lodging rates are relatively low Monday through Wednesday, but up to twice as much Thursday through Sunday. Many inns require a two- or three-night minimum stay on summer weekends. When you add the 5.7% state room tax and 4% Lenox room tax to weekend rates, that means a Lenox weekend can cost $280 to $500 just for lodging. Faced with such prices, many thrifty travelers opt to sleep in lower-priced communities such as Lee and Great Barrington. But if you can afford them, Lenox's inns provide charming digs and memorable stays.

Most inn rooms have private bath, and include a full breakfast and perhaps even afternoon tea. Prices are always quoted per double room. Very few Lenox inns accept children under 10 or 12, or pets.

Walker House (☎ 413-637-1271), 74 Walker St, convenient to everything in the town center, looks relatively modest from the front. Behind the classic facade are three acres of gardens and the friendliest innkeepers in town. Rooms with private bath cost $70 to $90 midweek, $100 to $170 weekends.

Amadeus House (☎ 413-637-4770, 800-205-4770), 15 Cliffwood St, is modest compared to some of Lenox's great houses, but very comfy and reasonably priced at $55 to $115 midweek, $85 to $175 weekends.

Hampton Terrace (☎ 413-637-1773), 91 Walker St, next to the Episcopal church and across from the Gables Inn, is big but not as grand as some of its neighbors. Prices are a bit lower as well, at $55 midweek, $85 to $100 on weekends.

The Village Inn (☎ 413-637-0020, fax 637-9756), 16 Church St, was built in 1771. The Federal-style inn has 32 rooms with bath priced from $85 to $175, a dining room serving breakfast, afternoon tea and dinner, and a tavern featuring English ales, draft beer and light meals.

The *Candlelight Inn* (☎ 413-637-1555),

35 Walker St, is well known for its candlelit restaurant. The guest rooms, at $60 to $155, are a less prominent feature, but comfy and well located.

The Gables Inn (☎ 413-637-3416), 103 Walker St (MA 183), was originally known as Pine Acre. Built in 1885, the Queen Anne-style "cottage" was the summer home of Mrs William C Wharton, whose son Teddy married Edith Newbold Jones (see The Mount, above). The house has been nicely restored, and now rents rooms for $90 to $195.

The Birchwood Inn (☎ 413-637-2600, 800-524-1646), 7 Hubbard St, across MA 183 from the Church on the Hill, dates from 1767. The mansard-roofed house is now quite a gracious inn enjoying fine views of the town. Rooms cost $50 to $195 per night.

If money is no object, the place for you is *Blantyre* (☎ 413-637-3556, fax 637-4282), three miles west of I-90 exit 2 along US 20. An imitation Scottish Tudor mansion built in 1902, Blantyre sits amidst 85 acres of grounds equipped with four tennis courts, croquet lawns, a swimming pool, hot tub and sauna. The 23 rooms, suites and cottages are priced from $263 to $688 per night, continental breakfast included.

Places to Eat

The chamber of commerce has a collection of menus from local restaurants, which is useful in choosing places to eat. Because many people take picnics to the Tanglewood concerts, most eateries can prepare your chosen food for take out. Start your restaurant roamings on Church St, which is lined with eateries.

Breakfast & Lunch Because of Lenox's city-sophisticate clientele, it's easy to find balsamic vinegar this and three-mustard that. So where does one find cheap, good food? At the *Village Snack Shop* (☎ 413-637-2564), 35 Housatonic St at Church St, breakfast and lunch are served at the lunch counter and won't bust your budget.

Berkshire Bagel (☎ 413-637-1500), 18 Franklin St, is more upscale but still rea-

sonable, with bagels and bagel-sandwiches for $1 to $4, and even a few outdoor tables. It closes at 5 pm. *Salerno's Gourmet Pizza*, in the same building, satisfies a different craving.

The *Lenox Pizza House* (☎ 413-637-2590), 7 Franklin St, serves pan pizza (whole pie or by the slice), grinders, Greek salads and pasta.

Carol's (☎ 413-637-8948), across from the Lenox Pizza House on Franklin St, has a long menu of light meals and snacks priced around $6, plus lots of take-out items.

Cheesecake Charlie's (☎ 413-637-3411, fax 637-1356) has 50 varieties of cheesecake and an espresso bar. The other side of Charlie's is *Wholesome Harold's*, with an organic juice bar, a healthy deli featuring organic greens and non-sugared desserts. They're both at 60 Main St in the Village Shopping Center.

Dinner Though some of these restaurants serve lunch and dinner, most do only the evening meal.

Church Street Café (☎ 413-637-2745), 69 Church St, has made diners happy for years with its reasonably priced lunches (under $10), and inventive dinners ($20 to $40) served in simple, attractive dining rooms and on the deck. The menu is eclectic and good.

Roseborough Grill (☎ 413-637-2700), 83 Church St, just down from the Church Street Café and similar in price, is a converted house with tables set out on the front porch. The emphasis here is on fresh local produce, home baking and grilled meats, poultry, fish and vegetables.

Café Lucia (☎ 413-637-2640), 90 Church St, serves classic Italian dinners indoors or out (closed Sunday and Monday), as does *Antonio's* (☎ 413-637-9894), around the corner on Franklin St.

A number of Lenox inns serve elegant dinners, see Places to Stay for details. *The Village Inn* has a good dining room at moderate prices. The *Candlelight Inn* has four dining rooms decorated in turn-of-the-century style, and a transatlantic menu. Come for dinner (outside in good weather), or after-performance drinks and desserts.

The *Gateways Inn & Restaurant* (☎ 413-637-2532), 51 Walker St, was the mansion of Harley Proctor (of Proctor & Gamble). The elegant dining room has a two-tier price policy similar to lodgings: Monday through Thursday you can have a table d'hôte dinner for $20 (plus drinks, tax and tip). On weekends, main courses are priced at $26.50 including salad, pasta, vegetable, bread and butter. The food is good and the surroundings plush.

Getting There & Away
The nearest airports are Bradley in Windsor Locks, CT, and in Albany, NY. Peter Pan Bus Lines (☎ 617-426-7838) operates buses between Lenox and Boston. See Tanglewood Music Festival for organized tours information. Trains stop in nearby Pittsfield; see that section for details.

Driving details for Lenox are:

Destination	Mileage	Hr:Min
Albany, NY	45 miles	1:00
Boston, MA	138 miles	3:10
Great Barrington, MA	16 miles	0:30
Hartford, CT	78 miles	1:30
Lee, MA	5 miles	0:12
Litchfield, CT	46 miles	1:15
New York, NY	147 miles	3:20
Pittsfield, MA	7 miles	0:15
Springfield, MA	40 miles	0:55
Stockbridge, MA	5 miles	0:12
West Stockbridge, MA	9 miles	0:20
Williamstown, MA	29 miles	0:50

STOCKBRIDGE
Stockbridge is the quintessential New England picture-postcard town, absolutely beautiful, almost too perfect – the way Normal Rockwell might have seen it.

In fact, Rockwell *did* see it, because he lived here. Whether it has always been this beautiful, or whether it has remade itself in Rockwell's image, we will never know.

Both the town and the artist attract the summer crowds. They come to stroll its streets, inspect its shops and sit in the rockers on the porch of the grand old Red Lion Inn. And they come (by the busload) to visit the Norman Rockwell Museum on the town's outskirts.

Also of interest in this pretty town are Chesterwood, the country home and studio of sculptor Daniel Chester French; Naumkeag, a lavish turn-of-the-century "Berkshire cottage" and the Berkshire Theatre Festival.

Orientation & Information
Stockbridge's Main St is MA 102. The central district is only a few blocks long.

An information kiosk on Main St is sometimes staffed by volunteers in the summer months. For accommodation information, contact the Stockbridge Lodging Association (☎ 413-298-5327), PO Box 224, Stockbridge, MA 01262.

Norman Rockwell Museum
Norman Rockwell (1894-1978) was born in New York City, and sold his first magazine cover illustration to the *Saturday Evening Post* in 1916. In the following half century he did another 316 covers for the *Post*, as well as illustrations for books, posters and many other magazines. His clever, masterful, insightful art made him the best-known and most popular illustrator in US history.

Rockwell lived and worked in Stockbridge for the last 25 years of his life. This new, modern museum has the largest collection of his original art. His studio was moved here from behind his Stockbridge home. The museum (☎ 413-298-4100) is open every day from 10 am to 5 pm May to October and 11 am to 4 pm on weekdays from November to April. Admission costs $18 per family, $8 adult, $2 child over five, under five are free. Picnic tables are set in a grove near the museum.

The museum is on MA 183 south of MA 102. Follow MA 102 west from Stockbridge, turn left (south) on MA 183, and look for the museum on the left-hand side.

Chesterwood
Daniel Chester French (1850-1931) is best known for his statue "The Minute Man"

(1875) at the Old North Bridge in Concord, MA, and his great statue of Lincoln sitting in the Lincoln Monument in Washington, DC (1922).

French's work was mostly monumental sculpture. He created over 100 great public works and became prosperous at it. His home was in New York City, but he spent most of his summers after 1897 at Chesterwood (☎ 413-298-3579), his gracious Berkshire estate. He continued work on his sculptures here while enjoying the society of the other "cottage" owners.

The sculptor's house and studio are substantially as they were when he lived and worked here, with nearly 500 pieces of sculpture, finished and unfinished, in the barn-like studio.

Chesterwood is open to the public daily from May through October from 10 am to 5 pm. The museum is on Williamsville Rd near the village of Glendale, off MA 183 south of the Norman Rockwell Museum. Follow MA 102 west from Stockbridge and turn left onto Glendale Middle Rd, proceed through Glendale to Williamsville Rd and turn left; the museum is on the right. Admission costs $16 for a family, or $6.50 per adult, $3.50 for youth 13 to 18, $1.50 for kids six to 12, under six free.

Naumkeag

This is another of those grand Berkshire "cottages" on Prospect Hill. It was designed in 1885 by Stanford White for attorney and diplomat Joseph Hodges Choate. Choate was a noted collector of art, so the summer house is filled with oriental carpets, Chinese porcelain and other luxury goods. The gardens are the work of 30 years of devotion on the part of Fletcher Steele, a prominent landscape architect, and the Choate family.

You can take a guided tour of the house (☎ 413-298-3239) and a stroll through the gardens from late May through early September daily except Monday from 10 am to 4:15 pm. From early September through mid-October the house is open on weekends and holidays. Admission costs $6.50 for adults ($5 for the gardens only), $2.50 for children six to 12, under six free. Follow Pine St from the Red Lion Inn to Prospect St.

Mission House

This historic residence (☎ 413-298-3239) on Main St was the home of the Reverend John Sergeant, the first missionary to the Native Americans in this area. He built the original part of the house in 1739. It's furnished with 17th- and 18th-century effects and houses a small museum of Native American artifacts. It's open from late May through early September from 11 am to 3:30 pm. Admission costs $5 for adults, $2.50 kids six to 12.

Merwin House

This late Federal-style brick residence (☎ 413-298-4703), 14 Main St, is furnished with an eclectic mix of European and American pieces. There are tours at noon, 1, 2, 3 and 4 pm on Tuesday, Thursday, Saturday and Sunday, June through mid-October. Admission costs $2 for adults, $3.50 seniors, $4 children 12 and under.

Berkshire Botanical Garden

Two miles from the center of Stockbridge, the 15-acre Berkshire Botanical Garden (☎ 413-298-3926), 5 W Stockbridge Rd (MA 102), is within walking distance of the Norman Rockwell Museum. Wildflowers, herbs, perennials and water plants, alpine forest and rock gardens are yours to enjoy from 10 am to 5 pm daily. Admission costs $5 for adults, $4 seniors; children 15 and under are free.

West Stockbridge

If Stockbridge is pure Norman Rockwell, West Stockbridge is Ye Olde Colonial Shoppinge Mall. Its aggressive cuteness has suffered some mild scuffing in recent years, but it's still popular with the youthful set as a place to hang out. Dining and shopping is why people come here.

Places to Stay

There are numerous inns and B&Bs in and around Stockbridge. The following are among the least expensive.

Williamson Guest House (☎ 413-298-4931), 32 Church St a mile from the town center, has four rooms with shared baths priced from $60 to $75.

The *Yesterhouse* (☎ 413-298-5509), 2 Lukeman Lane, RR 2, West Stockbridge, is near the Berkshire Botanical Garden. Its three rooms with shared baths cost $70 to $95.

Red Lion Inn (☎ 413-298-5545, fax 298-5130), on Main St, is the very heart of Stockbridge. A huge 108-room white frame hotel, it dominates the town center both by its size and activity. Founded in 1773, it was completely rebuilt after a fire in 1897. Rooms are priced at $117 and $142 midweek, $140 and $155 on weekends. Rooms with shared baths are only $70 midweek, $85 on weekends.

Places to Eat

The *Red Lion Inn* is also Stockbridge's premier place for dining. Besides the elegant formal dining room, there's the *Widow Bingham Tavern*, a rough-hewn colonial pub. The *Lion's Den*, downstairs, is the cocktail lounge with a sandwich and salad menu. Plan to spend about $35 or $40 per person for a luxurious continental dinner. In summer there's dining in the pretty courtyard in back.

Naji's (☎ 413-298-5465), 40 Main St, down an alley just north of the Red Lion Inn, has a marvelous selection of sandwiches, huge grinders, calzones and Middle East delicacies that are the favorites of owner Naji Nejaime. Naji will make up a sumptuous six-course picnic-to-go for $13.50 to $17.50, or you can eat here. It opens at 11 am in summer. If you saw the 1960s Arlo Guthrie antiwar movie *Alice's Restaurant*, which was set in Stockbridge, you may recognize Naji's as the site of Alice's.

Ali's (☎ 413-298-3550), in the Mews not far away, serves breakfast ($3 to $6) and lunch ($4 to $7) in clean, modern, bright surroundings.

Daily Bread Bakery (☎ 413-298-0272), "on the sunny side of Main St," sells cakes, cookies, bread and rolls good for snacks or picnics.

In West Stockbridge the menu at *Shaker Mill Tavern* (☎ 413-232-8565) is a youthful assortment of burgers, salads and pizza, with several main-course dishes priced from $8 to $11. It has pleasant dining areas both inside and out. At *Card Lake Inn* (☎ 413-232-0272), 29 Main St, the menu is fancier and more sophisticated, at moderate prices. *Caffe Pomodoro*, in the railroad station right next to the post office, is a pleasant bakery-cafe good for a cuppa, snack or light meal.

Entertainment

The *Berkshire Theatre Festival* (☎ 413-298-5576), PO Box 797, Stockbridge, MA 01262-0797, stages new and innovative plays from late June through early September at its Mainstage and smaller Unicorn Theatre. Tickets are priced from $12 to $28. There's a Children's Theatre ($3.50) as well. Call or write for current offerings.

Getting There & Away

Driving details for Stockbridge are:

Destination	Mileage	Hr:Min
Great Barrington, MA	7 miles	0:15
Lee, MA	5 miles	0:15
Lenox, MA	7 miles	0:20
West Stockbridge, MA	8 miles	0:17

GREAT BARRINGTON

Great Barrington is about as far as you can get from Boston and still be in Massachusetts. Unsullied by the crowds of city sophisticates flocking to Lenox and Stockbridge, Great Barrington maintains an engaging informal down-home how're-ya-doin' ambiance. There is a lot outdoors to explore here. It is an unfancy but not unattractive place, and it has been that way since its founding in 1761: a farming town that provides the surrounding villages with a commercial, social and cultural center.

Barringtonians have always asserted their independence. In 1774 local citizens,

Great Barrington native and Harvard graduate WEB Dubois edited the *Crisis* and wrote the book *Color and Democracy* (1945).

chafing under the abuses of the king's governors in Boston, prevented the royal judges from meeting in the local courthouse. Great Barrington saw the birth of the great African-American teacher and civil rights leader William Edward Burghardt DuBois (1868–1963). After receiving a PhD from Harvard, Professor DuBois became a pioneer for civil rights and a co-founder of the NAACP.

Today Great Barrington makes its living at tourism, health care, the antiques trade and education as well as farming. The local newspaper, the *Berkshire Eagle*, has won Pulitzer prizes, and a fountain (1895) near the railroad station commemorates "the newsboy," the link between the printing room and the reader.

Orientation & Information
The Housatonic River flows through the center of town just east of Main St (US 7), the main thoroughfare. Most lodgings and restaurants are on Main St in the town center, or on US 7 North, or MA 23/41 south of the town.

The Southern Berkshire Chamber of Commerce (☎ 413-528-1510), 362 Main St, Great Barrington, MA 01230, has lots of good maps, brochures, restaurant menus and other materials on area attractions and businesses.

Searles Castle
Mr and Mrs Edward Searles were Great Barrington's most wealthy and prominent citizens in the late 19th century. Mrs Searles, the widow of railroad tycoon Mark Hopkins, built an imposing mansion here in 1886. Now called Searles Castle, it stands behind high walls on Main St at the southern end of the town center. It must have seemed out of place in a town otherwise populated by sturdy peasants. Today the great house is the home of John Dewey Academy, a private school.

Monterey & Tyringham
Take MA 23 east out of Great Barrington eight miles to the village of Monterey. Its general store is only slightly updated. If you buy lunch at its deli, try the local Rawson Brook Farm goat cheese.

The village of Tyringham, several miles north along the back road, is the perfect goal for an excursion deep into the rural Berkshire countryside. Once the home of a Shaker community (1792-1870s), the village is now famous for its **Gingerbread House,** an architectural fantasy designed by sculptor Henry Hudson Kitson at the turn of the century. Kitson's best known work is the statue of Capt Parker as the minuteman which graces the Lexington Green. The thatched cottage, once Kitson's studio, now houses the **Tyringham Art Galleries** (☎ 413-243-3260), open daily from 10 am to 5 pm. For places to stay in Tyringham, see Inns & B&Bs, below.

Hiking
To residents of southwestern Massachusetts, a "cobble" is a high rocky knoll of limestone, marble or quartzite. These knobby hills, which were formed about 500 million years ago, are now a

curiosity. **Bartholomew's Cobble**, 10 miles south of Great Barrington along US 7 and MA 7A toward Ashley Falls, is a 277-acre reservation cloaked in trees, ferns, flowers and moss. Six miles of hiking trails provide routes for enjoying the cobble and the woods set beneath a flyway used by over 200 species of birds. This property of the Trustees of Reservations (☎ 413-229-8600) is open from mid-April to mid-October, 9 am to 5 pm, for a small admission fee.

Twelve miles south of South Egremont, right on the New York state line, is **Bash Bish Falls**, a pretty 50-foot woodland waterfall reached by either of two paths. Follow MA 41 south out of Great Barrington and turn right onto Mt Washington Rd following signs for the Catamount Ski Area. Then follow signs to the falls, taking East St, then West St and finally Bash Bish Falls Rd, deep in the Mt Washington State Forest.

The **River Walk**, a path along the western bank of the Housatonic River between Bridge and Cottage Sts, is a community work-in-progress. You can currently enjoy the walk via the entrance at 195 Main St.

On US 7 less than five miles north of the town center, **Monument Mountain** can be climbed by either of two trails. On a clear day, the view from the top is good, and the roundtrip hike takes between two and three hours.

Special Events
The Aston Magna Festival (☎ 413-528-3595) celebrates classical (especially Baroque) music each summer in July and August. If you like Bach, Brahms and Buxtehude, buy your tickets ($12.50 to $15) preferably well in advance. Concerts are held in St James Church, on Main St (US 7) at Taconic Ave, near the Town Hall.

Places to Stay
Though Great Barrington is not a busy tourist town, the crush of the crowds going to Tanglewood is so intense in summer that many people venture here looking for accommodations after Lenox, Lee and other central Berkshire towns have filled up. Weekend rates (Thursday, Friday, Saturday nights) are higher than midweek as well.

Camping *Tolland State Forest* (☎ 413-269-6002), on MA 8 in Otis, 16 miles east of Great Barrington, has 90 sites. *Beartown State Forest* (☎ 413-528-0904), on Blue Hill Rd in Monterey, eight miles east of Great Barrington along MA 23, has 12 simple sites. At *Mt Washington State Forest* (☎ 413-528-0330), on East St in the village of Mt Washington southwest of South Egremont, there are 15 wilderness sites for hikers.

Prospect Lake Park (☎ 413-528-4158), on Prospect Lake Rd in North Egremont, has 140 sites open May through mid-October. Most of the other campgrounds are in or near Otis, including *Camp Overflow* (☎ 413-269-4036), with 100 sites, and *Laurel Ridge Camping Area* (☎ 413-269-4804), in East Otis, with 140 sites.

Motels On the southern side of the town center, the conveniently located *Berkshire Motor Inn* (☎ 413-528-3150), right behind the chamber of commerce, has the best prices at $45/$50 a single/double, but is rather bleak, if serviceable. There's an indoor pool.

Lantern House Motel (☎ 413-528-2350), on Stockbridge Rd (US 7) just north of the center, is the best deal in terms of value. Rooms cost $50/$60 Sunday through Wednesday, higher Thursday through Saturday. There's a nice swimming pool.

The *Barrington Court Motel* (☎ 413-528-2340), 400 Stockbridge Rd, costs the same midweek, but $100 on weekends.

Monument Mountain Motel (☎ 413-528-3272), 249 Stockbridge Rd, charges $60 to $70 midweek, $95 to $105 Thursday through Saturday.

Inns & B&Bs *Littlejohn Manor* (☎ 413-528-2882), 1 Newsboy Monument Lane, is a nice big Victorian house with four guest rooms sharing baths. Rates, $70 to $85 in summer, include a full English breakfast and afternoon tea.

The Wainwright Inn (☎ 413-528-2062), 518 S Main St, terms itself "a country bed and breakfast," although it's a short walk from the center of town. It's a big house in which all guest rooms have private bath and cost $50 to $125, depending upon the season and the day of the week.

You might also have a look at *Turn-of-the-Century B&B* (☎ 413-528-6305), 18 Higgins St. *Baldwin Hill Farm B&B* (☎ 413-528-4092), RR 3, Box 125, on Baldwin Hill Rd (off MA 71) in South Egremont has four rooms priced from $70 to $104, a fine pool and beautiful views.

If you fall in love with Tyringham, you can spend the night at *The Golden Goose* (☎ 413-243-3008), 123 Main Rd, Box 336. Six rooms rent for $65 to $120, breakfast included. There's also the *Sunset Farm B&B* (☎ 413-243-3229), on Main Rd, with four rooms priced from $75 to $100.

There are many other inns on MA 23/41 South between Great Barrington and South Egremont.

Places to Eat

There are several good restaurants in the town center, and lots more on the northeastern outskirts along US 7.

Ruby's Diner, 282 Main St downtown, is open from 8 am to 8 pm and serves breakfast ($3 to $6) all day. Lunch and dinner are yours for $5 to $10, along with fruit pies and ice cream.

Berkshire Coffee Roasting Company, right near Ruby's, brews many varieties of coffee, and supplements them with a limited selection of cookies and sweet pastries – the coffee's the thing here.

Castle St Café (☎ 413-528-5244), 10 Castle St, just off Main St, is a storefront bistro serving upscale food in informal surroundings at moderate prices. Look for inventive but skillful cooking here. Chef/owner Michael Ballon uses lots of fresh local ingredients. Dinners are in the $30 to

$40 range. It's closed on Tuesday.

Captain Toss Seafood Restaurant (☎ 413-528-3512), 485 Main St, is the local fish place.

On US 7 North (Stockbridge Rd), two to three miles from the center of town, are the fast-food eateries such as Friendly's, Burger King and McDonald's, as well as the following places:

Jodi's Country Cookery (☎ 413-528-6064), 327 Stockbridge Rd, is an "old farmhouse" set on a commercial street. The homey interior of bright pine floors and rough-hewn beams is supplemented with front-porch dining (though the traffic can be noisy) and belied by servers wearing radio headsets to communicate with the kitchen. The menu is long and eclectic, from burgers through fettuccine puttanesca to grilled duck sausage with apple brandy. Expect to spend $17 to $36 per person at dinner. Jodi's is open every day from 8 am to 9 pm.

Boiler Room Café (☎ 413-528-4280), 405 Stockbridge Rd, serves quite fine New American cuisine from a changing menu. Dinner costs $20 to $35 per person.

Dos Amigos, near the motels on Stockbridge Rd, is the local Mexican place. For Chinese, try *Panda West Chinese Restaurant*, right nearby.

In South Egremont, *The Old Mill* (☎ 413-528-1421), 53 Main St (MA 23), is a 1797 grist mill and blacksmith's shop turned into an atmospheric restaurant serving American and continental cuisine. Dinners cost about $30 to $45; portions tend to be small. The neighboring *Gaslight Café* is cheaper and simpler.

Getting There & Away

Driving details for Great Barrington are:

Destination	Mileage	Hr:Min
Boston, MA	146 miles	3:00
Lenox, MA	13 miles	0:25
Litchfield, CT	33 miles	1:00
South Egremont, MA	4 miles	0:11
Stockbridge, MA	7 miles	0:15
Williamstown, MA	42 miles	1:20

PITTSFIELD

Pittsfield is the service city of Berkshire County. This is where the trains stop and where all the biggest stores are. For tourists, there are only two or three things to stop for.

Orientation & Information

Park Square, at the intersection of North, South, East and West Sts, is the center of Pittsfield. North and South Sts are also US 7.

The RSVP tourist information booth in Park Square is open every day in summer. The Central Berkshire Chamber of Commerce (☎ 413-499-4000), a half block west of Park Square in the Tierney Building, also provides information. The Berkshire Visitors Bureau (☎ 413-443-9186), in the Berkshire Common building by the Hilton hotel, has lots of information. Pittsfield Central (☎ 413-443-6501), 141 North St (US 7), 1½ blocks north of Park Square, has a brochure for a self-guided architectural walking tour of central Pittsfield.

Hancock Shaker Village

The Shakers were among the earliest and most admirable of the numerous millennial Christian sects that flourished in the fertile climate of religious freedom to be found in the New World. Hancock Shaker Village, five miles west of Pittsfield on US 20, gives you a studied look at their peaceful, prayerful way of life.

Twenty of the original Shaker buildings are carefully restored at Hancock Shaker Village, and are open to view. Most famous is the Round Stone Barn (1826), but other structures such as the Brick Dwelling (1830), the laundry and machine shop (1790), the trustees' office (1830-1895), the meetinghouse (1793) and the sisters' and brethrens' shops (1795) are of equal interest.

Hancock Shaker Village (☎ 413-443-0188), on US 20 southwest of Pittsfield center near the intersection with MA 41 (*not* in the village of Hancock), was known as the "City of Peace," and was occupied by

---

Shakes of Ecstasy

The United Society of Believers in Christ's Second Appearing, or the Millennial Church, popularly known as the Shakers, an offshoot of Quakerism, began in 1747 in England. Followers of the sect believed in and strictly observed the principles of communal possessions, pacifism, open confession of sins and equality – but celibacy – of the sexes.

Shakers believed that God had both a male and a female nature. Ann Lee, an ardent follower of the sect, proclaimed that she had been blessed with the "mother element" of the spirit of Jesus. Calling herself Mother Ann, she pressed her claim so zealously that she was imprisoned.

On her release she set sail with a handful of followers for New York. They founded the first Shaker community in the New World near Albany in 1774.

Mother Ann died in 1784, but her followers went on to found other Shaker communities in northern New England. Besides Hancock, there are surviving Shaker communities at Canterbury, NH (near Concord), and Sabbathday Lake, ME (north of Portland).

With celibacy as a tenet, Shakerism depended upon conversion for its growth and sustenance. Converts to the church turned over all their worldly possessions to the movement, and worked selflessly on its behalf, but members were free to leave at any time. Shaker worship services were characterized by a communal dance-like movement, during which some congregants would be overcome with religious zeal and suffer tremors ("shakes") of ecstasy.

Each community was organized into "families" of 30 to 90 members who lived and worked together. Though there was equality of the sexes, there was also a good deal of segregation. Communities were largely self-sufficient, trading produce and handicrafts with the rest of the world for the things they could not produce themselves. Work, among Shakers, was a consecrated act, an attitude reflected in the high quality of workmanship and design of Shaker furniture and crafts. In effect, every product was a prayer. ∎

Shakers until 1960. At its peak in 1830, the community numbered some 300 souls. Preserved as a historic monument, the village still gives you a good look at what the excellent principles of Shakerism could accomplish. Interpreters in the historic buildings demonstrate the quiet, kindly, hard-working Shaker way of life from 9:30 am to 5 pm May through October; in April and November there are guided tours between 10 am and 3 pm. Admission costs $25 for a family, $10 adult, $5 kids six to 17, under six are free. On Saturday evening, you can feast on a bountiful Shaker candlelight dinner while being entertained by Shaker music. Call for details and reservations.

Berkshire Museum

Pittsfield's major repository of art, history and natural science is the Berkshire Museum (☎ 413-443-7171), 39 South St (US 7), just south of Park Square. The museum's painting collection holds 19th-century masters such as Bierstadt, Church, Copley, Inness and Peale. The history collections are strong in regional artifacts, tools, firearms, dolls and costumes. The natural science section highlights the ecology, flora and fauna of the Berkshires, and has a rock and mineral collection numbering over 3000 pieces.

It's open every day in July and August from 10 am to 5 pm (Sunday from 1 to 5 pm); closed Monday in other months. Admission costs $3 for adults, $2 seniors and students, $1 youth 12 to 18, under 12 free.

Melville's Arrowhead

The novelist Herman Melville (1819-1891) lived in Pittsfield at 780 Holmes Rd from 1850 to 1863. It was here, in the house he called Arrowhead (☎ 413-442-1793) that he wrote his masterwork *Moby Dick*. The house is now a museum maintained by the Berkshire County Historical Society and is open to visits or by guided tour Friday to Monday from 10 am to 5 pm (last tour at 4:30 pm). Admission costs $15 for a family, $4.50 adult, $4 senior, $3 child six to 16.

Places to Stay & Eat

Pittsfield has the usual selection of business-oriented hotels and motels for a city of its size. Most visitors prefer to stay in one of the more picturesque communities such as Lenox or Great Barrington.

There are plenty of places to pick up a quick meal on North and South Sts (US 7) as you pass through, or around Park Square if you plan to stop.

Getting There & Away

Air The nearest airports are Bradley airport and at Albany, NY. For airport transportation, contact Peter Pan Bus Lines.

Bus The Pittsfield Bus Terminal (☎ 413-442-4451) is at 57 S Church St. Peter Pan Bus Lines (☎ 800-343-9999) operates routes connecting Pittsfield with Albany, Bennington, Boston, Hartford, Lee, Lenox, North Adams, Springfield, Toronto, Williamstown and Worcester. Many other destinations, including Amherst, Hyannis, New Haven, New York City, Philadelphia and Washington, are available via Peter Pan's Springfield hub.

Bonanza Bus Lines (☎ 800-556-3815) runs buses daily between New York City and Bennington via Great Barrington, Stockbridge, Lee, Lenox, Pittsfield (with a connecting service to Albany) and Williamstown. The ride between New York City and Pittsfield takes about four hours.

Train For Amtrak information, see the beginning of this chapter.

Car Driving details for Pittsfield are:

Destination	Mileage	Hr:Min
Albany, NY	38 miles	0:50
Bennington, VT	36 miles	0:50
Boston, MA	145 miles	3:20
Hartford, CT	85 miles	1:40
Lenox, MA	7 miles	0:15
Litchfield, CT	53 miles	1:25
New York , NY	154 miles	3:30
Springfield, MA	47 miles	1:10
Williamstown, MA	22 miles	0:40

WILLIAMSTOWN

After all of the domestic architectural extravagances of the central Berkshires, Williamstown comes as something of a surprise. The big buildings here are not palatial mansions, but marble-faced college halls. The northwestern corner of Massachusetts, though far from university-strewn Boston or the college-crowded Pioneer Valley, has its own prestigious institution of higher learning in Williams College. As well, Bennington College is only 30 minutes north in Vermont, making this area of the Berkshires something of a find.

History

Ephraim Williams, Jr, born in 1714, was a soldier in the British colonial army. He worked at surveying this area until he was given command of the line of British frontier forts facing the French North American territories. Fort Massachusetts, in North Adams, was one of these forts. Six miles to the west was the town of West Hoosuck.

In 1755, Williams led a column of Massachusetts troops toward Lake George and the French positions there. He died in the fighting. His will provided a substantial

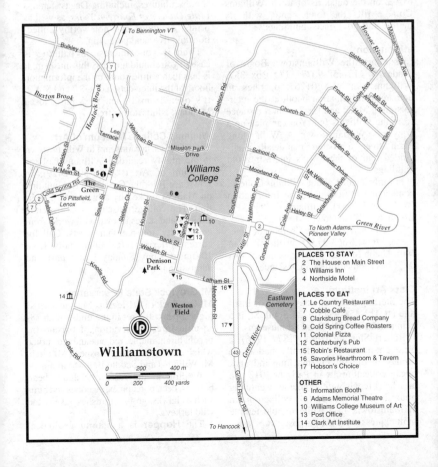

PLACES TO STAY
2 The House on Main Street
3 Williams Inn
4 Northside Motel

PLACES TO EAT
1 Le Country Restaurant
7 Cobble Café
8 Clarksburg Bread Company
9 Cold Spring Coffee Roasters
11 Colonial Pizza
12 Canterbury's Pub
15 Robin's Restaurant
16 Savories Hearthroom & Tavern
17 Hobson's Choice

OTHER
5 Information Booth
6 Adams Memorial Theatre
10 Williams College Museum of Art
13 Post Office
14 Clark Art Institute

Williamstown

To Bennington VT

MASSACHUSETTS

amount of money for the founding of a college in West Hoosuck, if the town would change its name to his. Luckily for future Hoosuckers, it did. Williams College, in Williamstown, enrolled its first students in 1793. The college is now, and has been for two centuries, the lifeblood of the town.

Orientation

US 7 and MA 2 (Main St) intersect at the western corner of the town center. The small central commercial district is off Main St on Spring St. Other businesses, including several motels, are on US 7 and MA 2 on the outskirts of town. Williams College fills the town center with its marble-and-brick-faced buildings.

Information

In summer, the Williamstown Board of Trade (☎ 413-458-9077), PO Box 357, Williamstown, MA 01267, operates an unmanned information booth at the intersection of MA 2 and US 7, a short distance from the Williams Inn. You can pick up a copy of "Williamstown: A Walk along Main Street," a brochure that details a self-guided tour of the town's interesting old buildings.

For information about Williams College, contact the Office of Public Information (☎ 413-597-3131), Williams College, PO Box 676, Williamstown, MA 01267.

The Northern Berkshire Chamber of Commerce (☎ 413-663-3735), in the Windsor Mill, Union St (MA 2), North Adams, MA 01247, is another information source.

Clark Art Institute

The Sterling and Francine Clark Art Institute (☎ 413-458-9545), 225 South St, is a gem among New England art museums.

Robert Sterling Clark (1877-1956), a Yale engineer whose family had made money in the sewing machine industry, began collecting art in Paris in 1912. He and his French wife Francine eventually housed their wonderful collection in Williamstown, in a white marble temple built expressly for the purpose.

The collection and its needs soon outgrew the original building. In 1973 the museum's space was greatly expanded.

The Clark's collections are particularly strong in the Impressionists, their academic contemporaries in France and the mid-century Barbizon artists, including Millet, Troyon and Corot. Contemporary American painting is represented by Cassatt, Homer, Remington and Sargent. From earlier centuries there are excellent works by Piero della Francesca, Memling, Gossaert, Jacob van Ruisdael, Fragonard, Gainsborough, Turner and Goya. There are some sculptures, including Degas' famous *Little Dancer of Fourteen Years*, as well as prints, drawings and noteworthy collections of silver and porcelain.

Even if your interest in painting is casual, you should not miss this museum. It is less than a mile south of the information booth at the intersection of US 7 and MA 2. It's open from 10 am to 5 pm, closed Monday; admission is free.

Williams College Museum of Art

The Clark's sister museum in Williamstown is the highly regarded Williams College Museum of Art (☎ 413-597-2429), in Lawrence Hall, the Greek Revival building on Main St backed by a big modern addition. The college museum hosts traveling exhibits and stages its own with works from community and regional artists. Call for current offerings. It's open daily from 10 am to 5 pm (Sunday 1 to 5 pm), and admission is free.

Mt Greylock State Reservation

Mt Greylock (3491 feet) is Massachusetts' highest peak. It's set in the midst of an 18-sq-mile forest reservation of balsam fir, beech, birch, maple, red oak and red spruce which also includes Mt Prospect, Mt Fitch, Mt Williams and Saddle Ball Mountain.

Wildlife in the reserve includes bear, bobcats, deer, porcupines, raccoons and birds such as hawks, grouse, thrushes, ravens and wild turkeys.

The **Hopper** is a natural geological

feature formed by Mts Greylock, Williams and Prospect and Stoney Ledge. Its forests have some old-growth trees (more than 150 years).

There's an access road to the summit which begins in North Adams, six miles east of Williamstown along MA 2. Several miles up the road, as you reach the summit, you see the 92-foot-high War Veterans Memorial Tower (1932), restored in 1975, and Bascom Lodge (☎ 413-743-1591), a mountain hostelry built by the CCC in the 1930s. Bascom Lodge is administered by the AMC; it can provide beds for 32 people from mid-May through mid-October. Reservations are essential.

The Mt Greylock State Reservation (☎ 413-499-4262) has some 45 miles of hiking trails, including a portion of the Appalachian Trail. Several state parks have campsites (see Camping below).

Special Events

From the third week in June to the third week in August, the Williamstown Theatre Festival (☎ 413-597-3399, tickets 597-3400), PO Box 517, Williamstown, MA 01267, mounts the region's major theatrical offerings, and tickets are usually inexpensive. The main works are acted out in the 500-seat Adams Memorial Theatre on Main St. Plays in the 96-seat Other Stage are new and experimental. There are also cabaret performances in area restaurants. On Sundays, the Clark Art Institute is the scene for special dramatic events.

Places to Stay

Camping *Mt Greylock State Reservation* (☎ 413-499-4262) in North Adams has 35 campsites ($4) and pit toilets, but no showers.

If you follow MA 8 north from North Adams you'll pass *Natural Bridge State Park* (☎ 413-663-6312), a day-use area for picnicking; a bit farther along MA 8 is *Clarksburg State Park* (☎ 413-663-6312), on Middle Rd, with 47 campsites ($4), pit toilets, but no showers.

Savoy Mountain State Forest (☎ 413-663-8469), Central Shaft Rd from US 2, Florida, has 45 sites, some of which may be

reserved in advance, priced at $6. There are showers and flush toilets.

Motels & Hotels There are hotels and motels on MA 2 East and US 7 North, as well as in the town center.

Northside Motel (☎ 413-458-8107), 45 North St, very near the information booth, charges $65 for its 34 rooms. There's a small pool and it's a short walk to the museums.

Williams Inn (☎ 413-458-9371), on the green, is the major hotel in the center of town, with a restaurant and indoor pool. Its 100 rooms have the standard luxury hotel comforts, and cost $100 to $140.

Out on US 7 North, *Cozy Corner Motel* (☎ 413-458-8006), 284 Sand Springs Rd, 1½ miles north of the information booth, charges $52 to $80 for its rooms, depending upon season, and prides itself on the fish and chips served in the adjoining restaurant.

Green Valley Motel (☎ 413-458-3864), 1216 Simonds Rd, just south of the Vermont-Massachusetts state line, has 18 rooms with bathtubs for $55 to $65, and a swimming pool. A light breakfast is included.

Going east from the town center along MA 2, you pass the following lodgings. *Four Acres Restaurant & Motel* (☎ 413-458-8158), 213 Main St, has 30 neat rooms for $62 to $75.

The Orchards (☎ 413-458-9611), 222 Adams Rd, is the area's most expensive place to stay, a modern hotel decorated as an old inn. The luxury rooms are priced from $150 to $215; the dining room is very good.

Chimney Mirror Motel (☎ 413-458-5202), 295 Main St, a mile east of the center, charges $49 to $80 for its 18 rooms with one or two double beds, includes a continental breakfast and has a picnic area.

The 16-room *Willows Motel* (☎ 413-458-5768), 480 Main St, charges $52 to $62 for its simple but adequate rooms.

The small, 15-room *Maple Terrace Motel* (☎ 413-458-9677), 555 Main St, on the outskirts, has a big old house with motel units priced from $49 to $83 behind it, light breakfast included. There's a secluded pool.

There are more inexpensive motels in North Adams, the next town to the east of Williamstown along MA 2.

Inns & B&Bs Most of these have a two-night minimum on weekends, and some require a three-night stay on holidays and for special college events. Breakfast is included in the rates.

My favorite of all is *River Bend Farm* (☎ 413-458-3121), 643 Simonds Rd, just off US 7 on the north side of the little bridge over the Hoosic River. A Georgian tavern since revolutionary times, it has been carefully and authentically restored. Rooms with bath cost $90 to $115 double.

Field Farm Guest House (☎ 413-458-3135), 554 Sloan Rd, was the country estate of art collectors Lawrence and Eleanore Bloedel. Built in the spare, clean-lined post-WWII style on 254 wooded acres, the estate was willed to the Trustees of Reservations, which now operates it. The five modern rooms with bath are priced at $90. There's a pond, walking trails, tennis court, swimming pool and blissful quiet. Follow US 7 south to MA 43 west, and, just past the intersection, turn on Sloan Rd. Field Farm is just over a mile down Sloan Rd.

The House on Main Street (☎ 413-458-3031), 1120 Main St, just down from Williams Inn, is a nice old Victorian once owned by the daughter of President Woodrow Wilson, with six rooms (three with private baths) priced from $65 to $85.

Williamstown B&B (☎ 413-458-9202), 30 Cold Spring Rd (US 7 south and MA 2 west), right in the center of town just off the green, charges $80 for its three rooms with private baths.

Places to Eat

Visitors to the Berkshires think nothing of driving 30 miles to reach a favorite restaurant, but there are a number of good eating places right in Williamstown itself. Many serve vegetarian dishes.

For pizza, a sandwich or a light meal, wander along Spring St, the main shopping street. *Colonial Pizza* (☎ 413-458-9009), 22 Spring St, has spaghetti, souvlaki, Greek giros and huge grinders as well as pizza.

Cobble Café (☎ 413-458-5930), 27 Spring St, has an interesting, eclectic menu great for any meal, and for late evening snacks at the wine bar. On Sunday, only breakfast is served.

Clarksburg Bread Company (☎ 413-458-2251), 37 Spring St, has fresh-baked biscuits, breads, coffee cakes, cookies, muffins, pies, rolls, scones and squares, as well as coffee, tea and juices. It's open Tuesday through Saturday from 7 am to 4 pm.

Canterbury's Pub (☎ 413-458-2808), 46 Spring St, features an Olde English decor, foreign beers, Guinness on tap, a salad bar, soups and sandwiches.

Cold Spring Coffee Roasters (☎ 413-458-5010), 47 Spring St, roasts, grinds, brews and serves its premium coffees in elaborate preparations, complemented by baked treats, daily.

Chopsticks Chinese Restaurant (☎ 413-458-5750), 412 Main St, across MA 2 from The Orchards in the Grand Union shopping center, can satisfy your craving for Asian cuisine at low to moderate prices.

Robin's Restaurant (☎ 413-458-4489), at the south end of Spring St, serves California-style cuisine with New England's seasonal ingredients in white-tablecloth style. For dinner, they might feature duck liver truffle pâté with grilled garlic bread to start, followed by shrimp and black lobster ravioli with tomatoes, pesto and cream. Lunch tends to cost $10 to $15, dinner $28 to $45. No dinner is served Sunday, no lunch Monday; call ahead in the off-season.

Savories Hearthroom & Tavern (☎ 413-458-2175), 123 Water St (MA 43) features fresh pasta, seafood, grilled steaks and homemade desserts. It's open Tuesday through Sunday evenings, and some nights there's live music (jazz, folk, bluegrass, pop). *Hobson's Choice* (☎ 413-458-9101), just down the street at 159 Water St is similar, and a locals' favorite.

Le Country Restaurant (☎ 413-458-4000), on US 7 North just down the hill from the information booth, serves traditional continental cuisine at moderate prices, about $30 to $45 per person. Lunch is served on weekdays, dinner every evening; closed Monday.

Entertainment

During the academic year, call Concertline (☎ 413-597-3146) of the Williams College Department of Music for information on concerts, recitals and performances. In summer, *Williamstown Chamber Concerts* (☎ 413-458-8273) stages concerts at the Clark Art Institute.

For pub action, head for *Canterbury's,* described above in Places to Eat. Or try the *Purple Pub* (☎ 413-458-3306), just off Spring St at 2-4 Bank St, which has shaded outdoor tables and a very Williamstown atmosphere – that is, it's very friendly.

Getting There & Away

North Adams has a small airport and the Mohawk Soaring Club, but no scheduled air service.

Williamstown's bus station is the lobby of the Williams Inn (☎ 413-458-2665), on Main St near the intersection of US 7 and MA 2.

Peter Pan Bus Lines (☎ 800-343-9999) runs daily buses between Bennington and Boston via Williamstown, Pittsfield, Lee and Springfield. The trip between Boston and Williamstown takes slightly over four hours.

Bonanza Bus Lines (☎ 800-556-3815) runs daily buses between New York City and Bennington via Great Barrington, Stockbridge, Lee, Lenox, Pittsfield and Williamstown. The bus ride between New York and Williamstown takes about five hours.

Driving details for Williamstown are:

Destination	Mileage	Hr:Min
Amherst, MA	61 miles	1:20
Bennington, VT	14 miles	0:30
Boston, MA	145 miles	3:30
Deerfield, MA	45 miles	1:10
Hartford, CT	107 miles	2:30
Lenox, MA	29 miles	1:05
Litchfield, CT	75 miles	2:00
New York, NY	165 miles	3:45

MASSACHUSETTS

Rhode Island

The "Ocean State," as Rhode Island is known, may be the smallest state in the USA, but that distinction doesn't do justice to its beauty and variety. This corner of New England has its own special character and charm.

Providence, the state capital and third-largest city in New England, is a pleasant, historic, manageable city that's recently undergone an ambitious facelift. Newport, the famed 19th-century summer play-

ground of the colossally wealthy, is now the region's yachting capital and summer home to the merely inordinately wealthy. Block Island is a junior version of Nantucket or Martha's Vineyard, perfect for a day trip or overnight. The hundreds of miles of seacoast ringing the convoluted shoreline of Narragansett Bay provide ever-changing scenery. The coast of south-western Rhode Island is laced with good, long and sandy beaches.

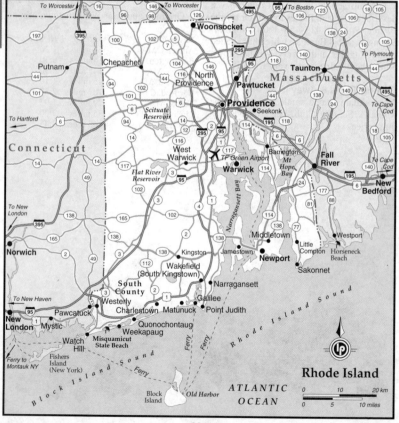

The Rhode Island Tourism Division (☎ 401-277-2601, 800-556-2484) is based at 1 Exchange St in Providence. The Rhode Island Traveler's Aid Society, also based in Providence, provides a Helpline (☎ 401-351-6500, 800-367-2700) that can help you with accommodations emergencies and directions.

Bed & Breakfast of Rhode Island (☎ 401-849-1298, 800-828-0000), PO Box 3291, Newport, RI 02840, can make reservations at over 200 B&Bs and inns in the state for a $5 postage and handling fee.

There's a Rhode Island Welcome Center as you head north on I-95, between exits 2 and 3; it's open daily, year round from 8 am to 5 pm, and from Memorial Day to Columbus Day to 6:30 pm.

Getting There & Around

See Providence for this information.

PROVIDENCE

Providence is a compact, walkable city of some 160,000 people. In size, it vies neck and neck with Worcester, MA, for the distinction of being the second-largest city in New England (after Boston).

While it is neither as populous or cosmopolitan as New England's hub city of Boston, nor as fun-loving and tourist-oriented as seaside Newport, Providence offers the discriminating visitor a sense of history and a wealth of fine architecture. For its size, the city is also well-endowed with excellent restaurants in all price ranges. (It is widely accepted among local "foodies" that Providence has better restaurants than Boston.)

Providence's high-profile universities and colleges (Brown, Rhode Island School of Design, Johnson & Wales) keep the city's social and arts scenes lively by providing an annual influx of new students.

For such a historic city, Providence is looking shiny and new these days. A multi-million-dollar downtown renovation project called Capital Center is nearing its final stages.

The city's skyline – punctuated by the Art Deco lines of the Fleet Bank building (often referred to as "the Superman building" because it evokes the one that the Caped One flew from in the old television show) – now sports a towering Westin Hotel, part of the Providence Convention Center complex in the heart of the new downtown.

Taking a cue from San Antonio (Texas), Providence has been busily reclaiming its long-neglected waterfront. The mammoth Waterplace Park project and its Riverwalk extensions, now largely completed, has moved the city's central rivers – the Moshassuck and the Woonasquatucket, which merge into the Providence River – back to their historic positions after more than a century of filling and dredging had reduced them to near invisibility.

Lining the "new/old" riverbanks are curvy, landscaped parks that invite strollers to see Providence's historic downtown from a new perspective. You can even rent kayaks and canoes for a paddle on the rivers themselves.

History

Ever since it was founded in 1636 by Roger Williams (1603-83), a religious outcast from Boston, Providence has been a city with an independent frame of mind. The gilded statue atop the Rhode Island State House even goes by the name *The Independent Man.*

Williams' guiding principle, the one that got him ejected from the Puritan Massachusetts Bay colony, was that all people should have freedom of conscience. He was an early advocate of separation between civil and religious authorities. With his new settlement of Providence, he put into practice these core beliefs, remaining on friendly terms with the local Narragansett Indians after purchasing from them the land for his bold experiment in tolerance and peaceful coexistence.

So it should perhaps not be surprising that Rhode Island became the first colony to declare independence from England in May, 1776. From that time until 1900, the state's two major cities – Providence and Newport – alternated as state capital, but Providence was the state's premier port city

RHODE ISLAND

following the devastation wrought by the British during the Revolutionary War.

The most significant name in Providence history after that of Roger Williams is that of the Brown family. John Brown, whose magnificent mansion on the East Side is open to the public, was a slave-trader who also opened trade with China to establish the family's wealth. John's brother Joseph was an architect whose fine buildings, including the First Baptist Meetinghouse, Market House and his brother John's mansion, still are among the most distinguished in the city. And Moses Brown, who unlike his slave-trader brother was an abolitionist and a pacifist, founded the Quaker school in Providence which is named for him. The last of the Brown brothers, Nicholas, was the founder of Brown University.

Like many small East Coast cities, Providence went into a precipitous decline in the 1940s and '50s as its manufacturing industries (textiles and costume jewelry) faltered. In the 1960s, preservation efforts led by Antoinette Downing salvaged the historic architectural framework of the city, and following a few stalls and starts in the decades since, Providence now appears to be on the comeback trail.

Even though much of Providence is new or even in progress, the city's main appeal is in its historic buildings. Its colorful colonial history is reflected in the multi-hued 18th-century houses that line Benefit St on the East Side. These are, for the most part, private homes, but many are open for tours one weekend each spring during the Providence Preservation Society's (☎ 401-831-7440) annual Festival of Historic Homes.

Benefit St itself is a story: rescued by local preservationists in the 1960s from misguided urban-renewal efforts that would have destroyed it, the street today offers a wealth of architectural and historical buildings, from the 1708 Stephen Hopkins House (open by appointment) to the clean, Greek Revival lines of the 1838 Providence Athenaeum, a privately operated subscription library and rare books collection that is a must-see for bibliophiles.

Downtown, the Beaux Arts style of City Hall makes an imposing centerpiece to Kennedy Plaza, and the stately white dome of the Rhode Island State House (designed by McKim, Mead & White in 1904) is visible from many corners of the city. America's first indoor shopping mall – the 1828 Greek Revival Providence Arcade – is an airy, tile-floored space with shops and cafes on three floors.

Victorian and Queen Anne-style houses line Broadway and Elmwood Aves in an area of Providence that fell into decay for several decades before reclamation in the early 1980s. These once-grand houses, though, are still jewels in the rough.

Orientation

Providence is situated at the head of Narragansett Bay astride two rivers, the Moshassuck and the Woonasquatucket, which merge into the Providence River at the new Waterplace Park. Surrounding Providence are the populous suburbs of Warwick, Cranston, Johnston, Pawtucket and East Providence, which are where most people who work in Providence actually live.

I-95 is the main north-south artery through Providence, with I-195 splitting from it eastward towards Cape Cod. Take the Downtown exit from I-95, or the Wickenden St exit from I-195, to reach the city center.

Kennedy Plaza, with the Omni Biltmore Hotel to one side, is the center of the city. The Rhode Island State Capitol looms above the plaza from its hilltop perch, with the Amtrak train station in between.

The heart of the city is a surprisingly compact area, and you'll get more of the flavor of Providence on foot than you will in a car. Remember to look up! Many of downtown's most architecturally interesting building facades are several stories above street level.

Information

Tourist Offices Call ☎ 800-556-2484 for the Rhode Island Tourism Division, who can

RHODE ISLAND

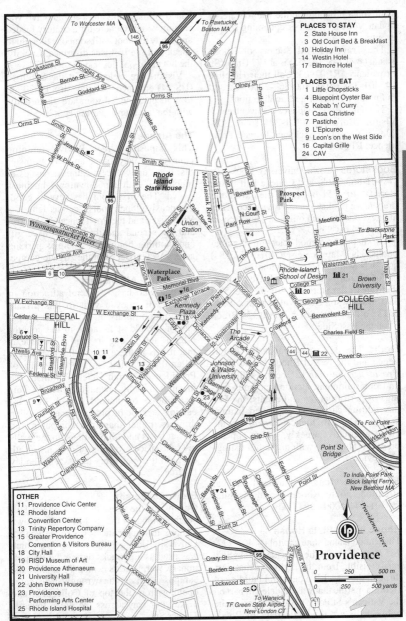

PLACES TO STAY
2 State House Inn
3 Old Court Bed & Breakfast
10 Holiday Inn
14 Westin Hotel
17 Biltmore Hotel

PLACES TO EAT
1 Little Chopsticks
4 Bluepoint Oyster Bar
5 Kebab 'n' Curry
6 Casa Christine
7 Pastiche
8 L'Epicureo
9 Leon's on the West Side
16 Capital Grille
24 CAV

OTHER
11 Providence Civic Center
12 Rhode Island
   Convention Center
13 Trinity Repertory Company
15 Greater Providence
   Convention & Visitors Bureau
18 City Hall
19 RISD Museum of Art
20 Providence Athenaeum
21 University Hall
22 John Brown House
23 Providence
   Performing Arts Center
25 Rhode Island Hospital

Providence

0   250   500 m
0   250   500 yards

send you a brochure on the whole state, or update you on current or upcoming special events.

The Travelers Aid Society of Rhode Island (☎ 401-521-2255) is at 177 Union St, Providence, RI 02903. Call their Helpline (☎ 401-351-6500, 800-367-2700) for aid in finding a room or getting directions.

The Greater Providence Convention & Visitors Bureau (☎ 401-274-1636, 800-233-1636) is at 30 Exchange Terrace, Providence, RI 02903.

Bookstores Brown University Bookstore (☎ 401-863-3168) and College Hill Bookstore (☎ 401-751-6404) are the most comprehensive bookstores in Providence. They are next door to each other on Thayer St on the city's East Side.

For maps and a good selection of guidebooks, The Map Center (☎ 401-421-2184) at 671 N Main St is a gold mine.

For a quality selection of used books, there are Cellar Stories (☎ 401-521-2665) at 190 Mathewson St downtown, and Seward's Folly (☎ 401-861-6271) at 139 Brook St on the East Side.

Media The daily newspaper for Providence and the rest of Rhode Island is the *Providence Journal*. Lifebeat, a daily arts and entertainment section, includes listings of performances and events; the Friday edition carries an expanded listings section. The Providence *Phoenix* is the city's alternative weekly, which appears on every Thursday with nightclub listings and reviews.

Medical Services If you need medical attention, go to Rhode Island Hospital (☎ 401-444-4000), 593 Eddy St.

Rhode Island State House

The Rhode Island state capitol (☎ 401-277-2357) rises above the Providence skyline, easily visible from the highways that pass through the city. It's a beautiful building of Georgia marble that was modeled in part on the Vatican's St Peter's Basilica. Inside the public halls are the battle flags of Rhode

Island military units and a curious Civil War cannon which sat here for a century loaded and ready to shoot until someone thought to check and see if it was disarmed. Luckily, the hot air of politics hadn't set it off.

Visitors are welcomed at the Smith St (US 44) entrance weekdays from 8:30 am to 4:30 pm. Guided tours are given daily, with the last tour departing at 3:30 pm.

The Arcade

This imposing Greek Revival building connecting Weybosset and Westminster Sts, open daily except Sunday, bustles at lunchtime with the downtown business crowd. The first floor has several good, inexpensive lunch spots, such as Jensen's, Villa Pizza and the Providence Cookie Co, and the second and third floors have gift and clothing boutiques. There is parking across Weybosset St in the Arcade garage.

Providence Athenaeum

Anyone who has a visceral attraction to books will enjoy a visit to this private subscription library at 251 Benefit St. It's one of the oldest libraries in the country (1831), and among its claims to fame is that it was in these stacks that poet Edgar Allan Poe carried on his courtship of Providence's Sarah Helen Whitman, the inspiration for his poem, *Annabel Lee*. This is a library of the old school: the card catalog is kept in old-fashioned wooden drawers, rather than in a computer, and plaster busts and oil paintings on the walls give the place a feeling of closeness with the past. It's open every day except Sunday for free.

Brown University

Occupying the crest of the College Hill neighborhood on the East Side, the Brown campus has authentic Ivy League charm. University Hall, a 1770 brick edifice which was used as a barracks during the Revolutionary War, is at its center. To explore the campus, start at the wrought-iron gates opening from the top of College St and make your way across the green towards Thayer St.

John Brown House

Called the "most magnificent and elegant mansion that I have ever seen on this continent" by John Quincy Adams, this brick residence at 52 Power St was built in 1788 for Providence merchant John Brown by his brother Joseph. It is now operated as a museum house by the Rhode Island Historical Society. It's closed Monday; admission is $5 adults, $3 students and seniors, $2 children. Tours run every half hour between 11 am and 3:30 pm.

RISD Museum of Art

Exhibits in the small but select Museum of Art of the Rhode Island School of Design (☎ 401-454-6500), 224 Benefit St, include 19th-century French paintings, classical Greek, Roman and Etruscan art, Medieval and Renaissance works, European and Oriental decorative arts and examples of 19th- and 20th-century American painting, furniture and decorative arts. Admission costs $2 for adults, 50¢ for seniors and children five to 18. Opening hours are complicated, but in summer are generally from noon to 5 pm, Wednesday through Saturday.

Neighborhoods

Federal Hill Among the most colorful of Providence's neighborhoods is Federal Hill, which is so fervently Italian that it paints the colors of the flag of Italy down its main street, Atwells Ave, each year for the Festival of St Joseph (usually the last week of April). While Federal Hill is especially vibrant for this event, it is always a great place to wander, taking in the aromas of sausages, peppers and garlic from a multitude of neighborhood groceries such as Tony's Colonial Market, Providence Cheese and Roma Gourmet. Scialo Bakery on Atwells is the prototypical Italian pastry shop, with its sweet confections displayed tantalizingly atop paper doilies in its glass cases. Many of Providence's best restaurants are on Atwells Ave as well.

Fox Point The city's substantial Portuguese population still centers in this waterfront section of the city, though some gentrification has taken place with influxes of Brown University professors and students and artists from RISD. But you can still find an Old World-style grocery like the Friends Market on Brook St tucked in among the trendy coffeehouses, salons and galleries. Most of the action in Fox Point centers around Wickenden St.

Blackstone Boulevard The Boulevard is not so much a neighborhood as an address that says you've arrived. Along this two-mile avenue divided by a park-like central strip of green space in Providence's East Side are some of Providence's most imposing residences, most dating to the 1920s and '30s and surrounded by lush landscaping. Joggers favor Blackstone Park, and it's also worthwhile to explore the lovely grounds of Swan Point Cemetery on the banks of the Seekonk River.

Waterplace Park & Riverwalks

Cobblestone paths lead along the Woonasquatucket River to this central pool and fountain, overlooked by a stepped amphitheater where outdoor performance artists liven up the scene in warm weather. Waterplace is the centerpiece of Providence's Capital Center reconstruction project, which is nearing completion after more than a decade. Take a look at the historical maps and photos mounted on the walls of the walkway beneath Memorial Drive to get an idea of how the massive project has changed the face of downtown Providence.

Prospect Terrace Park

A great spot from which to get an overview of the city, Prospect Terrace is a small pocket of green space off Congdon St on the East Side. In warm weather, you'll find students throwing Frisbees, office workers picnicking and people just gazing at the view, which is extra special at sunset. The monumental statue facing the city is that of Providence founder Roger Williams, whose remains were moved to this site in 1939.

Roger Williams Park

In 1871, Ms Betsey Williams, great-great-great granddaughter of the founder of Providence, donated her farm to the city as a public park. Today this 420-acre expanse of greenery only a short drive south of Providence includes lakes and ponds, forest copses and broad lawns, picnic grounds, the Planetarium and Museum of Natural History, boathouse, greenhouses, and Ms Williams' cottage.

Perhaps the park's most significant attraction is the **Roger Williams Park Zoo** (☎ 401-785-3510). The zoo, home to more than 600 animals, is open daily from 9 am to 5 pm (weekends until 6 pm). To reach the park, go south on I-95 from Providence to exit17 (Elmwood Ave). If you're heading north from Connecticut or the Rhode Island beaches, take exit 16.

East Bay Bicycle Path

Starting at India Point Park on the Narragansett Bay waterfront in Providence, the East Bay Bicycle Path wends its way 14.5 miles south along a former railroad track. The scenic, mostly flat, paved path follows the shoreline to the pretty seaport of Bristol. State parks along the route make good spots for picnics.

Boating

Kayaks and canoes may be rented from Baer's River Workshop (☎ 401-453-1633) at 222 Water St, downtown. Baer's offers an urban boating experience, with paddlers heading into the heart of the city along the newly landscaped riverways.

Places to Stay

Camping Camping areas are outside the city, but as Rhode Island is small, they aren't all that far away.

George Washington Management Area (☎ 401-568-2013), on US 44 two miles east of the Connecticut state line in Gloucester, has 45 simple tent and RV sites ($12 for out-of-staters/$8 residents) and two shelters ($20 per night) in a wooded area overlooking the Bowdish Reservoir.

If the state-operated campground is full,

try the neighboring private *Bowdish Lake Camping Area* (☎ 401-568-8890), with 450 sites priced from $14 to $25, depending upon location and facilities. There's also *Camp Ponagansett* (☎ 401-647-7377), two miles north of RI 102 on Rustic Hill Rd, with 40 RV sites open from mid-April through mid-October.

Inns & B&Bs Bed & Breakfast of Rhode Island (☎ 401-849-1298, 800-828-0000, fax 401-849-1306), 38 Bellevue Ave (PO Box 3291), Newport, RI 02840, has listings for the entire state, including Providence.

Old Court Bed & Breakfast (☎ 401-751-2002), 144 Benefit St, has 10 rooms in an elegant 1863 Italianate building in the heart of Providence's historic area. Rates are from $110 to $135.

The State House Inn (☎ 401-785-1235), 43 Jewett St, in a restored 1880s house close to the Rhode Island State House, is decorated in simple Shaker style. Rates are $99 to $109.

Hotels The *Westin Hotel* (☎ 401-598-8000), 1 W Exchange St, is the city's newest high-rise, opened in 1994. Its 363 rooms range from $165 to $200.

The *Biltmore Hotel* (☎ 401-421-0700), Kennedy Plaza, is a classic grand hotel of the 1920s. Rooms cost $150.

The *Holiday Inn* (☎ 401-831-3900), 21 Atwells Ave at I-95, has recently been refurbished and is conveniently located right next to the Civic Center between downtown and Federal Hill. Rates are $100 to $116 per room.

Places to Eat

Providence is a great place to find a good meal in almost any price range. Both Rhode Island School of Design and Johnson & Wales University have culinary programs that annually turn out creative new chefs to liven up the city's restaurant scene.

With its large Italian population, Providence is well-endowed with the proverbial "great little Italian places." For modestly priced hearty fare in a family-run place, *Casa Christine* (☎ 401-453-6255), 145 Spruce

St, is a top choice for locals, with main courses priced from $9 to $12.

At the higher end of the price scale, *L'Epicureo* (☎ 401-454-8430), 238 Atwells Ave, features wood-grilled meats and inventive pasta dishes for $17 to $22.

For seafood, the *Bluepoint Oyster Bar* (☎ 401-272-6145), 99 N Main St, is a chic little place at the base of College Hill that is renowned for its sophisticated wine list and fresh seafood dishes. Plan to spend about $100 for two at dinner with wine, tax and tip included.

The *Capital Grille* (☎ 401-521-5600), 1 Cookson Place, in the former Providence train station, is the place to go for a truly great steak. With the atmosphere of a posh men's club, the Capital Grille is where the city's movers and shakers go to see and be seen. Dinner costs $40 to $50 per person, all in; lunch is somewhat cheaper.

A casual bistro with modestly priced food, *Leon's on the West Side*, (☎ 401-273-1055), 166 Broadway, features inventively prepared entrees, salads, pizzas, and pasta dishes. Leon's also has great brunches on Saturday and Sunday. Most main courses are in the range of $8 to $19.

Another popular bistro is on the East Side: *Rue de l'Espoir* (☎ 401-751-8890), 99 Hope St, is not as French as it sounds. The menu is eclectic and ever-changing; prices are moderate, with main courses priced from $11 to $17. The Rue also does a great breakfast.

For Chinese food of the fiery Szechuan variety, *Little Chopsticks* (☎ 401-351-4290), 495 Smith St, is a good choice. You'll find a mixture of Thai, Vietnamese and Chinese at the *Gourmet House*, (☎ 401-621-9818), 787 Hope St.

Indian food is the specialty at *Kebab 'n' Curry* (☎ 401-273-8844), 261 Thayer St; Chicken Tikka Masala is a favorite here.

When you really want a special dessert and coffee, *Pastiche* (☎ 401-861-5190), 92 Spruce St, is the place to go. Tucked away on a side street of Federal Hill, Pastiche is a sweet little place, awash in soothing colors and warmed by a fire in winter. Other popular coffeehouses are the *Coffee Exchange* (☎ 401-273-1198), 207 Wickenden St, and *CAV* (☎ 401-751-9164), 14 Imperial Place. CAV also has live music and poetry readings in the evening.

For a down-home, diner-style breakfast, rather than a fancy brunch, try the *Modern Diner* (☎ 401-726-8390), 364 East Ave, on the Providence-Pawtucket town line.

Entertainment

The Providence Civic Center (☎ 401-331-6700), 1 LaSalle Square, is the place to see touring rock groups as well as sporting events (see Spectator Sports, below).

Theater *Trinity Repertory Company*, (☎ 401-351-4242), 201 Washington St, performs classic and contemporary plays in the historic Lederer Theater downtown. Trinity is a favorite try-out space for Broadway productions, and it's not unusual for stars such as Olympia Dukakis or Jason Robards to turn up in a performance. Over several decades, Trinity Rep has earned a reputation for adventurous productions, but mainstream audiences are satisfied as well.

Contemporary and avant garde productions are staged by several smaller theater companies in Providence. Check local listings in the newspaper or call Alias Stage (☎ 401-831-2919) at 31 Elbow St, or New Gate Theater (☎ 401-421-9680) at 134 Mathewson St, for upcoming performances. *Leeds Theatre at Brown University* (☎ 401-863-2838) offers productions ranging from traditional to contemporary, featuring student actors.

The Providence Performing Arts Center (☎ 401-421-2787) at 220 Weybosset St is a popular venue for touring Broadway shows such as *Cats* and *Phantom of the Opera*. The former Loew's Theater building, which dates to 1928, has a lavish, Art Deco interior that has been restored to its original splendor.

Cinemas The *Cable Car Cinema* (☎ 401-272-3970), 204 S Main St, invites its patrons to sit on couches while they enjoy the show. The Cable Car specializes in offbeat and foreign films. The popcorn is all-you-can-eat, and there are often informal performances by local talents to warm the audience up for the show.

The *Avon* (☎ 401-421-3315), 260 Thayer St in the heart of the college district, also has foreign films, cult classics and experimental movies.

Nightclubs With its large population of students, Providence has a lively nightclub scene. Refer to the Lifebeat section in the daily *Providence Journal* for listings of performers, venues and schedules.

Legendary in the city is *Lupo's Heartbreak Hotel* (☎ 401-272-5876), 239 Westminster St, which hosts national acts (progressive rock, R&B, blues) in an intimate space that usually accommodates some dancing. Nearby are the smaller *Met Cafe* (☎ 401-861-2142), 130 Union St, and the *Strand* (☎ 401-272-0444), 79 Washington St. The *G Clef* (☎ 401-273-0095), 580 S Main St, has jazz.

Brewpubs Providence has several fine brewpubs. The *Union Station Brewery* (☎ 401-274-2739), 36 Exchange Terrace, is always bustling with the downtown crowd, who come as much for the convivial atmosphere and fine food as for the selection of American-style home-brews.

Trinity Brewhouse (☎ 401-453-2337), 186 Fountain St, also brews its own, but its beer is more in the hop-heavy Irish/British style. Trinity also offers a hearty selection of food in a casual atmosphere.

Spectator Sports The *Pawtucket Red Sox* (☎ 401-724-7300), a Triple-A (minor league) farm team for the Boston Red Sox, play all spring and summer long at McCoy Stadium in Pawtucket, just across the city line from Providence. A night here, complete with ballpark franks and peanuts, is a favorite way for baseball addicts to get a fix without the hassle and cost of driving to and parking at Fenway Park in Boston.

The *Providence Bruins* hockey team, another farm team for Boston, play a regular schedule at the Civic Center in the fall and winter.

Things to Buy
Providence is not really a shopper's city. Over the past several decades, the once-vigorous downtown shopping district has emptied out as merchants fled the city for the more customer-friendly suburbs just a 15-minute drive from the city. Garden City in Cranston and the Warwick and Rhode Island Malls in Warwick are the places to head to find all the usual suspects: The Gap, The Limited, Victoria's Secret and the rest.

What's left downtown are some small shops, with a heavy concentration in men's business clothes. On the East Side, near Brown University, there are a few streets that merit a shopping stroll: Thayer St is a lively student strip which has a couple of fine bookstores, several music stores and a handful of cafes and inexpensive restaurants. Wickenden St has more cafes and a good selection of antiques shops and informal art galleries.

Getting There & Away
Air TF Green State Airport (☎ 401-737-4000) is in Warwick about 20 minutes south of Providence. Green is served by American Airlines, Continental, Delta, United and USAir. There is no airport bus. Taxi services include Airport Taxi (☎ 401-737-2868) and Checker Cab (☎ 401-273-2222).

Bus Rhode Island Public Transit Authority (☎ 401-781-9400) links Providence with the rest of the state for fares ranging from 85¢ to $2.50. Bonanza Bus Lines (☎ 401-751-8800) connects Providence with Boston and Cape Cod.

Train Ten daily Amtrak (☎ 800-872-7245) trains connect Providence's Union Station with Boston (one hour) and New York (four hours).

For information on Amtrak's *Cape Codder* trains between New York City and Hyannis, MA, via Providence, see the Getting There & Away chapter.

Boston's MBTA Commuter Rail (☎ 617-222-3200, 800-392-6100) trains also run between Providence and Boston's South Station.

Car All of the major car rental companies have offices at TF Green Airport in Warwick. Avis (☎ 401-521-7900) has an office downtown as well.

Driving details for Providence are:

Destination	Mileage	Hr:Min
Boston, MA	45 miles	1:00
Hyannis, MA	50 miles	1:10
Mystic, CT	40 miles	0:50
New Bedford, MA	32 miles	0:45
New Haven, CT	104 miles	2:10
New London, CT	55 miles	1:10
New York, NY	185 miles	4:00
Newport, RI	30 miles	0:45

Boat Interstate Navigation Co runs summer ferries to Block Island. The Block Island Ferry Terminal is at the southern terminus of Water St at India Street Dock, west of India Point Park. See Block Island for details.

Getting Around
With the Capital Center project still in its final stages, traffic patterns in downtown Providence remain disrupted, and it can be frustrating to try to get from Point A to Point B. The best solution is to have patience as you drive, or, better yet, to walk.

Should you want a taxi, you'll always find one in front of the Biltmore Hotel on Kennedy Plaza.

NEWPORT
Perfectly situated for access by sea, Newport was an important commercial port, a conquered war prize and a wealthy summer resort before becoming one of New England's busiest and most entertaining tourist destinations. It is thronged all summer by young day-trippers, older bus tourists, foreign tourists and families whose cars pack its narrow colonial streets, bringing traffic to a standstill.

Much of Newport is beautiful, with restored colonial buildings, cobbled streets and surprising sea views. The rest is humdrum, a collection of crowded residential areas, cheerless condominium developments and decaying maritime industry facilities.

Most people visit Newport to see the sumptuous mansions – disingenuously called "summer cottages" by their fabulously wealthy owners – ranged along Bellevue Ave, with peerless views of the sea. Others come by yacht to visit friends, who may still live in some of the more secluded mansions. Yet other tourists come to the music festivals – classical, folk, jazz – which are among the most important in the USA. In addition, Newport boasts several of New England's most beautiful and oldest religious buildings.

You'll enjoy Newport, especially in July and August, but only if you plan carefully where to park your car and your body.

Orientation
Newport occupies the southwestern end of Aquidneck Island. Adjoining it to the north is Middletown, which holds many of the services, less expensive residential areas and unsightly commercial strips not allowed in (but needed by) Newport. Most cheap motels and guest houses are in Middletown, several miles north of the center, while the more expensive inns and hotels are in Newport proper.

Downtown Newport's main north-south commercial streets are America's Cup Ave and Thames (that's thaymz not temz) St, just in from the harbor.

Your initial destination should be the Newport Gateway Transportation & Visitors Center, which holds the bus station and the tourist office. Biking around town is probably the best way to go; see Getting Around, below, for rentals.

Parking Note Parking is particularly difficult and expensive. The best place is at the Newport Gateway Transportation & Visitors Center, which gives you the first half-hour for free, each additional half-hour for 75¢, to a maximum of $8 per day. If you park at a meter (25¢ for 15 minutes, up to two hours), observe its time limit scrupulously or you'll end up with a ticket.

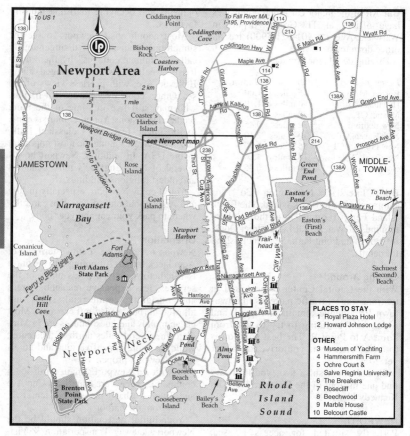

Newport Area

0   1   2 km

0   .5   1 mile

To US 1

Coddington
Point

*Coddington
Cove*

Bishop
Rock

*Coasters
Harbor*

To Fall River MA,
I-195, Providence

Coddington Hwy

Maple Ave

E Main Rd

Wyatt Rd

W Main Rd

E Main Rd

Valley Rd

Aquidneck Ave

Turner Rd

Green End Ave

Paradise Ave

Prospect Ave

Wolcott Ave

138A

MIDDLE-
TOWN

To Third
Beach

Purgatory Rd

Tuckerman Ave

Sachuest
(Second)
Beach

Girard Ave

JT Connell Rd

Admiral Kalbfus
Rd

Malbone Rd

Bliss Rd

Bliss Mine Rd

*Green
End
Pond*

*Easton's
Pond*

Easton's
(First)
Beach

Coaster's
Harbor
Island

Rose
Island

Goat
Island

*Newport
Harbor*

JAMESTOWN

*Narragansett
Bay*

Newport Bridge (toll)

Carrollus Ave

E Shore Rd

Ferry to Providence

see Newport map

Third St

Farewell St

America's Cup Ave

Broadway

Touro St

Mill St

Old Beach
Rd

Spring St

Memorial Blvd

Bellevue Ave

Cliff Walk

Trail-
head

Eustis Ave

Conanicut
Island

Castle
Hill
Cove

Fort
Adams

**Fort Adams
State Park**

3

Ridge Rd

Harrison Ave

Wellington Ave

Thames St

Narragansett Ave

Spring St

Leroy
Ave

Ochre Point Ave

Harrison
Ave

Ruggles Ave

Coggeshall Ave

6

Newport   Neck

Hammersmith Rd

Brenton Rd

Harard Rd

Ocean Ave

*Lily
Pond*

*Almy
Pond*

4

Harrison Ave

Ocean Ave

**Brenton
Point
State Park**

Gooseberry
Beach

Gooseberry
Island

Bailey's
Beach

Bellevue
Ave

7
5
8

9
10

*Rhode
Island
Sound*

Ferry to Block Island

PLACES TO STAY
1   Royal Plaza Hotel
2   Howard Johnson Lodge

OTHER
3   Museum of Yachting
4   Hammersmith Farm
5   Ochre Court &
    Salve Regina University
6   The Breakers
7   Rosecliff
8   Beechwood
9   Marble House
10 Belcourt Castle

Information

The Newport County Convention & Visitors Bureau (☎ 401-849-8048, 800-326-6030, fax 401-849-0291) operates the information office in the Newport Gateway Transportation & Visitor Center, 23 America's Cup Ave. It's open from 9 am to 6 pm (until 7 pm on Friday and Saturday). Information personnel won't make room reservations, but there are direct phones to hotels and inns and a list of vacancies.

For books on Newport and Rhode Island and especially the New England coast,

look for the Armchair Sailor bookstore (☎ 401-847-1219), 543 Thames St, which has an extensive nautical collection.

Mansions

During the 19th century, the wealthiest New York bankers and business families chose Newport as their summer resort. This was pre-income tax America, their fortunes were fabulous and their "summer cottages" – actually mansions and palaces – were fabulous as well. Most are ranged along Bellevue Ave. You must visit at least a few of them.

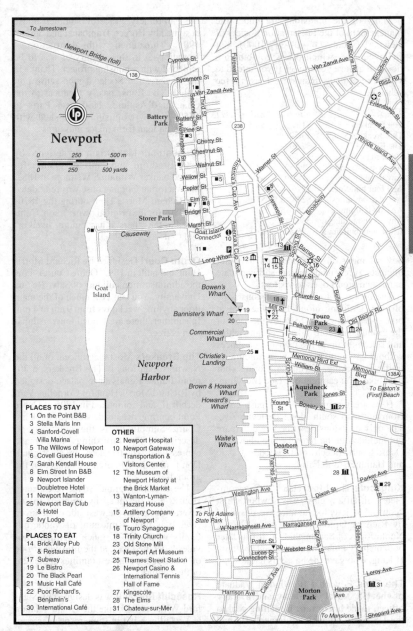

Newport

0   250   500 m
0   250   500 yards

Newport Harbor

Goat Island

Newport Bridge (toll)

To Jamestown

Battery Park

Storer Park

Causeway

Bowen's Wharf

Bannister's Wharf

Commercial Wharf

Christie's Landing

Brown & Howard Wharf

Howard's Wharf

Waite's Wharf

Touro Park

Aquidneck Park

Morton Park

To Fort Adams State Park

To Easton's (First) Beach

To Mansions

PLACES TO STAY
1 On the Point B&B
3 Stella Maris Inn
4 Sanford-Covell Villa Marina
5 The Willows of Newport
6 Covell Guest House
7 Sarah Kendall House
8 Elm Street Inn B&B
9 Newport Islander Doubletree Hotel
11 Newport Marriott
25 Newport Bay Club & Hotel
29 Ivy Lodge

PLACES TO EAT
14 Brick Alley Pub & Restaurant
17 Subway
19 Le Bistro
20 The Black Pearl
21 Music Hall Café
22 Poor Richard's, Benjamin's
30 International Café

OTHER
2 Newport Hospital
10 Newport Gateway Transportation & Visitors Center
12 The Museum of Newport History at the Brick Market
13 Wanton-Lyman-Hazard House
15 Artillery Company of Newport
16 Touro Synagogue
18 Trinity Church
23 Old Stone Mill
24 Newport Art Museum
25 Thames Street Station
26 Newport Casino & International Tennis Hall of Fame
27 Kingscote
28 The Elms
31 Chateau-sur-Mer

RHODE ISLAND

Many of the mansions are under the management of the Preservation Society of Newport County (☎ 401-847-1000), 424 Bellevue Ave, which offers combination tickets that save you money if you intend to visit several of its mansions. Here's a fee schedule:

Ticket	Adults	Kids 6 to 11
The Breakers	$10	$3.50
The Breakers Stable	$3.50	$2
The Elms	$7.50	$3
Other mansions	$6.50	$3
Any two buildings	$12.50	$4
Any three buildings	$17.50	$5
Any four buildings	$21	$6
Any five buildings	$24	$7
Any six buildings	$28	$8
Any seven buildings	$32	$9
All society buildings	$35.50	$10

Several mansions are operated by other interests. A few mansions are still in private hands and aren't open to visitors.

The best way to see the mansions is by bicycle. Cruising along Bellevue Ave at bike speed allows you to enjoy the view of the grounds, explore side streets and paths, and ride right up to the mansion entrances without having to worry about holding up traffic or parking. If you can't bring your own bike, you can rent one (see Bicycling, below).

Here are the mansions you pass going from north to south along Bellevue Ave. The only mansions described here that are not included in the fee schedule above are Ochre Court, Beechwood, Belcourt Castle and Hammersmith Farm.

Kingscote This Elizabethan fantasy, complete with Tiffany glass, was Newport's first "cottage" strictly for summer use, designed by Richard Upjohn in 1841 for George Noble Jones of Savannah, GA. It was later bought by China-trade merchant William H King, who gave the house its name.

The Elms Edward J Berwind, a graduate of the US Naval Academy and a Navy officer, made his fortune by selling coal to the US Navy after his retirement. He had this supremely graceful summer house designed by Horace Trumbauer and built in 1901. Threatened with destruction – incredibly – in this century, it was to be replaced with a housing project. Thanks to the Preservation Society, good sense prevailed. The Elms, nearly identical to the Chateau d'Asnieres built near Paris in 1750, is now exquisitely furnished with pieces on loan from major museums.

Chateau-sur-Mer Originally designed by Seth Bradford and built of granite for retired banker William S Wetmore in 1852, this Victorian Gothic house was remodeled by Richard Morris Hunt during the 1870s and '80s for the original owner's son. Compared to the others, it has a more "lived in" feel to it.

Ochre Court Designed by Richard Morris Hunt and built in 1892, Ochre Court is now the administration building of Salve Regina University. You can visit much of the main floor anytime weekdays from 9 am to 4 pm. In summer, there are guided tours. Admission is free.

The Breakers Most magnificent of all the Newport mansions is The Breakers, a 70-room Italian Renaissance palace designed by Richard Morris Hunt for Cornelius Vanderbilt II, and completed in 1895 at Ochre Point, a prime oceanside site next to Ochre Court. Sumptuous is the only way to describe it. The furnishings, most made expressly for The Breakers, are all original. Don't miss the Children's Cottage, on the grounds.

The Breakers' grand Stable & Carriage House, also designed by Hunt, is inland several blocks, on the west side of Bellevue Ave. It is now a museum of Vanderbilt family memorabilia, much of which provides a detailed look at the lifestyle of one of America's wealthiest families at the turn of the century.

Rosecliff Rosecliff was designed by Stanford White to look like the Grand Trianon at Versailles – but in some respects is even

Before Donald Trump, Martha Stewart and Bill Gates, America had the Astors, Carnegies and the Auchinclosses. Above, The Breakers is a Newport "cottage" built for the Vanderbilts.

grander. Its Marie Antoinette was Mrs Hermann Oelrichs (née Theresa Fair), an heiress of the Comstock Lode silver treasure. Mrs Oelrichs liked to entertain, so she saw to it that her house had Newport's largest ballroom.

Beechwood William B Astor built Beechwood (☎ 401-846-7288), 580 Bellevue Ave, in 1856. Today it is peopled by Beechwood Theater Company actors who portray a "typical" summer's houseful of family, staff and visitors. They bring the old house to life. Beechwood is open daily in summer from 10 am to 5 pm; November through mid-December until 4 pm; February through mid-May 10 am to 4 pm; it's closed mid-December through January. Admission costs $8, $6 for seniors and kids 12 and under.

Marble House Designed by Hunt and built in 1892 for William K Vanderbilt, younger brother of Cornelius II, Marble House takes its aspect from the palace of Versailles, complete with its original Louis XIV-style furnishings custom-made for the mansion.

The Gold Room (a ballroom) is aptly named. Have a look at the Chinese Teahouse as well.

Belcourt Castle Oliver Hazard Perry Belmont and his wife, the former Mrs William Vanderbilt, had Hunt design them a castle according to the 17th-century tastes of France's King Louis XIII. They then stocked it with period art, tapestries, glassware and even suits of armor from 32 countries. Tours at Belcourt Castle (☎ 401-846-0669), 657 Bellevue Ave, are offered daily for $7.50 for adults, $6 for seniors and recent college grads, $5 for students 13 to 18, and $3 for kids six to 12. Hours are 9 am to 5 pm from late May through mid-October, 10 am to 4 pm at other times.

Hammersmith Farm This "farm" (☎ 401-846-0420), on Ocean Ave southwest of Fort Adams State Park, is different from other Newport mansions. The 28-room house built in 1887 was the summer residence of the Auchincloss family. Mrs Hugh Auchincloss's daughter, Jacqueline Bouvier, was married to John F Kennedy in

Newport. The reception was held here at Hammersmith Farm. When Jack became president of the US and Jackie the First Lady, they visited the farm occasionally. It's now open to the public, with many of its original furnishings, from 10 am to 5 pm mid-April to mid-November, until 7 pm in summer. Admission costs $8 for adults, $3 for kids six to 12.

Museums

Newport has its share of museums, from the ponderous to the sublime and the ridiculous.

Housed in the Griswold Mansion (1864), a vast Victorian frame summer cottage at 76 Bellevue Ave, the **Newport Art Museum** (☎ 401-848-8200) has changing exhibits of paintings, sculpture, metalwork, ceramics, photography, etc. Call for current exhibits. It's open in summer daily from 10 am to 5 pm for $7, $4 for seniors and students 13 to 18; kids 12 and under get in for free. In winter it's open 10 am to 4 pm (Sunday 1 to 5 pm), closed Monday.

Located in Newport's historic Brick Market building, the **Museum of Newport History** (☎ 401-846-0813), operated by the Newport Historical Society (☎ 401-846-0813), traces the town's eventful history. It's open from 10 am to 5 pm (Sunday 1 to 5 pm), closed Tuesday. Admission costs $6, $5 for seniors, $3 for kids over five.

The **Wanton-Lyman-Hazard House**, 17 Broadway, is the oldest restored house in the city, having been built in 1675. Used as a residence by colonial governors and well-to-do residents, it's now a museum of colonial Newport operated by the Newport Historical Society. Call the society for hours of operation.

The **Old Stone Mill**, off Bellevue Ave in Touro Park, is a curious stone tower of uncertain provenance. Some people believe it was built by Norse mariners before the voyages of Columbus; others say by an early governor of the colony.

The **International Tennis Hall of Fame** (☎ 401-849-3990), 194 Bellevue Ave just south of Memorial Blvd, is in the historic Newport Casino building (1880),

once the wealthy Newporters' summer club. The forerunners of today's US Open Tennis Tournament were held here in 1881. If you have an interest in the game, or on playing on one of its 13 grass courts, pay $7 for adults, $4 for seniors, $3 for kids under 16 ($14 per family) and the pleasure is yours. It's open every day of the year from 10 am to 5 pm.

For decades Newport was the home port for America's Cup races, which is why it has a **Museum of Yachting** (☎ 401-847-1018) in Fort Adams State Park. It's open daily from 10 am to 5 pm, mid-May through October.

The **Artillery Company of Newport** (☎ 401-846-8488), 23 Clarke St, has an extensive collection of military uniforms, paraphernalia and memorabilia on view daily except Tuesday, June through September, from 10 am to 4 pm (Sunday noon to 4 pm). Admission costs $2.50 for adults, $1.75 for kids.

Touro Synagogue

This house of worship (☎ 401-847-4794), on Touro St near Spring St, was designed by Peter Harrison (who did King's Chapel in Boston) and built by the nascent Sephardic Orthodox Congregation Jeshuat Israel in 1763, and has the distinction of being North America's oldest Jewish house of worship. Inside, a letter to the congregation from President George Washington, written in 1790, hangs in a prominent spot. There's a historic cemetery just up the street.

The synagogue is open to visitors daily except Saturday from 10 am to 5 pm (until 3 pm on Friday) in summer; in spring and fall from 11 am to 1 pm (Sunday from 1 to 3 pm); in winter on Sunday from 1 to 3 pm, and by appointment.

Trinity Church

This Episcopal church (☎ 401-846-0660), Spring and Church Sts on Queen Anne Square, follows the design canon of Sir Christopher Wren's Palladian churches in London. Built in 1725-26, it has a fine wineglass-shaped pulpit, tall windows to let light flood in, and traditional box pews to keep out drafts of cold air. It's open daily from 10 am to 4 pm from mid-June through early September; from 1 to 4 pm in May and from early September through mid-October; and from 10 am to 1 pm the rest of the year.

Beaches
Newport's public beaches are on the eastern side of the peninsula along Memorial Blvd. Easton's Beach (☎ 401-848-6491), also called First Beach, is the largest, with bath houses and showers, snack bar and a fee of $7 per car ($10 on weekends). It's open from 9 am to 6 pm in summer.

East of Easton's Beach along Purgatory Rd is Sachuest (Second) Beach (☎ 401-846-6273) for $10, $15 on weekends, with showers and a snack bar; not far east of that for the same fee is Third Beach (☎ 401-847-1993), the favored spot for sailboarders.

Other "pocket" beaches exist along Ocean Ave, but most of these, such as Bailey's Beach, are fiercely private. An exception is Gooseberry Beach, open to the public for a fee of $8 per car, $2 for pedestrians and cyclists.

Cliff Walk
Cliff Walk is a footpath that runs along the eastern edge of the peninsula, with vast views of the sea to one side and the mansions along Bellevue Ave to the other. It starts at the inn called Cliff Walk Manor, just west of Easton's Beach, and goes south, then west almost to Bailey's Beach. It takes about an hour to stroll its entire length.

State Parks
Fort Adams, built between 1824 and 1857, crowns a rise at the end of the peninsula which juts northward into Newport Harbor. Like many American coastal fortresses, it had a short practical life as a deterrent, and a long life as a tourist attraction. It's the centerpiece of **Fort Adams State Park** (☎ 401-847-2400), the venue for the Newport Jazz and Folk Festivals and special events. A beach, picnic and fishing areas and a boat ramp are open daily from 6 am to 11 pm. The Museum of Yachting (see Museums, above), and the ferry to Block Island are here as well.

At the opposite end of the peninsula, **Brenton Point State Park**, due south of Fort Adams on Ocean Ave, is a prime place for gazing at the ocean and flying kites.

Bicycling
Newport is a fine town for bicycling. Rent your wheels at Firehouse Bicycle Company (☎ 401-847-5700), 25 Mill St, or at Ten Speed Spokes (☎ 401-847-5609), 18 Elm St, really on America's Cup Ave next to the Gateway Visitor Center.

You can rent mountain bikes and motorbikes (mopeds) at Adventure Sports Rentals (☎ 849-4400), 2 Bowen's Landing. Mountain bikes go for $5 per hour, $25 for eight hours, $140 per week. Motor bikes cost $16 for one hour, $35 for four, $45 for eight; two-person motorbikes are slightly less than twice those rates, but you need a motorcycle driver's license to rent them. An insurance fee is added to all rentals.

Special Events
Newport has always had many community celebrations, and since the town depends upon tourism, local leaders have designed a full schedule year round.

The most interesting and heavily-attended events are those in the summer. If you plan to attend, make sure you reserve accommodations and concert tickets in advance (tickets are usually on sale in mid-May). Newport is also home to many summer regattas and boat shows.

Newport Music Festival
    In July, this includes classical music concerts in many of the great mansions for $20 to $25 per ticket. For a schedule, write to the Newport Music Festival, PO Box 3300, Newport, RI 02840 or call ☎ 401-846-1133.
Int'l Tennis Hall of Fame Championships
    In July, this event hosts top professionals. Contact the Hall of Fame (☎ 401-849-3990), 194 Bellevue Ave, Newport, RI 02840.
Ben & Jerry's Newport Folk Festival
    In early August, this music fest has big-name

stars and up-and-coming groups performing at Fort Adams State Park and other venues around town. Call ☎ 401-847-3700 for information; tickets are from $25 to $40.

JVC Newport Jazz Festival

This event (☎ 401-847-3700) usually takes place on a mid-August weekend, with concerts at the Newport Casino (International Tennis Hall of Fame) and Fort Adams State Park.

Places to Stay

Newport's lodgings are expensive. The cozy inns and harborside hotels in the center of town generally charge $100 to $185 and up for a double room with breakfast in season. Rhode Island sales tax of 7% and Newport lodging tax of 5% will be added to your bill.

On weekend nights (Friday and Saturday) prices are highest; during the music festivals they're higher still. From Sunday through Thursday rates fall up to 30%.

Many lodgings require a two-night minimum on weekends, and on holidays a three-night minimum.

As rooms can be scarce in summer, you might want to use a reservations service. Anna's Victorian Connection (☎ 401-849-2489), 5 Fowler Ave, Newport, RI 02840, will make a reservation at no cost to you.

If you arrive without a reservation, go to the visitors center and ask to see their list of vacancies.

Camping The *Paradise Mobile Home Park* (☎ 401-847-1500), 459 Aquidneck Ave (RI 138A) in Middletown, northeast of Easton's Beach, takes self-contained RVs only, with full hookups.

The *Meadowlark Recreational Vehicle Park* (☎ 401-846-9455), 132 Prospect Ave (off RI 138A) in Middletown, has 40 RV sites open from mid-April through October for $21 per night.

There's also the *Melville Ponds Campground* (☎ 401-849-8212), 181 Bradford Ave (off RI 114), a municipal campground in Portsmouth, about 10 miles north of Newport center, with 57 tent sites ($13) and 66 RV sites ($18 to $22) open April through October. To find it, take RI 114 to

Stringham Rd, to Sullivan Rd, then north to the campground.

Across the Newport Bridge on Conanicut Island in Jamestown is the *Fort Getty Recreation Area* (☎ 401-423-7264), with 25 tent sites ($17) and 100 RV sites ($22). From RI 138, go south on North Rd, cross Narragansett Ave and continue on Southwest Ave, then merge into Beaver Tail Rd and turn right onto Fort Getty Rd.

Motels Compared to Newport's many wonderful inns, its motels lack character, but make up for it with modern conveniences and lower prices. Most are in Middletown on RI 114 (W Main Rd) and RI 138 (E Main Rd).

The *Best Western Mainstay Inn* (☎ 401-849-9880, 800-528-1234, fax 849-4391), 151 Admiral Kalbfus Rd (RI 138) near Newport Bridge, is a bit closer to downtown Newport and charges $129 for a room with two double beds on Friday and Saturday nights, but only $88 the rest of the week.

Howard Johnson Lodge (☎ 401-849-2000, 800-446-4656, fax 401-849-6047), 351 E Main Rd (RI 138), Middletown, charges $94 on weekdays, $134 on weekends.

Budget Host Inn (☎ 401-849-4700, 800-862-2006), also on W Main Rd (RI 114) in Middletown, charges $98 to $110 for rooms on Friday and Saturday, $68 to $78 Sunday through Thursday.

Royal Plaza Hotel (☎ 401-846-3555, 800-825-7072), on E Main Rd (RI 138), Middletown, is trim and well kept, with rooms for $109 Sunday through Thursday, from $159 to $175 on weekends.

Inns & B&Bs Unless otherwise mentioned, all inn and B&B rooms have private baths and come with breakfast.

Perhaps the best collection of small inns and B&Bs is in the neighborhood called The Point, north of the visitors center.

Sarah Kendall House (☎ 401-846-3979), 47 Washington St at Elm, is homey and nice. The rooms have air-con and cable TV, and most have water views for $135 to $185.

Stella Maris Inn (☎ 401-849-2862),

Church on the Hill, Lenox, MA

Peaceful Massachusetts

Berkshires harvest

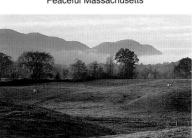
Amherst, Pioneer Valley, MA

A popular New England activity

KIM GRANT
The Breakers, Newport, RI

KIM GRANT
Narragansett Bay at Newport

KIM GRANT
Newport mansion

KIM GRANT
Block Island, RI

91 Washington St at Pine, is a big, quiet stone-and-frame inn with numerous fire-places. Its rooms with garden view rent for $125, with water view for $150 on summer weekends; during the week the rates fall to $95 and $110.

The Victorian "Stick-style" *Sanford-Covell Villa Marina* (☎ 401-847-0206), 72 Washington St at Walnut, was perhaps Newport's most lavish house when it was built in 1869. With a saltwater swimming pool and spa and a marvelous sunset-view, wrap-around veranda right over the water, it's still pretty lavish. Rooms range in price from $95 (small, no water view, shared bath) to $225 (large, lavish, grand water views). Some mid-price rooms have toilet and sink, but share showers.

On the Point B&B (☎ 401-846-8377), 102 3rd St between Sycamore and Van Zandt, is comfy and a bit farther from New-port's center, so rooms are reasonably priced at $95 to $105 on weekends, $75 to $90 on weekdays; the higher-priced rooms have private bath and color TV.

The Willows of Newport (☎ 401-846-5486), 8 Willow St, has four delicately, lav-ishly decorated rooms with private bath for $175 to $185 in-season, $88 to $98 off-season, breakfast in bed included.

In other neighborhoods, try: *Covell Guest House* (☎ 401-847-8872), 43 Fare-well St, several blocks east of The Point, was built in 1805 but renovated in 1982. Its five rooms cost $100 to $110.

Ivy Lodge (☎ 401-849-6865), 12 Clay St, is a block east of Bellevue Ave along Parker Ave, east of The Elms. Though not quite as grand as other Bellevue mansions, it is an impressive place, with guest rooms renting for $100 to $165, buffet breakfast included.

Hotels Newport's downtown hotels are convenient, elegant, beautiful and pricey.

The elegant *Newport Bay Club & Hotel* (☎ 401-849-8600, fax 846-6857), 337 Thames St (PO Box 1440), is a beautiful stone building right at the foot of Memorial Blvd on the waterfront. One-bedroom suites cost $169 on weekdays, $279 on weekends.

The posh 317-room *Newport Marriott* (☎ 401-849-1000, 800-228-9290, fax 849-3422), 25 America's Cup Ave, charges $199 to $219 during the week, $229 to $269 on summer weekends.

The 253-room *Newport Islander Double-tree Hotel* (☎ 401-849-2600, 800-222-8733), right out in the harbor on Goat Island (connected to the mainland via causeway), has all the amenities, which can be yours for $194 on weekdays, $244 on weekends.

Places to Eat

The cheapest breakfasts and sandwiches are at *Poor Richard's* (☎ 401-846-8768), 254 Thames St, where you can get two eggs, home-fried potatoes and toast for $2, and later a hamburger for under $3. The upstairs dining room, *Benjamin's* is a bit more expensive.

Cheap and fast salads and sandwiches are served at the local branch of the *Subway* chain of restaurants, Thames St at Mary St.

The ever-popular *Brick Alley Pub & Restaurant* (☎ 401-849-6334), 140 Thames St, has a huge menu of snacks, sandwiches, bar food, Mexican specialties and full meals, as well as Newport's most elaborate drinks list. Try the all-you-can-eat soup, salad and bread bar for $6 before 5 pm, $8 after. There are billiards and pinball in the back room, and an outdoor eating area.

The Black Pearl (☎ 401-846-5264), on Bannister's Wharf, is Newport's Old Reliable with three types of dining: the Tavern's sandwich board and seafood menu ($6 to $14) are long and varied, the atmos-phere suitably nautical. For traditional swordfish, steaks and rack of lamb ($12 to $24) in fancier surroundings, there's the Commodore's Room. The Hot Dog Annex supplies cheap snacks ($2). In my informal survey of clam chowder throughout New England, the Black Pearl's comes in first.

Music Hall Café (☎ 401-848-2330), 250 Thames St, is a Tex-Mex place where tacos, burritos, barbecue pork ribs and – incongruously – Italian pastas are priced less than $10, and most between $6 and $8.

For excellent food at moderate prices, get away from the crowds in the town center. The *International Café* (☎ 401-847-1033),

677 Thames St at Potter, serves a surprisingly varied dinner menu from 4:30 pm. Philippine egg rolls, sautéed lobster, Mexican salads, Thai specialties – you're never sure what'll be on the menu, but you can be sure the price will be reasonable, with full dinners below $20. Bring your own alcohol (which also keeps the price down). It's closed Monday and Tuesday.

Le Bistro (☎ 401-849-7778), on Bowen's Wharf, serves French country cuisine, and offers a great deal for those who want to dine early. Their Sunset Special, served between 5 and 6:30 pm, includes soup or salad, main course (which could be a one-pound lobster) and dessert for around $20, altogether.

Entertainment
This is a resort town, and in July and August it rocks at night (see Special Events). But really, any day is a good one for finding a congenial pub.

The Brick Alley Pub & Restaurant (see above) has an agreeable bar. The bar at *Salas'* (☎ 401-846-8772), 343 Thames St, draws a crowd of locals, boaters and fishers.

For dancing, check out *Thames Street Station* (☎ 401-849-9480), 337 Thames St, which features live entertainment Sunday through Thursday – everything from reggae to rock. The *Wharf Deli & Pub* (☎ 401-846-9233), 37 Bowen's Wharf, is a showcase for local talent seven nights a week.

Getting There & Away
Bonanza Bus Lines (☎ 401-846-1820), at Gateway Center, operates a half-dozen buses daily between Newport and Boston via Fall River, MA. The bus ride takes about 1¾ hours.

The Rhode Island Public Transit Authority (☎ 401-781-9400, 800-244-0444) runs buses on RI 60 between Newport (Gateway Center) and Providence (Kennedy Plaza, Francis St Terminus) at least every hour from around 5:30 am to 9:30 pm, for $3.

A summer ferry stops at Fort Adams Dock, taking on passengers to Block Island (a two-hour trip) from Providence; see Block Island for more information.

Getting Around
The Rhode Island Public Transit Authority (☎ 401-781-9400, 800-244-0444) runs limited service from the Gateway Center up Touro St, along Bellevue Ave and past Easton's Beach. Trips on Bus Route 61 run about every hour from morning to late afternoon, for $1.

See above for bicycling information.

BLOCK ISLAND
Ever since it was named one of 12 "Last Great Places" in the Western Hemisphere by the Nature Conservancy in 1991, Block Island has enjoyed a higher profile than ever before. Fortunately for those who love this quiet place adrift in the Atlantic, its notoriety hasn't gone to its head.

This 11-sq-mile island, shaped something like a pork chop, never had the celebrity cachet of Martha's Vineyard or Nantucket. Instead, it seems quietly content to be just what it is, a sleepy little island 13 miles off the Rhode Island coast with a Brigadoon-like air of otherworldliness.

History
In 1614, before the Pilgrims founded their settlement at Plymouth, MA, a mariner named Adriaen Block stopped at this island, giving it its name.

When colonists came to the region a decade later, relations with the local Pequot Indians were not particularly cordial. But by 1672 the thriving fishing town of New Shoreham was chartered on Block Island.

Fishing and farming were mainstays of the island's simple economy for almost two centuries. In the mid-1800s, the development of steam-powered vessels, and the wealth of the New England economy, made it possible for mainlanders to contemplate summer vacations on the island.

Block Island had its heyday as a summer resort in the 1890s, when steamboats made regular trips from New York and Boston, and the hotels were full of long-skirted ladies and men in straw-boaters. Today, the landscape has the spare, haunted feeling of an Andrew Wyeth painting, with stone walls

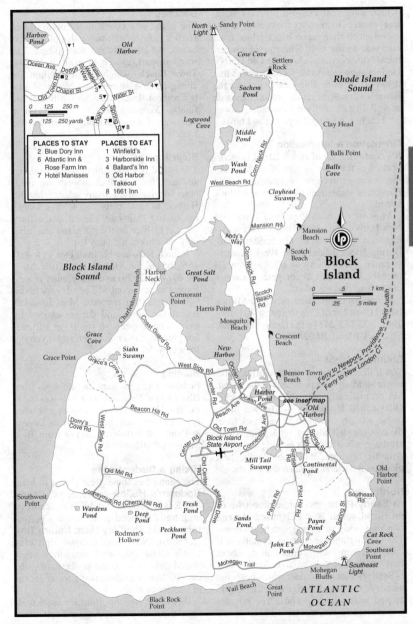

RHODE ISLAND

Block Island

North Light
Sandy Point
Cow Cove
Settlers Rock
Rhode Island Sound
Sachem Pond
Logwood Cove
Middle Pond
Clay Head
Balls Point
Balls Cove
Corn Neck Rd
Wash Pond
West Beach Rd
Clayhead Swamp
Mansion Rd
Andy's Way
Mansion Beach
Scotch Beach
Block Island Sound
Harbor Neck
Great Salt Pond
Cormorant Point
Harris Point
Mosquito Beach
Scotch Beach Rd
Crescent Beach
Grace Cove
Siahs Swamp
Grace Point
Grace's Cove Rd
Charlestown Beach
Coast Guard Rd
West Side Rd
New Harbor
Ocean Ave
Benson Town Beach
Ferry to Newport, Providence, Point Judith
Ferry to New London CT
Beacon Hill Rd
Center Rd
Beach Ave
Ocean Ave
Harbor Pond
see inset map
Old Harbor
High St
Spring St
Dorry's Cove Rd
West Side Rd
Old Town Rd
Connecticut Ave
Block Island State Airport
Mill Tail Swamp
Sunset Rd
Continental Pond
Old Harbor Point
Old Mill Rd
Center Rd
Old Center Rd
Lakeside Drive
Payne Rd
Pilot Hill Rd
Spring St
Southeast Rd
Cooneymus Rd (Cherry Hill Rd)
Southwest Point
Wardens Pond
Deep Pond
Fresh Pond
Sands Pond
Peckham Pond
Rodman's Hollow
John E's Pond
Payne Pond
Mohegan Trail
Cat Rock Cove
Southeast Point
Southeast Light
Mohegan Bluffs
Mohegan Trail
Vail Beach
Great Point
Black Rock Point
ATLANTIC OCEAN

Inset map (Old Harbor):

Harbor Pond
Old Harbor
Ocean Ave
Dodge St
Water St
Weldens St
Old Town Rd
Chapel St
Water St
High St
Spring St

0   125   250 m
0   125   250 yards

PLACES TO STAY
2 Blue Dory Inn
6 Atlantic Inn & Rose Farm Inn
7 Hotel Manisses

PLACES TO EAT
1 Winfield's
3 Harborside Inn
4 Ballard's Inn
5 Old Harbor Takeout
8 1661 Inn

demarcating centuries-old property lines, and few trees to interrupt the ocean views.

Not much changes on Block Island from one year to the next. The row of ginger-bread Victorian inns along the Old Harbor landing shows the same face to visitors that it did 50 or even 100 years ago, and the island's attractions remain much the same as well. In a nutshell (or a clamshell), those are beaches, boating, bicycling and birds.

Orientation & Information
It's confusing: all of Block Island is incorporated as the town of New Shoreham, but the main settlement is known as Old Harbor, or sometimes as the town of Block Island.

Most of the boating activity centers in New Harbor, the island's other main settlement on the shore of Great Salt Pond. During Block Island Race Week in early summer, yachtsmen come here from all over the East Coast to compete in a series of races around the island.

For tourist information, contact the Block Island Chamber of Commerce (☎ 401-466-2982, 800-383-2474), PO Drawer D, Water St, Block Island, RI 02807.

Southeast Light
You'll likely recognize this red brick lighthouse building from postcards of the island. Set dramatically atop 200-foot red-clay cliffs called **Mohegan Bluffs**, the lighthouse actually had to be moved back from the eroding cliff edge in 1993. With waves crashing below and sails moving across the Atlantic offshore, it's probably the best place on the island to watch the sun set.

North Light
At **Sandy Point**, the northernmost tip of the island, scenic North Light is at the end of a long sandy path lined with beach roses. The 1867 lighthouse contains a small maritime museum with information about famous island wrecks. Also at Sandy Point is **Settlers Rock** a boulder which bears the names of the island's original settlers, who arrived at this spot in 1661. The boulder was erected as a memorial in 1911.

Beaches
The island's east coast to the north of Old Harbor is lined with two miles of glorious beach, the Block Island State Beach. The southern part, closest to town, is Benson Town Beach, which has a pavilion for changing and showering. North of that is Crescent Beach, then Scotch Beach and finally Mansion Beach, named for a mansion of which nothing is left but the foundation.

Bicycling
The island is a convenient size for biking, and bicycles as well as mopeds are available for rental at many places in Old Harbor. In fact, many people save money by leaving their cars parked at the ferry dock in Galilee on the mainland and bring only their bikes for a day trip.

Rentals are available from Esta's (☎ 401-466-2651), the Old Harbor Bike Shop (☎ 401-466-2029) and many other places. Expect to pay about $15 per day for bikes, $40 per day for mopeds. Most islanders resent the noise and danger caused by tourists on mopeds, so you'll get a friendlier greeting (and more exercise) if you opt for a bicycle.

Boating
Fishing charters may be booked from Block Island Boat Basin (☎ 401-466-2631) in New Harbor. Kayaks, canoes and other types of boats may be rented from Oceans & Ponds (☎ 401-466-5131) or from Twin Maples (☎ 401-466-5547).

Hiking & Birdwatching
The island has some great places to hike: **Rodman's Hollow** (entrance off Cherry Hill Rd) is a 100-acre wildlife refuge laced with trails that end at the beach – perfect for a picnic. The **Clay Head Nature Trail** (off Corn Neck Rd) follows high clay bluffs along the beachfront, then veers inland through a maze-like series of paths cut into low vegetation that attracts dozens of species of birds.

Birdwatching opportunities are excellent, especially in spring and fall when migratory species are making their way north or south along the Atlantic Flyway. The island's verdant landscape and many freshwater ponds provide ample habitat.

Places to Stay

Camping is not allowed on the island, but there are some 35 B&Bs and small guest house-style inns. You should know, however, that many places have a two- or three-day minimum stay in summer, and advance reservations are a necessity. The chamber of commerce (see Orientation & Information, above) can advise on price ranges.

The *Rose Farm Inn* (☎ 401-466-2021), Box E, Roslyn Rd, is convenient both to Old Harbor and the beach on High St. The older part of the inn has fine views of the ocean; a newer addition called the Captain Rose House has nine rooms with more modern accouterments. Summer rates are $95 to $179 per room.

The *Blue Dory Inn* (☎ 401-466-2254, 800-992-7290), Box 488, Dodge St, has 14 small rooms decorated in Victorian style. It's a cozy little place located at the edge of Old Harbor near the beach. Summer rates are $135 to $195.

The 1879 *Atlantic Inn* (☎ 401-466-5883, 800-224-7422) on High St in Old Harbor, overlooks the activities at the ferry landing from a lofty perch high on a hill. The gracefully proportioned Victorian inn has 21 rooms and a wide porch, yours for $110 to $195 per room.

The fanciest hotel on the island is the *Hotel Manisses* (☎ 401-466-2063, 466-2421, 800-626-4773, fax 401-466-2858), Spring St, Old Harbor. With its high Victorian "widow's walk" turret and small but lushly furnished guest rooms, the Manisses combines sophistication with Block Island's relaxed brand of country charm. Summer rates are $150 to $300, buffet breakfast, wine and cheese hour and service (but not tax) included.

Places to Eat

For an inexpensive meal, *Old Harbor Takeout* (☎ 401-466-2935), Water St, is a good bet for sandwiches to take on a picnic.

The *1661 Inn* (☎ 401-466-2421), on Spring St, serves an excellent – if somewhat pricey – outdoor buffet brunch on a grassy hillside overlooking the Atlantic.

For lunch, the *Harborside Inn* (☎ 401-466-5504), on Water St, is a good choice. You can't miss the red umbrellas of its outdoor patio as you step off the ferry at Old Harbor. Expect to spend $10 to $20 per person for the pleasure, almost twice that at dinnertime.

Ballard's Inn (☎ 401-466-2231), in Old Harbor near the ferry landing, is popular with young people and the boating crowd. Lobster, seafood and standard fare is served in a cavernous dining room draped with flags.

For a classier dining experience, one of the best dining rooms on the island is at the Hotel Manisses (☎ 401-466-2421), on Spring St. Vegetables come from the hotel's garden, and the style of cooking is creative, often featuring fresh local seafood. Full dinners cost around $40 to $50 per person, all in.

Another classy place is *Winfield's* (☎ 401-466-5856), Corn Neck Rd, with exposed wood ceiling beams, white tablecloths and a menu that features such classics as rack of lamb and filet mignon, at prices similar to the Manisses.

Entertainment

No one goes to Block Island for the nightlife, but there are a couple of places that might keep you up past 10 pm. *McGovern's Yellow Kittens* (☎ 401-466-5855), on Corn Neck Rd just north of Old Harbor, has live music on weekends and jukebox music on weekday nights. It's been an island mainstay for decades, attracting New England-area bands and keeping patrons happy with pool, table tennis and darts.

The elevated porch of the *National Hotel* (☎ 401-466-2901) on Water St across from the ferry landing, has a relaxed "Margaritaville" atmosphere, with live music on most summer evenings.

There are two places to catch first-run movies on Block Island: *Oceanwest Theater* (☎ 401-466-2971) in New Harbor, and the *Empire* (☎ 401-466-2555) in a former rollerskating rink in Old Harbor.

Things to Buy
Opportunities for shopping are limited. Most shops are small, seasonal boutiques along Water and Dodge Sts in Old Harbor. Worth a look are the Ragged Sailor (crafts, paintings and folk art), the Scarlet Begonia (jewelry and craft items for the home) and the Star Department Store, a wood-floored classic that calls itself "Block Island's general store." This is the place to go for saltwater taffy and corny island souvenirs.

Getting There & Away
Air New England Airlines (☎ 401-596-2460, 800-243-2460) provides air service between Westerly State Airport, on Airport Rd off RI 78, and Block Island (25 minutes) for $56 per person, roundtrip.

Boat Interstate Navigation Co and Nelseco Navigation Co (☎ 401-783-4613 for reservations, for offices 203-442-7891, 442-9553), based in New London, CT, operate the ferry service to Block Island.

Interstate operates the car-and-passenger ferries from Galilee State Pier, Point Judith, to Old Harbor, Block Island, a voyage of just over an hour. Adults pay $10.50 for a same-day roundtrip ticket, children less. Cars are carried for $20 each way; reserve your car space in advance.

A daily Interstate passenger boat runs in summer from Providence's India Street Dock (four hours) via Newport's Fort Adams Dock (two hours) to Old Harbor, Block Island, for $8 per adult one way, half fare for kids, with greater parking hassles at the mainland ports. The boat takes bikes, but no cars.

Nelseco operates a daily ferry from mid-June to mid-September departing New London, CT, at breakfast time, returning from Old Harbor, Block Island, in the late afternoon. The two-hour voyage costs $15 for adults, $10 for kids, $50 roundtrip for a car (reserve in advance).

Getting Around
Block Island Car Rental (☎ 401-466-2297) rents cars, or you can hire a taxi. There are usually several available at the ferry dock in Old Harbor or in New Harbor. See Bicycling, above, for moped and bicycle rentals.

WATCH HILL
One of the toniest summer colonies in the Ocean State, Watch Hill occupies a spit of land at the southwesternmost point of Rhode Island, just south of Westerly. Drive into the village along winding RI 1A, and the place grabs you: huge shingled and Queen Anne summer houses command the rolling landscape from their perches high on rocky knolls. These houses show the wealth of their owners with subtle good taste: though they were built around the turn of the century, contemporaneously with Newport's mansions, they aren't flashy palaces. Perhaps partly because of that, Watch Hill's houses are still in private hands, while Newport's became white elephants, rescued only as tourist attractions.

Visitors not lucky enough to own a summer house here spend their time at the beach and browsing in the shops along Bay St, the main street. An ice cream cone from St Clair's Annex and a twirl on the Flying Horses Carousel make a summer day complete.

Flying Horses Carousel
The antique merry-go-round on Bay St dates from 1883. Besides being among the few historic carousels still in operation in the country, it boasts a unique design: its horses are suspended on chains so that they really do "fly" outward as the carousel spins. Rides cost 50¢.

Activities
For a long, leisurely beach walk, the half-mile stroll out to **Napatree Point** at the westernmost tip of Watch Hill is unbeatable. With the Atlantic on one side, and yacht-studded Little Narragansett Bay on the other, Napatree is a protected conserva-

tion area, so walkers are asked to stay on the trails and off of the dunes.

The nearest state beach to Watch Hill is **Misquamicut State Beach**, three miles to the east along RI 1A, but there is a fine beach right in Watch Hill, in front of the Ocean House Hotel. Access to the beach is by a right-of-way off of Bluff Rd, but there is no parking nearby, and neighboring property owners are vigilant about keeping beachgoers to the public area below the high tide line. There's also the small **Watch Hill Beach**, open to the public for a fee, behind the Flying Horses Carousel.

Places to Stay

The *Ocean House Hotel* (☎ 401-348-8161), 2 Bluff Ave, is the grand old lady of hotels in Watch Hill, the lone survivor of a series of fires and hurricanes that had destroyed its Victorian sisters by about 1950. While it's true that the imposing, yellow-clapboard Ocean House is looking a bit less than spiffy inside these days, the place does have the authentic ambiance of bygone days. The oceanfront porch is a great spot to sit with a drink after a day at the beach. Rooms cost about $200, breakfast and dinner included.

More modern and comfortable is the *Inn at Watch Hill* (☎ 401-596-0665), with motel-style rooms priced from $130 to $150 set above the row of shops on Bay St.

Places to Eat

The most atmospheric restaurant is the *Olympia Tea Room* (☎ 401-348-8211) on Bay St. The Olympia is an authentic 1918 soda fountain turned into a classy bistro, open in-season for breakfast, lunch and dinner. Varnished wooden booths, black-and-white checkered tiles on the floor and the antique marble-topped soda fountain all give the place an air of authenticity.

For more inexpensive food, including good take-out for picnics, there's the *Bay Street Deli* (☎ 401-596-6606), 110 Bay St. The *St Clair's Annex* ice cream shop across the street, run by the same family for more than a century, features over 30 flavors of homemade ice cream.

Things to Buy

Most shops are on Bay St, but one very special place is on RI 1A a few miles out of the center of town. Sun Up Gallery (☎ 401-596-3430), 95 Watch Hill Rd, has a wonderful selection of crafts by American artists, gifts, jewelry and women's clothes. The place has a summery setting on the banks of the Pawcatuck River.

Getting There & Away

Watch Hill is at the end of Watch Hill Rd, six miles south of Westerly, and 12 round-about miles east of Stonington, CT, by car.

Rhode Island Beaches

It's not by accident that Rhode Island is nicknamed the Ocean State. It's the little state with 400 miles of coastline – though most of those miles are actually on Narragansett Bay (which is better for boaters than for beachgoers).

Most public beaches in Rhode Island charge parking fees ranging from $5 to $15 for the day from mid-June to Labor Day. The best deals are the state beaches, for which state residents pay just $4 to $5 to park and out-of-staters $8 to $10. Reasonably priced season passes (which may be used at any state beach) are a good option if you're going to be spending more than a few days at the beach during your stay.

This is a selective look at some of the best beaches the Ocean State has to offer.

SOUTH COUNTY BEACHES

Rhode Island's topography means that it has two very different styles of ocean beaches. The best known beaches in the state are those in what is known as South County, the colloquial name for the southwestern coastline towns from Narragansett to Watch Hill in Westerly.

These beaches, which trace the coast like a necklace looped with tidal salt ponds, are similar in nature and, geologically speak-

RHODE ISLAND

ing, are all the same beach: a wide apron of pristine sand separating huge salt ponds such as Quonochontaug and Ninigret from the surfy, generally seaweed-free open ocean.

The salt ponds are home to multitudes of waterfowl and shellfish, and some (such as Trustom Pond in South Kingstown) have been designated as national wildlife refuges. If you're the type of person who gets bored just lying in the sun, take a bird-watching walk around the salt ponds instead. You're likely to see herons, egrets and sandpipers hunting for lunch, and, at low tide, clams squirting from beneath the muddy sand.

For information on South County beaches and attractions, contact the South County Tourism Council (☎ 401-789-4422, 800-548-4662), 4808 Tower Hill Rd, in Wakefield.

South Kingstown Town Beach
A fine, sandy beach that follows the South County model to a T, South Kingstown also has an attractive new pavilion and convenient parking in nearby Wakefield.

Roger Wheeler State Beach
Colloquially known as Sand Hill Cove, this has long been a favorite of families with small children. Not only does it have a playground and other facilities, but it also has an extremely gradual drop-off and little surf because it is protected by the rocky arms of a breakwater called the Point Judith Harbor of Refuge. Roger Wheeler State Beach is just south of Galilee.

Blue Shutters Town Beach
A Charlestown-managed beach, this is also a good choice for families. There are no amusements other than nature's, but there are convenient facilities, a watchful staff of lifeguards and generally mild surf.

Misquamicut State Beach
Misquamicut is one of the busiest beaches in the state because it's the closest to the Connecticut state line. It has a lot to offer families: it's inexpensive, has convenient

facilities for changing, showering and eating and it's close to a charmingly old-fashioned amusement area called Atlantic Beach Park. Here you'll find plenty to enjoy – waterslides, miniature golf, Dodge 'Em cars, kiddie rides and arcade games. Misquamicut is just south of Westerly.

Places to Stay
Camping The state-managed campgrounds in South County are among the prettiest spots in the state. Fees to camp at these campgrounds are $12, $16 for hookups.

Burlingame State Park Campsites, (☎ 401-322-7994, 322-7337), off US 1 in Charlestown, has more than 750 wooded sites near crystal-clear Watchaug Pond. First-come, first-served is the rule, but you can call ahead to check on availability.

There's also *Charlestown Beachway* (☎ 401-364-7000, 322-8910), off Charlestown Beach Rd, with 75 RV sites open from mid-April through October for $12 ($8 for RI residents).

At the *Legrand G Reynolds Horsemen's Camping Area* (☎ 401-539-2356, 277-1157), in Exeter, you must be on horseback to camp in one of the 20 sites ($3). To get there, take I-95 exit 5S, then follow RI 102, then RI 3 to RI 165 west, and north on Escoheag Hill Rd.

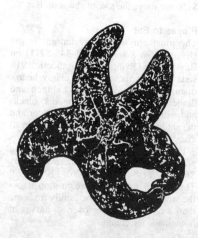

The *Ninigret Conservation Area* (☎ 401-322-0450), off East Beach Rd in Charlestown, has 20 RV sites for $12 ($8).

Private campgrounds include *Wakamo Park Resort* (☎ 401-783-6688), on Succotash Rd in South Kingstown, with 30 RV sites open from mid-April through mid-October for $40 each. From I-95 south, take RI 2 to RI 78 to US 1, then follow signs for East Natunck.

Worden's Pond Family Campground (☎ 401-789-9113), 416A Worden's Pond Road in South Kingstown, with 75 tent sites ($17) and 125 RV sites ($20). From US 1, follow RI 110 to the second left (Worden's Pond Rd), then it's less than a mile to the campground.

B&B Close to the beach town of Weekapaug in Westerly, the *Grandview Bed & Breakfast* (☎ 401-596-6384), 212 Shore Rd, Westerly, is a simply furnished but comfortable small guest house that's moderately priced for the area at $75 to $95 per night in summer.

Hotels In the beachy town of Matunuck, the *Admiral Dewey Inn* (☎ 401-783-2090), 668 Matunuck Beach Rd, South Kingstown, is an 1898 National Historic Register building whose 10 rooms range in price from $90 to $120.

At the upper end of the price scale in South County is the *Weekapaug Inn*, (☎ 401-322-0301), Spring Ave, Weekapaug. The vast shingled inn, with its wraparound porch and lawn sloping down to Quonochontaug Pond, is a classic shore hotel that caters to a rather sedate crowd, many of whom have been regulars for decades. The inn's setting, with its own private ocean beach, is one of the loveliest in New England. Double rooms cost about $300, including all meals.

Places to Eat

Not surprisingly, seafood is the order of the day in South County. Most spots are casual and beachy; shorts and T-shirts are far more common than suits and ties.

Aunt Carrie's (☎ 401-783-7930), RI 108

Beach Activities

South County's salt ponds and tidal rivers are ideal for **kayaking and canoeing**. It's even possible to venture out into the surf in a sea kayak. Outfitters in the area include Narragansett Kayak Co (☎ 401-364-2000), 2144 Matunuck Schoolhouse Rd, Charlestown; and Quaker Lane Bait & Tackle (☎ 401-294-9642), 4019 Quaker Lane, North Kingstown.

Narragansett Town Beach is considered to be among the top spots on the East Coast for **surfing**. You can rent surfboards, sailboards, and any other watersport gear you need at The Watershed (☎ 401-789-3399), 396 Main St, Wakefield. Owner Peter Pan also offers surfing lessons as well.

For the adventurous, **deep-sea fishing** trips – whole or half day – can be arranged with the Frances Fleet (☎ 401-783-4988, 800-662-2824), 2 State St, Galilee. The Frances fleet also runs whale-watching cruises in summer. If you want to charter a boat for a longer trip, contact Snug Harbor Marina (☎ 401-783-7766), Gooseberry Rd, Galilee. ∎

---

and Ocean Rd, Point Judith, has been a Rhode Island landmark for more than 60 years. Within a stone's throw of the ocean itself, the place is noted for its traditional shore dinners (steamed clams, corn on the cob and lobster), clam cakes and chowder.

Champlin's Seafood (☎ 401-783-3152), in Galilee's port is similarly casual, with an outdoor deck that overlooks the activity of the port. *George's of Galilee*, (☎ 401-783-2306), also at the port, has a take-out window where hordes of sandy people line up on summer afternoons for clam cakes that are crisp on the outside, doughy on the inside, and studded with bits of clams.

Things to Buy

Unusual is a mild way of describing The Fantastic Umbrella Factory, (☎ 401-364-6616), RI 1A, Charlestown. The place is a throwback to the '60s with a series of sheds filled with a wide variety of gift items: everything from flower bulbs and perennials to greeting cards, toys and handmade jewelry. You enter the place through a lushly unkempt garden and farm area where exotic birds and farm animals add to the commune-like ambiance.

Entertainment
Quiet, seaside South County is not noted for its nightlife, but there are a couple of places in the area that keep some folks up past 9 pm. *Theatre-by-the-Sea* (☎ 401-782-8587), Cards Pond Rd, South Kingstown, offers a summer schedule of easy-to-like musicals and plays in a simple, barn-like building in a scenic area close to the beaches of Matunuck. For live rock music geared to a younger crowd, there's *Ocean Mist*, (☎ 401-782-3740), 145 Matunuck Beach Rd, South Kingstown, which is set so close to the beach that if it weren't for the crashing bass, you might hear the crashing surf.

Getting There & Away
Though the Amtrak trains between Boston and New York via the *Shore Route* stop in Westerly, you really need a car to get to the beaches. Distances are not great (this is Rhode Island): from Westerly to Wakefield is only about 21 miles.

NARRAGANSETT BAY BEACHES
By contrast to the long straight beaches of South County, those on the east side of Narragansett Bay in Newport and Little Compton are more like coves. Often ringed with huge rocks, they are particularly lovely early and late in the day when the sun slants on the granite, stage-lighting the scene. Unfortunately, many of Little Compton's prettiest beaches are private, but in the evenings it's usually possible to stroll on them and take in the view.

For Narragansett area information, contact the Narragansett Chamber of Commerce (☎ 401-783-7121), The Towers, RI 1A, (PO Box 742) Narragansett, RI 02882.

Scarborough State Beach Scarborough (sometimes written "Scarboro") is the prototypical Rhode Island beach, and many

consider it the best in the state. A lovely, castle-like pavilion, generous boardwalks, a beachfront that is both wide and long, and great, predictable surf make Scarborough special. It tends to attract a lot of teenagers, but it's large enough that other people can take them or leave them.

Narragansett Town Beach Narragansett tends to be crowded because it is within an easy walk of the beachy town of Narragansett Pier. It is the only beach in Rhode Island that charges a per-person admission fee on top of a parking fee. Still, people – surfers in particular – adore it.

Newport
Easton's Beach Also known as First Beach, this is the beach that most Newport tourists go to because it's within walking distance of the center of town. The beach has an attractive new Victorian-style pavilion and a charming small aquarium where children can see and touch a variety of tide-pool creatures and fish.

Middletown
Sachuest Beach Named for the wildlife sanctuary close by, Sachuest (also called Second) Beach is a prettier, cleaner beach than First. It has a lovely setting, too, overlooked by the Gothic tower of St George's prep school.

Third Beach Popular with families because it is protected from the open ocean, Third Beach also appeals to windsurfers because the water is calm and the winds steady.

Little Compton

Goosewing Beach Lovely, remote Goosewing is the only good public beach in Little Compton, but access can be tricky. Due to an ongoing wrangle between the town and the Nature Conservancy over who controls the beach, parking and lifeguard coverage are perennially in question. Still, year after year since the dispute began, it has been possible to get onto Goosewing by the unusual means of parking at the town beach called South Shore and walking across a small tidal inlet to the more appealing Goosewing. What makes it so appealing will be immediately apparent: the long sand beach with its wide-open ocean view is backed by rolling farmland that seems a throwback to another era. With no facilities to speak of, Goosewing can't be called convenient, but it is a lovely place to spend a summer's day.

Places to Stay

Camping In the fishing port of Galilee, *Fishermen's Memorial State Park* (☎ 401-277-2632) off RI 108 is so popular that many families return year after year to the same site. There are only 180 campsites at Fishermen's, so it's wise to reserve early by contacting the park management: Division of Parks and Recreation, 2321 Hartford Ave, Johnstown, RI 02919. Sites cost $12 for a tent ($8 for Rhode Island residents), $10 to $16 for sites with hookups.

B&B *The Richards* (☎ 401-789-7746), 144 Gibson Ave, Narragansett, is built of locally quarried granite, and its Gothic English manor look sets it apart from other B&Bs. Rooms range in price from $65 to $90.

Places to Eat

Every beach has its collection of clam shacks and snack shops good for a quick lunch. Here are some of the better, less obvious places to dine.

For a fancy night out, *The Coast Guard House* (☎ 401-789-0700), 40 Ocean Rd, Narragansett, has traditional American favorites such as steak, veal and seafood. The place occupies a dramatic seaside site – one that has made it vulnerable to hurricanes in recent years. During Hurricane Bob in 1991, the dining room was washed away, but it has since been rebuilt.

Fancier still – featuring wood-grilled dishes and creative interpretations of local seafood – is the *South Shore Grille* (☎ 401-782-4780), 210 Salt Pond Rd, Wakefield. The restaurant, with its patio open in summer, overlooks Point Judith Pond, dotted with boats and marinas.

A good place for breakfast is *Main Street Foods & Bakery* (☎ 401-789-0914), 333 Main St, Wakefield. Hearty pancakes, waffles and all sorts of egg dishes are served daily except Sunday and Monday. Lunch and dinner are served also in a comfortable, bistro-style atmosphere.

Getting There & Around

Transportation around Narragansett Bay is by car. Ferries connect Block Island (see that section) to the mainland at Galilee, Newport and Providence.

RHODE ISLAND

Connecticut

Connecticut has a surprising variety of landscapes and cityscapes. The southeastern region looks to New York City. The coast is an ever-changing mix of historic towns and villages, and booming high-tech cities. Hartford, the capital, is an oasis of skyscrapers amid miles of farmers' fields. The northwestern corner is a more sedate, low-key version of Massachusetts' Berkshires.

Bisecting the state is the Connecticut River, called by the area's original inhabitants the Quinnehtukqut, or "long tidal river." Navigable all the way to Hartford, the great river was one of the reasons the colony, and then the state, prospered in the days before good highways and air transport.

Most of Connecticut's visitors come to visit Mystic Seaport, the historic recreation

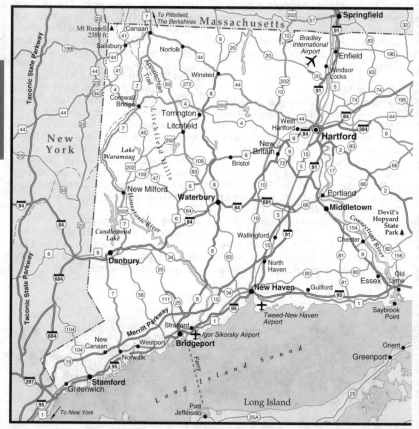

of a 19th-century working coastal town; to visit the campus and museums of Yale University at New Haven or the US Coast Guard Academy at New London; to relax in an historic inn along the coast or on the banks of the Connecticut River and to enjoy the scenery of the Litchfield Hills and their lakes.

The state tourism office (☎ 800-282-6863) provides a free brochure. With the same number, you can also reach the free statewide accommodations reservations service. Connecticut Welcome Centers are in Bradley Airport; on I-95 in North Ston-

ington (southbound) and Westbrook (northbound); I-84 at Danbury and Southington (eastbound) and Willington (westbound); I-91 at Middletown (northbound) and Wallingford (southbound).

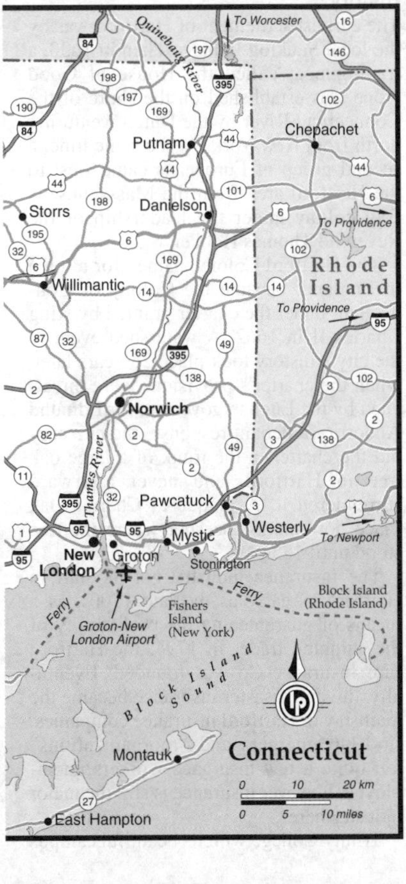

Getting There & Around

Air Bradley International Airport (☎ 860-292-2000), 12 miles north of Hartford in Windsor Locks (I-91 exit 40), serves the Hartford-Springfield area. Direct flights by American, Delta, Northwest, Continental, TWA, United and USAir connect Bradley with about 60 other US airports. Buses and limousine services shuttle passengers between the airport and major towns and cities in central Connecticut and Massachusetts.

Tweed-New Haven Airport (☎ 203-787-8283) in New Haven serves the southeastern part of the state with flights by United, USAir and others. See New Haven, Getting There & Away.

Groton-New London Airport (☎ 860-445-8549) in Groton, and Igor Sikorsky Memorial Airport (☎ 203-576-7498), closer to New York City in Bridgeport-Stratford, also serve the coast with commuter flights.

Train Metro North trains (☎ 212-532-4900, 800-223-6052, 800-638-7646) make the 1½-hour run between New York City's Grand Central Terminal and New Haven on weekdays almost every hour from 7 am to midnight, with more frequent trains during the morning and evening rush hours. On weekends, trains run about every two hours. There are frequent stops.

Other branches of Metro North service also have frequent stops and go north to Danbury (connect at South Norwalk), New Canaan (connect at Stamford) and Waterbury (connect at Bridgeport).

Connecticut Commuter Rail Service's Shore Line East service (☎ 800-255-7433) travels along the shore of Long Island Sound, connecting Old Saybrook, Westbrook, Clinton, Madison, Guilford, Branford and New Haven. At New Haven, the

CONNECTICUT

Connecticut

Shore Line East trains connect with Metro North and Amtrak routes.

Amtrak (☎ 800-872-7245) trains depart New York City's Pennsylvania Station to Connecticut on three lines: New Haven, Hartford, Springfield; New Haven, Hartford, Windsor Locks, Boston; and New Haven, New London, Mystic, Providence, Boston. Most tickets and trains allow stopovers along the way at no extra charge, so a ticket on the *Shore Route* between New York City and Boston may allow you to see New Haven, New London, Mystic and Providence for the same fare.

Bus Peter Pan Bus Lines (☎ 413-781-3320, 800-343-9999), with its hub in Springfield, MA, operates routes connecting Bridgeport, New Haven, Middletown and Hartford with New York City, Springfield and Boston.

Bonanza Bus Lines (☎ 401-331-7500, 800-556-3815), with its hub in Providence, RI, runs buses from New York City via Danbury and Hartford to Providence; and via New Milford, Kent and Canaan, CT, to Massachusetts' Berkshire hills and Bennington, VT. Connect at Providence with buses to Newport, RI, and to Boston, Falmouth, Hyannis and Woods Hole, MA, on Cape Cod.

Car Driver and front-seat passengers are required to wear safety belts in Connecticut. Children under one year of age must be in a child safety seat; children age one to four must sit in a back seat and wear a safety belt.

The use of radar detectors is illegal in Connecticut, and the fines are in the hundreds of dollars.

The maximum fine for a first speeding offense is about $350. Connecticut state police patrol the highways in marked and unmarked cars, and use radar frequently to catch speeders.

Connecticut gasoline prices are among the highest in the USA, and increase as you approach New York City.

Boat See Getting There & Away in New Haven and New London.

HARTFORD

It's a rare person who goes to Hartford on vacation – it's a work-a-day city rather than a tourist destination – but once you're here, for whatever reason, you'll be surprised at how much Connecticut's capital city has to offer visitors, with particular strengths in history and art.

With a population of about 124,000, Hartford's main business, aside from state government, is insurance. In fact, the city has long been known as the insurance capital of the nation, home to some 35 major insurance companies.

History

The earliest settlement of Hartford was by the local Saukiog Indians. Then in 1633, a trading post called the House of Good Hope was established on the shore of the Connecticut River by the Dutch, venturing north from New York. At the same time, a second group of Europeans came west to the Hartford area from the Massachusetts Bay colony under the leadership of the Reverend Thomas Hooker.

The Hartford Colony, named for a town in England, became the Colony of Connecticut under the charter granted by King Charles II in 1662. A watershed event in the city's history took place 25 years later, when the charter's provisions were threatened by the English governor, Sir Edmund Andorra. In defiant response, the citizenry hid the charter in the trunk of a large oak tree in Hartford, and never afterward surrendered it. A plaque at Charter Oak Place now marks the spot where the tree stood until 1856.

The insurance industry got its start in Hartford as early as the late 1700s, as a means of guaranteeing the profitability of the shipping trade. In 1794, the Hartford Fire Insurance Co was founded. Eventually, fire and disaster insurance became the mainstay of Hartford insurance companies. In 1996, mergers and "reorganizations" left quite a few insurance workers unemployed, however insurance is still the major industry here.

Trinity College with its beautiful campus

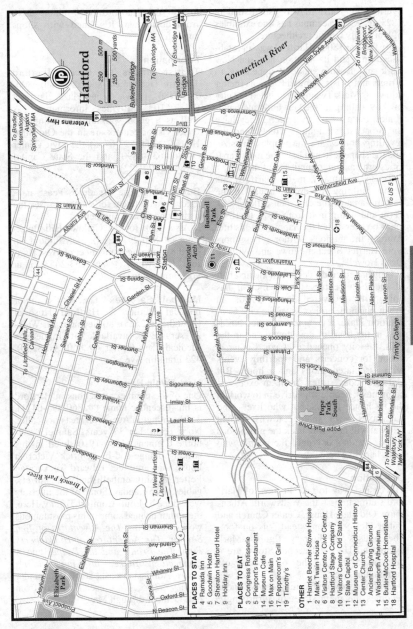

Hartford

Connecticut River

To Sturbridge MA
To Sturbridge MA
Bulkeley Bridge
Founders Bridge
To Bradley International Airport, Springfield MA
Veterans Hwy
To Litchfield Hills, Canaan
To West Hartford, Litchfield
To New Britain, Waterbury, New York NY
To New Haven, Bridgeport, New York NY
To US 5

N Branch Park River
Connecticut River

Bushnell Park
Memorial Arch
Pope Park South
Elizabeth Park
Trinity College

PLACES TO STAY
4 Ramada Inn
5 Goodwin Hotel
7 Sheraton Hartford Hotel
9 Holiday Inn

PLACES TO EAT
3 Congress Rotisserie
14 Pierpont's Restaurant
    Museum Cafe
16 Max on Main
17 Peppercorn's Grill
19 Timothy's

OTHER
1 Harriet Beecher Stowe House
2 Mark Twain House
6 Visitors Center, Civic Center
8 Hartford Stage Company
10 Visitors Center, Old State House
11 State Capitol
12 Museum of Connecticut History
13 Center Church,
    Ancient Burying Ground
14 Wadsworth Atheneum
15 Butler-McCook Homestead
18 Hartford Hospital

CONNECTICUT

overlooking Hartford was established in 1823. Its 96-acre campus has fine examples of University Gothic architecture.

By the late 1800s, Hartford was an established city, and its location between New York and Boston made it appealing to writers and artists. Samuel Clemens (better known as Mark Twain) first visited the city in 1869, calling it "the best built and handsomest town I have ever seen. They have the broadest, straightest streets, and the dwelling houses are the amplest in size, and the shapeliest, and have the most capacious ornamental grounds about them."

Twain eventually made Hartford his home, building his dream house in the pastoral area of the city then called Nook Farm and living in it from 1874 to 1891, years he later called the happiest of his life. Among the famous author's neighbors were Harriet Beecher Stowe and William Dean Howells.

Hartford entered a decline in the first half of the 20th century from which it has only partly recovered. In the 1960s, an urban planning project gave the city Constitution Plaza, a complex of office buildings in the heart of downtown, and in the '70s, the city opened its Civic Center, a venue for concerts and sporting events with associated shops and a hotel. But Hartford today suffers from an excess of commuters: people who drive in to work in the insurance towers, but who live – and pay taxes – in smaller towns. Urban renewal will not bring back the prosperous city of Twain's day until the people who work here live here.

Orientation

The easiest way to take in most of Hartford's attractions – the Wadsworth Athenaeum, Old State House, Center Church and Butler-McCook Homestead – is on foot. The houses of literary figures Mark Twain and Harriet Beecher Stowe are a mile or so west of the town center off Farmington Ave.

Continue west on Farmington Ave and it becomes the main street of surprisingly lovely West Hartford, a 10-minute drive from downtown. It's lined with shops and cafes.

Information

Tourist Offices The Greater Hartford Tourism District (☎ 860-520-4480, 800-793-4480), 1 Civic Center Plaza, Hartford, CT 06103, provides information, as well as a good walking-tour pamphlet. Other visitor centers are in the Old State House (☎ 860-522-6766), the Civic Center (☎ 860-633-6890) and the State Capitol (☎ 860-240-0222).

Bookstores The Reader's Feast is a unique environment for shopping – see the listing under Entertainment.

Also, look for the Gallows Hill Bookstore (☎ 860-297-5231), 300 Summit St. On the charming main street of West Hartford, Bookworm (☎ 860-233-2653), is at 968 Farmington Ave.

Medical Services The city's major medical facility is Hartford Hospital (☎ 860-524-2525), 80 Seymour St. Walk-in service is available at Immediate Medical Care Center (☎ 860-296-8330), 423 Franklin Ave.

Mark Twain House

One of the premier attractions in Hartford is this eccentric home (☎ 860-493-6411), 351 Farmington Ave, in an area once called Nook Farm. For 17 years, Samuel Langhorne Clemens (1835-1910) lived in this striking orange-and-black brick Victorian house that architect Edward Tuckerman Potter lavishly embellished with turrets, gables and verandas. Some of the interiors were done by Louis Comfort Tiffany. Here, the author penned some of his most famous works, including *The Adventures of Tom Sawyer*, *The Adventures of Huckleberry Finn*, *The Prince and the Pauper* and *A Connecticut Yankee in King Arthur's Court*. Admission costs $6.50; kids under 16 pay $2.75. It's closed Tuesday from mid-October through May.

Harriet Beecher Stowe House

Next door to the Twain house is this author's home (☎ 860-525-9317), 73 Forest St. Stowe was the woman that Abraham Lincoln said started the Civil War with her book, *Uncle Tom's Cabin*. Built in 1871 and reflecting the author's strong ideas about decorating (her book on the subject was nearly as popular as *Uncle Tom's Cabin*), the Stowe house is light-filled, with big windows draped in plants. It's open daily from June through mid-October, closed Monday the rest of the year. Admission costs $6.50; ages six to 16 pay $2.75.

State Capitol

The Connecticut State Capitol (☎ 860-240-0222), Capitol Ave and Trinity St, on Capitol Hill, is an imposing white marble building with Gothic details and a gold-leaf dome. Because of the variety of architectural styles it reflects, it has been unkindly dubbed "the most beautiful ugly building in the world." Designed by Richard Upjohn in 1879, it has recently been refurbished. You can visit any weekday from 8 am to 5 pm, for free.

Museum of Connecticut History

While you're up on Capitol Hill, have a look at this museum (☎ 860-566-3056), 231 Capitol Ave, housed in the State Library and Supreme Court Building across from the State Capitol. Nationally known for its genealogy library, it also holds a prime collection of Colt firearms (which were manufactured in Hartford), clocks and the table at which Abraham Lincoln signed the Emancipation Proclamation. The museum is open Monday through Friday from 9:30 am to 4 pm, and admission is free.

Wadsworth Atheneum

The nation's oldest continuously operating art museum, the Wadsworth Atheneum (☎ 860-278-2670), 600 Main St, is housed in a castle-like Gothic Revival building. Paintings by members of the Hudson River School, including some by Hartford resident Frederic Church, are an important part of the Atheneum's holdings. Also on exhibit are 19th-century impressionist works, 18th-century furniture and African-American art. The Atheneum contains some 40,000 pieces of art, including the Matrix Gallery of works by contemporary artists. The Atheneum is open from 11 am to 5 pm, closed Monday. Admission costs $5; kids under 13 get in free.

You can eat here too; see Places to Eat.

Center Church

Center Church (☎ 860-249-5631), 675 Main St, is the church that Reverend Thomas Hooker established when he came to Hartford from the Massachusetts Bay colony in 1636. The present building dates from 1807 and was modeled on the St Martin's-in-the-Fields in London. In the **Ancient Burying Ground** behind the church lie the remains of Hooker, and Revolutionary War patriots Joseph and Jeremiah Wadsworth. Some headstones date from the 1600s.

Butler-McCook Homestead

A single family occupied the Butler-McCook Homestead (☎ 860-247-8996, 522-1806), 396 Main St, for four generations, from 1782 to 1971. The museum house contains its original 18th and 19th-century furnishings, a collection of Japanese armor, toys, pewter plates and stoneware. A Victorian garden is part of the grounds. It's open Tuesday, Thursday and Sunday afternoons from mid-May to mid-October for $4 (kids under 18 get in for $1).

Bushnell Park

Hartford's 37-acre Bushnell Park (☎ 860-522-3668) was designed by Jacob Weidenmann in the 1850s. The Pump House Gallery in the downtown park features art exhibits and a summer concert series. Children will enjoy the park's 1914 carousel designed by Stein and Goldstein with 48 horses and a Wurlitzer band organ. Bushnell Park abuts the State Capitol building grounds on its north end; a memorial arch to soldiers and sailors frames the Trinity St entrance.

CONNECTICUT

Elizabeth Park

You'll find Elizabeth Park (☎ 860-722-6514) on Prospect Ave at Asylum Ave. It's a 100-acre preserve on the Hartford-West Hartford town line that is known for its fine collection of roses. More than 14,000 plants – some 900 varieties including climbers, American Beauties, ramblers and heavily perfumed Damasks – cover the grounds. June and July are the best months to see the roses in full flower, but they bloom, if less profusely, well into fall. Elizabeth Park also has greenhouses, landscaped walking paths and a pretty gazebo. Park greenhouses are open daily from 10 am to 4 pm.

Places to Stay

Just outside the center of Hartford are many of the usual chain motels, usually offering the best value in area accommodations.

Ten miles south of the city center off I-91 at the Silas Deane exit is a 146-room Motel 6 (☎ 860-563-5900), 1341 Silas Deane Hwy, Wethersfield. Rooms are comfortable and clean for $50, with a restaurant next door.

Also south of the city is the Courtyard by Marriott Hotel (☎ 860-683-0022, 800-321-2211), 1 Day Hill Rd, Windsor. The comfortable rooms are geared to business travelers and cost $50 to $80. There's an indoor swimming pool.

In the city, there's not much in the way of B&Bs, but one standout is the 1895 House (☎ 860-232-0014), 97 Girard Ave on the west side of the city, close to the West Hartford line. The graceful Victorian house has just three guest rooms. A suite ($75 per night) is on the 3rd floor in a space that was originally a billiard room. Two other rooms ($60) share a bath.

Overlooking the State Capitol grounds is the Ramada Inn (☎ 860-246-6591, 800-272-6232), 440 Asylum St, close to train and bus connections at Union Station. The Ramada is relatively small, with 96 rooms, many of which offer good views of the Capitol, for $50 to $80.

For convenience of location, the Shera-ton Hartford Hotel (☎ 860-728-5151, 800-325-3535), 315 Trumbull St, is hard to beat. The 382-room, 22-story hotel is directly across from the Hartford Civic Center, and within easy walking distance of everything downtown. Rates are $75 to $100.

Also close to the Civic Center is the Holiday Inn (☎ 860-549-2400, 800-465-4329), 50 Morgan St N. With 360 guest rooms, this is a typical chain hotel with many guest services including shuttle service to Bradley Airport, an outdoor swimming pool, on-site restaurant and baby-sitting services. Rooms are from $96 to $127.

The fanciest hotel address in Hartford is the Goodwin Hotel (860-246-7500), 1 Haynes St. Across the street from the Civic Center, this five-story, 124-room, 1881 red brick building looks historic on the outside, but inside it has been entirely remodeled to appeal to modern preferences for large, light-filled rooms. Decor is traditional, with antique reproduction furniture, in keeping with the age of the hotel. Afternoon tea is served in the lobby. Rooms cost $92 to $162.

Places to Eat

For picnic fare to eat among the roses at Elizabeth Park, the Congress Rotisserie (☎ 860-278-7711), 274 Farmington Ave, is a wholesome deli with creative sandwiches, soups and salads.

A convivial atmosphere is on tap at Hartford's first brewpub, the Hartford Brewery (☎ 860-246-2337), 35 Pearl St. The place has inexpensive pub-style food for lunch or dinner, as well as pool, darts and backgammon to pass the time.

In the Wadsworth Atheneum, the Museum Cafe (☎ 860-728-5989), 600 Main St, serves lunch daily except Monday. It's casual, but menu offerings tend to be light and sophisticated, with main courses for about $8.

Drawing a loyal crowd of students and faculty members from nearby Trinity College, Timothy's (860-728-9822), 243 Zion St, is renowned for its plentiful servings of home-style food at inexpensive prices. Hearty soups and fat sandwiches are good bets for lunch; try the blackboard specials for dinner (around $12). The place has an invitingly casual diner atmosphere, with a Formica-topped counter, vinyl booths and a black tin ceiling.

Classy and urbane, *Max on Main* (860-522-2530), 205 Main St, is the favorite spot of the downtown "in" crowd. Serving a wide selection of American bistro dishes and creative interpretations of regional classics in an Art Deco space, Max is open for lunch and dinner on weekdays, and dinner on Saturday as well. Full dinners cost $20 to $30 per person; you'll pay less at lunch.

Top choice for a romantic dinner on the town is *Pierpont's* (☎ 860-522-4935, 246-7500), in the Goodwin Hotel. Named for famous financier J Pierpont Morgan, a Hartford resident, Pierpont's offers expert traditional continental dishes. Dinner will cost about $30 to $40.

Modern American interpretations of Italian dishes are the specialty of the house at *Peppercorn's Grill* (860-547-1714), 357 Main St. In this family-run place, you might find anything from veal saltimbocca to a zesty dish of ravioli with scallops and lobster. Lunch ($12 to $17) is served weekdays, dinner ($28 to $45) weekdays and Saturday; it's closed Sunday.

For vegetarian fare, see the Reader's Feast bookstore and cafe, below.

Entertainment

The Hartford Civic Center is the venue for big shows.

Contemporary as well as classic plays are presented by the *Hartford Stage Company* (☎ 860-527-5151), 50 Church St, from September through June. The theater building is striking, designed by Venturi & Rauch of red brick with darker red zigzag details.

A gallery that combines contemporary works on paper and canvas with works on video, poetry and musical events, *Real Art Ways* (☎ 860-232-1006), 56 Arbor St, is always offbeat and adventurous. Admis-

sion is free; performances usually cost $5 to $10. The gallery is open on weekdays from 10 am to 5 pm, Saturday from noon to 5 pm

If you want to catch a movie, the gorgeous, velvet-seated *Cinestudio* (☎ 860-297-2463 for show times, 297-2544 office), 300 Summit St at Trinity College, shows first-run and art films – at lower-than-average prices.

For casual live music, check out the cafe culture at *Reader's Feast* (☎ 860-232-3710), 529 Farmington Ave near Whitney St. It's a cozy environment to grab a book, sip latte, munch vegetarian food and see a band.

The *Russian Lady*, 191 Ann St, is the fun and happening bar for locals (especially on the weekends) with an outdoor patio and area bands.

Getting There & Away

See Connecticut, Getting There & Around for more information.

Air Bradley International Airport (☎ 860-292-2000), 12 miles north of Hartford in Windsor Locks, is central Connecticut's regional airport, with service by American, Continental, TWA, United, USAir and several commuter airlines.

Bus Bus links from Hartford's Union Station to other Northeast cities are provided by Greyhound (☎ 860-247-3524), Peter Pan (☎ 860-724-5400, 800-343-9999) and Bonanza (☎ 800-556-3815). See the beginning of this chapter for details.

Train Amtrak (☎ 800-872-7245) trains connect Hartford to New York and Boston.

Car Driving details for Hartford are:

Destination	Mileage	Hr:Min
Boston, MA	102 miles	2:10
Litchfield, CT	34 miles	1:00
Mystic, CT	54 miles	1:00
New Haven, CT	36 miles	0:50
New London, CT	52 miles	1:00
New York, NY	117 miles	2:30
Providence, RI	71 miles	1:30

Outdoor Connecticut

The northern New England states – Vermont, New Hampshire and Maine – are justly noted for their outdoor activities, but that doesn't mean that Connecticut can't compete.

Northwest Connecticut's Housatonic River is particularly good for canoeing, kayaking, rafting and tubing. With the spring floods, the white water can reach Class III; in summer it's Class I and II.

Riverrunning Expeditions, Ltd (☎ 860-824-5579, fax 824-5286), 85 Main St, Falls Village (Canaan), CT 06031, can set you up with equipment, training and guides for an adventure on the Housatonic River. They'll rent you a two-person canoe ($45), a raft ($25 per person), a kayak ($35 per person) or a tube ($10) to run the Housatonic, as well as a guide ($80 per day for up to eight canoes) and shuttle service.

Clarke Outdoors (☎ 860-672-6365), 163 US 7, West Cornwall, CT 06796, can also equip you for a run down the Housatonic.

Farmington River Tubing (☎ 860-693-6465), in New Hartford, CT, a division of North American Canoe Tours, Inc (☎ 860-739-0791), of Niantic, will take you tubing down the Farmington River at Satans Kingdom State Recreation Area only a dozen miles west of Hartford on US 44. ∎

Getting Around

Bus service within the city is by Connecticut Transit (☎ 860-525-9181), which has an information booth at State House Square and Market St.

Taxis are available outside Union Station downtown, or call Yellow Cab Co (☎ 860-666-6666).

Lower Connecticut River Valley

Unlike New York's Hudson River and New London's Thames, the Connecticut River has escaped the bustle of industry and commerce that so often mar the heavily used rivers of the Northeast. That's because, even though the Connecticut is the longest river in New England (with its headwaters near New Hampshire's Canadian border), it is surprisingly shallow near its mouth at Long Island Sound. Lack of depth led burgeoning industry to look for better harbors elsewhere, and the lower end of the Connecticut has since remained so unspoiled that it was recently named one of the Northeast's "last great places" by the Nature Conservancy.

A string of old New England river towns include: Old Lyme, Essex, Ivoryton, Chester, Hadlyme and East Haddam. Each is charming on its own, and together they offer visitors a combination of attractions that include fine dining, river excursions, art museums, theater and more. The sections below on activities, places to stay and places to eat include information on all these towns.

Information

For information on the towns of the Connecticut River Valley, contact the Connecticut River Valley and Shoreline Visitors Council (☎ 860-347-0028, 800-486-3346), 393 Main St, Middletown, CT 06457.

Essex

Essex is a good starting point for an exploration of the Lower Connecticut River Valley. Established in 1635 and well-endowed with lovely Federal-period houses that are the legacy of rum and tobacco fortunes made in the 19th century, Essex today has the genteel, controlled air of an aristocratic place: everything from landscaping to street signage is scripted to look good, and it does.

The center of activity in Essex is always the riverfront, where glistening yachts nose the docks. The **Connecticut River Museum** (☎ 860-767-8269) at Steamboat Dock tells some of the history of the area, with exhibits including a reproduction of the world's first submarine, the *Turtle*, built here by Yale student David Bushnell in 1776. The unusual vessel looks something like a large wooden barrel. Admission is $4 for adults, $2 for children; it's closed Monday.

But the centerpiece of Essex is the **1776 Griswold Inn** (☎ 860-767-1776), 36 Main St, a hostelry since the time of the Revolutionary War. "The Griz," as the natives call it, is today both an inn and a restaurant, and its taproom is the obvious place to meet in town. Sunday morning "Hunt Breakfasts" are a renowned tradition that dates to the War of 1812, when British soldiers occupying Essex demanded to be fed in the manner to which they were accustomed. See Places to Stay, below.

Once you've seen the waterfront, take to the streets of Essex to find a host of attractive shops, many selling high-end antiques and art.

A good way to see some of the countryside around Essex is on the **Valley Railroad** (☎ 860-767-0103), which has its terminus on Railroad Ave in town. An authentic coal-fired steam engine powers the train, which rumbles north to the town of Deep River, where passengers may connect with a riverboat for a cruise on the Connecticut before heading back on the train. The ride takes about an hour, covering about 12 miles. Trains leave the Essex station five times daily in summer, six on weekends. Fall foliage runs are usually scheduled as well. Combination tickets for the train and riverboat cruise are $14 for adults, $7 for children. For the train ride alone, it's $8.50 and $4.25.

Old Lyme

For information about Old Lyme, contact the Lyme and Old Lyme Chamber of Commerce (☎ 860-434-1665), 70 Lyme St, PO Box 268, Old Lyme, CT 06371.

To the south of Essex are several venerable river towns that are well worth visiting. Southernmost is Old Lyme, which in the 19th century was hometown to some 60 sea captains. Since the early 1900s, however, Old Lyme has been better known as a center for the American impressionist art movement. Artists such as Charles Ebert, Childe Hassam, Willard Metcalfe, Henry Ward Ranger and Guy and Carleston Wiggins came here to paint, staying in the mansion of local art patron Florence Griswold. The house (which her artist friends

Lower Connecticut River Valley

Long Island Sound

CONNECTICUT

often decorated with murals in lieu of paying rent) is now a museum containing a good selection of impressionist and Barbizon paintings. The **Florence Griswold Museum** (☎ 860-434-5542), 96 Lyme St, is closed Monday in summer, Monday and Tuesday the rest of the year. Admission is $3.

Also in Lyme is the **Lyme Academy of Fine Arts** (☎ 860-434-5232) and the **Lyme Art Association Gallery** (☎ 860-434-7802). Both regularly feature contemporary works by local artists.

Ivoryton

A mile west of Essex is the sleepy river town of Ivoryton, named for the African elephant tusks imported during the 19th century by the Comstock-Cheney piano manufacturers, which turned them into piano keys. Today, that industry is gone, and the reason most people go to relaxed, quiet Ivoryton is to dine at the Copper Beech Inn or the Ivoryton Inn. (See Places to Eat, below.)

Chester

Another lovely, slow old river town is Chester, cupped in the valley of Pattaconk Brook. A general store, post office, library and a few shops pretty much account for all the activity in town.

Most visitors to the place come either for the fine dining at the Inn at Chester (see Places to Eat), or to browse in the antique shops and boutiques on the town's charming main street. A special place to buy handicrafts is Connecticut River Artisans (☎ 860-526-5575), 1 Spring St. This non-profit artists' cooperative has paintings, photographs, jewelry, pottery, prints, wearable art and more. The artist is often on site. It's closed Monday and Tuesday.

Hadlyme

From Chester, a car ferry (☎ 860-566-7635) crosses the Connecticut River to Hadlyme. The trip takes just about five minutes; the ferry – which carries just eight cars – is the second-oldest in continuous

operation in the state, operating daily April through mid-December.

Looming on one of the Seven Sisters hills above the river crossing is **Gillette Castle** (☎ 860-526-2336), 67 River Rd, East Haddam, a 24-room stone-turreted mansion that is one of Connecticut's leading attractions. Frankly, from the outside it looks as if the stones might crumble apart at any minute. Built from 1914 to 1919 by an eccentric actor named William Gillette, it was modeled on the medieval castles of Germany's Rhineland. Gillette made his name and his considerable fortune on stage in the role of Sherlock Holmes in a play that he wrote himself based on the famous mystery series by Sir Arthur Conan Doyle. In a sense, he made his castle/home part of the Holmes role as well: an upstairs room replicates Conan Doyle's description of the sitting room at 221B Baker St, London.

Following Gillette's death in 1937, his dream house and its surrounding 117 acres were designated a Connecticut state park. The castle is open daily from late May through mid-October, then on weekends until Christmas. The state park is open year round, with areas for picnicking and hiking.

East Haddam

The only town in Connecticut to span both sides of the river, East Haddam's claim to fame (beyond its obvious riverine beauty) is the **Goodspeed Opera House** (☎ 860-873-8668), CT 82, an American Gothic-style confection of a place that is known as "the birthplace of the American musical." It is today the only theater in the country dedicated to both the preservation of old and the development of new American musicals.

The shows *Man of La Mancha* and *Annie* premiered at the Goodspeed before going on to national fame. The six-story, Victorian-style theater, built in 1876, enjoyed a huge reputation before the Great Depression. It was saved from demolition in 1959 by a group of concerned citizens, then refurbished and reopened in 1963. Its schedule of productions runs from April to December.

Also in East Haddam is the **Nathan Hale**

Schoolhouse (☎ 860-873-9547), behind St Stephen's Church in the center of town. Hale taught in this one-room building from 1773 to 1774 when it was called the Union School. Hale (1755-1776) is famous for his patriotic statement: "I only regret that I have but one life to lose for my country," as he was hanged for treason by the British without trial. Today it is a museum of Hale family memorabilia and local history. The museum is open weekends and holidays in the summer, from 2 to 4 pm.

Activities

The **Devil's Hopyard State Park** (☎ 860-566-2304), East Haddam, has 860 acres of parkland great for hiking, with the 60-foot Chapman Falls.

The peaceful waters of the Connecticut lend themselves to canoeing. Down River Canoes (☎ 860-345-8355, 346-3308), CT 154, Haddam, offers one- to three-day outings on the river, including instruction and snacks.

Connecticut River Cruises (☎ 860-345-8373), 6 Marine Park, Haddam, offers cruises on the river daily during the summer months and on fall foliage weekends aboard the paddle-wheeler *Tom Sawyer*.

Places To Stay

Camping There are a few campsites in *Devil's Hopyard State Park* (☎ 860-566-2304), but there are better facilities at *Wolf's Den Campground* (☎ 860-873-9681) in East Haddam (235 sites), or *Little City Campground* (☎ 860-345-4886, 345-8489) in Haddam (50 sites).

Inns & B&Bs The *Griswold Inn* (☎ 860-767-1776), 36 Main St, Essex, is the area's landmark inn, with an inviting porch surrounding the classic green-shuttered, white-clapboard Colonial inn. Despite the Griz's antiquity (it has been an inn since the Revolutionary War), its 25 guest rooms have modern conveniences, and cost $90 to $175.

The *Inn at Chester* (☎ 860-526-9541, 800-949-7829), 318 W Main St, Chester, is another 1776 building that has been respect-fully transformed into a comfortable modern inn. Its 44 air-conditioned rooms cost $95 to $175; more for suites.

The *Bee & Thistle Inn* (☎ 860-434-1667), 100 Lyme St, Old Lyme, is a 1756 Dutch Colonial farmhouse with 11 rooms, some of which share baths. The dining room is excellent (closed Tuesday). Room rates are $85 to $225.

The *Copper Beech Inn* (☎ 860-767-0330), 46 Main St, Ivoryton, follows the Connecticut River Valley model of fine old inns with sophisticated restaurants, in the case of the Copper Beech serving French country cuisine. This inn, which was built in the 1890s as the residence of ivory importer AW Comstock, has four guest rooms in the main house and nine more luxurious rooms in the Carriage House, priced from $120 to $200. Be sure to make reservations well in advance.

The Connecticut, Housatonic and Farmington Rivers provide good canoeing in the state.

Places to Eat

Most experienced travelers know that hotel dining rooms often suffer in comparison to independent restaurants. But in the Connecticut River Valley, some of the best restaurants are in gracious old inns, such as the Copper Beech in Ivoryton, the Griswold in Essex, the Bee & Thistle in Old Lyme, and the Inn at Chester. For details, see Places to Stay, above.

For an inexpensive but well-prepared meal, *She Sells Sandwiches* (☎ 860-767-3288), in Brewer's Shipyard, Pratt St, Essex, is a good bet. A favorite stop of yachtsmen as well as landlubbers, She Sells serves breakfast from 7:30 am daily, lunch daily to 5 pm, and dinners in summer only.

Seafood is the main attraction at *Fiddler's* (☎ 860-526-3210), 4 Water St, Chester. Special favorites are the bouillabaisse and inventive lobster dishes. Lunch and dinner are served daily except Monday. The fixed-price dinner costs $15; a regular menu is served as well.

Restaurant du Village (☎ 860-526-5301), 59 Main St, Chester, is like a little piece of Provence. Painted blue with flower-filled window boxes beneath multi-paned windows, the restaurant has a country French menu of sophisticated dishes. Most entrees cost between $23 to $26, and a full dinner with wine might cost twice as much.

Connecticut Coast

Connecticut's coastline on Long Island Sound is long and varied. The western coast is crowded with industrial and commercial cities, and suburban bedroom communities, which are within the magnetic influence of New York City. The central coast, from New Haven to the mouth of the Connecticut River, is less urban, with historic towns and villages. The eastern coast includes New London and Groton, both important in naval history, and Mystic, where the Mystic Seaport Museum brings maritime history to life.

Here are the most interesting points along the coast, from west to east.

NEW HAVEN

Though home to one of America's most prestigious universities, this is no mere college town. Business and industry – shipping, manufacturing, health care, the telephone company – power New Haven's economy more than student dollars.

As you roll into town along I-95, New Haven appears bustling and muscular – it's still an important port, as it has been since the 1630s. But at the city's center is a tranquil core: New Haven Green, surrounded by graceful Colonial churches and the venerable Yale University.

History

The Puritan founders of New Haven established their colony in 1637-38 at a spot where the Quinnipiac and other small rivers enter Long Island Sound. The new town was to be no haven of religious freedom: this was a theocracy, only believers could be citizens, and the Bible was the law.

The strictness of religious law was softened somewhat in 1665 when New Haven reluctantly joined the larger province of Connecticut. It served as joint province capital (along with Hartford) from 1701 to 1875, testifying to its prominence during that time.

Its prominence first came from its port, but by the late 1700s and early 1800s, Yankee ingenuity made New Haven an important manufacturing city as well.

In 1702, a collegiate school was founded in Clinton, CT, by James Pierpont. It soon moved to Old Saybrook, and in 1716 to New Haven in response to a generous grant of funds by Elihu Yale. In 1718 the name was changed to Yale in honor of the benefactor.

Re-chartered in 1745, Yale grew extensively over the following century, adding schools of medicine, divinity, law, art and architecture, music, forestry, engineering, drama and a graduate school. By 1887 it was time to rename it Yale University. Now a member of the Ivy League, Yale has one of the finest libraries in the country, with many rare manuscripts.

Yale may be the best-known, but New Haven is also home to the University of New Haven and Southern Connecticut State College.

Orientation

I-95 skirts the shoreline of New Haven Harbor; I-91 splits off to the north and east. The center of the city can be reached by following CT 34, the Oak St Connector, west from I-95, or by taking I-95 exit 46 and following the signs to downtown. New Haven Green, with Yale to its west, is the town center.

Most hotels and sights are within a few blocks of the green. The bus and train stations are near I-95 in the southeast part of the city.

Information

Tourist Offices The New Haven Chamber of Commerce (☎ 203-777-8550, 800-332-7829) maintains an information office at 1 Long Wharf Drive on the waterfront, off I-95 exit 46 (follow the signs).

Yale University has a Visitor Information Office (☎ 203-432-2302) at Phelps Gate, 344 College St, on the west side of the green where you can get free campus maps and a self-guided walking tour pamphlet.

Bookstores To get in touch with the student population, the Yale Co-Op (☎ 203-772-0670), 77 Broadway, not only has a great number of books, but also Yale sweatshirts and other necessities. The Atticus Bookstore Café is a huge favorite; see Places to Eat.

Travel Agency There's a Council Travel office (☎ 203-562-5335) at 320 Elm St.

Safety As a working city, New Haven has urban pleasures and problems, including street crime. You should meet with no problems during the day in the center of the city, but avoid run-down neighborhoods and empty streets after dark, and don't leave *anything* visible in your parked car.

New Haven Green

New Haven's traditional town green, the spiritual center of the city, is spacious and framed by beautiful churches. The Georgian-style Center Church, a good example of New England's interpretation of Palladian architecture, harbors many colonial tombstones in its crypt. Trinity Church resembles England's York Minster. United Church is another Georgian-Palladian work.

Grove Street Cemetery, at 227 Grove St three blocks north of the green, has the graves of several famous New Havenites behind its grand Egyptian Revival gate (1845), including rubber magnate Charles Goodyear, telegraph inventor Samuel Morse, lexicographer Noah Webster and cotton gin inventor Eli Whitney.

Yale University

Crowded with University Gothic buildings, Yale's old campus dominates the northern and western portions of downtown New Haven. Tallest of its Gothic spires is Harkness Tower, from which a carillon peals at appropriate moments throughout the day. On the south side of I-95 is an extensive modern campus holding the Yale-New Haven Hospital and many other medical science buildings.

Stop at the Visitor Information Office at Phelps Gate (see Information), and pick up a free campus map and a walking tour brochure; or arrive weekdays slightly before 10:30 am or 2 pm, on Saturday or Sunday at 1:30 pm, for a free one-hour student-guided tour.

Yale's museums have outstanding collections, and the art museums are free.

Peabody Museum of Natural History

The museum (☎ 203-432-5050), at 170 Whitney Ave, five blocks northeast of the green along Temple St, has a vast collection of animal, vegetable and mineral specimens, including dinosaur fossils, wildlife dioramas, meteorites and minerals.

CONNECTICUT

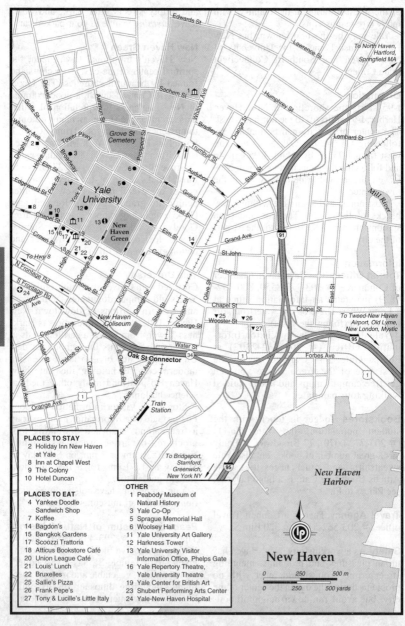

PLACES TO STAY
2 Holiday Inn New Haven
  at Yale
8 Inn at Chapel West
9 The Colony
10 Hotel Duncan

PLACES TO EAT
4 Yankee Doodle
  Sandwich Shop
7 Koffee
14 Bagdon's
15 Bangkok Gardens
17 Scoozzi Trattoria
18 Atticus Bookstore Café
20 Union League Café
21 Louis' Lunch
22 Bruxelles
25 Sallie's Pizza
26 Frank Pepe's
27 Tony & Lucille's Little Italy

OTHER
1 Peabody Museum of
  Natural History
3 Yale Co-Op
5 Sprague Memorial Hall
6 Woolsey Hall
11 Yale University Art Gallery
12 Harkness Tower
13 Yale University Visitor
  Information Office, Phelps Gate
16 Yale Repertory Theatre,
  Yale University Theatre
19 Yale Center for British Art
23 Shubert Performing Arts Center
24 Yale-New Haven Hospital

New Haven

0   250   500 m
0   250   500 yards

It's open from 10 am to 5 pm (Sunday noon to 5 pm), closed Monday. Admission costs $4 for adults, $3 for seniors, $2.50 for kids from three to 15.

Yale Center for British Art This museum (☎ 203-432-2800), 1080 Chapel St, corner of High St a block west of the green, holds the most comprehensive collection of British art outside the UK. The collections cover the period from Queen Elizabeth I to the present, with special emphasis on the period from Hogarth (born 1697) through Turner (died 1851). It's free and open from 10 am to 5 pm (Sunday noon to 5 pm), closed Monday.

Yale University Art Gallery Masterworks by Frans Hals, Peter Paul Rubens, Manet, Picasso and Van Gogh fill the Yale Gallery (☎ 203-432-0600), 1111 Chapel St between High and York, opposite the Yale Center for British Art. Besides the masterworks, there are important collections of American silver from the 1700s, and art from Africa, Asia, Europe, and the pre- and post-Colombian Americas: 75,000 objects in all. Admission to the gallery is free. It's open from 10 am to 4:45 pm (Sunday 2 to 4:45 pm), closed Monday, and all of August.

Places to Stay

Camping There are no campgrounds near New Haven. The closest are 21 miles east along I-95 near Clinton. *Hammonasset Beach State Park* (☎ 203-566-2304), on the coast between Madison and Clinton (I-95 exit 62), has 558 sites for $10 each and, despite its size, is crowded in high summer.

Riverdale Farm Campsites (☎ 203-669-5388), River Rd in Clinton, has 250 sites open mid-April through September. The nearby *River Road Campground* (☎ 203-669-2238), 13 River Rd, has 50 sites open from mid-April to mid-October.

Motels The *Motel 6 New Haven* (☎ 203-469-0343, 800-466-8356), 270 Foxon Blvd (I-91 exit 8), is a few miles north of the city,

with 58 rooms for $57. The *Quality Inn & Conference Center* (☎ 203-387-6651, 800-228-5151), 100 Pond Lily Ave, just off the Wilbur Cross Parkway (exit 59), offers its 125 rooms for $79 to $99, light breakfast included.

Hotels & Inns *Hotel Duncan* (☎ 203-787-1273), 1151 Chapel St at York, is New Haven's classic hostelry, a period piece over a century old. The decor and facilities of fin-de-siécle New Haven have been preserved (rooms have fans rather than air-conditioning). Prices also seem from an earlier time: $40 single, $60 double.

Only a few steps from the Duncan is *The Colony* (☎ 203-776-1234, 800-458-8810, fax 772-3929), 1157 Chapel St, a modernish hotel with 86 comfortable rooms within walking distance of everything, going for $88 single, $98 double.

Holiday Inn New Haven at Yale (☎ 203-777-6221), 30 Whalley Ave, has 160 rooms (the higher ones with good views) only a few minutes' walk from the green. Rooms are priced at $85 to $110.

The *Inn at Chapel West* (☎ 203-777-1201), 1201 Chapel St, New Haven, CT 06511, is a 19th-century house that's been well restored, and is a short walk to downtown. The 10 rooms are nicely decorated in period style (mostly Victorian), and rent for $175 per night, breakfast, refreshments and parking included.

Places to Eat

Cafes & Diners Yale students get their caffeine jolts at a number of coffeehouses within a few blocks of the green.

Koffee (☎ 203-562-5454), 104 Audubon St, serves only a few muffins; the bean-brew itself is the main event here. It's nice for its bright solarium and gardens in back.

Atticus Bookstore Café (☎ 203-776-4040), 1082 Chapel St between High and York, has been serving coffee, soups, sandwiches and pastries amid the stacks for over a decade. Mocking McDonald's, it proclaims "Millions of scones served since 1981." Prices are not low, and a slice of choice pastry or cheesecake might cost as

CONNECTICUT

much as $5, though there are things for less. The bookstore adjoins, and both are open true college-town hours: from 8 am to midnight daily.

Yankee Doodle Sandwich Shop, 258 Elm St at York, is a classic hole-in-the-wall American lunch counter – Formica countertop, chrome and plastic stools – with prices to match: hamburgers for $1.30, ham and cheese sandwiches for $2.50. They're open for breakfast and lunch except Sunday.

Louis' Lunch (☎ 203-562-5507), 261-263 Crown St between College and High, claims to be the place where the hamburger was invented – well, almost. Around the turn of the century, when the vertically grilled ground beef sandwich was first introduced at Louis', the restaurant was in a different location. It still uses the historic vertical grills, and serves other sandwiches as well, most for under $3.50. It's open from 11 am to 4 pm (Friday and Saturday until 1 am), closed Sunday.

Restaurants *Bangkok Gardens* (☎ 203-789-8684), 172 York St just off Chapel, is the center's most popular Thai eatery. At lunch, big plates of pork, beef and chicken with vegetables cost only $5. At dinner, main courses range from $7 to $11. It's open every day.

Bruxelles (☎ 203-777-7752), 220 College St, corner of Crown, is an upscale New American bistro just a short stroll from the green. Grilled beef, lamb, pork and fowl turn on the spits as diners quaff select wines and beers and exotic appetizers. Lunch comes to around $15 to $18, dinner $20 to $35. It's open daily for lunch and dinner, Sunday for brunch only from noon to 3 pm.

Another New American bistro is *Bagdon's* (☎ 203-777-1962), 9 Elm St, corner of State, with cutting-edge fare served in trendy black-and-white at similar prices.

Scoozzi Trattoria (☎ 203-776-8268), 1104 Chapel St at York next to the Yale Rep Theatre, serves trendy Italian fare with strong New American accents. Their little pizzettes and other appetizers are favorites with the before- and after-theater crowd, who combine them with wine by the glass

to make a light supper. More substantial fare includes creative pasta combinations and new variations on traditional Italian meat courses. Lunches cost from $10 to $18, dinners from $16 to $40. Scoozzi is closed Sunday.

The *Union League Café* (☎ 203-562-4299), 1032 Chapel St, is an upscale European bistro in the historic Union League building. Expect a menu featuring continental classics along with those of *nouvelle cuisine* for about $15 to $20 per person at lunch, twice that at dinner.

Wooster Square, six blocks east of the green, is a mostly residential neighborhood with a sprinkling of good Italian restaurants.

Frank Pepe's (☎ 203-865-5762), 157 Wooster St, serves good pizza, as it has for decades, in spartan surroundings. Prices range from $5 to $20 per pie, depending on size and toppings.

Challenger to Pepe's is *Sallie's Pizza* (☎ 203-624-5271), nearby at 237 Wooster St, younger but even more highly regarded by many New Havenites.

Tony & Lucille's Little Italy (☎ 203-787-1621), 150 Wooster St, is the restaurant to try if you want to go beyond pizza to a full Italian tuck-in.

Entertainment

As a college town and a city of some size, New Haven has a lively evening entertainment scene.

Theater & Ballet The well regarded *Yale Repertory Theatre* and the *Yale University Theatre* companies both perform in a converted church (☎ 203-432-1234) at 222 York St, corner of Chapel, with a full and varied program of performances from October to May.

The *Long Wharf Theatre* (☎ 203-787-4282), 222 Sargent Drive (I-95 exit 46), is down on the waterfront near the Howard Johnson's, with a season extending from October through June.

The Shubert Performing Arts Center (☎ 203-562-5666, 800-228-6622), 247 College St, is the venue for ballet and many musical performances from September through May.

For shows that command a large audience, it's the New Haven Coliseum (☎ 203-772-4200), 275 S Orange St.

Classical Music The *New Haven Symphony Orchestra* (☎ 203-776-1444, 800-292-6476) holds concerts each Tuesday evening at 8 pm from October through June in Yale's Woolsey Hall.

The *Chamber Music Society* at Yale (☎ 203-432-4158), 470 College St, sponsors Tuesday-evening concerts at 8 pm from September through April in the Morse Recital Hall of Sprague Memorial Hall, 470 College St.

Other concerts are hosted by the Yale School of Music (☎ 203-432-4157) and the Yale Collection of Musical Instruments (☎ 203-432-0822).

Folk & Rock Music *Toad's Place* (☎ 203-624-8623 recording, 562-5589 office), 300 York St, is a hot nightclub. Groups such as Black 47, Johnny Cash, Michael Bolton, and the Dave Matthews band headline there. Cover is free to $25.

The *Greater New Haven Acoustic Music Society* (☎ 203-468-1000) hosts folk concerts and performances during the summer in the Eli Whitney 1816 Barn; and in the winter in Dodds Hall, 300 Orange Ave, on the University of New Haven (not Yale) campus.

Getting There & Away
Air Tweed-New Haven Airport (☎ 203-787-8283), I-95 exit 50, is served by United; in addition, flights serving New York City (JFK airport) are handled by Continental, TWA and USAir, flights serving Boston by Continental and USAir.

Bus Peter Pan Bus Lines (☎ 800-343-9999) connects New Haven with New York City, Hartford, Springfield and Boston.

Connecticut Limousine (☎ 800-472-5466) runs buses between New Haven and New York City's airports (LaGuardia, JFK and Newark).

Train Metro North trains (☎ 212-532-4900, 800-223-6052, 800-638-7646) make the 1½-hour run between New York City's Grand Central Terminal and New Haven on weekdays almost every hour from 7 am to midnight, with more frequent trains during the morning and evening rush hours. On weekends, trains run about every two hours.

There are also several daily trains by Amtrak (☎ 800-872-7245) from New York's Pennsylvania Station, but at a higher fare.

Car Avis, Budget, Dollar, Hertz and Thrifty rent cars at the airport. Driving details for New Haven are:

Destination	Mileage	Hr:Min
Boston, MA	141 miles	3:25
Hartford, CT	36 miles	0.50
Litchfield, CT	36 miles	1:00
Mystic, CT	55 miles	1:15
New London, CT	46 miles	1:00
New York, NY	75 miles	1:30
Providence, RI	101 miles	2:15

Boat Bridgeport & Port Jefferson Steamboat Company (☎ 203-367-3043, 516-473-0286), 102 W Broadway, Port Jefferson, NY 11777, operates daily car ferries between Bridgeport, 10 miles southwest of New Haven, and Port Jefferson on Long Island about every 1½ hours. The 1½-hour voyage costs $8.50 to $11.50 per adult one way, $8.50 to $10.50 for seniors, $4.50 to $5.50 for kids six to 12. The price depends upon whether you're in a car (which is cheaper) or not. The fee for a car and driver is $27 to $32 in peak times (Friday noon through Sunday); off-peak, the highest fare is $36 for a car and all passengers. Call and reserve space for your car.

NEW LONDON
Across the Thames River from Groton and stretching six miles along the river's shoreline, the city of New London was a whaling town that in the 19th century rivaled Massachusetts' Nantucket and New Bedford for whaling activity. At its height in the mid-1800s, New London was home port to some 200 whaling vessels, more than

twice as many as were based at all other Connecticut ports together. Even after the whaling era ended, New London kept its ties to the sea.

Orientation

I-95 runs east-west through New London. Toward the west end of town, US 1 (Colman St) extends south from I-95, only to loop back to the interstate. The US Coast Guard Academy is north of I-95 on CT 32 (Mohegan Ave); most sites, including the Ferry Terminal and the Amtrak station, are south of I-95 on CT 32, called Water St as it narrows.

New London is on the west bank of the Thames River, Groton on the east.

Information

Contact the Chamber of Commerce of Southeastern Connecticut (☎ 860-443-8332), 105 Huntington St, New London, CT 06320.

Things to See

New London has a well laid-out walking tour that starts along the restored pedestrian mall called the **Captain's Walk** (State St). Among the major sites along it are the city's 19th-century railroad station and the nearby Nathan Hale Schoolhouse (☎ 860-426-3918), yet one more tiny two-story building where Hale taught before enlisting in George Washington's Colonial army in 1775 (see East Haddam). There is also the 1833 Custom House, whose front door was once part of the USS *Constitution*.

Between Federal St and Governor Winthrop Blvd, **Whale Oil Row** features four imposing mansions built for whaling merchants in 1830. The Hempstead House (☎ 860-443-7949) is a 1678 landmark maintained by the descendants of the original owners until 1937. It is one of few 17th-century houses remaining in the area, having survived the burning of New London by Benedict Arnold and the British in 1781. (The house is insulated with seaweed, of all things.)

More fine old houses are on Starr St; shops and cafes line Bank St near the waterfront.

At 325 Pequot Ave, **Monte Cristo Cottage** (☎ 860-443-0051) is the boyhood home of playwright Eugene O'Neill, open for tours. Located near Ocean Beach Park, the Victorian-style house is now a research library for dramatists, but many of O'Neill's belongings are on display, including his desk. You might recognize the living room: it was the setting for two of O'Neill's most famous plays, *Long Day's Journey into Night* and *Ah, Wilderness!* (Theater buffs should be sure to visit the Eugene O'Neill Theater Center in nearby Waterford, which hosts an annual summer series of readings by young playwrights.)

The **Lyman-Allyn Art Museum** (☎ 860-443-2545), 625 Williams St, is a Neo-Classical building with exhibits that include early American silver, Far Eastern, Greco-Roman, European and ethnic art of many cultures, as well as a collection of dolls and dollhouses. Included on the grounds of the museum is the Deshon-Allyn House, a whaling captain's Federal-style house, furnished with period antiques.

At the end of Ocean Ave is **Ocean Beach Park**, a popular beach and amusement area with waterslides, a picnic area, miniature golf, an arcade, a swimming pool and an old-fashioned boardwalk.

Visitors can tour the grounds of the **US Coast Guard Academy** (☎ 860-444-8270), whose museum is open daily May through October. When it's in port (usually on Sunday) you can climb aboard the tall ship *Eagle*, used for cadet training and in boat parades.

Places to Stay

Budget lodgings are at the *Red Roof Inn* (☎ 860-443-0001, 800-843-7663), 707 Colman St (I-95 North exit 82A, I-95 South exit 83), with 108 rooms ranging in price from $50 to $90. There's also a 135-room *Holiday Inn* (☎ 860-442-0631, 800-465-4329) here, and a 120-room *Radisson Hotel* (☎ 860-443-7000).

The *Queen Anne Inne* (☎ 860-447-2600, 800-347-8818), 265 Williams St, is a high-Victorian 1903 mansion with an art gallery as well as 10 guest rooms priced from $80 to $160, full breakfast and afternoon tea included. A 20th-century hot tub is also available.

Close to the beach is the *Lighthouse Inn* (☎ 860-443-8411), 6 Guthrie Place. The restored 1902 mansion has 51 rooms priced from $90 to $255.

Places to Eat
For good, medium-priced steaks, there's *Ye Olde Tavern* (☎ 860-442-0353), 345 Bank St. For great, inexpensive pizza (said to rival New Haven's famous Pepe's), New London has the *Recovery Room* (☎ 860-443-2619), 443 Ocean Ave, a family-run place near the beach.

Getting There & Away
Air The Groton/New London Airport (☎ 860-445-8549) is served by Continental and several other airlines. Flights serving New York City (JFK airport) are handled by TWA, USAir and American; TWA and USAir flights serve Boston.

Train Amtrak (☎ 800-872-7245) trains between New York and Boston on the *Shore Route* stop at New London.

Car Driving details for New London are:

Destination	Mileage	Hr:Min
Boston, MA	101 miles	2:00
Hartford, CT	52 miles	1:00
Hyannis, MA	104 miles	2:00
Mystic, CT	9 miles	0:15
New Haven, CT	46 miles	0:55
New York, NY	121 miles	2:30
Providence, RI	54 miles	1:00

Boat Cross Sound Ferry (☎ 860-443-5281, 516-323-2525), 2 Ferry St (PO Box 33), New London, CT 06320, operates car ferries year round between Orient Point, Long Island (NY) and New London, a 1½-hour run. From late June through Labor Day, ferries depart each port every hour on the hour from 7 am to 9 pm (last boats at 9:45 pm). Weekend voyages in June and September are almost as frequent. Off-season, boats tend to run every two hours. For one way/same-day roundtrip, adults pay $8.50/$13, children two to 12 pay

$4.25/$6.50. Cars are charged $28, bicycles $2 one way. Call for car reservations.

In summer, there are daily boats between New London and Block Island, RI, as well. See Block Island for details.

GROTON
West of Mystic, and across the Thames River from New London, Groton is known primarily as the home of the US Navy Submarine Base, the largest submarine base in the country. That's fitting, because just down the coast in Old Saybrook, the world's first submarine was launched in 1776 (see Old Saybrook).

Information
Contact the Chamber of Commerce of Southeastern Connecticut (☎ 860-443-8332), 105 Huntington St, New London, CT 06320.

Submarine Base
On Groton's Thames St, visitors can board the USS *Croaker* (☎ 860-448-1616), a vintage WWII submarine that was built by General Dynamics in Groton, served in the Pacific theater of the war and then returned to its birthplace. Displays show how a submarine moves, dives and surfaces; visitors can explore the sub's control room, torpedo rooms, conning tower and engine rooms.

At the USS *Nautilus* Memorial & Submarine Force Library and Museum (☎ 860-449-3174, 800-343-0079), visitors can board the world's first nuclear-powered submarine, the *Nautilus*, launched on January 21, 1954. Admission is free.

Fort Griswold State Park
At Groton's Fort Griswold State Park, a 130-foot obelisk marks the place where colonial troops were defeated by Benedict Arnold and the British in 1781, in a battle that saw the death of colonial Colonel William Ledyard and the British burning of Groton and New London. Monument House features the Daughters of the American Revolution's collection of Revolutionary and Civil War memorabilia. Admission is free.

CONNECTICUT

Places to Stay

Groton is not long on charming places to stay; most visitors choose to stay in the Mystic area instead. But there are some clean and comfortable motels, such as the *Gold Star Inn* (☎ 860-446-0660, 800-443-0611), 156 Kings Hwy (US 1), with 69 rooms for about $100 a double, or the *Groton Inn and Suites* (☎ 860-445-9784), CT 184 at I-95, with 115 rooms priced from $100 to $140.

Places to Eat

Family fare is mostly what you'll find in Groton. For a more elegant meal, head east on US 1 towards Mystic or Stonington. A couple of places worth trying in Groton are *G Williker's* (☎ 860-445-8043), 156 King's Hwy (US 1), and the *Fun 'n' Food Clam Bar* (☎ 860-445-6186), 283 CT 12.

Getting There & Away

See the New London section.

MYSTIC

No visit to the Connecticut coast would be complete without a stop at Mystic, a town name which by now has become synonymous with the Mystic Seaport Museum. Mystic was a lovely old seaport town centuries before the Seaport Museum became such a popular tourist attraction, and it's still a pleasant place to stroll, shop and dine. An appealingly nostalgic steel drawbridge spans the Mystic River, and it's part of the ritual of the place to wait while the bridge is raised for boat traffic.

Information

Contact the Mystic Chamber of Commerce (☎ 860-572-9578), 16 Cottrell St, PO Box 143, Mystic, CT 06355. Another source for area information is the Southeastern Connecticut Tourism Council (☎ 800-863-6569), PO Box 89, New London, CT 06320.

Mystic Seaport Museum

From simple beginnings in the 1600s, the village of Mystic grew to become one of the great shipbuilding ports of the East

Coast. In the mid-1800s, Mystic's shipyards launched clipper ships, many from the George Greenman and Co Shipyard, which is now the site of Mystic Seaport Museum, inaugurated in 1929.

Today, the Mystic Seaport Museum (☎ 860-572-5315), CT 27, covers 17 acres and includes more than 60 historic buildings, four ships and many smaller vessels. Some of the buildings in the Seaport are original to the site, but as at Old Sturbridge Village in Massachusetts, many were transported to Mystic from other parts of New England and arranged to recreate the look of the past. Seaport buildings are staffed by costumed interpreters who talk with visitors about their crafts and trades.

Visitors can board the *Charles W Morgan* (1841), the last surviving wooden whaling ship in America; the *LA Dunton*, a three-masted fishing schooner or the *Joseph Conrad*, a square-rigged training ship. "Fishermen" interpreters on the

KIM GRANT

A square-rigger at Mystic Seaport Museum

The haul in Stonington, CT

KIM GRANT

TOM BROSNAHAN
Haight Vineyard, Litchfield, CT

KIM GRANT
Stonington, CT

KIM GRANT

Upper Connecticut River Valley, VT

KATE MINER

Harvest Festival, VT

KIM GRANT

Manchester, VT

KIM GRANT

Nimms Farm, Dorset, VT

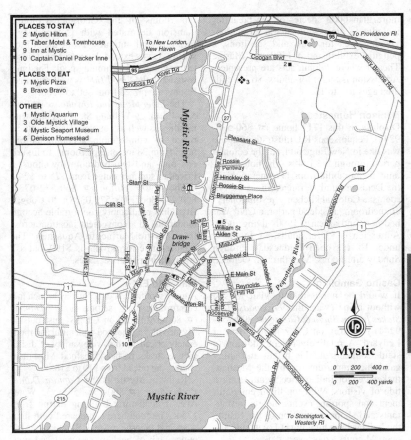

PLACES TO STAY
2 Mystic Hilton
5 Taber Motel & Townhouse
9 Inn at Mystic
10 Captain Daniel Packer Inne

PLACES TO EAT
7 Mystic Pizza
8 Bravo Bravo

OTHER
1 Mystic Aquarium
3 Olde Mystick Village
4 Mystic Seaport Museum
6 Denison Homestead

To New London, New Haven

Coogan Blvd

To Providence RI

Jerry Browne Rd

Bindloss Rd

River Rd

Mystic River

Pequotsepos Rd

Pleasant St

Rossie Pentway

Hinckley St

Rossie St

Bruggeman Place

Starr St

River Rd

Clift St

Clift Lane

Greenmanville Ave

Isham St

William St

Alden St

Mistuxet Ave

Drawbridge

Gravel St

Holmes St

Willow St

School St

E Main St

Broadway

Bobcdell Ave

Pequotsepos River

High St

W Main St

Pearl St

Cottrell St

E Main St

Lincoln Ave

Dennison Ave

Reynolds Hill Rd

Washington St

Roosevelt St

Williams Ave

Hatch St

Stonington Rd

Hewitt Rd

Water Ave

Noank Ave

Water Ave

Mystic Ave

Mystic River

To Stonington, Westerly RI

Mystic

0   200   400 m
0   200   400 yards

CONNECTICUT

Dunton show how cod was salted and demonstrate other skills essential to life at sea in the 19th century.

At the Henry B duPont Preservation Shipyard, visitors can watch large wooden boats being restored. In the Small Boat Shop, smaller-scale wooden boats are hand-built by skilled craftsmen using authentic 19th-century techniques, then either sold or used along the waterfront at the museum. The Seaport includes a general store, chapel, school, sail loft, shipsmith and ship chandlery – all the sorts of places that you'd expect to find in a real shipbuilding town of 150 years ago. The

Wendell Building has a display of ships' figureheads and carvings.

The *Sabino* (☎ 860-572-5315), a 1908 steamboat, takes visitors on excursion trips up the Mystic River from May through October.

All-day admission to Mystic Seaport Museum is $16 for adults, $8 for children six to 15. The museum is open from 9 am to 5 pm daily in summer.

Mystic Marinelife Aquarium
The family-oriented Mystic Marinelife Aquarium (☎ 860-572-5955), 55 Coogan Blvd (CT 27, use I-95 exit 90), has

more than 6000 species of sea creatures including a great white shark, an outdoor viewing area for seals and sea lions, a penguin exhibit and a 1400-seat Marine Theater where dolphin acts are presented. Admission is $9.50 for adults, $6 for children ages five to 12.

Denison Homestead

Displays in this 1717 home (☎ 860-536-9248), Pequotsepos Rd, illustrate what life was like in New England from the colonial period through the 1940s. The house contains memorabilia from 11 generations of the Denison family arranged in a series of rooms: a Colonial kitchen, a revolutionary-era bedroom, a Federal parlor, a Civil War bedroom and an early 1900s living room. Admission is $3 for adults, $1 for those under 16. It's open Wednesday through Sunday afternoons, May through October.

Casino Gambling

It would be impossible to visit Mystic without being aware that *Foxwoods High Stakes Indian Bingo & Casino* (☎ 800-752-9244) is nearby on CT 2 in the town of Ledyard. A relatively recent addition to staid Connecticut, this bright and shiny gambling emporium run by the Mashantucket Pequot Indian tribe is attracting a tide of visitors. With top-flight entertainment and sporting events, hotels, restaurants and shops in addition to the casino, the Indians have hit it big at Foxwoods. It's open 24 hours a day, every day.

Places to Stay

Many hotels and motels are clustered at I-95 exit 90. A few more motels are on the quiet US 1 to Stonington. Stonington itself is barely a 10-minute drive away.

The *Seaport Motor Inn* (☎ 860-536-2621), CT 27, Mystic, has 120 clean, simple rooms with motel conveniences and an outdoor pool. Prices range in summer from $40 to $100.

The *Inn at Mystic* (☎ 860-536-9604, 800-237-2415, fax 572-1635), US 1 and CT 27, has a variety of accommodations, from simple, clean motel-style rooms to inn rooms in the Georgian Colonial mansion decorated with Colonial-style furniture and antiques. From the hilltop setting, lawns extend down to a boat dock, tennis court and swimming pool. The inn's restaurant, the *Flood Tide*, is well-regarded. Rooms are priced from $60 to $200.

The *Taber Motel and Townhouse* (☎ 860-536-4904), 29 William St, is popular with families as well as couples. There's quite a range of comfortable accommodations here, from 28 motel-type rooms, to luxurious one- and two-bedroom townhouses. Prices in summer range from $75 to $240.

The *Mystic Hilton* (☎ 860-572-0731, 800-445-8667, fax 572-0328), 20 Coogan Blvd, has predictably comfortable accommodations in a convenient location across from Mystic Marinelife Aquarium. The standard rate for a room is $190, but ask about their special packages.

Places to Eat

A great spot for dinner or Sunday brunch in a comfortable barn setting is *JP Daniels* (☎ 860-572-9564) on CT 184 just outside Mystic village. The food is plentiful and moderately priced, with a wide variety of dishes such as steaks, pasta and seafood. Most main courses are priced from $10 to $18.

Right in Mystic is the *Captain Daniel Packer Inne* (☎ 860-536-3555), 32 Water Ave, in a historic building dating from 1754. The food here is prepared with flair. A special favorite is Steak Blackjack, a 16-ounce slab of beef in a sauce laced with whiskey. Expect to spend $25 to $45 for a very filling dinner.

On the east side of the drawbridge in downtown Mystic is *Bravo Bravo* (☎ 860-536-3228), serving nouvelle Italian food – flavorful and inventive pastas, seafood and beef (each about $15) – in a bright, sophisticated setting.

Lobster-lovers should check out *Abbott's Lobster in the Rough* (☎ 860-536-7719), on the waterfront in the neighboring town of Noank, just west of Mystic. Abbott's is as simple as it gets: order your lobster (or other seafood) at the window, get a number, pick out a picnic table by the water, and when your number is called, pay ($10 to $18 per meal) and eat. It doesn't get much better than this on a warm summer night. Abbott's is open daily for lunch and dinner, May through October.

Mystic Pizza (☎ 860-536-3737), 56 W Main St, calls its pizzas "little slices of heaven," and also serves salads and hearty grinders. If the name sounds familiar, it might be because it was a movie title a few years back. The low-budget comedy (one of Julia Roberts' first) was inspired by the pizza parlor, which has since become more popular than ever.

Things to Buy

Around the drawbridge, Mystic's Main St and Water Ave are lined with quaint shops, but some people feel compelled to go to Olde Mistick Village on CT 27 just off I-95 to browse the "shoppes" there. The shopping center is a pseudo-Colonial village that's set around a central green complete with Congregational church. Here you'll find stores selling sportswear, gifts, crafts, jewelry and Lladró porcelain. Nearby is Mystic Factory Outlets (☎ 860-443-4788), with 24 outlets for men's and women's clothes, leather, handicrafts, shoes and more.

Getting There & Away

Train Amtrak (☎ 800-872-7245) trains between New York and Boston on the *Shore Route* stop at Mystic.

Car Driving details for Mystic are:

Destination	Mileage	Hr:Min
Boston, MA	108 miles	2:00
Hartford, CT	54 miles	1:00
Hyannis, MA	95 miles	1:50
New Haven, CT	55 miles	1:05
New London, CT	9 miles	0:15
New York, NY	130 miles	2:40
Providence, RI	45 miles	1:00

STONINGTON

Five miles east of Mystic on US 1 is Stonington, unquestionably one of the most appealing towns on the Connecticut coast. Many of the town's 18th and 19th-century houses were once the homes of sea captains. One of the finest of these belonged to Captain Nathaniel Palmer, who earned fame at the tender age of 21 by discovering the continent of Antarctica.

It's best to explore this historic town – actually a "borough," Connecticut's oldest – on foot. Compactly laid out on a peninsula that juts into Long Island Sound, Stonington has wonderful streetscapes of period architecture. The short main thoroughfare, Water St, is lined with interesting shops, many featuring high-end antiques, colorful French Quimper Faience porcelain and upscale gifts. There are also a couple of good waterfront restaurants and delis. At the southern end of Water St is the "point" or tip of the peninsula.

History

It's hard to believe now, but tiny Stonington was once the hub of a network of steamships and trains that transported passengers between New York and Boston. At one time, in the mid-1800s, some 17 train tracks converged in the town. Train passengers from Boston boarded steamships in Stonington to New York.

Ironically, when the era of the steamships ended in the 1880s, and the Northeast Corridor trip could be made entirely by rail, the once-vital connection at Stonington was no longer needed. Then, a new railroad viaduct across the main north-south road into Stonington had the effect of cutting off the village from the commercial highway corridor of US 1. Many longtime Stonington residents credit (or blame, depending on their point of view) the railroad viaduct for leaving the mile-long peninsula and its little village in a kind of time-warp, in which it has remained ever since.

Stonington was a center of New England's whaling and sealing industry. In the first half of the 19th century, the borough's two main north-south streets, Water and Main, were lined with the fine houses of successful shipping merchants as well as bustling commercial buildings. Some of Stonington's earliest buildings were destroyed in the Battle of Stonington during the

War of 1812, but many more remain, including a sweet little Greek Revival Arcade.

The battle was a moment of high drama for the village: on August 9, 1814, four British ships used 158 Royal Navy guns to batter the town, which was suspected of harboring torpedoes. Forty buildings were destroyed, but miraculously there was only one human casualty on the American side. The Brits didn't fare so well, as Stonington men successfully defended the town with all they had in their arsenal: a pair of 18-pound cannons and one six-pounder hastily set up at the end of the point and aimed out to sea.

The Battle of Stonington is memorialized in the village's Cannon Square, where the cannons that served Stonington so well are on perpetual display. A plaque mounted at the end of the point bears the simple statement "This is To Remember." British cannonballs, recovered from all over the village after the battle, are fixed atop granite gateposts and hitching posts all over town.

Things to See

Stonington has had its share of famous residents over the years. The Colonel Amos Palmer House (1780) on Water St at Wall St, was the home of artist James McNeill Whistler, and later of poet Stephen Vincent Benét. (The house is not open to the public.)

Next door, the **Portuguese Holy Ghost Society** building is a reminder of the contributions made to Stonington by Azoreans who signed onto Stonington-bound whalers in the 1800s and eventually settled in the village. Today, their descendants still form a significant part of Stonington's population, though the village's ever-increasing appeal to wealthy New Yorkers seeking summer homes has had the effect of driving the locals out of the real estate market.

At the southern end of Water St, close to the point, the houses become plainer and simpler, many dating from the 1700s. These were the residences of ships' carpenters and fishermen.

At the end of the point, near a small shingle beach, is the **Old Lighthouse**

Museum (☎ 860-535-1440), 7 Water St. The octagonal-towered granite lighthouse, built in 1823 as the first government lighthouse in Connecticut, was moved to its present location in 1840 and deactivated 50 years later. In 1925, it was remodeled as a museum with exhibits on whaling, Indian artifacts, curios from the China trade, wooden boats, weaponry, 19th-century oil portraits, toys and decoys. The museum is open May through October from 11 am to 5 pm (closed Monday except in July and August). Adults pay $2, kids six to 12, $1.

Places to Stay

Stonington is the area's quaintest place to stay; see Mystic or New London for cheaper, or chain motels.

Camping *Highland Orchards Resort Park* (☎ 860-599-5101, 800-624-0829), in North Stonington, has 260 sites for $18 to $22. It's open all year.

MHG RV Park (☎ 860-535-0501), on CT 184 in North Stonington, is also open all year.

Motels The least expensive motels are along US 1 between Stonington and Mystic. The *Stonington Motel* (☎ 860-599-2330), US 1, Stonington, has 12 rooms priced from $50 to $80. The *Sea Breeze Motel* (☎ 860-535-2843), 812 Stonington Rd, has 30 rooms from $40 to $80.

Inns & B&Bs Calling itself "a quiet guesthouse" – the only one in the heart of Stonington, *Lasbury's* (☎ 860-535-2681), 24 Orchard St, is simple, unpretentious and conveniently within walking distance of everything in town. Double rooms cost about $75, including continental breakfast.

Randall's Ordinary (☎ 860-599-4540), PO Box 243, CT 2, North Stonington, is a centuries-old farmhouse (1685) that now is an unusual inn and restaurant (see Places to Eat). In the main house are three guest rooms; nine more are in the barn. All rooms have private baths, and four are suites. Rates in season range from $75 to $230, the latter being for a deluxe suite.

Places to Eat

Breakfast, lunch and dinner are served at *Noah's* (☎ 860-535-3925), 115 Water St. A pretty, informal place with two small rooms topped with original tin ceilings, Noah's has local art on the walls and an authentic old-fashioned atmosphere. Dinners cost about $12 to $18 per person; it's closed Monday.

Tucked away on the harbor behind the Harborview (see below) is *Skipper's Dock* (☎ 860-535-2000), a casual seafood restaurant with a waterside deck. This is the place to order steamers, lobster or what is locally known as a clam boil – the works, including clams, corn, lobster, fish and sausage, for $20 to $30 per person at dinner.

The fanciest restaurant in Stonington is the *Harborview* (☎ 860-535-2720), 60 Water St. Located, as its name suggests, right on the harbor, the Harborview has an intimate atmosphere perfect for a romantic evening ($40 to $50 per person). The cuisine tends towards French, but there's an English-style pub room decorated with old photographs and memorabilia of Stonington, and lower pub-food prices. The Harborview is open daily for lunch and dinner.

Hearth-cooking in the authentic colonial manner is the specialty at *Randall's Ordinary* (☎ 860-599-4540), CT 2, in North Stonington. There is just one dinner seating at 7 pm, for such fare as beef, fish, chicken and venison, hearth-baked cornbread and slow-simmered soups. Dinner is fixed price at $30, and reservations are necessary.

Litchfield Hills

The gently rolling hills in the northwestern corner of Connecticut are named for the historic town of Litchfield at their center. Sprinkled with lakes and dotted with state parks and forests, this beautiful, tranquil area offers an excess of natural beauty, but a paucity of accommodations. Only a handful of inns and campgrounds provide for travelers, an intentional curb on development which guarantees the preservation of the area's exceptional attractiveness.

LITCHFIELD

The centerpiece of the region is Litchfield, Connecticut's best-preserved late-18th century town.

Founded in 1719, between 1780 and 1840, Litchfield prospered on the commerce brought to and through the town by the stagecoaches en route between Hartford and Albany. In the mid-1800s, railroads did away with the coach routes, and industrial water-powered machinery drove Litchfield's artisans out of the markets, leaving the town to retreat into a torpor of faded gentility.

This proved to be its salvation. Its grand 18th-century houses were not torn down to build factories or Victorian mansions or shopping malls. With the advent of the automobile, Litchfield's economy was saved by tourism.

But it is mostly day-trip tourism. By plan, Litchfield and surrounding towns have very few beds for overnight visitors.

Orientation

US 202 goes right through the center of Litchfield along West St, the town's main street. CT 63 passes east of the center along North and South Sts. The town green is at the intersection of US 202 and CT 63. An 18th-century milestone stands on the green as it has since stagecoach days, informing passengers that they had another 33 miles to ride to Hartford, or 102 to New York City. Several restaurants face the green.

Information

From June through mid-September, an information booth on the town green is staffed daily by helpful locals; it's open weekends from mid-September through October.

The Litchfield Hills Travel Council (☎ 860-567-4506), PO Box 968, Litchfield, CT 06759, can send you an excellent booklet with precise route details on touring the Litchfield Hills by car, by boat, by bike or on foot.

Barnidge & McEnroe is the place to find books, see Places to Eat.

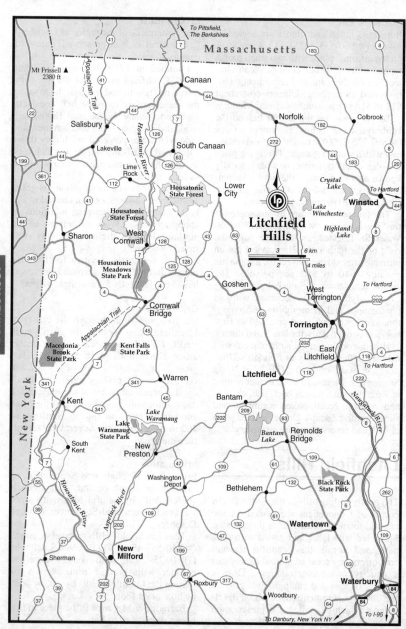

Things to See

A walk around town starts at the information kiosk on the town green. Just north across West St is the town's historic jail, adjoining – of all things – a bank. Stroll along North St to see the fine houses.

More of Litchfield's well-preserved 18th-century houses are along South St. Set well back from the roadway across broad lawns and behind old trees, the houses take you back visually to Litchfield's golden age.

The **Litchfield Historical Society** (☎ 860-567-4501), 7 South St, has set up a museum in its headquarters, open mid-April to mid-November, 11 am to 5 pm (Sunday from 1 to 5 pm), closed Monday. Admission costs $2 for adults, nothing for children under 16.

The **Tapping Reeve House** (☎ 860-567-4501), 82 South St, at the corner of Wolcott, now administered by the Historical Society, dates from 1773. Beside it is a tiny shed (1784) which once housed America's first school of law, established by Tapping Reeve in 1775. Lest it look too modest to have had any effect, you should know that John C Calhoun and 130 members of Congress were trained here. The school's most notorious graduate was Aaron Burr who, while serving as vice president of the US under Jefferson, shot Alexander Hamilton in an upstate New York duel in 1804. The house and the historical law school are open from mid-May to mid-October, 11 am to 5 pm (Sunday 1 to 5 pm), closed Monday. Admission costs $2 for adults, free for kids under 16.

At the southern end of South St is a house which may have been the birthplace of Ethan Allen, leader of Vermont's famous "Green Mountain Boys" during the Revolutionary War.

Activities

One mile southeast of the town center off CT 118, **Haight Vineyards** (☎ 860-567-4045, 800-325-5567), 29 Chestnut Hill Rd, makes tasty wines from vinifera and French-American hybrid grapes grown on the property. Grape varieties include Chardonnay, Maréchal Foch, Seyval Blanc, Vidal Blanc and Vignoles. They even make

a sparkling wine by the *méthode champenoise*, hand-riddling the bottles and disgorging by hand after resting on the lees. Winery tours and free tastings are available from 10:30 am to 5 pm (Sunday from 1 to 5 pm), year round.

The **White Memorial Conservation Center** (☎ 860-567-0857), 2½ miles west of town along US 202, has 35 miles of hiking and nature trails on 6¼ sq miles, open year round. The Natural History Museum is open from 9 am to 5 pm (Sunday noon to 4 pm).

Two miles east of the town green along CT 118, **Topsmead State Forest** was once the estate of Ms Edith Morton Chase. You can visit Ms Chase's grand Tudor-style summer home, complete with its original furnishings, then spread a blanket on the lawn and have a picnic while enjoying the view from this perch at 1230 feet. There are hiking trails as well.

Places to Stay

Camping The simple *Looking Glass Hill Campground* (☎ 860-567-2050), five miles west of Litchfield on US 202 in Bantam, is the most appealing, with 30 sites. The elaborate *Hemlock Hill Camp Resort* (☎ 860-567-2267), on Hemlock Hill Rd, has 125 pine-shaded sites open from May through late October. From Litchfield, go west along US 202 one mile, then right on Milton Rd.

Valley in the Pines (☎ 860-491-2032, 800-210-2267), has 35 sites open all year. Go west on US 202 almost to Bantam, turn north on Maple St and go 5½ miles to the campground.

Inn & B&B The *Litchfield Inn* (☎ 860-567-4503, 800-499-3444, fax 567-5358), two miles west of the green on US 202, has 30 elegant, luxurious rooms at premium rates.

Abel Darling (☎ 860-567-0384), 102 West St, is an early American house (1782) with two rooms to rent, continental breakfast included.

Places to Eat

Barnidge & McEnroe (☎ 860-567-4670), 7 West St facing the green, serves great

CONNECTICUT

coffee, good sweet buns and intellectual satisfaction – it's a bookstore cafe.

Aspen Garden (☎ 860-567-9477), on West St facing the green, serves a good selection of light meals with Greek accents: salads and sandwiches (around $5), and also baklava and tiramisu. Sit at an umbrella-shaded terrace table in good weather.

The *West Street Grill* (☎ 860-567-3885), on West St facing the green, is a sophisti-cated city grill and tavern serving creative New American cuisine, with full dinners going for about $30 per person. The wine and drink list is extensive.

The *Village Restaurant* (☎ 860-567-8307), on the green just a bit farther along West St, features gourmet sandwiches and similar lighter fare.

Difranco's Restaurant & Pizzeria (☎ 860-567-8872), is traditional and inexpensive, offering veal marsala for $12, pasta and sandwiches for $4 to $6.

Carrie's American Grill & Coffee House (☎ 860-567-8744), 342 Bantam Rd, a mile west of the center along US 202, is good for a cheap breakfast and a substantial lun-cheon sandwich at non-Litchfield prices. It's open daily from 8 am to 2 pm.

Getting There & Away
Bus Bonanza Bus Lines (☎ 800-556-3815) runs four buses between New York City and Bennington, VT, via Danbury, Kent and Cornwall Bridge, CT. No buses stop in Litchfield; these come the closest.

Car Driving details for Litchfield are:

Destination	Mileage	Hr:Min
Boston, MA	136 miles	2:00
Great Barrington, MA	33 miles	1:00
Hartford, CT	34 miles	1:00
Lake Waramaug, CT	15 miles	0:25
Lenox, MA	46 miles	1:15
New Haven, CT	36 miles	1:00
New York, NY	99 miles	2:30
Springfield, MA	58 miles	1:25

LAKE WARAMAUG
Of the dozens of lakes and ponds in the Litchfield Hills, Lake Waramaug, north of

New Preston, is perhaps the most beautiful. Gracious inns dot its shoreline, parts of which are protected as state parks.

As you make your way around the north-ern shore of the lake on North Shore Rd you'll come to the **Hopkins Vineyard** (☎ 860-868-7954), on Hopkins Rd in Warren, next to the *Hopkins Inn* (☎ 860-868-7295). The wines, made mostly from French-American hybrid grapes, are emi-nently drinkable.

The *Inn on Lake Waramaug* (☎ 860-868-0563, 800-525-3466), North Shore Rd, New Preston, CT 06777, is a posh resort inn with 23 rooms (some of them in modern motel-style units) and a long list of activities, including water sports on the lake.

Around the bend in the lake is **Lake Waramaug State Park** (☎ 860-868-0220), 30 Lake Waramaug Rd, with 88 beautiful lakeside campsites which are usually booked well in advance.

The Boulders (☎ 860-868-0541), East Shore Rd (CT 45), New Preston, CT 06777, was a grand summer house, and now makes a fine inn with a highly regarded restaurant. Rooms cost $175 to $200, breakfast included; for $50 more per room per night, you can have a full dinner as well.

NORTH TO SALISBURY
Almost every town in the northwest corner of Connecticut has a historic inn or two, a main street with a few antique and handi-craft shops and an art gallery.

From Lake Waramaug, go north on CT 45 via Warren to Cornwall Bridge, stopping for a look at its famous covered bridge.

North of Cornwall Bridge, flanking US 7, is **Housatonic Meadows State Park** (☎ 860-927-3238), famous for its two-mile-long stretch of Carse Brook set aside exclu-sively for fly fishing. The campground (☎ 860-672-6772) has 102 sites open from mid-April to mid-October.

The town of **Lime Rock**, west of US 7 along CT 112, is famous for its auto race-

track, the Lime Rock Park Raceway (☎ 860-435-0896).

The *Iron Masters Motor Inne* (☎ 860-435-9844), on CT 44 in nearby Lakeville, CT 06039, can provide moderately priced lodging for $75 Sunday through Wednesday, $120 Thursday through Saturday nights.

SALISBURY

This pristine New England village is Connecticut's answer to the gracious towns of Massachusetts' Berkshire hills just to the north across the state line. Salisbury prides itself on its beautiful inns, its good restaurants, and its wealthy real estate brokers.

The 23-room *White Hart Inn* (☎ 860-435-0030), on the village green right where CT 41 and US 44 meet, has the perfect front porch for watching the minimal activity in the town, and frilly chintz-filled rooms for $90 to $180. The dining room, called *Julie's New American Sea Grill*, serves all three meals.

Just across US 44 is the 10-room *Ragamount Inn* (☎ 860-435-2372), which also has a good restaurant. Rooms are a bit less expensive at *Alice's B&B* (☎ 860-435-8808), 267 Main St (US 44), a big Victorian with a wraparound porch.

Tea-lovers will want to know about *Chaiwalla* (☎ 860-435-9758), 1 Main St (US 44), a mail-order tea company which serves tea and light meals. Chaiwalla imports and sells unblended teas, which are a tea-drinker's equivalent to estate-bottled wines, brewpub beer and single malt scotches. If you develop a craving for unblended varietal teas, pick up a copy of their mail-order catalog.

CONNECTICUT

Vermont

Vermont is rural, beautiful and ecologically minded. Vermont is small, with a population of only about half a million people. Vermont is mountainous and green.

In fact, Vermont is one of the most rural states in the union. It has only one city worthy of the name – Burlington – with a population of a mere 50,000. It's a land of towns and villages, self-sufficient in the way of the old-fashioned America before jet planes and interstate highways.

Some of its towns bear the scars of the Industrial Revolution: once-proud 19th-century brick factories sit by the riverside now somewhat forlorn and dispirited, recycled for storage or retail space. But many Vermont towns and villages are proud inheritors of the New England traditions of hard, honest work, good taste and staunch patriotism. Some are pristine virtual museums of New England architecture and town planning.

Vermont is busiest with visitors in winter when its many ski slopes draw enthusiasts from Albany, Boston, Hartford, Montréal and New York. But summer is the more beautiful time, and fall is positively glorious.

To enjoy Vermont properly you must drive slowly, hike into the forests, canoe down a rushing stream. Don't rush it. Enjoy the land and the friendly people.

Statewide information is available from the Vermont Department of Travel & Tourism (☎ 802-828-3236), 134 State St, Montpelier, VT 05602, open weekdays during business hours. They'll also send you a good detailed road map for free. This organization maintains Vermont Welcome Centers at I-91 near the Massachusetts state line, on VT 4A near the New York state line and on I-89 near the Canadian border.

For information on fall foliage color and where it's at its best, call ☎ 802-828-3239 (fall only).

The Vermont Chamber of Commerce (☎ 802-223-3443), PO Box 37, Montpelier, VT 05601, has information on Vermont businesses, including hotels, restaurants and other tourist services. It's open during weekday business hours.

The Vermont Ski Areas Association (☎ 802-223-2439), PO Box 368, 26 State St, Montpelier, VT 05601, can provide you with information to help you plan a ski trip. For today's report on ski conditions (winter only) call ☎ 802-229-0531. Ski Vermont is also on the Internet's World Wide Web at http://www.cybermalls.com/cymont/vtski/vtski.html or contact them at their email address: vtski@cybermalls.com.

Getting There & Around

Air Vermont's major airport is at Burlington, which is served by large and small planes. There is a commercial airport at Rutland as well. Delta, Continental, Northwest and USAir service these airports. Other gateways to Vermont include Albany, NY; Montréal, Québec, Canada; Hartford, CT; and Boston.

Bus Vermont Transit (☎ 802-864-6811, 800-451-3292 in New England), based in Burlington, provides land transport to major towns in Vermont as well as to Manchester, NH; Keene, NH; Boston and Albany.

Greyhound Lines (☎ 800-231-2222) operates one bus daily between Burlington and Montréal. The three-hour trip costs $23.50 one way.

Train Amtrak's (☎ 800-872-7245) *Vermonter* and *Montréaler* provide the state's passenger rail service, but its funding is in doubt from year to year. Its route follows that of the same river valleys traversed by I-89 and I-91.

Car Though Vermont is not a particularly large state, it is mountainous. I-89 and I-91

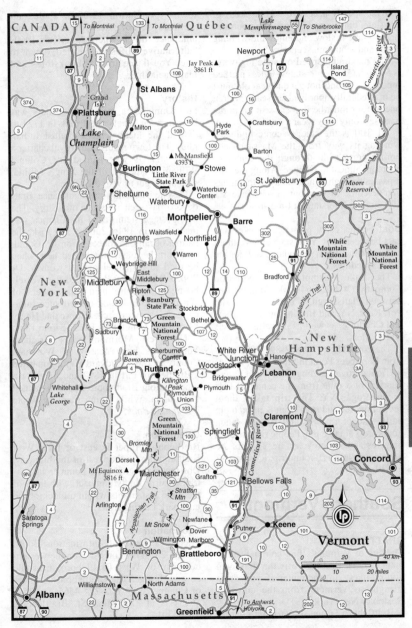

provide speedy access to certain areas of the state, but the rest of the time you must plan to take it slow and enjoy the winding roads and mountain scenery.

The maximum speed on state highways is 50 mph (55 on interstates) unless marked otherwise. Infants not yet one year old must be in a federally approved car seat; children one to four must be in a car seat or, in the back seat only, may wear a seat belt instead.

VT 100 is the state's scenic highway, winding its way from the Massachusetts border north right through the center of Vermont almost to Québec. Along the way it passes through or near many of the things you've come to Vermont to see. Take VT 100, not the Interstate, if time allows.

Boat Ferries carry passengers, bikes and cars between New York state and Vermont on Lake Champlain seasonally. Call for the latest schedules.

The Lake Champlain Transportation Company (☎ 802-864-9804) runs ferries between Plattsburgh, NY, and Grand Isle; Port Kent, NY, and Burlington; Essex, NY, and Charlotte, as well as operating cruises and charters.

The Fort Ti Ferry (☎ 802-897-7999) runs from Larrabees Point in Shoreham (VT 74) to Ticonderoga Landing (Ferry Rd), three-quarters of a mile from the center of Fort Ticonderoga, NY. The trip takes about seven minutes and runs from 8 am to 6 pm daily, except in July and August when hours are 7 am to 8 pm. People ride for 50¢, bicycles and motorcycles are $3, cars are $6 one way and $10 roundtrip. RVs cost $7 to $30, one way.

Southern Vermont

BRATTLEBORO

The site of Vermont's first colonial settlement (1724), Brattleboro is the first town you're likely to encounter if you drive straight to Vermont from the cities of Boston or New York.

Brattleboro is one of Vermont's larger towns (population 12,000), a pleasant workaday sort of place with an interesting ambiance: this is where America's 1960s "alternative" lifestyle settled down to live. You'll see lots of bookstores and male facial hair.

History

Fort Dummer, a wooden stockade, was built here on Whetstone Brook in 1724 to defend the local settlers against Indian raids. The town received its royal charter a year later. It was named for Colonel William Brattle, Jr, of the King's Militia, who never got to visit the town.

Despite its country-town ambiance, Brattleboro has seen its share of history. The first postage stamp used in America was made here in 1846. Jubilee Jim Fisk, the partner of railroad robber baron Jay Gould, was born here and was buried here when he died in a quarrel over a woman. Dr Robert Wesselhoeft developed the Wessel-hoeft Water Cure using the waters of Whetstone Brook, and treated such luminaries as Harriet Beecher Stowe and Henry Wadsworth Longfellow from 1846 to 1871.

The great Mormon leader Brigham Young was born nearby in Windham County in 1801. Rudyard Kipling married a Brattleboro girl in 1892 and lived for a time in a big Brattleboro house he named Naulaukha. While living there he wrote *The Jungle Book*.

Orientation

Brattleboro proper is east of I-91; West Brattleboro is to the west of the highway. Downtown Brattleboro's commercial district is surprisingly compact, with most of the good restaurants within a block of the landmark Latchis Hotel.

Information

There's a Vermont Information Booth (☎ 802-257-1112) on VT 9 on the western outskirts of West Brattleboro, near the covered bridge. The Brattleboro Chamber of Commerce (☎ 802-254-4565, fax 254-5675) is at 180 Main St, Brattleboro, VT 05301.

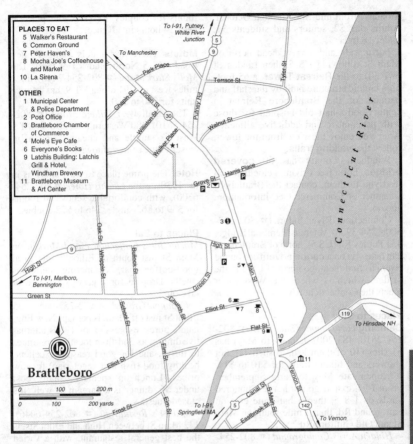

PLACES TO EAT
5 Walker's Restaurant
6 Common Ground
7 Peter Haven's
8 Mocha Joe's Coffeehouse
   and Market
10 La Sirena

OTHER
1 Municipal Center
   & Police Department
2 Post Office
3 Brattleboro Chamber
   of Commerce
4 Mole's Eye Cafe
6 Everyone's Books
9 Latchis Building: Latchis
   Grill & Hotel,
   Windham Brewery
11 Brattleboro Museum
   & Art Center

To I-91, Putney,
White River
Junction

To Manchester

Park Place

Terrace St

Chapin St

Linden St

Putney Rd

Walnut St

Walker Place

★1

Grove St

Harris Place

P

2

3

High St

4

P

5

Main St

Green St

Oak St

Whipple St

Bullock St

Church St

9

To I-91, Marlboro,
Bennington

Green St

School St

Elliot St

6

7

8

Flat St

9

10

Elm St

Elliot St

Brattleboro

0   100   200 m
0   100   200 yards

Frost St

To I-91,
Springfield MA

Canal St

S Main St

Vernon St

11

119

To Hinsdale NH

Connecticut River

To Vernon

142

Eastbrook St

5

VERMONT

Beneath the 2nd-floor restaurant Common Ground (see Places to Eat) is Everyone's Books, selling polit-lit, and also T-shirts, including one that reads "Discover Columbus's legacy – 500 years of racist oppression and stolen land."

Things to See & Do

At the center of the town's commercial district – and of its history in this century – is the pure Art Deco **Latchis Building**, including the Latchis Theatre, Latchis Hotel and Latchis Grille. Built in the 1930s by Demetrius Latchis, a Greek immigrant successful in the fruit business, it has been nicely restored. It still serves its original purposes. You can stay and dine in the hotel, and see first-run movies in the theater.

The **Brattleboro Museum & Art Center** (☎ 802-257-0124), in the Union Railroad Station, is right in the center of town near the intersection of VT 119 and VT 142. Besides the permanent collection of Estey reed organs made here in Brattleboro during the late 1800s, the museum hosts changing art and history exhibitions. It's open from 10 am to 6 pm (closed

Monday) from mid-May through October. Adults pay $2, seniors and students $1, under 18 free.

For a walk and a view, head north on Main St following US 5, then Linden St (VT 30) to the **Retreat Tower**, a 65-foot-high Gothic structure built by the staff and patients of the Brattleboro Retreat, a century-and-a-half old hospital for those with psychiatric and addictive ailments. After you enjoy the view from the tower, follow the **walking trails**.

Windham County has 30 **covered bridges**. For a free driving guide that will lead you to them, contact the Brattleboro Chamber of Commerce (see Information, above).

Connecticut River Safari (☎ 802-257-5008, 254-3908), Veterans Memorial Bridge, 451 Putney Rd (US 5), north of Brattleboro, can take you on a **canoe adventure** on the river. To find them, go north of US 5 to the bridge, which is where the West River meets the Connecticut River.

Places to Stay

Camping *Fort Dummer State Park* (☎ 802-254-2610, 483-2001 January to May) has 61 sites (10 of them lean-to shelters), hot showers and hiking trails for $10 to $14. It's open late May to early September. From I-91, exit 1, go north a few hundred yards on US 5, then a half-mile east on Fairground Rd, then a mile south on Main St and Old Guilford Rd.

Hidden Acres Campground (☎ 802-254-2098, 254-2724) has lots of services, even miniature golf, for a base rate of $16. It's on US 5 about 2½ miles north of I-91, exit 3. *Brattleboro North KOA* (☎ 800-468-8562) is a few miles farther north, and even more elaborate, for $18 to $26.

Hostel The nearest hostel is 25 miles north along VT 30, the *HI/AYH – Vagabond* (☎ 802-874-4096), VT 30, Box 224, East Jamaica, VT 05343. Vagabond serves as a hostel from late May through mid-October, and a ski lodge the rest of the year. Office hours are 5 to 9 pm; the 20 beds are priced at $12 plus tax; there are a few private rooms for couples. Reserve your place at least 24 hours in advance.

Motels There are motels along Putney Road (US 5 North) and VT 9 West. The *Molly Stark Motel* (☎ 802-254-2440), three miles west of I-91 along VT 9, has 14 nice units for $40 to $60.

The small *West Village Motel* (☎ 802-254-5610), 480 Western Ave, also on VT 9 West, is simple and cheaper, and a bit closer to the center of town.

Hotel The prime place to stay, today as in the 1930s, is the *Latchis Hotel* (☎ 802-254-6300), with comfortable renovated rooms for $39 to $62 single, $46 to $72 double.

Places to Eat

Mocha Joe's Coffeehouse and Market, on Main St just south of Elliot, is the local good-coffee bar, emanating delicious smells. Drop in for a java to sip here or take out.

Common Ground (☎ 802-257-0855), 25 Elliot St just off Main, is perhaps New England's purest expression of 1960s alternative dining. Its 2nd-floor location continues to thrive, and for good reason: excellent, healthy food (fish and vegetarian) for low prices. Luncheon specials usually cost under $6, dinner is a bargain as well. It's closed Tuesday.

Walker's Restaurant (☎ 802-254-6046), 132 Main St between High and Elliot Sts, is the best general restaurant, with a varied menu (hummus, fish and chips, teriyaki Delmonico steak) and good dinners for under $20, lunch for much less.

La Sirena (☎ 802-257-5234), on Main St right by Whetstone Brook, serves Mexican food at low prices, with lots of main courses for $7 or $8. Lunch is served Tuesday, Friday and Saturday, dinner Tuesday through Sunday.

Latchis Grille (☎ 254-4747), 6 Flat St, in the Latchis Hotel with views over Whetstone Brook, serves good New American cuisine such as roasted chicken breast stuffed with fresh greens, fennel, walnuts and currents, with a black currant velouté

($14). The Windham Brewery is here as well. Grille and Brewery are open for lunch and dinner every day.

Peter Haven's (☎ 802-257-3333), on Elliot St just up from Main St, has snowy white tablecloths, a quiet ambiance and main courses such as grilled loin lamb chops with rosemary mushroom sauce ($18.75). Main courses are priced from $13 to $20. This is among the fanciest places to dine in town.

Entertainment

The oak-paneled *Moles Eye Cafe* (☎ 802-257-0771), at the corner of Main and High Sts in the former Brooks Hotel, has live entertainment Wednesday through Saturday, and a well-stocked bar, as well as good meals at moderate prices.

The *Windham Brewery* is at the same address as the Latchis Grille. Try a pint of their Olde Guilford Porter, a dark, medium-bodied ale ($2.75).

Getting There & Away

Vermont Transit (☎ 802-864-6811, 800-451-3292 in New England) runs four buses daily between Hanover, NH, and Springfield, MA, with connections to Hartford, CT; New York, NY; Burlington and Montréal, Québec, Canada.

Driving details for Brattleboro are:

Destination	Distance	Hr:Min
Bennington, VT	40 miles	1:10
Marlboro, VT	8 miles	0:20
Springfield, MA	65 miles	1:30
Wilmington, VT	21 miles	0:45

MARLBORO

To the traveler, the village of Marlboro appears pretty but unremarkable: a white church, a white inn, a white village office building and a few white houses, all a short distance off the Molly Stark Trail (VT 9) eight miles west of Brattleboro.

To lovers of chamber music, Marlboro looms large as the home of **Marlboro Music Fest**, founded and directed for many years by the late Rudolf Serkin, and attended by Pablo Casals. On weekends

from mid-July to mid-August, the small Marlboro College is alive with music students, concerts and concert-goers in the small 700-seat auditorium.

Many concerts sell out almost immediately, so it's essential to reserve in advance. Write to Marlboro Music, 135 S 18th St, Philadelphia, PA 19103 for information; after June 20, call ☎ 802-254-2394. Tickets cost $5 to $20.

Heading west from Marlboro on VT 9 brings you up **Hogback Mountain** (2410 feet). There's a lookout at the high point, and also two restaurants, the *Summit Cafe* and the *Skyline Restaurant* (☎ 802-464-3536), moderately priced places to stop for a snack or a meal, with the marvelous "100-mile" view.

For **camping**, *Molly Stark State Park* (☎ 802-464-5460), three miles east of Wilmington on VT 9, has 34 sites (10 lean-tos) for $10 to $14, hot showers and hiking trails with panoramic views. It's open late May through mid-October.

WILMINGTON & MT SNOW

Though a pretty town in its own right, Wilmington is a crossroads where people on their way between Massachusetts and Vermont stop for a rest, a meal and perhaps some shopping. Mt Snow and Haystack are southern Vermont's twin ski resorts, with golfing in summer.

VT 100, Vermont's central north-south highway, goes north from Wilmington past Haystack and Mt Snow, and VT 9, the main route across southern Vermont, is Wilmington's main street.

The main street is lined with restaurants and clothing stores that cater to those passing through and also to those headed to the resorts just to the north.

Information

The Mt Snow-Haystack Chamber of Commerce (☎ 802-464-8092), PO Box 3, Wilmington, VT 05363, maintains an information booth on the eastern outskirts of Wilmington at the intersection of VT 100 South and VT 9, open from May through October.

Mt Snow & Haystack

Mt Snow, a popular family ski area, has 127 trails, 24 lifts, a vertical drop of 1700 feet and snowmaking ability to cover 83% of the trails. Cross-country routes cover over 60 miles. Haystack, the smaller area, has 43 trails (mostly intermediate, with a few short, steep expert runs). There are six lifts, a drop of 1400 feet and 85% snowmaking ability. Both ski areas have ski schools and, in summer, golf courses. You can get more information and book accommodations by calling ☎ 802-245-7669.

Places to Stay & Eat

Wilmington has numerous inns, motels and restaurants. This is a short listing.

Camping See Marlboro, above, for Molly Stark State Park.

Motels The *Vintage Motel* (☎ 802-464-8824, 800-899-9660), on VT 9 a mile west of the town center, has 18 tidy units open all year, and a heated pool. Rooms cost $52 to $76, light breakfast included.

The *Nutmeg Inn* (☎ 802-464-3351), on VT 9 west of Wilmington, is a larger, fancier motel charging $75 to $165 per room, depending upon the room and the season.

Inns *Trail's End* (☎ 802-859-2585), Smith Rd, about four miles north of Wilmington on a side road (watch for signs), has a country-home feel to it, and 15 cozy rooms with private baths for $110 to $170 double, full breakfast included.

The *Red Shutter Inn* (☎ 802-464-3768), on VT 9 in the village, is a grand old house dating from 1894 with seven guest rooms – all different – and two suites. All have private baths, and are priced from $88 to $165. The inn is more famous for its restaurant than its lodging, actually.

The *White House of Wilmington* (☎ 802-464-2135, 800-541-2135, fax 802-464-5222) crowns a hill on the eastern outskirts of the town. This grand, white Federal mansion has an indoor pool, a large outdoor pool, whirlpool and sauna, an excellent dining room and luxury guest

rooms priced from $190 to $240 a double, full breakfast and dinner included.

Getting There & Away

Wilmington is 21 miles (45 minutes on the curvy roads) west of Brattleboro, and 20 miles (40 minutes) east of Bennington.

BENNINGTON

Bennington, a felicitous mix of picture-perfect Vermont village (Old Bennington) and workaday town (Bennington proper), is the more refined of Vermont's two large southern towns. Home to Bennington College and the famous Bennington Museum, it is a historic place, famed for its tall monument commemorating the crucial Battle of Bennington in the Revolutionary War. Robert Frost, perhaps the most famous American poet of the 20th century, is buried here.

History

In August of 1777 during the Revolutionary War, British General John ("Gentleman Johnny") Burgoyne, his supplies depleted during the battle at Fort Ticonderoga, sent two units toward Bennington to seize military supplies held by the Colonials. He misjudged the size of the American defenses, and was unaware that General John Stark, battle-tested at Bunker Hill and a commander under Washington at the battles of Trenton and Princeton, was leading the defense.

Stark headed off the British advance in Walloomsac, NY, six miles west of Bennington. "There are the Redcoats!" he exclaimed. "They will be ours tonight or Molly Stark sleeps a widow!"

The two sides clashed on August 16, 1777. The ferocious pitched battle lasted two hours, with the Americans victorious, but British reinforcements threatened Stark's retreat to Bennington. The American victory was saved by Colonel Seth Warner and his Green Mountain Boys, who arrived in time to counter the British resurgence. The Americans captured more than 800 British regulars, about one-sixth of Burgoyne's total force.

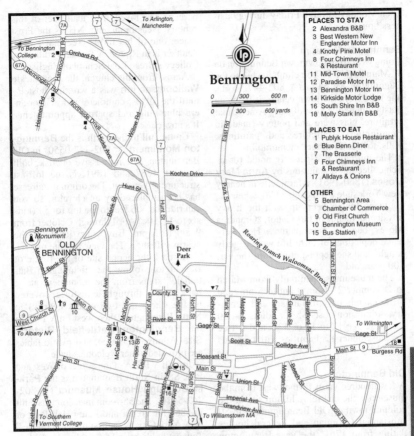

Bennington

0   300   600 m

0   300   600 yards

PLACES TO STAY
2 Alexandra B&B
3 Best Western New
   Englander Motor Inn
4 Knotty Pine Motel
6 Four Chimneys Inn
   & Restaurant
11 Mid-Town Motel
12 Paradise Motor Inn
13 Bennington Motor Inn
14 Kirkside Motor Lodge
16 South Shire Inn B&B
18 Molly Stark Inn B&B

PLACES TO EAT
1 Publyk House Restaurant
3 Blue Benn Diner
7 The Brasserie
8 Four Chimneys Inn
   & Restaurant
17 Alldays & Onions

OTHER
5 Bennington Area
   Chamber of Commerce
9 Old First Church
10 Bennington Museum
15 Bus Station

VERMONT

Unable to procure Bennington's supplies, and suffering badly from the loss of soldiers, Burgoyne's forces went into the Battle of Saratoga in October much weakened. After the disastrous defeat, General Burgoyne surrendered his entire command to the Americans, ending his drive down the Hudson Valley which would have cut the colonies in two.

Orientation
Converging in Bennington are US 7, VT 7A and VT 9, making it an important crossroads. Most businesses, lodgings and

restaurants are in downtown Bennington, but the monument, museum and prettiest houses are in Old Bennington, a mile from the center of town at the western end of Main St on the way to New York state. The actual site of the Battle of Bennington is in Walloomsac, NY, six miles west of the monument.

Information
The Bennington Area Chamber of Commerce (☎ 802-447-3311), Veterans Memorial Drive (US 7), Bennington, VT 05202, maintains an information office

open Monday through Friday during business hours.

Bennington Museum

Going west from downtown Bennington on W Main St (VT 9), you climb the hill to the Bennington Museum (☎ 802-447-1571), one mile from the town center. It holds an outstanding collection of early Americana: furniture, glassware and pottery (made in Bennington), sculpture and paintings, dolls, toys and military memorabilia.

The museum is especially noted for its rich collection of paintings by **Anna Mary Moses** (1860-1961), a farm wife in nearby New York state. At the age of 70, when she could no longer keep up with the heavy physical demands of farm labor, "Grandma Moses" began to paint pictures. Her lively naive depictions of farm life were eagerly sought, and she kept painting until she was 100 years old.

The museum is open daily from March to December 23 from 9 am to 5 pm, and on weekends only in January and February. Admission costs $5 for adults, $4.50 for those age 12 to 17 or 62+, and is free for those under 12. Families with two kids pay $12.

Old Bennington

A few hundred yards further west from the museum is the charming hilltop site of the colonial town of Old Bennington, with 80 substantial Georgian and Federal houses dating from 1761 (the year Bennington was founded) to 1830 arranged along a broad mall.

The **Old First Church**, towering at the village center, was built in 1806 in Palladian style. Its churchyard holds the remains of five Vermont governors, numerous Revolutionary War soldiers and poet **Robert Frost** (1874-1963). Frost was born in California of New England stock, lived and wrote in England for a time, but is famous for his poems of the New England experience, inspired by his life on several New England farms. Although never successful at farming, Frost became the best-known and

perhaps best-loved American poet of this century. Near Franconia, NH, is the Frost Place, one of his farms (see that entry). Another is in Ripton, VT, near Middlebury College's Bread Loaf School of English.

Across from the church, the ramshackle **Walloomsac Inn** was a working hostelry until the 1980s, complete with Victorian-era plumbing and spartan appointments. It's now closed.

Up the hill to the north is the **Bennington Monument** (☎ 802-447-0550) in Old Bennington. The impressive obelisk, built between 1887 and 1891, is the loftiest structure in Vermont. The original staircase has been replaced by an elevator, so you can ride the 306 feet to the top for $1 (kids six to 11, 50¢) April through October from 9 am to 5 pm. Buy your tickets at the nearby gift shop. The view is quite nice.

To reach the actual site of the Battle of Bennington, follow the "Bennington Battlefield" signs from the monument along back roads, through a historic covered bridge (there are two others nearby) to North Bennington, then west on VT 67 to the **Bennington Battlefield Historic Site**. Admission is free, and picnic tables are provided under welcome shade.

Just off VT 67A at the corner of West and Park Sts in North Bennington is the **Park-McCullough House Museum** (☎ 802-442-5441). The 35-room mansion was built in 1865 for Trenor and Laura Hall Park of New York City as their summer "cottage." Today it holds period furnishings and a fine collection of antique dolls, toys and carriages. It's open May through October from 10 am to 4 pm (last tour at 3 pm) for $4, less for seniors and students.

Canoeing

Batten Kill Canoe Ltd (☎ 802-362-2800, 800-421-5268), PO Box 65-1, VT 7A, Arlington, VT 05250, can fit you out for a day trip on the Batten Kill River, a lovely stream that winds through Vermont forest down to the Hudson River. They also arrange longer trips, from two to 10 days, combined with stays at inns.

Places to Stay

Camping *Woodford State Park* (☎ 802-447-7169), 10 miles east of Bennington on VT 9, has 102 sites (20 lean-tos) for $12 to $16, hot showers, a beach, boat and canoe rentals, and hiking trails.

Lake Shaftsbury State Park (☎ 802-375-9978), two miles south of Arlington on VT 7A, has only 15 sites, all lean-tos, for $10. There's a beach, boat and canoe rentals, and a nature trail. It's open from late May through early September.

Several other campgrounds are located near Pownal, off US 7 south of Bennington near the Massachusetts state line. *Shady Acres* (☎ 802-442-4960), on Jackson Cross Rd less than a half mile from Pownal, charges $11 to $14. *Pine Hollow* (☎ 802-823-5569) charges $12 to $16 for its 50 sites. From Bennington center, follow US 7 south 6½ miles, turn left on Barbers Pond Rd, go 1½ miles, then right on Old Military Rd for a half mile.

Other campgrounds are north of Bennington in Arlington. *Howell's* (☎ 802-375-6469), on School St one mile off VT 7A/313, has 70 sites for $14 each. *Camping on the Batten Kill* (☎ 802-375-6663), on VT 7A, has over 100 sites for $14. It's open from mid-April through October.

Hostel *Greenwood Lodge & Campsites* (☎ 802-442-2547), PO Box 246, Woodford, VT 05201, eight miles east of Bennington on VT 9 at Prospect Mountain, is the local HI/AYH hostel. It has budget dorms ($14 to $17 per person) and guest rooms ($30 to $36 single or double) as well as 20 campsites ($14) on 120 acres. Hot showers are free. For hostel accommodations, bring your own linens and soap, or rent theirs ($3). They provide clean pillows. Greenwood is open from mid-May to mid-October and during ski season. Office hours are from 8 to 10 am and 5 to 10 pm. Reserve by phone, no credit cards are accepted.

Motels *Harwood Hill Motel* (☎ 802-442-6278), on Harwood Hill along VT 7A two miles north of Bennington, has fine views of the Bennington Monument and the town, and charges an agreeable $46 to $60 for its rooms. No swimming pool, though.

Paradise Motor Inn (☎ 802-442-8351) is the big, fancy place in town, with 76 rooms and suites ($60 to $80), a restaurant and all services, right in the town center.

Mid-Town Motel (☎ 802-447-0189), 107 W Main St, Bennington, VT 05201, has 24 rooms, economy units as well as deluxe efficiencies, for $38 to $70. There's a pool and hot tub as well.

Bennington Motor Inn (☎ 802-442-5479, 800-359-9900), 143 W Main St, is within walking distance of most sights, and charges $67 to $70 for its rooms.

Kirkside Motor Lodge (☎ 802-447-7596), very near the marble church of St Francis de Sales, has 23 tidy rooms right in the center of town for $64 to $89.

Knotty Pine Motel (☎ 802-442-5487), 130 Northside Drive, on VT 7A in a commercial strip just off of US 7, has a fairly convenient location and decent rooms for $58 to $64.

Best Western New Englander Motor Inn (☎ 802-442-6311), 220 Northside Drive, near the Knotty Pine, has 51 rooms in a variety of styles priced at $60 to $90.

Lots more motels are south of Bennington along US 7 on the way to Williamstown, MA.

Inns There are lots more cozy inns and B&Bs north of Bennington in nearby Arlington, call the chamber of commerce for further information. The following listings are in Bennington:

Bennington Orchard Inn (☎ 802-447-1185), on VT 7A about two miles north of the town center, is a restored farmhouse perched on the hillside offering quiet guest rooms for $65 to $80.

Molly Stark Inn B&B (☎ 802-442-9631, 800-356-3076), 1067 Main St, is a big Victorian house (built in 1890), with an equally large sign and six comfy guest rooms priced at $70 to $90, some with private bath. A full breakfast costs extra.

Alex Koks and Andra Erickson, owners of the elegant Four Chimneys Inn, decided to start a small B&B as well. What to call it? *Alexandra B&B* (☎ 802-442-5619), of course! It's a tidy house about two miles north of Bennington on VT 7A North at Orchard Rd. Guest rooms cost $125, breakfast included.

South Shire Inn B&B (☎ 802-447-3839), 124 Elm St, is a Victorian inn furnished in antiques. Rooms have private baths, air-conditioning and, in some, fireplaces; they go for $110 to $160.

The Four Chimneys Inn & Restaurant (☎ 802-447-3500), 21 West Rd (VT 9 West) in Old Bennington, is known primarily for its elegant dining rooms, but it's also a treat to stay the night in this grand white mansion set amid verdant manicured lawns. Comfortable rooms with private bath cost $125.

Places to Eat

Alldays & Onions (☎ 802-447-0043), 519 Main St, encourages you to create your own sandwich from its bewilderingly long blackboard menu of ingredients. Salads, soups, quiches and other light fare rule at breakfast and lunch, with more substantial European-inspired cuisine in the evening (Thursday through Saturday, 6 to 8 pm). It's closed Sunday.

For a longer menu with several international dishes, try the *Blue Benn Diner* (☎ 802-442-5140), on North St. The standard diner fare is supplemented with Mexican, Asian and vegetarian dishes. An average meal costs around $10. Breakfast is served from 6 am on.

The Brasserie (☎ 802-447-7922), 324 County St, in Potters' Yard at the north end of School St, has been popular for years because of its bistro ambiance and good food at decent prices: antipasti, soups, quiches, excellent salads, breads, cheeses, crêpes – come and see. Arrive early or late for lunch to get one of the cafe tables on the marble terrace. It's open from 11:30 am to 8:30 pm, closed Tuesday.

The menu at the *Publyk House Restaurant* (☎ 802-442-8301), on VT 7A a mile or so north of the town center, is traditional American with lots of sirloin, shrimp, crab and chicken priced from $10 to $20 per main course. The setting is exceptional: through the greenhouse glass are great views of Mt Anthony and the lofty Bennington Monument.

For a super elegant lunch or dinner, head for the Four Chimneys Inn (see Places to Stay). A huge, gracious Georgian mansion is the venue for European and New American dishes. Try the duck salad with spiced pecans and melon, veal chops with morel mushrooms or tuck into a true beef Wellington. Expect to pay $25 to $30 per person.

Things to Buy

Farms in Bennington County produce lots of delicious maple syrup. Shops in town sell it, but it's much more interesting to visit one of the farms during maple sugaring (March and April) when the sap is collected and boiled in the sugar house to yield maple syrup. For a list of farms giving demonstrations, tastings and tours, contact the Bennington County Conservation District (☎ 802-442-2275), 118 South St, Bennington, VT 05201.

Getting There & Away

Vermont Transit (☎ 802-864-6811 800-451-3292 in New England) runs three buses daily between Albany, NY, and Burlington stopping in Bennington.

Driving details for Bennington are:

Destination	Distance	Hr:Min
Boston, MA	140 miles	3:10
Brattleboro, VT	40 miles	1:10
Manchester, VT	19 miles	0:30
Williamstown, MA	14 miles	0:25
Wilmington, VT	20 miles	0:40

NEWFANE & GRAFTON

Vermont has dozens of pretty villages, but Newfane and Grafton are near the top of everyone's list. All the beauties you expect in a Vermont town are here: tall old trees, white, high-steepled churches, excellent inns and gracious old houses. In spring both villages are busy making maple sugar, in summer with yard sales, in fall with "leaf peepers," in winter with couples seeking good food and cozy rooms in a cold-weather hideaway.

Newfane

A short stroll shows you all of Newfane – you'll see the stately Congregational Church (1839), the Windham County Courthouse (1825) in Greek Revival style and a few antique shops.

Places to Stay & Eat Most people stop here long enough for a meal or a night at the *Four Columns Inn* (☎ 802-365-7713), on West St in the town center (zip code 05345). The 1830s Greek Revival inn has a fine dining room serving New American cuisine with Vermont ingredients, and 15 guest rooms priced from $100 to $175; winter rates are lower.

The *West River Lodge* (☎ 802-365-7745), RR 1, Box 693, just outside the town, features its own watercolor and English riding workshops (it has its own stables) and farmhouse accommodations for $50 to $80, breakfast included.

Townshend State Park (☎ 802-365-7500), three miles north of Newfane along VT 30, has 34 tent sites ($10 to $14) open from early May through mid-October. Hiking trails include the sometimes steep, challenging path to the summit of Bald Mountain (1680 feet), a rocky climb that rises 1100 feet in less than a mile. Other trails are easier. There's swimming and boating at the nearby Army Corps of Engineers' Recreation Area at Townshend Dam. The West River is good for canoe trips.

Grafton

Graceful Grafton is not that way by accident. In the 1960s, the Windham Foundation established a program for the restoration and preservation of the entire village, and it has been eminently successful. It is virtually an open-air museum. The real museum, however, is the Grafton Historical Society (☎ 802-843-2584), south of the Old Tavern on Main St just down from the post office. It's open on weekend afternoons in summer.

The Grafton Village Cheese Company (☎ 802-843-2221), on the Townshend road a half mile south of the village, makes Covered Bridge Cheddar, and you can sample it and see it being made any weekday, as well as Saturday in summer; closed Sunday.

Places to Stay & Eat The central landmark is *The Old Tavern at Grafton* (☎ 802-843-2231, 800-843-1801), VT 35 and Townshend Rd, Grafton, VT 05146. The original inn is quite formal, the tavern restaurant in the adjoining barn less so. The 66 beautiful rooms cost $85 to $165.

The Inn at Woodchuck Hill (☎ 802-843-2398), Middletown Rd, Grafton, VT 05146, is a 1790s farmhouse on 200 acres with its own hiking and cross-country ski trails. The antique-filled guest rooms go for $79 to $160, full breakfast included.

Getting There & Away

Newfane is 12 miles northwest of Brattleboro, 19 miles northeast of Wilmington, and 15 miles south of Grafton.

Central Vermont

MANCHESTER

For almost two centuries, Manchester has been a summer resort. The mountain scenery, the equable summer climate and the Batten Kill River, one of Vermont's best trout streams, drew the crowds.

Now the draw is mostly winter skiing and shopping, but Manchester is also busy in summer with hikers, golfers and shoppers.

Two families put Manchester on the map. The first was that of native son Franklin Orvis (1824-1900), who became a New York businessman, but then returned to Manchester to found the Equinox House Hotel (1849). Orvis did much to beautify Manchester with the laying of marble

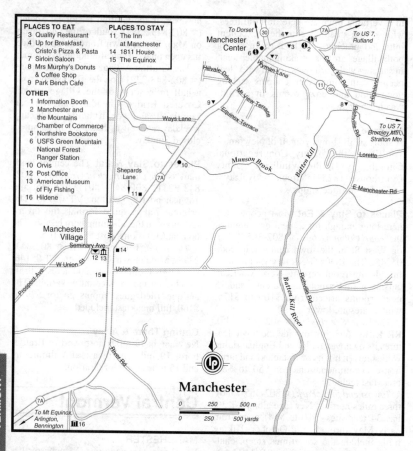

PLACES TO EAT
3 Quality Restaurant
4 Up for Breakfast,
   Cristo's Pizza & Pasta
7 Sirloin Saloon
8 Mrs Murphy's Donuts
   & Coffee Shop
9 Park Bench Cafe

OTHER
1 Information Booth
2 Manchester and
   the Mountains
   Chamber of Commerce
5 Northshire Bookstore
6 USFS Green Mountain
   National Forest
   Ranger Station
10 Orvis
12 Post Office
13 American Museum
    of Fly Fishing
16 Hildene

PLACES TO STAY
11 The Inn
    at Manchester
14 1811 House
15 The Equinox

Manchester

0   250   500 m
0   250   500 yards

sidewalks, the construction of public buildings and the opening of roads in the forest for excursions. Franklin's brother Charles founded the Orvis Company, makers of fly fishing equipment, in 1856. The Manchester-based company now has a world-wide following.

The second family was that of Abraham Lincoln (1809-1865), 16th president of the USA. His wife, Mary Todd Lincoln (1818-1882), and their son, Robert Todd Lincoln (1843-1926), came here during the Civil War, and Robert returned to build a mansion some years later.

Orientation

US 7 bypasses the town to the east; VT 7A goes right through the town's center.

Manchester has a split personality. When locals say "Manchester" or "Manchester Village," they're referring to the southern part of the town, a beautiful, dignified, historic Vermont village centered on the huge, venerable, posh Equinox Hotel. There are several other charming, expensive inns as well.

"Manchester Center," a few miles north along VT 7A, used to be called Factory Point, but this name did not fit well with

Manchester's resort image, so it was changed. Manchester Center has several moderately priced inns and cheap-to-moderate restaurants, but is devoted mostly to upscale outlet stores – Mark Cross, Giorgio Armani, Polo, etc – and ye olde Vermont-type shops.

Information

The Manchester and the Mountains Chamber of Commerce (☎ 802-362-2100) maintains an information office on the green in Manchester Center (open 9 am to 5 pm, Saturday 10 to 4, Sunday 10 to 2), located a few hundred yards north of the main intersections in town along VT 7A. They'll help you find a room if you need assistance.

The Northshire Bookstore (☎ 802-362-2200) on Main St in Manchester Center is a good stop.

Hildene

Abraham Lincoln, one of America's greatest presidents, had a tragic life. His wife went mad, and only one of his four sons lived to grow to manhood. That was Robert Todd Lincoln, who served on General Grant's staff during the Civil War before becoming a corporate lawyer in Chicago. He served as president of the Pullman Palace Car Company, Secretary of War and minister (ambassador) to Great Britain.

Robert Todd Lincoln built a 24-room Georgian Revival mansion, which he named Hildene, a short distance south of Manchester on VT 7A. He enjoyed the house until his death, and his great-granddaughter lived in the house until her death in 1975. Soon after, it was converted to a museum by the Friends of Hildene (☎ 802-362-1788).

Many of the Lincoln family's personal effects and furnishings are still in the house, which has been authentically restored. Guided tours are offered from mid-May through October from 9:30 am to 4 pm. Admission costs $6, or $2.50 for children.

American Museum of Fly Fishing

This museum (☎ 802-362-3300), at VT 7A and Seminary Ave, just north of Manchester Village, has perhaps the world's best display of fly fishing equipment, including historic rods used by Ernest Hemingway, Zane Grey and several US presidents. It's open daily from 10 am to 4 pm, May through October, and on weekdays from November through April.

To examine the new stuff, go further north about a half mile to the Orvis store (☎ 802-362-3750), on the opposite side of VT 7A, open daily from 9 am to 6 pm. They even have their own trout ponds on the grounds so you can try out a rod for real.

Mt Equinox

You can drive to the summit of Mt Equinox (3835 feet), a distance of just over five miles, departing from VT 7A south of Manchester. The private toll road, called Sky Line Drive (☎ 802-362-1114), is open May through October from 8 am to 10 pm. At the summit is the *Equinox Mountain Inn* (☎ 802-362-1113, 800-868-6843), with guest rooms ($85 to $140), a dining room (lunches $8 to $20, dinners $22 to $40) and lounge.

Activities

There's **Bromley Mountain** (☎ 802-824-5522, 800-865-4786), of Manchester on VT 11, a small family resort with 35 downhill ski runs, six chair lifts and three surface lifts, and 84% snowmaking capacity. In

VERMONT

summer there's an Alpine Slide, and the chair lifts operate to take hikers up to where trails lead even higher – or back down. Vermont's Long Trail goes right through Bromley.

Well known **Stratton Mountain** (☎ 802-297-2200, 800-843-6867), about 16 miles east of Manchester on VT 30, is larger, with 92 trails, 14 lifts (including a 57-cabin summit gondola), and a vertical drop of more than 2000 feet on a 3875-foot mountain. The longest downhill skiing trail is three miles, and there are 10 miles of cross-country trails. In summer, there's lots of golf, tennis and hiking. The gondola will take you and your mountain bike to the summit for an adventurous ride down.

The **Appalachian Trail** passes just east of Manchester, and in this area is the same as Vermont's **Long Trail**. There are shelters about every 10 miles; some are staffed. There are also a number of good day hikes, including the one to the summit of Bromley Mountain, and another to Stratton Pond. For details and maps, contact the USFS Green Mountain National Forest (☎ 802-362-2307), at the corner of VT 11 and 30 in Manchester Center.

The Batten Kill Sports Bicycle Shop (☎ 802-362-2734, 800-340-2734), on VT 11 and 30 between VT 7A and US 7, rents road, mountain and hybrid bikes for as little as $18 per day, including helmet, lock, trail recommendations and map. They do repairs, and are open every day in summer.

Green Mountain Adventures (☎ 802-362-1202, 375-2448), PO Box 1711, Manchester, VT 05255, organizes outdoor activities such as hiking, mountain biking, tubing in the river and canoe trips.

Places to Stay

Camping Emerald Lake State Park (☎ 802-362-1655), on US 7 just north of the village of East Dorset, has 105 sites, including 32 lean-tos. Sites cost $12 to $16, and are open from late May through mid-October. There's swimming and canoeing on the 80-foot-deep lake, and hiking through the mountains; some trails connect with the Long Trail.

Camping on the Batten Kill River, described above in the Bennington section, is not too far south of Manchester on VT 7A. There's also the Dorset RV Park (☎ 802-867-5754), five miles northwest of Manchester Center on VT 30 near Dorset, with 40 RV sites and a separate tenting area, mostly wooded.

Motels All of the motels are north of Manchester Center along VT 7A.

Wedgewood North Motel (☎ 802-362-2145), RR 1, Box 2295, on US 7 North, has 10 cozy little cottages trimmed in Wedgwood blue for $40 to $60, light breakfast included. The Chalet Motel (☎ 802-362-1622, 800-343-9900), on VT 11 and 30 east of the center, is also very reasonably priced. If these are full, try the Eyrie Motel (☎ 802-362-1208), RR 1, Box 501, East Dorset, VT 05253, seven miles north of Manchester Center on US 7.

The Stamford Motel (☎ 802-362-2342), PO Box 2320, VT 7A North, has 14 tidy units with the standard comforts for $50 to $60.

The Aspen Motel (☎ 802-362-2450), PO Box 548, Manchester, VT 05255, on VT 7A, is a sprawling place with 20 rooms priced from $50 to $80.

The Palmer House Motel (☎ 802-362-3600, 800-917-6245), on VT 7A north of the Barnumville intersection, is a lavish resort motel with lots of services and guest rooms priced from $50 to $100, a bit higher on holidays.

Inns Barnstead Innstead (☎ 802-362-1619), PO Box 988, Manchester, VT 05255, is among the town's best inns for charm, location and price. The 12 rooms are in a renovated 1830s hay barn, and have all the usual comforts for $65 to $90 in summer, somewhat more in foliage season.

Brook-n-Hearth (☎ 802-362-3604), PO Box 508, Manchester, VT 05255, is a B&B on VT 11 and 30 a mile east of US 7, offering cozy rooms with bath for $54 to $70 double, breakfast included.

Seth Warner Inn (☎ 802-362-3830), PO

Box 281, on VT 7A, has a country decor and rooms priced at $80 to $90.

The Inn at Manchester (☎ 802-362-1793, 800-273-1793), PO Box 41, on VT 7A, has 16 rooms and three suites in a restored house and carriage house for $80 to $130, breakfast, tea and Saturday wine and cheese included. The clientele is loyal.

1811 House (☎ 802-362-1811), PO Box 39, on VT 7A, is a grand Federal house built in the 1770s and surrounded by seven acres of lawns and gardens. It's been an inn since 1811. The antique-studded rooms cost $120 to $200 per night.

Resort You'll want to know about *The Equinox* (☎ 802-362-4700, 800-362-4747), VT 7A, Manchester's top place to stay, with its own 18-hole golf course, indoor and outdoor pools, three tennis courts and many other services. Elegant rooms cost $130 to $500 each, depending upon the season. The original building here, the Marsh Tavern, dates from 1769.

Places to Eat

The *Park Bench Cafe* (☎ 802-362-2557), VT 7A South, a half mile south of Manchester Center, is the most popular place in town. Its modern decor with gleaming brass is appealing, as is its long, eclectic menu on which only the steaks cost more than about $9, and the top steak (a 10-ounce New York sirloin) costs only $13. Come for lunch or dinner any day.

The *Quality Restaurant* (☎ 802-362-9839), 735 Main St, has been here since 1920, and was run by the same family for over half a century. Normal Rockwell used it for the setting of his painting "War News." The Quality has a long menu of breakfasts, salad plates and sandwiches for lunch, and dinner specials in the evening (until 9 pm), all at very good prices. *Christo's Pizza & Pasta* (☎ 802-362-2408), across the street, is a modern alternative.

Up for Breakfast (☎ 802-362-4204), above Christo's, is open from 6 am to noon for breakfast, 7 am to 1 pm on Sunday. Every breakfast dish from huevos rancheros to wild turkey hash is available from $4 to $8. Climb one flight of steps to reach the restaurant on the upper floor.

Manchester's down-home favorite for breakfast and lunch is *Mrs Murphy's Donuts & Coffee Shop* (☎ 802-362-1804), on VT 30 and 11, a few blocks east of VT 7A on the right (look for the pickup trucks). Come for fresh doughnuts, decent coffee and more substantial bacon-and-egg tuck-ins, too, at the lowest prices in town.

The *Sirloin Saloon* (☎ 802-362-2600), on VT 30 and 11 east of VT 7A, claims to be Vermont's oldest steakhouse, and that's still the specialty, though there's good seafood too. Wines are very reasonable in price, and a full dinner might cost $20 with drinks. It's open for dinner every day.

Manchester's many inns have excellent (though pricey) dining rooms. *The Restaurant at Willow Pond* (☎ 802-362-4733), in the Inn at Willow Pond, VT 7A North, serves northern Italian cuisine, with main dinner plates priced from $13 to $22, and a long list of Italian wines.

Entertainment

The Southern Vermont Art Center (☎ 802-362-1405), on West Rd, has a full program of summer concerts. Other concerts are organized by Hildene (☎ 802-362-1788), the Manchester Music Festival (☎ 802-362-1956) and Barrows House (☎ 802-867-4455) in Dorset.

Getting There & Away

Trains and stagecoaches brought early vacationers to Manchester. Now it's buses and cars. Vermont Transit (☎ 802-864-6811, 800-451-3292 in New England) runs three buses daily on the route Albany, Bennington, Manchester, Rutland, Burlington, Montréal. There's connecting service to and from New York City; connections from Boston are via Rutland or Albany.

Driving details for Manchester are:

Destination	Distance	Hr:Min
Bennington, VT	19 miles	0:30
Brattleboro, VT	46 miles	1:15
Rutland, VT	32 miles	0:55

DORSET

Dorset, six miles northwest of Manchester along VT 30, is a perfect Vermont village like many others, with its village green, stately inn and lofty church. The difference is that in Dorset the sidewalks, the church and lots of other things are made of creamy marble.

Settled in 1768, Dorset became a farming community with a healthy trade in marble. The quarry, about a mile south of the village center, supplied much of the marble for the grand New York Public Library building and numerous other public edifices. It's now filled with water.

Like Manchester, Dorset became a summer playground for well-to-do city folks more than a century ago. Today, besides the village's pristine beauty, the draw is the **Dorset Playhouse** (☎ 802-867-5777), on Cheney Rd down past the marble United Church of Christ. In summer the actors are professionals; at other times, community players.

Places to Stay & Eat

Dorset's lodging and dining places are upscale. The restored *Dorset Inn* (☎ 802-867-5500), at Church and Main Sts (zip code 05251), just off VT 30, faces the village green. Its 35 guest rooms cost $140 to $180 for two, breakfast and dinner in the excellent restaurant included.

Facing the village green from across the road, the *Dovetail Inn* (☎ 802-867-5747, fax 867-0246), VT 30, offers tidy, well-kept rooms and fresh-baked breakfast breads and muffins for $65 to $85 double, somewhat more in foliage season.

The Little Lodge at Dorset (☎ 802-867-4040), PO Box 673, is a B&B with five cozy rooms renting for $80 to $90, light breakfast included. It's set back from the road behind its own trout pond a short distance north of the green along VT 30, on the right (east) side.

Cornucopia B&B (☎ 802-867-5751), PO Box 307, is on VT 30. Its four perfectly kept guest rooms rent for $95 to $135 double, full breakfast included.

WOODSTOCK & BRIDGEWATER

Woodstock, VT, is the antithesis of that symbol of 1960s hippie living, Woodstock, NY. Vermont's Woodstock, chartered in 1761, has been the highly dignified shire town of Windsor County since 1766.

It prospered in this role. The townspeople built many grand houses surrounding the town common, and Woodstock's churches can boast no fewer than four bells cast by Paul Revere. Senator Jacob Collamer, a friend of President Abraham Lincoln's, once said, "The good people of Woodstock have less incentive than others to yearn for heaven."

In the 19th century, other New England towns built smoky factories, but the only pollution from Woodstock's industry of government was hot air, and it quickly rose out of sight.

Today Woodstock is still very beautiful and very rich. It demands at least some time spent just walking around the beautiful village green, admiring the Federal and Greek Revival houses and public buildings. The Rockefellers and the Rothschilds own estates in the surrounding countryside, and the well-to-do come to stay at the grand Woodstock Inn and Resort.

Woodstock is beautiful and fun. Despite its high-tone reputation, there are lodgings and meal possibilities at decent prices, and some interesting activities nearby.

Orientation

Woodstock is part of the Upper Connecticut River Valley community which includes Hanover and Lebanon, NH, Norwich and White River Junction, VT. People think nothing of driving from one to another of these towns to find a bed, a meal or an amusement.

Information

The Woodstock Area Chamber of Commerce (☎ 802-457-3555), 4 Central St, PO Box 486, Woodstock, VT 05091, operates a small information booth on the village green in summer. Parking places are at a premium in this town, and enforcement is strict, so obey regulations. Parking meters must be fed seven days a week.

For local guidebooks, maps and books in general, stop in at the Yankee Bookshop (☎ 802-457-2411), 12 Central St.

Billings Farm & Museum

After your walk pay a visit to the Billings Farm & Museum (☎ 802-457-2355), less than a mile north of the green along VT 12 at River Rd.

Railroad magnate Frederick Billings founded the farm in the late 1800s, and ran it on sound "modern" principles of conservation and animal husbandry. In 1871 he imported cattle directly from the Isle of Jersey in Britain, and the purebred descendants of these early bovine immigrants still give milk on the farm today.

Life on the working farm is a mix of 19th- and 20th-century methods, all of which delight curious children. There are daily demonstrations, audio-visual shows and special programs. Call for details. Admission costs $6 for adults, $3 for kids from six to 17. The farm is open daily, May through October, from 10 am to 5 pm, and on weekends in November and December to 4 pm.

Quechee Gorge

Eight miles east of Woodstock along US 4, the highway passes over Quechee (KWEE-chee) Gorge, a craggy chasm cut by the Ottauquechee River. Though less than 170 feet deep, the gorge provides romantic views, and Quechee Gorge State Park, on the east side of the gorge, has camping, hiking trails and picnic facilities (see Places to Stay). The walk down through the gorge to the river takes only 15 minutes.

Brewery Tours

At Bridgewater Mill, six miles west of Woodstock on US 4, is the **Marketplace** (☎ 802-672-3332), a collection of shops (crafts, clothing, books, etc) in a historic woolen mill built in the 1820s and restored in 1973. It's open from 10 am to 6 pm daily.

In the Marketplace basement, **Mountain Brewers** (☎ 802-672-5011) produces

Long Trail Ale, "Vermont's No 1 Selling Amber." You can stop in at the Marketplace from noon to 5 pm daily for a tour and a taste, both free. They also produce other European-style beers, including a stout and a kölsch, a German-style blond ale.

In White River Junction, 14 miles east of Woodstock along US 4, the **Catamount Brewing Company** (☎ 802-296-2248), 58 S Main St, also offers free tours and tastings (Saturday only in winter).

Vermont Raptor Center

A raptor is a bird of prey, and the Vermont Raptor Center (☎ 802-457-2779), 1½ miles southwest of the green in Woodstock along Church Hill Rd, in the Vermont Institute of Natural Science, can tell you all about them.

Over two dozen species of raptors are resident at the site, everything from the tiny three-ounce saw-whet owl to the mighty bald eagle. The birds have sustained permanent injuries which do not allow them to return to life in the wild. The three self-guided nature trails are a delight in good weather.

The center is open daily from 10 am to 4 pm, closed Sunday from November through April. Admission costs $5 for adults, $1 for children five to 15.

The Vermont Raptor Center is a good place to see the majestic bald eagle.

Summer Activities

There are three established walking trails within the town. The Billings Park Trails start on the far side of the Ottauquechee River from the village green, along the east edge of the cemetery. Stop in at the Woodstock Inn for maps. Be sure to look out for Woodstock's three covered bridges over the Ottauquechee.

There are also hiking trails and possibilities for swimming, boating and canoeing at nearby state parks. See Camping under Places to Stay for locations.

Bike Vermont (☎ 800-257-2226), PO Box 207, Woodstock, VT 05091, operates two-, three- and five-day bike tours, including inn-to-inn tours. Local bicycle shops, including Woodstock Sports (☎ 802-457-1568) and Cyclery Plus (☎ 802-457-3377) rent bicycles and provide maps of good local routes.

Green Mountain Horse Association & Youth Center (☎ 802-457-1509) in South Woodstock has steeds and knows the riding trails. Check also with Kedron Valley Stables (☎ 802-457-1480).

Skiing

Downhill In 1934, Woodstockers installed the first mechanical ski-tow in the USA, and skiing is still important here. **Suicide Six** (☎ 802-457-1666), three miles north of town on VT 12 in Pomret, is known for its difficult, challenging downhill runs. The lower slopes are fine for beginners, though. There are 19 trails, two double-chair lifts and a J-Bar.

Cross-Country Just south of town the **Woodstock Ski Touring Center** (☎ 802-457-6674), on VT 106, has 37 miles of groomed touring trails.

Places to Stay

Camping The Woodstock area has lots of state parks and, near them, many private campgrounds as well.

Quechee Gorge State Park (☎ 802-295-2990, 886-2434), 190 Dewey Mills Rd, White River Junction, VT 05001, is eight miles east of Woodstock, and three miles west of I-89, along US 4. The 54 pine-shaded sites (six lean-tos) are only a short stroll from Quechee Gorge, and cost $11 to $15.

Silver Lake State Park (☎ 802-234-9451, 886-2434), off VT 12 in Barnard, VT (05031), is 10 miles north of Woodstock, with 47 sites (seven lean-tos) for $12 to $16. It has a beach, boat and canoe rentals and fishing.

Ascutney State Park (☎ 802-674-2060, 886-2434), HCR 71, Box 186, Windsor, VT 05089, about 22 miles southeast of Woodstock, has 49 sites (10 lean-tos) at 3144 feet elevation for $10 to $14 each. There's a playground, hiking trails, hang-gliding and panoramic views. It's open late May to mid-October.

Wilgus State Park (☎ 802-674-5422, 866-2434), Box 196, Ascutney, VT 05030, is two miles south of I-91 exit 8 along US 5 (about 25 miles southeast of Woodstock). The 29 sites (nine lean-tos) next to the Connecticut River cost $11 to $15. There are hiking trails, and possibilities for fishing and canoeing.

Thetford Hill State Park (☎ 802-785-2266), Box 132, Thetford, VT 05074, has 16 sites (two lean-tos) for $10 to $16, plus hiking trails and a playground. From I-91 exit 14, go a mile west on VT 113A to Thetford Hill, then a mile south on Academy Rd.

Motels *Shire Motel* (☎ 802-457-2211), 46 Pleasant St (US 4), on the east side of town, is within walking distance of the town center and charges $45 to $125 for its 26 comfy rooms.

Woodstock Motel (☎ 802-457-2500), on US 4 (PO Box 141) on the east side of town, has comfortable rooms for $42 to $76.

Braeside Motel (☎ 802-457-1366), on US 4 (PO Box 411), east of town, has a nice situation, a swimming pool and 12 good rooms with light breakfast for $48 to $88.

A bit cheaper, because farther out of

town, are the *Quality Inn* (☎ 802-295-7600), on US 4 just east of Quechee Gorge, and the *Pleasant View Motel* (☎ 802-295-3485), a few miles farther east in Hartford, just west of White River Junction.

Inns

Barr House (☎ 802-457-3334), 55 South St (VT 106), a five-minute walk south of the green, is a handsome B&B with two rooms sharing a bath. A room with Vermont breakfast costs $45 to $60 single, $65 to $75 double.

Rosewood Inn (☎ 802-457-4485), Wood Rd (PO Box 125), South Pomfret, VT 05067, is a small five-room B&B two miles north of Woodstock. For a room with shared bath and country breakfast, you pay $55 to $75.

The *1830 Shire Town Inn* (☎ 802-457-1830), 31 South St (VT 106), is a cozy family B&B charging $55 to $95 double.

Woodstocker B&B (☎ 802-457-3896, 800-457-3896), 61 River St (US 4), offers nine spacious rooms for $90 to $125 (breakfast included) in a house dating from the 1830s.

Canterbury House (☎ 802-457-3077, 800-390-3077), 43 Pleasant St, is a restored 1880s Victorian B&B with eight charming guest rooms priced from $85 to $135; full breakfast is included.

Village Inn of Woodstock (☎ 802-457-1255, 800-722-4571), 41 Pleasant St, is a Victorian mansion owned by the chef who presides in the cozy dining room, where roast Vermont turkey dinners are the specialty. The eight guest rooms cost $60 to $135, full breakfast included.

Woodstock Inn & Resort (☎ 802-457-1100, 800-448-7900, fax 802-457-6699), 14 The Green, is a luxury hotel with extensive grounds, a formal dining room, indoor sports center and 146 rooms priced from $139 to $265 double.

Places to Eat

The Caffè Mill, on Central St right next to the river, is in an impressive stone building of gneiss, schist and marble. Besides a selection of coffees, teas, pastries and baked goods, they offer a good light lunch daily. The atmosphere is homey and comfortable; it's open from 9 am to 6 pm daily.

Dunham Hill Bakery & Cafe (☎ 802-457-3121), 61 Central St, is good for pastries and espresso, especially when taken at one of the few outdoor tables.

If you have a picnic lunch, take it to the George Perkins Marsh Man and Nature Park, a tiny hideaway right next to the river on Central St, across the river from the Caffè Mill. You can get a sandwich or other picnic fare at the *Mountain Creamery* (☎ 802-457-1715), a few steps west along Central St, serving breakfast and lunch.

Perhaps the best value in town is the roast turkey dinner served at the *Village Inn of Woodstock* (☎ 802-457-1255), 41 Pleasant St (US 4). For under $15 you get turkey, apple-sausage bread stuffing, gravy, homemade cranberry sauce, popovers, maple-bourbon candied yams, vegetable, potato, bread and salad. They serve several other main courses à la carte as well.

Bentley's of Woodstock (☎ 802-457-3232), 3 Elm St, is an eclectic Victorian labyrinth serving virtually everything from sandwiches and soup through pizza to duckling for $6 to $16. There's live jazz and folk music after dinner on Thursday and Sunday, and a dance club after 10 pm on Friday and Saturday.

The Prince & the Pauper (☎ 802-457-1818), 24 Elm St, is Woodstock's elegant New American bistro, serving a three-course prix fixe menu for $30. You can order things like apple wood smoked ruby trout with griddled corn cake and crème fraîche from the à la carte menu if you like.

Spooner's Restaurant (☎ 802-457-4022), US 4 at the eastern edge of town in a big red barn, is the local steak and seafood house serving hand-cut beef at lunch and dinner for $11 to $14, starch and salad included.

For Indian cuisine, try the *Star of India* (☎ 802-457-1177), 71 Central St, open for lunch and dinner. Most main courses, from biryani to vindaloo, cost under $10.

The village of Quechee, a few miles east of Woodstock north of US 4, has a few restaurants of its own, including *Rosalita's Southwestern Bar & Grill* (☎ 802-295-1600), at Waterman Place. The Mexican sampler plate costs $9, a huge chicken burrito even less.

Simon Pearce Restaurant (☎ 802-295-1470), in the Mill on Main St in Quechee Village, has a dramatic setting in an old mill overlooking the river and a covered bridge. The menu shows signs of New American cuisine influence, but maintains a refreshing simplicity: hickory-smoked coho salmon, followed by beef and Guinness stew, or grilled leg of lamb with garlic, rosemary and balsamic vinaigrette. Lunch (11:30 am to 2:45 pm) costs about $10 to $15, dinner (6 to 9 pm) $20 to $40. The stemware used at the restaurant was blown by hand in the Simon Pearce Glass workshops right in the mill, open for tours from 9 am to 9 pm daily.

Getting There & Away
Air The nearest airports are at Lebanon, NH (15 miles), and Rutland, VT (35 miles), served by Delta, Northwest and USAir.

Bus Vermont Transit (☎ 802-864-6811, 800-451-3292 in New England) has direct buses from Boston (downtown), Boston's Logan Airport, and Springfield, MA; and connecting service from New York, Hartford and Montréal to White River Junction; and one late-morning bus traveling the route between White River Junction, Quechee, Woodstock, Sherburne (Killington) and Rutland. If you take the bus to White River Junction on your way to Woodstock, you might find it easiest to take a taxi (they wait at the bus station) from there to Woodstock, a distance of 16 miles.

Train Amtrak's daily *Vermonter* between New York and St Albans, VT, stops at White River Junction.

Car Driving details for Woodstock are:

Destination	Distance	Hr:Min
Boston, MA	147 miles	3:10
Burlington, VT	89 miles	2:00
Hanover, NH	22 miles	0:35
Plymouth, VT	14 miles	0:25
Rutland, VT	31 miles	0:45
Sherburne (Killington), VT	20 miles	0:35
White River Junction, VT	16 miles	0:25

PLYMOUTH
The small farming village of Plymouth is known for two things: the Coolidge Homestead and the Plymouth Cheese Company, run by Coolidge descendants.

History
"If you don't say anything, you won't be called on to repeat it," said Calvin Coolidge (1872-1933), 30th president of the US. Coolidge was born in the village of Plymouth, VT, 14 miles southwest of Woodstock. He went to Amherst College, opened a law practice in Northampton, MA, ran for local office, then was elected to the state senate, followed by service as Massachusetts' lieutenant governor and governor. Elected as vice president of the US on the Harding ticket in 1920, he assumed the presidency upon Harding's sudden death in 1923.

Coolidge was visiting his boyhood home in Plymouth when word came of Harding's death, and his father, Colonel John Coolidge, the local justice of the peace, administered the presidential oath of office by kerosene lamp at 2:47 am on August 3, 1923.

Known for his simple, forthright New England style and his personal honesty, Coolidge had the good fortune to preside over a time of great prosperity. His laissez-faire business policies were well accepted, but contributed to the stock market crash of 1929. With wonderful *après-moi-le-déluge* luck, he declined to run for another term as president in 1928, although he probably would have won. Instead, he retired to Northampton to write articles for newspapers and magazines.

The burden of blame for the Depression thus fell hard on the shoulders of the 31st president, Herbert Hoover, who had engineered many of the Coolidge Administration's successes as its Secretary of Commerce. Hoover had only been in office a matter of months when the stock market crashed. In 1931, with many banks failed and a quarter of the nation's workers unemployed, Coolidge wallowed in understatement: "The country is not in good shape," he wrote.

Coolidge Homestead

The Coolidge Homestead (☎ 802-672-3773) is open from late May through mid-October, 9:30 am to 5:30 pm; adults pay $3, children under 12 are free; family tickets cost $8. Tour the Coolidge birthplace, the homestead, and Wilder Barn, a farmers' museum. Wilder House, once the home of Coolidge's mother, is now a lunchroom and shop. Calvin Coolidge is buried in the local cemetery.

Plymouth Cheese Company

Have you ever seen cheese made? You can see and taste at the Plymouth Cheese Company (☎ 802-672-3650), which makes a granular-curd cheddar from Vermont milk. Watch the process on weekdays from 11:30 am to 1 pm; the shop is open for tasting and selling daily from 9 am to 5:30 pm.

Places to Stay

Camping *Coolidge State Park* (☎ 802-672-3612, 886-2434), HCR 70, Box 105, Plymouth, VT 05056, is on VT 100A three miles northeast of Plymouth Union, and even closer to Plymouth itself. The 60 sites (35 lean-tos), located in a 25-sq-mile state forest at an elevation of 2100 feet, cost $10 to $14, and are open from late May to early October. There's a backcountry camping area, as well as hiking and fishing.

Sugarhouse Campground (☎ 802-672-5043), HCR 70, Box 44, Plymouth, is on the west side of VT 100 a half mile north of the junction with VT 100A (Plymouth Union). The 45 year-round sites have full hookups, and cost $12 and up.

Hostel *HI/AYH – Trojan Horse Hostel* (☎ 802-228-5244, 800-547-7475), 44 Andover St, Ludlow, VT 05149, is on VT 100 just south of Ludlow village, 11 miles south of Plymouth. It's open every month except April, and charges $12 each for its 18 beds in summer, $17 in winter, when it's crowded with skiers from the nearby Okemo Mountain ski area. Reserve in advance by phone December through March. Office hours are from 8 to 10 am and 5 to 9 pm.

A Taste of Vermont

Vermont is famous for its dairy farms, especially for Vermont cheddar cheese. Ben Cohen and Jerry Greenfield, founders of the Ben & Jerry's premium ice cream company, established themselves in Vermont because of its good dairy industry. You can visit their factory in Waterbury Center near Stowe.

The large number of dairy cattle has also given rise to another Vermont institution: the cow shop. A cow shop may be an elaborate store or a simple pushcart. It sells jokey gear based on the black-and-white mottle of the Holstein. The first time you see a cow shop it's funny, the second time boring, the third time depressing.

Vermont maple syrup and maple sugar candy are also big exports, even though maple trees can be tapped north well into Canada and as far south as Pennsylvania and west to Wisconsin.

Perhaps the best of Vermont products are its crafts: textiles, carvings of wood and stone, wrought ironwork and pottery. The Vermont Crafts Center organizes exhibits and sales outlets, the foremost of which is at Frog Hollow in Middlebury. ■

KILLINGTON

Killington is Vermont's prime ski resort, with 162 runs on six mountains, a vertical drop of more than 3000 feet, 20 lifts including the Skyeship gondola which lifts up to 3000 skiers per hour along the 2½-mile cable run in heated cars with closed-circuit radio. The Juggernaut Trail is the longest ski run in the USA – 10.2 miles, with a vertical drop of 3100 feet. The area has facilities for most winter activities, from ice skating to snow boarding. Ski season typically runs from mid-October through late May.

In summer, the Killington facilities are used for hiking, biking and other outdoor activities.

The Merrell Hiking Center (☎ 802-422-6708, 800-372-2007), in the Killington Base Lodge on Killington Rd, offers guided and self-guided nature interpretation hikes. For $10, you can ride the Skyeship gondola to the summit and walk your way down with a trail map and pocket field guide.

The Mountain Bike Center (☎ 802-422-6232, 800-372-2007) rents mountain bikes for $30 to $37 per day (helmet and trail map included). You and your bike can take a 1¼-mile chair lift ride to the 4241-foot summit of Killington Mountain and ride down, finding your way among 37 miles of trails.

Places to Stay

There are well over a hundred lodging places in the Killington area. The best way to find a bed is to call the Killington Travel Service at ☎ 800-372-2007. Package deals with sports activities and lodgings can be attractively priced: ask about them when you call.

Gifford Woods State Park (☎ 802-775-5354, 886-2434), Killington, VT 05751, has 48 campsites (21 lean-tos) on 114 acres just a half mile north of the intersection of US 4 and VT 100. Rates are $10 to $14, and the season lasts from late May through early October. There's a playground, hiking trails and fishing in Kent Pond.

RUTLAND

Only Burlington is larger than Rutland among Vermont's cities, but Rutland has none of Burlington's charms or attractions. US 7 bypasses the center of Rutland, and you will probably do the same.

In the 1800s, Rutland was important as a railroad town. The trains shipped Vermont marble out and the manufactured goods of the world in. But the city's main railroad station was torn down in the 1960s to be replaced by a nondescript shopping mall, leaving Rutland with not even a visual memory of its heyday.

If you need to find a big hardware store or automobile dealership, an airport or a hospital, Rutland will satisfy you. Otherwise, move on. For information on Rutland, contact the Rutland Region Chamber of Commerce (☎ 802-773-2747), 256 N Main St (US 7), Rutland, VT 05701.

MIDDLEBURY

Prosperity lives at the crossroads, and Middlebury obviously has its share. Aptly named, Middlebury stands at the nexus of eight highways, with the result that the center of town is always busy with traffic.

Despite its history of marble-quarrying, most buildings in the town's center are built of brick, wood and schist. Middlebury College, however, has many buildings of white marble and gray limestone.

History

Middlebury was permanently settled at the end of the 1700s. In 1800 Middlebury College was founded and ever since has been synonymous with the town.

The renowned liberal arts college is not Middlebury's only educational milestone. Education pioneer Emma Willard (1787-1870) moved here and, in 1814, founded a college-preparatory boarding school named the Middlebury Female Seminary. Its curriculum was organized to prepare women for college admissions, a radical idea in early 19th-century America. She moved her school to nearby New York state in

VERMONT

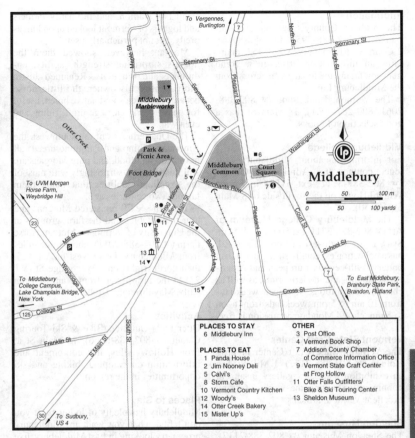

PLACES TO STAY
6 Middlebury Inn

PLACES TO EAT
1 Panda House
2 Jim Nooney Deli
5 Calvi's
8 Storm Cafe
10 Vermont Country Kitchen
12 Woody's
14 Otter Creek Bakery
15 Mister Up's

OTHER
3 Post Office
4 Vermont Book Shop
7 Addison County Chamber
   of Commerce Information Office
9 Vermont State Craft Center
   at Frog Hollow
11 Otter Falls Outfitters/
   Bike & Ski Touring Center
13 Sheldon Museum

VERMONT

1819, and continued her pioneering work for the educational advancement of women for another half century.

John Deere was an apprentice blacksmith in Middlebury during the 1820s. He soon moved westward to Illinois, and discovered that conventional plows had a hard time with the black prairie soils of the Midwest. He fashioned a plow with a one-piece steel plowshare and moldboard which proved to be a major advance in plow technology.

Robert Frost (1874-1963) had a farm in nearby Ripton, and he co-founded the now renowned Bread Loaf School of English of Middlebury College nearby.

Orientation

Middlebury stands on hilly ground straddling Otter Creek. Main St (VT 30) crosses the creek just above the Otter Creek Falls. The town green, Middlebury Inn and the Addison County Chamber of Commerce information office are on the north side of the creek; Frog Hollow and Middlebury College are to the south.

Information
The Addison County Chamber of Commerce (☎ 802-388-7951, fax 388-8066), 2 Court St, Middlebury, VT 05753, maintains an information office in a grand mansion facing the town green across from the Middlebury Inn.

The Vermont Book Shop (☎ 802-388-2061, 800-287-2061), 38 Main St, has a good selection of books.

Middlebury College
For information about Middlebury College, contact the Admissions Offices (☎ 802-388-3711, ext 5153) in Emma Willard House on the south side of S Main St (VT 30).

The **Middlebury College Museum of Art** (☎ 802-388-3711, ext 5007), on S Main St (VT 30) southwest of Porter Field Rd, has a collection especially strong in Cypriot pottery, 19th-century European and American sculpture, and modern prints, as well as changing exhibitions. It's open weekdays from 10 am to 5 pm, weekends from noon to 5 pm, closed Monday; admission is free.

Vermont State Craft Center
The Vermont State Craft Center at Frog Hollow (☎ 802-388-3177), 1 Mill St, has an exhibition and sales gallery in an old bobbin mill showing the works of many excellent Vermont artisans.

Sheldon Museum
The Sheldon Museum (☎ 802-388-2117), 1 Park St, is the work of Henry Sheldon, a town clerk, church organist, storekeeper, and avid collector of 19th-century Vermontiana. His collection of folk art, paintings, furniture and bric-a-brac is housed in a fine brick Federal-style mansion (1829), open all year weekdays from 10 am to 5 pm, Saturday from 10 am to 4 pm, closed Sunday. Tours are given from mid-May through October.

UVM Morgan Horse Farm
In 1789, Justin Morgan and his Thoroughbred-Arabian colt, Figure, came to Vermont from Springfield, MA. The colt grew to a small bay stallion, and the hardy farmers and loggers of Vermont looked upon him as pretty, but not particularly useful.

Morgan, however, showed them the horse's surprising strength, agility, endurance and longevity. Renamed Justin Morgan after his owner, the little horse became America's first native breed, useful for heavy work, carriage draft, riding and even war.

The Quarterhorses of the southwest, the American Albino and Palomino breeds all have Morgan blood, and pure Morgans are still raised today, surprisingly with most of the excellent qualities that made them famous two centuries ago.

You can see 70 registered Morgans and tour their stables and the farm grounds at the University of Vermont's Morgan Horse Farm (☎ 802-388-2011), about three miles from Middlebury. Drive west on VT 125, then north (right) onto Weybridge St (VT 23) to the farm, open from 9 am to 4 pm daily, May through October.

Activities
Otter Falls Outfitters/Bike & Ski Touring Center (☎ 802-388-6666), 74 Main St at Frog Hollow Alley, has equipment and information on camping, biking and ski opportunities in the region.

Places to Stay
Middlebury has plenty of lodgings. If you don't find what you want in Middlebury proper, try looking in East Middlebury, five miles southeast along US 7. The *Waybury Inn*, *The Annex B&B* and *By the Way B&B* are there, among others.

Camping There is little right near Middlebury, but several places are within an easy drive.

Branbury State Park (☎ 802-247-5925, 483-2001), RR 2, Box 2421, Brandon, VT 05733, is on the east side of Lake Dunmore on VT 53 between Brandon and Middlebury (as its name implies), about 10 miles south of Middlebury. With 44 sites (five lean-tos) on 96 acres, it charges $12 to $16 for camping, and is open from late May through early October. Hiking trails lead to spectacular views.

DAR State Park (☎ 802-759-2354, 483-2001), RFD 3, Box 3493, Vergennes, VT 05491, is on the shores of Lake Champlain between West Addison and Chimney Point, on VT 17 about 17 miles west of Middlebury. As befits a park in such a choice location, it has 71 campsites (21 lean-tos) priced from $11 to $15, as well as boating, fishing and a playground.

Elephant Mountain Camping Area (☎ 802-453-3123), RD 3, Box 850, Bristol, VT 05443, on VT 116 between East Middlebury and Bristol, has 50 sites with hookups priced from $10 to $15 and up, and is open all year.

Lake Dunmore Kampersville (☎ 802-352-4501, 388-2661), Box 214, Middlebury, VT 05753, has 210 sites with hookups, two swimming pools (one heated) as well as many other services, and is open all year. Sites with hookups start at $16.50.

Smoke Rise Family Campground (☎ 802-247-6472), two miles north of Brandon, on US 7, has 50 sites, most with hookups, for $10 and up. It's open from mid-May to mid-October.

Ten Acre Camping (☎ 802-759-2662), RD 3, Box 3560, Addison, VT 05491, has 90 sites (78 with hookups), a large tenting area, a heated pool and lots of amusements, for $10 and up. Ten Acre is 15 miles west of Middlebury on VT 125, a mile south of the Chimney Point Bridge to New York. It's open May to mid-October.

Motels *Maple Manor Motel* (☎ 802-388-3166, 800-852-2313), RD 4, Box 1150, Middlebury, VT 05753, is on US 7 South about a mile southeast of Middlebury center. Some units have kitchens; prices are $40 to $75 per room. The *Sugarhouse Motel* (☎ 802-388-2770), two miles north of the town center on US 7 North, is similar. Pets are welcome here.

The *Blue Spruce Motel* (☎ 802-388-4091), US 7 South, Middlebury, VT 05753, not far from the Maple Manor, is nice and charges $42 to $100 for its comfortable rooms.

Inns & B&Bs Liz Hunt's *Middlebury Bed & Breakfast* (☎ 802-388-4851), RD 1, Box 259, has four rooms (one with private bath) for $50 to $75 double, continental breakfast included. It's within walking distance of the town center along Washington St Extension.

The *Middlebury Inn* (☎ 802-388-4961, 800-842-4666, fax 388-4563), PO Box 798, has a fine old main building (1827) with formal public rooms, but much of the space is dedicated to sales. Many of the inn's guest rooms are modern motel units in the back. There are rooms in neighboring Porter House as well. Rates are $68 to $144 single, $75 to 144 double. Pets can stay with guests in the motel.

The *Swift House Inn* (☎ 802-388-9925, fax 388-9927), US 7 at Stewart Lane, is a grand white Federal house built in 1814, plus a large Gatehouse and Carriage House surrounded by fine lawns and gardens. Amenities include a steam room, sauna and Middlebury's best dining room. Luxury accommodations are priced from $85 to $155.

Places to Eat
Calvi's (☎ 802-388-9338), 42 Main St, has been here in this turn-of-the-century building since the 1950s, and has changed little since then. The authentic mid-century decor includes a real soda fountain and a balcony dining area overlooking Otter Creek. Deli sandwiches cost $4 to $5.

Storm Cafe (☎ 802-388-1063), in the basement of the stone Frog Hollow Mill, is popular with artists and artisans. Soups, salads, sandwiches and a short menu of organic produce are priced from $3 to $6. In good weather, find a table outdoors on the terrace overlooking Otter Creek.

Vermont Country Kitchen (☎ 802-388-8646), 3 Park St, serves latte, cappuccino, espresso, breakfast, lunch and muffins – good for a quick light meal.

Otter Creek Bakery (☎ 802-388-3371) is popular for take-out pastries, coffee and sandwiches.

In the Middlebury Marbleworks is the *Jim Nooney Deli* (☎ 802-388-0014),

VERMONT

a good place to pick up a sandwich, from 9 am to 9 pm, closed Sunday, to eat at a picnic table a few steps away at the riverside in the little Otter Creek Falls park. The footbridge across the river goes to Frog Hollow.

Also in the Marbleworks (at the end of the railroad tracks) is *Panda House* (☎ 802-388-3101), serving Chinese cuisine at lunch and dinner every day.

Woody's (☎ 802-388-4182, 800-346-3603), 5 Bakery Lane, has a fine location overlooking the creek just east of Main St. "Innovative international cuisine" is featured for lunch (11:30 am to 3 pm) and dinner (5 to 10 pm). At lunch, have a cup of soup and half a sandwich for under $5; main courses at dinner run from $11 to $17. The bar stays open until midnight.

Nearby is *Mister Up's* (☎ 802-388-6724), also overlooking the creek, with an up-tempo international menu, at similar prices.

Dog Team Tavern (☎ 802-388-7651), three miles north of Middlebury along US 7, is a local favorite here, serving hearty country fare: steaks, ham, chicken and the like for moderate prices.

Swift House Inn (☎ 802-388-9925), at the corner of Stewart Lane and US 7, has Middlebury's best and most expensive dining room. The menu changes daily, but usually dwells on classic dishes with a nouvelle twist. Dinner costs $30 to $50 per person.

Getting There & Away

Air There are airports at Burlington (34 miles) and Rutland (32 miles). The Burlington airport is much busier, with many national connections.

Bus Vermont Transit (☎ 802-864-6811, 800-451-3292 in New England) operates three buses daily on the Burlington, Rutland, Albany route, stopping at Middlebury. You can connect at Albany with buses for New York City, and at Burlington with buses for Montréal.

Car Driving details for Middlebury are:

Destination	Distance	Hr:Min
Boston, MA	210 miles	5:00
Burlington, VT	34 miles	0:50
Rutland, VT	32 miles	0:45
Stowe, VT	55 miles	1:30
Warren, VT	36 miles	0:55
Woodstock, VT	63 miles	1:30

RIPTON

Ten miles east of Middlebury on VT 125 is the village of Ripton, a beautiful little hamlet in the Vermont mountains. Two white churches, a few houses and the *Chipman Inn* (☎ 802-388-2390), Ripton, VT 05766, a big old country house turned into an inn – that's Ripton. Sit on the lawn in the sun, go down to the river and pitch stones, read, walk, think, talk. The inn, a beautiful Federal house built in 1828, is big on Frostiana, and also on the peace and quiet that Robert Frost sought. The nine guest rooms have private bath and are priced from $85 to $135, full breakfast included.

Frost spent 23 years on a farm nearby, and just east of Ripton is the **Robert Frost Wayside Recreation Area**. A forest trail less than a mile in length is marked with signs quoting the poet's works.

For information on the Bread Loaf School of English and Writers' Conference in Ripton, contact Middlebury College (☎ 802-388-3711).

The Texas Falls Recreation Area is a few miles east along VT 125, on the north side of the road.

SUGARBUSH, WARREN & WAITSFIELD

VT 100 continues north from the busy resort area around Killington to the small towns of Warren and Waitsfield.

Along the way, roads intersect from the west, coming across the mountains through four gaps, providing fine to superb views.

Warren and Waitsfield, though small, boast three significant ski areas: Sugarbush, Sugarbush North and Mad River

Glen, all in the mountains west of VT 100. There are also opportunities for bicycling, canoeing, horseback riding, kayaking, soaring and other activities.

Orientation

VT 73 comes across the Brandon Gap (2170 feet) from Brandon to Rochester and Talcville.

VT 125 comes across the Middlebury Gap from Middlebury (2149 feet) to Hancock.

A narrow local road comes across Lincoln Gap (2424 feet) from Bristol to Warren. The Lincoln Gap road is closed in winter due to heavy snowfall.

VT 17 comes across the Appalachian Gap (2356 feet) from Bristol to Irasville and Waitsfield, offering the best views of all.

Information

Sugarbush Chamber of Commerce (☎ 802-496-3409, 800-828-4748), PO Box 173, VT Route 100, Waitsfield, VT 05673, maintains an information office on VT 100 open during the summer, fall and winter tourism seasons, weekdays from 9 am to 5 pm, weekends from 10 am to 5 pm.

Local telephone calls from public phones are free in Warren and Waitsfield, courtesy of the Waitsfield-Fayston Telephone Company.

Skiing

Downhill Comprising New England's three highest skiable mountain peaks, **Sugarbush Resort** (☎ 802-583-2381 for information, 800-537-8427 for reservations), RR 1, Box 350, Warren, VT 05674-9993, has a 2600-foot vertical drop. There are over 110 ski and snow board trails, including 25 for beginners and 53 for skiers of intermediate skill. Three quad lifts, three triple lifts, six double lifts, three poma lifts and a rope tow get you up the slopes. The ski school has 85 full-time instructors to teach you skiing and snow boarding.

With a vertical drop of 2000 feet, **Mad River Glen** (☎ 802-496-3551), Route 17, Waitsfield, VT 05673, has 33 ski trails, many of them gladed, which meander over

a variety of terrain. A third of the trails are steep and for experts; less than a third for beginners.

Cross-Country Five local ski touring centers feature over 100 miles of groomed trails. Call the Sugarbush Chamber of Commerce for information. The two biggest ski touring centers are the **Blueberry Lake Cross Country Ski Center** (☎ 802-496-6687), and the **Inn at Round Barn Farm** (☎ 802-496-2276); see below for accommodations.

Bicycling

Mad River Bike Shop (☎ 802-496-9500), on VT 100 just south of VT 17 in Waitsfield, and the Blueberry Lake Cross Country Ski & Bike Center (☎ 802-496-6687) organize tours and races, and can advise you about rentals and routes, including mountain bike routes.

There are dozens of places to cross-country ski in Vermont.

VERMONT

Canoeing & Kayaking

Canoeing and kayaking is good on the Mad River (along VT 100) and White River (along VT 100 near Hancock) in April, May and early June, and on the larger Winooski River (along I-89) all spring, summer and fall.

Clearwater Sports (☎ 802-496-2708), on VT 100 in Waitsfield, rents bicycles, canoes, kayaks, river-floating tubes, in-line skates, and many other types of sports equipment, and organizes one-day guided canoe and kayak trips.

By the way, Waitsfield is home to Mad River Canoe (☎ 802-496-3127), New England's premier maker of canoes, open for factory tours weekdays from 10 am to 4 pm.

Soaring

You take off from Warren-Sugarbush Airport in an engineless sailplane towed by a conventional aircraft. After gaining altitude, you cast off the tow rope and soar quietly through the skies above the mountains and river valleys, kept aloft by updrafts of warm air. A sailplane can take one or two passengers as well as the pilot.

Rides last from 20 to 35 minutes, depending upon the weather, and cost from $60 to $85 for one person, $95 to $120 for two. For information on costs and soaring packages, contact Sugarbush Soaring (☎ 802-496-2290), PO Box 123, Warren, VT 05674.

Horseback Riding

Vermont Icelandic Horse Farm (☎ 802-496-6707), PO Box 905, Waitsfield, VT 05673, 1000 yards south of Waitsfield's town common, can take you on half-day, full-day or inn-to-inn rides in summer; half-day, full-day and skijöring rides in winter. Icelandic horses are fairly easy to ride, even for beginners.

Places to Stay

As the Sugarbush area is most active in the winter for skiing, there are no campgrounds nearby. Many of the accommodations in the area are condominiums marketed to the ski trade. The biggest collection of condos

is rented by Sugarbush Village (☎ 800-451-4326), right at the ski area, for $110 to $430 per day. Call for the proper rate, which depends upon condo size and location, date of arrival and length of stay.

Hyde Away (☎ 802-496-2322, 800-777-4933), RR 1, Box 65, Waitsfield, VT 05673, on VT 17, is an 1830 farmhouse, sawmill and barn with its own mountain bike touring center and 14 rooms going for $40 to $90, light breakfast included.

The Garrison (☎ 802-496-2352, 800-766-7829), VT 17, Waitsfield, is mostly condos, but the motel section has rooms for $40 in summer, $70 in winter.

The *Inn at Mad River Barn* (☎ 802-496-3310, 800-834-4666), Box 88, on VT 17, Waitsfield, is an old-time Vermont lodge with 15 rooms with private baths, some with queen-sized beds and TV sets, for $50 to $75.

Beaver Pond Farm Inn (☎ 802-583-2861), RD Box 306, Warren, VT 05674, is a restored 1840 farmhouse very near the Sugarbush Golf Course, charging $65 to $90 per room.

Places to Eat

Skiers' taverns abound in this area. Restaurants are quite busy in ski season, a bit sleepy at other times.

Miguel's Stowe Away (☎ 802-253-7574), Sugarbush Access Rd, Warren, serves Americanized Mexican recipes for $6.50 (tacos) to $13 (mole poblano). Miguel's opens at 4 pm; dinner is served from 5:30 to 10 pm daily.

If you need a dose of homemade pumpkin raviolini or linguini with white clam sauce, try *Bella Luna Pizzeria/Trattoria* (☎ 802-583-2001), in Sugarbush Village near the ski slopes, open from 5 to 10 pm daily. Main courses cost $8 to $10.50, pizzas $9 to $14.

The menu is longer, fancier and a bit cheaper at *Georgio's Cafe* (☎ 802-496-3983), at Tucker Hill Lodge, VT 17 in Waitsfield. They're proud of their traditional Italian stone oven here, which keeps a steady temperature of 700°F to cook pizza just right.

Among the area's fancy places, a long-time favorite is *The Common Man* (☎ 802-583-2800), opened in 1972 in a beautifully restored 19th-century barn on German Flats Rd in Warren. Despite its proletarian name, the restaurant specializes in intricate new American recipes and a fine wine cellar. Dinner is the only meal served, and costs between $25 and $40 per person.

Getting There & Away

Driving details for the Sugarbush area are:

Destination	Distance	Hr:Min
Boston, MA	190 miles	3:30
Burlington, VT	40 miles	1:00
Middlebury, VT	36 miles	0:55
Montpelier, VT	20 miles	0:35
Montréal, Canada	140 miles	3:00
Stowe, VT	22 miles	0:40
Woodstock, VT	55 miles	1:35

Northern Vermont

MONTPELIER

Montpelier (mont-PEEL-er), with its population of 8000 souls, would qualify as a large village in some countries. But in sparsely populated Vermont it is the capital city, complete with gold-domed State House (capitol) built of granite, quarried in nearby Barre, in 1836. You might want to visit Montpelier if you're intensely interested in Vermont history and affairs.

Orientation & Information

Montpelier is small. Look for the golden dome of the State House to find the three major sights.

There's an information kiosk on State St opposite the post office, open in the summer months. The Vermont Chamber of Commerce (☎ 802-223-3443, fax 229-4581), PO Box 37, Montpelier, VT 05601, issues information by phone, fax and mail.

You'll find Bear Pond Books (☎ 802-229-0774) well worth a stop at 77 Main St.

State Capitol

The front doors of the State House (☎ 802-828-2228), on State St, are guarded by a massive statue of Revolutionary War hero Ethan Allen. You can wander about on your own from 8 am to 4 pm on weekdays, or take one of the free tours given on the half hour from 10 am to 3:30 pm (Saturday from 11 am to 2:30 pm) from July through mid-October. The State House is closed on Sunday.

Vermont Historical Society

Next door to the State House, the Pavilion Building houses state offices and the Vermont Historical Society (☎ 802-828-2291), open Tuesday through Friday from 9 am to 4:30 pm, Saturday to 4 pm; the society's museum is also open on Sunday from noon to 4 pm. Admission costs $2, or $1 for students and seniors.

TW Wood Art Gallery

The TW Wood Art Gallery (☎ 802-828-8743), College St at E State St, on the Vermont College campus of Norwich University, was founded in 1895 by Thomas Waterman Wood (1823-1903), a native of Montpelier who gained a regional reputation for his portraits and genre paintings. The museum's collection is strong on Wood's art, and also Depression-era paintings. Changing exhibits, especially of arts made in Vermont, fill the main gallery. The gallery is open from noon to 4 pm for $2, and children under 12 are free. It's closed Monday.

Places to Stay & Eat

Montpelier has a range of accommodations and restaurants, but most tourists will be passing through. You might want to sample the wares of students from the New England Culinary Institute (☎ 802-223-6324), 250 Main St, which operates several restaurants:

The *Elm Street Cafe* (☎ 802-223-3188), 38 Elm St, serves New American cuisine and old continental favorites, and is closed Sunday.

VERMONT

Tubbs (☎ 802-229-9202), 24 Elm St, in Jailhouse Common, also serves innovative American fare served in Montpelier's historic old jailhouse.

La Brioche Bakery & Cafe (☎ 802-229-0443), 89 Main St, City Center, has the classic baked goods and light-meal menu of soups, salads and sandwiches, served indoors or outdoors.

Getting There & Away

Bus Vermont Transit (☎ 802-864-6811, 800-451-3292 in New England) runs four buses daily between Boston and Burlington stopping at Montpelier.

Car Driving details for Montpelier are:

Destination	Distance	Hr:Min
Boston, MA	182 miles	4:15
Burlington, VT	38 miles	0:45
Montréal Canada	132 miles	3:30
St Johnsbury, VT	39 miles	1:00
Stowe, VT	22 miles	0:30
Waitsfield, VT	20 miles	0:35

BARRE

Montpelier's even smaller neighbor, Barre (pronounced barry) touts itself as the "granite capital of the world."

Rock of Ages Quarries

The Rock of Ages quarries (☎ 802-476-3119), four miles southeast of Barre off VT 14, are the largest granite quarries in the world, covering 50 acres and mining a vein that's six miles long, four miles wide and 10 miles deep. The beautiful, durable, granular stone, formed over 330 million years ago, is used for tombstones, building facings, monuments, curbstones and tabletops.

The Rock of Ages Visitor Center is open daily from 8:30 am to 5 pm; closed Sunday mornings except during foliage season. You can see granite products being made – some with accuracy to within 25 millionths of an inch – at the Rock of Ages Manufacturing Division, open daily from 8 am to 3:30 pm. Follow a self-guided tour around the quarry, or take a guided tour for a small fee.

Hope Cemetery

Where do old granite carvers go when they die? In Barre, they end up in Hope Cemetery, on VT 14 just under a mile north of US 302.

To granite carvers, tombstones aren't dreary reminders of mortality, but artful celebrations of the carver's life. And what celebrations! A carver and his wife sit up in bed, holding hands and smiling at eternity; a granite cube balances precariously on one corner; a carver's favorite armchair is reproduced, larger than life and tellingly empty. If a cemetery can ever be fun, this one is. It's open all the time.

STOWE

Stowe, set in a cozy valley where the West Branch flows into the Little River, has a certain Vermont-style charm. Its small center is pretty without being prim. Its inns and hotels, ranged along the Mountain Rd up to the ski slopes of Mt Mansfield (4393 feet), adopt Central European names and architecture. Its visitors, who come from all over, find plenty to do outdoors in both summer and winter.

It also has Central European weather, with a lavish amount of rain and snowfall.

History

Founded in 1794, Stowe was a simple, pretty, backwoods farming town until 1859, when the Summit House was built as a

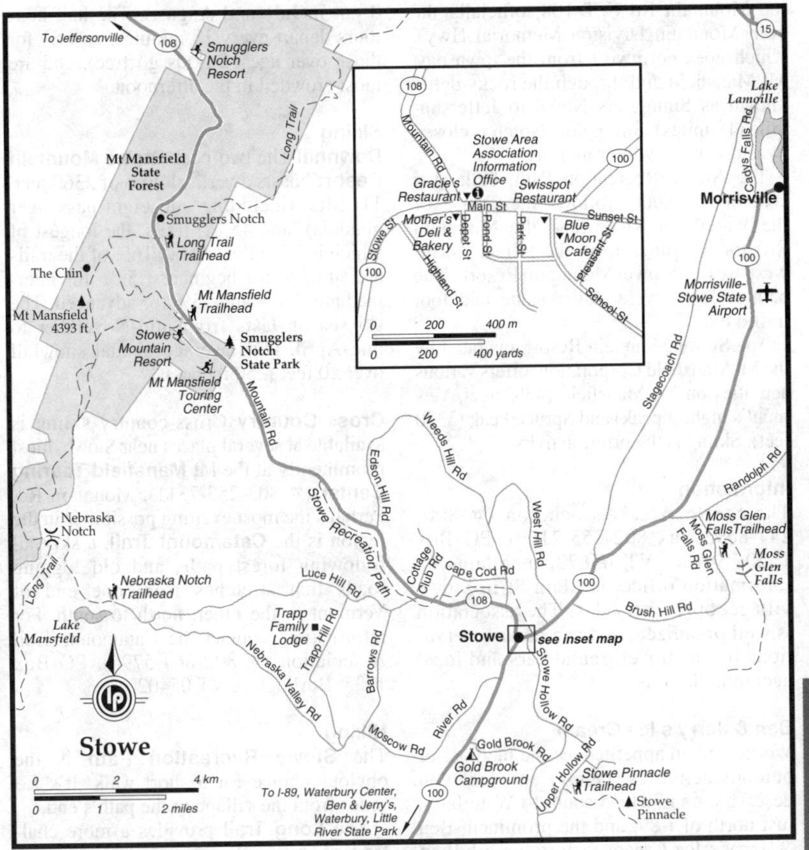

Stowe
To Jeffersonville
108
Smugglers Notch Resort
Long Trail
Mt Mansfield State Forest
Smugglers Notch
Long Trail Trailhead
The Chin
Mt Mansfield 4393 ft
Mt Mansfield Trailhead
Stowe Mountain Resort
Smugglers Notch State Park
Mt Mansfield Touring Center
Mountain Rd
Edson Hill Rd
Stowe Recreation Path
Weeds Hill Rd
West Hill Rd
Cottage Club Rd
Cape Cod Rd
Luce Hill Rd
Trapp Family Lodge
Trapp Hill Rd
Barrows Rd
Nebraska Valley Rd
Nebraska Notch
Nebraska Notch Trailhead
Lake Mansfield
Moscow Rd
River Rd
Gold Brook Rd
Gold Brook Campground
Stowe Hollow Rd
Upper Hollow Rd
Stowe Pinnacle Trailhead
Stowe Pinnacle
Stowe
see inset map
100
Brush Hill Rd
Moss Glen Falls Trailhead
Moss Glen Falls Rd
Moss Glen Falls
Randolph Rd
Stagecoach Rd
Morrisville-Stowe State Airport
Morrisville
Cadys Falls Rd
Lake Lamoille
15
To I-89, Waterbury Center, Ben & Jerry's, Waterbury, Little River State Park
0 2 4 km
0 1 2 miles
Mountain Rd
Stowe Area Association Information Office
Gracie's Restaurant
Swisspot Restaurant
Main St
Sunset St
Mother's Deli & Bakery
Depot St
Pond St
Park St
Blue Moon Cafe
Pleasant St
Stowe St
Highland St
School St
0 200 400 m
0 200 400 yards

summer resort atop Mt Mansfield. The resort business developed slowly. Skiing was introduced around 1912, and in the early 1930s Civilian Conservation Corps (CCC) workers cut the first real ski trails in the mountain's slopes.

In the late 1930s the Mt Mansfield Corporation was established, and it undertook installing the longest and highest chair lift in the USA. Skiing took off in Stowe.

An Austrian ski champion named Sepp Ruschp was hired as the resort's first ski school director, and eventually rose to become head of the corporation. At the time of Ruschp's death in 1990, Stowe was among the best-regarded ski resorts in the eastern US.

Orientation

Stowe is 10 miles north of I-89 exit 10, on VT 100. Waterbury Center, just three miles north of I-89 on the way to Stowe, is the home of Ben & Jerry's premium ice cream company.

Stowe village, at the intersection of VT 100 and VT 108, is small and easily negotiated on foot. However, many of the town's hotels and restaurants are spread out along the Mountain Rd (VT 108, officially the 10th Mountain Division Memorial Hwy), which goes northwest from the town past Mt Mansfield and through the rocky defile known as Smugglers Notch to Jefferson-ville (18 miles). Smugglers Notch is closed by snow in the winter months.

The Stowe Recreation Path, built at a cost of $680,000, follows the course of the Waterbury River (and the Mountain Rd) for 5.3 miles from the village north-west to the Stowe Mountain Resort. The path is for bicycle, roller skate and foot traffic only.

The Stowe Mountain Resort, operated by the Mt Mansfield Corporation, offers various activities on Mt Mansfield (4393 feet, Ver-mont's highest peak) and Spruce Peak (3320 feet). Skiing is the prime activity.

Information

The Stowe Area Association (☎ 800-247-8693, fax 802-253-2159), PO Box 1320, Stowe, VT 05672, maintains an information office on Main St in Stowe village, open every day. The association is well organized, and can make reserva-tions for air travel, rental cars and local accommodations.

Ben & Jerry's Ice Cream

Worked up an appetite (see the plethora of outdoor activities, below) and feel you deserve a treat? Head south to Waterbury, just north of I-89, and the prominent Ben & Jerry's Ice Cream factory, on a hilltop beside the road.

Many years ago, childhood buddies Ben Cohen and Jerry Greenfield sent away $5 for information about how to make ice cream. They opened up shop in a disused gas station in downtown Burlington, and the ice cream shop-cum-luncheonette pros-pered partly because of their original unorthodox flavor combinations. As super-premium (full-cream) ice creams became wildly popular, they abandoned the gas station and took to shipping their tasty product nationwide.

You can tour the factory (☎ 802-244-8687) between 9 am and 5 pm daily (until 8 pm in July and August). The half-hour tours depart every 15 minutes, cost $1 for those over age 12 (kids go free), and are most crowded in the afternoon.

Skiing

Downhill The two-peak **Stowe Mountain Resort** boasts a vertical drop of 2360 feet, 11 lifts (including an eight-passenger gondola), and 45 ski trails, the longest of which is 3.7 miles. About 16% of the trails are suitable for beginners, 59% for inter-mediate skiers and 25% for advanced. The ski season lasts from mid-November to mid-April, with average annual snowfall over 20 feet (250 inches).

Cross-Country Cross-country skiing is available at several places near Stowe, most prominently at the **Mt Mansfield Touring Center** (☎ 802-253-7311), Mountain Rd. Perhaps the most exciting possibility in the region is the **Catamount Trail**, a ski trail following forest paths and old logging roads that stretches from one end of Vermont to the other, north to south. For information, contact the Catamount Trail Association (☎ 802-864-5794), PO Box 1235, Burlington, VT 05402.

Hiking

The **Stowe Recreation Path** is the obvious choice for a short walk. It's 5.3 miles from the village to the path's end.

The **Long Trail** provides a more chal-lenging hike. It's a primitive footpath which follows the crest of the Green Moun-tains 265 miles from Canada to Massachu-setts, with 175 miles of side trails and 62 rustic cabins and lean-tos for shelter.

The Green Mountain Club (☎ 802-244-7037), RR 1, Box 650, Waterbury Center, VT 05677, with offices on the 1836 May Farm, on VT 100 a few miles south of Stowe, was founded in 1910 to maintain the Long Trail, which it still does. The club also publishes some excellent hikers' materials, including the *Guide Book of the Long Trail* ($10), complete with 16 color topographical maps. The guide book and other hiking information are available from the Green Mountain Club's offices or by mail.

The Green Mountain Club recommends the following day hikes around Stowe:

Moss Glen Falls
0.5 mile, 1/2 hour, an easy walk. Follow VT 100 three miles north of Stowe center and bear right onto Randolph Rd. Go 0.3 mile and turn right for the parking area, and walk along the obvious path to reach a deep cascade and waterfalls.

Nebraska Notch
3.2 miles, 2¼ hours, moderate difficulty. South of Stowe, go west on Moscow Rd 5.8 miles to the Lake Mansfield Trout Club. The trail follows an old logging road for a ways, then ascends past beaver dams and grand views to join the Long Trail at Taylor Lodge.

Stowe Pinnacle
2.8 miles, two hours, moderate difficulty. South of Stowe, follow Gold Brook Rd east 0.3 miles, cross a bridge, and turn left to continue along Gold Brook Rd. About 1.6 miles later you come to Upper Hollow Rd; turn right and go to the top of the hill, just past Pinnacle Rd, to find the small parking area on the left. The hike to Stowe Pinnacle, a rocky outcrop offering sweeping mountain views, is short but steep.

Mt Mansfield
seven miles, five hours, a difficult hike. Follow VT 108 east from Stowe to the Long Trail parking area, 0.7 miles past Stowe Mountain Resort Ski Area. Mt Mansfield is thought by some to resemble a man's profile in repose. Follow the Long Trail to the "chin," then go south along the summit ridge to Profanity Trail, and follow that aptly named route to Taft Lodge, then the Long Trail back down.

Bicycling

Several bike shops can supply you with wheels for cruising along the recreation path. Mountain Bike Shop (☎ 802-253-7919), on the Mountain Rd, rents bikes for $4 to $10 per hour, $12 to $40 per day, depending on how classy a bike you want, from single-speed to suspension mountain bikes. There's also AJ's Mountain Bikes (☎ 802-253-4593), which rents in-line skates as well.

Canoeing & Kayaking

Umiak Outdoor Outfitters (☎ 802-253-2317), Gale Farm Center, 1880 Mountain Rd, rents canoes for $30 per day, and offers lake and river shuttle trips for $20 per person. The full moon canoe tours ($25) are unforgettable.

Soaring

Stowe Soaring (☎ 802-888-7845, 800-898-7845), Morrisville-Stowe State Airport, on VT 100, will take two people up in a glider for any length of time from 10 minutes ($48) to an hour ($169).

Places to Stay

Stowe has a wide variety of lodging choices, with about 75 different inns, motels and B&Bs; many are along Mountain Rd. The Stowe Area Association (☎ 802-253-7321, 800-247-8693, fax 802-253-2159) will help you make reservations if you like.

Camping *Little River State Park* (☎ 802-244-7103, 479-4280), RD 1, Box 1150, Waterbury, VT 05676, just north of I-89, has 101 campsites (20 lean-tos) open from late May through early September for $12 to $16. The park is next to Waterbury Reservoir, with boating, fishing and swimming. To find it, go 1½ miles west of Waterbury on US 2, then 3½ miles north on Little River Rd.

Smugglers Notch State Park (☎ 802-253-4014), 7248 Mountain Rd (VT 108), eight miles northwest of Stowe, is a small park with 38 sites (14 lean-tos) on 25 acres priced from $11 to $15, open from late May to mid-October.

Gold Brook Campground (☎ 802-253-7683), on VT 100 7½ miles north of I-89, has 100 sites (half with hookups), free hot showers and many services. The rate for two in a tent is $12. It's open all year, and you may need to reserve in advance for the busy summer months.

Hostel The nearest hostel is on the opposite side of Mt Mansfield at Underhill Center. Though only about 12 miles away as the eagle flies, by road it's 38 miles. See the Burlington section for details.

Motels *Die Alpenrose Motel* (☎ 802-253-7277, 800-962-7002), 2619 Mountain Rd, has two rooms and three efficiency units priced from $40 to $50 in summer.

Innsbruck Inn (☎ 802-253-8582, 800-225-8582), 4361 Mountain Rd, is a modern interpretation of a traditional Alpine inn. Rooms are comfy and well equipped, and cost $70 to $90 in summer.

The Salzburg Inn (☎ 802-253-8541, 800-448-4554), Mountain Rd, has 42 rooms and eight efficiencies, a dining room, indoor and outdoor swimming pools, sauna, whirlpool and a game room. Rooms cost $68 to $78 double.

Stowe Motel (☎ 802-253-7629, 800-829-7629), 2043 Mountain Rd, has 16 efficiencies priced from $56 to $75 in summer. Services include a swimming pool, tennis court, badminton and lawn games. They'll lend you bicycles to ride on the recreation path as well.

Inns My favorite is the simple, traditional, reasonably priced *Ski Inn* (☎ 802-253-4050) – it's the farthest inn from Stowe's center on the Mountain Rd, near Smugglers Notch State Park. The Ski Inn, only a mile from the ski area, opened in 1941 just after the first chair lift was built. It has clean, simple rooms (some with private baths, others share) and a family atmosphere. Rates for a double room are $45 to $65 in winter, $5 per room cheaper in summer, continental breakfast included.

Fiddler's Green Inn (☎ 802-253-8124, 800-882-5346), 4859 Mountain Rd near the Ski Inn, has rustic pine walls, a field-stone fireplace and seven guest rooms priced from $40 to $60. Meals are served in the dining room.

Nichol's Lodge (☎ 802-253-7683), on Stowe St (VT 100) south of the town center, is a basic place with eight rooms and four dorms charging a low $32 to $42 per room.

Andersen Lodge (☎ 802-253-7336, 800-336-7336), 3430 Mountain Rd, Stowe, VT 05672, is a 17-room Tyrolean-style inn with a good dining room, swimming pool, tennis courts and sauna. Rooms cost $45 to $120 for two, breakfast included.

Bittersweet Inn (☎ 802-253-7787), on Stowe St (VT 100) just southwest of the town center, is a homey eight-room B&B with rooms for $54 to $64, a swimming pool and lawn games.

Vermont: Alive with the Sound of Music

Stowe has a more famous Austrian connection than ski champion Sepp Ruschp: the Trapp family immortalized in "The Sound of Music."

In Austria in the 1920s, Maria Augusta Kutschera (1905-87) was hired as governess to the seven children of Baron Georg von Trapp, a widower. The baron, who loved children and music, married the governess in 1927, and sired three more children, bringing the family to a neat dozen, just enough for a good choir.

By the mid-1930s the young ones were old enough to sing, and by 1937 they had made a European singing tour. When Hitler took Austria they fled to the USA, making singing tours around the country from 1940 to 1947, when Baron von Trapp died. Baroness von Trapp wrote the family history, *The Story of the Trapp Family Singers* (1949), and continued touring until 1955.

The Trapp story came to the attention of composer Richard Rogers and lyricist Oscar Hammerstein II, who romanticized it and made it into a wildly successful Broadway show (1959), followed by the movie *The Sound of Music*, starring Julie Andrews as the Baroness.

The Trapp family, aglow with fame and royalties, retired to the hills above Stowe on a 2000-acre farm. They built an Austrian-style inn, the Trapp Family Lodge, which now has become a large, luxurious country hotel and condominium resort. ■

Golden Kitz Lodge & Motel (☎ 802-253-7730, 800-548-7568), Mountain Rd, has nine cozy rooms and six motel units costing $46 to $66 per night.

The Siebeness Inn (☎ 802-253-8942, 800-426-9001), 3681 Mountain Rd, is an 11-room family country inn with a swimming pool and lots of other activity possibilities. Rooms are priced at $70 to $95 in summer, but ask about special package rates.

The dramatically rustic 46-room *Stowehof Inn & Resort* (☎ 802-253-9722l, 800-932-7136), Edson Hill Rd, has a hillside location, a good dining room, lots of services and amenities, and guest rooms priced from $135 to $222 a double, breakfast, tax and service charge included.

Topnotch at Stowe (☎ 802-253-8585, 800-451-8686, fax 253-9263), Mountain Rd, is Stowe's most lavish resort with all sorts of facilities and services for $140 to $291 a double per night in its 92 rooms.

Places to Eat

Food in Stowe seems to be somewhat expensive and often mediocre. Most of the motels and inns serve breakfast and dinner. There are plenty of independent restaurants as well.

Breakfast The locals traditionally take breakfast at *McCarthy's* (☎ 802-253-8626). The breakfasts are hearty: French toast, apple pancakes with maple syrup, lots of different omelets, each serving for $3 or $4. Look for McCarthy's in the shopping center by the Stowe Cinema, across Mountain Rd from Ye Olde England Inne.

If you want the cozy ambiance of an inn, *The Gables Inn* (☎ 802-253-7730), Mountain Rd, is the one for breakfast.

Other Meals *Mother's Bakery & Deli* (☎ 802-253-9044), Main St, is a good place to grab a quick muffin, sandwich or snack ($1.50 to $5). There are tables inside and outside.

Gracie's Restaurant (☎ 802-253-8741), off Main St behind Carlson Real Estate, features light meals such as burgers and sandwiches, tacos and burritos, fried onion rings and chicken dishes. Full meals cost $10 or less. Its menus change throughout the day, but it's open from 11:30 am to late-night 12:30 am.

Trattoria La Festa (☎ 802-253-8480), Mountain Rd near Topnotch at Stowe Resort, has great Italian fare made by real Italian chefs. Look for Roman and Tuscan classics here, priced from $7 to $17. Dinner (only) is served nightly.

Miguel's Stowe Away (☎ 802-253-7574), on the Mountain Rd near Edson Hill Rd, features Mexican cuisine with a good number of vegetarian dishes, all at moderate prices. The cantina is open from 4:30 pm to midnight; dinner is served from 5:30 to 10 pm.

Restaurant Swisspot (☎ 802-253-4622), on Main St in Stowe village, serves Swiss specialties such as fondue, raclette and Bündnerfleisch (air-dried beef), though most other dishes are more familiarly American. Expect to spend $12 to $30 for dinner, less for lunch.

Blue Moon Cafe (☎ 802-253-7006), on School St a half block off Main St in a converted house with a little sunporch, is among Stowe's newer and trendier eateries. The menu of New American dishes is short, serious, interesting and good, and spares diners the exuberant verbal embellishment. At lunch, the traditional sandwiches are vitalized with creative touches, but dinner is the time to come. You might spend about $30 per person, all included.

Partridge Inn (☎ 802-253-8000), Mountain Rd, specializes in seafood, and in a mountain town it's good to have your fish in a place where it's the main event.

Mr Pickwick's Pub & Restaurant (☎ 802-253-7064), in Ye Olde England Inne, is heavy on the Angloid decor and features 120 beers and ales, including rare Scottish malts. Amid familiar Yankee dishes are exotics such as Cornish pasty, bangers and mash, and steak and kidney pie. Dinners cost $12 to $30.

Whiskers (☎ 802-253-8996), Mountain Rd, is a steakhouse specializing in prime

VERMONT

rib of beef, including an 18- to 20-ounce monster portion for $19, but a bowl of soup and several trips to the salad bar can be had for under $10. The outdoor dining is nice in summer.

Getting There & Away

Air See the Burlington section for details.

Bus Vermont Transit (☎ 802-864-6811, 800-451-3292 in New England) buses going between Boston and Burlington (with connections for Montréal) stop at Waterbury, 10 miles south of Stowe, two or three times daily.

Train Amtrak's daily *Vermonter* stops at Waterbury. Some hotels and inns will arrange to pick up guests at the station.

Car Driving details for Stowe are:

Destination	Distance	Hr:Min
Boston, MA	205 miles	4:15
Burlington, VT	36 miles	0:45
Middlebury, VT	55 miles	1:30
Montpelier, VT	22 miles	0:35
Montréal, Canada	140 miles	3:15
New York, NY	325 miles	7:00
Waitsfield, VT	22 miles	0:40
Woodstock, VT	73 miles	2:00

Getting Around

If you don't have your own vehicle, look for the Stowe Trolley, a bus that runs daily during ski season from Stowe village along the Mountain Road to the ski slopes every half hour. For a schedule and list of stops, ask at your inn or at the Stowe Area Association's information office.

BURLINGTON

Vermont's largest city (population 55,000) would be a small city in most other states. Burlington's small size is one of its beauties, however. With the University of Vermont's (UVM) student population and a vibrant cultural and social life, Burlington has a spirited, youthful ambiance. As far as nightlife goes, Burlington is Vermont's center, often offering the only big-name acts in the state. A jazz festival and a

popular reggae fest are held in the summer; contact the chamber of commerce for more details.

Its location adds charm. Perched on the shore of vast Lake Champlain, yet less than an hour's drive from Stowe and other Green Mountain towns, Burlington can be used as a base for exploring much of northern Vermont.

Perhaps the best way to enjoy Burlington is to stroll along Church St Marketplace, have lunch or dinner, then spend the night. Spend the next day touring the famous Shelburne Museum of Americana, and Shelburne Farms, south of the city, before heading on.

Orientation

Take I-89 exit 14 to reach the city center; or exit 13 to I-189 west to go straight to Shelburne and the motel strip along US 7 south of Burlington.

Downtown Burlington is easily negotiated on foot. Parking is usually not a big problem. The heart of the city is Church St Marketplace, and the four blocks of Church St between Pearl and Main Sts are closed to vehicles as a pedestrian mall.

Four blocks west along College St is the city's nice Waterfront Park.

Information

The Lake Champlain Regional Chamber of Commerce (☎ 802-863-3489), Main St, Burlington, VT 05401, provides information, as does the information kiosk at the intersection of Church and Bank Sts.

Try Chassman & Bem Booksellers (☎ 802-862-4332), at 81 Church St, for books and guides. In the nearby town of Williston, east of Burlington on I-89, you'll find one of the great outdoor adventure stores, *Adventurous Traveler Bookstore* (☎ 800-282-3963). They have tons of guidebooks, and the staff is very outdoors-savvy.

Shelburne Museum

The Shelburne Museum (☎ 802-985-3346), seven miles south of Burlington off US 7, is a 45-acre estate once owned by the

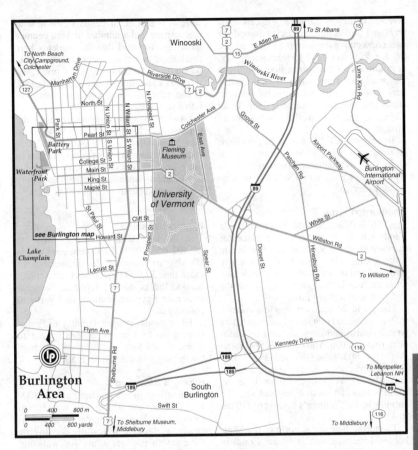

Burlington Area

0 400 800 m
0 400 800 yards

see Burlington map

To Shelburne Museum, Middlebury

To Middlebury

Havemeyer family. HO and Louisine Havemeyer were patrons of the arts and collectors of European and Old Masters paintings. Their daughter Electra's interests were for the more familiar and utilitarian. Electra Havemeyer (1888-1960) amassed a huge, priceless collection of American works of art and craft, which she put on display (1947) in the numerous buildings of the museum. Indeed the buildings themselves are exhibits. Many were moved here from other parts of New England in order to assure their preservation.

The collections, 80,000 objects housed in 37 buildings, include exhibits on folk art, transportation, decorative arts, Vermont history, tools and trades, and New England houses. There's a classic Round Barn (1901), a railroad station complete with locomotive (1915) and luxury private rail coach (1890), a Circus Building and 1920s carousel, a sawmill (1786), covered bridge (1845), lighthouse (1871) and even the Lake Champlain side-wheeler steamboat *SS Ticonderoga* (1906).

The museum is open from 10 am to 5 pm daily from late May through late October; at other times, a 90-minute guided tour of selected buildings starts daily except holidays at 1 pm. Admission tickets, good for two consecutive days, cost $15 for adults, $6 for kids six to 14, free under six. A minimal visit takes three hours, and you can easily (and pleasantly) spend all day here. Food is available at the refreshment stand and the more elaborate Dog Team Cafe restaurant, as well as in Shelburne village.

To get there, CCTA buses (75¢) run from Burlington's Cherry St terminal south along US 7 to Shelburne Museum 10 times on weekdays, and four on Saturday with no Sunday service.

Shelburne Farms

In 1886 William Seward Webb and Lila Vanderbilt Webb made a little place for themselves in the Vermont countryside on Lake Champlain. The 1000-acre farm, designed and landscaped by Frederick Law Olmsted, was both a country house for the Webbs and a working farm.

The grand 24-bedroom English country manor (1899), now an inn, is surrounded by working farm buildings inspired by European romanticism. You can visit Shelburne Farms (☎ 802-985-8686, 985-8442), buy some of the cheese, maple syrup, mustard and other items produced here, hike the walking trail (10 am to 4 pm) and visit the animals in the Children's Farmyard (10 am to 4 pm).

The farm, three miles north of the Shelburne Museum, opens at 10 am (9 am in summer) and closes at 5 pm. Guided tours lasting 90 minutes are conducted from mid-May through mid-October at 9:30 and 11 am, 12:30, 2 and 3:30 pm. A tour of the farm costs $6.50 for adults, $5.50 for seniors, $3.50 for kids two to 14. To hike the walking trail and/or visit the Children's Farmyard costs $4 for adults, $3 for kids.

UVM

The University of Vermont (☎ 802-656-3131), with its 10,400 students, is what brings Burlington its youthful vigor. The campus is east of the center of town, with green space and a number of 18th-century buildings. It's said that the students here drink more than the students at Dartmouth, which might be hard to actually prove, but if true is something of an accomplishment. If you go out at night, you'll no doubt run into a few of them.

From fall to spring, the main event at the Guterson Field House is UVM Hockey, which consistently sells out games: call ahead for information on getting tickets to these thrillers. Go online (www.uvm.edu) for a campus calendar of events including public speakers, art exhibitions and sporting events.

Fleming Museum

The Robert Hull Fleming Museum (☎ 802-656-2090), 61 Colchester Ave, is UVM's art museum. Its collections of more than 17,000 objects include African masks, Indian drums, Japanese Samurai armor, an Egyptian mummy and Vermont paintings.

The museum is open Tuesday to Friday from 9 am to 5 pm, weekends from 1 to 5 pm; closed Monday. Admission is free, but the suggested donation is $2.

Hiking & Bicycling

The Burlington Recreation Path (☎ 802-864-0123) runs along the waterfront through the Waterfront Park and Promenade, as does the nine-mile Burlington Bikeway, a popular route for walking, biking and in-line skating. You can rent bikes at the Community Boathouse (below).

Paragliding

Fight Gravity, Inc (☎ 802-862-3646), PO Box 191, Burlington, VT 05402, gives instruction in paragliding, the sport of sailing through the air following the air currents attached to a wide oblong "parachute." The paraglider fits in a backpack and weighs only about 20 lbs.

Paragliding is a sport you must learn; you can't just grab a paraglider and sail off

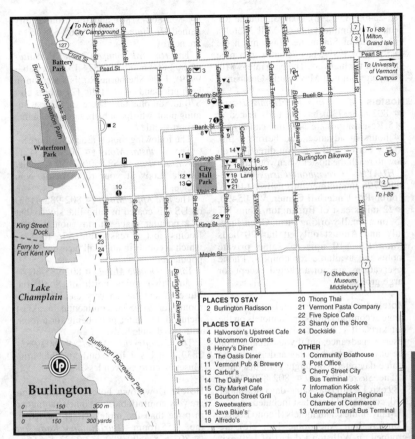

To North Beach
City Campground

127
Front St

Battery
Park

Pearl St

Lake St

Battery St

Burlington Recreation Path

Waterfront
Park

1

10

King Street
Dock

Ferry to
Fort Kent NY

Lake
Champlain

Burlington

0   150   300 m
0   150   300 yards

Champlain St

Park St

Pine St

George St

Elmwood Ave

St Paul St

Clark St

S Winooski Ave

Lafayette St

N Union St

Green St

Pearl St

7   2   To I-89,
Milton,
Grand Isle

To University
of Vermont
Campus

3

4

Cherry St

5   6

Bank St

7

8   9

College St

11

12   13

Main St

King St

Maple St

Church Street Marketplace

City
Hall
Park

14   16
15
17 18
19
20
21

22

Center St

Mechanics
Lane

Orchard Terrace

Buell St

Burlington Bikeway

Burlington Bikeway

Hungerford St

N Willard St

S Winooski Ave

N Union St

S Willard St

2

To I-89

To Shelburne
Museum,
Middlebury

7

Burlington Recreation Path

Burlington Bikeway

PLACES TO STAY	20 Thong Thai
2 Burlington Radisson	21 Vermont Pasta Company
	22 Five Spice Cafe
PLACES TO EAT	23 Shanty on the Shore
4 Halvorson's Upstreet Cafe	24 Dockside
6 Uncommon Grounds	
8 Henry's Diner	OTHER
9 The Oasis Diner	1 Community Boathouse
11 Vermont Pub & Brewery	3 Post Office
12 Carbur's	5 Cherry Street City
14 The Daily Planet	Bus Terminal
15 City Market Cafe	7 Information Kiosk
16 Bourbon Street Grill	10 Lake Champlain Regional
17 Sweetwaters	Chamber of Commerce
18 Java Blue's	13 Vermont Transit Bus Terminal
19 Alfredo's	

VERMONT

into the air for the day. Your first lesson costs $100; a six-lesson novice package is $400. Flights take place on Burlington's waterfront or at Cobble Hill in Milton, 10 miles north of the city.

Boating
Burlington's Community Boathouse (☎ 802-865-3377), on the lakeshore at the foot of College St, rents rowboats, sailboats, canoes and kayaks as well as bicycles and scuba equipment.

Places to Stay
Camping *North Beach Campground* (☎ 802-862-0942), 60 Institute Rd, is operated by the City of Burlington. With 98 sites (mostly for tents) on 45 acres near the city center, but right on Lake Champlain, it's the first choice for tent campers. Tent sites cost $14. To find it, get to the lakeshore in Burlington, then go north along Battery St and North Ave (VT 127), and turn left on Institute Rd.

The *Shelburne Camping Area* (☎ 802-

985-2540, 985-2296), 2056 Shelburne Rd, near the prominent Dutch Mill Motel a mile north of Shelburne Museum on the east side of US 7, has 76 sites in a pine grove off the highway. The base rate is $16; it's open from mid-May to mid-October.

Hostels *Mrs Farrell's Home Hostel* (☎ 802-865-3730) has six beds priced at $15. Reservations are essential; call at least 24 hours in advance, and before 8 pm. Nancy Farrell will give you directions on how to reach the hostel when you call.

HI/AYH – Greenmont Farms (☎ 802-899-1796 in summer only), Box 148, W Bolton Rd, Underhill Center, VT 05490, is 22 miles east of Burlington along VT 15, on a small working farm. Open June, July and August only, it has 20 beds going for $10 apiece. Some private rooms are available for couples. Phone reservations are not accepted except for large groups.

Motels Burlington's low end and middle-range accommodations are in motels on the outskirts. It's not usually necessary to reserve in advance, but if you call ahead on the day you intend to stay and ask for the "same-day rate," you might get a discount.

The *Susse Chalet* (☎ 802-879-8999), I-89 exit 12, offers a "same-day rate" under $50, continental breakfast included.

Many of the chain motels (Econo Lodge, Comfort Inn, Anchorage Inn, etc) are grouped on Williston Rd east of I-89 exit 14. There's another collection of lodgings along US 7 north of Burlington and Winooski in Colchester (I-89 exit 16).

Perhaps the best selection of low- and middle-end places is along Shelburne Rd (US 7) in South Burlington on the way to Shelburne. Here are some suggestions, listed in the order you'll come to them as you drive south from central Burlington.

The 37-room *Colonial Motor Inn* (☎ 802-862-5754), 462 Shelburne Rd, has the advantage of being near central Burlington, and moderate prices of $38 to $58 per room. The *Town & Country Motel*

(☎ 802-862-5786) and the wonderfully named *Ho Hum Motel* (☎ 802-658-1314) are nearby.

The *Howard Johnson Motel & Suites* (☎ 802-860-6000, 800-874-1554, fax 864-9919), 1720 Shelburne Rd, is a step up in both price and comfort. Its 121 rooms cost $70 to $80 plus tax. There's a nice swimming pool, whirlpool bath, sauna and a free airport shuttle.

The following motels are in Shelburne:

The *Northstar Motel* (☎ 802 863 3421) advertises rates of $22.50/$28.50 a single/double. Look at your room before you decide.

The *Red Apple Motel* (☎ 802-985-4153) on US 7 is coated in icing-like stucco, but is a popular place to stay nonetheless. Rooms cost a reasonable $35 to $45, which accounts in no small measure for its popularity.

Yankee Doodle Motel (☎ 802-985-8004) is just two miles north of Shelburne Museum and has 15 very clean and tidy rooms for $45/$55, continental breakfast included, the latter price being for a room with two double beds.

The *Countryside Motel* (☎ 802-985-2839), on US 7 just south of Shelburne Museum, charges even less.

Hotels Downtown hotels in Burlington are very comfortable and somewhat higher in price than the motels. Best-located is the 255-room *Burlington Radisson* (☎ 802-658-6500, 800-333-3333, fax 658-4659), 60 Battery St, with rooms for $79 to $112 double.

Inn If you've always dreamed of being lord of the manor, you can indulge your fantasies at the sumptuous *Inn at Shelburne Farms* (☎ 802-985-8498), formerly the Webb's summer mansion. Rooms vary in size and appointments, and are priced from $85 to $140 (shared bath), or $155 to $250 (private bath), plus 8% tax and 15% service charge. Meals are served (extra). The inn is open seasonally from mid-May to mid-October.

Places to Eat

Burlington is perhaps the only place in Vermont that has a full range of restaurants. There are dozens in and near the Church St Marketplace. Most serve alcoholic beverages.

Uncommon Grounds (☎ 802-865-6227), on Church St, is a local good-coffee mecca. Take your newspaper (or this guidebook), order a cup of joe and perhaps a muffin, and fit into the woodwork, or take over one of the sidewalk tables (in good weather).

Java Blue's (☎ 802-860-5060), 197 College St, is a coffee bar where the cool young have hot coffee. Closed Sunday.

Henry's Diner (☎ 802-862-9010), 115 Bank St, is a Burlington fixture, having opened in 1925. The daily special meal of soup, main course, dessert and beverage costs only around $5. (Compare this to $3.50 for a bratwurst with sauerkraut from a pushcart on the Church St Mall.) Everything on Henry's menu is priced under $8. The food is simple, the atmosphere homey and pleasant, the prices unbeatable.

Another old-time place is *The Oasis Diner* (☎ 802-864-5308), 189 Bank St just off Church St, a stainless steel diner serving breakfast and lunch from 5:30 am to 4:30 pm. Try it for Sunday brunch from 8 am to 3 pm.

City Market Cafe (☎ 802-658-5061), 211 College St, serves mostly vegetarian food, and has a huge, heavily foliated bulletin board for notices of local events, music, rentals, items wanted and for sale. There's live entertainment some evenings.

The Daily Planet (☎ 802-862-9647), 15 Center St, has big sandwiches for $6, and in the evening main courses such as potato-crusted salmon with Moroccan vegetable sautée, or Thai shrimp salad, for $11 to $16.

Sweetwaters (☎ 802-864-9800), 120 Church St, heavily nouveau-Victorian in decor, is a local watering hole for the young and upwardly mobile. In the evening the glass-covered eating area is loud with chatter and redolent of nachos and chicken wings; the beverage of choice is an exotic beer. Lunch is more for eating than meeting. Impress your companion: order the bison burger, medium-rare ($6).

Vermont Pasta Company (☎ 802-658-2575), corner of Church and Main Sts, has a long menu of "international" pasta dishes made with fresh (not dried) pasta priced from $7 to $11, and heartier meat dishes as well, at higher prices.

Halvorson's Upstreet Cafe (☎ 802-658-0278), on Church St just south of Pearl St, has a young and lively crowd and a trendy Southwestern menu. On my last visit it included a Mexican combination plate for $8 and lots of sandwiches. There's plenty of sidewalk seating, and live entertainment with no cover some evenings.

Alfredo's (☎ 802-864-0854), Mechanics Lane at Church St across from City Hall, is Burlington's longtime favorite for traditional Italian export cuisine. Main courses cost $9 to $13, and are consumed amid the equally traditional checked tablecloths and Chianti bottles. Thursday is veal night; Friday there are lobster specials. Luncheon special meals, for about $5, are great bargains.

Carbur's (☎ 802-862-4106), 115 St Paul St facing City Hall Park, is elaborate and hyper-American in every way: jokey purple menu prose, complicated mixed drinks, 80 exotic beers, over 100 varieties of complex gigantic sandwiches, decent prices and a small outdoor dining area in back.

Vermont Pub & Brewery (☎ 802-865-0500), 144 College St, has pints for $3 and an assortment of specialty and seasonal brews made on the premises such as Burly Irish Ale, Dogbite Bitter, Dr Walther's Wunder Pils, Vermont Smoked Porter, etc. There's plenty of bar food to go with the pints

Thong Thai (☎ 802-865-3663), 144 Church St, is a good choice for Thai cuisine. For Vietnamese, try *Sai-Gon Cafe* (☎ 802-863-5632), 133 Bank St. Main courses cost $6 to $12. It's open for lunch and dinner daily (dinner only on Sunday). For dim sum brunch on Sunday, you've got to go to *Five Spice Cafe* (☎ 802-864-4045),

175 Church St, which serves dishes from China, India and Indonesia as well as Thailand and Vietnam.

For American-style hot stuff, head for the *Bourbon Street Grill* (☎ 802-865-2800), 213 College St, which specializes in spicy Cajun food. There's jambalaya and Bourbon Street Fire Chicken, but also many dishes that won't bite back when you bite them. Main courses cost $5 to $7.50 at lunch, $13 to $16 at dinner.

For lakefront dining, try *Shanty on the Shore* (☎ 802-864-0238), 181 Battery St. It faces the car ferry dock and enjoys a fine view of the lake. This combined seafood market and eatery serves fresh lobster, fish and shellfish lunches and dinners for $8 to $20.

Dockside (☎ 802-864-5266), 209 Battery St, is fancier, with a nice patio overlooking the lake and a more varied menu that includes landlubber grub as well as nautical nourishment. Dinners cost $25 to $30, lunch much less.

Entertainment

The *Burlington Free Press*, the local newspaper, carries a special weekend entertainment section in its Thursday issue. This is perhaps the best source for up-to-date concert, theater, cinema, lecture and other program information.

Church St Marketplace, with its many restaurants and sidewalk cafes, is also the center of Burlington nightlife.

The Daily Planet is for the young and hip; thirtysomethings who have "made it" (or hope they have) go to Sweetwaters for the free snacks on weekday afternoons from 5 to 7 pm, though the action doesn't get heavy until 9:30 pm or so. Halvorson's, the City Market Cafe and the Vermont Pub & Brewery often have live music (see Places to Eat for information).

Reuben James (☎ 802-864-0744), 159 Main St, is a college hangout with loud music and fast dancing. Wednesday evenings there's live reggae. *Pearl's* (☎ 802-864-9800), 135 Pearl St, is the center of the gay scene.

Bambino's (☎ 802-863-1108), in South Burlington off Shelburne Rd (US 7) behind the Factory Outlet Mall, is a large entertainment complex with a sports bar and a nightclub ($3 to $6 cover charge) with a young crowd dancing to top-40 tunes, and *Rhinestones*, a country music club ($3 to $5 cover).

Getting There & Away

Bus Vermont Transit (☎ 802-864-6811, 800-451-3292 in New England), based in Burlington, provides transport to major towns in Vermont as well as to Manchester, NH; Keene, NH; Albany, NY and Boston. The Vermont Transit terminal, at 135 St Paul St, faces City Hall Park.

Greyhound Lines (☎ 800-231-2222) operates one bus daily between Burlington and Montréal. The three-hour trip costs $23.50 one way.

Car Driving details for Burlington are:

Destination	Distance	Hr:Min
Boston, MA	220 miles	4:35
Middlebury, VT	34 miles	0:50
Montréal, Canada	94 miles	2:15
New York, NY	339 miles	7:00
Plattsburgh, NY	26 miles	0:40
Stowe, VT	36 miles	0:50

Boat Lake Champlain Transportation Co (☎ 802-864-9804), King St Dock, Burlington, runs car ferries across the lake to connect Burlington with Port Kent, NY, departing 14 times daily in summer. There are fewer trips in spring (eight) and fall (11), and no service from mid-October to mid-May. The fare for the one-hour voyage is $12 for a car and driver, $3 for each adult, $1 for each child six to 12. Ferries depart from the dock at the foot of King St.

The company also operates ferries connecting Charlotte, VT, with Essex, NY (south of Burlington); and Grand Isle, VT (north of Burlington), with Plattsburgh, NY. The latter service runs year round.

Getting Around

CCTA Buses Chittenden County Transportation Authority (☎ 802-864-0211) operates buses from its Cherry St Terminal (at the corner of Church St) to Burlington Airport, the Amtrak station and south along US 7 to Shelburne Museum. Buses run about every half hour, departing Cherry St at quarter past and quarter to the hour. There is no service on Sunday.

Normal adult fare is 75¢, 50¢ if you're under 18, or 35¢ if you're 60+.

College St Shuttle A free College St shuttle bus runs a loop route from the Waterfront Park near the Community Boathouse stopping at Battery St, St Paul St, Church St Marketplace, Winooski Ave, Union St and Willard St, ending at the UVM campus. In summer, shuttles run every 10 minutes from 11 am to 6 pm.

NORTHEAST KINGDOM

Extreme northeastern Vermont, traditionally called the Northeast Kingdom, is a region of smaller and even more remote towns and villages. For many visitors, its remoteness is its charm: the uncrowded ski slopes at **Jay Peak** (☎ 802-988-2611) and **Burke Mountain** (☎ 802-626-3305, 800-541-5480) are attractive to the devoted skier.

Book lovers should seek out the American Society of Dowsers Bookstore (☎ 802 748-8565) in St Johnsbury. For a nice tour of the Northeast Kingdom, try the **Lamoille Valley Railroad** (☎ 802-888-7183) in Morrisville.

There's lots to explore here. For guidance, call on the Northeast Kingdom Chamber of Commerce (☎ 802-748-3678, 800-639-6379), 30 Western Ave, St Johnsbury, VT 05819.

New Hampshire

New Hampshire, like neighboring Vermont, is mountainous and beautiful. The state's White Mountain Range includes Mt Washington (6288 feet), one of the highest peaks east of the Mississippi River. The state's symbol is the "Great Stone Face" (also called the Old Man of the Mountain), a natural "profile" of a man formed by the granite of a rocky hillside at Franconia Notch in the White Mountain National Forest.

New Hampshire's earliest recorded inhabitants were the Abenakis, an Eastern Woodland people of the Algonquian group. In 1622 the Council for New England awarded the territory from the Merrimack to the Kennebec Rivers to Captain John Mason and Sir Ferdinando Gorges as "the Province of Maine." A year later the first English settlers arrived, setting up home at Portsmouth.

In 1629 Mason's land grant, which he renamed New Hampshire, was extended from the Merrimack to the Piscataqua River, and later it was enlarged even further, though these early borders were often in dispute. In 1641 four New Hampshire towns placed themselves under the protection of the royal governor of Massachusetts, but in 1679 New Hampshire received its own royal charter from King Charles II. The border disputes between the two provinces were only settled by royal decree in 1740. The following year Benning Wentworth of Portsmouth was appointed the colony's first royal governor. By this time, White settlers had long since penetrated to the fertile 211-mile-long Connecticut River Valley and the 100-mile-long Merrimack River.

Four months before the "shot heard round the world" rang out in Lexington, MA, April 19, 1775, the farmer-soldiers of New Hampshire had captured Fort William and Mary from its British garrison, signaling the start of the troubles. They seized the fort's military stores and sent them south to the Boston area, where they were later used at the Battle of Bunker Hill.

New Hampshirites provided important supplies, manpower and navy vessels for the Revolutionary War. The sloop *Ranger*, made famous through the exploits of captain John Paul Jones, was built and launched at Portsmouth.

On January 5, 1776, New Hampshire's provincial assembly adopted a constitution and within a half year had proclaimed its independence from Britain. On June 21, 1788, New Hampshire ratified the US Constitution and provided the ninth and final vote necessary to inaugurate the radically different form of government it described.

By 1790 New Hampshire had a population of almost 142,000. In the mid-1800s the Industrial Revolution brought considerable wealth to New Hampshire, which was blessed, like much of New England, with abundant water power. The great Amoskeag mills, built along the river at Manchester, are an impressive relic of this era. Perhaps in part because of its industrial wealth, New Hampshire produced two of America's best 19th-century sculptors, Daniel Chester French (1850-1931) and Augustus Saint-Gaudens (1848-1907).

New Hampshire received large numbers of foreign workers during the great migration to the eastern US at the beginning of the 20th century. In 1905 Portsmouth was the venue for the signature of the treaty ending the Russo-Japanese War. And in 1944 a United Nations conference at Bretton Woods designed the world's postwar economic model, resulting in the creation of the World Bank and the International Monetary Fund.

Today New Hampshire's farms produce part of the state's wealth, but tourism is a bigger industry. There's some light industry as well, but many New Hampshirites head south to Massachusetts to find work.

Known as the most politically conservative

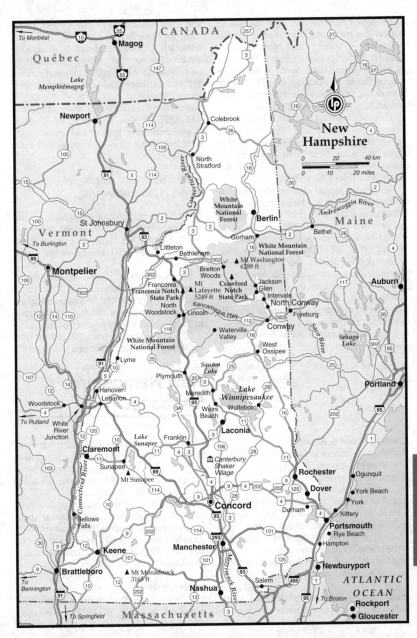

of the New England states, New Hampshire suffers the barbs and insults of its liberal neighbors in Vermont and Massachusetts. New Hampshirites take comfort in the words of native General John Stark, victor at the crucial Battle of Bennington (1777), "Live Free or Die," and live by their current tourism slogan, "It's *right* in New Hampshire."

There are 1300 lakes and ponds scattered across New Hampshire, the largest of which is vast Lake Winnipesaukee, a lake-lover's paradise. New Hampshire even has a seacoast for beach fun. If you like the outdoors, you'll love New Hampshire.

Besides its natural charms, the state has several cities, some good small museums and Dartmouth College in Hanover, one of the nation's best institutions of higher education.

The New Hampshire Office of Vacation Travel (☎ 603-271-2666), PO Box 856, Concord, NH 03301, is the statewide information source, but you'll get more complete information from the regional tourism offices. These offices, operated by a local chamber of commerce or tourism council, are mentioned below in each region.

Emergency numbers are as follows:

State Police	☎ 800-452-4664
Police or Ambulance	☎ 911 & consult local directory
Poison Control	☎ 800-562-8236
US Coast Guard & Rescue	☎ 603-436-4414

Getting There & Around

Air Most air access to the state is provided via Boston's Logan Airport. Manchester Airport is the state's largest, with frequent daily nonstop service to Boston, New York and Washington, DC, handled by Continental, Delta, United and USAir. Keene and several other smaller cities are served by Colgan Air (☎ 703-368-8880, 800-272-5488) with connections to national and international airlines at Boston, Manchester and Newark.

Bus Concord Trailways (☎ 603-228-3300, 800-639-3317) operates buses on routes to and from Boston and Logan Airport, stopping in Manchester, Concord, Laconia, Meredith, Conway, Jackson, Gorham and Berlin. There's also a route through Plymouth, North Woodstock/Lincoln, Franconia and Littleton and some other points along the way.

Vermont Transit (☎ 802-864-6811, 800-451-3292 in New England), operates a route connecting Boston and Portsmouth with the Maine cities of Portland, Bangor and Bar Harbor.

Train There is no Amtrak rail passenger service in New Hampshire.

Car New Hampshire's highways are among the best maintained in the region.

The Eastern NH Turnpike, Everett Turnpike and Spaulding Turnpike are toll roads (25¢ to $1).

Maximum speed limits, unless posted otherwise, are 30 mph in cities, 35 in rural residential districts, and 55 mph in all other areas. Some areas of the state's interstate highways have higher posted limits.

Children under five years of age must ride restrained by a seat belt or in a safety seat.

New Hampshire Seacoast

Many visitors are surprised to learn that New Hampshire has a seacoast. Even though it's only about 18 miles long, it provides New Hampshirites with access to the sea and, more importantly, to the beach.

The coast is mostly beach, with a few rocky headlands and coves. Several state beaches and parks along the coast provide orderly, well-regulated access to the beach. The rest of the beach is commercially developed.

Information

The Seacoast Council of Tourism (☎ 603-436-7678, 800-221-5623), 235 West Rd,

Nuclear Seabrook
Construction was begun in 1976 on a controversial nuclear electricity plant on the coast at Seabrook. Despite vociferous protests from local and regional groups and charges of inappropriate use of governmental powers, construction progressed. In 1989 the Nuclear Regulatory Commission approved emergency evacuation plans for the plant over the strenuous objections of the governor of nearby Massachusetts and many citizens groups. The plant began generating electricity commercially in 1990, after 14 years of construction and testing. Today New Hampshirites pay rates for electricity among the highest in the USA, due largely to the folly of Seabrook. ∎

No 10, Portsmouth, NH 03801, will provide maps and lists of places to stay and eat and things to do.

HAMPTON BEACH & RYE

At the southern end of New Hampshire's coastline is Hampton State Beach, two long stretches of sand along NH 1A with toilets and hookups for campers. To the north, North Beach and North Hampton State Beach have bathhouses and lifeguards. You must pay a small fee to swim here.

New England beachfront honky-tonk at its best (or worst): that's the town of Hampton Beach. Clam shacks, cheap motels, hot dog stands, coin-machine game arcades, free nightly entertainment and weekly fireworks, all spiced with lots of neon and noise, keep the crowds of mostly young sun-seekers happy in summer.

Accommodations are usually booked well in advance of the season. For information, contact Hampton Beach (☎ 603-926-8717, 800-438-2826), PO Box 790, Hampton Beach, NH 03842.

In Rye, Jenness Beach, north of the town of Rye, is a state beach with a bathhouse and lifeguards.

PORTSMOUTH

The New England coast is dotted with graceful old cities that grew to importance during the great days of New England's maritime ascendancy, when local merchants made fortunes trading with the world. Portsmouth (population 26,000) is New Hampshire's only such city, but it's one of the region's most attractive, with lots of historical interest.

Portsmouth's checkered history has left it with a particularly impressive and eclectic array of historic buildings from all periods. It is not a prissy, perfectly preserved "museum town," nor a modernized city, but an architectural museum of real life as lived on the New Hampshire seacoast from 1623 to the end of the millennium.

Because of its position an hour's drive north of Boston and an hour's drive south of Portland, with Manchester about the same distance away, Portsmouth has become something of a "restaurant resort." The selection of places to eat is excellent for a town of its size. People from other cities zoom up here on I-95 for a leisurely lunch and a stroll through town.

History

In 1623, only three years after the Pilgrims landed at Plymouth Rock, another band of intrepid settlers sailed to the mouth of the Piscataqua River. They landed and scrambled up a bank covered in wild strawberries – a good omen to hungry seafarers. They decided to stay, and named the place Strawbery Banke, changed in 1653 to Portsmouth.

Their colony had a purpose: fish. They caught fish and sold fish, built fishing boats and sold them and by the time of the American Revolution, Portsmouth was among the dozen largest cities in the English colonies. Its streets were lined with handsome houses built by merchants and ship captains, of which many remain today.

The War of 1812 was the beginning of the end for Portsmouth's greatness, however. Trade and shipping dropped off drastically during the war, and other ports grew to take up the slack after it. But the graceful

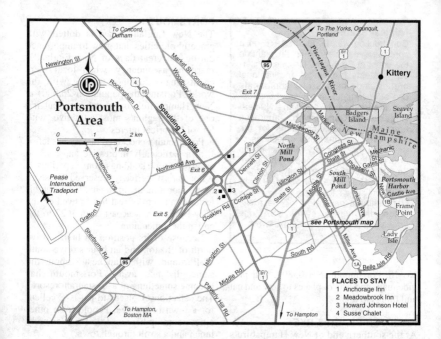

To Concord, Durham

To The Yorks, Ogunquit, Portland

Newington St

Portsmouth Area

0   1   2 km
0   .5   1 mile

Pease International Tradeport

Market St Connector

Woodbury Ave

Rockingham Dr

Spaulding Turnpike

Portsmouth Ave

Northwood Ave

Grafton Rd

Sherburne Rd

Islington St

Middle Rd

Peverly Hill Rd

Exit 7

Exit 6

Exit 5

Coakley Rd

Cottage St

Clifton St

Dennett St

Maplewood St

North Mill Pond

Islington St

State St

South Rd

Piscataqua River

Kittery

Badgers Island

Seavey Island

Maine New Hampshire

Market St

Congress St

State St

Pleasant St

Gates St

Mechanic St

South Mill Pond

Middle St

Summer St

Junkins Ave

Miller Ave

Portsmouth Harbor

Castle Ave

Frame Point

see Portsmouth map

Lady Isle

Belle Isle Rd

To Hampton, Boston MA

To Hampton

PLACES TO STAY
1 Anchorage Inn
2 Meadowbrook Inn
3 Howard Johnson Hotel
4 Susse Chalet

houses, fine churches and other great buildings from Portsmouth's heyday remain.

Today Portsmouth makes its living manufacturing computers and fiber-optic cable, and from tourism.

Orientation

Historic Portsmouth is surrounded on three sides by water. To the northeast is the Piscataqua River; to the northwest the North Mill Pond and to the southeast the South Mill Pond. Market St, reached from I-95 exit 7, is the main commercial street with shops, restaurants and two places to get information. Highway motels are clustered around I-95 exits 5 and 6.

Information

The Greater Portsmouth Chamber of Commerce (☎ 603-436-1118, fax 436-5118), 500 Market St (PO Box 239), Portsmouth, NH 03802-0239, can help with answers.

Stop at its information office on Market St just east of I-95 exit 7 (follow the signs), or at its information kiosk in the city center at Market Square, at the corner of Market and Daniel/Congress Sts. The chamber of commerce hands out a guide to the Portsmouth Harbour Trail which takes you to most of the city's sights, and also a Portsmouth Trail pamphlet highlighting the city's historic houses.

The Seacoast Council on Tourism (☎ 603-436-7678, 800-221-5623) can help with questions about activities along the New Hampshire seacoast.

Strawbery Banke Museum

Unlike New England's other historic recreations – Mystic Seaport, Old Sturbridge Village, Plimoth Plantation – Strawbery Banke Museum (☎ 603-433-1100) does not limit itself to one historical period. Like Portsmouth itself, it is an eclectic gathering

John Paul Jones

Born in Scotland the son of a gardener, John Paul Jones (1747–92) was America's first great naval commander.

At the age of 12, John Paul (his full name then) signed on as an apprentice aboard a merchant vessel bound for America. He later joined the British navy, but soon saw that a workingman could not get ahead there. He worked on a slave ship, then as an actor in the West Indies. On a trip back to Britain, the ship's captain and first mate both died of typhoid fever, leaving Paul the only man aboard who could navigate. He brought the ship safely to port, and the ship's owners made him its captain.

Troubled by several incidents in which he had disciplined sailors severely, Paul left his ship and, adding Jones to his name, disappeared into the colonies and set up as a planter.

When the Revolutionary War began, Jones rode to Philadelphia and signed on as first lieutenant aboard the *Alfred*, and later became commander of the *Providence*. In 1777 he outfitted the sloop *Ranger* in Portsmouth, NH, and took it to Europe, where he set about sinking British coastal ships.

In France he took command of the *Bonhomme Richard* and chased a British convoy in the North Sea. His ship was engaged on September 23, 1779, by HMS *Serapis*, a 44-gun frigate escorting the convoy. They fired at one another at close range for several hours. His ship in tatters, Jones had the bowsprit of the *Serapis* lashed to his own mizzenmast so it could not get away. The British commander called for Jones' surrender, to which Jones replied, "I have not yet begun to fight!"

The battle continued. When an American sailor lobbed a grenade into the *Serapis'* gunpowder magazine, Jones gained the victory.

After independence he served the new American government as an agent in Europe, and was later an admiral in the imperial Russian navy for a short time. He died in Paris in 1792. ∎

of 35 buildings spanning the town's history. Set on a 10-acre site in the Puddle Dock section, it includes Pitt Tavern (1766), a hotbed of American revolutionary sentiment, Goodwin Mansion and other grand 19th-century houses from Portsmouth's most prosperous time, Abbott's Little Corner Store (1943) and several other buildings.

Strawbery Banke is open from 10 am to 5 pm daily, May through October, Thanksgiving weekend and the first two weekends in December. An admission ticket good for two consecutive days costs $10 for adults, $7 kids seven to 17, $25 for families. Children six and under are free.

Prescott Park

The city's major waterfront park (☎ 603-431-8748) is just up Marcy St from Strawbery Banke at the northeastern end of the peninsula. It's a large formal garden with fountains and over 500 varieties of annuals.

Musical performances, part of the Prescott Park Arts Festival, are held throughout the summer. The park is open all day for free, and provides a haven of shade, flowers, quiet and fine views of the river mouth and harbor.

Historic Houses

Several of Portsmouth's grand old houses have been beautifully preserved. Most are open for tours from June through mid-October for $4 adults, $3.50 seniors, $2 children 12 and under.

The Governor John Langdon House (built 1784, ☎ 603-436-3205), 143 Pleasant St, was built for a prosperous merchant who later served as the state's governor.

The John Paul Jones House (1758, ☎ 603-436-8420), 43 Middle St at State St, was a boarding house when Jones lodged here during the outfitting of the *Ranger* (1777) and the *America* (1781). It's now the headquarters of the Portsmouth Historical

NEW HAMPSHIRE

Society, and is open Monday through Saturday from 10 am to 4 pm and Sunday from noon to 4 pm.

The Wentworth Gardner House (1760, ☎ 603-436-4406), 50 Mechanic St, is one of the finest Georgian houses in the USA. It's open daily from 1 to 4 pm (closed Monday).

The Rundlet-May House (1807, ☎ 603-436-3205), 364 Middle St, was built by a wealthy merchant in the Federal style, and is furnished with many pieces made in Portsmouth.

The Warner House (1716, 603-436-5909) is a fine brick town residence at the corner of Daniel and Chapel Sts.

The Moffatt-Ladd House (1763, ☎ 603-436-8221) on Market St was owned by an influential ship captain, and was later the home of General William Whipple, a signer of the Declaration of Independence. The gardens, which overlook the Piscataqua River, are particularly fine.

The 18th-century Wentworth-Coolidge Mansion (☎ 603-436-6607), on Little Harbor Rd south of the town center, was the home of New Hampshire's first royal governor. The 42-room mansion served as the colony's government center from 1741 to 1767. The lilacs on its grounds are descendants of the first lilacs planted in America, brought over from England by Governor Benning Wentworth.

USS *Albacore*

The USS *Albacore*, a 205-foot-long submarine, was launched from the Portsmouth Naval Shipyard in 1953. With a crew of 55 men, the underwater craft was piloted around the world for 19 years without firing a shot, then brought back home to become a museum. You can tour the 27-foot-wide sub, located off Market St near I-95 exit 7 and the chamber of commerce, from 9:30 am to 5:30 pm from May through mid-October for $3 per adult, $2 senior, $1 child seven to 17. Children six and under are free.

Children's Museum

The Children's Museum of Portsmouth (☎ 603-436-3853), 280 Marcy St, has changing exhibits, toys and experiments for children from one to 10 years old. Admission costs $3.50 for adults and kids, $3 for seniors. Children under 12 must be accompanied by an adult.

Cruises

Portsmouth Harbor Cruises (☎ 603-436-8084, 800-776-0915), Ceres St Dock, takes visitors on cruises up river, through the harbor, along the coast and out to the Isles of Shoals. Cruises last one to 2½ hours and cost $7.50 to $15 per adult, $1 less for seniors and $5 to $8 for kids older than two.

Oceanic Whale Watch Expeditions (☎ 603-431-5500, 800-441-4620), 315 Market St, working with the Isles of Shoals Steamship Company, at Barker Wharf off Market St, runs a variety of whale-watch, harbor and music cruises at $9 to $24 per adult. Call for details.

Places to Stay

Camping Most camping areas are privately run, and are inland from the seacoast. They're also very busy in the summer season, usually filled by RVs. Some campgrounds do not accept tents, only RVs.

Hotels & Motels Portsmouth's motels are clustered at I-95 exit 5 and 6, around the Portsmouth (or Interstate) Traffic Circle. Prices are generally lower during the week (Sunday through Thursday nights), rising by about 25% for Friday and Saturday nights. The low prices given here are for weekdays in summer, the high prices for weekends.

Susse Chalet (☎ 603-436-6363, 800-524-2538, fax 436-1621), 650 Borthwick Ave Extension, just off the Interstate Traffic Circle and the US 1 Bypass, has 105 simple rooms for $50 to $80, continental breakfast included.

The *Anchorage Inn* (☎ 603-431-8111, 800-370-8111), 417 Woodbury Ave, is very close to the Interstate Traffic Circle, with 93 rooms, an indoor swimming pool and sauna. Rates are $80 to $90 per double.

The 122-room *Meadowbrook Inn* (☎ 603-436-2700, 800-370-2727, fax 433-2700), has an older section with rooms for $60 to $90.

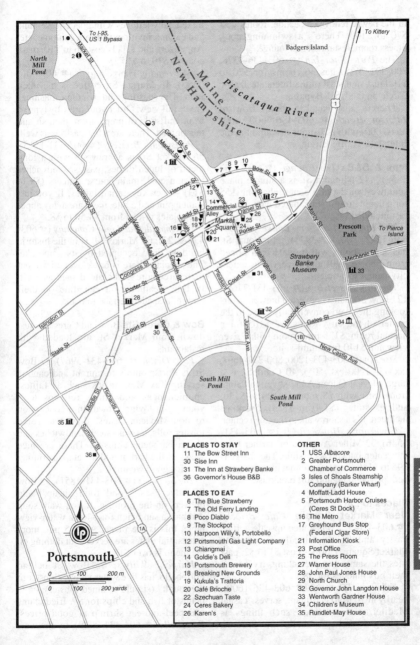

PLACES TO STAY
11 The Bow Street Inn
30 Sise Inn
31 The Inn at Strawbery Banke
36 Governor's House B&B

PLACES TO EAT
6 The Blue Strawberry
7 The Old Ferry Landing
8 Poco Diablo
9 The Stockpot
10 Harpoon Willy's, Portobello
12 Portsmouth Gas Light Company
13 Chiangmai
14 Goldie's Deli
15 Portsmouth Brewery
18 Breaking New Grounds
19 Kukula's Trattoria
20 Café Brioche
22 Szechuan Taste
24 Ceres Bakery
26 Karen's

OTHER
1 USS Albacore
2 Greater Portsmouth Chamber of Commerce
3 Isles of Shoals Steamship Company (Barker Wharf)
4 Moffatt-Ladd House
5 Portsmouth Harbor Cruises (Ceres St Dock)
16 The Metro
17 Greyhound Bus Stop (Federal Cigar Store)
21 Information Kiosk
23 Post Office
25 The Press Room
27 Warner House
28 John Paul Jones House
29 North Church
32 Governor John Langdon House
33 Wentworth Gardner House
34 Children's Museum
35 Rundlet-May House

NEW HAMPSHIRE

In the newly renovated section, rooms cost $70 to $100. There's a swimming pool, fitness room, restaurant and lounge.

The *Port Motor Inn* (☎ 603-436-4378, 800-282-7678) has 56 rooms for $70 to $100 just southeast of the Interstate Traffic Circle on the US 1 Bypass.

There's also a 135-room *Howard Johnson Hotel* (☎ 603-436-7600, 800-654-2000) with a 24-hour restaurant at the Interstate Traffic Circle.

Inns & B&Bs *The Cottage* (☎ 603-431-3353), 442 Islington St, is a simple place southwest of the city center charging $55 for a double room with shared bath, breakfast included.

The Inn at Strawbery Banke (☎ 603-436-7242, 800-428-3933), 314 Court St, has seven rooms with private bath priced from $80 to $90, and a very convenient city-center location.

The Bow Street Inn (☎ 603-431-7760), 121 Bow St, is in a converted brewery overlooking the river, conveniently close to the center of the city. Rates are $105 for a normal room, $125 for a room with a river view and $140 for a mini-suite.

Sise Inn (☎ 603-433-1200, 800-232-4667, fax 433-1200 ext. 505), 40 Court St, is a large, elegant Queen Anne-style inn dating from 1881 with 28 rooms ($100 to $130) and six suites ($150 to $185), breakfast included. It's a short walk to the town center.

Governor's House B&B (☎ 603-431-6546), 32 Miller Ave, is a bit farther from the center, but still accessible. The charge is $95 to $140 for a fine room with queen-size bed, private bath and full breakfast.

Places to Eat
Near Market Square *Cafe Brioche* (☎ 603-430-9225) is a nice upscale coffee, pastry and light-meal cafe overlooking Market Square. Coffees cost $1 to $2, pastries the same. For picnicking, try one of their box lunches for $8.

Kukula's Trattoria (☎ 603-436-1600), nearby at 10 Market Square, serves "casual Mediterranean cuisine," such things as asparagus and portobello mushrooms,

mixed baby lettuces with goat cheese, tuna and calamari with mushroom compote, etc. Appetizers and salads cost $6 to $10, main courses $10 to $15.

At *Breaking New Grounds* (☎ 603-436-9555), 16 Market St, coffee is the main item. The roasting and grinding machines are in full view. Order your brew by type of bean and style of preparation, then sit and talk or read. There are a few pastries as well.

Portsmouth Brewery (☎ 603-431-1115), 56 Market St, is a brewpub with a long menu of lunch dishes, pastas, sandwiches hot and cold, main-course dinners ($9 to $13) – even vegetarian fajitas. If you just want a pint and a bite, there are many appetizer plates priced from $4.50 to $8.

Portsmouth Gas Light Company (☎ 603-430-9122), 64 Market St, is in the historic building once occupied by its namesake. The specialty here is brick-oven pizza, but there are more elaborate dishes as well. In fine weather, you can dine on their umbrella-shaded terrace in back.

Bow & Ceres Sts Bow and Ceres Sts, just down from Market St, are loaded with restaurants.

Poco Diablo (☎ 603-431-5967), 37 Bow St, is Portsmouth's restaurant and cantina serving Tex-Mex dishes such as fajitas, chimichangas and chiles rellenos to a young, fun-loving crowd. In a concession to non-Mexican tastes, they also serve lobster rolls, teriyaki steak sandwiches and Cajun barbecue chicken. There are nice views of the harbor and a waterside dining area for good weather.

The Stockpot (☎ 603-431-1851), 53 Bow St, advertises "good food cheap," and delivers on the promise. If you want soup and half a sandwich for $4 at a water-view table, this is the place. After 5 pm, more substantial plates are served, but nothing on the menu is over $14.

Harpoon Willy's, 67 Bow St behind Portobello, has fine water views, "lobster in the rough" (simple steamed lobster), large plates of fish and chips for $7, fried clams and peel-and-eat shrimp at good prices. *Portobello* (☎ 603-431-2989), by the way, is Portsmouth's traditional Italian restaurant, with full dinners for $25 to $40.

The Old Ferry Landing (☎ 603-431-5510), 10 Ceres St (next to the tugboats), is lodged in what was the terminal for ferries connecting Portsmouth with other coastal points. It's an inexpensive seafood restaurant serving lunch plates for $6.50 to $9, and dinner plates for up to $13. Note the live lobster tank – always a good sign – just inside the door.

The Blue Strawberry (☎ 603-431-6420), 29 Ceres St, was among the early eateries that established Portsmouth's reputation, almost a quarter century ago, as a good food town. The food, a mixture of continental and New American dishes, is still very good, and still served as a six- to eight-course fixed-price table d'hôte dinner for $40 to $50 per person, plus drinks, tax and tip. You must have a reservation for a seating, so call ahead. They're usually closed Tuesday and Wednesday.

Chiangmai (☎ 603-433-1289), 128 Penhallow St just off Bow St, serves good Thai cuisine for lunch and dinner every day. Their luncheon specials give you a three-course meal for $6 to $7 (plus drink, tax and tip). Chicken satay is $5, pad Thai only a bit more. Try the Gourmet Madness: shrimp, scallops, mussels and squid stir-fried with mushrooms and vegetables in a very hot chili sauce. If you'd rather have Chinese food, *Szechuan Taste* (☎ 603-431-2226), a block southeast at 54 Daniel St, serves Szechuan, Hunan and Mandarin cuisine at similar prices.

Goldie's Deli, just up Penhallow from Chiangmai, has cheap sandwiches such as sausage for $3, and, of course, lots of bagels. *Ceres Bakery* (☎ 603-436-6518), 51 Penhallow St, is a good place to pick up fresh bread or pastry for a snack or picnic.

Karen's (☎ 603-431-1948), 105 Daniel St, always has several quite good vegetarian main courses on its New American lunch and dinner menus along with its fish, chicken, and lamb ($14). Breakfast is served daily; weekend brunch from 8 am to 2 pm is a specialty ($6 to $10). Dinner is not served Monday and Tuesday.

Entertainment
The Press Room (☎ 603-431-5186), 77 Daniel St, has live jazz and other entertainment most nights. There's a long menu of bar food with most items less than $7. Stop by or call to see who's performing.

Try also *The Metro* (☎ 603-436-0521), 20 High St, which sometimes has live jazz (and good seafood) in its cozy bar.

Getting There & Away
Bus Portsmouth's Greyhound bus station is the Federal Cigar Store (☎ 603-436-0163), 9 Congress St just off Market Square. The bus service is actually run by Vermont Transit on a route connecting Boston and Portsmouth with the Maine cities of Portland, Bangor and Bar Harbor. There are three or four buses daily, taking 80 minutes to Boston.

The Coach Company (☎ 800-874-3377) runs shuttles along the coast between Portsmouth and Boston, including Logan Airport, as does the Hampton Shuttle (☎ 603-926-8275, 800-883-6663). C&J Trailways (☎ 800-258-7111), at Pease International Tradeport (Portsmouth's airport) also has service to Boston's Logan Airport.

Car Driving details for Portsmouth are:

Destination	Mileage	Hr:Min
Boston, MA	57 miles	1:10
Concord, NH	47 miles	1:00
Kennebunkport, ME	28 miles	0:45
Manchester, NH	47 miles	1:00
New York, NY	275 miles	5:45
Portland, ME	55 miles	1:10

Merrimack River Valley

The Merrimack River Valley holds New Hampshire's two most important cities, Manchester and Concord.

MANCHESTER
Exploiting the abundant water power of the Merrimack, Manchester (population 100,000) became the state's manufacturing and commercial center in the 1800s. It's

now the banking center as well. Students crowd the campuses of New Hampshire Technical College, Notre Dame College and the University of New Hampshire.

Orientation

Manchester stretches along the east bank of the Merrimack; West Manchester is on the west side. If you enter Manchester from I-93, you miss the city view which defines it: the red-brick swath of the great Amoskeag textile mills stretching along the east bank of the river for over a mile. If you'd like to get the view, follow I-293 along the west bank of the river, and exit via the Amoskeag Bridge or the Queen City Bridge after you've passed the mills.

The heart of Manchester is ranged along Elm St (US 3), which runs north-south through the business and commercial district. The Currier Gallery of Art is six blocks east of Elm St along Orange St (there are signs); hotels are at the interstate exits.

Information

The Manchester Chamber of Commerce (☎ 603-666-6600), Manchester, NH 03101, is an information source, as is the Southern New Hampshire Convention & Visitors Bureau (☎ 603-635-9000, 800-932-4282), Windham, NH 03087.

Currier Gallery of Art

The state's premier fine arts museum is the Currier Gallery of Art (☎ 603-669-6144), 192 Orange St, with excellent collections of 19th- and 20th-century European and American glass, English and American silver and pewter, and colonial and early American furniture. Among European painters, Degas, Jan Gossaert and a follower of Meliore are represented. The museum underwent extensive renovation in 1995 and '96. Admission is free, and it's open from 10 am to 4 pm (Thursday until 10 pm), Sunday 2 to 5 pm, and is closed Monday. From Elm St (US 3) go east on Orange St for six blocks.

Amoskeag Mills

The great brick mills, lit by hundreds of tall windows, stretch along Commercial St on the riverbank for almost 1½ miles. Other mills face them across the river in West Manchester. For almost a century, from 1838 to 1920, the Amoskeag Manufacturing Company was the world's largest manufacturer of textiles. The mills employed up to 17,000 people a year (out of a city population of 70,000). Many of them lived in the trim brick tenements that stretch up the hillside eastward from the mills. The tenements have been restored, and are still used as housing.

As for the mills themselves, the company abandoned them when, hit hard by the Depression, it went bankrupt in 1935. Since that time the city has been searching for tenants. Many have been found, and there are now offices, college classrooms, restaurants, warehouses and storage rooms and broadcasting studios where noisy looms were once driven by water power and steam. But much of the vast extent of space remains empty still.

Unless you have business in the buildings, you will want to view them from the outside.

Anheuser-Busch Brewery

The Anheuser-Busch Company (☎ 603-595-1202), 221 Daniel Webster Hwy, has a large brewery in nearby Merrimack, one of a dozen located throughout the USA. The company that brews Budweiser and Michelob is the world's largest brewer of beer, making 86 million barrels annually.

You can tour the plant for free, watch the foamy stuff being made, then lift a sample glass yourself. Tours run throughout the day, departing from the alpine-looking building May to October from 9:30 am to 5 pm daily, and November to April, Wednesday through Sunday from 10 am to 4 pm.

Animal-lovers should not miss a visit to the **Clydesdale Hamlet** where a dozen of the huge, majestic Anheuser-Busch trade-

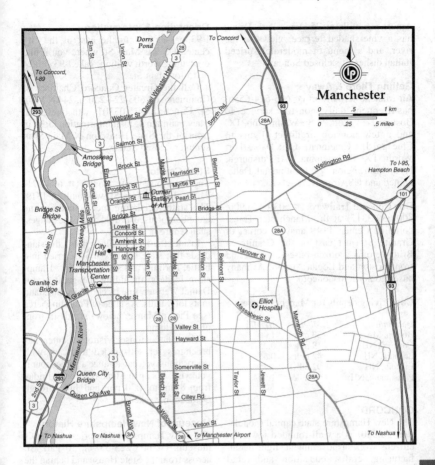

mark draft horses live. You may have seen an eight-horse hitch pulling an old-fashioned brewer's wagon in advertisements or parades.

To get to the brewery, go south on I-293 to the Everett Turnpike (US 3), and take exit 10 (Industrial Drive).

Places to Stay

There are no camping places convenient to Manchester.

Most of the city's lodging is for business travelers. The 102-room *Susse Chalet Inn* (☎ 603-625-2020, 800-258-1980, fax 623-7562), 860 Porter St, off I-293 exit 1 and S Willow St, is two miles from the city center. Rooms cost $50 to $75. The *Howard Johnson Hotel* (☎ 603-668-6426, 800-446-4656), 298 Queen City Ave, has 100 rooms and charges a bit more.

Places to Eat

There are several small restaurants along Elm St, and lots of fast-food places along US 3 in West Manchester (follow Elm St/US 3 south across the Queen City Bridge and turn left). The *Cafe Pavoné* (☎ 603-622-5488), down near the river and the

Amoskeag mills at 75 Arms Park Drive, has a vine-shaded terrace, views of the river, and a menu of moderately-priced Italian dishes. It's closed Sunday.

Getting There & Away
Air Manchester Airport (☎ 603-624-6556) has frequent daily nonstop service to Boston; New York City; Washington, DC and a few nonstop or direct flights to Chicago, IL; Cincinnati, OH; Dallas/Fort Worth, TX; Philadelphia, PA; Pittsburgh, PA and Burlington, VT. Continental, Delta, United and USAir provide service.

Bus Concord Trailways (☎ 603-647-6900, 800-639-3317) at the Manchester Transportation Center, 119 Canal St, corner of Granite St (just east of the Granite St Bridge), runs a dozen buses daily to and from Boston and Logan Airport. As many buses go north to Concord.

Car Driving details for Manchester are:

Destination	Mileage	Hr:Min
Boston, MA	53 miles	1:00
Concord, NH	19 miles	0:25
Laconia, NH	42 miles	0:55
Lincoln, NH	92 miles	1:45
Portsmouth, NH	51 miles	1:00

CONCORD
The New Hampshire state capital (population 36,000) is a well-rounded town. Its citizens work at government, light manufacturing, crafts, education and retail sales, as you'll see immediately when you approach the gigantic shopping mall beside I-93.

They also quarry granite, a suitable occupation in the Granite State. The facing stone for the Library of Congress in Washington, DC, was quarried at nearby Rattlesnake Hill. The state house, New Hampshire's capitol, and many of the buildings surrounding it, are also cut from the local stone.

Despite its modest charms, Concord will not grip you, and after a visit of several hours you may be on your way again.

Orientation & Information
I-93 passes just to the east of the city center. US 3 is Main St, where you'll find everything worth visiting. Take I-93 exit 14 or 15 for Main St.

Call the Greater Concord Chamber of Commerce (☎ 603-224-2508), 244 N Main St, Concord, NH 03301 with questions. They maintain a small information kiosk in front of the State House on N Main St in summer (closed Sunday).

State Capitol
The handsome State House (☎ 603-271-2154), 107 N Main St, was built in 1819. The state legislature meets in the same chambers it used in that year, the longest such tenure in the USA.

Inside, the Hall of Flags holds the standards that state military units carried into battle. Portraits and statues of New Hampshire leaders, including the great orator Daniel Webster, line its corridors and stand in its lofty halls. A statue of Franklin Pierce (see Pierce Manse, below) stands in front of the building.

The State House Visitors Center has brochures for self-guided tours, or with reservations, you can arrange a guided tour if you wish. It's open Monday through Friday from 8 am to 4:30 pm, and July through October on weekends.

Museum of New Hampshire History
The New Hampshire Historical Society's museum (☎ 603-225-3381), 30 Park St, across from the State House and behind the first lot of buildings, can fill you in on such Granite State topics as the Concord Coach, the stagecoach that provided transport to much of America's "Western Frontier."

There are also beautiful 19th-century paintings of the state's White Mountain scenes. The building itself – granite again – is good for strolling. The small park with a fountain and sidewalk cafe is the place to take a breather.

The museum is open weekdays from 9 am to 4:30 pm, weekends from noon to 4:30. Admission costs $10 for families, $3.50 adults, $1.75 youth six to 18. You're allowed in for free on Thursday evenings from 5 to 8:30 pm.

Pierce Manse

The home of Franklin Pierce (1804-69), 14th president of the US, is now a museum. The Pierce Manse (☎ 603-225-2068, 224-7668), 14 Penacook St, at the end of N Main St, was built in 1838-39 and saved from destruction a decade ago by the Pierce Brigade.

Pierce was the son of a two-term New Hampshire governor, a member and later Speaker of the New Hampshire General Court (legislature) and a representative and senator in Congress. He retired from the US Senate to practice law in Concord, maintaining an interest in politics, but having little interest in further public service. But during the Democratic party's convention of 1852, there were so many strong candidates for the presidency that none could achieve a majority vote. On the 49th ballot, Pierce, a compromise candidate, became the party's nominee and later won the presidency.

The manse was his family home from 1842 to 1848. It's open for visits from mid-June to mid-September, weekdays from 11 am to 3 pm. Admission costs $2 for adults, 50¢ children.

Christa McAuliffe Planetarium

This planetarium (☎ 603-271-7827), just northeast of I-93 exit 15 (follow the signs), is named in honor of the New Hampshire schoolteacher chosen to be America's first teacher-astronaut. McAuliffe and her fellow astronauts died in the tragic explosion of the *Challenger* spacecraft on January 28, 1986. Call for a schedule of shows, many of which are open to the public.

Places to Stay

There are several good highway hotels and motels to serve those staying in Concord on government business. Most tourists rocket through to the mountains or lakes. Far more camping and lodging choices in all price ranges are available not too far away in Laconia, Gilford and in other towns around Lake Winnipesaukee.

Rates at the 100-room *Comfort Inn* (☎ 603-226-4100), 71 Hall St, range from $50 off-season to $100 for summer holidays. The 122-room *Holiday Inn* (☎ 603-224-9534), 172 N Main St, is similar.

Places to Eat

The town layout tells you what goes on here: most of Concord's restaurants are on N Main St at Park St across from the State House, to catch the legislative lunch crowd. *Murphy's State House Tavern & Steakhouse* (☎ 603-224-1414), 130 N Main, and a few doors away, the *Brown Bag Deli* and the *Coffee Mill*, are all in the same row. The *Eagle Square Delicatessen* is behind these buildings off the park in front of the Museum of New Hampshire History; it's closed on weekends, though.

Perhaps the most interesting place to dine is the *Capital City Diner* (☎ 603-228-3463), at I-93 exit 13, an authentic diner from the 1950s serving breakfast, lunch, dinner and drinks.

Getting There & Away

Concord Trailways (☎ 603-228-3300, 800-639-3317) at the Trailways Transportation Center, on Storrs St by the Ames store, runs a dozen buses daily via Manchester to and from Boston and Logan Airport.

Driving details for Concord are:

Destination	Mileage	Hr:Min
Boston, MA	72 miles	1:30
Laconia, NH	23 miles	0:35
Lincoln, NH	73 miles	1:20
Manchester, NH	19 miles	0:25
North Conway, NH	73 miles	2:00

CANTERBURY SHAKER VILLAGE

Members of the United Society of Believers in Christ's Second Appearing were called "Shakers" because of the religious ecstasies they experienced during worship. (For a history of Shakers, see Facts about New England or the Pittsfield, MA, entry.)

NEW HAMPSHIRE

The Shaker community at Canterbury was founded in 1792, and was actively occupied for two centuries. Sister Ethel Hudson, last member of the Shaker colony here, died in 1992 at the age of 96. Now Canterbury Shaker Village (☎ 603-783-9511) is preserved as a non-profit trust to present the history of the Shakers. The lone surviving Shaker community, at Sabbathday Lake, ME, still accepts new members.

Canterbury Shaker Village has "interpreters" in period dress who still perform the tasks and labors of community daily life: fashioning Shaker furniture and crafts (for sale in the gift shop) and growing herbs and producing herbal medicines. The guided tour takes you to the herb garden, the Meetinghouse (1792), an apiary (bee house), the ministry, a "Sisters" shop, a laundry, horse barn, infirmary and the schoolhouse (1826).

On Thursday, Friday and Saturday evenings you can join in a traditional four-course candlelight dinner. The single evening seating at 7 pm sharp is family style, at long tables and you can choose from a poultry, meat or fish main course. Recipes, ingredients and cooking methods are all true to Shaker form and philosophy. After dinner has transported you to another era, you'll be guided through the village by candlelight, or if it's off-season and the village is closed, you'll be treated to an evening of folk singing. Dinner costs about $35 per person. Alternatively, *The Creamery* is a restaurant open for lunch daily from 11:30 am to 2 pm and for Sunday brunch from 11 am to 2 pm.

Canterbury Shaker Village is open for guided tours from May through October, Monday through Saturday from 10 am to 5 pm, Sunday from noon to 5 pm (last tour at 4 pm). In April, November and December, the village is open Friday through Sunday; it's closed January through March. Admission costs $7 for adults and $3.50 for kids six to 12.

To find the village, take I-93 exit 18 and follow the signs, or go 15 miles north of Concord on MA 106.

The Lakes Region

New Hampshire's Lakes Region, centered on vast Lake Winnipesaukee, is an odd mix of wondrous natural beauty and human commercial tawdriness.

The forest-shrouded lakes have beautiful, sinuous coastlines stretching for hundreds of miles. The roads skirting the shores and connecting the lakeside towns are a riotous festival of popular culture, lined with a mindless hodge-podge of shopping malls, gas stations, miniature golf courses, amusement arcades, auto dealerships, go-kart tracks, motels, private zoos, clam shacks, tourist cottages, junk food outlets, boat docks and gimcrack shops.

Most visitors to the Lakes Region are New England families who have cottages on or near the lake shore, or who take their annual vacations in one of the roadside motels and don't otherwise travel far from home on vacation.

Passing through on your way to the White Mountain Range to the north or Boston to the south, you can spend a day or two pleasantly enough here. Lake Winnipesaukee, the euphonious Indian name of New Hampshire's largest lake means "smile of the Great Spirit." Winnipesaukee has 183 miles of coastline, over 300 islands and, despite being landlocked, excellent salmon fishing.

Stop for a swim or a picnic at one of the two state parks on the lake. Take a ride on one of the several lake-cruising motor launches. Better yet, take a seaplane ride to view all the lakes from the air. Visit a museum. And, if you have children, don't miss a chance to prowl the video arcades, bowladromes and junk food cafes of Weirs Beach.

Orientation & Information
Laconia is the population center of the Lakes Region, the place you go to find a hospital, auto parts store or other service. Most visitors stay in the small towns near the lake.

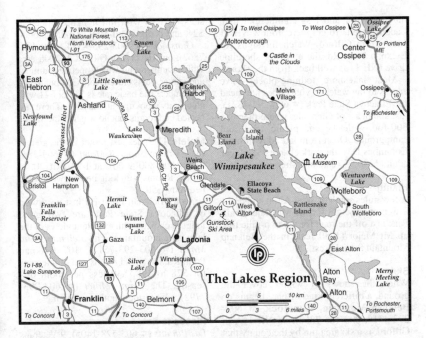

Meredith is a largish town with many lodging and dining possibilities. Weirs Beach is the place with the honky-tonk game arcades and boat rides. Glendale is sedate, with small hotels, motels and cottages shaded by pines. Wolfeboro, on the southeastern shore, is aristocratic.

Each of the larger towns has its own chamber of commerce information office found under each destination. You can also try the Lakes Region Association (☎ 603-253-8555), PO Box 589, Center Harbor, NH 03226.

Special Event

Winnipesaukee's annual Motorcycle Week, from June 12 to 18 or thereabouts, draws two-wheeled crowds to the New Hampshire International Speedway (☎ 603-783-4744), on NH 106 in Louden, for races, shows and other events. Bikers are everywhere, and lodgings (particularly camping and motels) can be difficult to find, so reserve ahead.

LACONIA, GILFORD & GLENDALE

The capital and largest town of the Lakes Region, Laconia occupies itself with light manufacturing of goods such as shoes and electrical components. Neighboring Gilford, in the shadow of Belknap Mountain (2384 feet, pronounced BELL-nap), is joined at the hip to Laconia, and is indistinguishable from Laconia to the casual visitor. Glendale, a neighborhood of Gilford, is the sedate lakeside area where you'll find Ellacoya State Park and its fine beach.

Information

The Greater Laconia & Weirs Beach Chamber of Commerce (☎ 603-524-5531, 800-531-2347), 11 Veterans Square, Laconia, NH 03246, maintains an information office in the old railroad station in the center of Laconia.

Lake Access

Lake Winnipesaukee is the big attraction, of course. The area around Glendale is much prettier and less commercial than Laconia itself. To get there, follow NH 11 south from Gilford. Watch for signs for Belknap Point Rd, the narrower shoreline drive (NH 11 is well back from the shore).

Most lakeshore lodging-places have access to the water. If yours does not, head for Ellacoya State Park (☎ 603-293-7821), just southeast of Glendale, where there's a 600-foot-wide beach, picnic area and campground. Open from late May through Columbus Day, the park charges $2.50 per adult (12 to 55 years old), free for others.

Hiking

A few miles south of West Alton on NH 11 a sign points right for the Mt Major Trail. Park just off the road for the two-mile trek up Mt Major (1780 feet) in the Belknap Mountain State Forest.

Skiing

When the snows of winter cover the ground, a different kind of play begins on Belknap Mountain. **Gunstock** (☎ 603-293-4318, 800-486-7862), on NH 11A in Gilford, is a ski area run by the county that has no lodging other than their campground (see below).

Gunstock sports 45 downhill runs on a vertical drop of 1400 feet. There are seven lifts, including a quad and two triples. They have a ski school, as well as day care facilities. Most of the mountain trails are intermediate, with a larger percentage of advanced than beginner trails.

Over 50 km of cross-country trails follow the wooded paths around Gilford. Of the trails, 25 are tracked, 37 are skate groomed and 13 are ungroomed for backcountry skiing.

Both downhill and cross-country skis are rented, with snowboards, snowskates (boots attached to shortened skis) and telemark skis also available. Call the main number to connect with the ski shop.

Places to Stay

Camping *Ellacoya State Park* (☎ 603-293-7821, 436-1552 for reservations), PO Box 7277, Laconia, NH 03247, has 35 unshaded sites for RVs with full hookups priced at $24, and is open mid-May to mid-October.

Gunstock (☎ 603-293-4344, 800-486-7862), on NH 11A in Gilford, is a ski area with a campground which operates summer and winter, but is closed from October to late November. The basic rate is $17 or $21 with electricity hookups at the site. There are heated bathrooms, but no water at the sites.

Motels The cheapest motel in the area is the 63-room *Super 8 Motel* (☎ 603-286-8882; 800-800-8000), at I-93 exit 20, at Tilton. Rooms with king bed or two double beds cost $50.

Along Belknap Point Rd just northwest of Ellacoya State Park are two good lodging choices with excellent views of the lake and mountains. The *Belknap Point Motel* (☎ 603-293-7511), 107 Belknap Point Rd, has motel rooms and efficiencies for $78 to $98, $40 less per room off-season. The *Estate Motel* (☎ 603-293-7792), a bit farther south, is similar.

Places to Eat

Las Piñatas (☎ 603-528-1405), 9 Veterans Square, in the old railroad station in downtown Laconia, has lots of traditional Mexican specialties as well as some Tex-Mex dishes. A full dinner need cost only $10 to $14.

Getting There & Away

Bus Concord Trailways (☎ 603-524-0530, 800-639-3317) at Week's Restaurant, 331 S Main St, runs three buses daily via Tilton Junction, Concord, and Manchester to and from Boston and Logan Airport. From Tilton Junction, just six miles southwest of Laconia at the Irving fuel station (☎ 603-286-3532) at the junction of US 3 and I-93 exit 20, there are one or two extra buses on weekends.

Car Driving details for Laconia are:

Destination	Mileage	Hr:Min
Boston, MA	95 miles	2:15
Concord, NH	23 miles	0:35
Lincoln/		
North Woodstock, NH	45 miles	1:10
Manchester, NH	42 miles	0:55

NEW HAMPSHIRE

Meredith, NH	8 miles	0:18
North Conway, NH	49 miles	1:25
Wolfeboro, NH	27 miles	0:55

WEIRS BEACH

Called Aquedoctan by its Native American settlers, Weirs Beach takes its English name from the Indian fishing weirs found here by the first White settlers and from the small sand beach which still draws swimmers.

Weirs Beach is the honky-tonk heart of Lake Winnipesaukee's childhood amusements. It's famous for its video game arcades and great variety of junk food offerings. But there is also a nice lakefront promenade, a small state park and beach, the dock for the MS *Mount Washington* cruise boat and a station on the local scenic railroad. You can even go up for a seaplane ride, one of the finer things to do here. As you ascend from the lake's surface, the tawdry commercial atmosphere drops away to reveal the verdant beauty of the countryside.

Information

The Greater Laconia & Weirs Beach Chamber of Commerce (☎ 603-524-5531, 800-531-2347), has an information booth on US 3 a mile south of Weirs Beach. They can help you find same-day accommodations.

Weirs Beach, the honky-tonk heart of Lake Winnipesaukee

Winnipesaukee Scenic Railroad

The Winnipesaukee Scenic Railroad (☎ 603-745-2135) has its terminus in Weirs Beach. Its season runs from March 15 to December 31, with trains running hourly every day in July and August, but in the spring, fall and winter, trains run at 11 am and 1 pm.

Seaplane Rides

Get up, up and away any day from 9 am to sunset in the summer from Seaplane Services, Inc's Paugus Bay Dock (☎ 603-524-0446), on US 3 between Weirs Beach and Gilford. Rides lasting 16 to 18 minutes are offered from 9 am to sunset daily for $20 per person ($40 minimum charge, kids under five fly free). There's a similar service available on the opposite side of the lake at Moultonboro Airport (☎ 603-476-8801), on NH 25.

Cruises

To see the lake from the lake, hop aboard one of the boats which depart Weirs Beach daily on scenic cruises. The MS *Mount Washington* (☎ 603-366-2628) steams out on 2¼- and 3¼-hour cruises several times daily for $12.50 per adult, $6.25 children four to 12. In the evening there are dinner cruises with entertainment ($26 to $32); ask what the night's theme will be.

The same company operates the sloop *Queen of Winnipesaukee* on 1½- to two-hour cruises from late May through early October. Adults pay $10, kids pay $6. Bring your own drinks; snacks are provided. If you prefer sail to motor, this is the cruise for you.

Other motor cruisers are the MV *Sophie C*, the US Mail boat, which takes the mail out to many of the lake's islands on 1½-hour morning and evening runs ($9 adult, $4.50 child); and the MV *Doris E*, making one-hour ($6.50, $3.25) and two-hour ($9, $4.50) cruises from Weirs Beach and Meredith.

Places to Stay

Camping Seasonal camping is available on US 3 south of Weirs Beach at *Weirs Beach Tent & Trailer Park* (☎ 603-366-4747),

1500 feet north of the beach. The 175 sites cost $16 to $26; some have hookups. It's open from mid-May to mid-September.

North of Weirs Beach along US 3 are several more campgrounds. *Pine Hollow Camping World* (☎ 603-366-2222) is a mile north of town, with sites for $20 and up open mid-May to mid-October.

Hack-Ma-Tack Campground (☎ 603-366-5977), 1½ miles north of Weirs Beach on US 3, has 75 sites (45 with hookups) going for $20 to $22. They're open from early May to early October.

Paugus Bay Campground (☎ 603-366-4757), on Hilliard Rd off US 3, has 130 wooded sites overlooking the bay priced at $23 and up.

Motels The *Half Moon Motel* (☎ 603-366-4494) PO Box 5183, Weirs Beach, NH 03247, just up the hill off the main street, has cottages and motel rooms for $50 to $75 per room, and is as close as possible to the arcade action here.

US 3 north from Gilford holds some of the nicer moderately-priced motels on this part of the shore. The 24-room *Birch Knoll Motel* (☎ 603-366-4958), 867 Weirs Blvd (PO Box 5172), Laconia, NH 03246, is among the better ones, with rooms for $78 to $92. Also try the *Bay Top Motel* (☎ 603-366-2225), US 3 Box 106, which is similar.

Places to Eat
Weirs Beach is all about eating: burgers, hot dogs, fried dough, lobsters, ice cream, doughnuts, anything sweet and anything fatty. Stroll the main street for the snack shops. For more substantial fare, try the *Weirs Beach Lobster Pound* (☎ 603-366-5713) on US 3 for chicken and steak as well as seafood. Kids' meals cost 5¢ per pound of kid. Wine and beer are served.

MEREDITH
A bit more sedate and upscale than Weirs Beach, Meredith is still a real Lakes Region town with a long lakeside commercial strip of restaurants, shops and places to stay.

Orientation & Information
US 3, NH 25 and NH 104 meet in Meredith, which is spread along the shore.

Meredith Chamber of Commerce (☎ 603-279-8897), PO Box 732, Meredith, NH 03253, maintains an information office right in the center of Meredith on US 3 facing the water.

Places to Stay
Camping *Harbor Hill Camping Area* (☎ 603-279-6910), on NH 25 1½ miles east of Meredith, has 140 sites, mostly wooded and with hookups, for $16 to $20.

The *Long Island Bridge Campground* (☎ 603-253-6053), 13 miles northeast of Meredith near Center Harbor, has a private beach and very popular tent sites for $14 to $20. In July and August you must rent a site for three days minimum; reservations are accepted from May through September. Follow NH 25 east from Center Harbor 1½ miles, then go south on Moultonboro Neck Rd for 6½ miles.

White Lake State Park (☎ 603-323-7350), PO Box 273, West Ossipee, NH 03890, is 22 miles northeast of Meredith at White Lake. It has 200 tent sites priced at $14 ($20 for waterfront sites), swimming and hiking trails.

Inns *Tuckernuck Inn* (☎ 603-279-5521), Red Gate Lane, off Water St, has five cozy guest rooms for $50 single, $55 double.

The *Red Hill Inn* (☎ 603-279-7001, 800-573-4455, fax 279-7003), RD 1, Box 99, Center Harbor, NH 03226, commands a fine view of the lakes region from its hilltop perch off NH 25B north of Meredith. Rooms in cottages and a farmhouse surrounding the main lodge cost $85 to $145. The dining room is excellent.

Places to Eat
Breakfast and lunch are good at the deli-cafe named *For Every Season* (☎ 603-279-8875), 67 Main St. Try an egg on wheels for breakfast ($2.25), or a grilled cheddar cheese and apple sandwich ($2.50) at lunchtime.

Getting There & Away

Meredith is eight miles north of Laconia, which has the nearest Concord Trailways bus station.

WOLFEBORO

Named for General Wolfe, who died vanquishing Montcalm on the Plains of Abraham in Québec, Wolfeboro claims to be "the oldest summer resort in America." Whether true or not, it is now the most pleasant resort town on the lake, with a fine lakefront situation, an agreeable bustle and plenty of services.

Information

The Wolfeboro Chamber of Commerce Information Booth (☎ 603-569-1817), is on S Main St at the intersection of NH 28 and 109, opposite the Exxon and Mobil gas stations. The chamber's main office (☎ 603-569-2200) is on Railroad Ave. Public toilets are at PJ's Dockside Restaurant (see below).

Walking Tours

Wolfeboro is a pretty town with some good examples of New England's architectural styles, from Georgian through Federal, Greek Revival and Second Empire.

The information office has several good suggestions for walks, including the half-mile-long Bridge Falls Path along the southern shore of Back Bay, the 10-minute walk to Abenaki Tower and the Wolfeboro-Sanbornville Recreational Trail which follows an abandoned railroad bed for 12 miles.

Clark House

The Clark House (☎ 603-569-4997), on S Main St (south of the information booth) opposite Huggins Hospital, is Wolfeboro's eclectic historical museum, with colonial artifacts, fire engines and equipment dating back to 1872, and a one-room schoolhouse from 1868.

Libby Museum

At the age of 40, Dr Henry Forrest Libby, a local dentist, began collecting things. Start-

ing with butterflies and moths, the amateur naturalist built up a private natural history collection. In 1912 he built a home for his collections, the Libby Museum (☎ 603-569-1035), on NH 109 in Winter Harbor, three miles north of Wolfeboro. Other collections were added, including Abenaki relics and early American farm and home implements.

The museum is open daily June through early September, for $2 per adult.

Cruises

The Wolfeboro Inn's 65-foot, diesel-powered launch, the MV *Judge Sewall* (☎ 603-569-3016), takes inn guests and others on tours of the lake daily in summer. You can board the quaint vessel, built in 1946, at the town dock off Main St, for $6.

The MV *Mount Washington* also has a daily 3½-hour cruise from Wolfeboro. See Weirs Beach, above, for details and fares.

Places to Stay

Camping *Wolfeboro Campground* (☎ 603-569-9881, 569-4029), on Haines Hill Rd (off NH 28 north of Wolfeboro), has 40 RV sites and 10 tent sites priced at $14 for a family of four. It's open from mid-May to mid-October.

Inns Best-known is the *Wolfeboro Inn* (☎ 603-569-3016, 800-451-2389), 44 N Main St, Wolfeboro, NH 03894, the town's main lodgings since 1812, with 43 very comfortable rooms priced from $119 to $139 per night.

A few hundred yards north up N Main St is the *Tuc' Me Inn* (☎ 603-569-5702), 68 N Main St, a nice B&B charging $60 to $75 for its rooms, country breakfast included.

Farther north along N Main (NH 28) are several good motels. The *Lakeview Inn & Motor Lodge* (☎ 603-569-1335), less than a mile north of Wolfeboro center, has very nice rooms priced from $55 to $90, breakfast included. The dining room here is a local favorite. The *Clearwater Lodges* (☎ 603-569-2370), 2½ miles north of Wolfeboro, are a collection of dark-wood cottages beneath tall trees on the lake shore.

Places to Eat

For breakfast or a light lunch, try the *Strawberry Patch* (☎ 603-569-5523), 30 N Main St, with a menu of pancakes, eggs, sandwiches and so forth priced from $2 to $6.

For a light breakfast or snack, the nearby *Yum Yum Shop* serves all sorts of baked goods, from doughnuts to wedding cakes, as well as good, strong coffee for low prices.

In the middle of the Main St shopping district, *Rumors Cafe* is the locals' favorite tavern hangout, and for good reason. The eclectic menu ranges from a basket of chicken and teriyaki steak sandwiches to pasta and clam rolls. Prices range from $4 to $9. The bar and rear terrace have fine lake views.

PJ's Dockside Restaurant, just off Main St in the center of town by the docks for the MV *Judge Sewall* and the MS *Mount Washington*, serves good seaside fare such as clam rolls and seafood combo plates for $9 to $12.

For a full restaurant, try the *Wolfeboro Inn*. In the rustic, colonial front of the inn is Wolfe's Tavern, with a bar and menu ranging from sandwiches to substantial tuck-ins for $6 to $18. In front of the tavern, terrace tables are set out in the open air in good weather. The inn's main dining rooms are more modern and formal, serving American and continental fare for $15 to $25 per person.

Getting There & Away

Driving details for Wolfeboro are:

Destination	Mileage	Hr:Min
Boston, MA	114 miles	2:50
Laconia, NH	30 miles	0:45
Lincoln, NH	75 miles	1:55
Manchester, NH	54 miles	1:35
North Conway, NH	43 miles	1:20
Portland, ME	60 miles	1:50
Portsmouth, NH	51 miles	1:25

Getting Around

Molly the Trolley (☎ 603-569-5257) trundles along Main St daily each hour from 10 am to 4 pm. An all-day pass costs $1.

White Mountains

The White Mountains are New England's greatest range and one of its prime outdoor playgrounds. Most of the range is protected from over-development by the White Mountain National Forest. Activities include hiking, rustic and backwoods camping, canoeing and kayaking and skiing.

Highlights of the White Mountain Range include Waterville Valley, a planned mountain resort community; the Kancamagus Hwy, a beautiful wilderness road over Kancamagus Pass; North Conway and Jackson, centers for downhill and cross-country skiing, canoeing and kayaking; Mt Washington, with Bretton Woods and its famous Mount Washington Hotel and the Franconia Notch area, with several ski areas and many dramatic geological formations (including New Hampshire's symbol, the Old Man of the Mountain).

Information

The headquarters of the White Mountain National Forest (☎ 603-528-8721), PO Box 638, Laconia, NH 03247, is the nerve center, but there's an information office in Lincoln just off I-93 exit 32.

Camping

The White Mountain National Forest covers a large area, but is also intensively used. Everyone camping in the backwoods should use common sense.

WATERVILLE VALLEY

Waterville Valley is a beautiful mountain valley developed to be a complete mountain resort community.

There was an incorporated town here in the shadow of Mt Tecumseh, on the banks of the Mad River, as early as 1829, but the valley took its present shape during the last decades of the 20th century. Hotels, condominiums, vacation villas, golf courses, ski runs, roads and services were all laid out according to plan and in conformity with

Geography of New Hampshire

Southern New Hampshire is a region of glacial lakes and low mountains, many of which are bathyliths – huge rounded granite domes formed deep underground and brought to the surface by upheavals and erosion. Mt Monadnock (3166 feet), southeast of Keene, is the most famous of New Hampshire's bathyliths.

The Merrimack River Valley drains the central and southern portions of the state. The river itself is easily traceable on any road map because it shares its valley with I-93 and I-293. Springing at Newfound Lake, it flows southeasterly through Concord, Manchester, Merrimack and Nashua-Hudson before turning northeasterly and entering the Atlantic at Newburyport, MA.

Southcentral New Hampshire's major feature is vast Lake Winnipesaukee, with 183 miles of shoreline. Surrounding lakes, which would be large in most other places, look small by comparison.

Northcentral New Hampshire has the White Mountain Range, the northern end of the Appalachian Highlands, which include the famous Presidential Range, with peaks named after many US presidents. Mt Washington (6288 feet) is the highest, of course.

Most of the White Mountain Range is included in the vast White Mountain National Forest. Several "notches" (narrow passes) provide passage between major mountains. Most famous of these is Franconia Notch, a five-mile-long gap within the serene and unwavering gaze of the Great Stone Face. ■

strict standards by the Waterville Company. The result is a harmonious but perhaps somewhat sterile resort with lots of organized sports activities.

Sports facilities include downhill and cross-country ski trails, hiking trails, tennis and golf, road and mountain bike routes, in-line skating routes and organized fun.

Orientation & Information

Waterville Valley is reached from I-93 exit 28 (Campton). Easily visible from the main road, there's an information office of the Waterville Valley Regional Chamber of Commerce (☎ 603-726-3804), RR 1, Box 1067, Campton, NH 03223. The road (NH 49) continues 13 miles northeast into the valley and to Waterville Valley resort.

Tripoli Rd (unpaved, closed in winter) goes northwest from Waterville Valley to I-93 exit 31, and thus north to Lincoln.

Town Square is the main service facility with the post office, bank ATM, information office, laundry, restaurants and shops.

Places to Stay

Camping Two national forest campgrounds are convenient to Waterville Valley. *Waterville Campground* (☎ 603-

536-1310), in Plymouth, has 27 very basic sites open all year for $8; some can be reserved in advance. *Campton Campground* (☎ 603-536-1310), also in Plymouth, has 58 sites near the Mad River for $11; some can be reserved in advance. There are pay showers and flush toilets.

Hotels All of the hotels in the valley proper are new and modern. The Waterville Valley resort has no cheap lodging, though there are economical lodgings in Campton, 13 miles to the southwest near I-93. Reservations for resort lodgings may be made through the central reservations service (☎ 800-468-2553, fax 603-236-4174).

The 80-room *Snowy Owl Inn* (☎ 800-766-9969) has a variety of accommodations. The simplest is modestly called Superior, and it goes up from there to Deluxe, Premium, Loft/Studio and Fireside. Prices range from $59 to $239, depending upon room and season.

Rooms at the Valley Inn & Conference Center (☎ 603-236-8336, 800-343-0969, fax 236-4294) are similar.

The *Black Bear Lodge* (☎ 603-236-4501) is a condominium hotel.

NEW HAMPSHIRE

Getting There & Away
Driving details for Waterville Valley are:

Destination	Mileage	Hr:Min
Boston, MA	139 miles	3:00
I-93 exit 28	13 miles	0:25
Laconia, NH	44 miles	1:15
Lincoln, NH	27 miles	0:45

KANCAMAGUS HIGHWAY
The Kancamagus Hwy is the stretch of NH 112 between Lincoln and Conway, through the White Mountain National Forest and over Kancamagus Pass (2868 feet). It's a beautiful paved road unspoiled by commercial development. Many USFS campgrounds are reached by this road.

History
About 1684, Kancamagus, "the fearless one," assumed the powers of *sagamon* (leader) of the Penacook Confederacy of Native American peoples in this region. He was the third and final sagamon, succeeding his grandfather the great Passaconaway and his uncle Wonalancet.

Kancamagus worked to keep the peace between the indigenous peoples and Euro-pean explorers and settlers. But provocations by the Whites pushed his patience to the breaking point. Kancamagus resorted to battle to rid the region of the Whites, but lost. By 1691 he and his followers were heading north to escape them.

Hiking
The White Mountain National Forest is laced with excellent hiking trails of varying difficulty. For detailed trail-by-trail information, stop at the Lincoln/Woodstock Chamber of Commerce (☎ 603-745-6621) information center in Lincoln just east of I-93 exit 32.

If you're the kind who plans ahead, get a copy of the *AMC White Mountain Guide* from the Appalachian Mountain Club, 5 Joy St, Boston, MA 02108, or from an outfitter or local bookshop.

Here are some hiking suggestions:

Lincoln Woods Trail
The trailhead (1157 feet elevation) is at the Lincoln Woods Trail parking lot on the Kancamagus Hwy five miles east of I-93. The 2.9-mile-long trail ends at the Pemigewasset Wilderness Boundary (elevation 1450 feet). This, along with the Wilderness Trail is

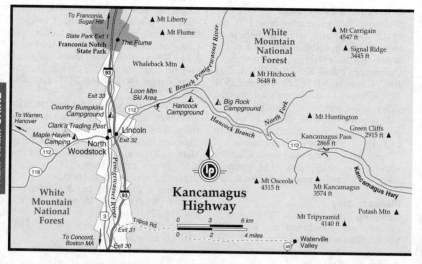

among the easiest and most popular trails in the national forest.

Wilderness Trail

The Wilderness Trail begins where the Lincoln Woods Trail ends and continues for six miles to Stillwater Junction (elevation 2060 feet). You can, if you like, follow the Cedar Brook and Hancock Notch Trails to return to the Kancamagus Hwy some miles east of the Lincoln Woods Trail trailhead parking lot.

Camping

The beautiful, heavily-wooded national forest campgrounds along the Kancamagus Hwy east of Lincoln offer primitive sites (pit toilets only) for $9; a few campgrounds have flush toilets and charge $10 per site. These campgrounds are under heavy demand in the warm months. Arrive in the morning to get a site, and on Thursday or Friday morning to pin one down for the weekend.

Here are the campgrounds, from west to east (Lincoln to Conway).

Four miles east of Lincoln, *Hancock Campground* (☎ 603-536-1310), in Plymouth, has 56 sites near the Pemigewasset River and Wilderness Trail. Hancock is open all year.

Big Rock Campground (☎ 603-536-1310) also in Plymouth six miles east of Lincoln, has 28 sites near the Wilderness Trail and is open all year.

Passaconaway Campground (☎ 603-447-5448), 15 miles west of Conway, has 33 sites on the Swift River, which is good for fishing. Camping season runs from mid-May through November.

Jigger Johnson Campground 12½ miles west of Conway, has 75 sites, flush toilets and nature lectures on summer weekends. It's open mid-May to mid-October.

Six miles west of Conway, the *Covered Bridge Campground* has 49 sites for $9, some can be reserved. And yes, you do cross the Albany Covered Bridge to reach the campground. The season runs from mid-May to mid-October.

Blackberry Crossing Campground, six miles west of Conway on the south side of the Kancamagus Hwy, is a former CCC camp with 26 sites going for $8 each. It's open all year.

NORTH WOODSTOCK & LINCOLN

The twin towns of North Woodstock and Lincoln serve a diverse clientele. Outdoorsy

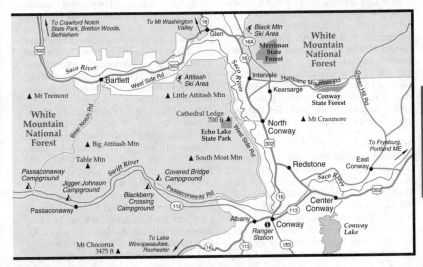

Moose Crossing

Signs at each end of the Kancamagus Hwy warn you to be careful to avoid hitting moose who wander onto the road. Moose weigh a lot, stand tall and will not necessarily get out of a speeding car's way. When a car hits a moose, the hood of the car goes beneath the moose's body, and the full weight of the animal crashes onto the windshield. This surprises the driver – if he or she lives long enough to register surprise. There are dozens of such accidents each year. ■

types in heavy boots stop here for provisions before heading out to camp and hike along the Kancamagus Hwy (NH 112). Retirees in huge peach-colored road cruisers stop for cocktails after photographing the Old Man of the Mountain in Franconia Notch State Park.

If you've come as far as North Woodstock and Lincoln, you must see the Old Man of the Mountain and enjoy the other natural wonders of the park. See the separate section on the park for details.

Orientation

The Pemigewasset River springs just south of Franconia Notch and runs southward parallel to I-93, and is joined by its East Branch at North Woodstock, west of I-93 exit 32. Lincoln, on the East Branch, is east of I-93. Both are pretty much one-street towns. The Kancamagus Hwy comes into the towns from Conway, which is 18 miles east of Kancamagus Pass (2860 feet).

Information

The Lincoln/Woodstock Chamber of Commerce (☎ 603-745-6621, 800-227-4191 for lodging reservations) has a big information center in Lincoln just east of I-93 exit 32. There's a rack with brochures detailing the hiking trails in the national forest, trail by trail.

Clark's Trading Post

Just north of North Woodstock on US 3, and just south of Franconia Notch State Park, is Clark's Trading Post, a traditional stop for families traveling in the White Mountains since 1928. If the kids are bored with too much time in the car, Clark's can help with its old-fashioned photo parlor, water-bumper boats, magic house, narrow-gauge steam locomotive and gift shop selling moccasins. Commercial? You bet, but fun.

Places to Stay

The information center has a large outdoor signboard with the names of motels and campgrounds on it. Signal lights indicate the motels and campgrounds with vacancies, a useful service.

Camping For the USFS campgrounds along the Kancamagus Hwy east of Lincoln, see Camping in the Kancamagus Highway section, above.

There's a very fine state-run campground at Lafayette Place in Franconia Notch State Park (see that section) with 97 wooded tent sites priced at $11, but it's in very heavy demand in summer. Arrive early in the day to claim a site.

As for commercial campgrounds, *Maple Haven Camping* (☎ 603-745-3350, 800-370-5678), a mile west of North Woodstock, charges $18 and up for tent and RV sites. *Lost River Valley Campground* (☎ 603-745-8321), three miles farther west, covers 200 acres (100 wooded), with lots of tent and RV sites on streams priced at $20 and up. *Country Bumpkins* (☎ 603-745-8837) has 46 sites near the Pemigewasset River and Bog Brook, for $16 and up. Take I-93 to exit 33, then go south on US 3 and look for it on the east side of the road, north of Lincoln.

Motels A few motels are in the center of Lincoln and east along the Kancamagus Hwy, but most are on US 3 between I-93 exits 32 and 33. First are those along the Kancamagus Hwy:

Lincoln Motel (☎ 603-745-2780), 5 Church St, has only 7 rooms, but it's convenient and priced well at $52 to $63. Look for it on the north side of the highway in the center of Lincoln.

Kancamagus Motor Lodge (☎ 603-745-3365, 800-346-4205), a bit farther east, has 34 modern rooms with private steam baths for $60 to $70, as well as a heated outdoor pool.

Going north from Lincoln and North Woodstock along US 3 brings you to many more motels, including:

Riverbank Motel & Cabins (☎ 603-745-3374, 800-633-5624), has motel rooms with and without kitchenettes and cabins for $40 to $56.

Cozy Cabins (☎ 603-745-8713) has passable little cabins for as little as $35, and as much as $75 with two bedrooms and full kitchen.

Red Doors Motel (☎ 603-745-2267) does indeed have red doors on its plain but comfy rooms which rent for $40 to $62.

Drummer Boy Motor Inn (☎ 603-745-3661, 800-762-7275) is a fairly luxurious place with nice indoor and outdoor pools, sauna, playground and comfortable rooms for $60 to $90.

Woodward's Motor Inn (☎ 603-745-8141, 800-635-8968) is the class act here with lots of facilities: an indoor pool, sauna, hot tub, racquetball court, tennis court and game room, as well as 80 good rooms for $68 to $89.

Franconia Notch Motel (☎ 603-745-2229) is very tidy, well-kept and attractive, with rooms for $45 to $75.

Inns The *Woodstock Inn* (☎ 603-745-3951, 800-321-3985), on Main St, North Woodstock, NH 03262, consists of three restored houses with lodging and dining rooms. The Victorian Main House has six rooms sharing three hall baths; Riverside

has 11 rooms with private bath and Deachman House has two rooms sharing a hall bath. Rates for bed and breakfast for two range from $54 to $140.

Places to Eat

The Kancamagus Hwy, NH 112, the highway through Lincoln, bears the usual assortment of fast food emporia – *Burger King, McDonald's* and the other franchise shops. The *Snow Goose* is a small local effort. *Gordi's Fish & Steak House* (☎ 603-745-6635) is a big place with a hearty menu to suit appetites sharpened by outdoor exercise. *The Garden Restaurant* in the Millfront Marketplace section of the Mill at Loon Mountain shopping center has a good selection of lighter meals and its bar is a gathering-place in the evening.

In general, eating possibilities improve west of the highway on Main St (US 3) in North Woodstock.

The Chalet Restaurant (☎ 603-745-2256), right at the intersection of US 3 and NH 112, is the touristy place. Right next door, *Peg's Breakfast & Lunch* (☎ 603-745-2740) is where the locals go for early breakfasts (from 5:30 am, 99¢ to $6) and late lunches (it closes at 4 pm) at low prices. Have the meatloaf sandwich with gravy for $6.25.

Truant's Taverne & Restaurant (☎ 603-745-2239), facing the chalet but entered around the back via Depot St, has a long list of bar food such as spare ribs, chicken fingers and peel-and-eat shrimp, but there's also vegetarian stir-fry for $8. Most main course dishes are priced under $12. There's live entertainment on weekends, including blues bands on Sunday night.

Woodstock Station & Stock Room (☎ 603-745-3951), on Main St in the Woodstock Inn, can probably satisfy any food craving you may have. They serve fish, pasta, steaks, Mexican food, sandwiches – just about everything. Most main courses cost $10 to $15. The restaurant's upscale Clement Room features such continental favorites as roast rack of lamb ($21) and steak Diane ($18) and offers perhaps the most elegant dining in the area.

Govoni's Italian Restaurant (☎ 603-745-8042), 1½ miles west of North Woodstock along NH 112, serves excellent Italian fare from late May through mid-October. It's difficult to get a table on summer weekends.

Getting There & Away

Driving details for Lincoln/North Woodstock are:

Destination	Mileage	Hr:Min
Boston, MA	140 miles	3:10
Franconia, NH	11 miles	0:20
Laconia, NH	45 miles	1:10
Montpelier, VT	65 miles	1:40
North Conway, NH	42 miles	1:05

FRANCONIA NOTCH STATE PARK

Franconia Notch is among the most dramatic of the state's several notches, a narrow defile shaped over the eons by a wild stream cutting through craggy granite.

The symbol of the Granite State, the natural rock formation called the Great Stone Face, or Old Man of the Mountain, gazes across Franconia Notch from its lofty perch high on the west wall of the defile. He doesn't even blink as thousands of tourists pass by daily looking up at him. South of the Old Man and to the east lies the undulant crest of Mt Liberty, which some think resembles George Washington lying in state. This is, after all, the Presidential Range.

There are a few AMC camping huts around here, contact their headquarters in Boston for more information.

Orientation

The most scenic parts of the notch are encompassed by and protected in Franconia Notch State Park. Lodging, meals and services are available in Lincoln and North Woodstock, south of the park, and also to a lesser extent in Franconia and Littleton to the north.

Franconia Notch is narrow. I-93 passes through it, reduced to two lanes and renamed the Franconia Notch Parkway. Stopping on the narrow road is not permitted. You must exit and park in a designated parking lot.

Information

There's a visitors center (☎ 603-745-8391) at The Flume (see below) which includes The Flume ticket office, a cafeteria, gift shop and auditorium, open from 9 am to 4:30 pm. Combination passes good for a visit to The Flume and other beauty spots, plus a ride on the Cannon Mountain Aerial Tramway, cost $11 for adults, $5 children six to 12. There's another visitors center at Lafayette Place, north of the Basin and south of Profile Lake.

For books and guides the Village Bookstore (☎ 603-444-5263), 81 Main St in Littleton, is worth a stop.

The Flume

Four miles north of North Woodstock is The Flume, a natural cleft in the granite bedrock. A two-mile self-guided nature walk takes you to and through the cleft – 12 to 20 feet wide – along an 800 foot boardwalk. The granite walls shoot up 70 to 90 feet above you, with mosses and plants growing from precarious toeholds in niches and crevices. Signs explain how nature formed The Flume, and point out interesting sights along the way. Near it is a covered bridge thought to be one of the oldest in the state, perhaps erected as early as the 1820s.

The Basin

The Basin is a huge glacial pothole 20 feet in diameter carved deep into the granite 15,000 years ago by the action of falling water and swirling stones. The Basin offers a nice (short) walk, a cool spot and a minor wonder of nature.

Lafayette Place

There's a visitors center here, as well as a campground (☎ 603-823-9513) with 97 wooded tent sites priced at $11 and in heavy demand in summer. Many of the state park's hiking trails start here.

Old Man of the Mountain

After 200 million years in the making, the Great Stone Face, a rock outcrop high up on the west wall of Franconia Notch, was

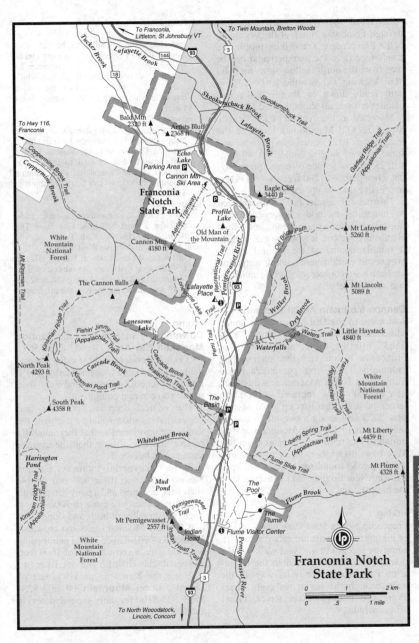

To Franconia,
Littleton, St Johnsbury VT

To Twin Mountain, Bretton Woods

Tucker Brook

Lafayette Brook

144

93

3

18

Skookumchuck Brook

Skookumchuck Trail

To Hwy 116,
Franconia

Coppermine Brook Trail

Coppermine Brook

Bald Mtn
2320 ft

Artists Bluff
2368 ft

Echo
Lake

Parking Area   P

Cannon Mtn
Ski Area

Franconia
Notch
State Park

Lafayette Brook

Garfield Ridge Trail
(Appalachian Trail)

Eagle Cliff
3440 ft

P

Aerial Tramway

Profile
Lake

P

Mt Lafayette
5260 ft

White
Mountain
National
Forest

Cannon Mtn
4180 ft

Old Man of
the Mountain

Recreational Trail

Pemigewasset River

Old Bridle Path

Mt Kinsman Trail

The Cannon Balls

Lafayette
Place

Lonesome Lake Trail

93

P

Walker Brook

Mt Lincoln
5089 ft

Kinsman Ridge Trail

Fishin' Jimmy Trail
(Appalachian Trail)

Lonesome
Lake

Pemi Trail

Dry Brook

Falling Waters Trail

Little Haystack
4840 ft

North Peak
4293 ft

Cascade Brook

Kinsman Pond Trail

Cascade Brook Trail
(Appalachian Trail)

Waterfalls

Franconia Ridge Trail
(Appalachian Trail)

White
Mountain
National
Forest

South Peak
4358 ft

The
Basin

P

Mt Liberty
4459 ft

Harrington
Pond

Whitehouse Brook

P

Liberty Spring Trail
(Appalachian Trail)

Flume Slide Trail

Mt Flume
4328 ft

Kinsman Ridge Trail
(Appalachian Trail)

White
Mountain
National
Forest

Mud
Pond

Mt Pemigewasset
Trail

The
Pool

Flume Brook

Indian Head Trail

Mt Pemigewasset
2557 ft

Indian
Head

The
Flume

Flume Visitor Center

Pemigewasset River

93

3

To North Woodstock,
Lincoln, Concord

Franconia Notch
State Park

0   1   2 km
0   .5   1 mile

NEW HAMPSHIRE

"discovered" by White settlers passing through Franconia Notch at the beginning of the 19th century. The striking profile of a man's face (à la Picasso, perhaps) can be seen from the north (follow signs for "Old Man Viewing"). From the parking lot, a path leads down to Profile Lake and plaques tell you all about the Old Man.

Marketed as the symbol of the Granite State, the Old Man looms larger in the imagination than in real life perhaps, and some viewers find it "small." A 40-foot-tall, 25-foot-wide face is indeed pretty big, but when perched 1200 feet above it is less impressive than its photographs.

This natural wonder has been stabilized by unnatural methods, however. As an important tourist attraction and New Hampshire symbol, it would not do to have it tumble down, so the natural consequences of earth tremors, wind, water and ice have been counteracted with (invisible) concrete and rebar.

Cannon Mountain Aerial Tramway

Just north of the Old Man is the Cannon Mountain Aerial Tramway (☎ 603-823-5563), offering a breathtaking view of Franconia Notch and the surrounding mountains. The first passenger aerial tramway in North America was installed here in 1938. It was replaced in 1980 by a larger cable car that lifts up to 80 passengers 2022 feet along a one-mile cable to the summit of Cannon Mountain in five minutes. The tramway operates from late May to mid-October, 9 am to 4:30 pm. Adults pay $8 roundtrip, kids six to 12 pay $4. The New England Ski Museum is in the base station.

Hiking

Franconia Notch State Park has a system of hiking trails; most are relatively short, some are steep. For a casual walk or bike ride, you can't do better than the Recreation Path which wends its way all the way through the notch for eight miles along the Pemigewasset River. Other hikes include:

Mt Pemigewasset Trail
This trail departs the Flume Visitor Center and climbs for 1.4 miles to the 2557-foot summit of Mt Pemigewasset (Indian Head), offering excellent views. You can return by the same trail or the Indian Head Trail, which joins US 3 after one mile, from there it's a one-mile walk north to the Flume Visitor Center.

Lonesome Lake Trail
Departing from Lafayette Place and its campground, this trail climbs 1000 feet in 1.5 miles to Lonesome Lake. Various branch trails lead farther upward to the several summits of The Cannon Balls and Cannon Mountain (3700 to 4180 feet) and south to The Basin.

Kinsman Falls
On the Cascade Brook, these falls are a good goal for a short half-mile hike from The Basin via the Basin Cascade Trail.

Bald Mountain and Artists Bluff Trail
Just north of Echo Lake off NH 18, this is a 1.5-mile loop that skirts the summit of Bald Mountain (2320 feet) and Artists Bluff (2368 feet), with short spur trails to the summits.

Skiing

Downhill The state operates the **Cannon Mountain Ski Area** (☎ 603-823-5563), I-93 exit 2. Besides the three cafeterias and the base station and lounges nearby, you'll find a ski school, a nursery and a ski shop where you can rent equipment.

The vertical drop is 2145 feet, and besides having snowmaking equipment, the slopes are positioned so that they naturally receive and retain more than the average amount of white stuff.

Besides the aerial tramway, Cannon Mountain has one triple and two double chair lifts, one quad and a pony lift, all with an hourly capacity of close to 7000 skiers. There are 26 miles of trails and slopes.

If Cannon Mountain gets too crowded, **Mittersill** (☎ 603-823-5511), its junior cousin on I-93, has a vertical drop of 1600 feet, and one double chair lift and one T-bar lift.

Along the Kancamagus Hwy east of Lincoln, **Loon Mountain** (☎ 603-823-5563, 823-8100 for daily snow updates) is another option.

Cross-Country Thanks to the extensive national forest, there are more than a few cross-country trails available, both at the downhill areas and elsewhere. Contact the Lincoln/Woodstock Chamber of Commerce (☎ 603-745-6621) for details on rentals and directions.

FRANCONIA

The town of Franconia, a few miles north of Franconia Notch along I-93, is a pleasant New England town with a poetic attraction: Robert Frost's farm. Franconia also has a good selection of motels and inns.

Orientation

Franconia is a small town, easily negotiable. Main St is also NH 18. Nearby Sugar Hill, a few miles west, has several fine country inns.

Information

The Franconia/Easton/Sugar Hill Chamber of Commerce (☎ 603-823-5661, 800-237-9007), PO Box 780, Franconia, NH 03580, maintains an information office on NH 18 just southeast of the town center.

The Frost Place

Robert Frost (1874-1963) was America's most renowned and best-loved poet in the middle of the 20th century. Born in San Francisco, Frost moved to Massachusetts with his mother after his father's death. He attended – but didn't graduate from – Dartmouth, then Harvard. He bought a small farm near Derry in southern New Hampshire, but didn't do well as a farmer.

After a sojourn of several years in England, Frost lived on this farm near Franconia with his wife and children during some of the most productive and inspired years of his life. He wrote many of his best and most famous poems to describe life on this farm and the scenery surrounding it, including "The Road Not Taken" and "Stopping by Woods on a Snowy Evening."

The farmhouse has been kept as faithful to the period as possible, with numerous exhibits of Frost memorabilia. Behind the house in the forest is a half-mile-long nature trail. Frost's poems are mounted on plaques in sites appropriate to the things they describe; in several places the plaques have been erected at the exact spots where Frost composed the poems.

The Frost Place (☎ 603-823-5510) has been preserved as a memorial to the poet's life and work. It's open weekend afternoons from late May through June from 1 to 5 pm, and from July through mid-October every day except Tuesday from 1 to 5 pm. The price of admission ($3 for adults, $2 for seniors, $1.25 for kids six through 15) includes a 20-minute slide show about Frost's early life and work and about the countryside here.

To find Frost's farm, follow NH 116 south from Franconia. After exactly a mile turn right onto Bickford Hill Rd, then left onto unpaved Ridge Rd, you'll find it a short distance along on the right.

Soaring

The Franconia Soaring Center (☎ 603-823-8881), on NH 116 south of the town across from the Franconia Inn, takes up one passenger at a time in a glider for $55 (15 minutes), $75 (25 minutes) or $95 (35

Frost's Accomplishments

In addition to writing very popular poetry, Robert Frost also garnered critical acclaim. In 1923 he won a Pulitzer Prize for his collection entitled *New Hampshire*, and won the same prize twice again for *Collected Poems* (1930) and *A Further Range* (1936).

In 1958, Frost was appointed the Poetry Consultant to the Library of Congress, and later received honorary doctorates from Oxford and Cambridge. At John F Kennedy's inauguration as President of the United States (1961), he read his poem "The Gift Outright." At the time of his death in 1963, Frost was considered the unofficial Poet Laureate of the United States. Not bad for a college dropout. ■

NEW HAMPSHIRE

minutes). Up to three passengers can take a plane ride for $55 (15 minutes) or $95 (25 minutes) for all three. Call and ask about flight conditions first.

Places to Stay & Eat
Camping is available in nearby Franconia Notch State Park – see that section. There's also *Fransted Family Campground* (☎ 603-823-5675), on NH 18 between Franconia and Franconia Notch, with sites for $14 to $17.

Most of the lodgings listed below have their own restaurants.

Motels *Hillwinds* (☎ 603-823-5551, 800-473-5299), on NH 18 at I-93 exit 38, is a comfortable motel with a riverside location, rooms going for $40 to $56 and a restaurant with moderate prices. Nearby *Stonybrook Motel & Lodge* (☎ 603-823-8192, 800-722-3552) on NH 18, has similar prices, as well as indoor and outdoor swimming pools. *Gale River Motel & Cottages* (☎ 603-823-5655, 800-255-7989), 1 Main St (NH 18) is a classic roadside motel with heated pool, hot tub and Jacuzzis.

Inns There are several dozen inns near Franconia. Here are some of the more interesting ones.

Pinestead Farm Lodge (☎ 603-823-8121), NH 116, is a working family farm with nine clean, simple rooms for rent, with a bath and kitchen/sitting room for each three rooms. The cost is $15 per person, double. You'll share your farm experience with Bob and Kathleen Sherburn, Jr, assorted cattle, pigs, chickens, ducks and horses. If you come in late winter you can help with the maple sugaring. The family's been renting rooms since 1899.

Blanche's B&B (☎ 603-823-7061), Easton Valley Rd, is, in the owners' words, a "19th-century farmhouse restored to a former glory it probably never had." Rooms cost $35 single, $60 to $85 double. The Kinsman Ridge Design Studio is here as well.

The 35-room *Franconia Inn* (☎ 603-823-5542, 800-473-5299; fax 823-8078), NH 116

south of Franconia, is a fine old inn set on 107 acres with cross-country ski possibilities in winter and hiking and horseback riding in summer. Rooms cost $58 to $180 depending upon the room, the season and meals included. In summer rates are $73 to $113 for a double room without meals.

Sugar Hill Inn (☎ 603-823-5621, 800-548-4748), on NH 117 in Sugar Hill, NH 03580, is a restored 1789 inn with lots of activities, an excellent dining room and 11 guest rooms with private bath priced from $90 to $125, breakfast included.

Lovett's Inn (☎ 603-823-7761), two miles south of Franconia on Profile Rd, is known for its dining, which is open to non-guests, as well as its good rooms.

Getting There & Away
Driving details for Franconia are:

Destination	Mileage	Hr:Min
Boston, MA	151 miles	3:30
North Conway, NH	44 miles	1:15
North Woodstock/		
Lincoln, NH	11 Miles	0:20
St Johnsbury, NH	25 miles	0:40

Mt Washington Valley

The Mt Washington Valley, stretching north from the eastern end of the Kancamagus Hwy, includes the towns of Bartlett, Conway, Glen, Intervale, Jackson and North Conway. The valley harbors a myriad of outdoor sports possibilities. The hub of the valley is the town of North Conway.

NORTH CONWAY
The Kancamagus Hwy's eastern terminus is the town of Conway, at the intersection of NH 16, 113, 153 and US 302. But the activities capital of the region is North Conway, five miles north along NH 16/US 302.

Orientation
North Conway is at the center of the Mt Washington Valley, which offers a great variety of hiking, camping, canoeing and

kayaking. Within a few miles' drive of the town are several alpine ski areas like Attitash, Black Mountain, Cranmore. Nearby Jackson and Intervale have miles and miles of cross-country ski trails.

Most of the time, the glut of auto traffic on Main St (NH 16/US 302) moves at a frustratingly slow pace. If your aim is to get around North Conway, not into it, take West Side Rd which follows the west bank of the Saco River between Conway and Glen. There's a short road connecting West Side Rd and NH 16 from Echo Lake into the center of North Conway.

Information

The Mt Washington Valley Chamber of Commerce (☎ 603-356-3171, 800-367-3364 for lodging reservations), PO Box 2300, North Conway, NH 03860, is the local information source. They maintain an office on North Conway's main street (NH 16/US 302) on the south side of the town center.

The State of New Hampshire maintains an information office in the rest area at Intervale, on NH 16/US 302 two miles north of the center of North Conway.

EMS (☎ 603-356-5433) on Main St in North Conway, is an outfitter that sells maps and guides to the White Mountain National Forest. They also rent camping equipment and, in the winter, cross-country skis. A climbing school operates year round and requires reservations. Call their number to get the "weather phone," a report updated daily.

The various ski areas – Attitash, Mt Cranmore, Black Mountain, Wildcat – can help you make lodging reservations.

Echo Lake State Park

Two miles west of North Conway off US 302 is Echo Lake State Park (☎ 603-356-2672), with its placid mountain lake at the foot of the sheer rock wall called White Horse Ledge. There's a scenic road up to the 700-foot-high Cathedral Ledge and panoramic views of the White Mountain Range. You can swim in the lake and use

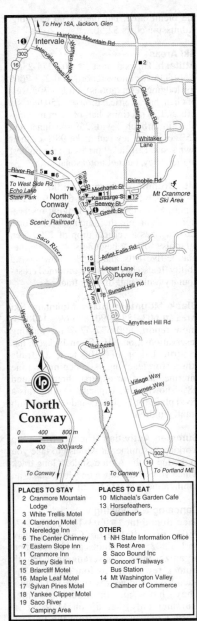

NEW HAMPSHIRE

PLACES TO STAY	PLACES TO EAT
2 Cranmore Mountain Lodge	10 Michaela's Garden Cafe
3 White Trellis Motel	13 Horsefeathers, Guenther's
4 Clarendon Motel	
5 Nereledge Inn	**OTHER**
6 The Center Chimney	1 NH State Information Office & Rest Area
7 Eastern Slope Inn	8 Saco Bound Inc
11 Cranmore Inn	9 Concord Trailways Bus Station
12 Sunny Side Inn	14 Mt Washington Valley Chamber of Commerce
15 Briarcliff Motel	
16 Maple Leaf Motel	
17 Sylvan Pines Motel	
18 Yankee Clipper Motel	
19 Saco River Camping Area	

the picnic area, but there's no camping. Admission costs $2.50.

Ski Areas

Attitash This ski area (☎ 603-374-2368, 374-0946 for snow report, 800-223-7669 for lodging reservations), on US 302 west of Glen, has a vertical drop of 1750 feet, six lifts and 28 ski trails, half of them intermediate in difficulty, with 25% beginner and 25% expert. They can make 98% of their own snow. Lift-ticket prices are the highest in the valley, but not unreasonable.

Mt Cranmore Cranmore Ski Resort (☎ 603-356-5543, 800-786-6754 for snow report, 800-543-9206 for lodging reservations), right on the outskirts of North Conway, has a vertical drop of 1200 feet, 30 trails (40% for beginners, 40% intermediate), five lifts and 100% snowmaking ability. It also has 66 km of groomed cross-country trails, half of them tracked.

Black Mountain Black Mountain Ski Area (☎ 603-383-4490, 800-698-4490 for snow report, 800-677-5737 for lodging reservations), on NH 16B in Jackson, has a vertical drop of 1100 feet, 22 trails (three for teaching, six beginner, nine intermediate, four expert), three lifts and 98% snowmaking capacity, making this a good place for beginners and families with small children.

Summer Activities The ski lifts keep working in summer at Attitash to take you to the top of the Alpine Slide, a long track which you schuss down on a little cart – an exhilarating ride safe for all ages.

Canoeing & Kayaking

Saco Bound Inc (☎ 603-447-2177, 447-3801), two miles east of Center Conway on US 302, rents cánoes and kayaks and organizes guided trips ranging in length from a few hours to four days on the Saco River and nearby rivers and ponds. They have an information center (summer only) set up on Main St in North Conway across from the Eastern

Slope Inn. Daily canoe rental ranges from $20 to $25. The season runs April through October.

Kayak Jack Fun Yak Rentals (☎ 603-447-5571), on NH 16 next to Eastern Slope Campground in Conway, rents kayaks for $22 a day.

Conway Scenic Railroad

The station for the Conway Scenic Railroad (☎ 603-356-5251, 800-232-5251) is a prominent feature on Main St in the center of town. Built in 1874 and restored in 1974, the station is the departure point for one-hour, 11-mile antique steam train rides through the Mt Washington Valley.

Fares are $7.50 (coach) or $9.50 (1st class) for adults, $5 to $7 for kids four to 12. Kids under four ride free in coach class, or for $3.50 in 1st class. Trains run twice daily on weekends from April to mid-May, then daily until late October and on weekends again until mid-December.

Places to Stay

Camping There are commercial campgrounds in Conway, North Conway and Glen. Here is a partial listing:

In Conway, look for the *Beach Camping Area* (☎ 603-447-2723), on NH 16 on the Saco River and the *Cove Camping Area* (☎ 603-447-6734), off Stark Rd on Conway Lake. The *Eastern Slope Camping Area* (☎ 603-447-5092), on NH 16, has 260 sites for $20 to $25 and long beaches on the Saco River.

In North Conway, try the *Saco River Camping Area* (☎ 603-356-3360), on the Saco River off NH 16.

Hostel The 44-bed *Albert B Lester Memorial HI/AYH Hostel* (☎ 603-447-1001, 617-731-8096 in the off-season), 36 Washington St (off Main St/NH 16), Conway, NH 03818, is on the edge of the White Mountain National Forest. This "sustainable living center" focuses on environmentally-friendly practices and conservation; the hostel is big on recycling and gives out information on how to apply "green" technologies to your daily life.

More importantly the facility offers six bedrooms with bunk beds ($16 per person) and three family-size rooms ($45, regardless of number). The cost includes linens and continental breakfast. Just outside the door is excellent hiking and bicycling, and canoers can easily portage to two close-by rivers.

Motels Most of North Conway's motels are south of the town center along NH 16/ US 302. Driving from south to north, here are some choices:

The *Yankee Clipper Motel* (☎ 603-356-5736) has standard rooms for $39 to $52. The *Sylvan Pines* (☎ 603-356-2878), set on spacious grounds, is nicer and a bit more expensive.

The *Maple Leaf Motel* (☎ 603-356-5388) is tidy and reasonably priced, with rooms going for $38 to $52. The *Briarcliff Motel* (☎ 603-356-5584, 800-338-4291) costs only a bit more.

There are also a few motels on the north side of North Conway along NH 16, including the *Clarendon Motel* (☎ 603-356-3551, 800-433-3551), with rooms for $42 to $88, and the similar *White Trellis Motel* (☎ 603-356-2492). *Perry's Motel & Cottages* (☎ 603-356-2214), on NH 16A in Intervale, two miles north of North Conway, charges $29 to $64 for motel rooms, $45 to $65 for cottages with kitchenettes.

Inns & B&Bs There are dozens of inns in this region, many of them affordable B&Bs. Some are members of an organization called Country Inns in the White Mountains, which has its own toll-free reservations line: ☎ 800-562-1300.

Sunny Side Inn (☎ 603-356-6239), on Seavey St, a quiet back street one block east of Main St, is a nice old house with nine rooms, all with private baths, for $50 to $100 double, breakfast included.

Cranmore Inn (☎ 603-356-5502, 800-526-5502), on Kearsarge St a block east of Main St, has been among North Conway's most reliable good values for decades. Rooms range in price from $75 to $100, depending upon privacy of bath and time of year.

The similarly-named *Cranmore Mountain Lodge* (☎ 603-356-2044, 800-356-3596) is farther east along Kearsarge Rd (the continuation of Kearsarge St). It has rooms in several price ranges that come with full breakfast, from $29 for a bunk in the dorm, through $82 to $102 for a double room in the Inn or the Barn Loft, to $190 to $220 for a suite or townhouse.

The Center Chimney (☎ 603-356-6788), on River Rd (turn at the Texaco station), was built in 1787 and now offers charming guest rooms for $44 to $55 double, continental breakfast included.

Nereledge Inn (☎ 603-356-2831), also on River Rd, has nice rooms for $60 to $80 double (full breakfast included), and its own White Horse Pub.

Places to Eat

Many inns – especially those in Jackson, north of North Conway – have good, elegant dining rooms.

Guenther's, at Main and Seavey Sts, is like your mother's kitchen: simple and homey, with big portions of food. Come for breakfast or lunch (7 am to 3 pm) for $4 to $11. It's located up one flight from Campbell's Bookstore.

Horsefeathers (☎ 603-356-2687), on Main St in the center of town, has a long, jokey menu featuring lots of bar food, sandwiches, snacks and light meals from $4 to $11.

Michaela's Garden Cafe, on Main St at Kearsarge St, has indoor and outdoor dining, lots of white lattice and white wine and Italian-American cuisine priced from $8 to $18 for an average meal.

Getting There & Away

Bus Concord Trailways (☎ 603-228-7266, 800-639-3317) runs a daily route between Boston and Berlin stopping at Manchester, Concord, points near Lake Winnipesaukee, Conway, Glen, Jackson, Pinkham Notch and Gorham. The trip between Boston and the Mt Washington Valley takes about 3½ hours.

The bus from Boston will drop you in North Conway on Main St across from the

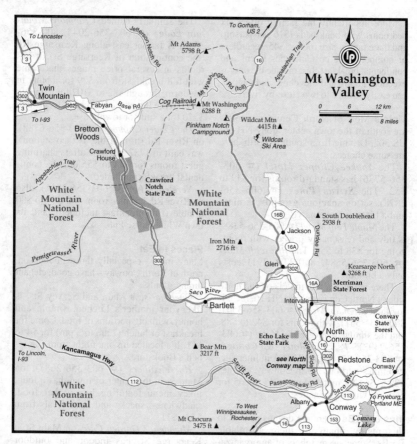

Mt Washington Valley

Eastern Slope Inn, but the bus to Boston will only pick you up in Jackson (Ellis Grocery Store, ☎ 603-383-9041), Glen (Storybook Motor Inn, ☎ 603-383-6800) or Conway (First Stop on W Main St, ☎ 603-447-8444).

Car Distances and travel times to North Conway are:

Destination	Mileage	Hr:Min
Boston, MA	144 miles	3:40
Bretton Woods, NH	32 miles	0:50
Franconia, NH	44 miles	1:15
Laconia, NH	49 miles	1:25
Lincoln, NH	39 miles	1:00

JACKSON

Seven miles north of North Conway just east of NH 16 across the Ellis River via a red covered bridge is the village of Jackson, the Mt Washington Valley's premier cross-country ski center. Jackson has many inns that provide charming accommodations summer or winter, but prices are fairly high.

Orientation & Information

NH 16A circles from NH 16 through the center of Jackson and back to NH 16. NH 16B heads into the hills.

The Jackson Resort Association (☎ 603-383-9356, 800-866-3334), PO Box 304,

see North Conway map

NEW HAMPSHIRE

Jackson, NH 03846, can help with lodging reservations. They have an information office on NH 16 south of the covered bridge.

Cross-Country Skiing

Jackson is famous for its 93 miles of trails. Each of the downhill ski areas in the valley (see Ski Areas in the North Conway section) has some cross-country trails ranging from easy to expert. There is a small fee for the use of the trails. Clinics, tours and rentals are available in Jackson and North Conway.

Places to Stay

Jackson's inns have character, charm, lots of activities and quite substantial price tags. One charming inn quotes prices from $125 to $270, breakfast included, but the small print adds 8% tax and 15% service charge, resulting in a daily price tag of $154 to $332. If you call for reservations, ask that prices be quoted with these extras added in.

Motels You can't miss the *Covered Bridge Motor Lodge* (☎ 603-383-6630, 800-634-2911) on NH 16 just south of Jackson's covered bridge. Comfortable rooms go for $50 to $88, depending upon the season.

Inns *The Village House* (☎ 603-383-6666, 800-972-8343), is the large house on the left just after you go east across the covered bridge. Ten comfy rooms with private bath cost $55 to $90 double with breakfast; some have kitchenettes. There's a swimming pool, hot tub and tennis court.

The Forest, A Country Inn (☎ 603-356-9772, 800-448-3534), has 11 rooms in a mansard-roofed Victorian going for $60 to $90, full breakfast included. There's a heated pool as well.

The *Wildcat Inn & Tavern* (☎ 603-383-4245, 800-228-4245), in the village center, has a dozen rooms, most with private bath for $59 to $76, but a few rooms sharing a hall bath go for $59 to $64. Add 8% tax and 10% "gratuities."

Places to Eat

Many of Jackson's inns have excellent (and expensive) dining rooms. For a simpler meal or snack, try *As You Like It* (☎ 603-383-6425), in Jackson next to the post office. They serve a hot buffet breakfast from 8 to 11 am and deli lunches with a salad bar from 11:30 am to 5 pm.

Getting There & Away

See the North Conway section, above.

PINKHAM NOTCH

In the 1820s, a settler named Daniel Pinkham attempted to build a road north from Jackson through the narrow notch on the eastern slope of Mt Washington. Torrential rains in 1826 caused mud slides that buried his best efforts, but not his name. The place is still called Pinkham Notch. It was almost a century later that an auto road was put through the narrow mountain gap and Pinkham's dream of easy transit realized.

Today this area is still known for its wild beauty even though useful facilities for campers and hikers make it among the most popular activity centers in the White Mountains. Wildcat Mountain and Tuckerman's Ravine offer good skiing, and an excellent system of trails provides access to the natural beauties of the Presidential Range, especially Mt Washington. For the less athletically inclined, the Mt Washington Auto Road provides easy access to the summit.

Orientation & Information

NH 16 goes north 11 miles from North Conway and Jackson to Pinkham Notch (2032 feet), then past the Wildcat Mountain ski area and Tuckerman's Ravine, through the small settlement of Glen House and past the Dolly Copp Campground to Gorham and Berlin. The AMC maintains a hikers' cafeteria and dormitory facilities at its excellent Pinkham Notch Camp.

The AMC's Pinkham Notch Camp is the intelligence center in these parts (see entry below). The AMC's main office (☎ 617-523-0636) is at 5 Joy St, Boston, MA 02108.

NEW HAMPSHIRE

Mt Washington Auto Road

The Mt Washington Summit Road Company (☎ 603-466-2222, 466-3988), operates an alpine toll road from Pinkham Notch to the summit at 6288 feet. Look for the entrance 2½ miles north of the AMC Pinkham Notch Camp off NH 16.

Private cars (no trucks or campers allowed) pay a toll of $15 for car and driver and $5 for each passenger (kids five to 12, $4). Vans operated by the company will take you to the top and back down again (1½ hours) for $19 per person (kids, $14) if you'd rather not drive. The auto road is open from mid-May to mid-October from 7:30 am to 6 pm; van tours run from 8:30 am to 4:30 pm. In severe weather, the road may be closed even in season.

Pinkham Notch Camp

Guided nature walks, canoe trips, cross-country ski and snowshoe treks and other outdoor adventures are organized by the AMC from the camp. Call the camp at ☎ 603-466-2727, 800-262-4455 for current offerings.

Here you can buy the *AMC White Mountain Guide*, with detailed maps and the vital statistics of each trail: how long and how difficult it is, the vertical rise, the average walking time, reference points along the way and what to see as you walk. There are individual trail map/guides sold as well.

The AMC also maintains two hikers' huts providing meals and lodging. Carter Notch Hut is on Nineteen-Mile Brook Trail and Lakes of the Clouds Hut is on Crawford Path (see Crawford Notch, below).

For lodging and meals information on the camp, see places to stay.

Mt Washington

The summit (6288 feet) of this tallest mountain in the northeast is the **Mt Washington State Park** (☎ 603-466-3347). The restored Tip Top House hotel no longer provides overnight lodging, but hikers and patrons of the Mt Washington Auto Road, and the Mt Washington Cog Railway described in Bretton Woods, can now find food, souvenirs and historical exhibits here at the top.

In good weather, the hike up Mt Washington is an exhilarating experience. If you're in good physical condition and you start early, you can make it to the top and back down in a day.

You can do several good short hikes from Pinkham Notch Camp, including the short walk to Crystal Cascade and the equally easy one to Glen Ellis Falls.

The Tuckerman Ravine Trail starts at the Pinkham Notch Camp and ends after 4.2 miles at the summit. It's the shortest hike to the top: just over four hours up, slightly less coming down.

Other trails to the peak are described in the Crawford Notch section, below.

Note Mt Washington's weather is notoriously severe. The highest wind ever recorded – 213 mph – was registered at the summit in April, 1934.

The summit of Mt Washington has a reputation for the most severe weather in the region. A weather monitoring station atop the mountain has enabled climatologists to measure the weather here for decades.

I hiked the Tuckerman Ravine Trail to the summit at the end of August some years ago. It was a warm T-shirt-and-shorts day at the base, but 20°F with snow, ice and 115-mph winds at the summit. Pack along warm windproof clothes and shoes even in high summer, always consult with AMC personnel at the huts and don't be reluctant to turn back if the weather changes for the worse. Dozens of hikers who ignored such warnings are commemorated by trailside monuments and crosses.

Ski Areas

Wildcat Mountain This ski area (☎ 603-466-3326, 800-255-6439, 800-643-4521 for snow report), whose mountain tops off at 4415 feet, is on NH 16 in Pinkham Notch north of Jackson. Its downhill skiing facilities sport a vertical drop of 2100 feet, 31 ski trails (30% beginner, 40% intermediate, 30% expert), six lifts and 90% snowmaking capacity.

Tuckerman Ravine The cirque at Tuckerman Ravine has several ski trails for ski purists. What's pure about it? No lifts. You climb up the mountain then ski down. Purists say that if you climb up you have strong legs that won't break easily in a fall on the way down.

Tuckerman is perhaps best in spring when the ski resorts are struggling to keep their snow cover, but nature conspires to keep the ravine in shadow much of the time, and thus in deep natural snow.

Park in the Wildcat Mountain lot for the climb up the ravine.

Summer Activities The Gondola Skyride at Wildcat Mountain, which was the first in the USA, operates in summer as well, just for the fun of the ride and the view. Adults pay $8, children five to 12 half price. Hours are 9 am to 5 pm daily (twilight rides from 6 to 8:30 pm Sunday and Wednesday) from late May through mid October.

Soaring
Mt Washington Sky Adventures (☎ 603-466-5822, 466-3374), 289 Main St, Gorham, at the junction of NH 2 and 16, will take you soaring over the summit of Mt Washington in a three-seat glider. Call for prices, wind conditions and reservations.

Places to Stay
The AMC *Pinkham Notch Camp* (☎ 603-466-2727, 800-262-4455) has the Joe Dodge Lodge with dorms with over 100 beds going for $38 per adult, breakfast included; children 12 and under get a discount. You must reserve your bunks in advance and pay a non-refundable deposit.

The *Dolly Copp Campground* (☎ 800-283-2267), a USFS campground six miles north of the AMC camp, has 176 simple sites priced at $10, and is open all year. Call for reservations during the summer and autumn.

CRAWFORD NOTCH
US 302 goes west from Glen, then north to Crawford Notch (1773 feet), through some beautiful mountain scenery. Crawford

Notch State Park has a system of shorter hiking trails (one-half to three miles), and trailheads for longer hikes to the summit of Mt Washington.

Crawford Notch State Park
In 1826, torrential rains caused massive mud slides in this steep valley, surrounding the home of the Willey family. The house was spared, but the family was not – all were outside at the fatal moment and were swept away.

The incident made the newspapers and fired the imaginations of painter Thomas Cole and author Nathaniel Hawthorne who used the incident for inspiration and unwittingly put Crawford Notch on the tourist maps. Soon visitors arrived to visit the tragic spot and to stay for the bracing mountain air and healthful exercise.

The Crawford family opened the Crawford House hotel in 1859 and set to work grooming mountain trails so their guests could penetrate the trackless wilderness. Their work was the basis for today's excellent system of trails. (The hotel was razed in 1977.) Crawford Notch State Park (☎ 603-374-2272) now occupies this beautiful, historic valley.

From the Willey House site, now used as a state park visitors center, you can walk the easy half-mile Pond Loop Trail, the one-mile Sam Willey Trail and the Ripley Falls Trail, a one-mile hike from US 302 via the Ethan Pond Trail. A half mile south of the Dry River Campground on US 302 is the trailhead for Arethusa Falls, a 1.3-mile hike in.

Mt Washington
Please read the warnings about severe weather (in the Pinkham Notch section, above) and consult with AMC personnel before attempting a hike to the summit of Mt Washington.

If you're in good shape and properly equipped, try the trails described below.

Ammonoosuc Ravine Trail This trail is among the shortest hiking routes to the summit, going via the AMC's **Lakes of the Clouds Hut** at 5000 feet elevation. It's one of the best routes to take in inclement weather because it is protected from the worst of the winds, and, if the weather turns very nasty, you can take shelter in the AMC hut. For overnight lodging and meals you must reserve in advance through the Pinkham Notch Camp (☎ 603-466-2727, 800-262-4455).

The trail starts at a parking lot on Base Station Rd near the entrance to the Mount Washington Cog Railway (2560 feet elevation) and climbs easily for two miles up the dramatic ravine to **Gem Pool.** From Gem Pool, however, the climb is far more strenuous and demanding, with a sharp vertical rise to the AMC hut.

From Lakes of the Clouds Hut, other trails ascend to the summit and the **Tip Top House**, a hotel that doesn't provide lodging, but does have other services.

Jewell Trail This trail is more exposed than the Ammonoosuc Ravine Trail and should be used only in fine weather. The last 0.7 mile is above treeline and very windy.

The Jewell Trail starts at the same parking lot as the Ammonoosuc Ravine Trail, but follows a more northeasterly course up a ridge. At 2.8 miles the trail comes above timberline and climbs by a series of switchbacks to meet the **Gulfside Trail** after 3.5 miles. The Gulfside continues to the summit.

Camping

Dry River Campground, just east of US 302 near the southern end of Crawford Notch State Park, has 30 tent sites for $11 each.

You can also stay at AMC's *Lakes of the Clouds Hut*, see the Ammonoosuc Ravine Trail entry for details.

BRETTON WOODS

Before 1944, the name Bretton Woods was known only among locals and the wealthy summer visitors who patronized the grand Mount Washington Hotel. After President Roosevelt chose the hotel as the site of the conference to establish a new world economic order after WWII, the whole world knew about Bretton Woods.

The mountainous countryside is still as beautiful, the hotel is almost as grand (if a bit past its prime), and the name still rings with history. At the very least you must stop to admire the view of the great hotel set against the mountains. You may want to stay a night or two. And to ascend Mt Washington in a train pulled by a cog-driven steam locomotive is fun for all, and a must for railroad buffs.

History

WWII devastated Europe and Japan, and this threw the world economy into a tailspin. Clearly, the economics of rebuilding these war-torn areas and restoring the world economy to health was going to be a principal concern of world leaders once the fighting stopped.

From July 1 to 22, 1944, world leaders and financial experts gathered here in the United Nations Monetary and Financial Conference to hammer out a model for the postwar world economy. Among the conference's products was the design of the International Monetary Fund and, out of it, the World Bank. Plans were also drawn up to provide for stable currency exchange rates and temporary assistance to member nations with balance-of-payments problems.

The Bretton Woods conference paved the way for the conference at Dumbarton Oaks in Washington, DC, in September and October 1944, at which a prototype for the United Nations charter was written. At Yalta in February 1945 the shape of the new organization was refined, setting the stage for the United Nations' founding conference in San Francisco from April to June 1945.

Though some elements of the economic world order formed at Bretton Woods – such as the gold standard – have been superseded, much of the conference's work has proven to be remarkably durable.

Information

The Twin Mountain Chamber of Commerce (☎ 603-846-5407, 800-245-8946) has an information booth in the center of Twin Mountain, several miles northwest of Bretton Woods at the intersection of US 302 and US 3.

Mt Washington Cog Railway

Purists walk, those out of shape or in a hurry drive, but certainly the quaintest way to reach the summit of Mt Washington is to take the Mt Washington Cog Railway (☎ 603-846-5404, 800-922-8825). A coal-fired, steam-powered locomotive follows a 3½-mile track along a steep trestle up the mountainside. A cog or gear wheel on its undercarriage engages pins between the rails to pull the locomotive and a single passenger car up the mountainside, burning a ton of coal and blowing a thousand gallons of water into steam along the way. Up to eight locomotives may be huffing and puffing at one time, all with boilers tilted to accommodate the grade, which at the "Jacob's Ladder" trestle is 37% grade – the second-steepest railway track in the world.

In operation since 1869, the three-hour roundtrip scenic excursion costs $36 per adult; there are discounts for seniors and children eight and under (or free for kids who sit on a parent's lap). Trains run from early May to early June on weekends, then daily through late October, and on weekends until early November. The first train puffs off at 8:30 am, the last at 4:30 pm. To be sure of a seat and to avoid a long wait, reserve in advance by phone. Also remember that the average temperature at the summit is 40°F in summer (it may be lower) and the wind is always blowing – bring a sweater and windbreaker.

The base station is six miles east of US 302. Turn at Fabyan, just northwest of the Mount Washington Hotel between Bretton Woods and Twin Mountain.

Places to Stay

Camping *Cherry Mountain KOA* (☎ 603-846-5559, 800-743-5819), north off US 302 along US 3 to NH 115, has lots of facilities and charges $18 and up for a site.

Motels *The Bretton Woods Motor Inn* (☎ 603-278-1000, 800-258-0330, fax 278-3457), run by the Mount Washington Resort, has the best view of the Mount Washington Hotel set against the mountains. The modern motel is the cheapest of the resort's four accommodations, with rooms priced at $60 to $95.

Boulder Motor Court (☎ 603-846-5437, 800-352-4556), on US 302 east of US 3 in Twin Mountain, NH 03595, has rooms for $50 to $59, $10 more if you want one with a fireplace. *Patio Motor Court* (☎ 603-846-5515), on US 3 North, has rooms for $50, two-bedroom units for $63 and duplex units for $73. *Carlson's Lodge* (☎ 603-846-5501, 800-348-5502), on US 302 a half mile west of US 3, has rooms for $40 to $70.

Hotels Prime of course is the *Mount Washington Hotel* (☎ 603-278-1000, 800-258-0330, fax 278-3457), US 302, Bretton Woods, NH 03575, with grand public rooms, thousands of acres of grounds, 27 holes of golf, 12 clay tennis courts, an equestrian center, indoor and outdoor heated pools, etc. It has 170 rooms priced from $125 to $230 single, $165 to $275 double, breakfast and dinner included. Add 8% for service and another 8% for tax to the bill.

Inns *The Bretton Arms Inn* (☎ 603-278-1000, 800-258-0330, fax 278-3457), run by the Mount Washington Resort, was built as a grand summer cottage in 1896, but has been an inn since 1907, restored extensively in 1986. Rooms cost $80 to $115.

Upper Connecticut River Valley

Hanover is part of the larger community of the Upper Connecticut River Valley which includes Lyme and Lebanon, NH, as well as Norwich, White River Junction and Woodstock, VT. When looking for services (including accommodations and dining possibilities), consider all of these places, not just Hanover.

NEW HAMPSHIRE

HANOVER
History
Chartered in 1761, settled in 1765, Hanover took the name of Britain's reigning dynasty. It was a frontier farming outpost with little to set it apart from others.

Hanover's future was determined when Reverend Eleazar Wheelock moved his Christian school for Native American youth to Hanover from Connecticut. One of Reverend Wheelock's former students had returned from a fund-raising mission in England with sufficient money to found a proper college, and the Earl of Dartmouth, King George III's colonial secretary, lent it his noble patronage.

Dartmouth College was chartered in 1769 primarily "for the education and instruction of Youth of the Indian Tribes," it was located deep in the forests where its prospective students lived. Only secondarily was it intended to serve "English Youth and others." In fact Dartmouth graduated few Indian youths, and was soon attended almost exclusively by colonists. Daniel Webster (1782-1852), Class of 1801, prominent lawyer, longtime US Senator, sometime Secretary of State and perhaps the USA's most esteemed orator, is the college's most illustrious alumnus.

Though it declines to call itself a university, Dartmouth is far more than a New England liberal arts college. It has well-regarded graduate schools of medicine, engineering and business administration. The BASIC computer language was developed here in its acclaimed mathematics department. Today, despite its graceful Georgian buildings and country-verdant campus, Dartmouth is very up-to-date and heavily wired for data transmission.

Orientation
To visit Hanover is to visit Dartmouth College, for the college dominates the town.

Hanover is fairly easily negotiable. Many services (including restaurants) are along Main St. Central reference to everything is the green, the broad lawn bounded by Wheelock, N Main, Wentworth and College Sts.

Information
The Hanover Area Chamber of Commerce (☎ 603-643-3115), 37 S Main St (PO Box 5105), Hanover, NH 03755, has maps, brochures and answers to your questions

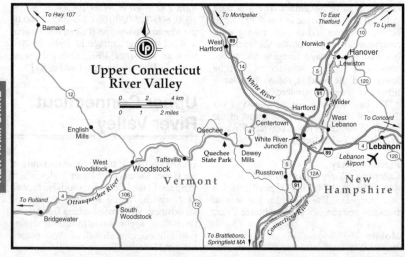

about Hanover and adjoining Norwich, VT. They maintain an information booth near the green in summer.

Dartmouth Bookstore (☎ 603-643-3616), 33 S Main St, comes highly recommended.

Dartmouth College

Free guided **walking tours** of the college tours depart from the college information booth during the summer at 9 and 11 am and 3 pm, and from the Hopkins Center at 2 pm. There are no tours on Sunday. In winter, tours depart from McNutt Hall, the admissions building on N Main St facing the green.

For a look at Dartmouth's prettiest and most historic buildings, start from the green. To the north is **Baker Memorial Library** (☎ 603-646-2560), the college's central library. In the basement reading room is a series of **murals** by José Clemente Orozco (1883-1949), the renowned Mexican muralist, who taught and painted at Dartmouth from 1932 to 1934.

The series follows the course of civilization in North America from the time of the Aztecs to the present century.

Along the east side of the green on College St is picturesque **Dartmouth Row**, four harmonious Georgian buildings named Wentworth, Dartmouth, Thornton and Reed. Dartmouth Hall was the original college building constructed in 1791. After it burned in 1904, it was wisely reconstructed in brick.

The **Hopkins Center for the Arts** (☎ 603-646-2422) is Dartmouth's outstanding venue for the performing arts. A long way from such cosmopolitan centers as Boston, New York and Montréal, Dartmouth must make its own entertainment to fill the long winter nights. Much of it takes place at the Hopkins.

South of the Hopkins Center is the **Hood Museum of Art** (☎ 603-646-2808), with fine collections ranging from ancient Greece and Rome through the European Renaissance to modern times.

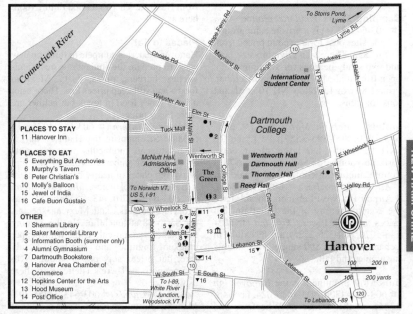

PLACES TO STAY
11 Hanover Inn

PLACES TO EAT
5 Everything But Anchovies
6 Murphy's Tavern
8 Peter Christian's
10 Molly's Balloon
15 Jewel of India
16 Cafe Buon Gustaio

OTHER
1 Sherman Library
2 Baker Memorial Library
3 Information Booth (summer only)
4 Alumni Gymnasium
7 Dartmouth Bookstore
9 Hanover Area Chamber of Commerce
12 Hopkins Center for the Arts
13 Hood Museum
14 Post Office

Hanover

NEW HAMPSHIRE

Special Events

Each February, Dartmouth celebrates its week-long Winter Carnival, the winter's major fun-and-social event, with special art shows, drama and concerts, an ice sculpture contest and other amusements. Call the chamber of commerce for dates and details.

Places to Stay

Hanover's economy has a split personality: eating places are designed and priced for students, while lodgings are designed for the (mostly) well-heeled parents who visit them here. So meals are cheap, but accommodations are surprisingly expensive.

Accomodations in this region (Hanover, Lebanon, White River Junction, Woodstock) are in greatest demand during foliage season, when virtually all are reserved in advance; there is also high demand in summer and at special college times. At times, visitors find themselves driving hours to find a room, so it's a good idea to reserve in advance if you can.

Camping *Storrs Pond Recreation Area* (☎ 603-643-2134) is a private campground with 35 sites on a 15-acre pond priced from $12 to $22. There's an Olympic-size pool and two sandy beaches for swimming. It's open from mid-May through mid-October. From I-89 exit 13 follow NH 10 north and look for signs.

Motels *Chieftain Motor Inn* (☎ 603-643-2550, 800-845-3557), 84 Lyme Rd (NH 10 North), has large, clean, comfortable rooms for $68 a single, $78 a double, including continental breakfast.

Airport Econo Inn (☎ 603-298-8888), 7 Airport Rd, West Lebanon, doesn't have the country setting of the Chieftain, but prices are a bit lower. *Days Inn* (☎ 603-448-5070, 800-325-2525), at I-89 exit 18 in Lebanon, charges $90 single, $110 double in summer and fall.

Inns Most prominent is the *Hanover Inn* (☎ 603-643-4300, 800-443-7024, fax 646-3744), at the corner of Wheelock and

Main Sts facing the green on its south side. Owned by Dartmouth College, the inn is colonial in decor, upscale in ambiance and high in price, with rooms going for $186 to $239.

Two Mile Farm (☎ 603-643-6462), 2 Ferson Rd off Etna Rd, is a farmhouse built in the late 1700s, now a B&B charging $75 for a double with shared bath, $90 with private bath.

Ten miles north of Hanover along NH 10 is Lyme, and facing its common are the *Lyme Inn* and *Dowd's Country Inn* (☎ 603-795-2222, fax 795-4220), under the same management. The Lyme Inn, built in 1809, has a very good restaurant and tavern as well as colonial guest rooms with modern facilities. The Dowd's Country Inn has 22 rooms. Rates range from $90 to $160 double, breakfast included, but when you add tax and 10% for service, it's more like $108 to $189.

Prices are similar at the *Norwich Inn* (☎ 802-649-1143), on Main St in Norwich, VT, just west across the Connecticut River from Hanover. There's a good dining room here as well.

Places to Eat

Hanover's eateries compete to think up new ways to prepare the student classics: sandwiches, burgers, pizza, pasta, Mexican food – and still keep prices low. There's not a lot of fancy food in town, but neither are there fancy prices.

Murphy's Tavern (☎ 603-643-4075), 11 S Main St, opposite the Hanover Inn, is where students and faculty meet over pints of Catamount amber ale ($2.50) and big, satisfying plates of hearty bar food.

Besides a cool name, *Molly's Balloon* (☎ 603-643-2570), 43 S Main St, has "gourmet burgers" and Mexican specials for $5 to $8 at lunchtime. In the evening the menu goes upscale a bit with pepper chicken linguine and similarly trendy fare, but prices stay put at about $9 to $15 per portion. There's a delicatessen here as well.

Peter Christian's (☎ 603-643-2345), 39 S Main St, is a student hangout serving lots of

Two of New Hampshire's covered bridges

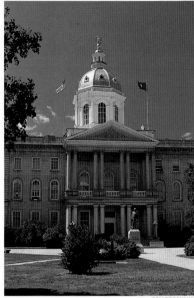

State Capitol, Concord, NH

Strawbery Banke Museum, Portsmouth, NH

KIM GRANT

"America's Oldest General Store," NH

KIM GRANT

Mt Washington Cog Railway, Bretton Woods, NH

sandwiches ($5 to $7), and old-time American favorites like turkey pot pie for $8.

Everything But Anchovies (☎ 603-643-6135), 5 Allen St between Main and School Sts, has luncheon sandwiches, salads and pastas to eat here or take out. It's a great place to pick up ready-made picnics.

Jewel of India (☎ 603-643-2217), 27 Lebanon St, varies the gustatory map by bringing in a whiff of curry. Try their Sunday brunch with lots of curry and 10 kinds of bread. For Chinese cuisine, the *Panda House* (☎ 603-643-1290) is two blocks away at 3 Lebanon St.

Cafe Buon Gustaio (☎ 603-643-5711), 72 S Main St, is the local Italian dining spot. The menu is short but sweet with updated classics: linguine with lobster and four cheeses in a spinach cream sauce, for example. A full dinner might cost you around $17 to $35.

The *Daniel Webster Room* at the Hanover Inn (☎ 603-643-4300), Main and Wheelock Sts, is perhaps the town's most elegant place to dine. Appetizers are priced from $6 to $9, main courses from $16 to $23, full dinners with wine from $35 to $65. The inn's *Ivy Grill* is a lot cheaper, with full meals for $22 to $30.

Getting There & Away

Air The short-haul "commuter" subsidiaries of Delta, Northwest, TWA, American Airlines and USAir link Lebanon Municipal Airport, six miles south of Hanover, with Boston, Montréal, New York and Hartford.

Bus Vermont Transit (☎ 802-864-6811, 800-451-3292 in New England) has direct buses from Boston (downtown), Boston's Logan Airport and Springfield, MA, and connecting service from New York, Hartford, and Montréal to White River Junction, VT. From White River Junction you can travel by taxi or Advance Transit bus (see Getting Around, below) to Hanover.

Car Driving details for Hanover are:

Destination	Mileage	Hr:Min
Boston, MA	135 miles	3:00
Burlington, VT	111 miles	2:35
Concord, NH	59 miles	1:10
Hartford, CT	155 miles	3:10
Laconia, NH	63 miles	1:35
Lebanon, NH	5 miles	0:10
Woodstock, VT	20 miles	0:40

Getting Around

Airport Dartmouth Mini Coach (☎ 603-448-2800, 448-1184) operates three shuttles daily between Hanover and the Manchester airport and Boston's Logan International Airport. The fare is $35 and reservations are required.

Bus Advance Transit (☎ 603-448-2815) operates buses in Hanover and between Hanover and Lyme; Lebanon and West Lebanon, NH and Norwich, Hartford and White River Junction, VT. Rides are free within Hanover and between Hanover and Lebanon; otherwise the fare is $1.25. Look for the blue-and-yellow AT signs to board.

Maine

Maine is a study in contrasts. It has the largest land area of the six New England states but the most sparse population of any state east of the Mississippi River.

The "rockbound coast of Maine" is about 228 miles long as the crow flies, but a tall-masted schooner sailing its tortuous course would cover almost 3500 miles. Bays, islands, inlets, peninsulas, isthmuses and coves make up the granite-strewn coast, along with a few stretches of sand beach.

When European explorers discovered Maine, it was populated by an Algonquian people known as the Abenaki, many of whom belonged to the Penobscot and Passamaquoddy tribes.

The Cabots, John and Sebastian, sailed the coast of Maine at the end of the 1400s, and an English colony was founded at Popham Beach in 1607, but it was short-lived. Many of the first European settlers were French coming south from Québec. English, Scots-Irish and German colonists followed. In 1614 John Smith charted the Maine coast, and in less than a decade there were settlements at Monhegan (1622), Saco (1623) and York (1624). York became the first chartered city in English America in 1641.

During the 1600s, while Maine was governed on and off by the colonial government of Massachusetts Bay at Boston, a series of wars raged between Maine's English colonists and Québec's French colonists with their Native American allies: King Philip's War (1675-1678), King William's War (1689-1697), Queen Anne's War (1702-1713) and King George's War (1744-1748). When the British defeated the French on the Plains of Abraham at Québec in 1759, there was finally peace among Maine's English, French and Native American inhabitants.

During the Revolutionary War, Benedict Arnold started out from Augusta on his expedition to capture Québec. In 1775, British forces burned Portland.

Maine was governed from Boston until 1820, when it became the 23rd state admitted to the union, with its capital at Portland. The capital was moved to Augusta in 1827, and the State Capitol completed in 1832.

Though the border between Maine and the Canadian province of New Brunswick had been set at the St Croix River in 1783, neither side had been happy with the decision. The dispute flared into the Aroostook War in 1838 – a war of words, not bullets. It was settled by the Webster-Ashburton Treaty in 1842.

Today, southern coastal Maine is thickly settled. The settlements vary from beautiful, well-preserved historic towns to miles of shopping malls and "factory outlet" stores. There are genteel summer resorts and honky-tonk beach resorts.

Northern, inland Maine is New England's wilderness, with vast (for New England) areas of trackless forest and thousands of glacial lakes inhabited only by fish and fowl. About 89% of Maine is covered in forests of white pine, fir and hardwood. See The North Woods for more information.

In winter, Maine feels isolated and distant from the cosmopolitan centers of New York City, Boston and Montréal. In summer, these cities seem to move en masse to Maine's coastal resorts, and city accents and attitudes drive out the simpler speech and ways of local folk.

The Maine Publicity Bureau, Inc (☎ 207-623-0363), 325B Water St, Hallowell, ME 04347, maintains information centers on the principal routes into the state at Calais, Fryeburg, Hampden, Houlton, Kittery and Yarmouth. Each facility is open from 9 am to 5 pm with extended hours in the summer.

Seat belts are required by law for those age 19 or younger, and recommended for all.

The legal age to buy or consume alcohol in Maine is 21 years; you must buy alcohol between 6 am and 1 am. The maximum amounts of liquor you are allowed to bring into Maine are one gallon of whiskey, one gallon of wine or other liquor and one case of beer.

Smoking is prohibited in all enclosed areas where the public is invited or allowed, and this includes restrooms.

In an emergency, for Maine State Police call ☎ 800-482-0730.

Getting There & Around

There is talk of reviving a passenger rail service route from Boston to Portland, but at present you are limited to transport by air, bus, car and ferryboat.

Air Portland International Jetport is the state's main airport, while a number of flights also serve Bangor.

Augusta, Bar Harbor (Hancock County Airport), Belfast, Camden (Knox County Airport), Caribou, Frenchville (Northern Aroostook Airport), Fort Kent, Houlton and Presque Isle (Northern Maine Regional Airport) have smaller airports served by commuter or charter aircraft.

The airlines serving these airports vary from year to year, but at the time of writing these included Colgan Air (☎ 800-272-5488) and Business Express (☎ 800-345-3400). In addition to those, Continental Express, Delta, United, Trans World Express and USAir Express serve Portland and Bangor.

Bus Concord Trailways (☎ 800-639-3317) operates daily buses between Boston and its Logan International Airport and Bangor, Bath, Belfast, Brunswick, Camden/Rockport, Damariscotta, Lincolnville, Portland, Rockland, Searsport and Waldoboro. Some Concord Trailways buses connect with the Maine State Ferry Service to islands off the coast.

Concord Trailways buses from Boston and Portland connect at Bangor with West Transportation Service buses to Ellsworth (for Bar Harbor) and towns along the Downeast coast to Perry, then inland to Calais.

SMT Line (☎ 207-767-9500) buses carry passengers from Bangor to St Stephen, New Brunswick, Canada.

Cyr Bus Lines (☎ 207-942-3354) runs from Bangor to Caribou via Orono, Houlton, Presque Isle and other towns in between.

Car In general, you must plan more travel time in Maine. Except for the Maine Turnpike (I-95 and I-495), Maine has no fast limited-access highways. Roads along the coast are often very heavy with traffic during the summer tourist season.

Note Moose are a particular danger to drivers in Maine, even as far south as Portland – they've been known to cripple a bus and walk away. Moose-vehicle accidents rose in Maine from 150 in 1981 to 658 in 1994. An increase was also seen in New Hampshire.

Be especially watchful in spring and fall and around dusk and dawn when the animals are most active. The same goes for other wildlife on the road.

Boat Maine State Ferry Service (☎ 207-596-2202) operates ferryboats between the mainland and several of the state's important islands. There's also car and passenger ferry service from Portland and Bar Harbor to Yarmouth, Nova Scotia, Canada, operated by Marine Atlantic (☎ 800-341-7981).

Southeast Maine

KITTERY

Entry to Maine along US 1 or I-95 at Kittery can be less than thrilling – unless you're going shopping. Kittery is famous for its shopping malls and outlet stores, all of which claim to offer deep discounts on everything from apparel to china to camping gear.

If shopping is not your thrill, you can head straight through Kittery, fast on I-95, much more slowly on US 1. Keep in mind

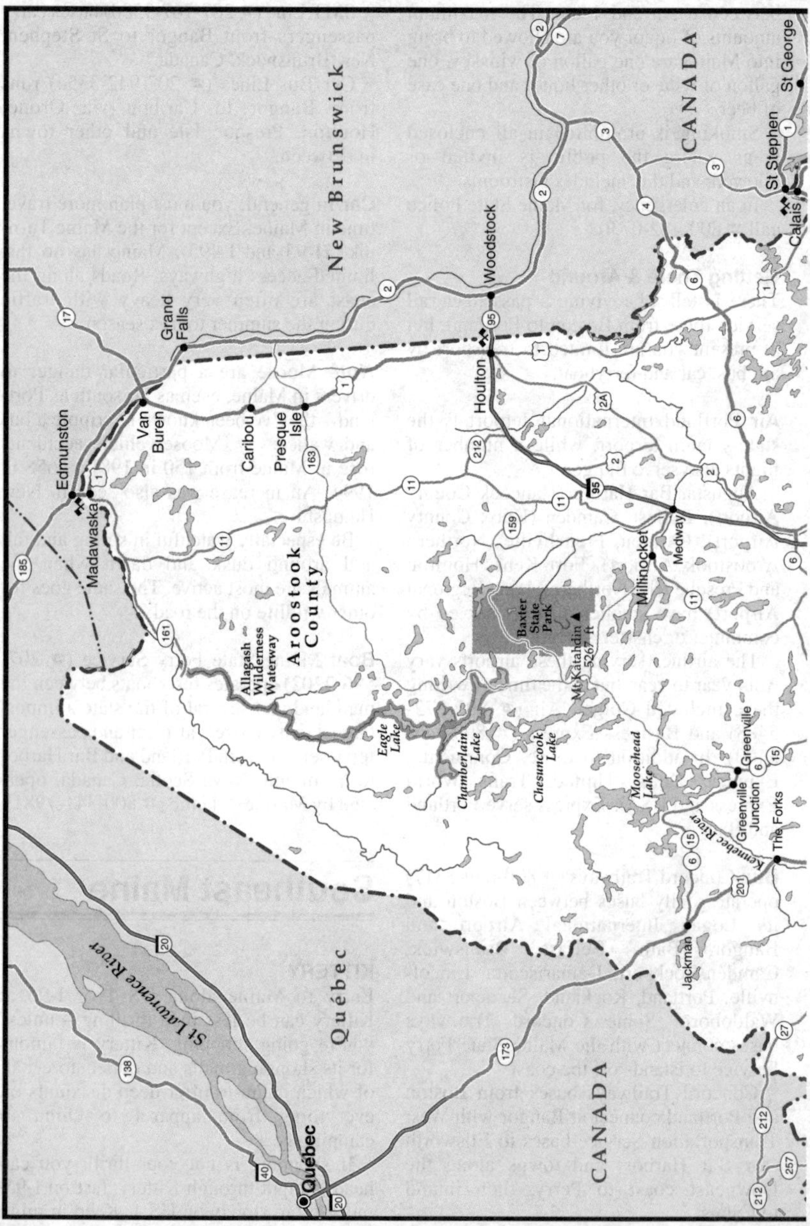
New Brunswick
CANADA
St George
St Stephen
Calais
Woodstock
Houlton
Grand Falls
Van Buren
Caribou
Presque Isle
Edmunston
Madawaska
Aroostook County
Allagash Wilderness Waterway
Baxter State Park
Mt Katahdin ▲ 5267 ft
Millinocket
Medway
Eagle Lake
Chamberlain Lake
Chesuncook Lake
Moosehead Lake
Greenville
Greenville Junction
The Forks
Kennebec River
Jackman
Québec
St Lawrence River
CANADA
Québec

MAINE

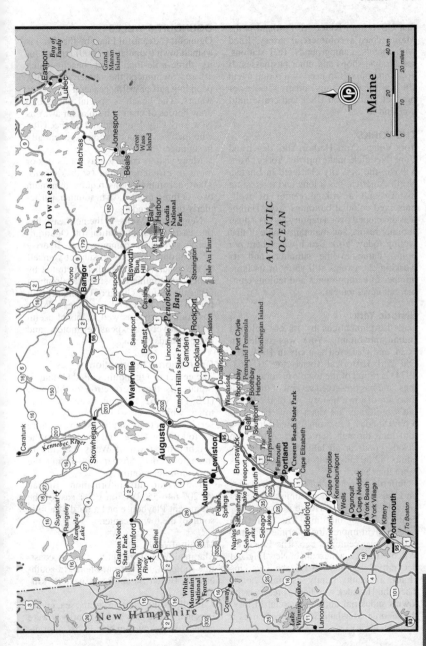

that US 1 from Kittery to Portland is the Maine coast's commercial artery, lined with motels, campgrounds, fuel stations, restaurants, shops and other businesses. If you find yourself in need of a room, a tent site, a meal or any other service or product, just get on US 1 and cruise until you find it.

THE YORKS
York Village, York Harbor, York Beach and Cape Neddick make up the Yorks. York Village, the first city chartered in English North America, has a long and interesting history and a village center of well-preserved colonial buildings. York Harbor was developed over a century ago as a posh summer resort, and maintains some of that feeling today. York Beach was where *hoi polloi* came in the summer, and its working-class roots still show in its large number of campgrounds and tedious commercial development.

Historic York
Called Agamenticus by its pre-colonial Indian inhabitants, York was settled in 1624, and chartered as a city in 1641. The Old York Historical Society (☎ 207-363-4974) is proud of the town's historic buildings, and has preserved several of them as a museum of town history. All of the museum's buildings are open from 10 am to 5 pm (Sunday 1 to 5 pm, closed Monday), mid-June through September. Admission tickets good for all buildings cost $6 for adults, $2.50 kids six to 16; no family pays more than $16.

Jefferds Tavern Visitor Center, off US 1A on Lindsay Rd, is where admission tickets are sold. The School House is a mid-18th-century school building. The Old Gaol gives a vivid impression of crime and punishment two centuries ago. The Emerson-Wilcox House is a museum of New England decorative arts, and the Elizabeth Perkins House a wealthy family's summer home. The John Hancock warehouse preserves the town's industrial and commercial history; the George Marshall Store now houses a research library.

OGUNQUIT & WELLS
Ogunquit ("Beautiful Place by the Sea") is a small town (population 1000) famous for its three-mile-long sand beach which affords swimmers the choice of chilly, pounding surf or warm, peaceful back-cove waters. The beach is special enough to draw hordes of visitors from as far away as New York City, Montréal and Québec City, who increase the population exponentially in summer.

Many visitors come to stay for a week or more in efficiency units (with kitchen). Many accommodations require minimum two- or three-night stays in summer, particularly on weekends.

Neighboring Wells, to the northeast, has the eastward continuation of Ogunquit Beach, and several camping areas. To drive US 1 through Wells is to subject yourself to the usual visual assault perpetrated by American commercial strip development (after the relative charm of Ogunquit). But for all its commercial tawdriness, Wells has good beaches as well as lots of useful and relatively inexpensive motels and campgrounds.

Orientation & Information
The center of Ogunquit, called Ogunquit Square, is the intersection of Main St (US 1), Shore Rd and Beach St. The town, which seems to be mostly tourist services, stretches southeast down Shore Rd to Perkins Cove, and northeast to the neighboring town of Wells. Parking in town lots costs $6 per day during the busy summer months.

The Ogunquit Information Bureau (☎ 207-646-5533) is on US 1 east of the prominent Playhouse and a third of a mile south of the town's center.

Marginal Way
Marginal Way, Ogunquit's famous coastline footpath, starts from Shore Rd southeast of Beach St and ends near Perkins Cove.

It follows the "margin" of the sea, giving it its name. The path and right-of-way were ceded to the town in the 1920s after its

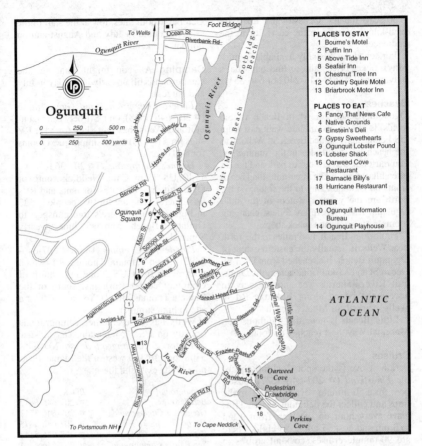

Ogunquit

0 250 500 m	
0 250 500 yards	

PLACES TO STAY
1 Bourne's Motel
2 Puffin Inn
5 Above Tide Inn
8 Seafair Inn
11 Chestnut Tree Inn
12 Country Squire Motel
13 Briarbrook Motor Inn

PLACES TO EAT
3 Fancy That News Cafe
4 Native Grounds
6 Einstein's Deli
7 Gypsy Sweethearts
9 Ogunquit Lobster Pound
15 Lobster Shack
16 Oarweed Cove
    Restaurant
17 Barnacle Billy's
18 Hurricane Restaurant

OTHER
10 Ogunquit Information
    Bureau
14 Ogunquit Playhouse

owner, Josiah Chase, sold off the valuable house lots with sea views. The scenic walk is slightly more than a mile, from the center of Ogunquit to Perkins Cove. If you don't want to walk back, you can take the trolley which runs in the summer.

Wells Auto Museum

In 1946 a resident of Wells was given a Stanley Steamer that his uncle found in the cellar of his barn in Vermont. The new owner restored the ancient car, built early in the century, and soon had a burgeoning collection of restored classic cars powered by steam, electricity and gasoline. The museum, a nonprofit organization, now has 70 cars of 45 different makes, including Rolls-Royce, Stutz, Cadillac, Packard, Pierce Arrow and Knox.

The Wells Auto Museum (☎ 207-646-9064), on US 1, is open from mid-June to mid-September from 10 am to 5 pm for $4 adult, $2 per child; kids under six are free.

Ogunquit Playhouse

The Ogunquit Playhouse lit up for the first time in 1933, and at its present site south of the center of town in 1937. The season begins in late June and offers three musicals and two plays each year in the small

MAINE

(750-seat) theater. Occasionally there are well-known names in the cast – or in the audience.

For schedules (usually available in mid-May), ticket prices and to find out what's playing, call ☎ 207-646-2402 or 646-5511.

Beaches

Ogunquit Beach (or Main Beach to the locals) is only a five-minute walk east from US 1 along aptly named Beach St. Walking to the beach is a good idea in the summer, as you must pay $2 per hour to park and the lot often fills up early. The three-mile-long beach fronts on Ogunquit Bay to the south; on the north are the warmer waters of the tidal Ogunquit River. There are toilets, changing rooms, restaurants and snack shops.

Footbridge Beach, two miles to the north near Wells, is actually the eastern extent of Ogunquit Beach. It's reached from US 1 by Ocean St and a footbridge across the Ogunquit River. There's yet another way to access the beach along Eldridge Rd in Wells, marked for Moody Beach.

Little Beach is near the lighthouse on Marginal Way, best reached on foot.

Cruises

Perkins Cove is the spot to climb aboard the *Finestkind* (☎ 207-646-5227) lobster boat for a 50-minute voyage to pull up the traps and collect the delicious beasts. Trips leave every hour on the hour from 9 am to 3 pm and cost $7 adult, $5 child. There are 90-minute cruises, cocktail cruises in the late afternoon and evening, and even a 9 pm starlight cruise as well.

You can take sailing yacht cruises aboard the *Silverlining* (☎ 207-361-9800), a 42-foot Hinckley sloop, out of Perkins Cove four times daily. The two-hour cruise costs $28 per person in high season. The *Cricket* (☎ 207-646-5227), a locally built catboat, sails away from Barnacle Billy's dock in Perkins Cove on 1¾-hour cruises four times daily for $15.

Places to Stay

Though a few places stay open all year, most open in mid-May and close by mid-October. Room rates, low at the start of the season, double in July and August and on holiday weekends.

Camping As you might imagine, the campgrounds fill up early in the day in July and August.

Elmere Campground and Guest House (☎ 207-646-5538), on US 1 between Ogunquit and Wells, has tent sites for $12, RV sites for $16 to $18 and simple guest rooms for $40 double.

Dixon's Campground (☎ 207-363-2131), 1740 US 1, in Cape Neddick south of Ogunquit, has 100 sites for tents and RVs on 40 acres. The fee for two people is $23 in high summer. There's free transport to Ogunquit Beach from late June to early September.

Pinederosa Camping Area (☎ 207-646-2492), is on Captain Thomas Rd, which goes north from US 1 one mile north of Ogunquit center (turn just south of the Captain Thomas Motel). You pay $20 for a site in high summer.

Wells has several other campgrounds (mostly on US 1), including *Ocean View Cottages & Campground* (☎ 207-646-3308) on ME 109 west of the Maine Turnpike Wells exit, and these:

Campground	Phone
Beach Acres	☎ 207-646-5612
Gregoire's Campground	☎ 207-646-3711
Ocean Overlook	☎ 207-646-3075
Riverside Park Campground	☎ 207-646-3145
Sea Breeze Campground	☎ 207-646-4301
Sea-Vu Campground	☎ 207-646-7732
Stadig Campground	☎ 207-646-2298
Wells Beach Resort	☎ 207-646-7570

Motels *Briarbrook Motor Inn* (☎ 207-646-7571), adjacent to the Ogunquit Playhouse south of the center of town on US 1, charges $72 to $77 for rooms in high summer.

Bourne's Motel (☎ 207-646-2823, 646-9093), at US 1 and Ocean St, is not far from Footbridge Beach and charges $60 to $80. The *Studio East Motor Inn* (☎ 207-646-7297) on US 1 is similar. The *Country Squire Motel* (☎ 207-646-3162), at US 1 and Bourne's Lane, is also good.

Inns & B&Bs The *Cape Neddick House B&B* (☎ 207-363-2500), 1300 US 1, Cape Neddick, ME 03902, is an 1880s Victorian that rents double rooms with private bath and full breakfast for $75 in summer, $65 in fall and $55 at other times of the year.

Seafair Inn (☎ 207-646-2181), 14 Shore Rd, Ogunquit, ME 03907, is a Victorian summer house on the way to the beach charging $60 for rooms with shared bath, $85 with private bath. Continental breakfast is included.

Chestnut Tree Inn (☎ 207-646-4529, 800-362-0757), 93 Shore Rd, on the way to Perkins Cove, was built in 1870 and has 22 guest rooms going for $68 to $80, continental breakfast included.

Puffin Inn (☎ 207-646-5496), 233 US 1, just north of the center of town, is another big Victorian with a convenient location and rooms with private bath and breakfast for $80 to $90.

The aptly named *Above Tide Inn* (☎ 207-646-7454), 26 Beach St, is perched on piles above the Ogunquit River only a stone's throw from Ogunquit Beach, and advertises "spectacular views." From mid-May to mid-June and mid-September to mid-October the price is good at $65 and up. In-season the price rises to $110, with a three-night minimum.

Places to Eat

The influx of New Yorkers has influenced Ogunquit's restaurant scene, so you can find good bagels everywhere. If you have lunch at *Einstein's Deli* (☎ 207-646-5262), 2 Shore Rd at Main St (US 1), you must note that the clam chowder served here is Manhattan-style (with tomatoes) and not New England-style (with cream).

Besides its catchy name, *Gypsy Sweethearts* (☎ 207-646-7021), 10 Shore Rd, serves the catch of the day and other seafood at moderate prices. Dinner with wine costs around $20 to $35 per person. They serve breakfast with fresh-ground coffee and fresh-baked bread from 7:30 am to noon.

Fancy That News Cafe, at the intersection of US 1 and Shore Rd, has an assortment of pastries, coffees and teas if you need a quick pick-me-up.

Across US 1, *Native Grounds* serves soups, sandwiches and similar light fare that you can eat on the terrace at umbrella-shaded tables right next to the busy intersection. This is Ogunquit's prime place to see and be seen. The pastries and confections are wonderful, for $3 to $6 with coffee.

In Perkins Cove the perennial favorite is *Barnacle Billy's* (☎ 207-646-5575), once a rough-and-ready eatery, now more refined, with prices to match. Lobsters are priced according to the season, but a big lunch or dinner here usually costs $20 to $30 with wine or beer. Alternatives are the *Lobster Shack* (☎ 207-646-2941), which has been serving lobsters here for 40 years, and the *Oarweed Cove Restaurant* (☎ 207-646-4022), which has its own parking lot at the beginning of Marginal Way.

Ogunquit Lobster Pound (☎ 207-646-2516), on US 1 only a quarter mile south of Ogunquit Square, is typically informal, with picnic tables set amidst pine trees and a big stone lobster steamer. Prices seem a bit high, but then, that's Ogunquit in summer.

For a fancy lunch or dinner, try the *Hurricane Restaurant* (☎ 207-646-6348), at Perkins Cove: "Our view will blow you away, our menu will bring you back." The specialty is Maine lobster chowder, but the menu always includes some elaborate New American dishes as well as daily seafood specials. Expect to spend $25 to $45 for dinner with wine.

Getting There & Away

Driving details from Ogunquit are:

Destination	Mileage	Hr:Min
Bar Harbor, ME	196 miles	4:30
Boothbay, ME	94 miles	2:25
Boston, MA	70 miles	1:30
Freeport, ME	51 miles	1:05
Kennebunkport, ME	11 miles	0:30
Portland, ME	35 miles	0:50
Portsmouth, NH	17 miles	0:25

Getting Around

"Trolleys" (disguised buses, 50¢) circulate through Ogunquit every 10 minutes from

MAINE

8 am to midnight in the summer months to take you easily from the center of town to the beach or to Perkins Cove.

The Shuttlebus (☎ 207-282-5408) runs a route four times daily connecting Kennebunk, Kennebunkport, Wells, Ogunquit, the Yorks and Kittery/Eliot during the summer (late June to early September). Fares are on a zone system, from $1 to $3 for adults, a flat $1 for kids five to 12.

THE KENNEBUNKS
Together the towns of Kennebunk, Kennebunkport and Kennebunk Beach make up the Kennebunks.

Kennebunkport, most famous of the three towns, is beautiful, historical and absolutely packed in the summer. Walk anywhere to see the pristine hundred and two-hundred-year-old houses and mansions, the manicured lawns, the sea views. Even in the autumn, when beach resorts such as Old Orchard Beach have closed down, visitors throng to Kennebunkport to shop in its boutiques, stay in its gracious inns and drive along the ocean to admire the view.

Ocean Ave presents the most dramatic vistas, but the back streets, inland from the Kennebunk River and the sea, are less busy. Follow Ocean Ave south, then northeast to get a view of the Bush estate on Walker's Point. It's not all that exciting, but it's something every visitor to Kennebunkport does.

Orientation
The epicenter of Kennebunkport activity is Dock Square, just over the bridge on the east side of the Kennebunk River. South of Dock Square is the historic district, with many fine old mansions, some of which are now inns. Ocean Ave goes south from Dock Square to the sea, then east to Walker's Point and the Bush compound. Follow Ocean Ave eastward, then northeast, to reach Cape Porpoise, a charming hamlet.

On the west side of the Kennebunk River Bridge is Kennebunk Lower Village, virtually part of Kennebunkport.

Information
The Kennebunkport Information & Hospitality Center (☎ 207-967-8600), just southeast of Dock Square, has toilets, brochures and maps, and will help you to find accommodations for the same night. It's open from 10 am to 9 pm in summer, 11 am to 4 pm in fall.

The Kennebunk-Kennebunkport Chamber of Commerce Information Center (☎ 207-967-0857), is on Port Rd (ME 35) in Kennebunk Lower Village, open from 10 am to 6 pm (until 4 pm Sunday); in September and October it's open weekdays from 10 am to 5 pm.

Seashore Trolley Museum
Trolleys, the light rail systems that provided most urban transport a century ago, are the strong suit of the Seashore Trolley Museum (☎ 207-967-2800), on Log Cabin Rd north of Dock Square. Founded as the Seashore Electric Railway, the museum now holds a variety of streetcars (including one named Desire), antique buses and public transit paraphernalia. The museum is open from May to October, but has a complicated schedule of hours. Call before you go.

Beaches
Kennebunkport proper has only Colony Beach, dominated by the Colony Hotel. But west of the Kennebunk River and south of Kennebunk Lower Village along Beach St and Sea Rd are three good public beaches: Gooch's Beach, Middle Beach and Mother's Beach, known collectively as Kennebunk Beach.

Bicycling
Bicycling is a good way to get around Kennebunkport. Bikes, Blades & Boards (known as B3, ☎ 207-967-3601), in the Shipyard complex behind the Mobil station just south of the bridge in Kennebunk Lower Village, rents bicycles for one ($15 to $25) or for two ($40) people, as well as in-line roller skates and skateboards. Helmet and lock are included with each rental.

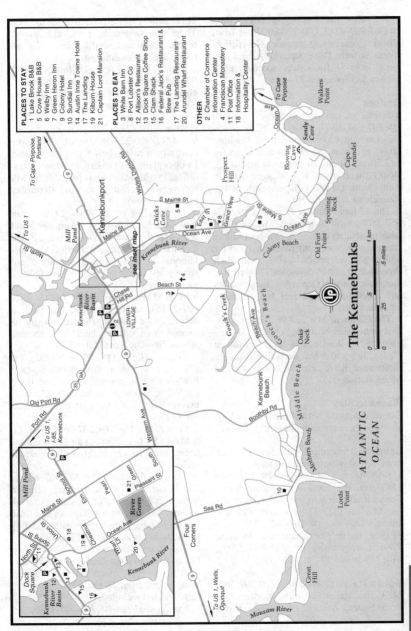

PLACES TO STAY
1 Lake Brook B&B
5 Cove House B&B
6 Welby Inn
7 Green Heron Inn
9 Colony Hotel
10 Sundial Inn
14 Austin Inne Towne Hotel
17 The Landing
19 Kilburn House
21 Captain Lord Mansion

PLACES TO EAT
3 White Barn Inn
8 Port Lobster Co
12 Allison's Restaurant
13 Dock Square Coffee Shop
15 Clam Shack
16 Federal Jack's Restaurant & Brew Pub
17 The Landing Restaurant
20 Arundel Wharf Restaurant

OTHER
2 Chamber of Commerce Information Center
4 Franciscan Monastery
11 Post Office
18 Information & Hospitality Center

The Kennebunks

MAINE

Try also the Cape-able Bike Shop (☎ 207-967-4382, 800-220-0907), at Town House Corners and Arundel Rd (follow North St from Dock Square). Rental fees range from $8 for a three-speed or kid's bike to $25 for a new 21-speed.

Cruises

You can go out on the *Second Chance* (☎ 207-967-5507, 800-767-2628), a 45-foot Downeast lobster boat for a 1½-hour cruise at 10 am, noon, 2, 4 and 7 pm for $12.50 per adult, $6 per child six to 12. Board the boat at 4-A Western Ave in Kennebunk Lower Village, south of the Kennebunk River Bridge.

The 42-foot schooner *Lazy Jack* (☎ 207-967-8809), built in Ipswich, MA, in 1947, takes passengers on two- or four-hour sailing cruises in the waters off Kennebunkport for $30 to $50 per person. Call Captain Rich Woodman or stop by Schooner's Wharf, near the southern end of Ocean Ave, for schedules and reservations, and feel free to bring a picnic.

The *Elizabeth 2* (☎ 207-967-5595), a 60-foot sightseeing boat which holds 118 passengers, has similar fares for its cruises at 11 am, 1, 3 and 5 pm, departing from the Kennebunk River near the bridge and the Mobil station.

Places to Stay

Kennebunkport is not a cheap place to stay, although there are many beautiful inns.

Camping The campgrounds here are open from mid-May through mid-October.

Salty Acres Campground (☎ 207-967-2483), on ME 9 north of Cape Porpoise on Goose Rocks Beach, has 225 sites going for $18 to $25. There's also *Kennebunkport Camping* (☎ 207-967-2732), with 82 sites, and in West Kennebunk, *Mousam River Campground* (☎ 207-985-2507), with 115 sites.

Motels The *Beechwood Motel* (☎ 207-967-2483), on ME 9 five miles northeast of Dock Square, has 112 rooms (some with

kitchenettes) priced from $42 to $78. There's a swimming pool, kids' pool, tennis court and shuffleboard. Not all rooms are air-conditioned.

The 20-room *Turnpike Motel* (☎ 207-985-4404), I-95 exit 3 in Kennebunk, charges $56 for a room in high summer, $37 to $45 off-season.

Hotels *Austin Inne Towne Hotel* (☎ 207-967-4241, 800-227-3809) couldn't be more centrally located, being just steps from Dock Square. It's modern, but done in traditional style, with rooms priced from $49 (off-season weekday) to $109 (Saturday night in-season).

The Landing (☎ 207-967-4221), Ocean Ave, is a big old wooden summer hotel right over the water on Ocean Ave, a prime location in the high-rent district. It's most famous for its restaurant, but there are some guest rooms going for $90 double.

Inns & B&Bs *Green Heron Inn* (☎ 207-967-3315), on Ocean Ave, has been a dependably comfy inn for decades. Its 10 rooms, all with private bath, color TV and air-conditioning, cost $60 to $86.

Kilburn House (☎ 207-967-4762), on Chestnut St, is a turn-of-the-century B&B with four rooms on the 2nd floor for $45 to $60 with shared bath, $75 with private bath, and a suite on the 3rd floor for $125.

Cove House B&B (☎ 207-967-3704), 11 S Maine St, has rooms in an 18th-century home for $70 per night, full breakfast included.

The *Lake Brook B&B* (☎ 207-967-4069), 57 Western Ave, Kennebunk Lower Village, is a nice turn-of-the-century farmhouse at the edge of a salt marsh and tidal brook. Rooms with private bath and full breakfast are priced from $75 to $90.

The *Welby Inn* (☎ 207-967-4655), on Ocean Ave, is a large gambrel-roofed house with seven guest rooms (all with private bath) priced from $80 to $95 in summer, full breakfast included.

The *Sundial Inn* (☎ 207-967-3850, fax

967-4719), 48 Beach Ave facing Kennebunk Beach, was built around 1891 and fully renovated in 1987. Bright, sunny rooms cost $106 to $150 in summer, continental breakfast included. The price depends on the room size, the view and the date.

If cost is no object, the *Captain Lord Mansion* (☎ 207-967-3141, fax 967-3127), on Ocean Ave, is the place for you. This great sea captain's house has been meticulously restored and is, if anything, more plush and beautiful than when lived in by its original occupants. Rooms are priced from $149 to $199 double, full breakfast included. On weekends, you must stay at least two nights.

Places to Eat

The tiny *Dock Square Coffee Shop* (☎ 207-985-4070) is usually packed all the time it's open from 7 am to 3 pm. Besides the usual array of fancy coffees, teas and some pastries, they offer one or two lunch items each day: hand-cut sandwiches, chilis or stews, priced at $6 or $7.

On the west side of the bridge in Kennebunk Lower Village, the *Clam Shack* has hamburgers for $2, clam and fish plates for $6 to $10. You can eat standing up on their long deck over the water, but beware the seagulls who will snatch your food.

Allison's Restaurant (☎ 207-967-4841), 5 Dock Square at the center of town, is crowded all day because of its decent food at very good prices, like these at lunch time: fried shrimp basket for $7, shepherd's pie for $5.50 or an extra-long lobster roll for $9. It's open for lunch and dinner every day.

Arundel Wharf Restaurant (☎ 207-967-3444), on Arundel Wharf just south of Dock Square, is moderately priced at about $5 to $15 for lunch, $30 to $45 for dinner (have the coastal paella or a seafood skewer for $16). The location, overlooking the Kennebunk River, is good.

Port Lobster Co (☎ 207-967-5411), Ocean Ave, is a lobster pound and fish market that also sells crab meat, shrimp and lobster rolls as well as boiled lobster.

Dining is decidedly informal, and prices are good.

The Landing Restaurant (☎ 207-967-4221), on Ocean Ave in the hotel, is a comfy old favorite among longtime residents of Kennebunkport. Seafood is the specialty, of course, and prices are moderate.

Federal Jack's Restaurant & Brew Pub (☎ 207-967-4322), above the Kennebunkport Brewing Co in the Shipyard complex in Kennebunk Lower Village, has a good menu of pub food, salads, sandwiches, pizzas and heartier main courses to go with its selection of "hand-crafted" ales on draft. The microbrews here are excellent. A meal may cost anywhere from $6 to $20. The *Lobster Deck Restaurant*, a bit fancier, is here as well.

The *White Barn Inn* (☎ 207-967-2321, fax 967-1100), on Beach St, is Kennebunkport's most renowned restaurant. The decor and ambiance are "country-elegant," the food New American. The menu changes weekly, and leans heavily on local seafood supplemented by locally grown herbs, fruits and vegetables and California greens. Dinner is served nightly. Make reservations, dress well and expect to pay $50 to $75 per person.

Getting There & Away

Driving details for Kennebunkport are:

Destination	Mileage	Hr:Min
Bar Harbor, ME	187 miles	4:20
Boothbay, ME	88 miles	2:15
Boston, MA	80 miles	1:45
Freeport, ME	45 miles	1:00
Ogunquit, ME	11 miles	0:30
Portland, ME	29 miles	0:40
Portsmouth, NH	28 miles	0:40

Getting Around

The In-Town Trolley (☎ 207-967-3686) circulates through Kennebunkport all day. Your ticket ($5 adult, $2 child) is good all day. You can stay on for the 45-minute narrated tour of the whole route, or hop on and off as you like at the designated stops, including along Beach Ave.

OLD ORCHARD BEACH

Old Orchard Beach is the quintessential New England beach playground, alive with lights, music and noise, and skimpily clad crowds of fun-loving sun worshippers making the rounds of fast food emporiums, mechanical amusements and gimcrack shops. Palace Playland, at the very center of town on the beach, is a fitting symbol, with its carousel, Ferris wheel and other children's rides, fried clams and pizza stands, T-shirt and souvenir shops.

Old Orchard Beach has long been a favorite summer resort of Quebeckers, who flock south in July and August. Many signs are bilingual (English and French) to accommodate the friendly Canadians.

Dozens of little motels and guest houses line the beaches north and south of the center of town, and all are full from late June through Labor Day. Before and after that, Old Orchard Beach slumbers. If you're driving by, you can spend an afternoon or evening pleasantly enough.

PORTLAND

Maine's largest city, largest port and commercial center is a small, manageable, safe, pleasant, relatively prosperous city of 64,000 people; if you include the suburbs, Greater Portland has about 230,000 in population.

Like London, Portland offers many surprising urban perspectives: turn a corner, look down a street and a grand building or view is framed neatly at the end of it.

The city center's architectural unity stems in part from tragedy. The city was ravaged by fire several times in its history, the latest and worst being the great fire of 1866. Built mostly of wood, the port area's buildings were reduced to ashes.

Portlanders resolved not to let it happen again, so they rebuilt their city in the style of the time using brick and stone. A providential lack of booming prosperity kept its old buildings from being torn down and replaced by sterile modern structures.

Today the Old Port is a charming area for a stroll, especially the blocks bounded by

Temple and Franklin Sts, and Commercial and Congress Sts. Many of the city's best restaurants, bars and shops are here.

Congress St is the city's main business and shopping thoroughfare with many office buildings and banks.

The neighborhoods just east of the Western Promenade have many grand Victorian mansions, Queen Anne cottages and Romanesque Revival houses, some with fine views. A few of these are now elegant B&Bs.

The neighborhoods of the Eastern Promenade have not fared as well: though some of the houses were once grand, most are no longer so, though the view is still fine.

Orientation

Portland is set on a ridge of hills along a peninsula surrounded by the Fore River, Casco Bay and Back Cove. Portland Harbor, where the Fore River meets Casco Bay, is its historical heart, where you'll want to spend your time. This, the Old Port, holds most of the city's good restaurants, hotels, galleries and shops.

Atop the hills at the southwestern end of the peninsula is the Western Promenade, a long stretch of green park framing a neighborhood of grand houses of stone or brick. At the opposite end of the peninsula, the Eastern Promenade serves the same function, with much finer views of Casco Bay and its islands, though the neighborhood is not quite so plush.

Downtown Portland, with its business district, museums, shops and galleries, is centered between the promenades. Congress St is the main thoroughfare along the top of the ridge, passing Portland's most imposing buildings: City Hall, banks, churches and hotels. Commercial St is the fitting name of the main business street in the Old Port, where tourists spend most of their time.

I-95 skirts the city to the west, while I-295 makes a detour into the city, and hooks back up with I-95 north of Back Cove. Approaching Portland from the south, follow I-95 to exit 6A, then I-295 to exit 4, then US 1 to US 1A North, which is Commercial St, and takes you right to the Old Port.

From the north, follow I-295 to exit 7, then US 1A South (Commercial St).

Information

The Convention & Visitors Bureau of Greater Portland (☎ 207-772-5800) has an information office at 305 Commercial St, at Foundry Lane, on the south side of the Old Port. It's open daily in summer from 8 am to 6 pm (weekends and holidays 10 am to 6 pm), with shorter hours in winter.

For information on arts and events, call "I Call" (☎ 207-797-1313).

In an emergency, call ☎ 911; for Portland police, call ☎ 207-874-8300; for Maine State Police call ☎ 800-482-0730.

Portland Museum of Art

Portland's fine arts museum (☎ 207-773-2787, 800-639-4067), 7 Congress Square, at Congress and High Sts, has an outstanding collection especially rich in the works of Maine painters Winslow Homer, Edward Hopper, Rockwell Kent, Maurice Prendergast and Andrew Wyeth. There are works by European masters such as Degas, Picasso and Renoir as well, though exhibit space is limited compared to the size of the collection. From time to time there are very good special shows (call for current offerings). The museum ($5) is open from 10 am to 5 pm (Thursday until 9 pm, Sunday noon to 5 pm), and is closed Monday.

Historic Houses

The **Morse-Libby House** (☎ 207-772-4841), 109 Danforth St at Park St, a few blocks southeast of the art museum, is known as the Victoria Mansion. This Italianate palace was built in 1859 and decorated sumptuously with rich furniture, frescoes, paintings, carpets, gilding and exotic wood and stone. It's open to visitors from late May through early September from 10 am to 5 pm (noon to 5 pm on Sunday), closed Monday, and from early September through mid-October on week-

ends only. Admission costs $4, and includes a 45-minute guided tour.

The **Wadsworth-Longfellow House** (☎ 207-879-0427), 485 Congress St, was built of brick (1786) in the Federal style. The builder was General Peleg Wadsworth, a hero in the Revolutionary War and later grandfather of poet Henry Wadsworth Longfellow. Longfellow grew up here, and the house's furnishings recall his 19th-century surroundings. Admission details are similar to those of the Morse-Libby House.

Children's Museum of Maine

The Children's Museum (☎ 207-828-1234), 142 Free St near Congress and High Sts, gives kids the opportunity to haul in traps on a kid-sized lobster boat, see what it's like to broadcast the news and to make stained glass. If you have kids and if it's raining, head for the Children's Museum. It's open in winter from 10 am to 5 pm (Tuesday and Sunday noon to 5 pm, Friday 10 am to 8 pm), with longer hours in summer. Admission costs $4 (kids under a year old enter free); admission is free on Friday from 5 to 8 pm.

Cape Elizabeth

South and east across the bay via the Million Dollar Bridge are the towns of South Portland and Cape Elizabeth. Fort Williams Park, four miles from central Portland in Cape Elizabeth, is worth a visit for its panoramas and picnic possibilities.

The vast rolling lawns of the park are dotted with WWII bunkers and gun emplacements. Fortification of Portland Head began in 1873, and the installation was named Fort Williams in 1899. The fort guarded the entrance to Casco Bay, and was active until 1964.

Right next to the park is Portland Head Light (☎ 207-799-5251), the oldest of Maine's 52 lighthouses. It was commissioned by President George Washington in 1791 and staffed until 1989, when machines took over. The keeper's house is now the **Museum at Portland Head Light**

MAINE

Portland

Casco Bay

Portland Harbor

Back Cove

Eastern Promenade

EAST END

To I-95, Falmouth, Freeport

Maine State Pier

Casco Bay Ferry/ Island Ferry

Custom House Wharf

Long Wharf

Custom House St

see inset map

Civic Center

OLD PORT

Civic Center

0   200   400 m
0   200   400 yards

Street labels

Eastern Promenade
Cumberland Ave
North St
Sheridan St
Washington St
Greenleaf St
Smith St
Boyd St
Mayo St
Wilmot St
Pearl St
Myrtle St
Chestnut St
Elm St
Preble St
Brown St
Casco St
Oak St
Forest Ave
Hanover St
Alder St
Mechanic St
Paris St
High St
State St
Park Ave
Grant St
Sherman St
Cumberland Ave
Deering St
Forest Ave
Deering Ave
Brighton Ave
St John St
Park Ave
Congress St
Mt Fort St
Morning St
Atlantic St
Hampshire St
India St
Franklin St
Pearl St
Federal St
Temple St
Union St
Exchange St
Center St
Cross St
Fore St
Commercial St
Market St
Congress St
Elm St
Silver St
Dana St
Wharf St
Moulton St
Milk St

Exit 7
Exit 6
26
295
1A
1
26
100
302
25
295
293

To South Portland I-95

To Portland International Jetport

1 4 2 3 5 6 7 8 9 10 11 14 15 16 17 18 19 27 28 29 30 31 32 33 34 35 36 37 38 39 40 41 42 43 44 45

Sawyer St
Pine St
To Spring Point Light
Pine St
Pine St
Broadway
Cottage St
To Fort Williams Park,
Portland Head Light
& Museum
Sawyer St

Mill
Cove

SOUTH
PORTLAND

Ocean St
(77)
Broadway
Highland Ave
To Crescent Beach
State Park, Cape Elizabeth
(77)

Ferry to Yarmouth, Nova Scotia

To US 1,
I-295

High St
Park St
State St
Danforth St
York St
Clark St
Brackett St
Pine St
Commercial St
Spring St
Gray St
Winter St

Carleton St
Neal St
Marshall Vaughn St
Chadwick St
WEST END
WESTERN
PROMENADE
Western Promenade
Carrol St
Bowdoin St
Gilman St

Valley St
St John St
WESTERN
PROMENADE

Ogdensburg St

Fore
River

Veterans Memorial Bridge

To Old
Orchard Beach

Million Dollar Bridge

Portland Harbor

1A

Danforth St

Commercial St

26

24

PLACES TO STAY
2 Inn at St John
4 Susse Chalet Portland In-Town
5 Portland Summer Hostel
10 Hotel Everett
20 West End Inn B&B
21 The Inn on Carleton
38 Portland Regency Inn

PLACES TO EAT
6 Bella Bella
7 Katahdin
12 Cafe Always
13 The Pepperclub
15 Gilbert's Chowder House
17 Porthole
22 West Side Restaurant
29 Bien Hong
30 Afghan Restaurant
31 Box Lunch
34 Portland Wine & Cheese
35 Perfetto
36 Walter's Cafe
37 Java Joe's
39 Hi Bombay
40 Brian Boru
41 The Baker's Table
42 Street & Co
43 Gritty McDuff's Brew Pub
44 Wharf Street Cafe
45 Port Bake House

OTHER
1 Concord Trailways Bus Station
3 Greyhound-Vermont Transit Bus Station
8 Portland Museum of Art
9 Children's Museum of Maine
11 Wadsworth-Longfellow House
14 Eagle Tours, Olde Port Marine Fleet
16 Casco Bay Lines Ticket Office
18 Island Ferry Terminal
19 Casco Bay Ferry Terminal
23 Mercy Hospital
24 Morse-Libby House (Victoria Mansion)
25 Convention & Visitors Bureau
    of Greater Portland Tourist Office
26 Prince of Fundy Cruises
27 Metro Pulse City Bus Terminal,
    Elm St Parking Garage
28 City Hall
32 Tommy's Park
33 Post Office Park

MAINE

(☎ 207-799-2661), tracing the maritime and military history of the region. It's open from 10 am to 4 pm, June to October.

Jogging

Back Cove, northwest of the city's center on the other side of I-295, is surrounded by a two-mile jogging trail. Take I-295 exit 6 and follow US 1 North; or take Bus 2 to Forest Ave Plaza, Bus 6 to Payson Park or Bus 8 to the Shop 'n' Save and you'll be near Back Cove.

Organized Tours

For a good look at the Eastern and Western Promenades, Congress St and the heart of downtown Portland, hop aboard Bus 1 ($1) and ride until you've had enough.

Starting from downtown Portland, you can peddle into the forest in about 20 minutes. Forest City Mountain Bike Tours (☎ 207-780-8155), 51 Melbourne St, will take you on guided tours through Portland, South Portland, Cape Elizabeth and other towns. Tours last from two to six hours and cost from $10 to $25 per person, depending upon the tour. Bike rental is an additional $10 to $15 each. Reservations are required.

Cruises

Just east of Portland is Casco Bay, crowded with islands. The motorboats of Casco Bay Lines (☎ 207-774-7871) cruise the islands delivering mail, freight and visitors. These are working boats, but they're comfortably outfitted. The cruises vary in length from 1¾ hours (roundtrip to the Diamond Islands) for $7.75 for adults, $6.50 seniors, $3 kids five to nine; the 5¾-hour (roundtrip) nature cruise complete with lecture to Bailey Island for $13.50, $12, $6. Two of the six cruises operate daily year round. All cruises depart from the Casco Bay Ferry Terminal at 56 Commercial St at Franklin St.

You can also cruise Casco Bay under sail aboard the *Palawan* (☎ 207-773-2163), a 58-foot ocean racing yacht designed by Sparkman & Stevens. There are cruises in the morning ($20 for three hours), afternoon

($30 for three hours) and evening ($20 for two hours). Seniors and kids 12 and under pay half fare.

Eagle Tours (☎ 207-799-6498), at Long Wharf on Commercial St, runs tours of Casco Bay, including trips to Eagle Island and Portland Head Light.

The Olde Port Marine Fleet (☎ 207-775-0727, 642-3270, 800-437-3270) has three boats departing Long Wharf on deep-sea fishing trips, whale watches, lobstering trips and one-hour harbor cruises. Call for details, or stop by the blue ticket booth next to the Key Bank on Commercial St.

Places to Stay

Camping There are no camping places in Portland, but there are several near Freeport, only 16 miles to the northeast. See the Freeport section for details.

Hostel From June through August the University of Maine's Portland Hall becomes the local HI/AYH hostel called the *Portland Summer Hostel* (☎ 207-874-3281, off-season 617-731-8096), 645 Congress St. Rooms are $15 per person, and most have two beds, so if you come alone there's a chance you'll be sharing. The price includes linens and a continental breakfast, as well as free parking in their gated lot – a plus in downtown Portland. There's no age limit.

Budget Hotels The *Inn at St John* (☎ 207-773-6481), 939 Congress St at St John, advertises itself as Portland's "low-fat" hotel, with rooms starting at $25 per night. In fact, prices are more like $35 to $50 double, and it's somewhat noisy, but it's right across the street from the Greyhound/Vermont Transit bus station, and on Buses 1 and 3. Continental breakfast is included.

The *Hotel Everett* (☎ 207-773-7882), 51A Oak St, Portland, ME 04101, off Congress St, is old-fashioned but central and reasonably priced. Some rooms have shared baths.

Motels Motels outside the city's center are moderately priced. There are several at I-95

exit 7, near the Maine Mall (Comfort Inn, Portland Marriott and Days Inn); and at exit 8.

The *Susse Chalet Portland/Westbrook* (☎ 207-774-6101, 800-258-1980), I-95 exit 8, charges $59.70 for up to four people, even less if you call and ask for the same-day rate.

The similarly priced *Howard Johnson* (☎ 207-774-5861, 800-654-2000), 155 Riverside St (I-95 exit 8), has 120 rooms, a restaurant and indoor pool. The *Holiday Inn West* (☎ 207-774-5601, 800-465-4329, fax 774-2103), 81 Riverside St, is at exit 8 as well.

Moderate Hotels The *Susse Chalet Portland In-Town* (☎ 207-871-0611, 800-258-1980), 340 Park Ave, charges $69.70 for a double room. Rooms with two double beds can sleep up to four, and if two are small children, the price is the same. They sometimes offer a same-day rate that's substantially less. From I-95, take exit 6A to I-295 to exit 5A (Congress St); at the end of the ramp turn right, then left at the signs for Stroudwater/Westbrook.

The *Portland Regency Inn* (☎ 207-774-4200, 800-727-3436, fax 775-2150), 20 Milk St, is housed in the port's substantial old red-brick armory right in the Old Port a block from the waterfront. Its 95 very comfortable rooms in this excellent, central location cost $120/130 a single/double during the week, $130/175 on weekends. It's undergoing major expansion reconstruction in '96 (beware of early morning hammering).

Inns & B&Bs Portland's West End, near the Western Promenade, is a pretty residential neighborhood with many grand houses, some of which have been converted to inns.

The *West End Inn B&B* (☎ 207-772-1377, 800-338-1377), 146 Pine St, Portland, ME 04102, was built in 1871. It has only five rooms, all with TV and private bath, for $109 to $149 double, depending on when you stay.

The Inn on Carleton (☎ 207-775-1910), 46 Carleton St, Portland, ME 04102, is a restored 1869 Victorian house with seven rooms priced at $85 (shared bath) to $105 (private bath).

Places to Eat

Most of the restaurants in the Old Port area will make you a sandwich to go. To buy your own provisions, head for upper Exchange St (between Middle and Federal) where there are several delicatessens, including *Box Lunch*. *Portland Wine & Cheese* (☎ 207-772-4647), corner of Middle and Exchange Sts, has high-quality sandwiches and salads to go.

The *Port Bake House* (☎ 207-773-2217), at Dana and Commercial Sts, is good for baked goods, pastries, sandwiches, soups and salads.

Portland is strong on bistros, little storefront restaurants with inventive and eclectic menus, simple but pleasant decor, friendly service and moderate prices. The larger, fancier restaurants along the waterfront and in the Old Port tend to have plush dining rooms and bland, even disappointing food. Vegetarian food can be found easily here, unlike around the rest of the state.

The main restaurant streets are in the Old Port: Exchange St between Fore and Federal, and Wharf St between Union and Dana. Other good restaurants are scattered about downtown. All serve wine and beer, most do not accept reservations except for large parties on weekends, so you may have to dine early or wait in line.

Java Joe's (☎ 207-761-5637), 13 Exchange St near Fore St, is the favored place for a cup of good joe, plain or fancy, for 85¢ to $3. They serve a selection of sandwiches, cookies and pastries as well. There's cool live music some evenings, and lots of whispered intellectual discussion.

Gilbert's Chowder House (☎ 207-871-5636), 92 Commercial St at Pearl St, is a simple diner with a lunch counter and tables, good for a load of fish and chips ($8) or a big bowl of their very thick clam chowder ($4).

Even cheaper prices are to be found at the *Porthole* (☎ 207-773-9348), 20 Custom

House Wharf, down a passage to the right of Gilbert's. Perched on a rundown but atmospheric wharf right in the middle of the workaday docks, the Porthole serves all three meals simply but very cheaply. Their all-you-can-eat fish fry costs $3.75 at lunch, $5 at dinner (after 4 pm). You can eat at a few outdoor picnic tables if the weather's good.

Afghan Restaurant (☎ 207-773-3431), 88 Exchange St, is among Portland's most exotic eateries, with various sorts of palaw (rice pilaf), many of them vegetarian. Prices are excellent, with many main courses priced under $10, and full table d'hôte meals for two priced under $25, for four under $45.

Bien Hong (☎ 207-879-1967), 106 Exchange St near Federal, is Portland's southeast Asian eatery, serving Thai and Vietnamese dishes such as spicy chicken and beef in oyster sauce. The food is good, the prices excellent, with full dinners priced around $10. It's open every day for lunch and dinner, but no lunch is served on Sunday.

The Pepperclub (☎ 207-772-0531), 78 Middle St, just northeast of Franklin Artery, serves dinner every night and is usually packed shortly after 6 pm. The reason is the eclectic menu – a Middle Eastern mezze plate for starters, then Jamaican jerked chicken burritos – and the low prices. Most main courses cost $8 to $10, making possible an excellent, interesting dinner with wine for about $20 per person. Service is friendly and good.

Bella Bella (☎ 207-780-1260), 606 Congress St, west of High St, is usually busy every night despite its location well away from the intense dining activity in the Old Port. The reason is plain: good food at low prices. Cannelloni with spinach ricotta costs only $8, roast duck only $9. The menu is short and sweet, the dining room is bright and simple but pleasant and it's only a few blocks' walk from several large downtown hotels. Saturday and Sunday it's open 9 am to 1 pm.

If your craving is for Indian food, try *Hi Bombay* (☎ 207-772-8767), 1 Pleasant St at

Center St, which serves lunch ($8 to $15) and dinner ($15 to $22) every day.

Katahdin (☎ 207-774-1740), 106 High St at Spring St, is a popular bistro named for Maine's tallest mountain. The menu puts a new twist on old American favorites, as in the pot roast with vegetables braised in red wine gravy, or wild mushroom ravioli in seasonal vegetable broth. The decor is simple American eclectic, with patchwork quilts and other crafts. Dinner, served daily except Sunday, might cost $25 to $30 with wine.

Street & Company (☎ 207-775-0887), 33 Wharf St, is the current favorite among Wharf St bistros. The cramped but congenial dining rooms are usually packed for dinner so reserve in advance. The blackboard menu lists specialties such as scallops Pernod in cream, and categories such as "grilled blackened," and "over linguine." Fresh ingredients and seafood are featured, and a normal dinner costs from $25 to $36.

Wharf Street Cafe (☎ 207-773-6667), 35 Wharf St, is another of these industrial buildings converted for fine dining: rough brick walls and smooth cuisine. You might start dinner with a crab and avocado quesadilla, then go on to eggplant and tomato bread pudding or shrimp and scallop fra diavolo. The wine list is good, and they serve local beers; total, the bill will be about $22 to $32. They also serve lots of luncheon sandwiches for $3 to $4, aiming at nearby office workers. The cafe is open Monday to Saturday in summer, closed Sunday through Tuesday off season.

The Baker's Table (☎ 207-775-0303, 773-3333) was the first restaurant on Wharf St, having opened more than a decade ago. Its interesting menu lists several appealing vegetarian dishes, such as veggie fajitas and hot basil vegetable stir-fry, but they also serve tournedos Oscar and similarly meaty dishes. Come for the weekend brunch.

Walter's Cafe (☎ 207-871-9258), 15 Exchange St, is one of Portland's coolest bistros, a narrow storefront dining room with a high ceiling and even higher culinary aspirations. They use Maine ingredients when they can, as in their grilled salmon in a blueberry basil oil over mixed greens. Vegetarians should try the Rasta pasta of linguine and julienne vegetables. This is a good place for a hot lunch. Closed Sunday. If it's too full, try *Perfétto* (☎ 207-828-0001), 28 Exchange St, right across the street.

Cafe Always (☎ 207-774-9399), 47 Middle St, one of Portland's first (1985) and best bistros, is northeast of Hampshire St in a drab neighborhood with a sausage factory belching smoky scents from across the street. The chef plans the menu according to this rule: there are no rules. Thus you may find French, Japanese and Mexican elements sharing space with Maine specialties such as grilled venison with sun-dried cherry sauce. It's worth the few blocks' walk to try the interesting menu. Dinner, which ranges in price from $24 to $35 all in, is served after 5 pm from Tuesday to Saturday.

You will no doubt hear about the *West Side Restaurant* (☎ 207-773-8223), 58 Pine St at Brackett St, near the Western Promenade, if you stay in any of the promenade's fine small inns. It's open daily for all three meals, with a menu that changes frequently. This is some of Portland's best dining, at moderate to high prices.

Entertainment
Fore St between Union and Exchange Sts is lined with restaurants and bars. Those near Union, like *Three Dollar Dewey's Alehouse* at Fore and Union, and *The Big Easy Sports Cafe* nearby, tend to be sports bars with large-screen TVs and pinball machines or billiard tables clicking nearby. *Cadillac Jack's* (☎ 207-774-7466), 442 Fore St, boasts 70 different kinds of beer, eight of them on tap, plus live music some nights. Amid the Fore St bars is Condom Sense, a shop specializing in condoms and related paraphernalia, including the inevitable tourist T-shirts.

The most popular spot for a pint is *Gritty McDuff's Brew Pub* (☎ 207-772-2739), 396 Fore St, "Portland's original brew pub." The half-dozen beers, ales and stouts served here are all brewed downstairs, and served up for $2.50 a pint. Pub food is served as well.

Portland's Irish pub is *Brian Ború* (☎ 207-780-1506), on Center St between Spring and Fore Sts.

Getting There & Away
There is currently no passenger rail service to Maine, but a Boston to Portland route is in the works; call Amtrak for details.

Air Portland International Jetport (☎ 207-874-8300) is Maine's largest and busiest air terminal. The "International" in the airport's name refers mostly to flights to and from Canada. For long-distance international flights you must connect through Boston or New York City (JFK airport).

Airlines serving the airport include Continental, Delta, Northwest, United and USAir.

City buses can take you to the center of town for $1 (see Getting Around).

Bus Vermont Transit (☎ 207-772-6587, 802-864-6811), in the Greyhound Terminal at 950 Congress St at St John St, is near I-295 exit 5. They run six buses daily to and from Boston (2½ hours), connecting with buses to Hartford (3¼ hours more) and New York City (4½ hours more).

Vermont Transit also runs three buses northeastward to Brunswick, and four up the Maine Turnpike to Lewiston, Augusta, Waterville and Bangor (3¼ hours), with one bus continuing to Bar Harbor (4 hours from Portland).

Concord Trailways (☎ 207-828-1151, 800-639-3317) has its terminal at 161 Marginal Way (the street running parallel to I-295) just southwest of Franklin Artery. They run six buses daily nonstop between Portland, Boston and Boston's Logan Airport.

From Portland, three buses go northeast to Bangor; one bus connects at Bangor with a Cyr bus headed north to Medway, Sherman, Houlton, Presque Isle and Caribou. There's also local service from Portland which runs along the coast stopping at the times of Brunswick, Bath, Wiscasset, Damariscotta, Waldoboro, Rockland, Camden/Rockport, Lincolnville, Belfast, Searsport and Bangor. On this route, the Portland to Bangor trip takes around four hours.

Car Driving details for Portland are:

Destination	Mileage	Hr:Min
Bar Harbor, ME	161 miles	4:00
Boothbay, ME	59 miles	1:15
Boston, MA	108 miles	2:15
Freeport, ME	16 miles	0:22
Kennebunkport, ME	29 miles	0:40
Ogunquit, ME	35 miles	0:50
Portsmouth, NH	52 miles	1:05

Boat For passenger ferry cruises between Portland and Bailey Island, see Cruises, above.

Prince of Fundy Cruises' MF *Scotia Prince* (☎ 207-775-5616, 800-341-7540, 800-482-0955 in Maine only) departs Portland each evening at 9 pm, arriving in Yarmouth, Nova Scotia, the next morning at breakfast time. The return trip departs Yarmouth at 10 am for Portland, arriving after dinner. The voyage takes approximately 11 hours. You must have proof of citizenship (your passport, or US citizen's birth certificate, or voter registration card) to enter Canada at Yarmouth.

The cruises operate daily (with some exceptions) from early May through late October for $55 for adults, $27.50 kids five to 14 ($75 and $37.50 in-season from late June through late September). Kids under five sail free. If you'd like a cabin, you pay $22 and up during the day, $20 to $60 at night ($32 to $95 in-season). Meals are not included in the price.

The fare to take a car is $80 ($98 in-season) one way. Car fares are reduced by half on certain days (mostly Tuesday and Wednesday); call for details. Thus for a couple with two children aged five to 14 with a car traveling in-season in two moderately priced cabins (at night, Portland to Yarmouth only), the roundtrip cost can reach around $1000, meals, taxes and tips included. Off-season, a couple without

children traveling with a car, using the cheapest cabin on the night sailing and bringing their own food can go roundtrip for about $400 minimum.

Getting Around
Portland's Metro (☎ 207-774-0351) is the local bus line, with its main terminus ("Metro Pulse") at the Elm St parking garage, on the corner of Elm and Congress Sts. The fare is $1.

Here are some useful routes serving the city center:

Destination	Bus
Airport	5
Back Cove	2, 3, 6
Casco Bay Ferry Terminal	8
Concord Trailways Bus Terminal	8
Eastern Promenade	1
International Ferry Terminal	8
Old Port	8
Portland Museum of Art	1, 3, 8
Vermont Transit/ Greyhound Bus Terminal	1, 3, 5
Western Promenade	1, 8

FREEPORT
Here amid the natural beauties of Maine's rockbound coast is a town devoted almost entirely to city-style shopping. Toney luggage, expensive china, trendy clothes and perfumed soaps are all available in its more than 100 shops backed by a maze of parking lots. The town's mile-long Main St (US 1) is a perpetual traffic jam of cars from all over the country and Canada, all in the name of nature.

Freeport's fame and fortune began a century ago when Leon Leonwood Bean opened a shop to sell equipment and provisions to hunters and fishers heading north into the Maine woods. LL Bean gave good value for money, and his customers were loyal. One foundation of their loyalty was his Maine Hunting Shoe, a rugged rubber bottom molded to a leather upper. It keeps your feet dry and warm in the chill air of dawn as you crouch in your duck blind.

Over the years the store added lots of other no-nonsense, good-quality outdoor gear, and some engaging retailing practices:

a catalog operation, perpetual open hours (the store *never* closes) and an iron-clad returns policy: send it back at any time if it proves unsatisfactory. Though the store fell on hard times in the 1960s, a shot of big-city marketing expertise soon boosted it to nationwide fame.

In summer the LL Bean store (☎ 800-341-4341 ext 7801), and indeed most of Freeport's shops, are busy with shoppers all day and into the night. See Things to Buy.

Orientation

Take I-95 exit 19 or 20 to reach downtown Freeport. The downtown shopping district along Main St (US 1) is easily negotiated on foot, but you might have to drive a short distance to your lodgings if you plan to stay the night.

The epicenter of Freeport shopping is the big LL Bean store which made Freeport what it is today, right on Main St.

South Freeport, south along US 1, is a sleepy residential community, but its Town Dock has a good local eatery and cruises of the bay.

Information

The State of Maine has a large information center at exit 17 off I-95, covering Freeport and indeed all of Maine. The Freeport Chamber of Commerce (☎ 207-725-8797) maintains information centers on Main St at Mallet St, and on Mill St a block south of Main St.

Hiking

Bradbury Mountain State Park, six miles west of Freeport on ME 9 just north of Pownal, has several miles of forested hiking trails, including an instant-gratification 10-minute hike from the picnic area uphill to the summit for a spectacular view reaching all the way to the ocean. There's camping as well (see below). Surprisingly, one sees very few Freeport shoppers testing their new outdoor gear in this pretty park.

Follow ME 125 and ME 136 north from Freeport, but turn left just after crossing I-95, following the state park signs.

Shopping

It's all around you, as are the shoppers.

Why should prices for luxury goods be lower here than in the major cities? The answer is rent and middlemen. The rent in Freeport is a fraction of that in Manhattan or Boston's Newbury St. And by establishing their own shops in this small Maine town, major purveyors of luxury goods avoid paying 50% and more of the retail price to the big-city department stores and specialty shops.

The car license plates are from Connecticut, Massachusetts, New York, Ontario, Pennsylvania, Québec and even farther afield. As for the shoppers themselves, many look to be outdoorsy types, but most seem to have more interest in the outdoors as a romantic idea than as a place to work up a sweat.

It's ironic that LL Bean, a store that built its fame on supplying outdoor sports enthusiasts, has led the transformation of Freeport into a mecca for urban shopping sophisticates. ■

Hot-Air Balloon Rides

Freeport Balloon Co (☎ 207-865-1712), 41 Tuttle Rd, Pownal, ME 04069, boasts "fair winds, soft landings and good crew." They'll take you aloft for a little over an hour for about $150 per person. Reserve in advance.

Cruises

A few miles south of the shopping frenzy, in South Freeport, is the Freeport Town Wharf, the departure point for several boats offering cruises around Casco Bay. *Freeport Sailing* (☎ 207-865-9225, 756-1230) will take you on a four-hour morning cruise for $30 per person. Atlantic Seal Cruises (☎ 207-865-6112) offers three-hour cruises for $20. Remember to pack a picnic lunch or ask about catered picnics when you make reservations.

Places to Stay

Camping Camping is available at a half-dozen campgrounds within a six-mile radius of Freeport. Choicest is the *Delia B Powers Winslow Memorial Park* (☎ 207-

865-4198), on Staples Point Road, a town park right on the ocean with water-view sites for $15, non-view for $13; there are no hookups. It closes after early September. Go south from Freeport along US 1, at the towering Lewinsky Indian statue turn left toward South Freeport, then right onto Staples Point Rd (there's a park sign) and go just under two miles to the park.

Next best is *Bradbury Mountain State Park*, with 41 forested sites ($15) on Route 9 north of Pownal. See Hiking (above) for details.

Closest to Freeport center is *Sandy Cedar Haven Campground* (☎ 207-865-6254), 19 Baker Rd, with 58 mostly wooded sites on Baker Rd (ME 125 North). On this same road is the *Florida Lake Campground* (☎ 207-865-4874), with 40 sites renting for $12 to $14 per day, three miles north of Freeport. A good alternative is *Blueberry Pond Campground* (☎ 207-688-4421), 355 Libby Rd in Pownal, four miles northeast of Freeport. It's a private place a few miles northeast of Bradbury Mountain (head for Bradbury Mountain, then follow the signs). *Flying Point Campground* (☎ 207-865-4569) has 38 sites on Lower Flying Point Rd four miles southeast of LL Bean via Bow St.

Motels Motels are mostly south of the city center on US 1 near I-95 exit 19. The highly visible *Super 8 Motel* (☎ 207-865-1408, 800-800-8000) is new and nice, and priced at $83 double. Facing the Super 8 across US 1, the *Dutch Village Motel* (☎ 207-865-6682) has a pool and little cottages as well as adequate motel units for $65 double. The *Eagle Motel* (☎ 207-865-4088, 800-334-4088), 291 US 1 South, is a handsome, classic American motel charging $80 per double, breakfast included. *Casco Bay Motel* (☎ 207-865-4925), 317 US 1 South, a few minutes' drive south of the town center, right next to the gigantic Lewinsky's Indian statue, charges $69 for a room with a double bed and a single.

Inns & B&Bs Several B&Bs are on Main St just north of the big Harraseeket Inn.

Others are within an easy walk of the city center. Most charge from $70 to $100 for a double room with bath and breakfast in summer.

The *Captain Josiah A Mitchell House* (☎ 207-865-3289), 188 Main St, is a historic ship captain's house with Victorian furnishings. Rooms, with full- or half-bath, cost $68 to $98, breakfast included.

Holbrook Inn (☎ 207-865-6693), 7 Holbrook St, charges $75 for a double with bath and breakfast. Note that no credit cards are accepted.

Bayberry Bed & Breakfast (☎ 207-865-1868), 8 Maple Ave, dates from the mid-1800s, with recent renovation. Rooms with private baths cost $75 to $95, breakfast included. *Country at Heart B&B* (☎ 207-865-0512), 37 Bow St, is 2½ blocks from LL Bean, and charges $75 to $85 for a double with bath and breakfast.

There are also some nice, quiet B&Bs on Main St in South Freeport near the Town Dock. The *Atlantic Seal B&B* (☎ 207-865-6112) at 25 Main offers boat cruises as well as lodging. Nearby is the *Harborside B&B*.

Freeport's classiest (and priciest) place to stay is the *Harraseeket Inn* (☎ 207-865-9377, 800-342-6423), 162 Main St, charging $140 to $180 for its elegant rooms. Manhattan prices here in the Maine woods.

Places to Eat

Freeport's Main St (US 1) has a dozen places to eat. The *Lobster Cooker* (☎ 207-865-4349), 39 Main St, is a fast-food place with excellent clam chowder ($3.95 a bowl), good cole slaw and boiled lobster lunches for about $15. Dine inside or on the deck.

Ocean Farms Restaurant (☎ 207-865-3101), 23 Main St at the south end of town, has a menu ranging from mozzarella sticks to New York sirloin, with lots of salads and sandwiches in between. Dine on the covered terrace in good weather. If you're not on a diet, try a bowl of lobster stew ("just lobster, cream and butter") for $10, or Cajun chicken for the same.

Crickets Restaurant (☎ 207-865-4005), on Lower Main St (US 1) just north of I-95 exit 19, a Freeport institution, has a lengthy menu of soups, salads, sandwiches ($5 to $9), seafood ($12 to $20), Italian specialties, fajitas ($9 to $10), lobsters, vegetarian dishes – almost everything. It's open for every meal, all week.

Harraseeket Lunch & Lobster Co (☎ 207-865-4888), on the Town Dock in South Freeport, serves a full menu of lunch items to be eaten at shaded picnic tables overlooking the bay. Get twin one-pound lobsters for $10, a clambake for $13 or a good lobster roll with French fries for $10. Live and cooked lobsters to take out are sold as well.

Getting There & Away
For bus transport, see the Portland section; buses do not stop in Freeport. Driving details for Freeport are:

Destination	Mileage	Hr:Min
Bar Harbor, ME	145 miles	3:45
Kennebunkport, ME	45 miles	1:00
Ogunquit, ME	51 miles	1:10
Portland, ME	16 miles	0:22
Portsmouth, NH	73 miles	1:20

BRUNSWICK
Settled in 1628 and incorporated in 1738, Brunswick was named in honor of the British royal house. Today it's most famous as the home of highly regarded Bowdoin College.

A short drive through the city center reveals stately Federal and Greek Revival houses and mansions built by wealthy sea captains. Stowe House (☎ 207-725-5543), 63 Federal St, is where Harriet Beecher Stowe wrote *Uncle Tom's Cabin*. This story of a runaway slave, published in 1852, was hugely popular. The poignant story fired the imagination of people in the northern states, who saw the book as a powerful indictment of slavery. It was translated into numerous foreign languages. Stowe House is now a restaurant.

Brunswick's green, called the Town Mall, is along Maine St. Farmer's markets are set up on Tuesday and Friday, and there are band concerts on Wednesday evenings in summer. In early August, the four-day Maine Arts Festival is held a short distance east of Brunswick in Cooks Corner at Thomas Point Beach.

Orientation & Information
Driving along US 1, the commercial center of Brunswick does not present a very attractive prospect. In fact, as the home of Bowdoin College, Brunswick is the cultural center for this part of the state. Turn off US 1 onto aptly named Pleasant St for a completely different view of Brunswick.

The Brunswick Area Chamber of Commerce (☎ 207-725-8797), 59 Pleasant St, can provide you with a map and help you with a room reservation if you need one.

Bowdoin College
Founded in 1794, Bowdoin is among the oldest colleges in the USA, and is the alma mater of Longfellow, Hawthorne and President Franklin Pierce. For general campus information call ☎ 207-725-3375. For a campus tour, follow the signs from Maine St to Moulton Union.

Smith Union is the student center, with an information desk on the mezzanine level, as well as a cafe, pub, small convenience store, lounge and small art gallery. There's also the requisite bookstore where you can buy a sweatshirt, and a mailroom where you can get stamps and send off your letters. There's also a bulletin board with information on local events, concerts and potential inexpensive transportation: ride shares.

Among visitable sites on campus are the Bowdoin College Museum of Art (☎ 207-725-3275), strong in 19th- and 20th-century European and American painters.

The Peary-MacMillan Arctic Museum (☎ 207-725-3416), in Hubbard Hall, holds memorabilia from the expeditions of Robert Edwin Peary and Donald Baxter MacMillan, Bowdoin alumni who were among the first explorers to reach the North Pole.

MAINE

Pejepscot Museums

Local history is preserved in the museums of the Pejepscot Historical Society.

The Pejepscot Museum (☎ 207-729-6606), 159 Park Row, has exhibits and old photographs of Brunswick, Topsham and Hartwell. The Skolfield-Whittier House, 161 Park Row, a grand 17-room brick mansion adjacent to the museum, is a virtual time capsule, having been closed up from 1925 to 1982. Even the receipts for the building's construction, and the spices in the kitchen racks, are authentic.

The Joshua L Chamberlain Museum, 226 Maine St, holds artifacts from the owner's eventful life as college professor, Civil War hero, president of Bowdoin College and four-term governor of Maine.

Entertainment

During the summer months, Bowdoin's Pickard Theater hosts the *Maine State Music Theater* (☎ 207-725-8769), a summer musical comedy series running eight performances a week from June through August.

Getting There & Away

Brunswick is the point at which I-95 heads north and inland toward Augusta, Waterville and Bangor, and US 1 heads east and north along the coast. It's about nine miles to Brunswick from Freeport, and eight from Bath. For bus information see the Portland section.

THE HARPSWELLS

Several narrow, wooded peninsulas dotted with small settlements jut southward into Casco Bay from Brunswick. Together the settlements, comprising the township of Harpswell, are known to locals and to summer residents as the Harpswells.

If you have a few hours and want to get away from the mad traffic on US 1, venture south for a meal or even a night. There are several B&Bs, inns and motels and enough restaurants to provide dependable sustenance.

Want to go the distance? Head all the way south on ME 24 to Bailey Island,

reached from Orrs Island over a cribstone granite bridge (1927) which allows the tides to flow right through it.

The village dock on Bailey Island is a stop on the Casco Bay cruise circuit, and can be more crowded than one expects when the cruise boats are tied up for their lobster bakes. If you want a lobster lunch, try *Cook's Lobster Pound* (☎ 207-833-2818) on ME 24.

BATH

In colonial times, the forested coasts of Maine were thick with tall trees just right for making masts for the king's navy. Indeed, for a time the king forbade anyone to cut the trees in Maine for anything else.

In 1607 the pinnace *Virginia*, among the earliest vessels built by Europeans on this coast, was launched into the Kennebec River at Phippsburg, south of Bath. Later the shipyards on the Kennebec turned to building coastal freighters, then tall clipper ships and grand multi-masted schooners.

Today Bath continues the tradition by building steel frigates, cruisers and other navy craft at the Bath Iron Works (BIW), one of the largest and most active shipyards in the USA. The Maine Maritime Museum, south of the shipyard, is Bath's biggest attraction.

Orientation & Information

The ironworks sprawls to the south of US 1. At 3:30 pm on weekdays, when the workshift changes at the ironworks, US 1 chokes with cars, and traffic throughout the town comes to a virtual halt. It's best to prepare for this, and to be on your way past Bath by 3:15, or be parked downtown for a walk around.

Bath has an attractive small commercial district north of US 1 centered on Front St.

The chamber of commerce information office (☎ 207-443-9751) is at 45 Front St.

Maine Maritime Museum & Shipyard

The Maine Maritime Museum (☎ 207-443-1316), 243 Washington St, south of the ironworks on the western bank of the

Kennebec, preserves the Kennebec's long shipbuilding tradition.

In summer, the preserved 19th-century Percy & Small Shipyard still has boatwrights hard at work building wooden boats. The Maritime History building holds paintings, models and hands-on exhibits that tell the tale of the last 400 years of maritime history. In the Apprenticeshop, boat builders restore and build wooden boats using traditional tools and methods.

A cruise boat called the *Hardy II* takes visitors for a 50-minute ride on the Kennebec in summer.

There's a play ship and picnic area as well as the Mariners' Fare restaurant. The museum is open from 9:30 am to 5 pm. Admission costs $6 for adults, $2.50 kids, $16 family; the river cruise is not included in the price.

Places to Stay

Camping *Ocean View Park Campground* (☎ 207-389-2564), on ME 209 at Popham Beach, is south of Bath at the end of the peninsula near Popham Beach State Park.

B&Bs Bath has a number of reasonably priced B&Bs in nice 19th-century houses.

The *Glad II B&B* (☎ 207-443-1191), 60 Pearl St, Bath, ME 04530, charges $45 for its three double rooms with shared bath.

Packard House (☎ 207-443-6069), a 1790s Georgian house at 45 Pearl St, charges $50 to $80 for double rooms with semi-private bath.

The Front Porch B&B (☎ 207-443-5790), 324 Washington St, costs $55 per night; the Carriage House sleeps four for $75. *The Fairhaven Inn* (☎ 207-443-4391), N Bath Rd near the Bath Country Club, is a bit out of the city center, set on spacious grounds. You pay $50 to $80 for a double with full breakfast.

Five miles south of Bath in Phippsburg, the *Riverview B&B* (☎ 207-389-1124), Church Lane, Phippsburg, ME 04562, charges $30/$40 a single/double with shared bath, $50 for a double with dressing room and private bath.

Getting There & Away

For bus information see the Portland section. Bath is eight miles east of Brunswick, and 10 miles southwest of Wiscasset.

WISCASSET

"Welcome to Wiscasset, the Prettiest Village in Maine." That's what the sign says as you enter Wiscasset from the west along US 1.

Other villages may dispute this claim, but certainly Wiscasset's history as a major shipbuilding port in the 1800s has left it with a legacy of exceptionally grand and beautiful houses.

Like Bath, Wiscasset was a shipbuilding and maritime trading center. Great four-masted schooners set off down the Sheepscot River for England and the West Indies in the Triangle Trade, shipping timber, molasses, rum, salt and salt fish. Two relics of Wiscasset's vanished maritime importance are the wrecked and weather-beaten hulks of the schooners *Hesper* and *Luther Little*. Built to haul lumber to Boston and coal back to Wiscasset, they ran aground in 1932 and have been slowly dissolving in the mud along the Sheepscot's west bank ever since.

Any town with lots of old houses is also liable to have a thriving antiques trade, and Wiscasset does. You can admire the houses and shops as you pass through along US 1 or, better, stop for a meal or a night.

Orientation & Information

The village straddles US 1 and most of it is easily accessible on foot. If you're just passing through by car, you'll still get to see quite a bit of the village as traffic is normally very slow in summer.

The Wiscasset Regional Business Association, PO Box 150, Wiscasset, ME 04578, is the local chamber of commerce.

Things to See

The **Old Jail Museum** (☎ 207-882-6817), on Federal St (Route 218 North) about a half mile north of US 1, is a hilltop structure of granite, brick and wood built in 1811 to house Wiscasset's rowdier citizens. It's now a museum open daily in July and August.

Wiscasset's grandest and best-sited mansion is **Castle Tucker** (☎ 207-882-7364), at High and Lee Sts, a five-minute walk uphill starting opposite the Bailey Inn. Judge Silas Lee had the house built to resemble a mansion in Dunbar, Scotland; he moved into it in 1807, then moved on to that great mansion in the sky a mere seven years later. Acquired by Captain Richard Tucker in 1858, it is still owned by his descendants. The house commands beautiful views which you can enjoy whether you tour the house or not. It's open ($3) in July and August from 11 am to 4 pm (closed Monday), and in June, September and October by request.

On the way from the Bailey Inn to Castle Tucker, stop at the **Musical Wonder House** (☎ 207-882-7163), 16-18 High St, a short walk from the town's central commercial district. It has an outstanding collection of antique music boxes, player pianos and early talking machines displayed in period rooms. Come and listen on a guided tour any day from Memorial Day to October 15, from 10 am to 5 pm; the gift shop stays open until 6 pm.

The **Nickels-Sortwell House** (☎ 207-882-6218), on US 1 at the corner of Federal St (ME 218) just a few steps downhill from the Bailey Inn, is one of the town's finest Federal mansions (1807), open June through September from Wednesday to Sunday afternoons. Tours are given on the hour starting at noon; the last tour is at 4 pm. Admission costs $4, $3.50 for seniors, $2 for kids six to 12.

A half mile south of the eastern end of the bridge over the Sheepscot, **Fort Edgecomb** (☎ 207-882-7157) is an octagonal wooden blockhouse built in 1808-9 to protect the valuable and strategic shipbuilding trade of Wiscasset. Commanding the riverine approach to the town, it is now the area's prime picnic site ($1).

Maine Coast Railroad

Rail service, both for freight and passengers, is slowly being restored on some sections of the old Maine Central Railroad, which used to run from Portland along the coast to Rockland, with a spur up to Augusta.

The Maine Coast Railroad (☎ 207-882-8000, 800-795-5404, fax 563-5261), runs restored 1930s coaches hauled by a diesel locomotive from Wiscasset to Newcastle (40 minutes) and back. A roundtrip rail excursion takes 1½ hours and costs $10 for adults, $5 children five to 12, $9 seniors, $25 for families. Trains depart Wiscasset at 11 am and 1 pm on weekends from late May through mid-June, 11 am, 1 and 3 pm daily in summer, 11 am and 1 pm from early September through mid-October, with an extra 3 pm train on weekends. The station is at Wiscasset Harbor, at the southern end of the town.

Places to Stay

Camping is available at *DownEast Family Camping* (☎ 207-882-5431), with 43 sites four miles north of Wiscasset along ME 27.

Wiscasset Motor Lodge (☎ 207-882-7137, 800-732-8168), on US 1 west of the city center, charges $40 to $60 for its comfy rooms and cottages. A light breakfast is included.

The *Bailey Inn & Restaurant* (☎ 207-882-4214), on US 1 at High St, has comfy guest rooms with bath for $85 including a full breakfast. The cozy tavern dining room is good for any meal, from waffles ($2) to filet mignon ($14). All the sights of Wiscasset are within walking distance.

The *Edgecomb Inn* (☎ 207-882-6343), US 1, Edgecomb, ME 04556, on the east side of the bridge, has inn rooms ($79 to $99), motor lodge suites ($89 to $110) and tidy little frame cottages ($79 to $89) in a pine grove overlooking the river. The inn's Muddy Rudder Restaurant shares the good view.

Places to Eat

Hearty breakfasts are served early (from 6 am) at *The Coffee Shop* (☎ 207-882-7148) on the right side of US 1 as you approach the bridge across the Sheepscot River. The long, homey dining room with flowered wallpaper is crowded straight through lunch time, except in winter, when it closes at noon.

Sarah's Pizza, in the center of town on US 1 at the corner of Middle St, serves its namesake as well as antipasto, spaghetti and meatballs and similar simple fare for $4 to $7 per plate.

Le Garage (☎ 207-882-5409) overlooks the wrecks of the wooden schooners *Hesper* and *Luther Little* from its perch at the end of Water St. This is the place for a filling, reasonably priced lunch ($5 to $10) or dinner ($10 to $25). Try the sautéed Maine shrimp with herbs and garlic ($14), or the finnan haddie (salt cod in a cream sauce). Come for lunch or dinner any day except Monday; Le Bar is open every day in summer.

Getting There & Away

Wiscasset is 10 miles northeast of Bath, seven miles west of Damariscotta, 13 miles north of Boothbay Harbor and 23 miles south of Augusta. For bus transport, see the Portland section.

AUGUSTA

Maine's capital city is small (population 22,000). Founded as a trading post in 1628, it was later abandoned, then resettled in 1724 at Fort Western (later Hallowell). Lumber, shingles, furs and fish were its early exports, sent down the Kennebec River to the world in sloops built right here. Augusta became Maine's capital in 1827, but was only chartered as a city in 1849.

Augustans do the work of government in a rural state, and then head for Portland for excitement.

Information

You can call the Kennebec Valley Chamber of Commerce (☎ 207-623-4559), University Drive, Augusta, ME 04332, with questions.

Things to See & Do

The granite **State House** (capitol) designed, like Boston's, by Charles Bulfinch, was built in 1832, and remodeled and enlarged in 1909-10.

You should have a look at the **Maine State Museum** (☎ 207-289-2301), in the Maine State Library and Archives next to the State House on State St. The museum traces Maine history through an astounding 12,000 years, and includes prehistoric arrowheads and tools as well as artifacts from more recent centuries. It's open every day from 9 am to 5 pm (Saturday from 10 am to 4 pm, Sunday from 1 to 4 pm).

In its own riverside park, **Old Fort Western** (☎ 207-626-2385) is across the river. Originally built as a frontier outpost in 1754, the restored 16-room structure is now a museum. Other sights worth a look include the Blaine House, the family home of US presidential candidate James G Blaine. The house is now Maine's governors' mansion.

Getting There & Away

Augusta, 23 miles north of Wiscasset, is best visited on a day excursion, or while passing through along I-95. Colgan Air (☎ 207-623-1684, 800-272-5488) flies between Augusta and Boston.

BOOTHBAY HARBOR

A beautiful little seafarers' town on a broad fjord-like harbor – that's Boothbay Harbor. Large, well-kept Victorian houses crown its many small hills, and a wooden footbridge ambles across the harbor to the far side.

Cross the Sheepscot River on US 1 from Wiscasset, turn right onto ME 27 and head south to reach Boothbay Harbor.

Boothbay Harbor is a beautiful town, which is why in summer its narrow, winding, hilly streets are choked with cars, and its sidewalks thronged with visitors boarding boats for a coastal cruise or browsing Boothbay's boutiques.

It's definitely a walking town. After you've strolled the waterfront along Commercial St, and the business district along Todd and Townsend Aves, walk to the top of McKown Hill along McKown St for a fine view. Then take the footbridge across the harbor to the town's East Side, where there are several huge seafood restaurants.

MAINE

Orientation

There are several towns with similar names: Boothbay, East Boothbay, etc. Boothbay Harbor is the largest and busiest. Follow ME 27 south to the town, which you will enter along Oak St (one way), which runs into Commercial St, the main street.

Parking can be very difficult in the summer months. It's best to park farther out and shuttle into the city center rather than to get caught in the slow-moving river of cars that flood the narrow, hilly streets.

Information

The Boothbay Chamber of Commerce (☎ 207-633-4743), ME 27, Boothbay, ME 04537, maintains an information office on ME 27 in the town of Boothbay. A short distance to the south along ME 27 is another office run by the Boothbay Harbor Region Chamber of Commerce (☎ 207-633-2353), PO Box 356, Boothbay Harbor, ME 04538.

Boothbay Railway Village

On ME 27 in Boothbay, the Railway

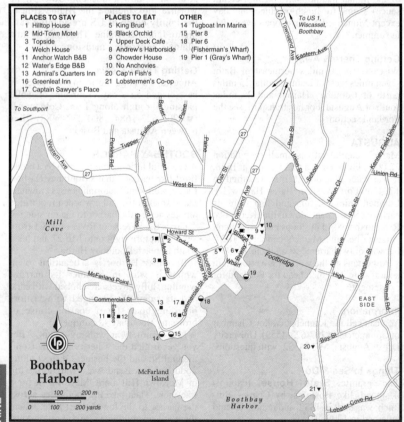

PLACES TO STAY
1 Hilltop House
2 Mid-Town Motel
3 Topside
4 Welch House
11 Anchor Watch B&B
12 Water's Edge B&B
13 Admiral's Quarters Inn
16 Greenleaf Inn
17 Captain Sawyer's Place

PLACES TO EAT
5 King Brud
6 Black Orchid
7 Upper Deck Cafe
8 Andrew's Harborside
9 Chowder House
10 No Anchovies
20 Cap'n Fish's
21 Lobstermen's Co-op

OTHER
14 Tugboat Inn Marina
15 Pier 8
18 Pier 6
　(Fisherman's Wharf)
19 Pier 1 (Gray's Wharf)

To US 1, Wiscasset, Boothbay

To Southport

Mill Cove

West St

Howard St

Boothbay Harbor

0　100　200 m
0　100　200 yards

McFarland Point

Commercial St

McFarland Island

Boothbay Harbor

EAST SIDE

MAINE

Village (☎ 207-633-4727) is a recreated New England village of 27 buildings with a narrow-gauge (two-foot) steam train line running through it. This nonprofit educational park also has a collection of more than 60 antique steam- and gasoline-powered motor vehicles.

Cruises

Boothbay's fine natural harbor features a variety of possibilities for maritime excursions.

You can take a 2½-hour sail-powered cruise aboard the 64-foot windjammer *Appledore* (☎ 207-633-6598) for $20 per person. There are four trips daily in summer departing from Fisherman's Wharf.

The *Bay Lady* (☎ 207-633-2284, 800-298-2284) is a 31-foot friendship sloop, the kind of boat once favored by lobstermen. The *Bay Lady* departs four times daily from Pier 8.

Yankee Clipper (☎ 207-633-4574, 633-4925), an aluminum craft designed for whale watching, departs the Tugboat Inn Marina (100 Commercial St) three times daily in summer. You're guaranteed to see a whale, or you can try again for free. Call for reservations, or buy your tickets from the office at 21 Commercial St. Food and drink are available aboard.

Cap'n Fish's Boat Trips (☎ 207-633-3244, 633-2626), in the red ticket booth at Pier 1, sails a variety of routes along the coast and among the islands in search of whales, puffins, seals and other wildlife. Voyages last from one to three hours. And yes, the owner's name really is Cap'n Bob Fish.

Balmy Days Cruises (☎ 207-633-2284, 800-298-2284) will take you out to Monhegan Island (see separate entry) for a day's visit, leaving after breakfast and returning before supper, for $26 adult, $15 child. They also run one-hour harbor tours ($7 and $4), night lights tours and supper cruises, all from Pier 8.

Places to Stay

Boothbay has campgrounds, motels, inns and B&Bs for every taste.

Camping There are several large campgrounds north of Boothbay Harbor along ME 27. Most campgrounds in the area cater to gigantic land yachts in need of 30-amp electricity and metered LP gas hookups, but all accept tenters as well.

Little Ponderosa Campground (☎ 207-633-2700), on ME 27 six miles north of Boothbay Harbor, has big open fields for games, and 90 campsites ($16 to $20) among tall pine trees, as well as 30 sites along the shore. There's a shuttle bus from the campground into Boothbay Harbor.

Smaller and quieter is *Camper's Cove Campground* (☎ 207-633-5013), 3¼ miles west of Boothbay with 56 sites on Back River Rd. *Gray Homestead* (☎ 207-633-4612), south of Boothbay Harbor in Southport, has 40 sites for $14 to $21.

Motels Boothbay and Boothbay Harbor also have lots of comfortable motels. Those on Townsend Ave (ME 27) north of the town are less expensive than the elaborate places on Atlantic Ave on the east side of the harbor.

Mid-Town Motel (☎ 207-633-2751) is a tidy little place in the very center of town near the intersection of Todd Ave and McKown St. Open from May through October, its simple but adequate rooms rent for $62 double.

Seagate Motel (☎ 207-633-3900, 800-633-1707), 124 Townsend Ave (ME 27), at the entrance to Boothbay Harbor coming from the north, is well kept and not badly located. Rooms have all the comforts, including refrigerators, and cost $70 to $75. A trolley shuttles you to the city center so you don't have to deal with the frightful parking.

The *Howard House B&B Motel* (☎ 207-633-3933, 633-6244), also on Townsend Ave, is modern, attractive, comfortable and reasonably priced at $65 to $80 double in summer, breakfast included.

Inns & B&Bs Boothbay Harbor has dozens of small inns and B&Bs. Some have only two or three rooms, others have up to a dozen. From mid-July through early September, reservations are a must. The chamber of commerce will help you with same-day reservations if you have trouble finding a room.

Hilltop House (☎ 207-633-2941), 44 McKown St, is a homey place renting a few simple rooms near the top of McKown Hill for very reasonable prices: $40 double with shared bath, $50 with private bath. A family unit rents for $60 to $80, depending upon the number of guests.

Sleepy Lobsterman B&B (☎ 207-633-5565), 57 Oak St, is a nice old house north of the Thistle Inn charging $60 double for either of its two rooms with semi-private bath, or $75 for the queen-bed room with private bath. It's a pleasant five-minute walk to the city center.

Atop McKown Hill, *Topside* (☎ 207-633-5404) has unparalleled views of the town and the harbor. The 30 rooms, in the original sea captain's house or adjoining motel, cost $50 to $95 in summer. All have private baths and refrigerators.

Welch House (☎ 207-633-3431), 36 McKown St, is another charming inn with fine views. All 16 rooms have private baths.

Captain Sawyer's Place (☎ 207-633-2290), 87 Commercial St, is the big yellow house overlooking the harbor right in the midst of everything. All rooms have private bath, and the captain's suite ($95) has its own deck. Rooms at the back without the sea view cost $60, those in the front $85.

Right next to Captain Sawyer's Place, the *Greenleaf Inn* (☎ 207-633-7346), 91 Commercial St, is similarly priced. The five rooms have private baths.

Admiral's Quarters Inn (☎ 207-633-2474), 105 Commercial St, is a large clapboard house on the side of McKown Hill overlooking Commercial St and the harbor. Built about 1820, the house has 20 rooms; the two-room suites rent for $85; single rooms cost $70. A light breakfast is included.

Anchor Watch B&B (☎ 207-633-7565), 3 Eames Rd, and *Water's Edge B&B* (☎ 207-633-4251), 8 Eames Rd, are at the western end of Commercial St, past Sea St,

right out on Signal Point. Water's Edge (six rooms for $65 to $90) has the best views; Anchor Watch (four rooms for $75 to $95) is the more interesting building. Both enjoy a superb location.

If you don't mind staying outside of town, there are several very fine choices.

The village of East Boothbay, two miles from Boothbay Harbor, is not as touristy or commercialized as Boothbay Harbor. It's a lot more like the real Maine. The *Sailmaker's Inn* (☎ 207-633-7390, in winter 501-925-2930), on ME 96 at Church St, East Boothbay, ME 04544, is a fine, cupola-topped Victorian charging $75 to $90 for its two rooms with private bath, breakfast included. *Five Gables Inn* (☎ 207-633-4551, 800-451-5048), Murray Hill Rd, just off ME 96, is a 125-year-old summer hotel with wraparound porch and 15 rooms with private bath for $80 to $115 double, breakfast included.

The *Lawnmeer Inn* (☎ 207-633-2544, 800-633-7645), PO Box 505, West Boothbay Harbor, ME 04575, is on Southport Island southwest of Boothbay Harbor on ME 27. The nice old inn set on spacious lawns is at the water's edge but away from it all. Rooms cost $54 to $110 in summer and have private baths.

Places to Eat

Most Boothbay Harbor restaurants are open from early May through mid-October.

King Brud has been selling hot dogs ($1) in the center of Boothbay Harbor for over 50 years. You'll see his cart at the corner of McKown and Oak Sts any day in summer. Veterans, ladies and others who ask politely may get a free autographed King Brud color picture postcard.

Andrew's Harborside (☎ 207-633-4704), just down Townsend St toward the footbridge, has country-style chicken pie for $10, scallops for $14, lots of sandwiches and great views of the traffic on the footbridge. If you'd rather have something lighter (and cheaper), the adjoining *Upper Deck Cafe* has a long sandwich and salad menu ($6 to $10) and some water views.

Walk down the hill and toward the foot-

Cape Neddick, The Yorks, ME

Cracking crab

Acadia National Park, ME

KIM GRANT
Maine blueberry harvest

KIM GRANT
New Harbor, ME

KIM GRANT
Lobster Pound, Seal Harbor, ME

TOM BROSNAHAN
Boothbay Harbor, ME

KIM GRANT
Pemaquid Point Light, ME

bridge, but before reaching the bridge bear left through the parking lot to find the rough-board *Chowder House* (☎ 207-633-5761), fraught with nautical paraphernalia and serving gallons of its namesake daily. A simple chowder-based lunch can be had for about $5, a more elaborate tuck-in for three or four times as much.

Right nearby, *No Anchovies* (☎ 207-633-2130) serves Italian cuisine at moderate prices, and anchovies are available if you really want them.

The *Black Orchid* (☎ 207-633-6659), 5 Byway, is Boothbay's fancy bistro, serving pasta primavera, mushrooms Gorgonzola and lobster fra diavolo in attractive modern dining rooms. There's a raw bar and an airy deck. Dinner is served every night except Tuesday, and costs about $30 to $40.

Lobster Dinners On the east side of the bay, the *Lobstermen's Co-Op* (☎ 207-633-4900), on Atlantic Ave, serves the traditional shore dinners of steamed soft-shell clams, boiled lobster and corn on the cob for $14 to $20, depending upon

the seasonal price of the catch. This is an informal place with lots of outdoor seating. *Cap'n Fish's*, also on Atlantic Ave, is similar. For a full sit-down restaurant, also with outdoor tables, try the *Lobsterman's Wharf* (☎ 207-633-3443) on ME 96 in East Boothbay.

To get the full nautical ambiance, have a *Clambake at Cabbage Island* (☎ 207-633-7200). You sail out of Boothbay Harbor from Pier 6 at Fisherman's Wharf aboard the motor vessel *Argo*. When you arrive at Cabbage Island, the captain and crew prepare a traditional clambake with steamed lobsters and clams, clam chowder, corn on the cob, onions and Maine potatoes, followed by Maine blueberry cake and coffee. Voyages depart Monday through Friday at 12:30 and 5 pm, Sunday at 11:30 am and 1:30 pm, returning about four hours later, from late June through early September. The cost is under $40 per person, all included.

Getting There & Away

Driving details for Boothbay Harbor are:

Destination	Mileage	Hr:Min
Bar Harbor, ME	125 miles	2:45
Boston, MA	167 miles	4:00
Camden, ME	48 miles	1:10
Freeport, ME	43 miles	1:00
Portland, ME	59 miles	1:20
Wiscasset, ME	13 miles	0:25

DAMARISCOTTA

Damariscotta is a pretty Maine town with numerous fine churches and an attractive downtown commercial district that serves the smaller towns and villages of the Pemaquid Peninsula to the south.

West of the town center on US 1 is a tourist information center run by the Damariscotta Region Information Bureau (☎ 207-563-3176). Follow US 1B ("Business") to reach the center of town. There's another tourism information office run by the Damariscotta Region Chamber of Commerce (☎ 207-563-8340) at the southern end of town just after ME 129/130 goes off to the right. Try also the Maine Coast Book Shop (☎ 207-563-3207) on Main St.

KIM GRANT

Pemaquid Point Light

PEMAQUID PENINSULA

ME 130 goes south from Damariscotta through the heart of the Pemaquid Peninsula to Pemaquid Neck, the southernmost part of the peninsula. On the west side of Pemaquid Neck are Pemaquid Beach and Fort William Henry, a relic of the colonial period. At the southern tip of Pemaquid Neck is Pemaquid Point, one of the most beautiful, atmospheric places in Maine.

Pemaquid Beach & Trail

Yes! There are a few stretches of sand beach along this rockbound coast, and Pemaquid Beach is one of them. As ME 130 approaches Pemaquid Neck, watch for signs to the right (west) for Pemaquid Beach along Huddle Rd or Snowball Hill Rd.

The beach is set in a park and both are open in summer for a small fee. The water is usually very cold for swimming. This is Maine.

The Pemaquid Trail, a paved dead-end road, heads south from Snowball Hill Rd just east of the Pemaquid Beach access road.

Fort William Henry

A quarter mile north of Pemaquid Beach are the remains of Fort William Henry, a reconstructed circular stone fort with commanding views (off to the left as you enter),

many old foundations, an old burial ground with interesting tombstones, an archeological dig and a small museum ($2 for adults, 50¢ for kids five to 11, seniors free).

English explorers set foot on this spot early in the 1600s: then Weymouth in 1605, Popham in 1607. But France claimed the land as well because the great Samuel de Champlain had been here (1605). Captain John Smith came for a look around in 1614. By the 1620s there was a thriving settlement here with a Customs House.

The first fortress to be built, Fort Pemaquid, was overcome and looted by pirates in 1632. Its replacement, Fort Charles, fell to the French and Indians, allied at the time, in 1689. Fort William Henry (1689), equally luckless, fell to a French force led by Baron de Castine. The fort was later restored and renamed Fort Frederick (1729). The Old Fort House, nearby, was built about this time and still stands.

Pemaquid Point

Along a 3500-mile coastline famed for its natural beauty, Pemaquid Point stands out because of its tortured, grainy igneous rock formations pounded by restless, treacherous seas.

Perched atop the rocks in Lighthouse Park ($1 for adults, 50¢ for seniors) is the 11,000-candlepower Pemaquid Light, built in 1827. It's one of the 61 surviving lighthouses along the Maine coast, 52 of which are still in operation. The keeper's house now serves as the Fishermen's Museum at Pemaquid Point, open from 10 am to 5 pm (from 11 am on Sunday; donations accepted). Lighthouse and fishing paraphernalia are on display, and there's a nautical chart of the entire Maine coast with all the lighthouses marked, and photographs of many.

By all means take photographs here at Pemaquid. But also take a few minutes to fix the view in your mind, as no photo can do justice to its wild beauty. If you clamber over the rocks beneath the light, do so with great care. Big waves sweep in unexpectedly, and tourists are swept back out with them periodically, ending their Maine

MAINE

vacations in a sudden, dramatic and fearfully permanent manner.

Places to Stay & Eat
Pemaquid Beach *Sherwood Forest Campsite & Log Cabins* (☎ 207-677-3642), PO Box 189, New Harbor, ME 04554, is on the Pemaquid Trail about a quarter mile from Pemaquid Beach. Tent and RV sites cost $14 to $18. There's a swimming pool, and they'll sell you live lobsters and clams for your own private clambake.

Right in between Pemaquid Beach and Fort William Henry, the *Apple Tree Inn* (☎ 207-677-3491), on Snowball Hill Rd, is a cozy yellow Cape Cod cottage with three guest rooms (one with a fireplace) priced from $55 to $70. It's open all year; no credit cards are accepted.

Right next to Fort William Henry, with sweeping views of the water, is the *Pemaquid Chart House Restaurant*, good for a drink or a meal.

Pemaquid Point The *Hotel Pemaquid* (☎ 207-677-2312), HC 61, Box 421, New Harbor, ME 04554, a hundred yards from Lighthouse Park, is a century-old frame hotel with a grand front porch, period guest rooms and housekeeping cottages priced from $44 to $125, depending upon the room and the season.

The *Bradley Inn* (☎ 207-677-2105), 361 Pemaquid Point, New Harbor, ME 04554, a few hundred yards inland, has 12 luxury rooms decorated with Victorian and nautical antiques priced from $85 to $140, as well as a restaurant and pub.

If you need refreshments, the *Sea Gull Restaurant and Gift Shop* (☎ 207-677-2374) is right next to the lighthouse park, serving breakfast, lunch and dinner with those same beautiful views.

THOMASTON & PORT CLYDE
Once among the wealthiest communities in New England, Thomaston's wooden shipbuilding business faded away with the coming of ironclads. The town's stately homes dating from the mid-1800s have fallen into dowdiness, though it's still possible to imagine their former glory.

Just east of Thomaston, ME 131 goes south from US 1 to St George, Tenants Harbor and Port Clyde.

The village of Port Clyde is the mainland port for the Monhegan Boat Company's (☎ 207-372-8848) vessels to Monhegan Island (see below).

MONHEGAN ISLAND
This rocky outcrop off the Maine coast due south of Port Clyde is a popular goal for summer excursions. The small island (1½ miles long by a half mile wide) was known to Basque and Portuguese fishers and mariners even before the English cruised these waters, but it came into its own as a summer resort around the turn of the century. When the great cities of the eastern seaboard were sweltering in summer's heat, cool sea breezes bathed Monhegan and those fortunate enough to have taken refuge here.

Early in its history as a resort it became popular with artists, who admired its dramatic views and agreeable isolation. The island village is small and very limited in its services.

Adding to the island's Victorian charm is the near-total absence of motor vehicles. The island is really too small to need many cars; the ones it has for essential jobs are few and old. Thus Monhegan is laid out for walking, with 17 miles of trails.

Unless you've made reservations well in advance at one of the island's few lodgings, you cannot plan on finding a room upon arrival. Plan to take a day excursion from Port Clyde or Boothbay Harbor, and allow yourself at least half a day (four hours or more) to walk the trails over the rocks and around the shore. Stop at the **lighthouse** (1824) for a look at the museum set up in the keeper's former house.

Places to Stay & Eat
The *Island Inn* (☎ 207-596-0371, 800-722-1269), Monhegan Island, ME 04852, is a typical Victorian mansard-roofed summer hotel with 45 small, simple rooms, eight of

them with private bath. The big front porch offers marvelous views, and the dining room provides three meals a day. Breakfast and dinner are included in the room rates of $112 to $154. Reserve early in the spring for dates in July and August.

Tribler Cottage (☎ 207-594-2445) has one room with bath and four efficiency apartments (room with kitchen and bath) priced from $55 to $90 double.

Other accommodations on the island include the *Monhegan House* (☎ 207-594-7983), *The Trailing Yew* (☎ 207-596-0440), *Shining Sails* (☎ 207-596-0041) and the *Hitchcock House* (☎ 207-594-8137).

Getting There & Away
From Port Clyde The Monhegan Boat Company's (☎ 207-372-8848) vessels to Monhegan Island depart Port Clyde, south of Thomaston, year round, with schedules and fares varying according to the season. You must make advance reservations to journey on these boats.

In high summer there are four trips daily departing Port Clyde at 7 and 10:30 am, and 1:30 and 4:30 pm; return trips depart Monhegan at 9 am and noon, and 3 and 6 pm. The first voyage of the day takes 70 minutes, the later ones, in the *Laura B*, take 50 minutes. The roundtrip fare is $24 for adults, $12 for children 12 and under. Parking in Port Clyde costs $4 per day.

From New Harbor The motor vessel *Hardy III* (☎ 207-677-2026) departs New Harbor, on the east side of the Pemaquid Peninsula, at 9 am daily during the warm months bound for Monhegan. It returns to New Harbor at 4 pm. The roundtrip fare is $26 for adults, $15 for children under 12; parking is free.

From Boothbay Harbor You can also visit Monhegan on a day excursion from Boothbay Harbor aboard one of the boats run by Balmy Days Cruises. See the Harbor Cruises entry in Boothbay Harbor for details.

Acadia National Park Region

The best-known feature of the coastal area south of Bangor is Acadia National Park, the only US national park in New England. Acadia is the centerpiece of the region which is quintessentially Maine: "Downeast."

Penobscot Bay, to the west of Acadia, is world-famous for its yachting ports of Camden, Rockport and Rockland, from which tall-masted windjammers take passengers on cruises of the beautiful coast. Blue Hill Bay and Frenchman Bay frame Mt Desert Island, a choice summer resort area for a century, and now the center of Acadia National Park.

To the east of Acadia, the coast of Downeast Maine is less traveled but all the more scenic and unspoiled, all the way to the town of Lubec where Maine, USA, meets New Brunswick, Canada.

ROCKLAND
Rockland was the birthplace of poet Edna St Vincent Millay (1892-1950), who grew up in neighboring Camden. Today Rockland is, with Camden, at the center of Maine's busy windjammer sailing business. Windjammers, the tall-masted sailing ships descended from those long built on these shores, cruise up and down the Maine coast in summer to the delight of their paying passengers. For details on windjammer cruises and places to stay in the area, see the Camden section below.

Farnsworth Art Museum
Rockland is also famous for its Farnsworth Art Museum (☎ 207-596-6457), on Elm St, one of the best small regional museums in the country. Its collection of 5000 works is especially strong in landscape and marine artists who have worked in Maine such as NC, Andrew and Jamie Wyeth; Louise Nevelson; Rockwell Kent and others. The

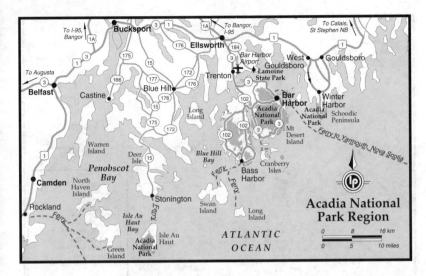

Acadia National Park Region

museum is open daily from 10 am to 5 pm (Sunday from 1 to 5 pm) in summer, closed on Monday off-season.

Getting There & Away

Air Rockland is served by Colgan Air (☎ 207-596-7604, 800-272-5488), a regional carrier, via their route from Boston to Bar Harbor.

Bus Concord Trailways (☎ 800-639-3317) runs buses from Boston and Logan Airport via Portland to Rockland, terminating right at the Maine State Ferry Service docks for boats to Vinalhaven. The trip from Boston to Rockland takes 4½ hours.

Car Driving details for Rockland are:

Destination	Mileage	Hr:Min
Camden, ME	8 miles	0:15
Damariscotta, ME	26 miles	0:40
Port Clyde, ME	19 miles	0:45
Portland, ME	81 miles	2:00

Boat Rockland is the port for the Maine State Ferry Service (☎ 207-596-2203) to the islands of Vinalhaven and North Haven. Ferries depart Rockland three times daily year round on the one-hour trip to North Haven; six times daily from April through October, with at least three boats for Vinalhaven daily at other times of the year.

CAMDEN

Home to Maine's large and justly famed fleet of windjammers (sailing ships), Camden continues its historic close links with the sea. Most vacationers come to sail on their boats, or on somebody else's boats, or just to look at boats. But Camden is a pretty town in its own right, worth a stop or an overnight whether you plan to sail or not. Camden Hills State Park, adjoining the town to the north, has hiking, picnicking and camping.

Like many communities along the Maine coast, Camden has a long history of shipbuilding. The mammoth six-masted schooner *George W Wells* was built here, setting the world record for masts on a sailing ship.

Camden was the girlhood home of Edna St Vincent Millay (1892-1950), one of America's most popular poets during the

MAINE

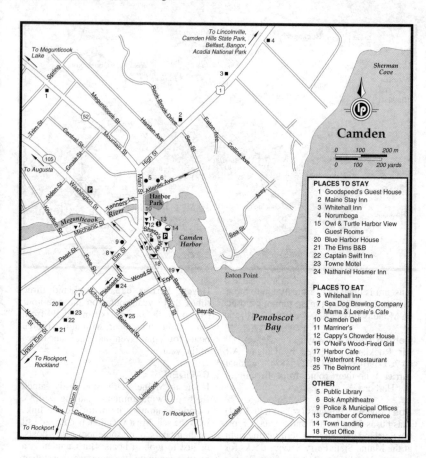

To Lincolnville,
Camden Hills State Park,
Belfast, Bangor,
Acadia National Park

To Megunticook
Lake

To Augusta

To Rockport,
Rockland

To Rockport

To Rockport

Sherman
Cove

Camden

0   100   200 m
0   100   200 yards

Harbor
Park

Megunticook
River

Camden
Harbor

Eaton Point

Penobscot
Bay

PLACES TO STAY
1   Goodspeed's Guest House
2   Maine Stay Inn
3   Whitehall Inn
4   Norumbega
15 Owl & Turtle Harbor View
     Guest Rooms
20 Blue Harbor House
21 The Elms B&B
22 Captain Swift Inn
23 Towne Motel
24 Nathaniel Hosmer Inn

PLACES TO EAT
3   Whitehall Inn
7   Sea Dog Brewing Company
8   Mama & Leenie's Cafe
10 Camden Deli
11 Marriner's
12 Cappy's Chowder House
16 O'Neil's Wood-Fired Grill
17 Harbor Cafe
19 Waterfront Restaurant
25 The Belmont

OTHER
5   Public Library
6   Bok Amphitheatre
9   Police & Municipal Offices
13 Chamber of Commerce
14 Town Landing
18 Post Office

first half of this century. Camden figures in some of the poet's work, as in these lines from *Renascence*:

All I could see from where I stood
Was three long mountains and a wood;
I turned and looked another way,
and saw three islands in a bay.

She later lived in Provincetown, MA, and New York City.

Camden is beautiful, and the windjammers are romantic and upscale, attracting a well-to-do crowd. Thus Camden's prices

for lodgings and food during the summer are higher than in less posh Maine communities.

Orientation

US 1 snakes its way through Camden, and is the town's main street, named Elm St to the south, Main St in the center and High St to the north. Though the downtown section is easily walkable, it is several miles from one end of town to the other. Some accommodations are up to 15 minutes' walk from the center of town.

Information

The Rockport, Camden & Lincolnville Chamber of Commerce (☎ 207-236-4404), PO Box 919, Camden, ME 04843, has an information office on the waterfront at the public landing in Camden, behind Cappy's Chowder House.

The Owl & Turtle Bookshop (☎ 207-236-4769) is the place to stop for books.

Windjammer Cruises

Camden is at the center of windjammer cruise country. Many boats dock at Rockport and Rockland as well.

Cruise itineraries vary with the ship, the weather and the length of the cruise.

Daysailers These are boats that take passengers out for two- to four-hour cruises in Penobscot Bay. Usually you can book your place on a daysailer the same day, even the same hour. Try these, which depart from Camden's Town Landing or adjoining Sharp's Wharf:

Olad
  (☎ 207-236-2323), $15 per adult (kids six to 12, $10) for a two-hour sail
Appledore
  (☎ 207-236-8353), $20 per adult for two hours
Surprise
  (☎ 207-236-4687), $25 per adult, includes snacks; no children under 12 are accepted

Overnighters A few boats, such as the schooner *Wendameen* (☎ 207-236-3472), take passengers out for a day and a night. The *Wendameen* charges $143 per person, all meals included, for this good taste of a Maine coastal cruise.

All about Windjammers

Windjammer Facts A windjammer is an ocean-going sailing ship such as a schooner, ketch or yacht, usually 60 to 135 feet in length, with two or three masts. These graceful vessels crowd the coves and harbors around Rockland, Rockport and Camden in summer, waiting for passengers for cruises. They are sometimes joined by several motor-powered yachts which, though not windjammers, make comparable cruises.

A windjammer normally sleeps between 20 and 45 passengers in single, double, triple and quad cabins. Many have sinks with hot and cold water. Showers are usually shared.

Passengers dine aboard and the prices for cruises usually include all three meals. Often one of these meals is a traditional clam or lobster bake on a coastal island.

Seasickness is rarely a problem on windjammer cruises as the ships sail mostly in protected waters, without the heavy wave action of vessels on the high seas.

Windjammers welcome passengers of all ages, except for young children. Usually a child must be at least 10 or 12 years of age to sail on a cruise.

When to Cruise The cruising season actually starts on Memorial Day weekend, the last in May, and continues right through the autumn foliage season.

The month of **June** is good because the days are very long, the harbors uncrowded, the fog rare and light and the rates low. However, days can be cool and nights even chilly. Forget swimming, unless you're a polar bear.

Then **July** is warmer, with daytime temperatures in the 70°s F; cruise rates are highest in July and August.

In **August**, the sea water gets as warm as it's going to, as does the air. Rates are at their highest and ports at their busiest, but when city dwellers are sweltering, cruisers are cool and happy.

After early **September** the coastline begins to show signs of autumn color. Days are shorter, rates are lower and the crowds have gone. The weather in early September can be as good as in August, with luck.

In **October** you can count on the shortest days, coolest weather, coldest water, but best foliage color and lowest rates of the season. The season usually ends after the Columbus Day weekend in mid-October. ■

Three to Six Days Longer cruises last from three to six days. Many six-day cruises visit points along the Maine coast from Boothbay Harbor in the southwest to Mt Desert Island (Acadia National Park) in the northeast. Stops may be made at Stonington, at the tip of Deer Isle; at the village of Castine; at various small islands offshore and at points in and around Acadia National Park.

Three-day cruises cover less of the coast, but are still delightful. There are numerous sail and motor craft offering day cruises as well.

Many three- to six-day cruises are priced from $300 to $700 per person, accommodations and all meals on board included.

Reservations are a must for overnight cruises. For detailed information on the various vessels available, contact these offices:

Maine Windjammer Association
  (☎ 207-374-2955, 800-807-9463,
  fax 207-374-5272), PO Box 1144,
  Blue Hill, ME 04614
Windjammer Wharf
  (☎ 800-999-7352), PO Box 1050,
  Rockland, ME 04841
North End Shipyard Schooners
  (☎ 207-594-8007, 800-648-4544,
  fax 207-594-8015), PO Box 482,
  Rockland, ME 04841

Other Cruises

You can take a two-hour lobster-fishing trip on the *Lively Lady* (☎ 207-236-6672), for $12 ($5 for kids under 15), from Sharp's Wharf.

To cruise the coast under your own speed, contact the Mt Pleasant Canoe & Kayak Co (☎ 207-785-4309), in West Rockport, to rent a sea-touring canoe or kayak for $65 a day, $35 a half-day, $30 for a sunset paddle.

Ducktrap Sea Kayak Tours (☎ 207-789-5950), at The Spouter Inn on US 1 in Lincolnville, will take you on a 2½-hour harbor tour by sea kayak for $25/40 single/double, or full-day trips for $50/80. Call for reservations.

Camden Hills State Park

The park, with an entrance just over 1½ miles northeast of Camden center, has an extensive system of well-marked hiking trails, from the half-mile, 45-minute climb up Mt Battie to the three-mile, two-hour Ski Shelter Trail.

Admission to the park costs $2 for adults, 50¢ for kids five to 12. Simple trail maps are available at the park entrance. The picnic area is on the south side of US 1, with short trails down to the shore.

Places to Stay

Camping *Camden Hills State Park* (☎ 207-236-3109) has a camping area with hot showers, flush toilets and 112 forested tent and RV sites (no hookups) for $15 each. Reservations are advised for high summer. A few sites are unreservable and are held on a first-come, first-served basis. Plan to arrive by lunch time to claim one.

If the park is full (as it often is), try *Megunticook by the Sea* (☎ 207-594-2428, 800-884-2428), three miles south of Camden off US 1, which rents sites for $15 to $22. There's also *Robert's Roost Campground* (☎ 207-236-2498), two miles west of Rockport on ME 90, charging $10 to $15 for a site.

The *Old Massachusetts Homestead Campground* (☎ 207-789-5135) is seven miles north of Camden on US 1 at Lincolnville Beach. The 60-acre forested site includes rental cabins with decks and private baths, as well as 68 sites for tents and RVs starting at $15.

Farther to the north, *Searsport Shores Camping Resort* (☎ /fax 207-548-6059), a mile south of Searsport on US 1, with 70 RV sites in a waterfront location. Rates range from $13 for a tent to $25 for a humongous motorhome.

Motels & Hotels Most of the area's motels are along US 1. There's a particularly large concentration in Lincolnville Beach, the next town to the north of Camden. Rates range from $30 for the cheapest places off-season, to about $100 for the choicest rooms in-season.

Birchwood Motel & Cottages (☎ 207-236-4204), Belfast Rd (US 1) north of Camden, has 16 motel rooms for $60 to $70.

Towne Motel (☎ 207-236-3377), 68 Elm St, has 18 rooms priced from $75 to $100, light breakfast included, right in the center of town.

Inns & B&Bs Camden has over 100 places to stay, most of them small inns or B&Bs priced from $75 to over $300 for a double room. If you want help in making reservations, call Camden Accommodations & Reservations (☎ 207-236-6090, 800-236-1920), PO Box 858, Camden, ME 04843. Like travel agents, they don't charge you for this service; the inns and hotels pay a commission to Camden Accommodations.

Goodspeed's Guest House (☎ 207-236-8077), 60 Mountain St (ME 52), a half mile uphill from the city center, has nine nicely decorated rooms, four with bath, for $50 to $85, breakfast included.

Owl & Turtle Harbor View Guest Rooms (☎ 207-236-9014), 8 Bayview St, has three rooms above the Owl & Turtle Bookstore overlooking the harbor, for $75 to $85 with bath. This is a great deal.

Elm St (US 1) just south of the city center has a number of nice B&Bs.

Captain Swift Inn (☎ 207-236-8113), 72 Elm St, is an 1810 Federal house with four rooms, all with bath, for $65 to $85, breakfast included.

Blue Harbor House (☎ 207-236-3196, 800-2348-3196), 67 Elm St, is a cozy New England Cape Cod-style house built in 1810 with 10 guest rooms, all with private baths, for $85 to $125, breakfast included.

The Elms B&B (☎ 207-236-6250), 84 Elm St, built in 1806, has three rooms with bath and breakfast for $75 to $100.

Bread & Roses Inn & Bakery (☎ 207-236-6116), 297 Commercial St (US 1) at Beech, between Camden and Rockport, is just what its name says: a B&B in an 1860s farmhouse, with a bakery open to the public from noon to 5 pm. Its seven rooms (three with bath) go for $50 to $80.

Maine Stay Inn (☎ 207-236-9636) is a fine Greek Revival house and carriage house at 22 High St. The eight guest rooms, four with bath, cost $75 to $110, full breakfast included.

Nathaniel Hosmer Inn (☎ 207-236-4012, 800-423-4012), 4 Pleasant St, is a block off the main street in a quiet residential neighborhood. The seven rooms, five with bath, rent for $80 to $140, full breakfast included.

Whitehall Inn (☎ 207-236-3391, 800-789-6565), 52 High St, has an old-time proper New England ambiance behind the Ionic columns on its broad front porch. Most of the 50 rooms in the main inn, the Maine House, and the Wicker House have private baths, and are priced from $70 to $170. Breakfast and dinner are served in the elegant dining room.

A listing of Camden lodgings would not be complete without a mention of *Norumbega* (☎ 207-236-4646), 61 High St, a fantastic, castle-like stone Victorian mansion with a dozen rooms renting from $195 to $425. The inn's brochure uses such words as "exceptional," "sumptuous" and "magnificent," which, for the price, it should be – and is.

Places to Eat
As in its lodgings, so in its restaurants: Camden prices tend to be higher than in most other towns.

The town's old reliable fish house is *Cappy's Chowder House* (☎ 207-236-2254), 1 Main St, at Bayview, right in the very center of town. The long menu lists just about everything, from sandwiches and light meals to hearty tuck-ins, but chowders ($3 to $8) and fish plates ($10 to $20) are the specialties.

Another good place out of the downtown bustle, with a view of the water, is the *Harbor Cafe* (☎ 207-236-6011), 3 Sharp's Way, off Bayview St. All three meals consist of locally grown and baked ingredients, many organic. Hummus with homemade bread is a great light lunch ($3.50). In the evening the international menu lists Maine lobster, enchiladas, fajitas and pad thai for $8 to $14.

MAINE

Just down the street in the midst of the shopping district is *Marriner's* (☎ 207-236-2647), 35 Main St, an old-fashioned inexpensive lunchroom serving a big fish and chips plate for $6, a bowl of chili with biscuits and salad for $5, and a huge plate of fried clams with potato, salad, bread and butter for $10.

For a picnic down by the water or atop Mt Battie, pick up a substantial sandwich at the *Camden Deli* (☎ 207-236-8343), 37 Main St. Sandwiches are priced from $3.60 to $6; there are several vegetarian choices.

The quaint *Mama & Leenie's Cafe* (☎ 236-6300), 27 Elm St, across from the flagpole park, opens at 7 am with down-home charm and serves breakfast all day (try Eggs in a Frame), excellent pies, strong coffee and lots of sandwiches for around $5.50. Dine on the hidden patio in good weather.

O'Neil's Wood-Fired Grill (☎ 207-236-3272), 21 Bayview St, has a good menu of salads, sandwiches and wood-grilled burgers, pizzas and calzones for $6 to $8. Fancier dinner plates go up to $15. This is a good value.

Waterfront Restaurant (☎ 207-236-3747), on Bayview, has atmospheric waterfront dining rooms and a spacious deck right next to the boats. Try the salade Niçoise ($8) for a light lunch, or the Penobscot Bay seafood platter (clams, crabs, lobster, etc) for $16. There's a raw bar for fresh clams and oysters as well. Lunch is served from 11:30 am to 2:30 pm, dinner from 5 to 10 pm.

Several of Camden's inns have fine dining rooms serving fancy fare. Try the *Whitehall Inn* (☎ 207-236-3391) for an excellent dinner in formal surroundings for $30 to $60 per person; or Jerry Clare's *The Belmont* (☎ 207-236-8053), at 6 Belmont Ave, serving "late 20th-century cuisine in late 19th-century surroundings."

Entertainment

The *Sea Dog Brewing Company* (☎ 207-236-6863), 43 Mechanic St in the Knox Mill, is a spacious restaurant/pub/nightspot serving sophisticated bar food ($5 to $10) and locally made beer, brown and pale ales. One lofty wall, all glass, looks out on the crashing waterfall of the old mill race. This is one of Camden's coolest places to see and be seen.

Getting There & Away

Driving details for Camden are:

Destination	Mileage	Hr:Min
Bangor, ME	53 miles	1:15
Bar Harbor, ME	77 miles	1:45
Boothbay, ME	48 miles	1:10
Boston, MA	195 miles	4:00
Portland, ME	85 miles	2:00

Getting Around

Fred's Bikes (☎ 207-236-6664), 53 Chestnut St, across from the YMCA, rents bikes for $15 a day, $9 a half day; they can rent other biking paraphernalia such as kid's seats and trailers as well. They'll deliver the bike to your B&B or motel for free.

BELFAST & SEARSPORT

Motels, campgrounds, restaurants, antique shops and flea markets dot the road north of Camden near Belfast and Searsport, providing dining, lodging and shopping opportunities. The establishments along here are considerably cheaper, and more likely to have vacancies in high summer, than comparable tourist meccas such as Camden, Blue Hill and Bar Harbor.

BUCKSPORT

A crossroads for highways and rail lines, Bucksport is a workaday town with light industry and a big Champion paper mill. There are numerous motels, restaurants and other services. The Bucksport Chamber of Commerce has an information office (☎ 207-469-6818) next to the municipal offices in the center of town.

Fort Knox

Just out of town on the west side of the river is the Fort Knox State Historic Site (☎ 207-469-7719), on ME 174 just north of the bridge. This huge granite fortress dominating the Penobscot River narrows comes as a surprise in peaceable rural Maine, but only until you learn the spot's history.

This part of the Penobscot River Valley was the riverine gateway to Bangor, the commercial heart of Maine's rich timber industry. It was held by the British in the Revolutionary War and the War of 1812.

In 1839 it appeared that the US and the UK might once again go to war over the disputed boundary between Maine and New Brunswick, and the US government feared that Bangor might once again fall into British hands. To protect the river approach to Bangor, construction was begun on Fort Knox in July of 1844. Work continued for almost a decade.

The elaborate fortress mounted 64 cannons, with an additional 69 defending the outer perimeter. Though it was garrisoned from 1863 to 1866 during the Civil War, and in 1898 during the Spanish-American War, it never had to use its firepower. Fort Knox was either a great waste of money or an effective deterrent, depending on your point of view.

Like so many of the world's elaborate military constructions, it is now a tourist attraction, open from 9 am to sunset in summer, to 6:30 pm in spring and autumn. Admission costs $2 for adults, 50¢ for kids five to 12, and is free to toddlers and those 65+. Bring a flashlight if you plan a close examination, as the fort's granite chambers are unlit. There's a nice picnic area outside the admissions gate.

CASTINE

At Orland, a few miles east of Bucksport along US 1, ME 175/166 goes south to the dignified and historic seaside village of Castine. Following an eventful history, Castine today is charming, quiet and refreshingly off the beaten track. It's the home of the Maine Maritime Academy and its big training ship, the *State of Maine* (1952), which you can visit.

Both Castine and Blue Hill are good places to get the feel of pre-tourist boom

Maine – these are gorgeous villages with none of the kitsch you might find in Boothbay or Bar Harbor.

History

It was the great French explorer Samuel de Champlain who first mapped the peninsula which was then called Pentagoët.

His countryman, Sieur Claude de Turgis de la Tour, founded Fort Pentagoët here in 1613. His goal was to trade with the Tarratine Indians of the region, which he did until the English came and conquered this part of the Maine coast in 1628, renaming Pentagoët as Majabagaduce. The village was back in French hands in 1635, put there by treaty, but it was to change hands many times between then and 1674, when the Dutch took it for two years.

In 1676 Jean Vincente d'Abbadie de St Castin, the second son of a French nobleman, claimed the land after military service in Québec and re-opened the trading station. He maintained excellent relations with the Native Americans, moving upriver to live with them and marrying the daughter of the Tarratine Sagamore Madockawando. Castin returned to France in 1701 to claim the baronial title left vacant by his older brother's death.

By 1760, however, the British ruled throughout the former French lands, and "Castin's Fort" was in their hands.

During the Revolutionary War, Bagaduce's citizens were split between those loyal to the British crown and those supporting the American cause. In 1779, a British naval force from Nova Scotia occupied the town and built a fortress, taunting the Americans by naming it Fort George. They hoped to force the fledgling US to set its northern boundary here, at the Penobscot River, leaving eastern Maine to the crown.

Rising to the challenge, the Great and General Court (legislature) of the Commonwealth of Massachusetts, which then controlled Maine, outfitted the Penobscot Expedition force at the enormous cost of $8 million and sent it off to take Fort George. Bad leadership and bad luck doomed the expeditionary force to ignominious defeat, and the Commonwealth to near-bankruptcy. The Brits held on.

What bullets could not claim, diplomacy gained, however. The Treaty of Paris that ended the Revolutionary War set the boundary at the St Stephen River, where it remains. The king's zealously loyal Bagaducians were to become rebel Americans.

So distasteful was this prospect that many loyalists put their houses onto rafts and sailed them to New Brunswick, plunking their homes down safely in British Canada. A few of these houses still exist in and near St Andrews, NB, Canada.

In 1796 Bagaduce became Castine, and in 1814, during the War of 1812, British forces occupied it yet again, though there was little military action. They left in April 1815, and Castine set to work once more as a farming and shipbuilding town.

Orientation & Information

Castine, at the southern end of ME 166, is small enough to be easily comprehensible. A free map entitled "A Walking Tour of Castine" is readily available at establishments in town.

Castine's Forts

After such an embattled history, you'd expect Castine to have old forts. These are not great stone citadels like Fort Knox at Bucksport, but rather low earthworks now park-like and planted with grass.

Close to the Maine Maritime Academy campus, **Fort George** is near the upper (northern) end of Main St where it meets Battle Ave and Wadsworth Cove Rd. **Fort Pentagoët** is on Perkins Rd at Tarratine St. The American **Fort Madison** (earlier Fort Porter, 1808) is farther west along Perkins St opposite Madockawando St.

Take a look also at the **Wilson Museum** on Perkins St near Fort Pentagoët, which holds a good collection of Native American artifacts, historic tools and farm equipment, and other relics of past centuries in Maine.

Places to Stay & Eat

The *Castine Inn* (☎ 207-326-4365), on Main St (PO Box 41, Castine, ME 04421), is a 20-room Victorian summer hotel beautifully maintained as an inn. Rooms with private bath cost $75 to $110, full breakfast included. From July through early September, you must stay at least two nights.

The Pentagoët Inn (☎ 207-326-8616, 800-845-1701), on the other side of Main St, has 16 rooms with bath at similar rates. Other gracious inns include *The Manor* (☎ 207-326-4861) on Battle Ave, *Holiday House* (☎ 207-326-4335) on Perkins St and *The Village Inn* (☎ 207-326-9510) at Main and Water Sts, which costs less than the others.

Getting There & Away

Castine is 18 miles south of US 1 at Orland, 56 miles northeast of Camden, 23 miles west of Blue Hill and 56 miles west of Bar Harbor.

BLUE HILL

Blue Hill is a dignified small Maine coastal town with tall trees, old houses and lots of culture. Many outstanding handicrafts artisans live and work here, and a summer chamber music series draws fine musicians.

Orientation & Information

Blue Hill is at the junction of ME 15, 172, 175, 176 and 177. The town is small enough for easy walking with a few inns, a few restaurants, a few antique stores and lots of lofty trees. You can tour Blue Hill on foot in a half hour or two hours, as you wish, though a few inns and restaurants are on the outskirts.

The Blue Hill Chamber of Commerce (no ☎), PO Box 520, Blue Hill, ME 04614, issues a map available for free at establishments in town.

Special Events

From early July through mid-August, the Kneisel Hall Chamber Music Festival (☎ 207-374-2811) attracts visitors from Portland, Bar

Harbor and beyond. Concerts are held in Kneisel Hall on Pleasant St (ME 15) on Friday evenings and Sunday afternoons.

The Blue Hill Fair (first week in September), held at the fairgrounds on ME 172 northeast of the town center, has oxen and horse pulls, sheepdog trials, livestock shows, fireworks, auto thrill shows, a petting zoo and other country-like things to do.

Places to Stay

Blue Hill is decidedly charming and decidedly upscale. Accommodations in town are wonderful but pricey.

Camping For camping you must travel some distance. The *Gatherings Family Campground* (☎ 207-667-8826)), on ME 172 four miles southwest of Ellsworth, has tent sites for $12 and RV hookups for $17 on a wooded lakefront.

The *Balsam Cove Campground* (☎ 207-469-7771, 800-469-7771), off ME 15 south of East Orland, is a mile south of US 1, then another mile east along an unpaved road. Tenters are welcomed particularly at this forested lakefront campground.

Inns *Mountain Road House* (☎ 207-374-2794), Mountain Rd (RR 1, Box 2040, Blue Hill, ME 04614), offers rooms with private bath ($55 to $75) in a fine 1890s farmhouse with views of the bay a few miles outside of the village. Mountain Rd runs between ME 15 and ME 172; look for the inn's signs.

The long-time favorite lodging place is the *Blue Hill Inn* (☎ 207-374-2844), on Union St (PO Box 403, Blue Hill, ME 04614), a few steps from the village center across from the George Stevens Academy. Dignified period rooms dating from 1840 cost $80 to $125 single, $110 to $165 double, breakfast and dinner included.

Blue Hill's newest B&B is the *Captain Isaac Merrill Inn* (☎ and fax 207-374-2555), 1 Union St, right in the center of things. Though opened in 1994, it has the feel of a 19th-century hostelry. Rates are $75/$85 with shared/private bath.

Places to Eat

For a quick bite or picnic sandwiches, stop at the *Red Bag Deli* (☎ 207-374-8800), on Water St across from the firehouse, open 9 am to 5 pm (Sunday 10 am to 3 pm).

Sarah's Restaurant (☎ 207-374-5181), on Main St just northeast of the post office, serves all three meals. Have soup and quiche for lunch, or southern fried chicken ($8) for a break from lobster and high prices.

Blue Hill's best restaurants are very busy at dinner, and reservations may be necessary.

Firepond (☎ 207-374-9970), by the creek on Main St, opens at 10 am for muffins and coffee, serves lunch (quiche, quesadillas) from 11 am and dinner from 5 pm. The dinner menu is classic with a modern twist: veal with morel mushrooms, Black Angus sirloin with peppercorn sauce. Full dinners cost $30 to $40. The choicest place to sit is the screened porch at creekside.

Jonathan's Restaurant (☎ 207-374-5226), on Main St right in the town's center, has an equally interesting and similarly priced menu featuring Maine crabcakes and lamb shank braised in beer and bourbon.

The *Left Bank Baker & Cafe* (☎ 374-2201), on ME 172 northeast of the village, serves everything from paella to pad thai, charging $25 to $34 for a full dinner. There's live entertainment some evenings.

Getting There & Away

Blue Hill is 23 miles east of Castine, 13 miles southwest of Ellsworth, 18 miles southeast of Bucksport.

DEER ISLE & STONINGTON

Travel south along ME 15 by pristine farms and stretches of rocky Maine coast with sailboats moored offshore. Deer Isle is a collection of islands joined by causeways and connected to the mainland by a picturesquely tall and narrow suspension bridge near Sargentville.

MAINE

TOM BROSNAHAN

The harbor at Stonington

Information

The Deer Isle-Stonington Chamber of Commerce (☎ 207-348-6124) maintains an information booth a quarter mile south of the suspension bridge, open from 10 am to 4 pm (Sunday 11 am to 5 pm) in summer.

Stonington is a departure point for Isle au Haut; see that entry.

Deer Isle Village

The small village of Deer Isle is a collection of shops and services near the Pilgrim Inn. Seven miles east of the village is the **Haystack Mountain School of Crafts** (☎ 207-348-2306), founded in 1950 and now open to public tours June through August on Wednesdays at 1 pm. The several galleries in Deer Isle and neighboring Stonington testify to the fascination this beautiful area has for fine artists.

Places to Stay & Eat *Sunshine Campground* (☎ 207-348-6681), RR 1, Box 521D, is nearly six miles east off ME 15, with tent sites for $10, RV hookups for $14.

Deer Isle Village Inn (☎ 207-348-2564), PO Box 456, Deer Isle, ME 04627, provides shared-bath lodging and breakfast in a typical Maine house just outside the village center for $60. It's open all year.

Pilgrim's Inn (☎ (207)-348-6615), Main St, dates from 1793 and has 13 quite elegant guest rooms, all with baths and water views. Two parlors have eight-foot-wide fireplaces, the library is well stocked and the barn has been converted to a rustic dining room where non-guests can also reserve space for dinner. Room rates run from $140 to $155 a double, breakfast and dinner included.

Stonington

At the southern tip of Deer Isle, Stonington is a granite-quarrying, fishing and tourist town, the three industries thriving close together but separately. Signs warn tourists not to park on the town dock, which is for pickups hauling lobster traps and refrigerated trucks laden with fish. Art galleries and shops alternate with auto

MAINE

parts stores and ship's chandleries on the main street.

Stonington got its name and its early prosperity from the pink granite quarried here. The rocky islets in the harbor show you the color of the stone, and small-scale quarrying continues.

Stonington calls itself "the ideal coastal Maine village," and is proud that it is "a real place, with a real working harbor," rather than a fantasy tourist village.

There's not much to do in Stonington but enjoy Stonington, which is easy enough, as a short walk around will prove.

Places to Stay Right in the town center on Main St, the recently refurbished *Inn on the Harbor* (☎ 207-367-2420) has doubles for $75 to $100, all with private bath. Cheaper rooms face the street. The seaside terrace serves breakfast, coffee and snacks with the best harbor view in town.

Across Main St, *Boyce's Motel* (☎ 207-367-2421, 800-224-2421), PO Box 94, ME 04681, a cedar-shake-covered hostelry, looks more like an inn and rents simple but suitable rooms for $37 double, up to $60 for apartments.

Près du Port B&B (☎ 207-367-5007), just up the hill at the west end of Main St (PO Box 319, Stonington, ME 04681), has three harbor-view rooms for $40 to $60 each, breakfast included.

Burnt Cove B&B (☎ 207-367-2392) on Whitman Rd (RR 1, Box 2905, Stonington, ME 04681), a short distance northwest of the center, has charming rooms for $45 single, $55 to $80 double, breakfast included.

Places to Eat For picnics, the place to stock up is *Penobscot Bay Provisions* (☎ 207-367-2920), on west Main St opposite the post office.

For breakfast, a light meal or snack, go for the view at the *Captain's Quarters Inn* on Main St. Across the street, the *Downtown Diner* (☎ 207-367-5099) serves breakfast from 5 am, 7 am on Sunday, and features a welcome list of sandwiches for around $2. They close at 2 pm.

The *Fisherman's Friend Restaurant* (☎ 207-367-2442), north up the hill on School St, is a general purpose dining spot with a full menu.

Getting There & Away
Deer Isle and Stonington are about five miles apart. Stonington is 23 miles south of Blue Hill, 36 miles southwest of Ellsworth and 78 miles from Camden.

Boats depart Stonington for Isle au Haut. See below.

ISLE AU HAUT
Much of Isle au Haut (that's aisle-a-ho), a rocky island six miles long, is in the keeping of Acadia National Park. More remote than the parklands near Bar Harbor, it is not flooded with visitors in summer. Serious hikers can tramp the island's miles of trails and camp the night in one of the five shelters maintained by the NPS.

For information on hiking and camping on Isle au Haut, contact Acadia National Park (☎ 207-288-3338), PO Box 177, Bar Harbor, ME 04609. Reservations for shelters must be accompanied with a fee of $5; reservations are not accepted before April 1 for the summer season.

Getting There & Away
The Isle au Haut Company (☎ 207-367-5193, evenings 367-2355) operates daily mail boat trips from Stonington's Atlantic Ave Hardware Dock to the village of Isle au Haut year round. In summer, except for Sunday and major holidays, there are at least three trips a day on the 45-minute crossing, for $9 per adult, $4.50 per child under 12 ($11 and $5 on Sunday). On Sunday and major holidays there is only one boat a day. Bicycles, motorcycles, boats and canoes can be carried to the village of Isle au Haut.

From late June through mid-September the company also makes the one-hour crossing to Duck Harbor, the entrance to the Isle au Haut territory of Acadia National Park. No bicycles, canoes or kayaks are transported on this run; no dogs are allowed in the Acadia campground.

MAINE

MT DESERT ISLAND

Samuel de Champlain, intrepid French explorer, sailed along this coast in the early 1600s. Seeing the bare, windswept granite summit of Cadillac Mountain, he called the island on which it stood *L'Île des Monts Déserts*. The name is still pronounced duh-ZERT almost 400 years later.

Mt Desert Island holds Bar Harbor, Maine's oldest summer resort, and Acadia National Park, the only national park in New England. Because of its dramatic Maine scenery and outdoor sports possibilities, it's one of the state's most popular and busiest summer resorts. Acadia is among the most heavily visited national parks in the country.

Visitors come, first and foremost, for the beautiful Maine coastal scenery. They hike the 120 miles of trails on the island, bike the 50 miles of unpaved carriage roads, camp in the park's 500+ campsites or stay in country inns, and seek out the 200 species of plants, 80 species of mammals and 273 kinds of birds that live here.

Orientation

The resort area of Bar Harbor and Acadia extends from the town of Ellsworth, on US 1, to the southern tip of the large mountainous island of Mt Desert. The island's major town, Bar Harbor, is on its northeast side, 20 miles southeast of Ellsworth. Acadia National Park covers much (but not all) of the land on the island, and includes large tracts of land on the Schoodic Peninsula south of Winter Harbor, across the water to the east, and on Isle au Haut, far to the southwest. The Schoodic Peninsula and Isle au Haut areas are not easily accessible from Mt Desert Island.

Information

In summer, the Thompson Island Information Center (☎ 207-288-3411), a joint effort of the NPS and three area chambers of commerce, is about 7½ miles south of Ellsworth. Acadia National Park's Hulls Cove Visitor Center (☎ 207-288-3338) is 16 miles south of Ellsworth, three miles north of Bar Harbor, and is open May

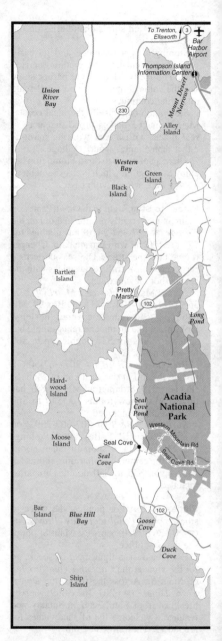

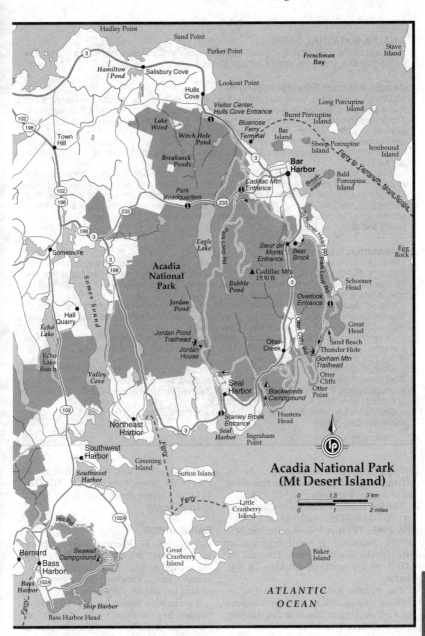

Acadia National Park
(Mt Desert Island)

ACADIA NATIONAL PARK

Acadia National Park covers over 62 sq miles and offers activities for everyone from the couch potato to the hyperactive sports enthusiast.

Acadia National Park Establishment

Mt Desert Island was a booming summer resort for the wealthy by the late 19th century, but it was a more workaday development which caused the creation of Acadia National Park. The invention of the "portable sawmill" meant that the forests of Acadia might be stripped of trees for cheap lumber, so in 1901 summer residents, led by Harvard University president Charles W Eliot, formed a land trust. Wealthy landowners donated land to the trust, and Acadia grew in extent. By 1916 the trust was a national monument, and in 1919 a national park.

John D Rockefeller donated 10,000 acres of land to the park. Alarmed at the prospect of its being overrun with automobiles (which some would say it now is), he ordered construction of 50 miles of one-lane gravel-topped carriage roads throughout the park. The carriage roads, built between 1918 and 1940, were to provide access to the park's more remote areas by horse-drawn carriage rather than automobile. Today they're popular with hikers and bikers as well.

Orientation & Information

The park's main entrance is at Hulls Cove, northwest of Bar Harbor off ME 3. The visitor center (☎ 207-288-3338) is here, and opens at 8 am in summer. From the visitor center, the 20-mile-long Park Loop Rd circumnavigates the northeastern section of the island. The road is one way for much of its length.

The admission fee to the park is $5 per vehicle and is good for seven consecutive days. The fee is collected at a booth just north of Sand Beach on the Park Loop Rd. If you enter the park by bike or on foot, the fee is $2 per person.

Other entrances to the park and the Park Loop Rd are the Cadillac Mountain entrance just west of Bar Harbor, the Overlook Entrance to the south of the town and the Stanley Brook Entrance east of Northeast Harbor.

Cadillac Mountain (1530 feet), the highest point in the park, is a few miles southwest of Bar Harbor. The summit can be reached by auto road, which is a pity. Most of the carriage roads (closed to motor vehicles) are between Bubble Pond and Somes Sound, to the west of Cadillac Mountain.

Call the visitor center for camping, road and weather information. For park emergencies, call ☎ 207-288-3369.

through October. Follow the signs. In the off-season go to Park Headquarters three miles west of Bar Harbor on ME 233.

The Bar Harbor Chamber of Commerce (☎ 207-288-3395, 800-345-4617, fax 288-2565), PO Box 158, Bar Harbor, ME 04609, maintains a small information office at the Bluenose Ferry Terminal on ME 3 on the northern outskirts of Bar Harbor.

The Acadia Area Association has an "official lodging office" at 55 West St near the Golden Anchor Motel in Bar Harbor, open weekdays from 10 am to 6 pm.

In Somesville, west of Bar Harbor, the Port in the Storm bookstore (☎ 207-244-4114) is a choice destination simply for its tranquil beauty.

BAR HARBOR

Bar Harbor is Maine's most popular summer resort. It's a pleasant town of big old houses, some of which have been converted to inns, a variety of restaurants and a relaxed but purposeful way of life.

Bar Harbor's busiest season is late June through August. There's a bit of a lull just before and just after Labor Day, but then it

MAINE

Maps & Guides
Free NPS maps of the park are available at the information and visitor centers. The *AMC Guide to Mt Desert Island & Acadia National Park* by the Appalachian Mountain Club (available from Globe Pequot publishers) has descriptions of all the trails as well as a good trail map. *Acadia's Biking Guide* by Tom St Germain has descriptions of numerous good bike tours to be made along the park's carriage roads. These guides and others, as well as a variety of maps, are sold at the Hulls Cove Visitor Center and at bookshops in Bar Harbor.

Touring Highlights
Start your tour with a drive along the Park Loop Rd. On the portion called Ocean Drive, stop at Thunder Hole, south of the Overlook Entrance, for a look at the surf crashing into a cleft in the granite (the effect is best on a strong incoming tide). Otter Cliffs, not far south of Thunder Hole, is a wall of pink granite rising right from the sea.

At Jordan Pond there's a self-guiding nature trail. Here you're in the midst of the trail and carriage roads systems. Stop for tea and popovers at *Jordan House* (☎ 207-276-3116), as visitors have been doing for over a century. Lunch is served on the porch, tea on the lawn and dinner by the fireplace.

For swimming, try either Sand Beach or Seal Harbor for chilly salt water, or Echo Lake for fresh water.

Finish your first explorations with a stop at the windy summit of Cadillac Mountain.

Outfitters
Acadia is great for all sorts of outdoor activities, including hiking, rock climbing, mountain biking, canoeing and sea kayaking. Numerous outfitters in Bar Harbor provide guide service, equipment for rent or sale and sports lessons. Many are found at the west end of Cottage St near ME 3, including Acadia Bike & Canoe (☎ 207-288-9605, 800-526-8615) at No 48, across from the post office; Acadia Outfitters (☎ 207-288-8118), No 106 across from the Exxon station; Bar Harbor Bicycle Shop (☎ 207-288-3886), No 141; National Park Outdoor Activities Center and Acadia Mountain Guides (☎ 207-288-0342, 288-8186), No 137.

Campgrounds
There are two campgrounds in the park. *Blackwoods Campground*, open all year, requires reservations in summer (☎ 207-288-3338); *Seawall Campground*, open from May through September, rents sites on a first-come, first-served basis. No backcountry camping is allowed. There are private campgrounds outside the park. See Bar Harbor Places to Stay for details. ∎

---

gets busy again in foliage season, through mid-October.

History
Bar Harbor was chartered as a town in 1796, while Maine was still part of the Commonwealth of Massachusetts. In 1844 landscape painters Thomas Cole and Frederick Church came to Mt Desert and liked what they saw. They sketched the landscape, and returned with their art students. Soon the wealthy families who purchased their paintings were asking them about the beautiful land they painted. They were told, and those families began to spend summers here.

Soon Bar Harbor rivaled Newport, RI, for the stature of its summer-colony guests. A rail line from Boston and regular steamboat service brought even more visitors. By the end of the 19th century, Bar Harbor was established as one of the eastern seaboard's most desirable summer resorts.

WWII damaged the tourist trade, but worse was to come. In 1947 a vast forest fire torched 17,000 acres of park land, along with 60 palatial "summer cottages" of wealthy summer residents, putting an

MAINE

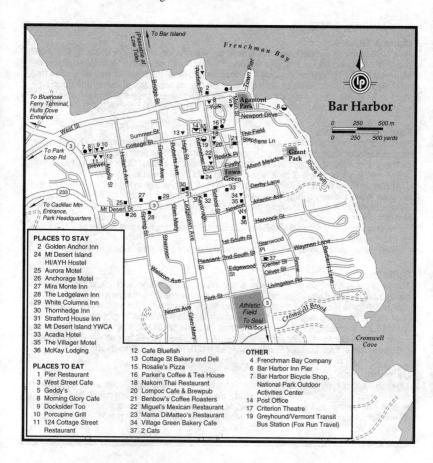

Bar Harbor

PLACES TO STAY
2   Golden Anchor Inn
24 Mt Desert Island
    HI/AYH Hostel
25 Aurora Motel
26 Anchorage Motel
27 Mira Monte Inn
28 The Ledgelawn Inn
29 White Columns Inn
30 Thornhedge Inn
31 Stratford House Inn
32 Mt Desert Island YWCA
33 Acadia Hotel
35 The Villager Motel
36 McKay Lodging

PLACES TO EAT
1   Pier Restaurant
3   West Street Cafe
5   Geddy's
8   Morning Glory Cafe
9   Docksider Too
10 Porcupine Grill
11 124 Cottage Street
    Restaurant

12 Cafe Bluefish
13 Cottage St Bakery and Deli
15 Rosalie's Pizza
16 Parker's Coffee & Tea House
18 Nakorn Thai Restaurant
20 Lompoc Cafe & Brewpub
21 Benbow's Coffee Roasters
22 Miguel's Mexican Restaurant
23 Mama DiMatteo's Restaurant
34 Village Green Bakery Cafe
37 2 Cats

OTHER
4   Frenchman Bay Company
6   Bar Harbor Inn Pier
7   Bar Harbor Bicycle Shop,
    National Park Outdoor
    Activities Center
14 Post Office
17 Criterion Theatre
19 Greyhound/Vermont Transit
    Bus Station (Fox Run Travel)

end to Bar Harbor's gilded age. But the town recovered as a destination for the new automobile-equipped mobile middle class of the postwar years.

Although Mt Desert Island still has a number of wealthy summer residents, they are far outnumbered by us common folk. There is an especially large contingent of outdoor sports lovers.

Orientation & Information

ME 3 approaches Bar Harbor from the north and west, and passes right through the town. Main St is the principal commercial thoroughfare, along with Cottage St. Mt Desert St has many of the town's inns, just a few minutes' walk from the town green.

See Information under Mt Desert Island for tourist facilities.

Rock Climbing

With all that granite, Acadia National Park is a mecca for rock climbers. If you'd like to learn the sport, Atlantic Climbing (☎ 207-288-2521) offers guide and instruction services. Acadia Mountain Guides (☎ 207-288-0342), at the National Park Outdoor Activities Center, 137 Cottage St, also gives instruction and can guide you to the best climbs.

Soaring

Island Soaring (☎ 207-667-7627), at the Hancock County-Bar Harbor Airport on ME 3 north of the Trenton Bridge, will take you soaring above Mt Desert Island for as little as $100 per couple. Call for reservations.

Cruises

Frenchman Bay Acadia National Park is the lure to Bar Harbor, but there are several worthwhile things to do outside the park as well. Cruising is one of them. Remember when you cruise that it is often 20°F cooler on the water than on land, so bring a jacket or sweater and windbreaker.

The Frenchman Bay Co (☎ 207-288-3322, 800-508-1499), 1 West St at Main, next to the town pier, will take you out for a two-hour cruise on the *Bay Lady*, an 85-foot schooner, for $15 for adults, $11 for kids six to 15; kids five and under cruise free. There are four cruises daily in summer.

Frenchman Bay also runs the *Whale Watcher*, a 105-foot steel vessel with three main engines, designed expressly for whale watching. There's also the *Acadian*, a steel-hulled, motor-driven sightseeing vessel which explores the coast and islands on two-hour cruises with a naturalist aboard.

The "Three Historic Vessels" (☎ 207-288-4585, 288-2373) depart from the Bar Harbor Inn Pier on two-hour cruises. The vessels are the 129-foot, three-masted schooner *Natalie Todd*; the 101-foot, two-masted schooner *Francis Todd* and the 65-foot, 1920s-era motor vessel *Chippewa*. Cruises cost from $15 to $17.50 for adults, or $8 to $10 for children under 12. Buy your tickets on the pier, or from the Natalie Todd Ticket Office at 27 Main St.

Friendship IV (☎ 207-288-2386) is a fast, modern 92-foot motor-driven catamaran which sets out from the Bluenose Ferry Terminal north of Bar Harbor on whale-watching cruises daily in summer. The catamaran design and spacious cabin are comfortable and stable, and there's a restaurant and bar aboard.

Nova Scotia Marine Atlantic's seagoing car ferry *Bluenose* (☎ 207-288-3395, 800-341-7981) provides a maritime link between Bar Harbor and Yarmouth, Nova Scotia, Canada. On board there are buffets, bars, duty-free shops and gambling devices such as slot machines. The voyage between Bar Harbor and Yarmouth takes six hours, so in a long day you can cruise there and back, though an overnight stay makes more sense.

Places to Stay – Bar Harbor

Bar Harbor has 2500 guest rooms in dozens of motels and inns. Many lodgings close from mid-October to mid-May.

The nicest places to stay are the campgrounds of Acadia National Park, or in one of Bar Harbor's Victorian inns. The first is cheap, the second expensive and in July and August, if you have not made reservations in advance, finding a place in either can be difficult.

Campgrounds Camping in Acadia National Park is covered under that heading in the sidebar. Commercial campgrounds are ranged along ME 3 from Ellsworth, and clustered near the entrances to the park.

There's also good camping at *Lamoine State Park* (☎ 207-667-4778), in Lamoine Beach at the southern end of ME 184, about 30 miles away by road, but only a few miles over the water. From Ellsworth, follow US 1 East past ME 3 to ME 184 South. Lamoine is open from mid-May to mid-October.

Hostels The *Mt Desert Island HI/AYH Hostel* (☎ 207-288-5587), 27 Kennebec St (PO Box 32, Bar Harbor, ME 04609), in the parish hall of St Saviour's Episcopal Church, has 20 beds going for $10 each. It's open from 7 to 9 am and 4:30 to 11 pm, mid-June through August.

The *Mt Desert Island YWCA* (☎ 207-288-5008), 36 Mt Desert St, offers lodging to women only for $15/$18/$25 in a dorm/shared double/single, with reductions for longer stays.

Motels The *Anchorage Motel* (☎ 207-288-3959, 800-336-3959), 51 Mt Desert St, is amidst the inns on the town's grandest street. Modern rooms cost $68/72 a single/double, somewhat higher at very busy times.

The nearby *Aurora Motel* (☎ 207-288-3771, 800-841-8925), 51 Holland Ave, is small, simple and well located, charging $75 to $90, with discounts if they're not busy.

The Villager Motel (☎ 207-288-3211), 207 Main St, charging $69 to $92 in high summer, is a block south of the town green, within walking distance to everything. Rates drop on August 25.

Among the best-situated and most expensive is the *Golden Anchor Inn* (☎ 207-288-5033, 800-328-5033), on West St, convenient to everything. Rates range from $95 to $185 double, with water views starting at $135.

Inns Most of the huge old "summer cottages" along Mt Desert St in Bar Harbor have been converted to inns. Prices are usually the same for one or two persons.

Cheapest by far is the *Acadia Hotel* (☎ 207-288-5721), 20 Mt Desert St, just off the green. Rooms in this well-kept old house cost $55 to $72 in high summer and they're usually all reserved in advance; call early.

McKay Lodging (☎ 207-288-3531, 800-866-2529), 243 Main St, is a short hop south of the green, with 23 recently renovated rooms in a Bar Harbor house for $65/$75 with shared bath, $10 more with private bath.

Bar Harbor's grandest downtown inn is *The Ledgelawn Inn* (☎ 207-288-4596), 66 Mt Desert St, a vast Colonial Revival summer "cottage" built in 1904 for a Boston shoe magnate. Well kept to this day, it reeks of charm and grandeur, which can be yours for $75 to $175 (more for suites), depending upon the day and the room.

Across the street, the *Mira Monte Inn* (☎ 207-288-4263, 800-553-5109, fax 288-3115) is particularly well kept and gracious, with rooms for $90 to $145 per night, suites for more.

Nearby, the *White Columns Inn* (☎ 207-

288-5357, 800-321-6379), 57 Mt Desert St, and the *Thornhedge Inn* (☎ 207-288-5398, 800-580-0800), 47 Mt Desert St, are under related management and charge $80 to $140 double for grand Victorian accommodations just a short walk from the park.

Half-timbered and aptly named, the *Stratford House Inn* (☎ 207-288-5189, 800-550-5189), 45 Mt Desert St, is a Tudor fantasy in the midst of Bar Harbor. Built by a wealthy Boston publisher, it now rents rooms for $75 to $135.

Places to Stay – Ellsworth
ME 3 from Ellsworth to Bar Harbor is dotted with cheaper motels, some charging as little as $40 double in summer. If everything in Bar Harbor is full, which happens sometimes on weekends in high summer, you should be able to locate a motel room along ME 3 without prior reservation. Start your search by early afternoon on weekends, though.

KIM GRANT

Schooners moored at Bar Harbor

Places to Eat

Coffeehouses For an authentic and elaborate cappuccino, latte or mocha, try *Parker's Coffee & Tea House* (☎ 207-288-2882), 37½ Cottage St, next to the Criterion Theater. Choose by the bean and the preparation for $1 to $3. Also good are *Benbow's Coffee Roasters* (☎ 207-288-5271), right in the center of town at 99 Main St, and *2 Cats* (☎ 207-288-2808), a few blocks south of the green at 318 Main St. All serve muffins and other pastries as well as java, but no liquor or large meals.

Breakfast & Lunch Several bakery-cafe-deli places are good for breakfast, lunch and box lunches for your picnic in Acadia.

Morning Glory Cafe (☎ 207-288-3041), 133 Cottage St, serves good pastries ($1), huge blueberry pancakes ($3), sandwiches and salads in a homey setting from 7 am to 2 pm. They'll make up a good box lunch for $5.50.

A hundred yards west, the *Cottage St Bakery and Deli* (☎ 207-288-3010), 59 Cottage St, has a wonderful front patio with umbrella-shaded tables where blueberry pancakes and other breakfast specialties are served from 6:30 am to 11 pm, along with lots of pizzas and deli sandwiches ($5.50).

Village Green Bakery Cafe (☎ 207-288-9450), 125 Main St, is just south of the park, serving fresh baked goods, sandwiches, salads, pasta and, as the menu says, "lobster of course."

Cheap Lunches & Suppers *Rosalie's Pizza* (☎ 207-288-5666), at the corner of Cottage and Rodick Sts, serves hearty sandwiches such as baked cheese steak for $3 and $4, and a myriad of fresh pizzas in varying sizes from $5 to $13. They do what they say: "We really s-t-r-e-t-c-h your dough."

The best place for a lobster picnic is at one of the lobster pounds clustered north of Trenton Bridge on ME 3, about 6½ miles south of Ellsworth on the road to Bar Harbor. You'll see them as you come in: *Bob's Chowderhouse* is first, across from the airport. Just south of Bob's is *Lunts*, and across from Lunts is the *Gateway. Trenton Bridge Lobster Pound*, with a pretty waterview picnic area, is at the north end of the causeway which leads over to Mt Desert Island. At any of these places a lobster dinner with steamed clams and corn or cole slaw, should cost only $7 or so. Prices are usually posted on highway signboards.

You needn't pay much more for a lobster dinner in town. Many restaurants have early bird specials: you get a full dinner, with perhaps slightly smaller portions, if you order before 6 or 6:30 pm. The West Street Cafe is one of these, as is Mama DiMatteo's (see below).

Dinner Rodick St, and Cottage St east of it, hold Bar Harbor's most interesting dining possibilities.

The bright, simple *Docksider Too* (☎ 207-288-9087), 131 Cottage St, is a branch of a well-known lobster house in Northeast Harbor. Take a table on the big, bright front porch and have light lunch for $6 to $8, or a lobster with salad, vegetable and bread for $13 to $16, depending upon the size of the lobster.

Across the street, the atmospheric *124 Cottage Street Restaurant* (☎ 207-288-4383) has a wonderful front porch dining area, and interesting dining rooms in an old house. The specialty is seafood served from 5 pm onward. The fish – sautéed, blackened, almandine – is as good as the setting, and full dinners go for around $30.

Cafe Bluefish (☎ 207-288-3696), 122 Cottage, is a storefront bistro which opens at 5:30 pm and offers an interesting menu featuring such things as chicken with apricots, and a vegetarian mushroom bean stroganoff. Full dinners cost about $30. Across the street, the *Porcupine Grill* (☎ 207-288-3884), 123 Cottage, has formal dining rooms in a small house, and a refined menu and wine list. It opens at 6 pm, and dinners cost about $35 to $40.

On Rodick south of Cottage is the *Lompoc Cafe & Brewpub* (☎ 207-288-9392), 36 Rodick, with a short but eclectic international menu – Indonesian peanut chicken shares space with shrimp étouffé ($10 to $13) – but most people come for the ingenious pizzas (Greek, goat cheese, etc, $6 to $8) and a glass of Bar Harbor Real Ale ($2.50 and up). Most evenings, there's live entertainment (see that section).

Right next door is the *Nakorn Thai Restaurant* (☎ 207-288-4060), 30 Rodick, serving familiar Thai dishes (some vegetarian) for $8 to $11. Farther south (up the hill), *Miguel's Mexican Restaurant* (☎ 207-288-5117), 51 Rodick, serves quesadillas with various fillings for $2.50 to $9.50, big combination dinners for $9.50 to $13, lots of other Mexican fare and beers as well. It opens at 5 pm for dinner only.

At the top of Rodick St, *Mama DiMatteo's Restaurant* (☎ 288-3666) serves nouveau Italian cuisine: smoked chicken ravioli, shrimp sautéed with prosciutto, capers and olives, and the like. Early bird specials (slightly smaller portions) are served from 4:30 to 6 pm for only $9. Basil and mint grow in abundance by the door.

The *West Street Cafe* (☎ 207-288-5242), at Rodick and West across from the Golden Anchor Inn, has sidewalk dining, and features cheap lobster from 11:30 am to 6:30 pm, after which prices rise a bit. The best deal is the Maine dinner of seafood chowder, steamed lobster and blueberry pie for $15.

Down by the harbor, the *Pier Restaurant* at the Golden Anchor Inn (☎ 207-288-5033) is usually busy because of its breezy setting at the end of a pier with a spectacular sunset view of the water and the pine-fringed coast. Have a drink in the open-air Topsider bar while you wait for a table. Fish courses cost around $13, vegetable lasagna is $10. The Pier opens for breakfast at 7 am and stops serving dinner at 9:30 pm.

Entertainment

Perhaps the most interesting venue is the Lompoc Cafe & Brewpub (see above) on Rodick St, which has a variety of performers playing jazz, blues, folk and classical. Check the signboard at the corner of Rodick and Cottage Sts for who's on when. The cover charge varies. Food and Bar Harbor Real Ale are available.

Other music spots include *Geddy's* on Main St, and the West Street Cafe (see above).

Getting There & Away

Air Colgan Air (☎ 207-667-7171, 800-272-5488) connects Bar Harbor and Boston with daily flights year round. The Hancock County-Bar Harbor Airport is at Trenton off ME 3 just north of the Trenton Bridge.

Bus Vermont Transit/Greyhound (☎ 207-288-3366, 802-864-6811) runs an early morning bus daily from Bar Harbor to Boston and New York City via Bangor and Portland. Likewise, a bus starts out from New York at breakfast time, reaching Boston by lunch time, and Bar Harbor by dinnertime.

The Bar Harbor bus stop is at Fox Run Travel, 4 Kennebec St, at Cottage St. You can also flag the bus down in the parking lot of the McDonald's in Ellsworth at the junction of US 1 and ME 3.

Car Driving details for Bar Harbor are:

Destination	Mileage	Hr:Min
Bangor, ME	34 miles	0:50
Boothbay, ME	125 miles	2:45
Boston, MA	269 miles	6:30
Calais, ME	132 miles	3:15
Camden, ME	77 miles	1:45
Freeport, ME	145 miles	3:50
Lubec, ME	103 miles	2:30
New York, NY	470 miles	12:00
Portland, ME	161 miles	4:00
Northeast Harbor, ME	13 miles	0:30
Southwest Harbor, ME	15 miles	0:35

Boat For details on the *Bluenose* to Yarmouth, Nova Scotia, see Nova Scotia Cruises, above.

NORTHEAST HARBOR

The aptly named vacation village of Northeast Harbor has a marina full of yachts, a main street populated with art galleries and boutiques, and back streets dotted with comfortable summer hideaways good for a brief visit.

Information is available at the marina, as is a shop selling soft drinks and snacks.

On the main street, the *Outback Cafe & Deli* (☎ 207-276-3335) sells light meals and drinks.

SOUTHWEST HARBOR

More laid-back and less wealthy than Northeast Harbor, Southwest Harbor also has more to do in a brief visit.

Cruises

From the Upper Town Dock – a quarter mile along Clark Point Rd from the flashing light in the center of town – boats venture out into Frenchman Bay to the Cranberry Isles, and on whale-watching expeditions. Cranberry Cove Boating Co (☎ 207-244-5882) operates the 47-passenger *Island Queen* on four cruises daily in summer. The 1½-hour voyage to and from the Cranberry Isles costs $8 per adult, half-price for kids three to 12.

Acadia Cruises' (☎ 207-244-7399) 63-foot, 49-passenger *Ranger* goes out looking for whales four times daily for $12 per adult, $8 senior, $6 child under 12.

Places to Stay & Eat

Penury Hall (☎ 207-244-7102), PO Box 68, Southwest Harbor, ME 04679, will put you up for the night (two nights minimum in summer) and give you breakfast for $55/60 a single/double. *Island House* (☎ 207-244-5180), on Clark Point Rd, is comparably priced, as is *Heron House* (☎ 207-244-0221), at ME 102 and Fernald Point Rd. For sustenance, try the *Cafe Drydock & Inn* (☎ 207-244-3886), on Main St.

BANGOR

Though Bangor figures large in present-day Maine, it is off the normal tourist routes. A boomtown during Maine's 19th-century lumbering prosperity, it was largely destroyed by a disastrous fire in 1911. Bangor today is mostly a modern, workaday town most famous as the home-town of best-selling novelist Stephen King (look for his appropriately spooky

mansion – complete with bat-and-cobweb fence – among the grand houses along Broadway). Bett's Bookstore (☎ 207-947-7052), 26 Main St, specializes in Stephen King's books.

The Bangor Historical Society (☎ 207-942-5766) has a museum at 159 Union St (closed mid-December through February). The Cole Land Transportation Museum, 405 Perry Rd, has exhibits of antique vehicles and photographs.

Places to Stay

Camping The *Pleasant Hill Campground* (☎ 207-848-5127), with 105 spaces for everything from tents to giant motorhomes, is 5½ miles west of I-95 exit 47 along Union St (ME 222). The 52 sites at the *Paul Bunyan Campground* (☎ 207-941-1177), 1862 Union St, are available year round.

Hotels The 35-room *Phoenix Inn* (☎ 207-947-0411, fax 947-0255), 20 Broad St, Bangor, ME 04401, is in the West Market Square Historic District, a row of buildings dating from 1837, when Bangor was Maine's lumbering capital. Tidy rooms cost $65/$75; buffet breakfast is included.

The *Best Western White House Inn* (☎ 207-862-3737, 800-528-1234, fax 862-6465), 155 Littlefield Ave, Bangor, ME 04401, is at I-95 exit 44, charging $74 for good rooms (some with two queen beds), breakfast included.

The similarly priced *Hampton Inn* (☎ 207-990-4400, 800-998-7829), 10 Bangor Mall Blvd, is at I-95 exit 49. The cheaper *Super 8 Motel* (☎ 207-945-5681, 800-337-8737), 462 Odlin Rd, is at I-95 exit 45, as is the *Fairfield Inn* (☎ 207-990-0001, 800-228-2800).

B&B *Hamstead Farm* (☎ 207-848-3749), RD 3, Box 703, Bangor, ME 04401, is an 1846 Cape Cod-style farmhouse on 150 acres of woods and pastures which are home to a small herd of black Angus cattle, as well as pigs and turkeys. Three guest rooms share two baths, and cost $40/$50, full farm breakfast included.

Places to Eat

Dining options are limited, but *Seguino's Italian Restaurant* (☎ 207-942-5766), 737 Main St, serves good Italian fare at moderate prices. Dinner is served every day, lunch Tuesday through Friday.

The Daily Grind (☎ 207-990-3138), 32 Broad St, serves eight different varieties of brewed coffee each day, and sells up to 60 different varieties by the pound. They serve lunch as well.

Getting There & Away

Air Bangor International Airport (☎ 207-947-0384) is the air transportation hub of the region, served by regional carriers associated with Continental, Delta and USAir.

Bus See Getting There & Away in the Portland section for bus routes. Vermont Transit Lines (☎ 207-945-3000), at the Bangor Bus Terminal, 158 Main St, runs four direct buses daily between Bangor and Boston via Portland and Portsmouth, NH. Concord Trailways (☎ 800-639-3317), Trailways Transportation Center, 1039 Union St, has three more, as well as service south along the Maine coast to Portland, and connecting service north and east to Calais and St Stephen, NB, Canada.

DOWNEAST MAINE

The Sunrise Coast is the name given by Maine's tourism promoters to the area east of Ellsworth to Lubec and Eastport. To Mainers, this is Downeast Maine, the area downwind and east of the rest of the state. It's sparsely populated, slower-paced and more traditional than the Maine to the south and west. It also has more frequent and denser fog.

If you seek quiet walks away from the tourist throngs, coastal villages with little impact from tourism and lower travel prices, explore the 900-plus miles of coastline east of Bar Harbor. But be mindful of the weather.

Highlights of Downeast Maine include the **Schoodic Peninsula** territory of Acadia National Park; **Jonesport** and **Beals Island**, with the largest fleet of lobster boats in Maine; **Great Wass Island**, a large nature preserve with walking paths and good opportunities for bird watching (including puffins).

The county seat of Washington County, **Machias** has a branch of the University of Maine, thereby making it the center of commerce, culture and art along this stretch of coast.

Lubec, a fish-processing center, is just across the bridge from Canada and Roosevelt Campobello International Park. Franklin Roosevelt's father James bought land here in 1883 and built a palatial summer "cottage." The future US president spent many boyhood summers here, and was later given the 34-room cottage. He and Eleanor made brief but well-publicized visits during his long tenure as president.

At the northern end of US 1, **Calais** (pronounced callous) is a twin town to St Stephen, New Brunswick, Canada. During the War of 1812, when the USA and Britain (including Canada) were at war, these two remote outposts of nationalism ignored the distant battles. Their citizens were so closely linked by blood and family ties that politics – even war – was ignored.

St Stephen is the gateway to Atlantic Canada, covered in the Lonely Planet's *Canada*.

Western Lakes & Mountains

Northern and western Maine is far less visited than coastal Maine. This suits the outdoorsy types who love northern Maine just fine. The fine old town of Bethel and the outdoor pleasures of the Rangeley Lakes are relatively accessible to city-dwellers in Boston, Providence and New York, and even closer to the outdoor playground of the White Mountain National Forest, in New Hampshire and in Maine.

SEBAGO LAKE

Sebago, a mere 15 miles northwest of Portland, is among Maine's largest and most accessible lakes. There are some small settlements along the eastern shore of the lake, best reached by US 302 from Portland. The town of Sebago Lake at the lake's south end is small and sleepy. Along the western shore, at East Sebago, are a few inns and cabins for rent.

At the northern tip of the lake, southeast of Naples, is Sebago Lake State Park (☎ 207-693-6615), with camping, picnicking, swimming, boating and fishing.

SABBATHDAY LAKE

Take Maine Turnpike exit 11, then ME 26 to reach the town of Sabbathday Lake, 30 miles north of Portland near the lake of that name. Sabbathday has the nation's only active Shaker community. It was founded in the 1700s, and a small number of devotees (perhaps four or five) keep the Shaker tradition of prayer, simple living, hard work and fine artistry alive.

Among the plain white, well-kept buildings of the community are a welcome center, museum and shop selling the community's crafts. Most other buildings, including the impressive Brick Dwelling House, are not open to visitors.

A few miles to the north is the village of Poland Spring, famous for its mineral water, which is now shipped throughout the USA. In the 1800s a visitor was miraculously cured by drinking water from Poland Spring. Not known to miss a good thing, the locals opened hotels to cater to those wanting to take the waters.

BETHEL

For a small town in the Maine woods, Bethel, 63 miles northwest of Portland on ME 26, is surprisingly refined. Part of its backwoods sophistication comes from its being the home to Gould Academy, a well-regarded prep school founded in 1836.

Orientation & Information

The town is small enough to find your way around easily. The Bethel Area Chamber of Commerce (☎ 800-442-5826) can answer any questions.

Things to See & Do

While in Bethel, stop by the **Dr Moses Mason House** (☎ 207-824-2908), 15 Broad St, for a look at the house of Dr Mason (1789-1866), a prominent local physician and state representative. The house is now the museum and research library of the Bethel Historical Society, and is open in July and August from 1 to 4 pm, closed Monday.

Bethel Outdoor Adventures (☎ 207-836-3607, 800-533-3607, fax 836-2708), 646 W Bethel Rd, can rent you a canoe and arrange lessons and shuttles to and from the Androscoggin River, and guided trips.

The Great American Bike Renting Company (☎ 207-824-3092), on Sunday River Rd, rents tandems and mountain bikes for excursions into the countryside.

There's golf at the Bethel Inn (see below), hiking in the nearby forests and scenic drives all around. If you head west toward New Hampshire on US 2, be sure to admire the **Shelburne birches**, a high concentration of the white-barked trees between Gilead and Shelburne. **Grafton Notch State Park**, north of Bethel along ME 26, has hiking trails and pretty waterfalls, but no camping.

In the winter, visitors come to ski at the recently expanded **Sunday River Ski Area** (☎ 207-824-3000, 800-430-0771), six miles north of Bethel along ME 5/26, and at several cross-country ski centers.

Places to Stay

For its size Bethel has a surprising number of places to stay, which testifies to its importance as a crossroads town at the junction of routes between the Maine coast, northern Maine and New Hampshire.

Among the nicest and most economical lodgings is *The Chapman Inn* (☎ 207-824-2657), on the common (PO Box 206, Bethel, ME 04217), with dorms, single, double and family rooms. The *Holidae Inn* (☎ 207-824-3400), on Main St, is another good choice. *Bethel Bed & Breakfast*

(☎ 207-824-4000, 800-423-8435, fax 824-4001), 20 Church St, charges $50 to $65 for its rooms in summer. *Abbott House* (☎ 207-824-7600, 800-240-2377) is over two centuries old, and charges $60 double for its four rooms sharing two baths.

At the junction of US 2 and ME 26, the *River View Motel* (☎ 207-824-2808) is a bit cheaper.

The *Bethel Inn & Country Club* (☎ 800-654-0125), which dominates the town common, is popular with golfers who happily pay $200 to $300 double, breakfast and dinner included.

RANGELEY LAKES

Driving from Bethel via US 2 and ME 17 to Rangeley Lake, the road climbs through country that's exceptionally beautiful – even for Maine. Around the turn of the century, the lakes in this region were dotted with vast frame hotels and peopled with vacationers from Boston, New York and Philadelphia.

The hamlets of **Oquossoc** and **Haines Landing** have several traditional North Woods sporting camps nearby, rustic collections of cabins used by hunters and fishers.

In the village of Rangeley proper, a few vestiges of the region's time of glory remain, such as the *Rangeley Inn* (☎ 207-864-3342) and the *Country Club Inn* (☎ 207-864-3831). The *Northwoods B&B* (☎ 207-864-2440), on Main St (PO Box 79, Rangeley, ME 04970), will put you up for $60/$75 double with shared/private bath.

The North Woods

On the map, the farther north you go in Maine, the fewer roads you have to choose from.

On paper it looks as though this is trackless wilderness. In fact this vast area is owned by large paper companies who harvest timber for their paper mills. The land is crisscrossed by a matrix of rough logging roads. Logs used to be floated down the region's many rivers, but this practice increased the tannin levels in the rivers and threatened the ecological balance. With the advent of the internal combustion engine came the roads.

Now that the logs are out of the rivers, white-water rafters are in. The **Kennebec River** below the Harris Hydroelectric Station passes through a dramatic 12-mile gorge that's among the country's prime rafting places. Outflow from the hydroelectric station is controlled, which means that there is always water, and that periodic big releases make for more exciting rafting.

The Kennebec Valley Tourism Council (☎ 800-778-9898), 179 Main St, Waterville, ME 04901, will help with information.

CARATUNK & THE FORKS

These two villages on US 201 south of Jackman are at the center of the Kennebec rafting area. White-water rafting trips down the Kennebec and nearby rivers are wonderful adventures. Trips cost from $75 to $95 per person, and are suitable for everyone from children (eight and older) to seniors in their 70s (see sidebar). No experience is necessary for many trips.

Reserve your rafting trip in advance, and bring a bathing suit, wool or polar fleece sweater, windbreaker or rain suit. Avoid cotton clothing (such as T-shirts and blue-jeans) because cotton dries slowly and will make you feel cold. Wear more clothing than you think you'll need, and bring a towel to dry with and a dry change of clothes for the end of the trip. Sneakers or other soft-soled footwear are required in the inflatable rafts. Before June 30th and after September 1st, you may be required to have a wetsuit for the trip. Rafting companies often rent the suits and booties.

The rafting company supplies the raft, paddles, life vest, helmet, life preserver and first-aid kit. There will be a pre-trip orientation meeting with instruction about rafting and white-water safety. Your rafting company usually provides lunch (often grilled on the riverbank) as well.

Numerous companies will make arrangements for your rafting trip and lodging on

"Woooo-Hoooo!"

the Kennebec, Dead or Penobscot Rivers. Trips range in difficulty from Class II (easy enough for children age eight and over) to Class V (intense, difficult rapids, minimum age 15). See the Activities section in Facts for the Visitor for more details on rafting. Here is some local information:

Crab Apple Whitewater
    (☎ 207-663-4491, 800-553-7238), HC 63, Box 25, The Forks, ME 04985, runs trips on rivers in western Massachusetts as well
Downeast Rafting, The Forks
    c/o Downeast Whitewater (☎ 603-447-3002, 447-3801), PO Box 119, Center Conway, NH 03813, runs rafting trips on the Rapid River as well
Maine Whitewater
    (☎ 207-672-4814, 800-345-6246), PO Box 633, Bingham, ME 04920
New England Whitewater Center
    (☎ 207-672-5506, 800-766-7238), PO Box 21, Caratunk, ME 04925
Northern Outdoors
    (☎ 800-765-7238), PO Box 100, The Forks, ME 04985, runs rafting, mountain biking, fishing and sea kayaking trips in Maine and other areas
Professional River Runners of Maine
    (☎ 207-663-2229, 800-325-3911), PO Box 92, West Forks, ME 04985, runs rafting trips on these and other rivers in the eastern US
Voyagers Whitewater
    (☎ 207-663-4423, 800-289-6307), US 201, The Forks, ME 04985

ONWARD TO QUÉBEC CITY
North of the Kennebec Valley, US 201 heads through Jackman to the Canadian border. Continuing as Québec Route 173, it makes its way directly through the lush farm country of the St Lawrence Valley to Québec City, 111 miles from Jackman, 280 miles from Portland. For travel in Canada, get a copy of Lonely Planet's *Canada*.

MOOSEHEAD LAKE
Moosehead Lake, north of the town of Greenville, is huge; it's the largest lake totally within any New England state (Lake Champlain is bigger, but shares a border with New York). This is lumber and backwoods country, which is what makes Greenville the region's largest seaplane station. The pontoon planes will take you even deeper into the Maine woods for fishing trips or on lumber company business.

For answers to questions about the region, contact the Moosehead Lake Region Chamber of Commerce (☎ 207-695-2702), PO Box 581, Greenville, ME 04441. For information on wilderness canoe adventures, contact Rick and Judy Givens at Allagash Wilderness Outfitters (☎ 207-695-2821), Route 76, Box 620, Greenville, ME 04441 (December through April, ☎ 207-723-6622 at 36 Minuteman Drive, Millinocket, ME 04462).

Though once a bustling summer resort, Greenville has since reverted to a backwoods outpost. A few old summer hotels limp on in some form. But most visitors today are camping or heading through on their way to Baxter State Park and Mt Katahdin, with only a brief visit to the famous *Road Kill Cafe* (☎ 207-695-2230) in Greenville Junction.

The SS *Katahdin* (☎ 207-695-2716, 695-3764), a 115-foot steamboat built in 1914, still makes the rounds of the lake from Greenville twice daily in summer at 10 am and 2 pm as it did in Greenville's heyday. The three-hour cruise costs $12 for adults, $10 seniors, $6 kids five to 15. The lake's colorful history is preserved in the Moosehead Marine Museum.

VIA Rail Canada's trains between Montréal and Halifax follow a corridor route through northern Maine, and stop at Greenville Junction. This is more of a curiosity than a useful service to most visitors.

BAXTER STATE PARK

Mt Katahdin (5267 feet), Maine's tallest mountain and the northern terminus of the 2000-mile-long Appalachian Trail, is the centerpiece of Baxter State Park, which has 46 other mountain peaks, 1200 campsites and 180 miles of hiking trails as well. It offers the wildest, most unspoiled wilderness adventures in New England and Katahdin has a reputation as being a real rock climber's mountain.

Despite its relative inaccessibility – deep in the Maine woods over unpaved roads – Baxter hosts over 100,000 visitors annually, mostly during its summer season from mid-May through mid-October. It's open December through March for winter activities as well.

To enjoy Baxter State Park, you must arrive at the park entrance early in the day (only so many visitors are allowed in on any given day), and you should be well equipped for camping and perhaps for hiking and canoeing. Campsites in the park must be reserved well in advance by contacting Baxter State Park (☎ 207-723-5140), 64 Balsam Drive, Millinocket, ME 04462. You might also want to get information from the Maine Appalachian Trail Club, PO Box 283, Augusta, ME 04330 and the Millinocket Chamber of Commerce (☎ 207-723-4443), 1029 Central St.

If you are unable to get a reservation at one of the park's campsites, you can usually find a site at one of the private campsites just outside the Togue Ponds and Matagamon gates into the park. There are several campgrounds in Medway (just off I-95 exit 56), in Millinocket and in Greenville.

Getting There & Away

Medway is at I-95 exit 56; Millinocket is 11 miles northeast; and the southern border of Baxter State Park is about 20 miles

northeast from Millinocket. Here are distances and driving times from various places to Medway:

Destination	Mileage	Hr:Min
Bangor, ME	58 miles	1:15
Boston, MA	311 miles	7:00
Houlton, ME	68 miles	1:30
Presque Isle, ME	111 miles	3:15
New York, NY	512 miles	12:30
Portland, ME	203 miles	4:30
Montréal, Canada	346 miles	8:30
Québec City, Canada	284 miles	7:00
Halifax, Canada	359 miles	9:30

AROOSTOOK COUNTY

Aroostook County is huge, covering over 6400 sq miles, which makes it substantially larger than the entire state of Connecticut. "The County," as it's called, has more than 2000 lakes, ponds, streams and rivers. The western half of the county is deep forest owned by the timber and paper companies. The long eastern half, however, is good farming country, though the growing season is short. That makes it perfect for growing potatoes. The people of Aroostook County take advantage of this fact by producing 1½ million tons of potatoes every year.

If you're into potatoes or forests, Aroostook is heaven. Sit down at a diner in Houlton, Presque Isle or Madawaska, and you'll find potatoes on the menu in all sorts of original ways. The names of the many varieties of the noble spud *(Solanum tuberosum)* – Kennebec, Katahdin, Norchip, Superior, Ontario, Russet Burbank, Norgold Russet – are bandied about over breakfast.

Unless you're in the business, the fascination provided by tubers fades fast. You may well find Aroostook to be just a pretty place to pass through on your way to somewhere else.

I-95 ends at Houlton, on the border with the Canadian province of New Brunswick Route 95 continues on the other side, and links you to CN 2, the Trans-Canada Hwy.

From Houlton, US 1 goes north to Presque Isle, Caribou and Van Buren before crossing into New Brunswick. You can continue on NB 17 to Campbellton and Québec's beautiful Gaspé Peninsula, or head northwest on CN 185, the Trans-Canada, to Riviére-du-Loup, Québec, then southwest up the St Lawrence to Québec City; though the fastest route from Maine to Québec City is to take I-95 to Fairfield, just north of Winslow, then US 201 north via Skowhegan, Bingham, the Kennebec Valley and Jackman. But this way you don't get to see several thousand square miles of potatoes.

Various local information offices include the Aroostook County Tourist Hotline (☎ 800-487-1369), and the chambers of commerce in most towns, including **Caribou** (☎ 207-498-6156), **Houlton** (☎ 207-532-4216), **Presque Isle** (☎ 207-764-6561) and **Van Buren** (☎ 207-868-5059).

Glossary

Abenaki – a New England Native American tribe

Alpine Slide – a concrete chute navigated for fun on a simple wheeled car or, if it's a water slide, in an inflatable cushion

Amoskeag Mills – textile company that once thrived in New Hampshire. Its abandoned mills, which once covered over eight million sq feet, can still be seen along the banks of the Merrimack River in Manchester, NH.

AMC – Appalachian Mountain Club

Boonies or Boondocks – the most rural of rural locations: "That place is way out in the Boonies."

Brahmin – one descended from an old New England family; an Anglo Saxon or Yankee. As many English settlers acquired wealth, they settled together in Boston's Beacon Hill section.

The Cape – Cape Cod

chandleries – ships' outfitting stores

cobble – a high rocky knoll of limestone, marble or quartzite found in western Massachusetts

cod cheeks – delicacy along with cod tongue. Cod cheeks don't include the gill or any other bony parts. They're soft oyster-like bits of meat found on the sides of the "face."

cod tongues – a delicacy found in New England, but most popular in Newfoundland. If fresh and cooked properly (sautéed in a bit of hot butter), they are quite tasty.

CCC – Civilian Conservation Corps

CCNS – Cape Cod National Seashore

DAR – Daughters of the American Revolution, a service organization

dry town – a town in which municipal ordinances prohibit the sale (but usually not the possession, consumption or service of) alcoholic beverages

Equity playhouse – "Equity" is the US actors' union. "Equity actors" are professionals, members of the union.

gap – mountain pass with steep sides; called a notch in New Hampshire

gimcrack – a small item of uncertain use, perhaps frivolous; a gizmo

green – the grass-covered open space typically found at the center of a traditional New England village or town, originally used as common pastureland ("the common"), but now serving as a central park. The green is often surrounded by community service buildings such as the town hall, library, court house and churches.

grinder – a large sandwich of meat, cheese, lettuce, tomato, dressing, etc in a long bread roll; called a submarine, po boy or hoagie in other US regions

hidden drive – a driveway entering a road in such a way that visibility for approaching drivers is impaired; signs warn of them

housekeeping cabins/units – a hotel or motel room or detached housing unit equipped with kitchen facilities, rented by the day, week or month

Indian Summer – a brief warm period in autumn before the cold weather sets in for the winter

ironclads – a term for warships with iron sheathing

The Islands – Martha's Vineyard & Nantucket

leaf peepers (-peeping) – recreational touring to enjoy autumn foliage colors

lean-to – a simple shelter for camping, usually without walls, windows or doors, consisting of a roof with one side on or near the ground, the other slanting upward

lobster roll – a hot dog bun or other bread

roll filled with lobster meat in a mayonnaise sauce and sometimes dressed with celery, lettuce, etc

Lower (or Outer) Cape – the long, narrow extension of Cape Cod north and east from Orleans to Provincetown

Mid-Cape – region of Cape Cod roughly from Barnstable and Hyannis eastward to Orleans

minuteman – a colonist armed and pledged to be ready at a moment's notice to fight against the British just before and during the Revolutionary War

NPS – National Park Service

OSV – Old Sturbridge Village, MA

P-Town – Provincetown, on Cape Cod, MA
package store – liquor store
pitched battle – a general term for fighting without respite; the times in a battle when both sides are actively engaged in fighting
ploughman's lunch – an English term for a simple lunch of bread and cheese

rush tickets – sometimes called "student rush," these are discounted tickets bought at the box office usually no more than an hour or two before performances (usually theater or traditional music)

sachem – Native American cheiftan. Massasoit was sachem of the Wampanoags
shire town – county seat
sugaring off – the springtime (March) harvest of sap from maple trees, which is collected and boiled to reduce it to maple syrup
soaring – term for glider (sailplane) rides
Southie – someone from the town of South Boston, which is south of Boston across Fort Point Channel

The "T" – Boston's MBTA Rapid Transit System (subway or underground)
tall ships – tall-masted sailing transport vessels
tin ceilings – short for "stamped tin ceilings," which are stamped tin squares assembled on a ceiling to give an added texture to a room; a feature left over from the late 19th and early 20th centuries
tuck-in – a good, "square" meal

UMass – University of Massachussetts
Upper Cape – Cape Cod region near the canal and the mainland
USFS – United States Forest Service
USGS – United States Geological Survey
UVM – University of Vermont

The Vineyard – pronounced (VIN-yerd) Martha's Vineyard

weirs – fishnets of string, bark strips, twigs, etc, placed in a current to catch fish; the oldest known method of fishing

Yankee – an inhabitant or native of New England; one from the northeastern USA. Though its origin is hard to determine, the British were the first to attribute it to all Americans; during the Civil War, American Southerners attributed it specifically to Northerners.

Appendix I: Climate Charts

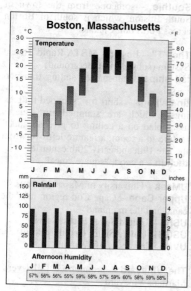

Boston, Massachusetts

Temperature

J F M A M J J A S O N D

Rainfall

Afternoon Humidity
J F M A M J J A S O N D
57% 56% 56% 55% 59% 58% 57% 59% 60% 58% 59% 58%

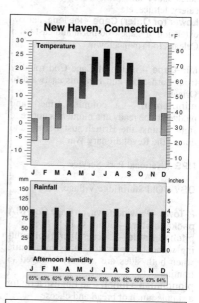

New Haven, Connecticut

Temperature

J F M A M J J A S O N D

Rainfall

Afternoon Humidity
J F M A M J J A S O N D
65% 63% 62% 60% 60% 63% 63% 62% 60% 63% 64%

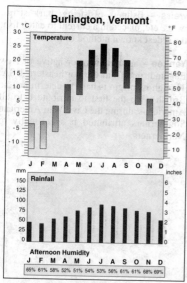

Burlington, Vermont

Temperature

J F M A M J J A S O N D

Rainfall

Afternoon Humidity
J F M A M J J A S O N D
65% 61% 58% 52% 51% 54% 53% 56% 61% 61% 68% 69%

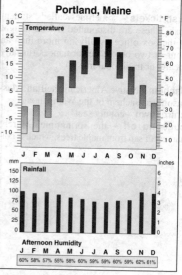

Portland, Maine

Temperature

J F M A M J J A S O N D

Rainfall

Afternoon Humidity
J F M A M J J A S O N D
60% 58% 57% 55% 58% 60% 59% 59% 60% 59% 62% 61%

514

Appendix II: State Abbreviations

The following is a list of the official US Postal Service state abbreviations that are used in mailing addresses and sometimes in general reference.

AK	Alaska	**KY**	Kentucky	**NY**	New York
AL	Alabama	**LA**	Louisiana	**OH**	Ohio
AR	Arkansas	**MA**	Massachusetts	**OK**	Oklahoma
AZ	Arizona	**MD**	Maryland	**OR**	Oregon
CA	California	**ME**	Maine	**PA**	Pennsylvania
CO	Colorado	**MI**	Michigan	**RI**	Rhode Island
CT	Connecticut	**MN**	Minnesota	**SC**	South Carolina
DC	Washington, DC	**MO**	Missouri	**SD**	South Dakota
DE	Delaware	**MS**	Mississippi	**TN**	Tennessee
FL	Florida	**MT**	Montana	**TX**	Texas
GA	Georgia	**NC**	North Carolina	**UT**	Utah
HI	Hawaii	**ND**	North Dakota	**VA**	Virginia
IA	Iowa	**NE**	Nebraska	**VT**	Vermont
ID	Idaho	**NH**	New Hampshire	**WA**	Washington
IL	Illinois	**NJ**	New Jersey	**WI**	Wisconsin
IN	Indiana	**NM**	New Mexico	**WV**	West Virginia
KS	Kansas	**NV**	Nevada	**WY**	Wyoming

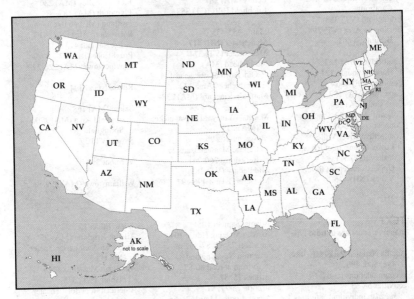

Index

LONELY PLANET PHRASEBOOKS

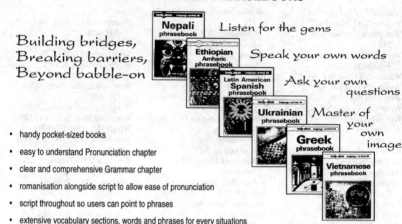

Building bridges,
Breaking barriers,
Beyond babble-on

Listen for the gems

Speak your own words

Ask your own
questions

Master of
your
own
image

- handy pocket-sized books
- easy to understand Pronunciation chapter
- clear and comprehensive Grammar chapter
- romanisation alongside script to allow ease of pronunciation
- script throughout so users can point to phrases
- extensive vocabulary sections, words and phrases for every situations
- full of cultural information and tips for the traveller

'...vital for a real DIY spirit and attitude in language learning' – Backpacker

'the phrasebooks have good cultural backgrounders and offer solid advice for challenging situations in remote locations' – San Francisco Examiner

'...they are unbeatable for their coverage of the world's more obscure languages' – The Geographical Magazine

---

Arabic (Egyptian)
Arabic (Moroccan)
Australia
  Australian English, Aboriginal and Torres Strait languages
Baltic States
  Estonian, Latvian, Lithuanian
Bengali
Burmese
Brazilian
Cantonese
Central Europe
  Czech, French, German, Hungarian, Italian and Slovak
Eastern Europe
  Bulgarian, Czech, Hungarian, Polish, Romanian and Slovak
Egyptian Arabic
Ethiopian (Amharic)
Fijian
French
German
Greek

Hindi/Urdu
Indonesian
Italian
Japanese
Korean
Lao
Latin American Spanish
Malay
Mandarin
Mediterranean Europe
  Albanian, Croatian, Greek, Italian, Macedonian, Maltese, Serbian, Slovene
Mongolian
Moroccan Arabic
Nepali
Papua New Guinea
Pilipino (Tagalog)
Quechua
Russian
Scandinavian Europe
  Danish, Finnish, Icelandic, Norwegian and Swedish

South-East Asia
  Burmese, Indonesian, Khmer, Lao, Malay, Tagalog (Pilipino), Thai and Vietnamese
Spanish
Sri Lanka
Swahili
Thai
Thai Hill Tribes
Tibetan
Turkish
Ukrainian
USA
  US English, Vernacular Talk, Native American languages and Hawaiian
Vietnamese
Western Europe
  Basque, Catalan, Dutch, French, German, Irish, Italian, Portuguese, Scottish Gaelic, Spanish (Castilian) and Welsh

PLANET TALK

Lonely Planet's FREE quarterly newsletter

We love hearing from you and think you'd like to hear from us.

*When...*is the right time to see reindeer in Finland?
*Where...*can you hear the best palm-wine music in Ghana?
*How...*do you get from Asunción to Areguá by steam train?
*What...*is the best way to see India?

For the answer to these and many other questions read PLANET TALK.

Every issue is packed with up-to-date travel news and advice including:

- a letter from Lonely Planet co-founders Tony and Maureen Wheeler
- go behind the scenes on the road with a Lonely Planet author
- feature article on an important and topical travel issue
- a selection of recent letters from travellers
- details on forthcoming Lonely Planet promotions
- complete list of Lonely Planet products

To join our mailing list contact any Lonely Planet office.

Also available: Lonely Planet T-shirts. 100% heavyweight cotton.

LONELY PLANET ONLINE

Get the latest travel information before you leave or while you're on the road

Whether you've just begun planning your next trip, or you're chasing down specific info on currency regulations or visa requirements, check out Lonely Planet Online for up-to-the minute travel information.

As well as travel profiles of your favourite destinations (including maps and photos), you'll find current reports from our researchers and other travellers, updates on health and visas, travel advisories, and discussion of the ecological and political issues you need to be aware of as you travel.

There's also an online travellers' forum where you can share your experience of life on the road, meet travel companions and ask other travellers for their recommendations and advice. We also have plenty of links to other online sites useful to independent travellers.

And of course we have a complete and up-to-date list of all Lonely Planet travel products including guides, phrasebooks, atlases, Journeys and videos and a simple online ordering facility if you can't find the book you want elsewhere.

www.lonelyplanet.com
or
AOL keyword: lp

LONELY PLANET PRODUCTS

Lonely Planet is known worldwide for publishing practical, reliable and no-nonsense travel information in our guides and on our web site. The Lonely Planet list covers just about every accessible part of the world. Currently there are eight series: *travel guides*, *shoestring guides*, *walking guides*, *city guides*, *phrasebooks*, *audio packs*, *travel atlases* and *Journeys* – a unique collection of travel writing.

EUROPE

Amsterdam • Austria • Baltic States phrasebook • Britain • Central Europe on a shoestring • Central Europe phrasebook • Czech & Slovak Republics • Denmark • Dublin • Eastern Europe on a shoestring • Eastern Europe phrasebook • Estonia, Latvia & Lithuania • Finland • France • French phrasebook • German phrasebook • Greece • Greek phrasebook • Hungary • Iceland, Greenland & the Faroe Islands • Ireland • Italian phrasebook • Italy • Mediterranean Europe on a shoestring • Mediterranean Europe phrasebook • Paris • Poland • Portugal • Portugal travel atlas • Prague • Russia, Ukraine & Belarus • Russian phrasebook • Scandinavian & Baltic Europe on a shoestring • Scandinavian Europe phrasebook • Slovenia • Spain • Spanish phrasebook • St Petersburg • Switzerland • Trekking in Greece • Trekking in Spain • Ukrainian phrasebook • Vienna • Walking in Britain • Walking in Switzerland • Western Europe on a shoestring • Western Europe phrasebook

Travel Literature: The Olive Grove: Travels in Greece

NORTH AMERICA

Alaska • Backpacking in Alaska • Baja California • California & Nevada • Canada • Florida • Hawaii • Honolulu • Los Angeles • Mexico • Miami • New England • New Orleans • New York City • New York, New Jersey & Pennsylvania • Pacific Northwest USA • Rocky Mountain States • San Francisco • Southwest USA • USA phrasebook • Washington, DC & the Capital Region

CENTRAL AMERICA & THE CARIBBEAN

Bermuda • Central America on a shoestring • Costa Rica • Cuba • Eastern Caribbean • Guatemala, Belize & Yucatán: La Ruta Maya • Jamaica

SOUTH AMERICA

Argentina, Uruguay & Paraguay • Bolivia • Brazil • Brazilian phrasebook • Buenos Aires • Chile & Easter Island • Chile & Easter Island travel atlas • Colombia • Ecuador & the Galápagos Islands • Latin American Spanish phrasebook • Peru • Quechua phrasebook • Rio de Janeiro • South America on a shoestring • Trekking in the Patagonian Andes • Venezuela

Travel Literature: Full Circle: A South American Journey

ANTARCTICA

Antarctica

ISLANDS OF THE INDIAN OCEAN

Madagascar & Comoros • Maldives • Mauritius, Réunion & Seychelles

AFRICA

Africa - the South • Africa on a shoestring • Arabic (Moroccan) phrasebook • Cape Town • Central Africa • East Africa • Egypt • Egypt travel atlas • Ethiopian (Amharic) phrasebook • Kenya • Kenya travel atlas • Malawi, Mozambique & Zambia • Morocco • North Africa • South Africa, Lesotho & Swaziland • South Africa, Lesotho & Swaziland travel atlas • Swahili phrasebook • Trekking in East Africa • West Africa • Zimbabwe, Botswana & Namibia • Zimbabwe, Botswana & Namibia travel atlas

Travel Literature: The Rainbird: A Central African Journey • Songs to an African Sunset: A Zimbabwean Story

MAIL ORDER

Lonely Planet products are distributed worldwide. They are also available by mail order from Lonely Planet, so if you have difficulty finding a title please write to us. North American and South American residents should write to Embarcadero West, 155 Filbert St, Suite 251, Oakland CA 94607, USA; European and African residents should write to 10 Barley Mow Passage, Chiswick, London W4 4PH; and residents of other countries to PO Box 617, Hawthorn, Victoria 3122, Australia.

NORTH-EAST ASIA

Beijing • Cantonese phrasebook • China • Hong Kong • Hong Kong, Macau & Guangzhou • Japan • Japanese phrasebook • Japanese audio pack • Korea • Korean phrasebook • Mandarin phrasebook • Mongolia • Mongolian phrasebook • North-East Asia on a shoestring • Seoul • Taiwan • Tibet • Tibet phrasebook • Tokyo

Travel Literature: Lost Japan

MIDDLE EAST & CENTRAL ASIA

Arab Gulf States • Arabic (Egyptian) phrasebook • Central Asia • Iran • Israel & the Palestinian Territories • Israel & the Palestinian Territories travel atlas • Istanbul • Jerusalem • Jordan & Syria • Jordan, Syria & Lebanon travel atlas • Middle East • Turkey • Turkish phrasebook • Turkey travel atlas • Yemen

Travel Literature: The Gates of Damascus • Kingdom of the Film Stars: Journey into Jordan

ALSO AVAILABLE:

Travel with Children • Traveller's Tales

INDIAN SUBCONTINENT

Bangladesh • Bengali phrasebook • Delhi • Hindi/Urdu phrasebook • India • India & Bangladesh travel atlas • Indian Himalaya • Karakoram Highway • Nepal • Nepali phrasebook • Pakistan • Rajasthan • Sri Lanka • Sri Lanka phrasebook • Trekking in the Indian Himalaya • Trekking in the Karakoram & Hindukush • Trekking in the Nepal Himalaya

Travel Literature: In Rajasthan • Shopping for Buddhas

SOUTH-EAST ASIA

Bali & Lombok • Bangkok • Burmese phrasebook • Cambodia • Ho Chi Minh City • Indonesia • Indonesian phrasebook • Indonesian audio pack • Jakarta • Java • Laos • Lao phrasebook • Laos travel atlas • Malay phrasebook • Malaysia, Singapore & Brunei • Myanmar (Burma) • Philippines • Pilipino phrasebook • Singapore • South-East Asia on a shoestring • South-East Asia phrasebook • Thailand • Thailand travel atlas • Thai phrasebook • Thai audio pack • Thai Hill Tribes phrasebook • Vietnam • Vietnamese phrasebook • Vietnam travel atlas

AUSTRALIA & THE PACIFIC

Australia • Australian phrasebook • Bushwalking in Australia • Bushwalking in Papua New Guinea • Fiji • Fijian phrasebook • Islands of Australia's Great Barrier Reef • Melbourne • Micronesia • New Caledonia • New South Wales & the ACT • New Zealand • Northern Territory • Outback Australia • Papua New Guinea • Papua New Guinea phrasebook • Queensland • Rarotonga & the Cook Islands • Samoa • Solomon Islands • South Australia • Sydney • Tahiti & French Polynesia • Tasmania • Tonga • Tramping in New Zealand • Vanuatu • Victoria • Western Australia

Travel Literature: Islands in the Clouds • Sean & David's Long Drive

THE LONELY PLANET STORY

Lonely Planet published its first book in 1973 in response to the numerous 'How did you do it?' questions Maureen and Tony Wheeler were asked after driving, bussing, hitching, sailing and railing their way from England to Australia.

Written at a kitchen table and hand collated, trimmed and stapled, *Across Asia on the Cheap* became an instant local bestseller, inspiring thoughts of another book.

Eighteen months in South-East Asia resulted in their second guide, *South-East Asia on a shoestring*, which they put together in a backstreet Chinese hotel in Singapore in 1975. The 'yellow bible', as it quickly became known to backpackers around the world, soon became *the* guide to the region. It has sold well over half a million copies and is now in its 9th edition, still retaining its familiar yellow cover.

Today there are over 240 titles, including travel guides, walking guides, language kits & phrasebooks, travel atlases and travel literature. The company is the largest independent travel publisher in the world. Although Lonely Planet initially specialised in guides to Asia, today there are few corners of the globe that have not been covered.

The emphasis continues to be on travel for independent travellers. Tony and Maureen still travel for several months of each year and play an active part in the writing, updating and quality control of Lonely Planet's guides.

They have been joined by over 70 authors and 170 staff at our offices in Melbourne (Australia), Oakland (USA), London (UK) and Paris (France). Travellers themselves also make a valuable contribution to the guides through the feedback we receive in thousands of letters each year and on our web site.

The people at Lonely Planet strongly believe that travellers can make a positive contribution to the countries they visit, both through their appreciation of the countries' culture, wildlife and natural features, and through the money they spend. In addition, the company makes a direct contribution to the countries and regions it covers. Since 1986 a percentage of the income from each book has been donated to ventures such as famine relief in Africa; aid projects in India; agricultural projects in Central America; Greenpeace's efforts to halt French nuclear testing in the Pacific; and Amnesty International.

'I hope we send people out with the right attitude about travel. You realise when you travel that there are so many different perspectives about the world, so we hope these books will make people more interested in what they see. Guidebooks can't really guide people. All you can do is point them in the right direction.'

– Tony Wheeler

LONELY PLANET PUBLICATIONS

Australia
PO Box 617, Hawthorn 3122, Victoria
tel: (03) 9819 1877 fax: (03) 9819 6459
e-mail: talk2us@lonelyplanet.com.au

USA
Embarcadero West, 155 Filbert St, Suite 251,
Oakland, CA 94607
tel: (510) 893 8555 TOLL FREE: 800 275-8555
fax: (510) 893 8563
e-mail: info@lonelyplanet.com

UK
10 Barley Mow Passage, Chiswick,
London W4 4PH
tel: (0181) 742 3161 fax: (0181) 742 2772
e-mail: lonelyplanetuk@compuserve.com

France:
71 bis rue du Cardinal Lemoine, 75005 Paris
tel: 1 44 32 06 20 fax: 1 46 34 72 55
e-mail: 100560.415@compuserve.com

World Wide Web: http://www.lonelyplanet.com
or *AOL* keyword: lp